THE PICADOR BOOK OF

CRICKET

THE PICADOR BOOK OF

CRICKET

Edited by Ramachandra Guha

PICADOR

First published 2001 by Picador
an imprint of Macmillan Publishers Ltd
25 Eccleston Place, London SW1W 9NF
Basingstoke and Oxford
Associated companies throughout the world
www.macmillan.com

ISBN 0 330 39612 9

3 5 7 9 8 6 4 2

A CIP catalogue record for this book is available from
the British Library.

Typeset by Intype London Ltd
Printed and bound in Great Britain by
Mackays of Chatham plc, Chatham, Kent

for Rukun

Contents

viii CONTENTS

CONTENTS   ix

Martin Johnson – *King of the Willow* 212

B. C. Pires – *Emperor of Trinidad* 215

Frank Keating – *Final Fling for the Fizzer* 217

Mike Selvey – *Sachin of Mumbai* 220

Suresh Menon – *Tendulkar of the World* 222

Alan Ross – *Watching Benaud Bowl* 225

LITTLE HEROES

A. A. Thomson – *Bat, Ball and Boomerang* 229

John Arlott – *Rough Diamond* 237

Neville Cardus – *Robinson of Yorkshire* 241

David Foot – *Character in the Counties* 244

Rowland Ryder – *The Unplayable Jeeves* 249

C. L. R. James – *The Most Unkindest Cut* 252

Matthew Engel – *A Great Fat Man* 261

Dale Slater – *Abed and Apartheid* 268

Philip Snow – *The Fijian Botham* 273

Sujit Mukherjee – *A Jesuit in Patna* 282

Neville Cardus – *A Shastbury Character* 286

Alan Gibson – *The Unmasking of a Dashing Oriental Star* 290

N. S. Ramaswami – *Iverson and the Lesser Arts* 293

Introduction

The Picador Book of Cricket is both homage and epitaph, a tribute to the finest writers on the game and an acknowledgement that the great days of cricket literature are behind us. 'Show me the Tolstoy of the Zulus,' said Saul Bellow once, bringing the wrath of the politically correct upon his head. Far less contentious would be the remark, 'Show me the Neville Cardus of one-day cricket.' Watching a one-day match is like smoking a good cigar – fine while it lasts, but difficult to write about afterwards. One limited-overs game is much like the next: played to a strict script, limited in its variations, lacking the long-drawn-out intensity and drama of the Test match. Meanwhile, live television and the greater frequency of international matches have also dealt a body blow to cricket writing as literature. When one has just watched England play Australia on the box, or at any rate is preparing to watch England play South Africa on the morrow, why bother to read an account, however evocative, of a tour through the Caribbean last winter?

The cricket-book market nowadays is cornered by ghosted autobiographies and statistical compendiums. The essayist, the biographer, the traveller and the roving correspondent: there is scarcely any space for these kinds of writers any more. There was a time when major English novelists or poets – P. G. Wodehouse, Arthur Conan Doyle, Francis Thomson, Alec Waugh and numerous others – took time off to play and write about cricket. Now they are more likely to celebrate football (as with Nick Hornby and Ian Hamilton), or accept commissions to report on Wimbledon (like Martin Amis).

Modern cricket writing was founded, more or less, by Neville Cardus. The son of a Manchester prostitute, his father unknown to him, Cardus educated himself in the streets, libraries and sports grounds of the city. He was a fair player himself, and for a time was assistant cricket coach at a minor public school. He found a job on the *Manchester Guardian*, where, remarkably, he was asked to fill in for the cricket correspondent, who had fallen ill. He stayed for twenty years. In his writing, the portrayal of character and the evocation of context take precedence over the analysis of technique. He dramatized the great team rivalries of the day, investing Lancashire v. Yorkshire or England v. Australia with a cosmic significance that his readers came to share. He humanized the players, finding distinctions of character in each, whether great international star or humdrum county professional. His hallmark was the capsule biography, the 2,000-word essay on how a cricketer bowled, batted, walked and talked. His taste for verbal embroidery, though deplored by the academic-minded, made him immensely more readable than those who had come before him.

When Neville Cardus died, in 1975, Alan Gibson remarked at his memorial service that 'all cricket writers of the last half century have been influenced by Cardus, whether they admit it or not, whether they have wished it or not, whether they have tried to copy him or tried to avoid copying him'. This is certainly true of the English writers who followed him, the best of whom have included R. C. Robertson-Glasgow, John Arlott, Alan Ross and Gibson himself. These men were all writers first and cricket writers second. It was Cardus who showed them that cricket could be a vehicle for literature. Without him, they might instead have made a career writing poetry or plays. They knew and loved the game, and brought to their writing a range of reading and experience denied to the workaday journalist.

The Cardus style has had less influence abroad. He stands above all English writers, true, but two Australian contemporaries also made major contributions to the literature of cricket. These were Ray Robinson and J. H. Fingleton – the latter a former Test player himself. In their writings there are few literary flourishes, no quoting of poets or evocations of the colour and fragrance of summer. The strength lies rather in the command of the game's technique, in the careful reconstruction of an innings or a spell or an entire match. Their books are marked by economy of expression and precision of analysis, based on a first-hand knowledge of the game. Cardus was also read, but not copied or avoided, by the Trinidadian historian and revolutionary C. L. R. James. His *Beyond a Boundary* – commonly acknowledged to be the most influential of all cricket books – mixes close knowledge of the game with an awesome command of colonial history and metropolitan literature.

Cardus, Robinson, Fingleton, James – all are richly represented in this anthology. So are numerous other writers. The first two sections of the book profile the truly great, from W. G. Grace to Sachin Tendulkar; the third honours those who have excited a more parochial passion (often the source of the finest writing); the fourth remembers some epic matches; and the fifth collects reflections on styles, themes and attitudes. In my selections I have preferred the classic to the kitsch, exposition to exclamation, the out of print to the readily accessible, the style of the broadsheet to that of the tabloid, and literature to journalism.

Wherever possible, I have chosen celebrations by a writer from one country of a cricketer from another. In a more general sense, *The Picador Book of Cricket* aims to challenge the self-centred chauvinism of previous collections of cricket literature. These have tended to under-represent writers as well as players from lands other than England. However, as sport and spectacle, cricket is now vastly more important in the erstwhile colonies than in the Mother Country. Indeed, an obscure town in the Arabian Gulf, Sharjah, hosts matches viewed by millions more people than would view an Ashes Test at Lord's. Moreover, for some time now the England team has been one of the weaker sides in world cricket. Other anthologists, usually English themselves, have shown a magisterial disregard of this decline. By contrast, this collection seeks to be truly international, its writers and subjects being chosen from across the great and growing territory of the game.

Ramachandra Guha

Cricket at Worcester: 1938

Dozing in deckchair's gentle curve,
Through half-closed eyes I watched the cricket,
Knowing the sporting press would say
'Perks bowled well on a perfect wicket.'

Fierce midday sun upon the ground;
Through heat haze came the hollow sound
Of wary bat on ball, to pound
The devil out of it, quell its bound.

Sunburned fieldsmen, flannelled cream,
Seemed, though urgent, scarce alive,
Swooped, like swallows of a dream,
On skimming fly, the hard-hit drive.

Beyond the scorebox, through the trees
Gleamed Severn, blue and wide,
Where oarsmen 'feathered' with polished ease
And passed in gentle glide.

The backcloth, setting off the setting,
Peter's cathedral soared,
Rich of shade and fine of fretting
Like cut and painted board.

To the cathedral, close for shelter
Huddled houses, bent and slim,
Some tall, some short, all helter-skelter,
Like a skyline drawn for Grimm.

This the fanciful engraver might
In his creative dream have seen,
Here, framed by summer's glaring light,
Grey stone, majestic over green.

Closer, the bowler's arm swept down,
The ball swung, swerved and darted,
Stump and bail flashed and flew;
The batsman pensively departed.

Like rattle of dry seeds in pods
The warm crowd faintly clapped,
The boys who came to watch their gods,
The tired old men who napped.

The members sat in their strong deckchairs
And sometimes glanced at the play,
They smoked, and talked of stocks and shares,
And the bar stayed open all day.

JOHN ARLOTT

FROM
GRACE
TO
HUTTON

Our first extract honours the first cricket travellers – the intrepid Englishmen who ranged far and wide in search of competition, heroes masquerading as mercenaries. Alan Gibson's account of the early tours reminds me of what an old Oxford historian (Cecil Headlam) once said: 'First the hunter, the missionary and the merchant, next the soldier and the politician, and then the cricketer – that is the history of British colonization. And of these civilizing influences the last may, perhaps, be said to do least harm.'

ALAN GIBSON

Great Men Before Agamemnon (1975)

Vixere fortes ante Agamemnona
Multi; sed omnes illacrimabiles
Urgentur ignotique longa
Nocte, carent quia vate sacro.
                                    – Horace

which may be roughly translated and abbreviated to 'There were great men before Agamemnon, but the press hadn't got round to it.'

The first English sporting team to tour abroad (or so I imagine) left our shores in 1586, under the captaincy of John Davis. Its destination was the Arctic Circle, where it took part in a series of athletic contests against the Eskimo. Like most touring teams, it won some and it lost some, though no detailed results survive. There were newspapers of a kind then, but they did not run to sports correspondents, and in any case there might have been a shortage of volunteers: intrepidly though our pressmen may now venture to Australia or America,

Greenland in the sixteenth century might have daunted the bravest. The expenses would no doubt have been good, but you could not be sure of surviving to claim them, and an occasional whale steak did not represent much in the way of free-loading.

This is not just a little joke. Davis, one of the most courageous and selfless of the great Elizabethan sailors, had visited the Arctic before, and had tried to establish friendly relations with the Eskimo, without much success. He had taken out some musicians, who played old English folk tunes, while the seamen danced to them. The Eskimo were only mildly interested, and did not seek to compete with these early Cloggies.

But Davis had noticed they were an active people, who enjoyed wrestling, jumping and other sports; so on his second trip he took some athletes with him. This did establish some kind of bond with the natives. 'Our men did overleape them, but we found them strong and nimble, and to have skil in wrestling, for they cast some of our men that were good wrestlers.' As many of Davis's men came from Devon and Cornwall, famous wrestling counties, we may take it that the Eskimo standard was high. They were not, however, so good at football, of which they already had a version. 'Divers times did they weave us on shore to play with them at the foot-ball, and some of our company went on shore to play with them, and our men did cast them downe as soon as they did come to strike the ball.' Clearly the Eskimo had not learnt to tackle.

This tour is worth remembering, as an illustration (there are many to the contrary) of the hopeful belief that if different peoples can be brought to play games together, they will understand each other better, and grow fonder of each other. But there is no record of anything like cricket being played. It is not quite impossible, because cricket and similar bat-and-ball games were known in England at the time, but the records are scanty, and mostly refer to the south-east of the country. So, reluctantly, I cannot grant John Davis the honour of being our first touring captain.

That distinction would have gone to the third Duke of Dorset, J. F. Sackville, at the end of the eighteenth century, but for an unhappy misadventure. He was one of the many nobility and gentry who were enthusiasts for the game, and used to gather at Hambledon: a great backer of sides, and a considerable player himself. At one time he was Ambassador in Paris, and in 1789 he asked the Foreign Secretary, the Duke of Leeds (another cricketer), for a token of goodwill towards the French. Between them they planned a tour of English cricketers to Paris. It seems odd, because there was nobody obvious for them to play, but that is what they did. Unfortunately the French Revolution broke out, and the first the Duke of Dorset saw of his team was at Dover, they wondering whether to embark and he flying homewards. As Major Rowland Bowen has pointed out, this was the first cricket tour to be cancelled because of political events, though not the last.

By this time, plenty of matches were being played at home by sides called 'England v. Kent', 'England v. Hambledon' and so on; but if we started taking these into account we should soon be in trouble, as in many cases we do not know the detailed scores or the teams. We may, however, moving on to the nineteenth century, pause on the name of William Clarke. Clarke was born in 1798. He was a Nottingham bricklayer. He played for his county at the age of eighteen but he was nearly fifty when he was first employed as a practice bowler at Lord's, where he soon made a reputation as one of the best in the country. In 1847, he and William Lillywhite took all twenty wickets for the Players against the Gentlemen. He spun the ball from leg, bowling at about the height of the hip, and there are many tales of his cunning. He was the founder of 'The All-England XI', which played its first match in 1846, against Twenty of Sheffield. The idea was that the best cricketers in the country should tour together, playing against local sides. It was a business enterprise, though occasionally a leading amateur, such as Mynn or Felix, would play.

In order to make an even game of it, All-England customarily played against odds, usually twenty-two. If the local sides still did not feel strong enough, they would engage a spare professional or two to play for them. One or two professionals, perhaps those who did not fit easily into the disciplines of a touring side, specialized in taking engagements for the opposition. Of one of these, William Caffyn tells a story in his capital book, *77 Not Out*. (Caffyn was a member of Clarke's team, and later had much to do with the advance of the game in Australia, where he coached.) The player concerned, he recalls, was about to be arrested for debt. The sum was only £12, and so he arranged with his creditor to be seized just before the start of play, on the ground of the club for whom he was playing. As both debtor and creditor had calculated, the club was so alarmed at the prospect of playing without their star guest that a whip-round raised the money.

The All-England XI had many adventures and many successes. F. S. Ashley-Cooper worked out that in the seven years 1847–53 Clarke himself took 2,385 wickets for them, an average of 340 per season. A booklet was published, for the benefit of local cricketers, entitled *How to Play Clarke*. He did not like taking himself off, and of course he had plenty of batsmen to bowl at, but it is still a lot of wickets. Batting twenty-two may not have made much difference to the scores of the local side, but it did make a difference to the England batsmen. Imagine the difficulty of scoring runs, against any sort of bowling, with twenty-two men in the field, especially when everything has to be run out, and with the crowd on the side of the fieldsmen, eager to return the ball (quite the opposite when their own side was batting). The grounds were often small, the pitches almost inevitably rough. In 1855, for instance, Caffyn averaged 22 in eleven-a-side matches, which would usually be played on better grounds, but only 16 for the whole season. In the same season John Wisden took 223 wickets in all matches at an average of 5, and averaged 23 with the bat, and it was the second figure that was considered more remarkable.

It was Wisden, with Jemmy Dean (two Sussex men), who founded the United England XI in 1852. Old Clarke was a bit of an autocrat, and was reputed to be making money out of all proportion to the £4 a match (which usually lasted three days) which he paid his players. In any case, now that the career of a travelling cricket professional had been shown to be feasible (it could not have been done without the railway), more good players were coming forward than one eleven could accommodate. The matches between the All-England and United XIs became the most important matches of the season, more so even than North v. South, much more so than Gentlemen v. Players – for this development of professional strength was too much for the amateurs, who between 1850 and 1865 lost very match but one. The England–United match first took place in 1857. Clarke, so long as he was in charge, would have nothing to do with it, and of course from his own point of view he was right, because the unique status of his side had gone. It is reported that 10,000 people at a time would attend these matches, which were sometimes played for the Cricketers' Friendly Fund ('after deducting all expenses', Caffyn says, a somewhat uncertain qualification). These two great elevens, which had a number of less successful imitators, undoubtedly did the game of cricket service, spreading it all over the

British Isles. The wide interest they created proved to be, as county clubs emerged, their own undoing. But they lasted a long time, and no discussion of English cricket captains should omit the name of crusty old Clarke.

Nor should it omit that of George Parr. The formula which had worked so well for the professionals at home might surely be tried out abroad, and so it was that a representative team left Liverpool for North America in 1859. Six players were from the All-England XI, and six from the United. Fred Lillywhite accompanied them as scorer, reporter and mentor, not to say Nestor. George Parr of Nottinghamshire was the captain. There were two other Nottinghamshire players, three from Cambridgeshire, two from Sussex, and four from Surrey. Wherever it went, the party was distinguished by Fred Lillywhite's portable scoring-booth and printing-press. The team were photographed before they started, against a suitable background of rigging (not actually on the ship they sailed on), in spotted shirts and striking attitudes. They had a rough passage, and Parr, a bad traveller, had consumed large quantities of gin-and-water before they arrived at Quebec.

Cricket was very popular then in the United States and Canada. At New York, 'ten thousand people' (though one must always mistrust such conveniently rounded figures) watched the match, all the ground could hold. The band played 'Rule, Britannia!' as the English began their innings. This was only forty-five years after the Second American War, and only three years before the *Alabama* sailed from Liverpool, nearly producing a third. At Philadelphia the crowds were even larger.

All the matches were played against odds, and if the match ended early, as often it did, the Englishmen would divide forces and play an eleven-a-side match, sharing the locals. In one of these additional matches, Parr was badly hit on the elbow by Jackson, the dreaded English fast bowler, and was unable to bat again during the tour. He did, however, make a public appearance in the last match, against a Combined Twenty-Two of Canada and the United States, when he volunteered to umpire. It was now the second half of October, and bitterly cold, and it has to be said that soon the umpire/captain abandoned his duties, retiring to the comforts of *hot* gin-and-water in the pavilion. His colleagues fielded in overcoats and gloves. On the second day there was no play because of snow, but the teams played a match at baseball instead.

In spite of the formidable travelling, and the fearful difficulties in transporting Lillywhite's scoring-booth, Parr's team won all its matches. They made themselves very popular, saw the Niagara Falls, and took home a profit of £90 a head. They had an even rougher passage back, and one of them, Jemmy Grundy, had a misunderstanding with the Customs over a box of cigars.

Parr had succeeded Clarke as the captain of the All-England XI, and was reckoned the champion of batsmen between Fuller Pilch and Richard Daft. He came to be called 'The Lion of the North', and he was a fine, courageous player, especially strong on the leg side. 'George Parr's tree' at Trent Bridge used to mark the spot where his favourite leg hits went, and when he died, in 1891, a branch from it was placed among the wreaths upon his grave at Radcliffe-on-Trent, his lifelong home. He was a nervous and choleric man, but popular with his teams. He had bright blue eyes, ginger hair, mutton-chop whiskers with moustache (or without either, according to his mood), and was not much good at administration and not very patient with those who had to do it. I would guess that he was the kind of man who, in any period, would turn out to be a captain of England at something or other.

Two years later, in 1861, the first English team went to Australia. It would probably have gone to North America, had it not been for the outbreak of the American Civil War, which among rather more important consequences set back American cricket severely. This was not, as English standards then went, a very good side. The 'northern players' were unhappy about the terms offered by the sponsors, the Melbourne caterers Spiers & Pond. These were £150 a head, plus – that word which could mean so much then, as now – 'expenses'. 'The northern players' meant, in effect, Parr and his Nottinghamshire men. They refused to go. The team was raised principally through the efforts of Surrey, whose secretary came to an amiable arrangement with the representative of Spiers & Pond. There were seven Surrey players in the twelve. Two Yorkshiremen, Iddison and Ned Stephenson, were enlisted – they would hardly at that stage of their careers have been first choices – and added much to the joviality of the tour, as well as its success. One cannot say quite so much, especially respecting the first part, of all the Yorkshiremen who have toured Australia since. Iddison wrote back home: 'We are made a great fuss of; the Queen herself could not have been treated better.' Ned made the witty remark, as they travelled through the Red Sea, that it looked no redder than any of the others he had seen, and stuffed a towel into the trombone of the cook at the ship's concert. Roaring Yorkshire stuff.

But it was Surrey's tour, essentially, and a Surrey man, H. H. Stephenson, was captain. They won 6 and lost 2 matches out of 12, all against odds. Stephenson, the captain, had much success as an after-dinner speaker, an accomplishment which many other captains had to learn, often painfully. Large crowds attended them. Stephenson was a notable cricketer, chiefly for his bowling, and his fast break-back (the arm had of course been getting above the shoulder by now, though an overarm delivery was not legalized until 1864). He was also a powerful hitter and probably the second-best English wicketkeeper, Lockyer being, it was recognized, the best. He became coach at Uppingham, where he produced many admirable cricketers, and seems, towards the end of his life, to have been the most influential, not to say bossy, man in the school. No doubt a man who had led the first England side in Australia was entitled to be a little authoritative.

In 1863, the American Civil War was still on, never more so, and the second English side to Australia set out, a better and more representative side than the first, Parr captain. Again, all matches were against odds, and England were unbeaten, though they only scrambled home by one wicket, almost at the end of their tour, against Twenty-Two of New South Wales. An amateur went on this tour, the youthful E. M. Grace of Gloucestershire.

Now in 1854 old Clarke had brought the All-England down to Bristol to play against the West Gloucestershire club, on the Downs at Durdham. This was the first important match that W. G. Grace, aged six, remembered watching. In 1855, Clarke brought the side again, though he did not play himself, and was impressed by the play of W. G.'s eldest brother, E. M. E. M. Grace was then thirteen years old. When he was asked to go to Australia, as the result of some extraordinary batting late in the season, he was twenty-one. After watching the boy E. M., Clarke gave him a bat, and gave his mother a copy of a book which bore his name, inscribing it

Presented to MRS. GRACE
By William Clarke,
Secretary All-England XI

The book ultimately came into the possession of W. G. Thus does one England captain edify and encourage another.

There was a lull in tours from England after this. Australia was such a long way away, and America, even when the war there was over, was bothered and restless and thinking of other things. But a lot of cricket was played, increasingly, in various parts of the world. Parr's second side had been the first from England to visit New Zealand. In the same year, cricket clubs were founded in the Transvaal and in Kingston, Jamaica, and in 1864 there took place the first known match between Madras and Calcutta. They were playing cricket in Valparaiso, and in 1866 came the first Argentinian hat-trick. In 1868 a team of Australian Aborigines visited Britain, and played a lot of cricket among their other entertainments, such as throwing boomerangs, but this, while a pleasing event both at the time and in retrospect, was one of history's freaks, and led to nothing.

In the same year a second English side went to North America. They drew against Twenty-Two of Canada, and beat Twenty-Two of the United States. Their captain was Edgar Willsher, who had caused such a stir at the Oval in 1862, when playing for 'England' against Surrey. He did not trouble to conceal the height at which his arm went over, well above shoulder height, and was no-balled five times running by his old pal John Lillywhite, whereupon he flung down the ball upon the pitch and left the field. The game was resumed the following day, after dropping the umpire, which as any cricketer to this day will tell you, is a plan with a lot to be said for it. Whether Willsher, in this unimportant tour, had any trouble with American umpires, I do not know.

In 1872 there came the third English tour to North America. The captain was R. A. Fitzgerald, although the dominating figure was that of W. G. Grace, now twenty-four and established as England's leading batsman: indeed, 'leading' does not quite fit the case. It was widely thought in England that there had never been a cricketer like him; it is still. But we shall have to deal with him again. Fitzgerald was secretary of the MCC, and all the team were members of MCC, and therefore amateur, so this tour was a departure from precedent, when the professionals had made all the running. Fitzgerald wrote an amusing book about it, *Wickets in the West*, but I must not dwell upon it, for even with Grace, the absence of professionals made it hopelessly far from an England XI. Not that it did badly, in terms of either results or attendance.

The following winter, 1873–4, Grace took a side to Australia, which played fifteen matches, all against odds, and lost three. They won the most important one, against a combined Fifteen of New South Wales and Victoria. This was a strong team, which included four amateurs besides the captain. It was clear that Australian cricket had made great strides, especially in bowling.

And so we come to the tour of 1876–7. Two tours to Australia were planned that summer. James Lillywhite, Junior – yet another member of that famous cricketing family – was intending to take out a band of professionals, and G. F. Grace one which was to include some amateurs. Grace's fell through, after many of the preliminary arrangements had been made. Now this was to prove a matter of some importance. To English cricketers, this was just another tour, but Lillywhite's men were to play two matches against a Combined Australian *Eleven*, the first time such a thing had happened. As the years went by, and cricketers began to develop their passion for statistics, it became desirable to decide which matches should count in the records as 'Test matches', and 1877 was the obvious place to start. But if there had been *two* touring sides, the status of the eleven-a-side matches would have been demonstrably reduced, and perhaps a different starting point would have been found.

However, Fred Grace did not go, and Lillywhite did, and so the match at Melbourne in 1877 became recognized as 'the first Test', and a hundred years later the centenary Test was played on the same ground, with exactly the same result, victory to Australia by 45 runs. From this point I have followed the generally recognized practice as to what was, and was not, a Test match. It leads to some absurdities. For instance, the standard of cricket on some of the early tours, particularly to South Africa, was a long way from a true international standard. I can, again, see no real reason why the 1929–30 England tour to New Zealand (captain, A. H. H. Gilligan) should be counted, and not that of 1935–6 (captain, E. R. T. Holmes). In February 1930, England began two Test matches on the same day, one at Auckland and one at Georgetown. But if you want to have statistics, you must agree on which matches to base them, or everyone would have his own, and it is more convenient to follow the accepted list. It does mean, however, that 'Test career records', at least up to the Second World War, are not quite always what they seem.

So they were making history, though they did not know it, the party of twelve professionals who set out in 1876. Let us consider these hardy pioneers a little.

Lillywhite, who was promoter and manager as well as captain, was a Sussex man, from West Hampnett, and thirty-five years old at the time of the first Test. He was a medium-paced left-arm bowler, in the steady, persistent style much admired at the time, and a good enough left-handed batsman to score the occasional century. He had visited Australia with the previous side. In the Tests (England won the second by 4 wickets, thus sharing the honours) he scored only 12 runs, but took 8 wickets, and only Alfred Shaw took as many. They were the only two Tests that Lillywhite played in. Alfred Shaw was vice-captain, and assistant manager. There were two other Sussex men besides the captain, Charlwood and Southerton (though Southerton at the time was playing for Surrey). Jupp and Pooley were Surrey-born, Selby and Shaw from Nottinghamshire. There were five Yorkshiremen: Greenwood, Armitage, Hill, and – two of the great all-rounders – Emmett and Ulyett, Emmett growing old but Ulyett with many Tests in front of him. So the south, the Midlands and the north were all represented. Lillywhite paid them £150 each for the trip, except for Shaw, who was paid £300 because of his extra responsibilities. Lillywhite also paid them travelling expenses, first class. This was an important point. W. G. Grace's side had caused some unfavourable comment, especially in Australia, because the professionals had travelled second class, and the amateurs first. This even extended to the hotels where they stayed. It was for this reason that Shaw had declined the trip. Now W. G., perhaps unfairly, was said to have cost the Australians a lot of money by his requirements for 'expenses': so an all-professional team, with the terms set out, suited both the hosts and the guests well. They knew where they were.

It was beginning to be possible, and the Australians were soon to recognize the possibilities, for a man to be a professional cricketer all the year round: £150 for the winter, with free living, and colonial hospitality, was not so bad, even though the travelling was severe. It was better than a man might do at home as a bricklayer, or a stonemason, or even a publican (half Lillywhite's team were publicans at some stage of their lives). Such men were letting the future take care of itself, but nearly all working men had to do that anyway, in those unpensioned days.

Sea travel was becoming safe (as important a fact in the growth of tours as the railway had been to the All-England XI). You could expect to get to Australia on the new P. & O. steamships which came into service in the 1870s, but it would take you a long time: forty-eight days was an average. If you went, first class, by P. & O., you would be comfortable, by the standards of the time. The P. & O. put their first-class cabins on the top deck, surrounding a central dining room, where there were long tables, with benches which could face either way, because you could switch their backs, and look at the table or the sea as you chose. Refrigeration was beginning, but livestock were still carried: cows, to provide fresh milk for the children, and sheep for meat, and hens for eggs.

I am indebted to Basil Greenhill, Director of the Greenwich Maritime Museum, for these details of how Lillywhite's men, and all the other touring sides of that period, travelled. 'The P. & O. really did their first-class passengers pretty well,' he concludes. But forty-eight days was a long time, however many runs round the deck you took, and at the coaling stops – Malta, Suez, King George's Sound – the cricketers conceivably went ashore in pursuit of more urgent interests than keeping fit. They must have felt weary when at last they got there.

It was not, therefore, surprising that they soon lost a match (against odds). After this they were given a ticking off in *The Australasian*. The English, it said,

> . . . are by a long way the weakest side that have ever played in the colonies, notwithstanding the presence of Shaw, who is termed the premier bowler of England. If Ulyett, Emmett, and Hill are specimens of the best fast bowling in England, all we can say is, either they have not shown their proper form, or British bowling has sadly deteriorated.

It is not uncommon, to this day, for touring sides to be hailed as heroes on arrival, and dismissed as nobodies when things go wrong.

However, the attendances were good, and the early matches suggested that Lillywhite would make a profit, as he ultimately did – on this tour, though not on later ones. But they still had much travelling ahead, even when they had settled to form. Apart from their journeys within Australia, they had undertaken to go to New Zealand (in the middle of the tour, with the big matches still to come). Touring in New Zealand then was even tougher than touring in Australia. It was in New Zealand that the English lost their wicketkeeper, Ed Pooley, in unfortunate circumstances. Pooley was a capable cricketer, and a popular one, but not one of Queen Victoria's more reliable citizens. He was to die in the workhouse, though he battled on for another thirty years. Alfred Shaw describes how

> We were playing against Eighteen of Canterbury, and in a discussion of the prospects of the match that occurred in an hotel bar at night, Pooley offered to take £1 to a shilling that he named the individual score of every member of the local team. It is a trick familiar to cricketers, and in the old days of matches against local eighteens and twenty-twos it was not infrequently worked off against the unwary. The bet being accepted, Pooley named a duck as the score of each batsman on the local side. A fair proportion of ducks was recorded, and Pooley claimed £1 for each of them, while prepared to pay one shilling for the other scores. The man with whom the bet had been made said it was a catch bet, and he declined to pay. The man's name was Donkin. His refusal to pay led to a scene of disorder. We next had to go to Otago, and at the close of the match there, Pooley was arrested on a charge of 'having at Christchurch maliciously injured property above the value of £5'; and another charge, of assaulting Donkin. For the assault he had £5 and costs to pay. In the other charge he had as partner in trouble Alf Bramall, a supernumerary attached to our team. The two were committed for trial, bail being allowed of £100. We never saw Pooley again during that tour.

Pooley's bail did not allow him to leave the country, and though he was acquitted of the major charge, and even had a public subscription raised for him by the New Zealanders – many of whom felt he had been inhospitably treated – the rest of the English team had to leave him behind, because they had to be back in Australia. Pooley ultimately trailed home on his own, thus missing playing in the first Test match. As it happened, he never had a chance to play in another.

It was suggested during this tour, both in Australia and New Zealand, that the English were too fond of diddling an innocent colonial, and of looking upon the girls when they were bonny, and the wine when it was red – even more when it was sparkling. This complaint also, whether true or not, remains a recognized accompaniment of any touring team which is not doing too well. The English would no doubt have pleaded justification for at least the last of these offences, because the travelling problems did give a man a thirst. After they had spent eighty hours on the road in New Zealand, wading and swimming through swollen streams on the way, they arrived in Christchurch just in time for the start of play. George Ulyett, no weakling he, but as strapping a man as ever came out of Yorkshire, said that 'We were so stiff, cold and sore with being wet and cramped up in the coach that we could scarcely bowl or run.' They only just managed to get the Eighteen of Canterbury out on the first day, and the local opinion was that the English might as well have stopped at home, instead of coming all that way to teach Canterbury folks how to play cricket. Ulyett goes on (A. W. Pullin took down his recollections):

> In the evening I told Lillywhite that we had been up to our necks in water, had no bed and nothing to eat, it was worth stretching a point, so we got him to allow us a case of champagne and we had a merry evening. The next day we went on to the field new men.

The early English touring sides were very fond of champagne, surprisingly – or so it seems to us, today, accustomed to watching the pints of beer go down. There are many instances of early English cricketers, in forlorn moments far from home, clamouring for champagne. I sometimes wonder if this is the origin of the term 'Pommy' (all the *Shorter Oxford* says is 'origin obscure'). Pommery was a well-known brand before the end of the century. After all, we were called 'Limeys' by the Americans because our seamen drank lime juice, as a precaution against the scurvy.

Well, while I am indulging in such speculations, the 1876–7 tourists are on their way back to Australia, and another rough trip they had, arriving several days late with no proper time to rest. 'Not one of us was fit to play cricket,' writes Shaw: 'I was simply spun out of myself.' There was probably some substance in this excuse. Armitage, who was the fattest member of the side, and a particularly bad traveller, bowled a ball to Bannerman which went for an overhead wide; and then rolled the next one along the ground. But only two wides were bowled in the innings, and Armitage was not primarily a bowler. It was more important that he dropped Bannerman, a simple catch at mid-off, before the Australian No. 1 had reached double figures. Bannerman went on to 165 (retired hurt) and effectively settled the match. This was a most extraordinary performance as scores went in those days. No other Australian, in either innings, scored more than 20, and the highest English score was 63, by Jupp.

If Lillywhite's men were not the best eleven cricketers in England, they were not so far from it, a tried professional eleven, and whatever their handicaps, they had had to give the colonials best. The *Melbourne Age* had no doubt of the significance of the victory:

> Such an event would not have been dreamed of as coming within the limits of possibility ten or fifteen years ago, and it is a crushing reply to those unpatriotic theorists who would have us believe that the Australian race is deteriorating from the Imperial type, or that lengthened existence under Australian suns would kill out the Briton in the blood.

Readers of *The Times* in London had to wait two months for their account, which ultimately came in their 'Melbourne Letter', immediately after a description of a first-class rumpus in the Victorian Parliament, and just before the latest population statistics. It is a shade patronizing.

> You know the result of our great cricket match. To use Mr Trollope's word, Australians will 'blow' about it for some time to come. It was played on the ground of the Melbourne Club, between Lillywhite's eleven and a combined eleven of New South Wales and Victoria. We are told that it is the first match in which an English professional eleven has been beaten out of England. The game was watched with intense excitement by enthusiastic crowds, and those who could not get to the ground clustered round the newspaper offices to see the last dispatches from the seat of war placarded on the door posts. It began and ended in good temper, and Lillywhite's pecuniary success must have consoled him for his defeat.

The reference to Trollope concerns some unflattering remarks he had made in a book about his Australian travels. After the victory, some triumphant verses appeared in the *Australasian*, called 'The Brazen Trumpet', and beginning

> Anthony Trollope
> Says we can wallop
> The whole of creation at 'blowing'.

It's well in a way,
But then he don't say
We blow about nothing worth showing!

Shaw, in his reminiscences, gives the full score of the match, but is careful to refer to the English eleven as 'Lillywhite's Eleven'. The excitement in England was not great, especially as the second Test, a fortnight later on the same ground, was won.

That brings me to a last curious point about this famous occasion. When G. F. Grace was still planning his tour, he had booked the Melbourne ground, the big ground, the home of the Melbourne Cricket Club. Lillywhite's agent had to be content with booking the East Melbourne ground, and the East Melbourne club duly went to much trouble and expense in making preparations. However, when Grace withdrew, Lillywhite naturally wanted to switch grounds, and this did not please the East Melbourne club at all. There were threats of legal proceedings. In the end an amicable settlement was reached. Lillywhite paid East Melbourne £230, and gave free admission to their members, of whom there were 500. He was not a mean man, which was one reason why he never made much money out of his various cricketing ventures. So Test cricket might have begun upon a relatively obscure ground, not at its most famous home, barring possibly one. There were several arguments during the tour, about such matters as rolling the pitch, and the hours of play. The Englishmen, their thoughts directed to the financial benefits, usually gave way. Nevertheless, there were times when feeling ran high. During the match against Fifteen of New South Wales, a lady wrote to Lillywhite imploring him to win, 'as it would not be safe for any Englishman or woman to walk the streets of Sydney if New South Wales were victorious'.

James Lillywhite, for all his adventures and misadventures, was England's first Test captain, as these things came to be reckoned, and he ended with a 50–50 record, slightly above average. What is more, he lived long enough to realize something of what he had started. He outlived all the other members of his team, and died in 1929, aged eighty-seven, when A. P. F. Chapman had just been to Australia (Lillywhite was nearly sixty when Chapman was born), and beaten them, 4–1, before record crowds.

*　*　*

William Gilbert Grace was the pre-eminent Victorian, better known
in his day than Disraeli or Gladstone. He was so venerated by the
common people of England that when he died of a heart attack, in
July 1915, the Germans, hoping to deliver a knockout blow to British
morale, claimed he was a victim of a Zeppelin raid. The memorial
to Grace at Lord's called him 'the Great Cricketer', the definitive
article and the capitals rightly setting him apart from the rest. Grace
had a fine tactical brain allied to a relentless will to win; it was he
who brought gamesmanship into the game. But he also revolution-
ized modern batsmanship

Some of the best cricket writers have expended ink on 'W. G.'.
Two chapters of C. L. R. James's *Beyond a Boundary* masterfully set
the cricketer in his social context. There have also been fine lives by
A. A. Thomson, Eric Midwinter and, most recently, Simon Rae.
I have chosen here a study of his batsmanship written by C. B. Fry,
who opened the batting for England with W. G., followed by a
charming sketch of the man by Bernard Darwin.

C. B. FRY

The Founder of Modern Batsmanship (1939)

W. G. always reminds me of Henry VIII. Henry VIII solidified into
a legend when he had already involved himself in several matrimonial
tangles and had become overweighted with flesh and religious controversies. Yet Henry in his physical prime had been, even allowing for
the adulation of courtiers, the premier athlete of England, a notable
wrestler, an accomplished horseman, and a frequent champion in the
military tournaments of his time. So it is with W. G. He figures in
the general mind in the heavy habit of his latter years on the cricket
fields, a bearded giant heavy of gait and limb, and wonderful by
reason of having outlived his contemporaries as a giant of cricket.
Even when disputes in clubs and pavilions canvass the relative merits
of W. G., Ranji and Don Bradman, the picture in the minds of the
disputants is of a big, heavy Englishman, a slim, lithe Oriental and
a nimble, lightweight Australian. Even those of us who wag our
heads and utter the conventional and oracular statement, 'Ah, W. G.!
There will never be his like again,' do not properly realize who it is
who will never be like whom. Incredible as it may appear, I myself

never saw W. G. till I played against him for Sussex at Bristol at the age of twenty-two and the great man himself was forty-six. So my own memory of him begins only five years before he retired from Test-match cricket, and he was already corpulent and comparatively inactive, though he was yet to enjoy one of his most successful seasons as a batsman and score 1,000 runs in May. But I came into first-class cricket soon enough to meet many of the leading cricketers who had played with W. G. in his early prime, and who talked first-hand of the W. G. we ought to have in mind when we institute comparisons between him and Don Bradman . . .

One saw him at his best against fast bowling. In the days of Richardson, Mold, Lockwood and Kortright, I once asked him who was the fastest bowler he had played. He answered without hesitation, 'George Freeman.' If W. G. in his youth treated George Freeman as I saw him in middle age treat Tom Richardson, all I can say is that George Freeman went home a wiser if not a better bowler. There were no fireworks or extravagances. W. G. just stood at his crease to his full height (and everyone who wishes to play fast bowling well should so stand) and proceeded to lean against the ball in various directions and send it scudding along the turf between the fielders. No visible effort, no hurry; just a rough-hewn precision. He was not a graceful bat and he was not ungraceful; just powerfully efficient.

For a very big man specially addicted to driving he was curiously adept at cutting fast bowlers very late. He did not cut with a flick like Ranji or a swish like Trumper. Before the stroke he seemed to be about to play the ball with his ordinary back stroke, but at the last moment he pressed down quickly with his wrists, with an almost vertical swing, and away sped the ball past all catching just clear of second or third slip. I remember seeing him make about 80 at the Oval against Richardson and Lockwood at their best; he scored at least half his runs with this late cut peculiar to himself, and eventually he was caught in the slips off it. When he came up to the dressing room, hugely hot and happy, he sat down and addressed us: 'Oughtn't to have done it . . . Dangerous stroke . . . But shan't give it up . . . Get too many runs with it.' He then changed his shirt and his thick under-vest and went away to have a chat with Charlie Alcock, the Surrey secretary, who was a crony of his.

In his later years, when he was handicapped by his weight, he went in for one unorthodox stroke. W. G. never played the glance to leg or the modern diversional strokes in that direction. The ball just outside the leg stump, if he could reach it, he hit with a plain variant of his great on drive, and the ball went square with the wicket a little in front of the umpire. If the ball pitched on his legs, he played the old-fashioned leg hit with an almost horizontal sweeping swing – but, ye moderns, with his weight fully on his front foot. This was the stroke with which in his later years he hit the ball from outside his off stump round to square leg. The young Gloucestershire bloods used to call this the 'Old Man's cow shot'. What actually W. G. did was to throw his left leg across the wicket to the off ball and treat it as if it were a ball to leg bowled to him from the direction of mid-off or extra cover. I fancy he introduced this stroke to himself in his great year of revival in the latter part of some of his big innings. The original exponent was the noted Surrey batsman W. W. Read, who used it with much effect on fast wickets against accurate slow bowlers such as Peate, Peel and Briggs. In fact, the stroke is the genuine leg hit. Ranji told me that Walter Read had shown him how to do it at the nets and that it was an easy stroke, but I never saw Ranji try it in a match; he had plenty of strokes without it.

Thinking back on what I have written, I am wondering whether I have succeeded in conveying the individuality of W. G.'s batsmanship, his tremendous physique, his indomitable precision, and the masterful power of his strokes. At any rate, there they were, these characters, and no one who ever saw W. G. play will admit the near equality of any other batsman, even though he thought, as I do, that in pure technique Ranji was a better.

BERNARD DARWIN

Genial Giant (1934)

'W. G.', said an old friend of his, 'was just a great big schoolboy in everything he did.' It would be difficult in a single sentence to come nearer to the clue to his character. He had all the schoolboy's love for elementary and boisterous jokes; his distaste for learning; his desperate and undisguised keenness; his guilelessness and his guile; his occasional pettishness and pettiness; his endless power of recovering his good spirits. To them may be added two qualities not as a rule to be found in schoolboys: a wonderful modesty and lack of vanity; an invariable kindness to those younger than himself, 'except', as one of his most devoted friends has observed, 'that he tried to chisel them out lbw' . . .

It has been said that W. G. liked simple jokes, and if they were familiar ones of the 'old grouse in the gunroom type' so much the better. There seems to me something extremely characteristic about a story, very small and mild in itself, told by Mr C. E. Green in the *Memorial Biography.* Mr Green was Master of the Essex Hounds, and had the hounds brought for W. G. to look at after breakfast. He liked the hounds, and he liked the Master's big grey horse, and, Mr Green goes on, 'For years afterwards whenever we met he would sing out "How's my old grey horse?"' That is perhaps hardly worthy of the name of joke, but, whatever it was, it was the kind of friendly chaff that pleased W. G. He liked jokes to do with conviviality, for he was a convivial soul. Essentially temperate in his everyday private life, he enjoyed good things on anything in the nature of an occasion; he had, as I fancy, a kind of Dickensian relish for good cheer, not merely the actual enjoyment of it but also the enjoyment of thinking and talking about it, and he combined with this, of course, a much greater practical capacity than Dickens ever had. A whole bottle of champagne was a mere nothing to him; having consumed it he would go down on all fours, and balance the bottle on the top of his head and rise to his feet again. Nothing could disturb that magnificent constitution, and those who hoped by a long and late sitting to shorten his innings next day often found themselves disappointed. His regular habit while cricketing was to drink one large whisky and soda, with a touch of angostura bitters, at lunch, and another when the day's play ended; this allowance he never varied or exceeded till the evening came, and, despite his huge frame, though he never dieted, he ate sparingly. His one attempt at a weight-reducing regimen was the drinking of cider. As he believed in a moderate amount of good drink, so he disbelieved strongly in tobacco. He had been brought up in a non-smoking family (though his brother Alfred became a backslider), and stuck to its tenets religiously all his life. It was an aphorism of his that 'you can get rid of drink, but you can never get rid of smoke'. He constantly proclaimed it as his own private belief, but he never made any attempt to put his team on any allowance of tobacco.

Mr A. J. Webbe tells me that he remembers at his mother's house in Eaton Square, W. G. marching round the drawing room after dinner, bearing the coal scuttle on his head as a helmet, with the poker carried as a sword. It is an agreeable picture, and we may feel sure that W. G. was ready to go on marching just a little longer than anyone else, for his energy was as inexhaustible as his humour was childlike; he must be playing at something – billiards or cards, dancing or coal scuttles, anything but sitting down. The simplicity of his humour often took, naturally enough, a practical direction; in one corner of his mind there probably lurked all his life amiable thoughts of booby traps and apple-pie beds, and he was even known in an exuberant moment on a golfing expedition to hurl rocks at a boat like another Polyphemus.

He carried his practical joking into the realms of cricket, as when, according to a well-known story, he caused the batsman to look up at the sky to see some imaginary birds, with the result that the poor innocent was blinded by the sun and promptly bowled. With this we come to one of the most difficult questions about W. G.: did he at all, and, if so, how far, overstep the line which, in a game, divides fair play from sharp practice? There is one preliminary thing to say, namely that there is no absolute standard in these matters, and that standards differ with times and societies. The sportsmen of the early nineteenth century did, naturally and unblushingly, things that would be considered very unsportsmanlike nowadays. In those days everything was a 'match': each party must look after himself; it was play or pay, and the devil take the hindermost. Anybody who reads the autobiography of the Squire, George Osbaldeston, will get an insight into the sporting morals of that day. 'A noble fellow, always straight,' said Mr Budd of the Squire: but he deliberately pulled a horse in order to get the better of those who in his estimation had overreached him, and, generally speaking, it was one of his guiding principles in all sports not to let the cat out of the bag. He never did what he thought a dishonourable thing, but he had a different standard of honour from our own. I believe that in W. G. was found something of a survival of this older tradition. He had his own notions of what was right and permissible, and I am convinced that he would never willingly have done anything contrary to them; the difficulty arose when other people did not think something permissible and he did. He would never have dreamed of purposely getting in the way of a fieldsman who might otherwise have caught him, but to shout cheerfully to that fieldsman, 'Miss it,' was – at any rate in a certain class of cricket – not merely within the law, but rather a good joke.

The law was the law, though in his intense keenness he could not wholly rid himself of the idea that it was sometimes unjustly enforced against him; what the law allowed was allowable. It was always worth appealing; if the umpire thought a man was out lbw, it did not matter what the bowler thought. 'You weren't out, you know,' he was sometimes heard to say to a retiring batsman against whom he had appealed, and thought no shame to do so: everything was open and above board; if the umpire decided you were out – and he sometimes decided wrong – that was all about it. He wanted desperately to get the other side out, and any fair way of doing so was justifiable; he never stooped to what he thought was a mean way. No man knew the law better, and it could seldom be said against him that he was wrong, but rather that he was too desperately right. Sometimes the fact that he had the reputation of wanting his pound of flesh caused him to be unjustly criticized when his claim was an entirely proper one. There was a certain match between Gloucestershire and Sussex, in which, at the end of the second innings of Sussex, the Sussex total for two innings was exactly equal to that of Gloucestershire's one innings, and there were left some eleven or eleven and a half minutes of time. Ten minutes' interval left a minute or so in which to get the one run for a 10-wicket victory. W. G. properly declared that Gloucestershire should go in. Sussex to some extent seem to have demurred on the ground that there was not time for an over. However, they went out to field. Ranji had changed into ordinary clothes, and W. G. went out to field as substitute for him. Tate bowled the one over to Jessop, and nothing could be done with three balls. The fourth was pushed gently towards W. G. at point, and the run gained almost before he had had time to stoop. It is a subject for irreverent speculation what would have happened if the batsmen had been caught in two minds in the middle of the pitch. Would that ball have gone straight to the wicketkeeper or is it possible that there would have been an overthrow? . . .

It is idle to deny, I suppose, that he led umpires rather a hard life; some of them may have been frightened of giving him out, but if he ever intimidated them it was certainly not of malice aforethought; it was rather that irrepressibly keen boy in him that had never quite grown up, and would break out now and then on the impulse of the moment. A boy naturally and properly thinks the umpire a beast who gives him out, and if there was a Peter Pan in the world it was Dr W. G. Grace. On the whole it was fortunate for him that umpires are not a revengeful race; indeed they probably stood so much in awe of him as to give him sometimes the benefit of the doubt. I am afraid of retelling old stories, but here is one new at any rate to me. Gloucestershire were playing Essex, and, when he had made three or four, W. G. was, in the general estimation of both sides, caught and bowled by Mead. He stoutly declared it was a bump ball, and, after some palaver, he went on batting. In due course, Kortright knocked his middle and leg stumps down, and, as the Old Man made ready to depart, exclaimed, 'What, are you going? There's still one standing.' W. G. said he had never been so insulted in his life, 'but', as the Gloucestershire narrator added, 'he'd made enough runs to win the match' . . .

In writing a personal sketch of a famous man, it is usual to say something of his appearance. In the case of W. G. as a cricketer, this must be unnecessary. We all know the vast bulk, the black beard in later years streaked with grey, the red and yellow cap. There is, however, another aspect of him that is not familiar – W. G. as a private person in mufti, and not a flannelled general on the battlefield. One proud and lucky man possesses a photograph, which will remain unique, since the plate is broken. It shows W. G. in his everyday clothes just before he is going into the pavilion to change. It is the first morning of the deciding Test match at the Oval in 1896; he has been looking at the wicket, and discussing with F. S. Jackson what is to be done if he wins the toss. On his head is one of those square felt hats which we generally associate with farmers. He wears a black tailcoat and waistcoat, built on easy-going lines with an expanse of watch chain, dark trousers, a little baggy at the knee, and boots made for muddy lanes. In one hand is a solid blackthorn stick with a silver band round it. Future generations who see that photograph will protest that this cannot be a mighty athlete about to lead the chosen of England to victory. It must be, they will say, a jovial middle-aged doctor discussing the price of oats with a patient or neighbour that he has met in the marketplace. The man in that picture is W. G., but it is the one we do not know, the country doctor who had followed his father's business, and could never quite understand why not one of his three sons wanted to be a country doctor too.

The W. G. that we know best is not merely a celebrity but the central figure in a cricketing mythology. The stories about him are endless, and this can hardly be explained by the fact that he was the best of all cricketers, that he looked the part of a Colossus, and had an amusing way of saying characteristic things. There have been many other mighty players if admittedly below him; yet the sum of the stories about them all is, by comparison, negligible. Many of them, though very famous in their day, live for us now only as minor personages in the W. G. legend; they are remembered because they come incidentally into stories about him. In point of his personality, as it will be handed on by tradition for years to come, he towers as high above them as he towered above them in stature when he was alive. If this is not greatness, it is something for which it is hard to find another name. May we not say that, with all his limitations, his one-sidedness, his simplicity, W. G. possessed in an obscure and unconscious way some of the qualities of a great man?

⋆　⋆　⋆

Wicketkeepers are truly the game's underclass: seldom honoured, seldom written about, noticed only when they make a mistake. Yet to keep wickets is indisputably the most difficult job in cricket. The demands of the job greatly exceed those of batting, bowling or fielding. There is the additional weight one carries, the pads and gloves not required by your teammates. There is the low posture, sometimes made more uncomfortable by smelly and unwashed batsmen. A wicketkeeper must be vigilant and he must be fearless, prepared to go up or sideways, willing to be hit on heart or head. The job, in sum, requires the concentration of a heart surgeon, the reflexes of a fighter pilot and the guts of a boxer.

Here Ray Robinson pays tribute to a man known with reason as 'the Prince of Wicketkeepers'.

RAY ROBINSON

The Second Most Famous Beard in Cricket (1951)

Wicketkeepers are like office boys in at least one way – few people take notice of them until something gets in a mess, a folder or a chance is lost, an inkpot or a catch spilt, a mail or a stumping missed.

For hours on end wicketkeepers may do their duty well and truly, but mostly they are out of focus, so to say. The onlookers' gaze is held between wicket and wicket by the principals in the encounter, bowler and batsman; the keeper might as well be a second with towel and sponge, close at hand but on the non-combatant side of the ropes. Some even think of him as neutral; when the Deputy Speaker, James Joseph Clark, left the chair of the House of Representatives to speak on the bill to nationalize banks in Australia he said he had been the wicketkeeper for the greater part of the debate.

Yet the wicketkeeper is the most important of them all, the cricket field's VIP. If you think that is going too far, reflect on what is the most grievous loss a side can suffer. A team can survive loss of a batsman, even the greatest of them all; when Bradman (twisted ankle) did not bat against South Africa in the Melbourne Test in February 1932, other Australians did well enough to win by an innings. Loss of a bowler is usually more serious – there are fewer to spare – but is not always fatal. Though Voce broke down in the 1947 New Year Test at Melbourne and Edrich was out of action for most of a day, England still dismissed Australia for 365 and the match ended in a draw. But when the wicketkeeper falls out confusion usually sets in. Dropped catches and missed stumpings blunt the bowling and boost the score, overthrows make the fielding increasingly ragged, and extras find form entitling them to a higher place in the batting order. When Frank Woolley, in his last Test, deputized for Ames (lumbago) at the Oval in 1934, 37 byes got past the tall veteran's hands, hidden in unaccustomed gloves. Replacing Oldfield (head injury) in England's second innings in the Adelaide Test, 1932, Victor Richardson kept byes down to 17 but missed five chances. As stand-in for Sismey through the Australian Services' second unofficial Test against India, 1945, opening batsman Keith Carmody was eluded by 41 byes and took only one of ten stumping and catching opportunities on the Calcutta wicket. Carmody's candid comment: 'If I had accepted all the chances I'd have broken Don Tallon's record.' None of their fellow players blamed these three attractive batsmen for such costly inefficiency. For a non-keeper to be put behind the stumps is as bad as being called up from the stalls to replace a ballet dancer who cannot appear because of an awful headache. If the Americans ever take to cricket I guess that the first change they would make in the laws of the game would be to give a team the right to call a relief keeper into the job the moment anything went amiss with the first-priority timber-tickler.

Yet it is true that a retired cricketer, choosing a Test team in a newspaper, named eleven without a keeper. Next day an acquaintance accosted him: 'What about that team you picked, George?'

George: 'Pretty good side – isn't it?'

The acquaintance: 'No keeper.'

George (quickly remembering the opposing batting strength): 'They won't need one.'

As with William the Conqueror, the first of the line of great Test keepers, John McCarthy Blackham, has since been talked about more than most of those who have succeeded him in the monarchy that rules behind the stumps. Blackham was reputed to have been the first to take fast bowling without a longstop behind him to have a second go at the balls wicketkeepers found too hot to handle.* He said to one captain: 'What's that man doing behind me? Put him where he'll be of some use.' Blackham wore the gloves in the first seventeen Test matches on end. In all, he kept in 33 Tests, catching 36 Englishmen and stumping 24 with such speed and style that he earned the title Prince of Wicketkeepers. I was too young to see him keep, but in junior cricket in the Melbourne suburb of Brighton in the 1920s I had the privilege of being stumped by his younger brother, Fred; a member of the royal family, as it were. When I asked Fred whether the Prince had given him any hints about keeping wickets, he replied: 'Only one – to give it up and take on bowling.'

Jack Blackham was a brown-eyed bank clerk with a black beard pruned more to the shape of King Edward VII's than the unrestrained ziff that screened W. G. Grace's bronchial zone. He stood 5 ft 9½ in, weighed 11 st 3 lb, and walked to the wickets and between them with a quick step suggesting impetuosity. That appearance must have been deceptive, because no impulsive man can even begin to become a great wicketkeeper; snatching hands often rebuff the ball. Blackham played before keepers began to squat to await the bowling. He bent forward, rather like a man peeping through a keyhole. If prints of 1877 give a true picture, he spread his feet wider than most present-day keepers, the point of his beard was just outside the line of the

---

* George Pinder (Yorkshire) was credited with having been the first in England to do without a longstop to fast bowling.

off stump, and his hands were poised apart in front of his knees. A striped, narrow-peaked cap was set well back on his head, either to let a wave of dark forelock be seen or because the artist popped it on as an afterthought. More startling are two other things he is depicted wearing : a tie and the gloves. A modern keeper, who has 1¾ lb of gloves in his 6½ lb of equipment, would shy at the sight of Blackham's hand coverings: they look more like the light gauntlets motorists use. Yet with only this flimsy protection, Blackham usually stood right up to the stumps to the fast bowlers of his time, catching batsmen off Spofforth the Demon and Turner the Terror as confidently as he stumped them off Giffen the flighty. No wonder his hands became so severely damaged that in two of his thirty-five Tests and one innings of another he had to be rested from his post of danger and was played as an ordinary fieldsman. In the end, a broken finger finished his Test career in 1894, when he was thirty-nine.

His brother told me that Blackham, as a boy, had been taken by their father, a member of the Press Cricket Club, to see a match against a country team. Young Jack was called in to fill a vacancy and was sent to field in the slips. Some lure of the stumps soon began to work. As if drawn by a magnet, the boy edged closer to the wicket until he was taking the team's quickest bowlers with his bare hands, while behind him the Press backstop's gloves waved and flapped abortively. Among teammates watching the youth at close quarters was John Conway, captain of South Melbourne, who became manager of the Australian XI. The sequel was that at the age of eighteen Blackham was keeping for Victoria, and at twenty-one for his country in the first of all Test matches. The Demon and he became such a famous combination and Blackham's brilliance in taking fast balls at beard's length from the stumps so stirred the crowds that years afterwards men said the game of cricket had produced no greater spectacle. They say that for the remainder of his life Blackham had a cavity in his chest where one of Spofforth's fastest staved in his ribs.

Blackham's manner of appealing to umpires was quiet. Sometimes he merely raised his hand questioningly to bring the matter up for decision. Playing in a Victorian country town, he brought off an unprecedented feat by stumping a batsman off a fastish leg ball of the kind that usually had longstop at full stretch near the boundary

to save four byes. To Blackham's tenor 'How's that?' the square-leg
umpire replied: 'Wonderful.'

★ ★ ★

Victor Trumper was a batsman of dash and daring, his style memorial-
ized for posterity in the famous photograph, by G. W. Beldham, of
him jumping out to drive. He was the best loved of Australian
sportsmen, as much for his personality as for his batsmanship. The
Australian cricket writer and one-time Test opening batsman J. H.
Fingleton grew up on stories of Trumper. Here he recollects some
of them.

J. H. FINGLETON

Never Another Like Victor (1958)

On 28, June 1915, Victor Trumper died at Sydney in his thirty-eighth
year. His funeral caused the streets of the city to be blocked and he
was carried to his grave by eleven Australian cricketers. In London,
in the midst of World War I and all its momentous happenings, the
event was featured on newspaper posters, as, for example, 'Death of
a Great Cricketer'.

Men said then – and some in both Australia and England still say
it – 'There will never be another like Vic Trumper.'

I never saw Trumper bat; I was only a few years old when he
died. But so often have I listened to stories of him, so often have I
seen a new light come into the eyes of people at the mention of his
name, so much have I read of him, that I am prepared to believe
that nobody, before or since, ever achieved the standards of batsmanship set by Trumper. Sir Pelham Warner, Warren Bardsley, Vernon
Ransford and others saw all the great moderns and near-moderns –
Bradman, Ponsford, Hobbs, Hammond, Hutton, Compton, McCabe
and the like – yet there was more than loyalty to their own generation
when they cast their minds back over the years and said, 'There will
never be another like Vic.'

Many players, it is true, made more runs; but runs can never be accepted as the true indication of a player's greatness. A fighting innings of 30 or so under difficult conditions is lost in cold statistics, yet its merits may far outweigh many staid (and unnecessary) centuries that are recorded for all time. The longer I live, I am pleased to say, the less nationalistic I become. The outcome of a match is interesting but not, on the scales of time, of any great moment. What *is* important is whether a particular contest gives to posterity a challenge that is accepted and won, or yields in classical technique an innings or a bowling effort that makes the game richer, so that the devotee can say years afterwards, with joy in his voice, 'I saw that performance.'

Trumper went to bat one day against Victoria in Sydney on a wet pitch. The first ball from Jack Saunders (a terror on such pitches) beat him completely. Saunders' eyes lit up. His fellow Victorians grinned in anticipation. Trumper smiled broadly. 'Why, Jack,' he called down the pitch, 'what a thing to do to an old friend. Well, it's either you or me for it.'

And then, by dazzling footwork and miraculous stroke play, Trumper hit a century in 60 minutes.

At the beginning of 1904, in Melbourne, Trumper faced up to Rhodes and Hirst on a wet pitch. These Yorkshiremen were two of the greatest left-handed bowlers of all time and a wet Melbourne pitch was known as the worst in the world, with balls from a good length lifting quickly around the chin.

Trumper was first in and last out, for 74, in a total of 122. Hopkins made 18 and Duff 10. Noble, Syd Gregory, Trumble and Armstrong made 9 between them!

That innings caused Charles Fry, in one of his unpredictable moments, to rise suddenly from a reverie during a dinner in London and say: 'Gentlemen, charge your glasses. I give you the toast of the world's greatest batsman. Drink to Victor Trumper, first man in, last man out, on a bad pitch and against Hirst and Rhodes.'

Fry knew the full value of such an innings on such a pitch and against two skilled left-handers. His short and unexpected speech brought down the house.

No less interesting is the fact that Mrs Fry (who may or may not have had some knowledge of cricket) shared her famous husband's admiration of Trumper. My information on this point comes from the Sydney *Bulletin* of the period. It appears that Mrs Fry declared in a London periodical that Vic Trumper was an artist and that some day someone would paint his portrait and have it hung in a National Gallery. 'He will be', the lady said, 'dressed in white, with his splendid neck bared to the wind, standing on short green grass against a blue sky; he will be waiting for the ball, the orchestra to strike up.' . . .

My formative days in cricket were spent in the Sydney suburb of Waverley. We adjoined Paddington, the club of Trumper and Noble, but we yielded to no Sydney club in the proud possession of internationals and other first-class players. Carter, all the twentieth-century Gregorys, Kippax, Hendry, Collins, Frank O'Keefe (one of our very best batsmen who, denied opportunities, went to Victoria, hit two centuries in a game against New South Wales, and then went to the Lancashire League, there dying soon afterwards) and many other proficient players figured with Waverley and established the high standards of the district. One of the great sources of the club's strength was that cricket, and talk of it, flowed through the life of the district. All the internationals I have mentioned showed themselves on the local oval at practice during the week and played there in the club games on Saturday afternoons.

Saturday evenings and Sunday mornings were given over to post-mortems. We had four grade sides and promising youngsters, if unable to make the grade, were fitted in with the Veterans team where they played under the leadership of men such as Syd Gregory, Australian captain, and Tom Howard, treasurer of the 1934 team to England.

The returning warriors, coming from their games in distant suburbs, would meticulously report in at Bondi Junction on Saturday evenings and at Waverley Park on Sunday mornings – unless, of course, dire personal disaster induced them to go to ground for a week. At those rendezvous both players and critics gathered and form and happenings were first reported and then dissected and judged. It was a hard and discerning school of criticism. Those no longer able to play were in their element as they passed solemn judgment upon some 'shyster' or 'grubber' – Waverley terms for the lowly cricketer. Few merited the accolade of a 'great' performance. Even 'good' was seldom used. In the main, ranking varied from 'fair' to 'quite good'.

These critics – some lovely characters among them – knew their cricket. When they had disposed of the present they drifted, fondly, to the hallowed ground of the past, and always, I found, the day's reminiscences ended on Victor Trumper.

As I walked home I used to wonder how one cricketer could so capture the imagination above all others; and the imagination, moreover, of men so steeped in the game that they were the severest of critics. Yet even years after Trumper's death they spoke wistfully of him and would brook no interlopers. Nor criticism. Trumper was unique in that nobody ever criticized him as a cricketer or as a man. In England, in Australia, in South Africa, listening to men who knew and played against him, I never at any time heard a derogatory word said against Trumper. That could not be said of any other cricketer of any generation.

A mark of a great man is the power of making lasting impressions upon people he meets. Winston Churchill once wrote of F. E. Smith, the first Earl of Birkenhead: 'Some men when they die after busy, toilsome, successful lives leave a great stock of scrip and securities, of acres or factories or the goodwill of large undertakings. F. E. banked his treasure in the hearts of his friends, and they will cherish his memory until their time is come.'

That could also have been written of Trumper. He left no stock or securities. He was a singularly unsuccessful businessman. He ran a sporting-goods firm in the city of Sydney but he was too generous with his gifts to accumulate money. Once, on the morning of a Test, he was working in his shop and allowed time to elude him. He hurried into his coat, took down a new bat from the rack, caught a taxi to the Sydney Cricket Ground – and made 185 not out!

It has been said that this was the most brilliant and versatile innings ever played by the Master. The match was the famous one in which R. E. Foster, the Englishman, hit a brilliant 287 in his first Test and Clem Hill was concerned in the most tumultuous run-out in the history of Test cricket . . .

An admirer of Trumper came into his shop after the match and asked whether he could buy a bat Trumper had used.

Yes, he was told. There was the bat used in the recent Test.

The admirer's eyes sparkled. How much would it be?

'Well,' said the impractical Victor, 'it was a forty-five-shilling bat but it is now second-hand. You can have it for a pound.'

What a difference, this, from a modern I know who swapped a bat with which he had made a record for one of the most fabulous cars seen on a roadway . . .

Another tale of Trumper – there are dozens – was told me by Vernon Ransford, his comrade in many Australian XIs.

The Australians were dressing at Melbourne for a Test, against Sherwell's South Africans, when there came a knock at the door. Was Mr Trumper available?

Trumper went to the door and found a young man, a complete stranger, holding a bat. He was anxious to begin in the bat-making business. This was one of his bats and he wondered whether Mr Trumper would use it in the Test.

This usage of material is one of the niceties of 'amateur' sport. A successful player is retained to use the material of a certain sports outfitter. Not only, by his play, is he expected to bring glory and advertisement to the firm's goods, but he must also be well practised in presenting the name on his equipment whenever his photograph is being taken. Thus, when you see a triumphant winner of Wimbledon in a photograph, you have a fair chance of seeing also the name of the racquet used as the hero pushes it to the front. Strictly speaking, of course, amateurs are not allowed to associate their names with sporting goods – and knowing editors now sometimes help them to observe the proprieties by blacking out the name in the printed photograph!

That angle on sport was not developed in Trumper's day. He would have had in his bag several bats that suited him in weight and balance but, nevertheless, he didn't hesitate about accepting the young applicant's gruesome-looking bat. It weighed almost 3 lb 6 oz and it staggered his teammates.

'Surely', one of them said, 'you won't use that blunderbuss, Vic?'

'He's only a young chap and he's starting out in business,' replied Trumper. 'If I can get a few runs with this it might help him.'

He made 87 (probably wearying of lifting it!), inscribed it on the back with a hearty recommendation, and gave it back to the delighted young man.

Hanson Carter, the great wicketkeeper, was my first club captain. 'You must never', he once sternly told me, 'compare Hobbs, Bradman or anybody else with Trumper. If you want to try and classify the great batsmen in the game, put Victor Trumper way up there – on his own – and then you can begin to talk about the rest.'

So, too, with Charlie Macartney, upon whose shoulders the mantle of Trumper was supposed to have descended. He revelled in talking of the things Trumper did. So did Ransford. I sat with him in his office a few years ago when he was secretary of the Melbourne

Cricket Ground and he went into rhapsodies regarding the dismally wet season in England in 1902 when Trumper made 2,570 runs.

'If Vic had been greedy, it could have been 4,000,' said Ransford. 'His highest score, despite all the centuries he scored, was only 128. He could, obviously, have turned many of those centuries into double ones had he wished. But he was too generous. He looked around for some deserving character, a youngster maybe, or some player down on his luck, and unostentatiously gave him his wicket. That was Vic.'

Wisden's wrote of Trumper and that tour: 'Trumper stood alone. He put everybody else into the shade. No one, not even Ranjitsinhji has been at once so brilliant and so consistent since Dr W. G. Grace was at his best.'

The English bosie bowler, Bosanquet, clean bowled Trumper with the first bosie he sent down to him. 'Plum' Warner describes it:

It was in Sydney in 1903. Trumper and Duff had gone in first and in 35 minutes had scored 72 runs by batting, every stroke of which I remember vividly to this day. Bosanquet went on to bowl and his first ball pitched a good length just outside the off stump. Trumper thought it was a leg break and proceeded to cut it late, as he hoped, for four, but it came back and down went his off stump. Subsequently, he used to 'murder' Bosanquet but it is worth recording that the first 'googly' ever bowled in Australia bowled out the man who, in spite of all the fine deeds of Don Bradman, many Australians regard as the finest batsman their country has ever produced.

It is very doubtful if there has ever been a greater batsman and his wonderful deeds would have been even greater but for indifferent health, which, in the end, cut short his life.

No one ever played so naturally, and he was as modest as he was magnificent. To this day in Australia, he is regarded as the highest ideal of batsmanship. He was, I think, the most fascinating batsman I have seen. He had grace, ease, style and power and a quickness of foot both in jumping out and in getting back to a ball that can surely never be surpassed.

He had every known stroke and one or two of his own. When set on a good wicket it seemed impossible to place a field for him. He was somewhat slightly built, but his sense of timing was so perfect that he hit the ball with tremendous power. Most bowlers are agreed that he was the most difficult batsman to keep quiet. I have heard a great bowler remark, 'I could, in the ordinary way, keep most people from scoring quickly, but I always felt rather helpless against Trumper, for he was so quick, and he had so many strokes.' His brilliant batting stirred cricketing England. His unrivalled skill and resource will never be forgotten. No cricketer was ever more popular, and he deserved it, for he preserved the modesty of true greatness and was the beau idéal of a cricketer.

On one occasion, after batting brilliantly at Kennington Oval, Trumper 'ducked' an official dinner at night. The fact was, simply, that he didn't want to be talking 'shop' among cricketers and receiving plaudits. He was duly fined for missing an official engagement!

The South Africans had a quick introduction to Trumper. An Australian team called at the Union on the way home from England, where Trumper had had a most successful tour. There were opinions that Trumper wouldn't find the matting pitches of South Africa too easy and money changed hands to say that, in the few matches played there, Trumper wouldn't make a century. He hit a double-century in his very first game on the mat!

The South Africans in Australia in 1910–11 were mesmerized by his skill. This was the team with all the bosie bowlers, but Trumper cut, hooked and drove at will. He had a fascinating stroke against a fast yorker. He lifted his back foot, jabbed down on the ball with his bat at an angle and it streaked away to the square-leg boundary. Somewhat naturally, they called it the dog stroke.

He teased Percy Sherwell, the Springbok captain. When a fieldsman was shifted, Trumper deliberately hit the next ball where that man had been. He was a consummate master at placement. Later, somebody commiserated with Sherwell at having his captaincy, his bowlers and his fieldsmen torn to tatters while Trumper made 214; whereupon the Springbok said, 'Ah, don't talk about it. We have seen batting today.'

Neville Cardus, the Trumper of cricket writing, once wrote, 'The art of Trumper is like the art in a bird's flight, an art that knows not how wonderful it is. Batting was for him a superb dissipation, a spontaneous spreading of fine feathers.'

How unfortunate it is that Trumper slightly preceded the movie-camera age!

Posterity has the chance of seeing all the moderns in action, as it has of hearing all the great singing voices. Mr Menzies, our Prime Minister, has a thrilling film of Don Bradman – there are a number of copies of the same film in existence – and to see Bradman on the screen is to realize again, instantly, his great stature as a batsman. The speed of his footwork, the flay of his bat, the manner in which he 'smelt' the ball, so over the ball was his head – all this has been caught and kept for the years to come and, in the evidence of the film, there can be no possible disputation over Bradman's status in the game.

With Trumper it is different. All we have, so far as I know, are the several photographic 'stills' of him at the beginning of an off drive and at the finish and, also, of his stance at the crease. But these do portray his art. The two of him playing the off drive are technically perfect in every detail – his feet, his shoulders, his head, his back swing, his follow-through with the proper transfer of weight and then, finally, the full, flowing arc of the bat. His stance is perfection.

Those who saw and knew Trumper used to say that Macartney, Jackson and Kippax were reminiscent of him; but that even when they were at their greatest they served only to rekindle memories of the Great Man. He was, obviously, supreme on the field; and a man of kind and generous nature, of consideration for his fellow man, off the field. He embodied, to those who knew him, all that was good and noble in cricket and life.

'Where would you like your field placed?' 'Plum' Warner, as captain, once asked George Hirst. And Hirst replied, 'It doesn't much matter, sir, where we put 'em. Victor will still do as 'e likes.'

The evidence, then, would seem to be conclusive. Many of Trumper's greatest innings were played in the full face of adversity, the true test of worth. He rose to heights on wet wickets where others tumbled to earth. Although some half a dozen or so players down the years could be regarded as really great, Trumper, as Carter said, merits a niche of his own. He brought to the game an artistry, a talent, and an inherent modesty not manifested by any other cricketer. In short, he possessed all the graces.

*   *   *

Sydney Francis Barnes is generally reckoned to be the greatest of all bowlers. He took 189 wickets in 27 Tests: 7 a match – an average no one else has remotely approached. But he could easily have played twice as many Tests had he bent more willingly to authority, or played for a fashionable county. His magnificent bowling and truculent spirit are both captured in this remembrance. Its author, Bernard Hollowood, played with Barnes for Staffordshire, and himself ended up as editor of *Punch*.

BERNARD HOLLOWOOD

The Greatest of Bowlers (1970)

Easily the greatest of Staffordshire cricketers was Sydney Francis Barnes, who was born on 19 April 1873.

Three years ago, on the Saturday of a Lord's Test, I spotted him in the pavilion. He was alone, puffing at his pipe and glaring out through the Long Room window at the sun-drenched arena. I had not seen him since 1935 and I was amazed to find so little change in him. He stood as straight as a guardsman, and was as lean and leathery as in his heyday. As I watched him I remembered the profound shock I had experienced on first seeing him strip for action at Birkenhead Park. He then had seemed indecently ancient, senile almost . . . One corner of the changing-room was roped off by his paraphernalia, his shirts, liniments, embrocations, bandages, elastic supports; and a fearful odour seeped from this clutter. It was the smell of hospitals. I looked for formaldehyde and other embalming fluids, for crutches, wooden legs and scars of operations.

Barney was already a legend in my family. He was a contemporary of my father's and because I thought of my old man as . . . well, old, I naturally enough considered Syd as having one and a half feet in the grave. But he was a spry old bird and kept himself in good condition by regular exercise, moderation in all things, an enquiring mind and steady application in his civilian job as clerk and calligrapher.

But that was more than thirty years ago. Now, here he was, the same man, still glaring from furrowed brows, still stiff enough to suggest *rigor mortis*. After five minutes of nostalgic rumination I approached him.

'Mr Barnes,' I said, 'you won't know me, but . . .'

His head jerked from the cricket, his eyes twinkled and his face broke into the familiar smile of truculent superiority.

'Hollowood,' he said, 'Bernard Hollowood, Albert's lad. How are you?'

We shook hands and I congratulated him on his state of preservation. He began to talk about my father, about what Albert would have done to the rubbishy bowling being served up by the Test idols in the middle, and then he was suddenly engulfed by fans, young codgers of seventy and eighty, who descended on him like a pack of cub reporters. And of course I lost him.

My father regarded Barnes as the greatest bowler of all time, though he invariably spoke disparagingly of him in other contexts than cricket. They had played together for Staffordshire during Syd's golden years and had battled against each other on numerous occasions in the League. Barnes, my father said, was as mean as they come, and 'difficult' – by which I understood him to mean that he didn't care very much for Barnes's brand of heavy sarcasm and bitter comment. But there was no doubt whatever about his genius. 'Oh, yes, he could bowl 'em all, but he got his wickets with fast leg breaks. Marvellous, absolutely marvellous, he was. Fast leg breaks and always on a length.' Others, Barnes included, have claimed that he bowled every known ball except the googly – swingers, off breaks, top spinners, the lot. But undoubtedly his *chef d'œuvre* was the leg break. He took a long run, a bounding, springy run, and as his arm came over in a perfect action, mid-on and mid-off could hear the snap of his long fingers as they rolled and squeezed the ball into its revolutionary parabola. There has been no one like him. O'Reilly could bend them from leg, but not with Barnes's consistency or devil: Douglas Wright could bowl fastish leg breaks, but not on the length that destroys and goes on destroying.

He was a strange man, a social misfit in the cricket scene of Victorian, Edwardian and Georgian days. He might have been a Keir Hardie or a George Lansbury or a Frank Cousins if he had turned his mind to politics, for he was forever kicking against the pricks and quarrelling with the Establishment. He considered himself under-valued by his employers, insufficiently recognized, and overworked, and he would down tools as readily as an East End docker. Throughout his long playing career he carried outsize chips on his shoulder, and not one of the many clubs he played for could ever be certain of his unqualified loyalty and cooperation.

He resented discipline not because he wanted complete freedom but as a matter of principle. At all levels of the game he had to be handled with kid gloves – by captains, colleagues and committees. Outspoken himself, he resented outspokenness in others and displayed acute sensibility to any word or deed that slighted his personal Bill of Rights. Put on to bowl at the 'wrong' end, he would scowl and sulk and develop mysterious physical disorders, sprains and strains. Time and time again his career was broken by some real or imagined injustice. He would be on top of the world, the master bowler wanted by his country, a dozen counties, scores of league clubs: and then he would disappear from public view. At the height of his powers he dropped out of the England team for years at a stretch. He sampled county cricket, played a match or two and quit.

The most common reason for these surprising exits was finance. Cricketers are poorly paid today: in Barnes's time they scratched a living and unless they found jobs during the winter – which wasn't easy – those with family responsibilities existed only marginally above the subsistence line. The old pro of the sentimental school of cricket writers is a dear fellow, nut-brown and salty-tongued, who reminisces cheerfully with pipe and pint at every opportunity. In reality, a majority of the county cricketers who ended their careers before the Hitler war found their middle and old age blighted by poverty. There were no pension funds for them, no large lump sums from benefit matches, and only a handful, the spectacularly successful, picked up good money on the side from journalism, authorship, lecturing, advertising, coaching and sponsoring. There was no money in radio, and television was not yet in action.

The players had no union to protect them, so that they were more or less compelled to accept whatever wage their counties thought reasonable, and the counties were governed by autocratic amateurs who treated the professionals with the kindly condescension that they reserved for their domestic servants, gardeners and local tradesmen. And it was this that made Barnes see red. His trouble, at root, was that he demanded equality of opportunity and the abolition of class distinctions fifty or sixty years before the rest of the country, and at a time when the lot of the vast majority was docile servitude.

His take-it-or-leave-it attitude of no compromise was a new

phenomenon in industrial relations – on the employees' side – and obviously it produced deadlock when matched by similar obstinacy from the bosses. Barnes asked for travelling expenses on top of his wage; the county told him that the wage included the travelling expenses; Barnes said that if they didn't meet his modest request he would leave the club; the county said they couldn't be dictated to by players. End of contract. Barney retires fuming to his tent. He told the Lancashire secretary that he expected the county to find him a decent job during the winter and was rebuffed, the secretary saying that 'it couldn't be bothered'. Barnes was promised a benefit match if he served the club dutifully and successfully for eight years, and Syd asked for the Roses Match, Lancashire v. Yorkshire, at Old Trafford on a bank holiday. The secretary explained that the club had never done as much for other players and couldn't make an exception for Barnes. So Barnes walked out.

On the field he was always a trier, always active mentally and physically. He wanted the game to be run his way and was openly critical of almost every captain he played under. If his advice was not heeded he grumbled and then retreated into cold fury. He set himself the highest standards of play and could not tolerate inefficiency in others. His masters paid by results and Barnes sweated and schemed to achieve rewarding figures, and anyone who reduced the effectiveness of his efforts through slackness, inability or misfortune had to suffer the consequences, scathing looks and words and a display of icy scorn.

His colleagues admired his skills, but were terrified of incurring his displeasure and found games with him a sore trial. So there was no great outcry when the selectors omitted the name Barnes, S. F., from their national elevens. I suspect that on these occasions – and they were numerous – all the more easy-going Players and most of the Gentlemen breathed a sigh of relief . . .

Barnes was always certain that he knew better than the umpire, and his method of registering displeasure with a decision was to stare at the official hard and long, his lean features loaded with disgust and contempt. These staring sessions seemed to last for minutes on end and were acutely embarrassing to everyone except Barnes. I was batting with him in his last match for Staffordshire at Castleford in 1935 when he was given out, lbw, to the Yorkshire fast bowler Hargreaves. From the other end he looked dead in front, but Barnes stood his ground and glowered at the umpire for so long that

I honestly thought he had refused to go. The fielders watched, immobile and fascinated, and the umpire looked distinctly uncomfortable. Then, with the passing of aeons, old Syd turned and marched to the pavilion with a face like that of Mr Hyde.

Thirty years ago I wrote a piece for the *Boy's Own Paper* in which I described Barnes's method of psychological warfare against tremulous batsmen.

All who have been fortunate enough to play with him . . . are agreed that as a bowler of length and spin, Barnes has no equal. Even one of our youngest cricketers, the record-breaking Len Hutton, has said, 'One of my best innings was against Sydney Barnes when I was sixteen; I scored 69 not out.' I remember that innings of Hutton's, and I recall the warm praise it received from Barnes. The master, or the 'maestro' as he is known in Staffordshire, turns the ball with equal facility from leg or off without ever losing a perfect length. His field placing is a work of art. It is not a matter of 'a bit deeper' or 'round a little'. When Barnes moves him a fieldsman must proceed to an appointed spot, mathematically determined, *and stay there.*

Denbighshire were batting and near 'stumps' on the first day had lost three wickets – all to Barnes. The game had been held up by rain and Staffordshire badly wanted another wicket before the close. The last over was called and the spectators moved to the gates. Barnes was bowling. The batsman defended stubbornly. Five balls were played carefully. Then, in the middle of his long springy run for the last ball, Barnes stopped. He motioned to me at point (two yards from the bat). His long fingers made some sign which I did not understand, but I moved round to silly mid-off. After all, there was only one ball. Once again Barnes turned to bowl, and once again his eyes swept the field as he began his run up to the wicket. I was watching, my hands cupped. His delivery arm was almost over when he halted suddenly, and looked at me with a face as black as thunder. Then, while the crowd laughed derisively, he walked up the pitch and led me (almost by the hand) to the position he had in mind. 'The old buffer,' I thought. 'How does *he* know what the batsman will do?'

By this time the poor batsman was in a terrible state. He looked hard at me, and I saw panic in his eyes. Barnes bowled.

The batsman prodded forward and the ball popped, so gently, into my waiting hands. It was typical of the 'maestro'.

... My last memory of him will always be of Barnes sitting late at night in the lounge of a Manchester hotel. He is surrounded by young Staffordshire players and we are begging him to reveal some of his secrets. We buy him drinks and he twinkles and chuckles. He rolls a ball in his long fingers and manipulates it like an Epstein fondling a clay bust. The topspinner like this, see! The leg break like so. The outswinger, well, hold the ball this way . . . It is obvious that he considers the demonstration a waste of time. He can tell us what to do, but we couldn't possibly do it. There was only one Barnes. 'Whatever you do,' he adds, 'don't bowl outside the off stump. Don't wait for the batsman to get himself out – always attack, and always bowl at the stumps.'

Finally, let me quote from Ian Peebles on Barnes. In his excellent book *Batter's Castle* Ian writes:

Walter Robins was playing for Sir Julien Cahn's team, a very strong side, against Staffordshire at Stoke, and was amongst those shot out for less than 80 by the youthful sixty-year-old Barnes. The position was indeed parlous when they came in to bat again, well behind, and Sir Julien took desperate counsel of Walter, who recommended one and all having a bash. To this suggestion Sir J. replied that he had better lead the way, so that Walter in due course took middle and leg and awaited his first experience of Barnes with the new ball. It was quite something; in fact, Walter recalls it as one of the most beautiful overs he has ever seen bowled. The first was the outswinger, which just missed the off stump. The second was an in-dipper, and the defender pulled his umbilicus smartly out of the way as it shot over the leg stump. The next was a leg break and, just to keep things symmetrical, this missed the off stump again; a yorker, an off break and then the last ball of the over, another leg break. Trying to smother it, the batsman just snicked it and almost before it arrived in the wicketkeeper's gloves all present appealed. To their astonishment, and that of the striker, the umpire said, 'Not out,' and Walter lived to fight another day, or at least another over. Be it said for Sir Julien, who liked to win, that on seeing his adviser in such a tangle he laughed until he cried. Meanwhile Walter had come to a powerful decision, and at the start of the next over, abandoning all thought of trying to parry this superb artistry, he rushed down the wicket and let the bat go. In the circumstances it was sheer vandalism, but it worked, and 16 runs came from the face, edges and back of the bat. This was too much for Barnes, who, with the temperament inseparable from genius, snatched his sweater and left the battle to lesser fry.

* * *

A question the Yorkshire writer A. A. Thomson liked to ask was: 'Who was the finest all-rounder in the history of the game?' Thomson would then supply the answer himself: 'No one can say for certain, but we know that he batted right-handed and bowled left, and that he was born in Kirkheaton.'

In time the career of Garfield Sobers would consign this question to the realm of antiquity, but until about 1960 it remained a clever one to ask. For those vital statistics fitted both George Herbert Hirst and Wilfred Rhodes. Hirst bowled left-arm fast-medium, and was a master of late inswing. Rhodes bowled slow left-arm, with consummate control and artistry. Hirst batted in the middle order, an attacking player whose particular glory was the pull shot. Rhodes was a careful batsman, a sharp runner of short singles who for both Yorkshire and England steadily worked his way up from No. 11 to No. 1. And both were born in the stone village of Kirkheaton.

The Kirkheaton twins took Yorkshire to many a county championship, but it was Rhodes who had much the better Test record. He also lived longer. On his ninetieth birthday he was the subject of this loving portrait by the former England wrist-spinner Ian Peebles.

IAN PEEBLES

The Colossus of Rhodes (1967)

In Spain, when they found a champion bullfighter, they used to say there must have been a lot of salt in the air the day he was born. In days gone by there must have been more sulphur than salt in the air of Kirkheaton, but it seems to have been equally stimulating. In this small Yorkshire village were born two of the greatest cricketers of all time.

If Yorkshire cricket ran to canonization it is pretty certain that the senior of these, George Hirst, would be its patron saint. Apart from his cricketing ability, he was a man of such integrity, courage and completeness of character that, on his death, after thirty years in retirement, the *Daily Mail* devoted its leader to him, citing his life as an example to the nation. This must be almost unique among tributes to sportsmen.

It is perhaps an equally unusual tribute to a man to start by acclaiming his elder, but Wilfred Rhodes would be the first to do so. Ninety years old on 27 October, he would have no other peer in the Yorkshire Hierology.

Only on referring again to Mr Sydney Rogerson's admirable biography was I reminded that he started life cleaning railway engines. Any cricketing lover of the steam locomotive would see that in robust, practical, purposeful character there must have been a profound bond between the cleaner and his charges. Ironically, he lost his job largely because of his single-minded devotion, otherwise the name of Rhodes might well have been coupled with those of Gresley and Stanier, rather than linked with those of Hirst and Hobbs.

All the world knows what Rhodes achieved in his long and astonishing career and, to some extent, what he said and thought. In writing of him the little I can add is of random personal glimpses and stories of him over forty years of intermittent encounters and conversations with mutual friends. These I will retail exactly as the subject would have them related – 'warts and all'.

The first time I saw this august figure close to was at Scarborough, just a year after he had won a Test match for England at the age of forty-eight. He played Bob Wyatt hard on to his left leg, whence the ball rebounded on to his right and, after a scuffle like a man trying to chop a rat lodged between his ankles, on to the stumps. The young smirked, but avoided the keen, unsmiling blue eye.

There were no frills about his batting. He had taken good sound basic materials and, by unremitting application, turned himself into a Test-match opening batsman. His attitude to the job was perfectly illustrated by Aubrey Faulkner's description of the Englishmen's first encounter with the South African googly quartet on matting wickets. Hobbs conquered them by sheer skill. Rhodes refused to be defeated.

Thus, when Hobbs had scored 50 out of the first 60 runs with elegant ease, Rhodes would have held them at bay by crowding everything into action, from the toe of his boot to the point of his thumb. Rueful jesters who addressed him as a lucky old so-and-so received the terse unarguable reply 'I'm still 'ere.'

He was not an effusive man while an active cricketer. When he spoke it was very much to the point, and sound sense. The listener was expected to respond in like vein and he was not a man for flippant banter. On tour in the West Indies he grew irritated with Ewart Astill, a musician who liked to joke, and ended one exchange with the stern reproof 'Tha's nowt but roody piano sergeant.' Which, incidentally, goes to show that the arts had their proper, but not exaggerated, place in a sensible man's scale of things.

It was on this tour of 1929–30 that Rhodes showed that his stamina and uncanny skill made him, at the age of fifty-two, still a most potent force. Illness and injury elsewhere threw an immense amount of work upon him, and he bowled over 500 overs in the heat. Never did the dashing West Indian batsmen get hold of him on their shirt-front wickets. Nigel Haig used to recall Wilfred bowling one end throughout a humid day, dropping unerringly into a bowler's footmark just outside the off stump. This was not to the home supporter's taste and there were great shouts of 'You no sportsman, Mistah Rhodes – you hidin' de ball.' They might as well have appealed to the Rock of Gibraltar. 'I'll give 'em hiding the ball,' he said, and dropped the next over all on the same tiny patch.

It was after this tour that one England cricketer, Greville Stevens, said that it was not until he had played with Wilfred that he realized how little he knew about the game. This great knowledge Rhodes would pass on to the young who were prepared to take pains. He instructed and guided and, although he would on occasions give measured encouragement, he did not indulge youth. Once, when a lad, I got him caught at the wicket off what I thought was rather a good ball. As he passed by he put the matter in proper perspective. 'Can't see 'em like I used to,' he said. Never mind, I knocked Emmott Robinson's castle down next ball, surely a right royal brace.

Wilfred Rhodes was certainly never a man to court popularity. He did and said what he thought was right, and he commanded immense respect. Perhaps because of this even his own side, being human, would occasionally enjoy the mishaps that cricket can bring to the most august, when they befell him. I was brought up on the

tale of Frank Mann hitting him thrice into the upper regions of
the Lord's pavilion, to the ill-concealed glee of the fielders. Apparently the victim bore this affront, if without pleasure, at least without
comment until his eye fell on Roy Kilner bent double with merriment
at mid-off. It was too much. The bowler stopped in his run. 'What
the bludy 'ell are you laffing at?' he demanded.

My last encounter with him on a cricket field was in somewhat
similar circumstances, I desperately holding up an end at Bradford
while Pat Hendren raced along at the other. Pat hit a couple of sixes
into the football ground then, chasing down the wicket, slipped and
fell yet got the bat to the ball. At the end of the over the great
man collected his sweater and, for the moment, we stood together,
separated from the rest of the field. He gave me a sinister smile.
'You're backing up a bit too soon, Mr Peebles,' he said. 'You don't
mind if we roon you out.' It was only right that someone should be
rebuked at that moment, and I felt rather proud that I should have
been the only one available.

His humour had the same realistic ring as his general demeanour,
penetrating but without cynicism. He was the first man I ever heard
describe a benevolently contrived contest as 'coostomer's game'.
I also liked his revealing tale of the visiting league pro sitting on
the bench with his opposite number when assailed by a scruffy little
dog. 'Git away, tha' dirty little rat,' says the visitor. 'Look out,' says
the host, 'that's president's dog.' 'Eh – president's dog,' says the
visitor. ''Ere – Spot, Spot, Spot.'

Now at ninety Wilfred Rhodes is completely blind and revered
in every cricketing country. He is more loquacious than in days of
yore, and wonderful company. I have said he was never one to court
popularity. Yet he is an enormously popular man – for affection can
readily grow from respect, even if the reverse is seldom true.

Next time we meet I shall ask him about railway engines.

* * *

All the major sports played by North Americans are of their own
invention – baseball, basketball and American football. Oddly enough,
the first international cricket match was played between the United
States of America and Canada – in 1844, thirty-three years before the

first England–Australia Test. Cricket was played here and there on that vast continent, but with most intensity and focus in the Anglophilic city of Philadelphia. It was in this city that, at the turn of the century, John Barton King made his bid to be recognized as one of the game's greats. The case is well made by Ralph Barker in this celebration of the bowler and wit.

Incidentally, the old Quaker college of Haverford, located just outside Philadelphia, has one of the finest cricket libraries in the world. And the city still has a cricket league, although the teams are likely to be made up of West Indians, Indians and Pakistanis.

RALPH BARKER

The American Lillee (1970)

Cricket is not much of a game for shooting a line. The 'first-baller' and the 'nought-for-plenty' are always waiting round the corner. Even the most ebullient chatterer is usually silent for a time after dropping a catch. Yet confidence in one's ability is perhaps the main requisite for success. 'I'm fastest bowler in England,' Freddie Trueman used to say, and because he believed it, he probably was. And it is this cocksure confidence which is the Yorkshireman's strength and which makes him so feared an opponent. 'Give me the ball,' says the Yorkshire bowler, 'and I'll bowl the boogers out.' And because he believes it, he probably will.

Whatever would happen if the Americans took up cricket as their national game? With their unshakeable belief in themselves and the American way of life, they would surely be unbeatable.

The Americans, of course, *did play* cricket – and a few of them still do. Seventy-five years ago, in the city of Philadelphia, a race of native American cricketers, whose ancestors had introduced cricket into America 200 years earlier, came to maturity and flourished for a brief but glorious span of twenty years. They had beautiful grounds, splendid pavilions and good wickets. The standard of their inter-club competition was not far below that of the English first-class game. They undertook five tours of England, including three major ones in 1897, 1903 and 1908, when they played many of the first-class counties, and they were visited by many touring sides, including Australian teams on their way home from England, whom they sometimes beat. They had many great players, batsmen and bowlers, at least half a dozen of whom would have been successful – indeed, were successful – in any company. And coinciding exactly with this great era was the career of the greatest of all American cricketers, one whose achievements may be said to demand a place for him among the immortals, John Barton King . . .

Bart King was born in Philadelphia on 19 October 1873, and as a boy his game was baseball. He had had no coaching as a cricketer when he played his first match for the Tioga juniors at the age of fifteen, in 1889. He was then played as a batsman. Tioga were one of the senior clubs who competed for the Halifax Cup, the cricket championship of Philadelphia, and King was chosen occasionally for the senior side. Because of his physique – he was nearly six feet tall and still growing – he was soon tried as a bowler in junior matches, and he showed such promise that he was urged to practise and to develop this side of his game. The result was that in junior cricket that year he took 37 wickets at an average of 2.40. He bowled just above medium pace at this time, with an orthodox action.

In common with many other young Americans, King had learned to put swerve on the ball when pitching at baseball. The simplest form of baseball swerve was the 'roundhouse' which was pitched with an action and grip similar to the off break in cricket, but which, when thrown with a bent elbow, curved outwards all the way. But such a uniform curve was not very effective, and all the best baseball pitchers discarded it and developed a delivery which stored up its swerve until the last fifteen feet of flight. This they knew as the 'hook', because it travelled straight for most of its flight and then curved in late in the form of a hook. To achieve such a swerve when throwing was, King knew, comparatively easy, but to produce it with a legitimate bowling action at cricket was another matter.

For his first two or three seasons with Tioga, King developed his pace until by the time he was eighteen he was genuinely fast. And it wasn't until he found genuine pace that he discovered that he could sometimes make the ball swerve. The fact that he was swerving was pointed out to him by the Tioga wicketkeeper, and King, realizing from his knowledge of baseball that if he could produce this swerve at will he would have a formidable weapon, began to analyse his methods and, in cooperation with the wicketkeeper, to try to isolate the characteristics that seemed to accompany swerve . . .

Every major American club at this time had its pair or more of swing bowlers, so it was not difficult for King to learn as he went along. Yet these bowlers admitted that curving the ball, although undoubtedly a science, remained something of a mystery and was not always effective. King determined to develop a method which was effective always, and before the end of his career he was able to declare that he could make even an old ball swing to some extent under all conditions. He could, at least, always swing the ball in. Because of his long arm and supple body he was able to bowl the inswinger from a point so far overhead that his hand and wrist were actually over his left shoulder, with the seam pointing roughly from mid-off to long leg: thus he approached the trajectory of a left-arm bowler bowling round the wicket, slanting the ball in with the arm.

King believed in those early days that the ball that curved outwards was of less value than the inswinger; yet he bowled both. He bowled the outswinger with a lower arm, but he found that it tended to lose pace off the pitch, and he used it mainly for variation.

This was the bowler who emerged as a permanent member of the Tioga senior eleven in the summer of 1892 – tall, strong, self-confident, fast, accurate and with a late swerve that soon began to take batsmen by surprise. He was not yet, perhaps, quite the powerful, compact figure that he became in his twenties, and he still retained something of the untidy angularity of youth, but with his long, bounding run up to the wicket, the ball gripped in both hands high above the head in the manner of the baseball pitcher in the final stride, he was a terrifying sight to batsmen. At the end of that wild gyration of arms there was a beautifully smooth shoulder and body swing as the ball was delivered at a great pace.

King's bowling for Tioga that year earned him his first chances in representative cricket; he played in the annual match for the United States against Canada, and he played for the Gentlemen of Philadelphia against the Gentlemen of Ireland, who were the tourists that year. Against Canada he made a successful start, taking 3 for 6 and 2 for 15, and in three representative matches against the Gentlemen of Ireland he was the leading American bowler, taking 19 wickets at an average of 13.53. He was still under nineteen.

In the following year, 1893, the Australians visited Philadelphia on their way home from their English tour that summer. They were a strong all-round side, but they were stale after an arduous tour, and they unwisely agreed to play a representative match against the full strength of Philadelphia the day after landing from a rough crossing of the Atlantic. But – the full strength of Philadelphia! What did that amount to? Australian teams had stopped at Philadelphia before, and although they had had one or two surprises, they knew that the opposition was not strong. Representative Philadelphian sides had toured England, it was true, but their standard had not been above club level, and it had been against the clubs and teams of amateurs that they had played. An Australian Test-match eleven could be in no possible danger.

The ground at Elmwood, Philadelphia, seemed small to the Australians; the leg boundary on one side was especially short. The grass at this time of year – September – was coarser than in midsummer, but the wicket looked good. The Philadelphians won the toss and batted first; and the Australians soon realized their mistake. The ground seemed to them to roll like the deck of the liner on which they had so recently crossed the Atlantic. In the circumstances they were glad they were in the field, but they dropped numerous catches, seemed unable to devise a plan to cope with the short boundary and allowed the Philadelphians to run up the huge total of 525. King, not yet recognized as a batsman, went in last and made 36. The Australian bowling was completely collared, and for long periods the only hope of a wicket seemed to be a run-out; three of the Americans were in fact dismissed in this way. The leading Australian bowlers, George Giffen and Hugh Trumble, took, respectively, 0 for 114 and 2 for 104!

By the time the Australians' turn came to bat, it was expected that they would have recovered from their ocean crossing. But they now encountered another problem in the swerve bowling of Bart King, so that they felt they were back in the middle of the Atlantic. They were all out for 199, and King took 5 for 78, his victims including Bannerman, Giffen, Harry Trott, and W. Bruce, who had topped the Australian Test-match averages in England that year. Following on, the Australians were all out a second time for 258, so the Gentlemen of Philadelphia, as their team was always styled, had won by an innings and 68 runs. It was a result that created a major sensation throughout the cricket world, and indeed it was astonishing that a single American city could turn out a side capable of beating the full strength of Australia.

The Australians won the return match by 6 wickets, and many people were inclined to shrug off the first result as a freak. But not

Blackham, the Australian captain. 'You have better players here', he told the Philadelphians, 'than we have been led to believe. They class with England's best and reflect great credit on your country. With some improvement, you should soon be able to beat England at her own game.' . . .

It was in the 1896 season that King moved to Belmont, which was to remain his club for the next seventeen seasons, and for whom his greatest performances in American cricket were to be achieved. And it was in 1896 that he won the Childs Bowling Cup, the premier award for bowling in American cricket, for the first time.

Then, in 1897, came the first major tour of England. Exciting as the prospect was to Philadelphian cricketers, who believed that it would be the finest possible way of improving and publicizing their cricket, it aroused little general interest in America. 'Cricket has never been popular here as a field sport,' said the *New York Herald* in an editorial wishing the team luck just before it sailed. 'It is too slow for the average American, but Philadelphians like it.' The American temperament, it seemed, was better suited to the individual and personal clash involved in tennis or golf. These two games, indeed, were getting a strong hold even in Philadelphia, and all the leading cricket clubs were becoming social clubs where all three games could be played. Philadelphians hoped, however, that their successes on the cricket field would encourage young Americans to take up the game. The Philadelphian tour, which was to be of two months' duration and to include fifteen first-class matches, began modestly. Their games did not attract the crowds, and few people were inclined to take them seriously as cricketers. The Americans play cricket? Not against the first-class counties, surely. It was not until the Sussex match at Brighton on 17 June that the Philadelphians established themselves on the English cricket scene. Sussex fielded a strong side – a compliment that was not paid by some of the other counties – and the Philadelphians, batting first, made 216, thanks largely to a fourth-wicket stand of 109 between King and the best of the American batsmen, J. A. Lester. Then, in less than an hour, and on a perfect wicket, Sussex were bowled out for 46. A strong breeze was blowing across the ground, and King, choosing the end where the wind came over his left shoulder, bowled 10 overs, 5 maidens, and took 7 Sussex wickets for 13. He clean bowled Ranji first ball, and he also clean bowled Murdoch and Vine. Ranji afterwards described how King's bowling seemed to spring at him from the wicket, and the ball that bowled him in this innings swung so late as to be unplayable.

Sussex followed on, and this time they scored 252, Ranjitsinhji getting 74, by which time the respect between batsman and bowler was mutual. Indeed King admitted that when Ranji got going he had no idea how to bowl to him. 'One ball may be pitched up and hit for four between cover point and extra cover, and the next, pitching in exactly the same place, may go for four between square and fine leg.' But Ranji's innings could not save Sussex, and the Philadelphians won by 8 wickets.

King on this tour was genuinely fast, and an indication of this came in a telegram that was sent on 5 July by the touring side to the committee in Philadelphia, asking for another wicketkeeper to be sent 'as Mr Ralston's hands are quite used up'. A replacement sailed two days later.

Another fine Philadelphian victory was against Warwickshire in the ninth match of the tour. Warwickshire made 296 (King 5 for 95) and 201 (King 7 for 72). The Philadelphians made 269 in their first innings, 27 runs behind, and then, after being set 229 to win, they got them for five wickets, King making 46 not out.

Like all bowlers, King had days when nothing would go right for him, when the ball wouldn't swing and when batsmen became established and he couldn't break through. One such instance on this tour was in the match against Gloucestershire at Bristol. King beat W. G. Grace before he had scored, but Grace got an inside edge and the ball streaked through for four: Grace made no further mistake and went on to get a hundred. Jessop followed and did the same, and Gloucester made 363. King's figures, though, did him credit – 36 overs, 7 maidens, 2 for 100.

Nothing impressed English cricketers so much as the manner in which the Philadelphians played their cricket. Cricket in Philadelphia was played because the men who took part in it loved it for itself and not because of any public demand; thus it was purely amateur. In addition, the Americans were so obviously determined to learn and to improve their cricket: their zest and enthusiasm were refreshing, and they played the game in the best possible spirit. On one occasion, for instance, against Somerset, when the wicket was dangerous, King was taken off. The Bath wicket had its terrors even then. 'They have made friends everywhere,' said the magazine *Cricket*, adding, apparently in some astonishment, 'and not a single word has been said in their disfavour; there has been no necessity for it.'

On this tour King averaged 20 with the bat, finishing fifth in the Philadelphian averages, and in the fifteen matches he bowled 655.4 overs and took 72 wickets at an average of 24.02. These were good figures in a side in which he was called upon to bowl for long periods and in which the standard of catching was not high.

Long before the end of the tour, several counties were casting covetous eyes on Bart King. He was a splendid and colourful all-rounder, deadly serious about his cricket and yet full of personality, and he received several offers to stay in England to play in county cricket. To observe the niceties, these offers were generally made through intermediaries, and as no one imagined that King would play as a professional, other inducements had to be offered. A prominent member of one county, notoriously thin in fast bowling, asked whether King would be likely to consider an offer of what he termed 'a cricket clerkship', under which his financial status would be assured outside the game. Several such 'clerkships', however, had already been offered and rejected, so the county's intermediary was obliged to produce his trump card.

'How would he like to marry a rich woman?'

The intermediary for King raised his eyebrows; here was some-thing new. 'We have a widow', went on the county's intermediary, 'with £7,000 a year. That would leave him nothing to do but shoot in the winter, and play cricket all the summer.'

'What would the widow say about that?'

'She is very fond of the county,' was the reply, 'and a liberal subscriber.' Liberal indeed! But this offer, like all the others, was declined . . .

The Philadelphians did not tour England again until 1903, but King's performances in the intervening years, in the Halifax Cup and against touring sides, were often astonishing. In 1901, for instance, an English team led by Bosanquet played two matches against the Gentlemen of Philadelphia, and King's figures were 8 for 78, 6 for 57, 6 for 74 and 3 for 28 – 23 wickets in four innings at an average of 10.3. When his swerve was acting right no one could cope with him; but even more important, he was still a great bowler when the conditions were not in his favour.

It was on their second tour of the English counties that the Philadelphians reached, perhaps, their highest standard as an all-round side. Of their 16 first-class matches they won 7, lost 6, and drew 2 (the other match being abandoned), putting themselves in the category of a good average county side. And in the course of their tour they brought off two really outstanding victories, one against Lancashire and the other against Surrey. Lancashire, it is true, were not at full strength, four of their players being engaged in the Gentlemen v. Players match at Lord's, but Surrey fielded a strong side . . .

In first-class matches on the 1903 tour King bowled 451 overs and took 78 wickets at an average of 16.06 each. He also scored 614 runs for a batting average of 29.23. This was in only thirteen first-class matches, and had he played anything like a full season he would certainly have done the double. 'King is so strong at all points', wrote one critic, 'that one would like to see him pitted at single wicket against one of our men such as Hirst or Jackson, or Jessop.' King in that 1903 season, in a period when both English and Australian cricket were exceptionally strong, had clearly established himself in world class. 'Is there a greater bowler today?' asked 'Short Leg', of the *Wakefield* (Yorkshire) *Express*. 'I cannot think of him.'

Having reached such a pinnacle, it was a tragedy that King's talents should be confined almost entirely to inter-club cricket in Philadelphia in the next five years. In the Halifax Cup, however, he was more dominating than ever. From 1904 to 1908 he won the Batting Cup three times and the Bowling Cup four times, and he twice exceeded 300 in an innings, once in 1905 against Germantown and again in 1906 against Merion. One of his best performances was in the play-off for the Halifax Cup of 1905: Belmont had tied with Merion, and in the play-off Merion won the toss and were dismissed for 56, King taking 6 for 30. King then went in first and hit 18 off the first over and 24 off the first 28, and Belmont won by 9 wickets.

It was during this period that the greatest of all stories about J. B. King had its origins. It has been told many times, and there are several versions of it, but there seems no doubt, in spite of past scepticism, that it is basically true. Belmont, Bart King's club, were playing at Elmwood in the Halifax Cup. The Trenton captain missed his train, and when he arrived on the ground about an hour late he found that in his absence his side had won the toss and batted and were doing badly; by the time he had changed and got ready to bat, nine of the side were out and he was obliged to bat No. 11.

On his way to the wicket the Trenton captain apologized to the

Belmont captain for being so unpunctual, adding somewhat unwisely that his team wouldn't have been in such a mess if he hadn't missed his train. This remark was overheard by King, whose sense of show-manship and the absurd was stimulated. King enjoyed nothing more than the comedy which deflates; a boast like that made by the Trenton captain called for a bathetic pay-off.

It was a popular stunt of a famous baseball pitcher of the day, Rube Waddell, to send all his catchers off the field as an act of showmanship towards the end of a game and to dismiss the striker without their help. The idea appealed to King, and as the Trenton captain took guard King called his fielders together and sent them to the pavilion. They needed some persuading at first, but such was King's personality and renown that they finally did as they were asked.

The Trenton captain watched all this uneasily; King must have something up his sleeve. King walked back to begin his run, but as he turned he saw that the wicketkeeper was still in his place.

'Why, Eddie,' he called, 'whatever are you doing there? I won't need you either, Eddie. You'd better join the others.'

The wicketkeeper left the field, leaving just the two batsmen, the two umpires, and Bart King. The Trenton captain was meanwhile torn between many emotions. King was clearly trying to make a fool of him, but at the same time he must surely have a unique opportunity of scoring in every sense off King. Fear of being made to look silly, however, was the dominant emotion, and he decided to protest to the umpires. Cricket was a game for two sides of eleven men; King's action was outside the laws and ought not to be allowed.

After going into a huddle, the umpires, with some prompting from King, decided that, while the law demanded that the fielding side should consist of not more than eleven men, there was nothing to prevent King from dispensing with his entire field if he wished. The Trenton captain was thus obliged to meet King's challenge.

King went back to his mark again, but this time he paused. His sense of occasion demanded some further gesture, and he called to the pavilion that he would want one fieldsman. A fieldsman duly appeared, and King proceeded to place him with elaborate care, twenty yards behind the wicket and four paces to leg.

This pantomime of field-placing puzzled the Trenton captain so much that he rose to the bait. 'For heaven's sake,' he demanded, 'you said you didn't want a wicketkeeper, but what do you want *him* for?'

'He's not a wicketkeeper,' said King. 'He's not even a fielder.'

'What is he, then?'

'I've given the umpires enough trouble already,' said King. 'He's there to pick up the bails.'

King, so the story goes, then ran up and hit the stumps with a fast 'angler'. The fieldsman bent down and gathered up the bails, which had fallen at his feet, and handed them courteously to the umpire, and the Trenton innings was over.

Other versions of the story have it that the fieldsman was placed at fine leg to pick up the ball, and that he duly did so. Efforts in later years to get confirmation of the story from surviving Belmont players, however, have met a tight-lipped loyalty. 'You heard what Bart said, didn't you?' was all the answer one could get. However, there is another version, one that King himself would have enjoyed. It was related many years later by the man who, if his story can be believed, was the Trenton captain on that day.

'When I went in to bat that afternoon,' said the Trenton captain, 'King had four balls left in his over. I hit his first delivery to cover point but of course there was no one there. The ball stopped within three feet of the boundary, and King had to chase it. By the time he got back we had run six.

'I drove the fourth ball of the over past mid-on and this time it stopped only inches from the boundary, and again we ran six. The same thing happened next ball, and by this time King's tongue was hanging out and I began to feel sorry for him. Besides, my partner was getting tired too. When King lobbed up his last ball – he was too exhausted now to bowl fast – I took pity on him and lifted it over the pavilion. That was 24 runs in four balls. I think I must be the only player ever to hit four successive sixes off Bart King.

'I would be the first to admit, though,' went on the man who claimed to have been the Trenton captain, 'that King was a great bowler, but I think he would have to take second place to me in one respect.'

'You mean as a batsman?'

'No, I don't think so. He was a much better bat than I was.' The man edged a bit closer. '*You see, the fact is, I happen to be the world's champion liar.*'

The inference was that Bart King himself was pretty good at telling the tale.

★ ★ ★

Although it was an Englishman, B. J. T. Bosanquet, who first invented the googly, it has since been Australians who have been its foremost practitioners. The three great googly bowlers between the wars were A. A. Mailey, C. V. Grimmett and W. J. O'Reilly. Sadly, space only permits the inclusion of this piece on Mailey (the other two do, however, make cameo appearances elsewhere in the book).

Neville Cardus's essay on his friend has some good stories, though one has been left out. This concerns an argument between Mailey and Cardus that took place some fifteen years after the (for England) disastrous series of 1921. At a posh club in London, the critic was telling the practitioner that he could 'read' him, even if the English batsmen of long ago could not. A bystander then procured a tennis ball, and the disputants (both in dinner jackets) left the party for the nearby Piccadilly Circus, a few fans following behind. At the roundabout Cardus took up his position as wicketkeeper, while Mailey began to bowl. The ball was tossed up, and the keeper, expecting a leg break, moved over smartly to the off. But it was the wrong-un, as cleverly disguised as ever, and Cardus was left stranded as the ball went gambolling the other way, down in the direction of Leicester Square.

NEVILLE CARDUS

The Millionaire of Spin (1970)

The most fascinating cricketer I have known was the Australian Arthur Mailey, an artist in every part of his nature. On the field of play, he bowled leg spin, with the 'googly'. A man of his gift for fantasy could never have contented himself with 'seaming' a new ball. Mailey would tell me how much he revelled in the 'feel' of a ball spinning from his fingers. 'I'd rather spin and see the ball hit for four than bowl a batsman out by a straight one.' Such a view or attitude was not exactly attuned to the main idea (the only idea nowadays) obsessing a cricketer: the lust for victory, the fear of defeat. Yet Mailey could win a match devastatingly, spinning the greatest batsmen to immobile helplessness. Once he bowled Gloucestershire out single-fingered, or rather, with three fingers and a thumb. He took all ten wickets in a Gloucestershire innings for 66. Then, later, when he wrote his autobiography, he called the book *10 for 66, and All That.*

His life as a boy was not unlike my own, born in a semi-slum, the so-called Surry 'hills', a Sydney excretion, eighty years ago. He was 'dragged up', and worked as a labourer, a plumber's mate, at any casual job. All the time he educated himself, learned not only the most difficult sort of bowling; also he cultivated a talent to paint pictures and draw cartoons. He became, at the height of his career as cricketer, a well-liked cartoonist in Sydney newspapers. He sketched in the manner of the 1890s, broad and unsubtle, yet humorous. He painted landscape canvases, with trees and skies recognizably green, brown or blue. In London, he had a private exhibition of his paintings. Queen Mary did him the honour of inspecting these landscapes. She was graciously approving, on the whole; but she paused in front of one canvas, saying; 'I don't think, Mr Mailey, you have painted the sun quite convincingly in this picture.' 'Perhaps not, Your Majesty,' replied Arthur, 'you see, Your Majesty, in this country I have to paint the sun from memory.'

'If ever I bowl a maiden over,' he assured me, 'it's not my fault, but the batsman's.' He enjoyed himself; he explored himself; he was whimsical. One Saturday in Sydney I saw him on the ferry boat going to Neutral Bay, a mile or two's journey – it couldn't be called a voyage. We chatted and parted at our suburban destination. A few days later, I read in a newspaper that he had arrived in London – in wartime. Not a word had he spoken, as we journeyed that Saturday afternoon to Neutral Bay, of his flight to London. I would run into him at Lord's, not during a tour of an Australian team here, run into him and cry out in surprise, 'Good Lord, Arthur, what are you doing in London? When did you come?' 'Oh,' he would say, 'I've just dropped in from Hong Kong – via Neutral Bay.' He was slender of physical build, well-shouldered; his face good-looking, with a touch of Aboriginal, was wrinkled with incipient fun. He never laughed loudly; he smiled, as the play of his whimsical mind tickled his nerve of risibility. He was one of the New South Wales bowlers pitted against Victoria at Melbourne, in the Australian summer of 1926–27, in the match in which Victoria amassed 1,107 runs in a single innings. Mailey contrived to take 4 wickets for round about 350 runs; but, he maintained to his life's end, the scorer's analysis on the occasion did him less than justice, because three catches were missed off his bowling – 'two by a man in the pavilion, wearing a bowler hat'.

He tossed up his spin to the batsman slow and alluringly; never have I seen on a cricket field such undisguised temptation as was presented to the batsman by Mailey's bowling. It was almost immoral. He once clean bowled the incomparable Hobbs with a slow full toss, also at Melbourne, after the Master and Herbert Sutcliffe had scored 283 together, undefeated, on the third day of the second Test match of the 1924–25 rubber. First ball next day Hobbs missed Mailey's full 'floater'. Mailey needed to double-up his body to express the humour of it. If a catch was dropped from his bowling, he seldom complained; he would go to the unhappy fieldsman and say: 'I'm expecting to take a wicket any day now.' No bowler has spun a ball with more than Mailey's twist, fingers and right forearm and leverage. He lacked the accuracy of, say, Grimmett, another Australian leg-spinner; but Mailey bowled his spin with the lavishness of a millionaire. Grimmett bowled it like a miser – as Ray Robinson, Australia's wittiest cricket writer, once put it, or suggested the simile, to me.

At the end of March 1948, I was one of the company of Bradman's Australian team sailing by Orient line to England, Bradman's last summer in England as cricketer. His team was indeed powerful, for in it were two great fast bowlers, Lindwall and Miller, with Johnston in support. The batsmen collaborating with Bradman included Morris, Barnes, Hassett, Harvey, Brown, Miller and Loxton. During the voyage, one evening after dinner, Bradman sat talking to a number of his players. One of them said, in an excess of pride that he was one of the chosen few, 'You've got a great side for this trip, Don. I doubt if Victor Trumper could have got a place in it.' The Don contemplated this remark for a few seconds. 'I don't agree,' he said quietly, 'no, I don't agree. Victor could have got in it all right.' 'But,' persisted the proud one, 'who could you drop out of this present team for Trumper?' Like a flash Bradman replied, 'You – to begin with.' Memorable and ruthless.

Arthur Mailey had now, of course, retired from active service on the field, but he was with us on the way to England in that spring of 1948. We sat at the same dining table throughout the five weeks' voyage from Sydney to Southampton. With us, each evening, was a lovely auburn-haired Sydney girl, who had ambitions as a ballet dancer. Under the sky of the Pacific and Indian Oceans she would dance for Arthur and myself, at midnight, on the high 'D' deck; I can see her yet, luminous in the moonlight and, apparently, as immaterial. Arthur and I both fell for her. Always the three of us took coffee together after dinner. At Colombo, a young judge came aboard. And the girl left us to dance with him, 'just one dance', she explained. But she did not return; she danced with this young judge persistently. We waited. At last I said to Mailey: 'Arthur, let's go to bed. We'll teach her a lesson. She'll come back here for a drink, and find we've gone. Come.' Arthur agreed. So we departed to our own cabins, which adjoined. I waited till I heard Arthur's electric light click. I listened. Not a sound. After a while, giving him time really to get off to sleep, I crept up to the dancing deck. I stealthily tiptoed, watching the dancers through the window. Soon, surely, the dancing would come to an end. Then I would . . . I saw her, still with the judge. Still, soon I would . . . I turned the corner of the dance hall, in the outside dark. And I collided with Arthur. He, too, had imagined he had heard *my* electric light click and thought I was safely asleep. He was the kind of blithe spirit that causes comical things like this to happen.

He took to cricket in the manner of nearly every Australian boy in his period of penniless nonage, playing with a kerosene tin for the wicket. At once he discovered that he could, with the sensitive education of his fingers, persuade a cricket ball to go through a kaleidoscope of changing curving flight and capricious gyrations from the earth; he could by spin and flight express his own mazeful mind. He was a romantic in the sense which is regarded as completely outmoded these days, a time of history described by Sir Thomas Beecham as 'the most barbaric since Attila' – and that is going back somewhat. Mailey when young was staggered one Saturday, in his head and his heart, to learn that he had been chosen to play in the First XI of his district 'grade' contingent. (In Australia every suburban community has two or three cricket teams.) Moreover, young Arthur would, this very Saturday, be playing against Victor Trumper's

side. And Victor then was in his prime, the idol worshipped by all
Australian boys – and by English boys, myself included – the most
chivalrous batsman of all time, the most gallant, versatile and
youthful. His grave, in a churchyard outside Sydney, is to this day
covered by fresh flowers. Young Mailey spent this Saturday morning,
preceding the afternoon of his personal contact with Apollo, in an
utter misery of anxiety. No; he wasn't worrying about his own
likelihood or unlikelihood of performing ably in his baptism into
top-class Sydney cricket, first rung on the ladder to Test matches.
His concern was all for Victor – was he well, not afflicted by a
chill? Would he get run over in the streets by a cab? People, sixty
or so years ago, did somehow get run over by four-wheeled cabs, so
Arthur's fears could be justified, considering the way God had made
him, responsive to any romantic suggestion. Victor survived the
morning's dangers; he did not cut himself dangerously while shaving,
did not scald his hand with hot water, did not get run over in the
streets. He played for his eleven v. the eleven containing the tyro
Mailey. And Mailey couldn't believe it when his captain asked him *to
bowl at Victor*! Arthur did bowl at the Incomparable. Victor enchanted
Arthur by some strokes from his bowling which, Arthur remembered
years after, were like strokes made by a bat of conjuration. Then,
incredibly, Arthur clean bowled Victor. And, wrote Mailey, in his
autobiography: 'I was ashamed. It was as though I had killed a dove.'
Language to bring a blush to the cheeks of the latest of cricket's
sophistical fellow workers.

Mailey really was an incorrigible romantic. Throughout his life
(and he passed his eightieth year), he remained, for all his show of
worldliness, the poor boy of the Sydney slums, never stale at whatever
life brought to him, always *experiencing* events with the boy's wonder
– 'how has all this happened to me?' On board ship, on his many
voyages to England and back to Sydney, his crowning moments
occurred whenever he gave a champagne cocktail party. Champagne
was, for him, the symbol of the miracle which had changed him
from a ragged urchin to one of the best-beloved and most magical
of cricketers. He would often, in his cabin on the ship, listen to a
gramophone record; Tauber singing about Vienna. He rented a flat in
Park Lane during one of his summer visits to London. He gravitated
naturally, on holiday, to Montmartre. He died happy. In his last
moments of delirium, he imagined he was on board the Orient liner
Orion, entertaining the ship's captain and officers to a champagne

party. He squandered his imagination to the end, even as he tossed up his spin, with the millionaire's generosity. In heaven he has probably already clean bowled the Holy Ghost – with a 'googly'.

★ ★ ★

I have a theory that the best cricket writers have been competent but not outstanding cricketers. They must have played good enough cricket to understand its technical complexities. But they must also have known what it is to fail, and to fail disastrously.

R. C. Robertson-Glasgow played for Oxford and Somerset without ever remotely approaching Test standard. He then became one of the foremost cricket writers of his time. His playing experience, as well as his previous classical education, are both manifest in these marvellously concise appreciations of three great batsmen. Observe the subtle way in which the author brings in his own experience of bowling at them.

<h1 style="text-align:center">R. C. ROBERTSON-GLASGOW</h1>

Three English Batsmen (1945)

J. B. Hobbs – Surrey

Hobbs was the greatest English batsman that I've seen and tried to remove. He was the most perfectly equipped by art and temperament for any style of innings on any sort of wicket against any quality of opposition. He was thirty-seven years of age when I first had the pleasure of bowling to him. Misleading suggestions are sometimes heard that a cricketer, after the age of thirty, is tottering on the brink of decline. This is humbug; not only in a Pickwickian sense. Tom Hayward was in his thirty-sixth year when, in 1906, he scored 3,518 runs in first-class cricket, which still stands as a record.

The early Hobbs, before the last war, may have had all the brilliance and daring, but he would be a rash man who denied that his meridian of skill was shown about the years 1919–26. In the 1924–5 tour to Australia, under A. E. R. Gilligan, he and Herbert Sutcliffe formed an opening pair which many regard as the greatest the game has seen. Back in England for summer 1925, Hobbs scored sixteen centuries. Of these, two were made in one match, against Somerset at Taunton. By them he equalled, then passed, Dr Grace's record of 126 centuries. In the next summer he and Sutcliffe made the memorable stand on a difficult wicket against Australia at the Oval in the fifth Test, the first match of six running in which A. P. F. Chapman led England to victory. Sutcliffe made 161, Hobbs exactly 100; then had his bails flicked off by a beauty from J. M. Gregory. But, apart from the runs, Hobbs showed himself the master tactician. He foxed A. J. Richardson, who was bowling off-spinners, and the Australian captain into thinking he was in difficulties. He was not. So, while the pitch remained difficult, he contrived to keep on and, for the most part, to keep the strike against the spin bowler whom he least feared.

At Taunton, the year before, on a hot August Saturday, I saw him nervous for the only time that I can remember. There was a large crowd, as crowds go in the West; a newsreel cinematograph was perched on the reluctant roof of the little pavilion. The match was 'news'. For Hobbs had made his 125th century some time before, and had been followed round by ill-luck and most of the cricket correspondents. We batted first – more waiting! – and fared poorly. Then the struggle began. He was anxious; the strokes were calculating, even stuffy; he was twice nearly lbw, once at each end. At about 30 he gave a chance to wide mid-on, which went wrong. But throughout these embarrassments his instinctive excellence of method saved him from those faults of execution which another man in the same circumstances would, fatally, have committed. At the close of play he was in the early nineties. Then – a Sunday, for more waiting. But nice for the Somerset gate.

On the Monday morning J. J. Bridges and I were the bowlers. I bowled a no-ball in the first over, which Hobbs hit to the square-leg boundary. Someone afterwards suggested that the no-ball was bowled on purpose! It wasn't. Hobbs never needed any presents at the wicket. In Bridges's second over Hobbs scored a single to leg that gave him what he has told me was the toughest century of the lot! His second hundred was a beauty, care-free and brilliant of stroke, and he began with a four past cover that I can still see.

I have seen Hobbs described as a frail man. Actually he had strength of thigh and forearm far above the average, a strength which was concealed in the art of method and grace of movement. His footwork was, as nearly as is humanly possible, perfect. In every stroke he moved into the line of the ball with so little effort that he could bat for hours without overtaxing energy of mind or body. I never saw him unbalanced in a forward stretch, or 'hopping' on a back stroke. The interplay between judgement and execution was wonderful to see and baffling to attack. He covered his wicket much in defence. So did 'W. G.', according to one of his greatest admirers and opponents, S. M. J. Woods.

There was no one stroke of which you could say that it was less strong than another. You will hear someone remark – 'What a glorious square cut Headley has!' or, 'Do you remember Hendren hooking?' You will not hear that of Hobbs. All his strokes, that is, all the strokes in the game, were equally strong and easy; they were of an even perfection. He would hook bumpers off his nose; and, as to leg-breakers, which can find out the faults of the best, he mastered them all in turn, from the South Africans on their matting, when he was young, to Mailey, Grimmett, and Freeman, when he was in early middle-age.

To crown all, he had the gift of smiling quietly at failure and triumph alike.

H. Sutcliffe – Yorkshire

Herbert Sutcliffe is the serenest batsman I have known. Whatever may have passed under that calm brow – anger, joy, disagreement, surprise, relief, triumph – no outward sign was betrayed on the field of play. He was understood, over two thousand years in advance, by the Greek philosophers. They called this character megalo-psychic. It is the sort of man who would rather miss a train than run for it, and so be seen in disorder and heard breathing heavily.

He sets himself the highest available standard of batting and deportment. His physical discipline equals his mental; shown in the cool, clear eye and the muscularity of frame. If he is bowled, he appears to regard the event less as a human miscalculation than some temporary, and reprehensible, lapse of natural laws. There has been a blunder, to which he is unwillingly privy and liable. The effects of this blunder will be entered, with other blunders, in a scorebook, and the world may read of it in due time. He does not regret that it has occurred, for he is never sorry for himself; but he is sorry that Nature should have forgotten herself. To the later comers to the ground he would, so to speak, announce: 'Mr Sutcliffe regrets he's unable to bat today, being, ludicrously enough, already out.' Yet he is not proud. He leaves pride to little cricketers. There is nothing little in Sutcliffe. He is great. Great in idea and great in effect.

In the matter of round numbers he has scored over 50,000 runs in twenty-one years at an average of 52. In Test matches against Australia his average stands at nearly 67 for 2,741 runs – easily the highest average among English batsmen. On his first appearance against Australia, at Sydney, he played an innings of 115. He took part with Holmes (P.) in the world's record first-wicket stand of 555 for Yorkshire at Leyton in 1932. These are but a few of the feats in a career of resounding triumph.

When I first saw him, in 1919, he was a debonair and powerful stylist. He didn't look Yorkshire; even less a Yorkshire No. 1. He looked, rather, as if he had remembered and caught something of an earlier and not indigenous grace of manner. Pudsey was his home, but his style was not Pudsey. He had easy off-side strokes and a disdainful hook. I would not say that with the years he lost this manner, but it was increasingly seldom seen in its fullness. Two visits within five years to help Hobbs for England against Australia must mark any batsman of Sutcliffe's will and intelligence. It became hard to discern which predominated, the pleasure of batting or the trick of staying in.

As you bowled opening overs to the later Sutcliffe you noticed the entire development of every defensive art: the depressingly straight bat, the astute use of pads (as with Hobbs), the sharp detection of which outswinger could be left; above all, the consistently safe playing down of a rising or turning ball on leg stump, or thighs. This last art you will, I think, find only in the best players; Makepeace, Holmes (P.), Hutton, D. R. Jardine, Sandham and Hobbs as a matter of course, spring to the mind's eye. Professionals generally acquire it more readily than amateurs, whose early coaching often tends to a neglect of the on-side strokes.

Sutcliffe added a defensive stroke of his own; not exactly pretty, nor easily imitable. It was often played to a rising ball on about the line of the off stump. The bat started straight, on a restricted forward stroke; then with a swivel or overturn of the wrists he caused the ball to lie 'dead' a few yards down the pitch, or where a silly point would have stood if such a liberty had been taken; as if Sutcliffe had thought: 'Ball, you irk me. There. Be strangled, and lie quiet.'

He has always been capable of scoring at a great speed, especially from fast bowling. His hook is imperious. Some remark that this stroke has often been his downfall. They forget the many hundreds of runs that it has brought him, from balls which make lesser batsmen dodge and murmur of danger. I hope we shall soon see his batting again.

F. E. Woolley – Kent

Frank Woolley was easy to watch, difficult to bowl to, and impossible to write about. When you bowled to him there weren't enough fielders; when you wrote about him there weren't enough words. In describing a great innings by Woolley, and few of them were not great in artistry, you had to go careful with your adjectives and stack them in little rows, like pats of butter or razor blades. In the first over of his innings, perhaps, there had been an exquisite off drive, followed by a perfect cut, then an effortless leg glide. In the second over the same sort of thing happened; and your superlatives had already gone. The best thing to do was to presume that your readers knew how Frank Woolley batted and use no adjectives at all.

I have never met a bowler who 'fancied himself' against Woolley, nor heard one who said, with conviction, 'Woolley doesn't like an off break on the middle stump or a fast bumper on the leg stump.' I never heard Woolley confess that he preferred or disliked any bowler whatsoever. But then he is a very quiet man. I have a belief that he was particularly fond of them fast and short. They went that much more quickly to the boundary.

It has been said that he was not a good starter. Like other great batsmen, he would sometimes miss in the first minutes. But equally he could kill two bowlers in the first six overs of any match. His own innings might be only about 50 or so, but he had fathered the centuries that followed. Only a few years ago, when he was some forty-seven years old, I saw him 'murder' Voce and Butler, the Nottinghamshire bowlers, in the first overs of a match at Canterbury. They were pitching a little, only a little, too short, and they extracted an exhibition of cutting and hooking which was . . . but we have refused the use of adjectives.

Merely from a personal aspect, I never knew so difficult a target as Woolley. His great reach, and the power of his pendulum, made a fool of length. Balls that you felt had a right to tax him he would hit airily over your head. He was immensely discouraging. The only policy was to keep pitching the ball up, and hope. He could never be properly described as being 'set', since he did not go through the habitual processes of becoming set. There was no visible growth of confidence or evident strengthening of stroke. He jumped to his meridian. He might hit the first ball of the match, a good ball too, if left to itself, crack to the boundary over mid-on; then, when he had made 60 or more, he might snick a short one past slip in a sudden freak of fallibility, a whim of humanity.

Sometimes he is compared with other famous left-handers, such as the late F. G. J. Ford. But these comparisons seem to be concerned only with attack. It is often forgotten, I think, that Woolley's defence was as sure and correct as that of Mead or Bardsley. Of its kind it was just as wonderful to see, on a sticky wicket, as was his attack. It had a corresponding ease and grace, without toil or trouble. For this reason I think that Woolley will rank as the greatest of all left-handers so far seen in the game. None has made so many runs while giving so much delight.

For many years Woolley was a great part of the Canterbury Festival. Myself, I preferred to watch him or play against him on some ground not in Kent. Praise and pride in home-grown skill are natural and right; but at Canterbury, in the later years, these had degenerated into a blind adulation that applauded his strokes with a very tiresome lack of discrimination. They had made a 'raree' show of a great batsman.

No one, when county cricket is resumed, will fill the place of Frank Woolley. I have tried to avoid metaphor and rhapsody; but there was all summer in a stroke by Woolley, and he batted as it is sometimes shown in dreams.

*   *   *

When Walter Hammond scored 905 runs in the Ashes Tests of 1928–9 he was hailed as the most accomplished cricketer of his generation. People thought he would dominate world cricket for the next decade or more. He was the best batsman in the world, the best slip fieldsman in the world, and a first-rate swing bowler too. But within a year and a half Hammond had his crown wrested from him. In the next Ashes series, played in England in 1930, Bradman scored 974 runs. No one had scored runs faster or with less effort or with more certainty. So infallible did Bradman seem that a duck by him was deemed more newsworthy than a double hundred by someone else.

In any other epoch Walter Hammond would have been top dog. He continued to score runs, and take wickets and catches, always with a classical elegance. Some of his own innings, such as the 240 he hit at Lord's in 1938, were acknowledged masterpieces. But he would inevitably be compared with Bradman. Theirs was one of the great rivalries of cricket, and it was usually the Australian who came out on top. Hammond had done enough nonetheless to become an icon to a whole generation of English schoolboys, of which the literary historian Ronald Mason was one.

RONALD MASON

Imperial Hammond (1955)

One day early in the Australian summer of 1928–9 a press photographer at Sydney, squinting through his sights for a suitable action snap, released the shutter at one precise and infinitesimal instant that gave him (all unknowing, it is to be supposed) the most striking action picture of a batsman that has ever been put on record. For poise, grace, symmetry, composition and power it might be a picture of a statue by Pheidias; there is a flawless balance in the distribution of every line and every mass in the field of vision, and moreover it conveys an infinite potentiality of strength. It is Hammond at the finish of an off drive; or, rather, not at the relaxed finish, like the classic Trumper snap where you can feel the delicious release of the sprung muscles after contained effort, but a split instant of time after the maximum of productive tension. The head, beautifully poised, is still tucked down over the point of impact; the bat has come up in a great arc to finish over the left shoulder; the left toe, giving direction to the stroke, is pointed as lightly and as weightlessly as a ballet dancer's. This dancer's lightness, expressed in the poise of the left foot, gives the whole bodily attitude a strange and lovely ease of movement. I never saw Nijinsky, but I doubt if any gesture of his could convey the power and the glory of motion as this superb snapshot of Walter Hammond does. Compositionally the picture has built itself up most happily in the form of a pyramid; the wicket-keeper, who is Oldfield and therefore adds an instinctive grace of his own, is bent alertly in such a way that the line of his back and the transverse one of his arms and outstretched gloves exactly lead into and answer the corresponding lines of the batsman's figure. All these lines point to the centre; to the great shoulders and whipcord sinews at the hub of this explosive activity. All else is just as the imagination hears and sees, the rich thunderous crack and the red flash, and the straight line shot through the covers to the fence.

More often than not, when pictures of Hammond are required, that is the one that does duty; and it is appropriate enough, for it shows him on the very threshold of his greatest period of renown. All in all his career in first-class cricket lasted from 1920, when he played, I think, three matches, to 1951, when he emerged from a sickeningly early retirement to play one more; yet it never excelled in consistency of success the greatness of his tour of Australia in 1928–9 under Percy Chapman. In the series of five Tests he made 905 runs, a record were it not for Bradman, who hardly counts; he seemed unbeatable and unbowlable and, though he curbed them of necessity, he commanded ferocious aggressive powers, of which the epitome is for all to see in the magnificent photograph I have described. On that tour he entered into possession of a kingdom for which, seasons before, he had begun to make insistent bids. I say 'kingdom' with considered stress on the word; about him and his cricket was a perennial air of cool domination. Where Hobbs seemed *primus inter pares*, chief servant of the state in an idyllic republic, Hammond lorded it unabashed like an emperor. I know nothing of his personal temperament; from hints I have gathered here and there he seems to have been gifted with a modesty and charm which make his public character even more attractive; but as a public figure he displayed the pride of a commander, a pride without frills and flounces, a direct and uncontradictable pride. 'Hammond', said Denzil Batchelor, 'never walked to the wicket. He strode'; and when he came down the steps and out on to the grass, you could hear in your ears the trumpets and the drums of an imperial salutation. His very name sounded like a ceremonial discharge of cannon.

He was not tall, but in his youth he was so proportioned as to give the effect of height together with a sinuous mobility concealing strength. I saw him first in a Champion County match at the Oval in 1925, in a team resplendent with all the batting talents, where his place was at 7 or 8. For Gloucestershire he had had a false start, owing to qualification trouble, and on resuming after an interval had begun to impress everyone with the astonishing power and correctness of his back play, his intensely aggressive off-side hitting, and (thrown in as if casually) bowling and fielding beyond the useful. That same season he had roused northern hackles by battering into impotent pulp, on its own ground, a Lancashire attack which included Macdonald, Dick Tyldesley and Parkin, to the value of 250 runs. In the match I saw his batting performance was negligible, and in any case I did not see it; but he bowled with an exciting swirling run-up and arched action; and he stood close up in the slips and held on to a buzzing cut with a practised ease that I was to get to know.

That winter he went on a tour to the West Indies, collected over 200 in an unofficial Test match, and came home with a serious illness that put him on his back during the crucial year of 1926, when he would otherwise have been fledging himself against the Australians. I, who under the spell of Hobbs took little note of him, let him slip from my memory and concentrated on the main issues; one young batsman the more or less did not matter. Hobbs, Sutcliffe and Rhodes had won us the Ashes, and what need had I to grieve for the loss of a promising all-rounder? It was true that when the next season began I looked for his return with some interest, remembering his great promise and feeling for him in an ordeal, that of re-establishing his confidence in himself, that must have been at that crucial stage in his career (he was not yet twenty-four) a rather unnerving one.

He answered my interested curiosity in the best possible manner. It was a filthy season, strewn with rains and ruins, a tattered squally ragbag of a summer conspicuous for abandonments and butt-ends of drowned cricket matches; it abides in my memory (I was in the Fourth XI at school, batting nervously and ineffectively, and I remember it well) as canopied with low racing clouds and bespattered with vile blowing showers. In this shambles of a season Walter Hammond came back into the game and instantly scored a thousand runs in May. His long rest had filled out his figure and, apparently, given him renewed confidence. From the very first match, which was against Yorkshire, he laid into the bowling with a power quite out of this world; it was in this dim and dripping May of 1927 that cricket first found itself enriched by the storming beauty of those murderous off drives. Many can now remember the iron summer of 1947 and the bushels of runs gathered in by Edrich and Compton on the brown baked grounds on the sweating sweltering afternoons of high June. We held our breath at their rapacity then, it is true, but it was nothing to the sensation that hit us like a planet twenty years before under the curtains of cloud, as Hammond in his billowing shirt with buttoned-down sleeves raced to his thousand between the freezing showers. Yorkshire, Lancashire, Surrey, Middlesex – all were met and massacred; and if the unconscionable weather had not entirely collapsed in June he would have tacked on another thousand by the end of that month to match the fruits of the first. In that marvellous first season of his true fulfilment he was established for good and all as one of the great. From that time forward he never lost his place in the world's esteem or in mine; and from the first Test in the next season against the West Indies at Lord's, until the last Test in 1946 against India at the Oval, when I saw him bat for the last time on a cheerless windy wet day in just such another season as that of his first blaze of splendour, no England side, in England, ever took the field without him, save once when he was suffering from throat trouble and could not be considered . . .

There never was an athlete, in his younger days especially, so lightly and delicately poised; yet there was no tension in his attitude, only a limber felicitous disposal of the limbs in poses that seemed to fall instinctively into attitudes of grace. His delicacy had nothing of affectation about it; it was a muscular strength that carried with it not a pose or a presumption. He stood in the slips on legs planted firmly, rather wide apart, the body flexing from the hips, the hands alert; his walk from one end of the wicket to the other was enough to reveal the grace of those compact muscles; his cap slightly askew, his nose in the air, he distilled a certain detached indifference into his manner. When he came to bat he injected into this detachment a suspicion of what might be called hostility; the better the opposition the intenser this became. On rare and special occasions it was reinforced by a flavour of insolent contempt. His eyes narrowed; as he stood at the wicket he seemed all shoulder and bat and pad. And when he moved from the static to the dynamic his feet slid as quietly and as inevitably as a dancer's dancing in tune. As the years proceeded and his frame thickened there seemed no corresponding slowing down of his footwork; only an increasingly obvious source of power behind the stroke, where previously there had been surprise at the stinging unexpectedness of its violence.

Two particular strokes of his I do remember out of the long

panorama of the innings I saw him play; neither of them strokes for which he was renowned. Eleven years separated them; September 1928, on the eve of his great progress through Australia, and August 1939, on the eve of something quite other. On the first occasion, willowy and fresh with the assurance of powerful youth, coming in after Hobbs and Woolley in a thunderous batting order for the Rest of England against Lancashire the champion county, he received in his first over a rasping break-back from Macdonald off the line of the middle and off stumps. It was a swine of a ball to have to counter so early in his innings; it would have picked the leg stump from behind most batsmen before they were aware of its lethal last-minute dip. Hammond tucked his nose down over it and glanced it clean off the bat's middle for four, a stroke that he did not play often and which with the apotheosis of the inswinger and the leg trap few batsmen remember to use nowadays. The ball glittered like a jewel as it went to the rails in a streak; and although he was caught at the wicket not many minutes later, and a fabulous innings built itself around our ears with centuries by Hobbs and Sutcliffe and Hendren, and various lashings-about by Woolley and Leyland and Ames, yet that one stroke is the sole enduring legacy, for me, of the day's play.

I sat in the pavilion then, high behind his back; eleven years later family necessities had stronger demands and I had discontinued my membership; and I watched the last first-class match that the Oval staged before Hitler invaded Poland from the bob seats alongside the Vauxhall stand, far in the distance and remote from my accustomed contacts. In this last Test match the West Indies strove and stormed with some success to break an England side that harboured the remnants of the one that had beaten Australia on that ground twelve months before; and Hammond for a long time made strangely heavy weather of fast bowlers, notably Constantine and Martindale, whose bite was every bit as bad as their bark. All of a sudden, out of a patch of somnolence, came a thunderbolt of memorable force. Hammond had leaned back and hit a short ball on the off stump with fearful power into the unguarded areas about long on – down to my very feet, in fact. I have rarely seen a ball travel quicker; at one moment it was going normally down the pitch from the bowler to the batsman; at the next it was fearsomely among us, cutting a smoking path through the grass. Just an ordinary pull, but with the impact of a steam hammer.

It may be that these isolated strokes surprised and dazzled by their unexpectedness, and that it is on that account that they have outlived in my memory the more characteristic delights with which he normally adorned his play. It was true of Hobbs that his strokes all round the wicket were so consummately skilful that he did not possess one that materially outshone the others, nor were any of the normal orthodoxies lacking; and that therefore you thought of Hobbs without particular reference to any one favourite shot, but in the context mostly of his departure from the usual . . . It would not have been wrong to say the same of Hammond: I have a photograph of a match in Australia in 1928 in which he has just executed the most delicate tickle of a late cut; he excelled in the towering full-shouldered clump straight back over the bowler's head, with which he once hit the ball clean through the pavilion door at Lord's and landed it first bounce crack against the far wall of the Long Room; and, as I have already shown, a leg glide of his is immortal in my memory. The difference between him and a master like Hobbs was that no wile of bowler, eccentricity of pitch or vicissitude of game could ever induce the latter to drop a single stroke out of his repertoire; he used them all with great safety and penetration, whatever the circumstances. Hammond, on the other hand, felt compelled to trim his sails to the prevailing wind; and it is said that experience of one kind and another led him quite early in his career to dispense with the hook. At least that is what we are told, and I admit I did not, so far as I can remember, see him execute this stroke; yet there remains the wry remark of Robertson-Glasgow to the effect that Hammond may possibly have dispensed with the hook but he had never noticed the lack of it when he bowled him a long hop. But if he did go lightly on certain on-side shots it is a matter of resonant history that he made up for it on the off.

Between backward point and mid-off Hammond is for all time undisputed king. On the ground or in the air they went from the rich middle of his bat like bombs. His methods of attack varied, his footwork never. That was always light and pliant, manoeuvring his powerful frame to a nicety at a split second's notice; but in attack he would bring into play the colossal tension of his great shoulders and reinforce it with the whipped uncoiling of his wrists – or he would stand erect and use the wrists alone, as he levered the shot off his back foot with all the muscular power that he could gather into the action. If he went out and drove off the front foot, God help mid-off or extra cover if it went along the ground and they got

a touch to it; it must have been like being handed for a moment or
so a ladleful of melted steel. More often it would beat all fielders
running all ways, or if he raised his head a fraction early, as he
sometimes did, it would whizz like a golfer's drive over extra cover's
head with a strong bending swing to it; at other times it went
straight, with a long hanging carry. But the gem was the upstanding
slash off the back foot. Bowl Hammond a quick good-length ball on
the off stump or outside it and either mid-off, extra cover or cover
himself would have to dash or dive; bowl the same ball further up
or shorter, it did not matter, and he would crack it square as it
passed him, rising on his toes and thrashing across the flight with
an uncanny precision of timing, so that elders with their heels on
the very fence were lucky if they had moved when the ball hit the
rails. Woolley's off drives were perhaps smoother and sweeter; but
for power and glory and grace Hammond's off-side play was the
major delight of twentieth-century cricket.

I am one of his most devoted, not to say fanatical, admirers; and
yet the full irony of frustration was reserved for me by fate; before
me indeed his superb panoply of batsmanship was never displayed
in its full splendour. I saw his greatness fitfully like the sun on a
cloudy day. As for so many tantalizing years Jack Hobbs had done,
so Hammond excelled in incredible feats the day before or the day
after I watched him vainly for full measure of success. The first time
I saw him in the full tide of his mature greatness, in his destroying
summer of 1927, he had (would you believe it?) been out the very
last thing the night before, the very last thing. Later in the barren
day he came out to field with the rest, impeccably laundered I
remember, and treading with the assurance that he was beginning
to wear as a trademark; but I never saw him bat that season, and in
the next, when he was if anything even more consistent, I watched
him scrape 3 two days before he launched himself on that fantastic week of all-round proficiency at Cheltenham of which I have
already made breathless mention. Then in his last innings before
he went through Australia like a withering flame I saw him make 9.
On the one occasion in the next season when I saw him bat he was
caught one-handed in the slips for 8.

For better or worse this kind of experience continued throughout
his career. I did see him make one century, and a satisfying proportion
of another; and I would like a pound note for every day on which I
had leisure to watch him in the field. In the early part of his career

indeed there was plenty of opportunity to consider him as a bowler; and I accept these visions of his out-cricket as valuable substitutes in my own experience for the prime satisfaction of watching him at his batting. For Hammond's greatness was spread evenly over all his play; it was in his slip fielding as much as in his batting, in his bowling as much as in either of the other two. By this I do not intend to write him down as a great bowler – only as a great cricketer bowling, who could indicate by his bowling that he was out of the ordinary, even if his bowling was not. And sometimes it was. His bowling had the Hammond mark of assured distinction upon it. His action was the most beautiful I have ever seen among medium-paced bowlers; for grace and felicity Larwood and Macdonald were better among fast men and Verity among the slows, but Hammond's run-up like a bird's flight curve, and the splendid arching back of his body as he went into his action, were only extensions, variations, comments indeed on his great cover drive or his back-foot slash. He swung the new ball viciously away from the bat and he was said to come off the pitch as unexpectedly quickly as Maurice Tate. An all-rounder of such commanding vigour and competence as Hammond could not fairly be expected to practise all departments of the game with equal assiduity, and it was his bowling that quite fairly and naturally was allowed to fall into disuse. It was a young man's art; and if I want to recapture quickly to my imagination the young Hammond it is that swallow-swerve run-up I remember most readily and the arched enchantment of the free light action following it.

The rest of his art he preserved unjaded into near middle age. It is a deplorable chance, and I believe it to be only a chance, that decreed that on the tour of Australia which concluded his career he should have been in his own special context a failure. We think of him therefore as petering out and retiring not a moment too soon. We forget that in the streaming wet season of 1946, the prelude to his last tour, he topped the English averages by the height of the stratosphere with an average of over 80. We forget that he had just as disastrous a Test series as far back as 1934; we forget easily enough that his performance on the ill-fated tour gave him an all-over average of 41 and included two masterpieces of innings of 32 and 23 on the spitting swamp of a Brisbane wicket where hardly anybody else got double figures. It is true that in the Tests that followed he did not do very well; but there were preoccupations in his mind, and he was leading a side of patchy and experimental quality. Let us remind ourselves that in what was virtually his last first-class match, a Test against New Zealand (though twice later he played in first-class games, one of which was as recent as 1951), he scored a splendid and selfless 79 and held a peach of a catch at slip.

A peach of a catch at slip; almost an inevitability when Hammond was playing. In the early part of his career he paraded the covers and the outfield, and I have seen him sprint like a stag with a real runner's rhythmic action to cut off a four; but all his Test-match days were spent at slip, and as for Gloucester – what Charlie Parker owed to him is only matched by what he owed to Charlie Parker. Close up on the bat's shoulder for Parker; back fifteen yards for Larwood, within chatting distance of the wicketkeeper; for twenty years that was his inevitable post. In Test-match action pictures from 1928 to 1947, with England in the field, there he is, receptive and alert, cheek by jowl with Ames or Duckworth or Evans, flanked by Chapman or Hendren or Compton. In action pictures of Bradman or Woodfull or McCabe or Barnes, there he is brooding in the background, distinctive, unfussy, virtually infallible. It was highly characteristic of him that he never in his life made a spectacular catch, though it is probable he took a hundred or two in his time that no one else could have touched. Where Chapman, wonderful fielder, might have hurled his vast weight sideways and flicked the ball one-handed an inch from the grass while rolling desperately over, Hammond would have taken the very same catch in his two hands, ankle height, to suit himself, with apparently time to roll up his sleeves first. Those exquisite light feet had taken him by antici-pation plumb into the right place as the bat met the ball. He was the greatest slip fielder I have ever watched, and I watched him for long enough. He could absorb a cannonball slash or pick a bounding snick off the bat's corner with an air of deepest unconcern.

Although not without gifts of showmanship, he was without showiness. He excelled, in the field, at understatement. In this manner he understated his way to over 800 catches in his career; of which one, a most uncommon affair, I remember to this instant as a blazing masterpiece. It was in a Test against India in 1936; in which, after ascertaining that I would not be present until the next day, he made 217. In the second innings of India in which many brave and inexperienced attempts were made, notably I remember by Amar Singh, to hit the not very formidable England attack off its length, a rather erratic G. O. Allen was bowling with great energy to a very erratic and equally energetic Mushtaq Ali – a batsman of freedom and beauty whose charm was expansive and evanescent, like candy-floss. This good batsman, faced with a rearing long hop outside the off stump, thrashed heartily across the line without bothering to get his foot to it, with the result that instead of going through cover like one of Hammond's own specials it rocketed at fearful speed at the height of about eight feet through the gap between first and second slip, standing I thought a little on the close side for a bowler of Allen's pace. Second slip was Voce, and the ball was by him in a blink, going like the dogs of war; but instinctively he leaped to it, grunting, at full stretch of his left arm, and as luck ordained got a touch on it with, I take it, his stretched little finger. The deflection was instantaneous and dramatic; the ball ricocheted like a shot off a shovel in the rough direction of the square-leg umpire; from eight feet in the air it shot steeply downwards like the hypotenuse of a rather erect right-angled triangle, its speed hardly decreased and its power to disconcert unexpectedly augmented. Hammond at first slip pivoted gracefully on his right foot, and with his back to the wicket and the batsman gathered in the catch just below his right armpit, one-handed, as it sped across his chest on the way to the opposite boundary. The surprise was not for the breathless speed of the manoeuvre, which was indeed breathless enough, but for the fact that Hammond accepted it as if it were part of some pre-rehearsed ritual carried out with care and elegance and watchfulness, but with no possible need for haste or surprise.

What was it about this man without warmth, this detached artist with the heavy-lidded eyes, this ruthless and efficient destroyer, to endear him so closely to his public? Jack Hobbs had the common touch and the common humours; Hammond, in public at least, walked like an emperor and walked alone. Yet England and English crowds thrilled to him as to few others; the welcoming roars broke more violently round his indifferent head than they did round any of his contemporaries. They tried to effect familiar relationships by calling him Wally. This may have been all right for his private character, but as far as his public face is concerned it was, for me, like calling Dr Johnson Sammy. For me he is always Walter Hammond; stern and majestic names for a stern and majestic man. Yet on his very last appearance, in 1951, when he played for Gloucestershire against Somerset in the August Bank Holiday game, he confessed that he had been hardly able to see the first few balls bowled to him, so moved had he been by the tremendous reception given him by the crowd. Abiding admiration, yes; immense respect, yes. But popularity, affection, a welcome to stir the heart? It is strange, and it is very good. It shows beyond doubt that the British public recognized and warmed to the character and artistry of an unusual man, not caring whether he troubled to pay court to them with his personality or not.

For Walter Hammond brought to the highest reaches of the game a stability and an assurance administered with stunning power. Nothing that he did was without grace; nothing that he did was without authority. He was orthodox, but he expressed his orthodoxy in rich chorded tones. His on drive was right out of the book; his off drive was right out of this world. To magnify the good and the right to Titanic dimensions; this is to behave after the high Roman fashion. Jack Hobbs was a fifth-century Greek; Walter Hammond an imperial Roman, of the days of the great Augustan empire. The Latin language has come down to us with its four great qualities plain: clarity, strength, weight, precision. Those, in his lesser field, are Walter Hammond's qualities too.

*   *   *

Donald George Bradman was the most phenomenal of cricketers. He was unquestionably the greatest batsman of all time, and one of the best captains. In his youth he also fielded brilliantly at cover point. But it was not so much the records he broke as how he broke them that attracted notice. No other cricketer, before or since, has been so successful in the pursuit of success. No other cricketer has had a revolutionary new strategy worked out by his opponents against him. In its own terms this strategy, 'bodyline', worked well – it brought Bradman's average, normally in excess of 100, to a mere 56. However, 'bodyline' also very nearly led to Australia's premature exit from the Empire.

From the huge and ever proliferating literature on Bradman I have chosen two essays – one on the promising youngster, the other on the veteran at the end of his career. Each is written by a man who played much cricket with the Don, who vastly respected his cricketing genius but who, nonetheless, had reservations about the damage done to the game by his single-minded pursuit of personal success.

W. J. O'REILLY
Young Don Bradman (1985)

I have often wondered about the strange fact that I still have the clearest possible recollection of the very first time I heard Don Bradman's name.

The strangeness of it comes from the present knowledge that the name must have meant absolutely nothing whatever then to a young Sydney Teachers' College student, as I was, just reaching the final stages of his two years' scholarship course and preparing to take up a job as a primary school teacher with the New South Wales Department of Public Instruction, as the Education Department was then known.

A small group of us were making our way past the 'Greasers' School', as we called Sydney University's School of Engineers, on our way down to the Forest Lodge exit from the University grounds, en route to the Jubilee Oval at Glebe Point, where we were due to take part in some sporting programme. To make some sort of appropriate conversation I mentioned that I would be returning to my Wingello home, where I hoped to take part in some of the cricket fixtures in the Southern Tablelands Cricket Competition during the coming two months' summer vacation. Len Kelsey, who hailed from Bowral and who had spent his two years' training at the College in close association with me, informed me that it would probably pay some dividends if I were to keep a wary eye open for a young man named Don Bradman, whom he had known as a fellow pupil at Bowral High School, and who was presently scoring lots of runs in the local competition. I passed the matter over in the same way a good chairman in a humdrum public meeting skims over the general business, setting it aside for later consideration.

But my meeting with Bradman came much sooner than I had anticipated. Boarding a passenger train leaving Sydney's Central Station for Goulburn one Saturday morning in December 1925, I travelled peacefully for eighty miles, blithely unaware of what was to happen to me before I arrived at my little home town, situated 104 miles south. As the train came to a halt at Bowral, an attractive township popular as a health resort and holiday mountain town, I was startled out of my peaceful reverie by the weird sensation of imagining that I heard my name being called. I jumped up, leaned my long frame from the carriage window and called out 'Here I am.'

It was the stationmaster from Wingello doing the bellowing. His instructions were terse and forceful. 'Grab your bag and get out.'

My reluctance to obey him must have been plain for him to see, for he added in explanation, 'We are all down here to play Bowral this afternoon and you are going to get the new ball.' I jumped out smartly. And that was a dreadful mistake, I must admit.

The stationmaster, with the same organizing ability which had induced the Railway Commissioners to promote him to his dizzy height of responsibility, put my fears to rest by informing me that he himself had been in close contact during the week with my dear mother, who had packed my cricket gear and given it to him to set me up for the afternoon. Misguidedly I silently gave three hearty cheers for the good luck which had given me such a welcome start to the Christmas holidays.

On the way to the Bowral Oval in an old 1918 Model T Ford truck I was well and truly briefed on the growing reputation of a kid named Don Bradman – there it was again – who had been showing such unusual skill that they had decided to enlist my services at short notice.

We were a motley-looking crew I suppose as we began to peel off under cover of a clump of gum trees beside the ground. Young and old, all shapes and sizes. Moustaches were popular with the more mature members, but no youngster dared then to run the risk of wholesale criticism by encouraging the reluctant growth of a few goose-down hairs on the top lip to give the false impression that he had entered the state of manhood. It wasn't done then. There were no beards. It was long since the days when cricketers found it necessary to add to their ferocity, glamour, sex appeal – call it what you will – by hiding behind a thatch of fearsome whiskers.

Bowral won the toss and batted. I got the new ball.

You might well ask, 'Why did O'Reilly get the new ball? He wasn't a fast bowler who thrashed them down at headlong speed. There has never been any suggestion that he could move the new ball in the air sufficiently to claim recognition as a worthwhile new-ball operator.'

Quite true.

O'Reilly got the new ball regardless. The reasons were basic. O'Reilly could bowl consistently at the stumps. He had earned himself a noticeable reputation as a wicket-taker in the Sydney Moore Park Saturday-morning competition. Furthermore the Wingello captain and the entire team – including O'Reilly himself – thought that O'Reilly was a good bowler.

Play began.

In my first over I hit the stumps of one of Bowral's openers. That warmed me up for the entrance of a diminutive figure, approaching with what appeared to be the diffident gait of a stopgap performer sent in to hold the fort long enough for the real No. 3 in the batting order to get his pads on. What struck me most about him was the difficulty he seemed to be having in taking normal steps as he approached. His pads seemed to reach right up to his navel. His bat was small and had reached the sere and yellow stage, where the yellow was turning to dark tobacco.

Still, he shaped up as though he knew what the game was all about, and the expression on his face publicized the fact that he felt quite at home and was ready to cope with anything that I had in store for him.

The battle was joined. As the game proceeded I was quick to realize that I had come into contact with my very first 'problem child'. My training as a prospective primary school teacher was supposed to have prepared me for dealing with the occasional hard case who would turn up from time to time, but nothing could have prepared me for the confrontation with this particular youth.

As the precocious lad began to handle my quickish leg breaks, bouncing high off the coir mat which always favoured spin, I was made aware that here at last I had a real job of work on my hands, and I wondered what I should have to say to Len Kelsey the next time I saw him.

I had a bit of bad luck early in that memorable afternoon. Twice before he had reached 30 the youngster was dropped in the slips off my bowling. To elucidate, it is necessary that I give an honest pen-picture of the captain who led Wingello in that great struggle.

Selby Jeffery was a railway fettler. He had worn the Australian uniform which proudly displayed the big brass 'A' denoting the fact that he was present on the Sunday morning of 25 April 1915, when the Australian and New Zealand forces went into action at Gallipoli in their attempt to open up the Dardanelles. Selby was an Anzac, and as such held the unbounded respect of every man on the field. He sported a fairly robust black moustache. His face was rosy with blatant good health and his persistent good humour was heralded by the most pleasant smile one could wish to see.

His snow-white shirt and duck trousers were immaculate, as were his rubber boots. He wore a black waistcoat, unbuttoned, over the shirt. The idea of the waistcoat was quite original – it held his pipe, his tobacco and his matches. It was not unusual in those far-off days for a country cricketer to light up and take a few draws on a pipe or cigarette. Nobody took umbrage at it. I saw it happen outback many times. Indeed I once saw it in first-class cricket on the Sydney Cricket Ground, when Freddie Mair, the gifted all-rounder and Balmain captain for many years, playing for New South Wales against Victoria, let his craving for a few draws get the better of him at the fall of a Victorian wicket. And I seem to recall that he had to get a match from the man fielding at short leg, but I can't remember who that was.

Selby used to slip his big-bowled bent-stemmed Captain Peterson pipe into the top pocket of his unbuttoned waistcoat. His tobacco pouch fitted snugly into the other top pocket, with the tin box holding his Wax Vestas matches in the bottom pocket along with a penknife for cutting the plug of dark 'Conqueror' tobacco.

It would have been senseless for him to field in any position where it might have been necessary to raise an occasional canter. Had he run there would have been a scattering of smoking parapher-nalia in all directions. Wisely therefore he placed himself invariably at first slip, where he was spendidly covered by a magnificent keeper named Tommy Lynam and always supported by an active and mobile second slip.

Very early in the day I got one to lift and bite. Young Bradman edged it and the ball travelled speedily and straight in the direction of Selby's midriff. It would have been an extraordinary effort had the catch been taken. It struck him in the solar plexus just at the moment when he was, with both hands well and truly occupied, lighting his pipe.

Bradman soon gave our skipper a chance to redeem himself by snicking my quicker ball straight to him again. This second time

Selby made a manful attempt with both hands to make the catch, but he had blown such a dense cloud of bluish smoke from his startled lungs that he must have lost sight of the ball well before it reached him.

'Sorry Bill,' he called, as if nothing untoward had happened. Selby's inconsistencies in the slips were part and parcel of the Wingello team's programme. I was probably the only one among us who felt that he might have been wise to deny himself just a little longer.

Who in the name of all that is holy could ever possibly hope to get away unscathed when Don Bradman had been given two lives? If I said earlier that I experienced some early worries as the boyish Bradman started his innings by methodical employment of the middle of his bat, I could certainly go much further in describing my own mental reactions as this young man tore the Wingello attack apart. Even though his size suggested that he would have been better fitted physically to have been riding winners at Randwick racecourse, he summoned up the energy required to land the ball right over the fence on half a dozen occasions. One wondered where he was hiding the battery that generated the power.

To draw a convenient veil over the desolate scene, Selby Jeffery's team finished the day a crestfallen crowd who listened more to the rattles of the old Model T Ford than to any animated flow of conversation on the thirty-mile return trip by road to Wingello. Their chief bowling hope had nothing whatever to say. The boy Bradman was 234 not out.

Back at home I questioned my mother's wisdom in aiding and abetting my downfall by so carefully collecting my gear, but she seemed to think I had come to little harm, really, and that I should have considered myself lucky to have spent such a lovely day out in the fresh air playing cricket.

As the game was to be continued on our Wingello wicket the following Saturday afternoon, I could not help feeling that I was due to face up to another hammering from this pint-sized powerhouse a week later. I saw no hope ahead for me. All was gloom. I began to count my blessings in that I had other sports to choose from. As an athlete I had spent two happy years with Botany Harriers, where I had done reasonably well without ever having really tried to train assiduously for the three events – high jump, triple jump and shot put – in which I competed. I had done well enough in tennis to promise myself some sort of a future there if I cared to concentrate.

All these thoughts went through my troubled boyish mind, but it was difficult to find one alleviating premise upon which to base my deep-dyed love for cricket. Having been belted unmercifully by a schoolboy was a pill too bitter for me to swallow. My pride had been badly injured.

The next Saturday afternoon arrived. I lined myself up manfully for another serve of what the game I had loved so much might have to offer.

The first ball again was mine to bowl, and the not out Bradman was there to deal with it. I let go my accustomed leg break, aimed at the leg stump. It spun sharply past the Bradman bat and crashed into the top of the off stump. Suddenly, I thought, the grass round our Wingello ground began to look greener than ever it had done before. The birds began to sing. The sun shone becomingly. One ball changed my whole sporting outlook. Gone were the dismaying plans to give the game away for ever. I was prepared to go on and take whatever it had in store for me, and I made the personal pledge that as I was taking it on the chin in future I would be unsparing in my efforts to deal out as much as I could of what I was getting.

There were lots of encounters for the two of us in the years that were to follow. There were times when I felt the full weight of Don Bradman's bat – many of them indeed – but there were many occasions too when I had ample reason to rejoice in the lesson I learned on those afternoons at Bowral and Wingello in 1925.

Fifty years later I had the privilege of bowling a ball to Sir Donald Bradman when we both appeared at the ceremony to open the Sir Donald Bradman Memorial Oval built on the very site of the little park in which we met for the first time ever – long before our first-class cricket careers began.

To cap this long story off I must tell you that on 26 August 1983, the day before Don's seventy-fifth birthday, Benson & Hedges invited me to attend a function at the New South Wales Cricketers' Club in Barrack Street, Sydney, where the company presented the bat used by Bradman in the game I have described to the NSW Cricket Association. It was the first bat he ever owned. His mammoth scores were shown thereon. That score of 234 led all the rest.

I was called upon to add a few words to the pleasant ceremony, and took the opportunity to pay a compliment or two to Sir Donald, and to his father, who had so beautifully dowelled a section of willow into the edge of the bat. I am afraid that I dwelt longer than I should have on that inside-edge repair job, which told of many snicked deliveries, and I claimed that many more than my actual share of these errors were committed by the maestro that memorable afternoon while I was bowling to him.

I was certainly not confident that I had convinced my listeners with that particular line of argument. Nor did I convince myself.

On the cricket field Bradman and I had the greatest respect for each other. I certainly did for him, and I know he did for me, but I might as well come straight out with it and let you know that, off the field, we had not much in common. You could say we did not like each other, but it would be closer to the truth to say we chose to have little to do with each other.

I don't really think that this arose from the ego-laden encounters of our younger days. It was more the product of the chemistry arising from our different backgrounds. Don Bradman was a teetotaller, ambitious, conservative and meticulous. I was outspoken and greg-arious, an equally ambitious young man of Irish descent.

J. H. FINGLETON

Brightly Fades the Don (1949)

On the sunny afternoon of 10 September 1948, Don Bradman was dismissed for the last time on English soil in a first-class match. Indulging in a hectic splurge of boundaries and running his score to 153, thus topping Barnes's 151 for the highest score in the match, Bradman singled out Bedser for his wicket and hit a ball high into the covers. By fate, it was Len Hutton, who, ten years before at the Kennington Oval, had taken the record score for the Test series from Bradman, who stood underneath the catch, but while the ball was yet soaring Bradman turned, took off his cap and ran full pelt for the pavilion.

By the time that Hutton's two safe hands had closed on the ball, Bradman was halfway to the pavilion. He did not turn to see whether the catch had been taken. He continued running, gloves, cap and bat fluttering from his hands, and almost before this huge Yorkshire crowd at the Scarborough Festival had had time to warm its hands in appreciation to him, Bradman was lost to view for ever as a first-class batsman on an English ground. It was the end of his 120th innings in England. He had scored the last run of his mammoth total in four tours of 9,837 runs; the statisticians were already discovering that he had averaged 96 runs per innings.

This was a most significant moment in cricketing history. Devotees of a game in a country in which many of its most illustrious players had continued long after [Bradman's] forty years of age could not credit that one so brilliant and so chockful of runs could possibly think of retirement when still lord and master of the cricketing domain. But the grim, purposeful Bradman had stated, before leaving Australia in March, that this would definitely be his last tour of England, no matter what happened. Not for him a repetition of the closing career of another illustrious Australian, Dame Nellie Melba, whose indefinite 'definite farewell appearance' became the joking butt of the country.

'Never,' said Sir Norman Birkett, at a London dinner in April, after Bradman, in a speech, had reiterated his intention to make this his final tour, 'never have I heard more tragic words fall from the lips of any man – but there is given to all men a chance to repent and, maybe, Bradman will yet repent words and an intention that seem intolerable to us.'

But those of us who knew Bradman knew full well at Scarborough that September day that we were watching him leave an English field as a batsman for the last time. It was, as I have written, a most significant moment in cricketing history. We had seen the thousands gather in front of the blitz-scarred Kennington Oval pavilion and applaud him most generously when he appeared and spoke to them at the end of his last Test match against England. Exactly a week later, he came, after hundreds had whistled and cheered and called for him, on to the pavilion balcony at Lord's and waved to the crowd below. This was at the finish of the game against the Gentlemen of England and everybody knew then that Lord's was seeing Bradman for the last time. A few minutes before he had fled from the field at the head of his Australian team as the match finished in yet another hollow victory. Bradman invariably fled from an English ground where, unlike the Australian grounds, there are no pickets to keep out the invading throng, and the invaders, as one, always made straight for Bradman at the game's finish.

He was burning, in this summer of 1948, his English pavilions behind him. On all famous grounds, as he made his farewell appearance, he was clapped to the centre as he walked slowly – always, all his cricketing lifetime, had he walked slowly to the middle as a batsman – but, at the finish of the game, a quick sprint took him soon from view. At Leeds, the most famous of all his happy hunting grounds, there was that lovely but practically unnoticed gesture of the English man in the street to Bradman as a very old and very squat Yorkshireman stood clapping, gnarled pipe in mouth and the most intent look and smile of appreciation on his face, as Bradman sprinted past him to the dressing room. 'Ah,' said the aged Yorkshireman, forgiving in a trice all the humiliation which Bradman had showered on his bowling heroes, 'you ——!' In Australia you may call a man such a name and it is a compliment when you say it with a smile. At Leeds, this day, this simple old Yorkshireman epitomized what the English cricketing public thought of Bradman over the years. The smile; the clap; the all-embracing look of intense pleasure which the retreating form had given him and, finally, the complimentary epitaph which spoke so well the thought that Bradman had been just too good – too good for every country and everybody if we except the turbulent period of bodyline when the most vicious form of attack known to the game was devised to curb the greatest batting automaton the game of cricket had produced.

Scarborough was the end of all this. Scarborough was the end of what Sir Pelham Warner has aptly termed . . . 'the Bradman era'. English cricket was free, at long last, of the Bradman plague, the Bradman scourge, the Bradman blight, call it what you will. On this lovely September afternoon, the cricket world far removed from that outside world of trouble and limitless and abortive peace talks, Bradman yielded up his batting ghost for the last time to English cricket, and his remark on returning to the pavilion, made in all good humour, was typical of the man.

On his entry, a sleepy Hassett stretched on a form.

'Ahhuum,' yawned Hassett, 'what happened? Did you chuck it away?'

'Well,' said Bradman, with a wide smile, 'I worked it out that to average 100 for every innings I have had in England, I would have had to make about 500 not out – and this game, as you know, is limited to three days.'

A few days later, at Balmoral, in Scotland, the Australian cricketers were entertained by their Majesties, the King and Queen.

'Tell me, Mr Ferguson,' said the King, with a twinkle, to 'Fergie', the official Australian scorer, 'do you use an adding machine when the Don comes to bat?'

'Fergie' laughed and was stumped for an appropriate answer but he knew that, over the years, the King's suggestion would have been a good one. 'Fergie' is a wizard scorer. He has a system all his own. He not only notes the bare details but he keeps diagrams which show, at a glance, where the batsman's runs have flowed and off which particular bowler; and, for good measure, he sketches on his sheet during the game a view he might have of steeples or trees or nearby houses. His scoring sheets, therefore, are things of rare attraction but, over the twenty years he scored during the Cricket King's Reign, 'Fergie' had no time for extraneous sketches. The Don kept him too busy for that and often, too, 'Fergie' had seen scoring boards go hay-wire in trying to keep up with Bradman's phenomenal flow of runs. It might be here that the scoring-board had not sufficient numerals in the hundreds to register after the second or third one; it might be there that the total got out of hand while a demented scoring attendant on the board tried to do justice by Bradman's and the side's totals at the same time. For never in the history of the game, Grace, Trumper, Hobbs and all the others notwithstanding, had the game known a batsman to approach Bradman's profligacy in the scoring of runs . . .

People will tell you that figures do not do justice to the superlative art that was Trumper's. Macartney was another whose skill was not revealed by figures, and the same, in my time, applied to McCabe. But as long as cricket lives, figures *will* tell the revealing story of Bradman. They will not tell, perhaps, of the murderous upsurge which happened whenever a ball was pitched short and Bradman fell into his very individual pull shot, but they will tell for all time how Bradman made runs and how he went on and on making runs.

In his pen picture of Bradman . . . Major Vincent, of *The Times*, tells how many people found themselves with a desire to go and have a beer after watching Bradman bat for some time. That was true but it applied more to Bradman in the post-bodyline period than before the days when Jardine and Larwood, the decision having been made that his batting technique was above them, decided to probe him on the physical side. Bodyline *did* leave its imprint on Bradman – as it did on all other Australian class batsmen who struck its full fire. Seldom, if ever, afterwards did Bradman's batting have the same jaunty air, if one may so term it, which distinguished his batting in 1929, 1930 (in England) and 1930–1 and 1931–2 in Australia. The bodyline sear was still there in 1934 in England when he experienced the only known run of outs in his whole first-class career.

Nothing I have experienced or read since has influenced me to alter, in the slightest, the bodyline story which I told in *Cricket Crisis*, and that historic happening in cricket was unimpeachably because of Bradman's influence and dominance in cricket. Bodyline was specially prepared, nurtured for and expended on him and, in consequence, his technique underwent a change quicker than might have been the case with the passage of time. Bodyline plucked something vibrant from his art.

It so happened, too, that soon after the bodyline period, Bradman became the Australian captain. This has to be considered in the general picture of Bradman's change of technique because it can be accepted that Bradman the batsman often became subservient to Bradman the captain. This was so, particularly, in the Australian season of 1936–7 when he had an uphill captaincy fight after Australia had lost the first two matches of the rubber. I batted almost the whole of one Test day with him in Melbourne when he refused to take the slightest risk because of the state of the game, and he did that again, often, in the series of 1938 (in England), 1946–7 (Australia) and, finally, this last season of 1948 in England.

Yardley quietened him for over after over in the first Test at Nottingham with leg theory. The 1930 Bradman would have thrived on such stuff; nor would the 1930 Bradman have adopted the 1948 technique of pushing his pads at the ball in negative answer to Bedser's threat of the fine-leg trap.

This, of a certainty, is not a criticism of Bradman. It is but another way of asserting that (a) nobody would have gone for a glass of beer while Bradman was batting in 1930 and (b) how successfully he changed his run-getting technique to suit requirements and the passage of years.

There were, I think, three periods of the Bradman era. One was pre-bodyline; the other was from then to the beginning of the world war, and the final was from 1945 to the end of 1948. In his first post-war game against England (for South Australia in Adelaide) Bradman found that his mind was moving quicker than his legs. He accommodated his technique to that, but in all periods of his era, though his technique changed considerably, Bradman retained to the last the most remarkable appetite for runs that the game of cricket has surely ever known.

As at Scarborough in his last innings, Bradman threw his wicket away on a number of occasions in England in 1948, but never until he had reached his objective, and Bradman, in all his career, never began an innings in any game without an objective. As I read his mind, he had two objectives before this 1948 tour started. One was to lead an unbeaten team through England (which had never happened before) and the other was to be cock of the batting walk until the very last. And he achieved both. No side beat this twentieth Australian XI, and Bradman, with 2,428 runs, was well ahead of the next batsman, Morris (1,922), though Morris and Barnes beat him in the Test averages.

I retain one vivid picture of Bradman's insatiable appetite for runs. It was late in the tour at Manchester and on the final day, when Bradman's decision to bat on denied the game any reasonable chance of a decision. All competitive interest had long since flown the game. Bradman had left his mark on it and Old Trafford by making a century, but in the 120s he scuttled as hard to run a three as a tyro would in running a three to make his first century in any type of a game. That was typical of Bradman. He never tired of making runs, even in his fortieth year. There was one previous occasion in this game when Bradman might have had a quick two, but the inimitable Sydney Barnes had his own ideas about the sharing of the strike. As Bradman turned for the two, Barnes had his broad back turned at the other end. It was a clear case of disagreement and, from the outside, it was apparent that Bradman rebuked Barnes down the length of the pitch.

Barnes, not easily rebuked, motioned to Bradman and made as if to walk out while the Lancashire men enjoyed the general situation. It transpired that Barnes said to Bradman: 'Here, you come and have it all. I'll have none.'

Bradman planned everything and, in his long career, I saw his complacency only twice rattled. Once was during the bodyline days and the other whenever a 'sticky' pitch happened along. Sir Pelham Warner writes of when Bradman scored a masterly 71 on a bad Sydney pitch in 1932. To be true, that was a lovely innings, but there was no fast English bowler playing that day, and for each of the few times Bradman succeeded on a bad pitch one could name half a dozen times when he failed. It was reputed of Dr Grace ('Strange to say, champion and all as W. G. was, he was not in any way a wonder on a sticky pitch' – Jack Worrell) that he had his limitations when the pitch was not good, and Bradman, though possessed of all the fundamentals to succeed, certainly had his. Bradman's limitations on a bad pitch were, I think, largely psychological. His whole demeanour changed on a sticky pitch and the psychologist had something to work on at Old Trafford on the final day of the third Test when Bradman, after every ball, walked down the pitch and energetically patted it, whereas, at the other end, Morris barely worried about it. This pitch was not bad. Something has happened to English pitches so that nowadays one rarely gets a bad one, and the turf certainly did not lift at Old Trafford this day. It was a sodden pitch, but Bradman's exaggerated patting of it was as if to suggest that it was a nasty business. Not a single ball flew.

That was one side to Bradman's batting nature and, to the student and historian, an interesting one, but, on good pitches, none will deny that this most amazing cricketer was the *greatest* personality the game has ever known. Much has been said and written of the 'jealousy' of those who played with and against Bradman, but those best qualified to speak are those who played with him, and I have never met a single first-class cricketer of Bradman's age who was not ever ready, indeed eager, to declare that the game of cricket had never known his like before. He had his critics, and will always have, I suppose, for his somewhat indifferent, cold and unfriendly attitude towards most of those with whom he played, but not one, I repeat, has ever denied the greatness which rightly belongs to Bradman. On good pitches, he stood in a class of his own as a scoring machine; and, moreover, the game has never known one to approach, yes, even approach, his miraculous consistency. When you boiled Bradman down, when you analysed his eyesight, his footwork, his judgement, his range of strokes, there was still something left in which he was also superior to all others, and that was consistency.

What was the secret of Bradman's consistency? That is a subject which will be always fresh as long as cricket is played, but I am inclined to think that the answer is to be found not so much in anything physical as in the mind. With the exception of those two perturbing instances I have mentioned, Bradman's mind was always cool, calm and analytical and, in its sphere, was as great a taskmaster of the body as man could possess. His mind gave his body no rest. His mind called the tune and his body, gifted as it was in peerless footwork, eyesight, judgement and a perfect dynamo of ceaseless energy, danced to it. The only times the dance became agitated were against bodyline and on sticky pitches.

One does well to try and analyse Bradman's mind because, in all cricket, I met no other like it. He was the only cricketer I knew who never tired of the game, who never became bored by it, who never became stale – or, if his body did, his mind would not allow it to be so.

Trumper, it was said, looked about for some deserving fellow after he had made a century and, unobtrusively, allowed him his wicket. It was said, further, that some English professional down on his luck often found himself back in the good books with Trumper's wicket against his name. A batsman like McCabe, after a run of good scores, would find himself bored and allow himself to become careless, but Bradman never allowed himself to relax or relent until his objective had been achieved. After a good day, the average cricketer, feeling at peace with the world, would seek out his comrades for a yarn and a little jollification in the evening, but Bradman either denied himself or did not want such mundane pleasures. He was not to be found.

Bradman's ways were not those of the ordinary cricketer. In the 1930 days of youthful rectitude, he made a very strong public statement against strong drink. Somewhat unkindly, impassioned zealots blazoned that statement out from noticeboards wherever Bradman went in England in 1948. He had changed somewhat in that direction but he had not changed in his general mixing. Down the Suez Canal, in October of 1948, a hot and dusty RAF lad bawled across the canal to the ship on which Bradman and his men were travelling: 'Hey, there, where are those Ashes? We'll get them from you next time, Don.' A day later came a lovely wireless message from Aden, arid, barren, rocky, sizzling Aden of all places, and in its message of greetings to Bradman and his men it concluded with a challenge to play the cricket-weary Aussies at cricket. It was from the RAF there, the RAF in one of the grimmest outposts in the whole world, and the day the *Orontes* arrived at Aden an RAF launch bobbed up and down, officers in cummerbunds and white mess jackets, waiting to take the cricketers off and entertain them.

Almost as one, but without Bradman, the Australians tumbled into the launch. Late at night they returned to the ship, singing 'Waltzing Matilda' and good cobbers for life with the men of the RAF. They had had a champion time. A few minutes after entering the mess, the CO dropped all formality by doffing his black tie and cummerbund. 'They were such good fellows', said one of the team, 'that, bless me, if we had stayed another day in Aden, we jolly well *would* have played them a game of cricket.'

It was a warm thought that the game of cricket should have its ties in such outlandish places and, thinking of the desolate lives the RAF must endure there, of what the British Empire owes to such men and how they worshipped and venerated him, it might be thought that Bradman, for once, would have yielded and gone to give, and have, pleasure. But here again was an instance of that mind which would not allow him to depart from a set course.

Do these interludes reveal anything of Bradman and his attitude towards cricket? I think they do because they show his mind and how he would never allow it to relax. Probably he reasoned that if he relaxed, if he became, mixed and lived like one of the ordinary cricketers, his concentration would be spoilt. You gathered that same concentration in conversation with him. There was the long pause, the slow, studied and concise reply . . .

These little facets of Bradman's character have to be written and understood so that we can interpret the mind which he brought to the game of cricket – a mind the game of cricket has surely not known before. D. R. Jardine was one of the few who did not give Bradman bouquets for his captaincy in England in 1948 but that might have been a hark back, on Jardine's part, to bodyline days. 'To suggest', wrote Jardine, in his cold, austere manner, 'that the captaincy of 1948 was brilliant or inspired would be flattery, but it was adequate and more than adequate.'

Bradman, in 1948, was a very sound captain. He had the advantage of leading a side that was overpowering in all directions, and that against very weak opposition, but just praise must be given him for moulding that side and for being equal to emergencies. He had one fault, I thought, as a captain and that was in having his favourites, particularly when it came to bowling out the tail-enders. Those not in the beam of his smile often received scant opportunities, so that this English tour was not a happy one for some. Midway through the tour, those who did not make the Test side, rightly thinking they might have been given more chances in other games, devised a song which they sang with rare gusto in the dressing room:

Ground-staff bowlers is our name,
Ground-staff bowling is our game.
At the nets, we bowl all day;
In a match, we're never asked to play.
We're the heroes of the dressing room;
Ground-staff bowlers is our name.

So weak was English cricket in 1948 that Bradman could well have given the 'Ground Staff' more opportunities without risk of defeat, but he had set his heart on an unbeaten record and never once took a risk with it. The Australian Board of Control, not regarding kindly what are called Festival Games in England, stipulated that there should be only a certain number of English Test players included against the Australians. Bradman 'policed' the opposing Scarborough selection pretty closely and then entered the field with his very own Test side. He was particularly 'toey' in these two Festival games, being anxious that the unbeaten record should not topple at the end, and he remembered, also, that it was in one of these games that Armstrong's great side of 1921 came to grief.

As a captain, he had good control of his side. There was the occasion at Manchester in the third Test when he apologized to Edrich ('Sorry, Bill, but these chaps get out of control when they get excited') after Miller had given Edrich four roaring bouncers in succession, but that was the time when Miller and Lindwall were stung into hectic bouncer offensive after Edrich, earlier in the day, had bowled bouncers at Lindwall. He had more conferences on the field than any other captain I knew. He took longer to place a field and was constantly in attendance on most of his bowlers during an over, but he always knew what he was striving for and always had something in mind. I can remember only two occasions on this tour when the game got away from him. Once was the Saturday at Manchester, in the third Test, and the other during the Leeds Test, in England's first innings, when, strangely, he had Johnson emulating Yardley's defensive 'wheel' field on the very first day of play. But, perhaps, there was some retaliation in this. In the final analysis, Bradman was, in every sense, a brilliant captain.

In calibre, Bradman's batting on this tour was, generally, only a shadow of what it had once been. He had some very jittery periods, particularly at the beginning of an innings and, often, against slow bowlers. He had difficulty in detecting the bosie, more difficulty than at any time of his career, but this, probably and naturally, was because his eyesight had lost its keen edge.

One day at Lord's, I stood with 'Buster' Nupen, the South African player, who had never seen Bradman bat and had flown specially to England to do so. This was Bradman's most jittery period. Laker turned him almost inside out but the little chap battled it through – and Nupen was satisfied at the end that he had seen something pretty good.

In absolute brilliance, Bradman might have been only a flicker of his 1930 self, but we must remember that those who knew him then were judging him in 1948 by his highest standards. The post-war generation were seeing him for the first time and they were satisfied, too, that he fulfilled every expectation. In this year of 1948 he had centuries on every ground of note – Lord's, the Oval, Old Trafford, Leeds, Trent Bridge, Worcester, Southend, Brighton and the rest. The post-war generation in Australia were sadly disillusioned by what they saw of Hammond in 1946–7 but Bradman, his hesitant periods apart, knew only fame and success wherever he went in England.

This 1948 tour of England was, in every way, a fitting end to the greatest career the game has known. Bradman not only again made runs unlimited but he stood out, with another Australian in the golfer von Nida, as England's sporting personality of the year. His speeches were bright and witty; he was fêted and received by the highest in the land. Together with all other cricketers of our generation, I salute him as the greatest player of his age, the greatest attraction the game of cricket has known. He did not make the friends in the game which others did but, possibly he reasoned, he would not have been the player he was had he allowed his concentration to be upset in the slightest manner. He brilliantly and decisively achieved the objective he set himself when he found his feet in first-class cricket – and that was to be, by far, the greatest run-getter and the greatest holder of records the game has known. And, in doing that, he gave to the man-in-the-street the greatest possible value for his admission money and he brought to cricket the most pronounced publicity the game had ever known.

*   *   *

With Learie Constantine, George Headley held together the West
Indian side in its early years of playing Tests. If he failed with the
bat, his side normally got out for under 100. Headley carried his
team on his shoulders: a later biography was entitled *The West Indian
Atlas*. So accomplished was his batsmanship that Anglo-Australian
writers liked to call him 'the Black Bradman'. His own compatriots,
such as Constantine, thought this inexact as well as patronizing: they
would rather refer to the Don as 'the White Headley'.

Headley's character and cricketing style are vividly evoked here
by C. L. R. James. James, however, omits one significant detail. When
England toured the West Indies in 1929–30, Headley's family (the
cricketer included) was due to emigrate to the United States of
America. But his passport was unaccountably delayed, this allowing
him to appear for Jamaica against the tourists. He scored a century,
was chosen for the West Indies, and never looked back or, shall we
say, never looked northward again. So, were it not for an indolent
bureaucrat, George Headley would have been lost to the world of
cricket.

C. L. R. James

The Black Bradman (1963)

To think about Constantine between the wars is to conjure up the
other West Indian master of the period, the one and only George
Headley. I write of him purely as a cricketer. And I do so . . . because,
first, this West Indian narrowly escapes being the greatest batsman I
have ever seen. Pride of place in my list goes to Bradman, but George
is not far behind. In fact, it is my belief that if he had lived his
cricketing life in England or Australia he would not be behind anyone.
Everyone is familiar with his scores. On a world scale his average is,
I believe, exceeded only by Bradman and Merchant. His average of
one century in every four Test innings is second only to Bradman.
In those days there were no Test matches against India and Pakistan
and New Zealand. George had to meet the full strength of
England and Australia. The second reason why I write about him is
that he is a remarkable individual. I believe that every great batsman
is a special organism; it must be so, for they are very rare, as rare

as great violinists – I doubt if I have known many more than a dozen.

There is a third reason, but that I shall reserve.

I saw George in 1930, I saw him in 1934, I played cricket with him in Lancashire. He had to a superlative degree the three cardinal qualities of the super batsman. He saw the ball early. He was quick on his feet. He was quick with his bat. The most important of all, in my view, is seeing the ball early. In 1953 George told me that from the time he began to play cricket he saw every ball bowled come out of the bowler's hand. He added that if he did not see it out of the bowler's hand he would be at a loss how to play. The conversation began by his telling me of a bowler in league cricket, of no importance, who had bowled him two balls in succession neither of which he saw out of the hand. The experience left him completely bewildered.

He was as quick on his feet as any player I have seen except Don Bradman. To see Bradman get back, his right foot outside the off stump, pointing to mid-on, and hook a fast bowler was to witness not cricket but acrobatics: you knew he had got there only after he had made the stroke. George's speed of foot was of the same kind. He was as quick with his bat as any. Bowlers, seeing the ball practically on his pad, appealed against him for lbw, only to grind their teeth as the bat came down and put the ball away to the fine-leg boundary. Any single one of these three qualities makes a fine batsman, and courage and confidence are the natural result of having all three.

What I want to draw special attention to here is George's play on wet or uncertain wickets. Here are his scores on such wickets in England.

1933   *Other high scores in the innings*

v. Northamptonshire	52 out of 129	32 and 15
v. Yorkshire	25 out of 115	25 and 16
v. Nottinghamshire	66 out of 314	54 and 51
v. Lancashire	66 out of 174	29 and 18
v. Leicestershire	60 out of 156	22 and 19
v. Leveson-Gower's XI	35 out of 251	70 and 44

1939

v. Surrey	52 out of 224	58 and 52
v. Yorkshire	61 out of 234	72 and 28

v. England	51 out of 133	47 and 16
	5 out of 43 (4w)	13 and 11
v. Somerset	0 out of 84	45 and 17
v. Gloucestershire	40 out of 220	50 and 28
	5 out of 162	43 and 26

In those thirteen innings George passed 50 seven times. Three times only he scored less than double figures, and in his other three innings his scores were 25, 35 and 40. I believe those figures would be hard to beat. Look at a similar list made for Bradman by Ray Robinson in his fascinating book *Between Wickets*.

	Match	Total	Bradman	Top Scorer
1928	Brisbane Test	66	1	Woodfull 30 n.o.
1929	Sydney	128	15	Fairfax 40
1930	Notts Test	144	8	Kippax 64 n.o.
	Northants	93	22	Bradman 22
	Gloucester	157	42	Ponsford 51
		117	14	McCabe 34
1932	Perth	159	3	McCabe 43
	Melbourne	19 (2w)	13	
1933	Sydney	180	1	Rowe 70
		128	71	Bradman 71
1934	Lord's Test	118	13	Woodfull 43
1936	Brisbane Test	58	0	Chipperfield 36
	Sydney Test	80	0	O'Reilly 37 n.o.
1938	Middlesex	132	5	Chipperfield 36
	Yorkshire	132	42	Bradman 42

In fifteen innings Bradman passed 50 only once, 40 only twice and 15 only four times. His average is 16.66. George's average is 39.85. You need not build on these figures a monument, but you cannot ignore them.

Bradman's curious deficiency on wet wickets has been the subject of much searching comment. George's superior record has been noticed before, and one critic, I think it was Neville Cardus, has stated that Headley has good claims to be considered *on all wickets* the finest of the inter-war batsmen. I would not go so far. It is easy to give figures and make comparisons and draw rational conclusions.

The fact remains that the odds were 10 to 1 that in any Test Bradman would make 150 or 200 runs, and the more the runs were needed the more certain he was to make them. Yet if Bradman never failed in a Test series, neither did George. I believe Bradman and Headley are the only two between the wars of whom that can be said. (Hammond failed terribly in 1930 in England and almost as badly in the West Indies in 1934–5.)

But there is another point I wish to bring out. Between 1930 and 1938 Bradman had with him in England Ponsford, Woodfull, McCabe, Kippax, Brown, Hassett. All scored heavily. In 1933 and 1939 West Indian batsmen scored runs at various times, but George had nobody who could be depended on. In 1933 his average in the Tests was 55.40. Among those who played regularly the next average was 23.83. In 1939 his average in the Tests was 66.80. The next batsman averaged 57.66, but of his total of 173 he made 137 in one innings. Next was 27.50. It can be argued that this stiffened his resistance. I don't think so. And George most certainly does not. 'I would be putting on my pads and sometimes before I was finished I would hear that the first wicket had gone.' This is what he carried on his shoulders for nearly ten years. None, not a single one of the great batsmen, has ever been so burdened for so long.

He had characteristics which can be attributed to less than half a dozen in the whole history of the game. He has said, and all who know his play can testify, that he did not care who bowled at him: right hand, left hand, new ball, old ball, slow, fast, all were the same. He loved the bad wickets. And his reason is indicative of the burden he carried. 'On a bad wicket it was you and the bowler. If he pitched up you had to drive. If he pitched short you had to turn and hook. No nonsense.' I sensed there a relief, a feeling that he was free to play the only game which could be successful under the circumstances, but this time his own natural game.

George was a quiet cricketer. So quiet that you could easily underestimate him. One day in 1933 West Indies were playing Yorkshire at Harrogate, the wicket was wet and Verity placed men close in, silly mid-off and silly point I think. The West Indian players talked about bowlers who placed men close in for this batsman and the other batsman. George joined in the reminiscences. Someone said, 'George, if Verity put a man there for you—'

A yell as of sudden, intense, unbearable pain burst from George, so as to startle everyone for yards around.

'Me!' he said. 'Put a man there for me!'

They could talk about it for other players. Test players, but that anyone should even think that such fieldsmen could be placed for him – that was too much for George. The idea hurt him physically.

George was a great master of the game in many senses. He landed in Australia (1931–2) a boy of twenty-one who had never played or seen cricket out of the West Indies. As he has told me in great detail: 'I was an off-side batsman, drive, cut and back stroke through the covers. Of course, I also could hook.' Australian critics were startled at his mastery of batting and of an innings of 131, played at Victoria in less than even time, one critic who had seen all the great players of the previous thirty years said that no finer innings had ever been seen on the Melbourne ground. An innings of 82 against New South Wales evoked the same admiration. Then, as he says, the word went round: keep away from his off stump and outside it, you will never get him there. Henceforth in every match, on every ground, it was a leg-stump attack and an on-side field. George was baffled and I remember how anxious we were at a succession of failures. What he did, under fire, so to speak, was to reorganize his batting to meet the new attack.

This is what happened to George in Australia: 25, 82, 131, 34. Then he failed steadily: 27 run out and 16; 0 and 11 (Test, to Grimmett both times); 3; 14 and 2 (Test); 19 and 17. Nine successive failures. It is only by the third Test that George is once more in control of the situation: 102 not out out of 193 (next highest score 22), and 28 out of 148 (again top score); 77 and 113; 75 and 39; 33 out of 99 (top score) and 11 out of 107 (fourth Test); 70 run out and 2; 105 and 30 (fifth Test).

He had so mastered the new problems that Grimmett considers Headley to be the greatest master of on-side play whom he ever bowled against, and he bowled against both Hobbs and Bradman. Yet of George's 169 not out in the Manchester Test of 1934, A. Ratcliffe, reviewing modern cricket (*The Cricketer Annual*, 1933–4), says, 'His cuts off the slow bowling were a strange sight to see and I had only seen such strokes once before when Woolley cut Roy Kilner's slow deliveries to the boundary time after time.'

George Headley, this West Indian, would be my candidate for a clinical study of a great batsman as a unique type of human being, mentally and physically. So far as I know no one has probed into this before.

Mentally. George is batting against an Australian slow bowler, probably Grimmett. To the length ball he gets back and forces Grimmett away between midwicket and mid-on or between mid-wicket and square leg. He is so quick on his feet and so quick with his bat that Grimmett simply cannot stop ones and twos in between the fieldsmen. Every time Grimmett flights the ball, out of the crease and the full drive. Grimmett, that great master of length, can't even keep George quiet. He has a man at fine leg. He shifts him round to square and moves square to block up the hole. Next ball is just outside the leg stump. George, gleeful at the thought that fine leg is no longer there, dances in front of the wicket 'to pick up a cheap four'. He glances neatly, only to see Oldfield, the wicketkeeper, way over on the leg side taking the catch. The two seasoned Australians have trapped him. That sort of thing has happened often enough. Now note George's reaction.

'I cut that out.'

'What do you mean, you cut it out?'

'I just made up my mind never to be caught that way again.'

'So you do not glance?'

'Sure I glance, but I take care to find out first if any of these traps are being laid.'

'Always?'

'Always.'

And I can see that he means it.

Mark Twain was once a pilot on the Mississippi. The bed of that river is always changing and a man is sounding all the time and calling out the changes. Mark Twain says that a pilot, whether on duty or not, is always hearing these soundings. Even when playing poker his mind registers them automatically and days after uses the latest results when piloting. Great batsmen are the same, they are not like you or me. An experience is automatically registered and henceforth functions as a permanent part of the organism.

Similarly with placing. For George, to make a stroke was to hit the ball (he had a loud scorn for 'the pushers') and to hit it precisely in a certain place. He couldn't think of a stroke without thinking of exactly where it was going. Whenever he had scored a century and runs were not urgent, he practised different strokes at the same ball, so as to be sure to command the placing of the ball where there was no fieldsman. Those who know George only after the war don't really know him. In 1939 he was, in addition to on-side play, a master of the cut, both square and late, and though he was, like Bradman, mainly a back-foot player, half-volleys did not escape him. This placing to a shifting field must also be to a substantial degree automatic. Having taken a glance round, *and sized up what the bowler is trying to do*, the great batsman puts the ball away more by reflex than conscious action.

George had one quality that was paralleled by no one except Bradman. When he was run out in the Oval Test in 1939 he had scored 65 and, as one reporter wrote, if he hadn't been run out nothing was more certain than that he would make a century. He was not on the defensive but, according to *Wisden*, was cutting, forcing off his legs and driving.

Now physically. Headley has told me that the night before a Test he rarely slept more than an hour or two. (The night before the second century in the Test at Lord's he never slept at all.) But he isn't suffering from insomnia, not in the least. This fantastic man is busy playing his innings the next day. The fast bowler will swing from leg. He plays a stroke. Then the bowler will come in from the off. He plays the stroke to correspond. The bowler will shorten. George hooks or cuts. Verity will keep a length on or just outside the off stump. George will force him away by getting back to cut and must be on guard not to go too greedily at a loose ball – that is how in Tests he most fears he will lose his innings (a revealing commentary on his attitude to bowlers). Langridge will flight the ball. Down the pitch to drive. So he goes through every conceivable ball and makes a stroke to correspond. This cricket strategist obviously works on Napoleon's maxim that if a general is taken by surprise at anything that occurs on a battlefield then he is a bad general.

Morning sees him in the grip of processes he does not control. He rises early and immediately has a bowel motion. At ten o'clock he has another. And then he is ready. He is very specific that these automatic physiological releases take place only on big-match days. He is chain-smoking in the dressing room. But once he starts to walk down the pavilion steps he would not be able to recognize his father if he met him halfway. Everything is out of his mind except batting. Bumpers? Bodyline? He is not concerned. He gets out to good balls (or bad), but such is his nervous control that no bowler as such has ever bothered him. Near the end of an English tour he is physically drained except for batting. He has a few days' leave, he sits and smokes. His companions plan expeditions, make dates to go out with girls. George sits and smokes. From where he sits he doesn't want to budge an inch. But when they return to the tour, as soon as he has a bat in his hands, he is as fit as ever; fit, however, for nothing else except batting. When the season is over the fatigue remains and it takes him weeks to recover his habitual self. I watched the West Indians in the nets at Lord's in 1933 before the tour began. George never to my knowledge practised seriously. He fooled around playing the ball here and there. It was his first visit to England, but he was as sure of himself as if he were in Jamaica. In 1933 he ended the season with scores of 79, 31 (run out), 167, 95, 14 and 35. He was third in the averages for the season, Hammond and Mead averaging 67 to his 66. If he had thought about it in 1933 he would have made the runs needed. With him batting was first, not second, nature. In 1939 he was 72 with Hammond next at 63. He was a fine fieldsman and of the great batsmen of his day only Bradman was faster between the wickets.

His only unhappiness on the cricket field was that he was allowed to bowl only on the rarest occasions. George used to watch batsmen and detect their weak points. But from there he went on to think that he could get them out with his leg break. Which does not at all follow. In 1933 he took 21 wickets. Alas! in 1939 he was allowed to bowl only ten overs for the whole season. He spoke of it with feeling. In 1948, in a series of intercolonial matches in Jamaica, George made, out of 356, 203 not out; out of 151 for 5, 57 not out; out of 456, 79 retired hurt. But he also took 4 for 40 and 3 for 53. Whereby I deduce that George captained the Jamaica side.

What does he remember most? Or rather what do I remember most about his talk on cricket? George rarely raises his voice. He never raised it louder than when he spoke of the West Indian failure in Australia to deal with the bumpers of Lindwall and Miller. 'West Indians couldn't hook,' he says, his eyes blazing. 'West Indians!' To this day he remains adamant in his view that as far as he is concerned bowlers can drop the ball where they like and put fieldsmen where they like. 'If they catch it when I hit it they are welcome.' There is not the slightest trace of braggadocio; I have not known a more genuinely modest cricketer. For all I know, George may be quite wrong in his views of short fast balls, though he had plenty of them in his time and dealt faithfully by them. He speaks as he does because it is part of his outlook: never to have his equanimity disturbed by anything that a bowler may do.

That is why he speaks so soberly of the two balls which he did not see out of the bowler's hand. He had a kind of nightmare vision of having to bat without seeing the ball out of the hand. And one more catastrophe, a real one. A celebration match in one of the leagues. Mayors and corporations, dignitaries and their ladies. George, the star attraction, opens the innings, taking the first ball. An unknown medium-paced bowler sends one right up on middle and leg. Right up. George plays comfortably forward, a thing he rarely does, only to see the ball move away in the last inches and hit his off stump. George is horrified. He has disappointed everybody. But there is more to it. He goes behind and observes the bowler carefully. Yes, it was not an accident, he is swinging the ball very late. George makes enquiries. Yes, he is a good league bowler, always moves the new ball well. It is years since it has happened. But George cannot get over it. He has been caught napping. He should never have assumed that any bowler with a new ball in whatever kind of cricket was not able to move it so late. Ordinary humans don't play cricket that way. Few people in this world do anything that way.

Such strange human beings as George Headley fascinate me not only for what they do but in themselves. There was a time when I read every biography of Napoleon I came across, and I still read some. He looks over a map of gun emplacements on the coast of France and points out that the investigators have left out two. I have known a few men who could do similarly. He could sleep instantaneously at any time for any length of time available. I have never met a man who could do that. And I have met very few men who can concentrate on anything as George concentrated on batting. I am sure he never had to learn it. I wonder if he had gone to America to study medicine (and had got interested in it) whether he would have become a great surgeon, seeing everything, remembering everything, hands deft and sure, without nerves before the most distressing case. These qualities were not remote from those which made George the batsman he was . . .

No, I have not forgotten the third reason why I wanted to write about George Headley. And note it well, you adventurous categorizers. I know Constantine and Headley pretty well, as crick-eters and as human beings. Contrary to all belief, popular and learned, Constantine the magician is the product of tradition and training. It is George the maestro who is an absolutely natural cricketer. We West Indians are a people on our way who have not yet reached a point of rest and consolidation. Critics of a sociological turn of mind had proved that we were a nation which naturally produced fast bowlers, when in 1950 Ram and Val, both under twenty-one, produced the greatest slow-bowling sensation since the South African team of 1907. We are moving too fast for any label to stick.

★   ★   ★

In the epic bodyline series of 1932–3, Don Bradman was reduced to human scale by the bowling of Harold Larwood. Larwood was a superb bowler of sharp pace, with a beautiful flowing action and a late outswing. Under instructions from his captain, D. R. Jardine, he eschewed his normal methods in favour of short, bumping balls aimed at the batsman's body. These tactics brought England the Ashes, but when they became too controversial to be repeated the bowler was made a scapegoat, and was never chosen for his country again.

The following essay describes the visit, years later, to Harold Larwood of one of his foremost opponents. The bowler himself regarded Fingleton as the bravest batsman he had bowled to. Appositely, it was 'Fingo' who later arranged for the bowler and his family to be resettled, with honour, in Australia.

J. H. FINGLETON

My Friend, the Enemy (1949)

It was in a side street in Blackpool that we found him. George Duckworth, one of his best friends in his playing days, knew the way. 'It is a neat little mixed shop,' said George, 'but you won't find his name on it.' And we didn't, which was strange, because in his day his name was possibly even as famous as Bradman's, but he had not only finished with all that. He had not the slightest wish to be reminded of it.

His eldest daughter saw us first. She recognized George and gave him a great welcome, smiling broadly and motioning towards the back of the house. And there in a homely room, its walls festooned with photographs of some of the most stirring times known to the game of cricket, he gave me a quiet but a warm welcome. He recognized me immediately, though I was the first Australian cricketer he had met since those stormy days of 1932–3 when his name was sprawled across the columns of newspapers in much the same manner as he sprawled his victims across the cricket field, but in 1948 he was much thinner. Walking behind him, one would never guess that here was the greatest fast bowler of the modern age; the possessor, in his time, of as lovely a bowling action as the game has ever known. But his face, though thinner, had not changed much. He was still the same Harold Larwood.

The conversation, for a time, was circumspect. Not only was I one of the 'enemy' of 1932–3 but I was a newspaperman, and Larwood had memories of how he had been publicized over the years by the stunting gentry of my profession. Then, in addition, he wanted to bury the dead. You saw that, clearly, in his refusal to have his name shown in the slightest manner over his shop. Dozens of former cricketers throughout the world, whose claim to fame could not compare with his, have capitalized their glory by having their names over balls or bats, by having it in books, by having it up in big letters outside their places of business, but not in the slightest manner, and certainly not by having his name blazoned to the outside world, did Harold Larwood wish to recapture the past. He wanted only to forget it, and so his business, to all appearance, was no different to thousands of similar businesses throughout England that are run by the Joneses, the Browns, Williams and Smiths.

It was a pinch of snuff, so to speak, that broke the ice. He took his box out and offered it to me. I declined. Not so George Duckworth. 'Aay, laad,' said George, taking a copious pinch. He placed it on the back of his hand, slapped it with the other, sniffed simultaneously and forthwith began to sneeze so vigorously that tears ran from his eyes. Larwood smiled and took his with the air of a man long accustomed to the art.

'You know,' he said to me, 'I always had snuff in my pocket when I was bowling. I often used to take a pinch of it on the field in Australia. It used to freshen me up. And it's much better for you than cigarettes.'

An eminent medical authority in the last century, Dr Gordon Hake, would have approved of that. 'Snuff', wrote Dr Hake to a critic of his habit, 'not only wakes up that torpor so prevalent between the nose and the brain, making the wings of an idea uncurl like those of a newborn butterfly, but while others sneeze and run at the eyes my schneiderian membrane is impervious to the weather or, to be explicit, I never take a cold in the head.' Soon after the introduction of snuff into Britain in the eighteenth century, the *Gentlewoman's Companion,* noble production, was advising its gentle readers whose sight was failing to use the right sort of Portugal snuff 'whereby many eminent people had cured themselves so that they could read without spectacles after having used them for many years'.

As Larwood was snuffing, I thought his Australian opponents might have been a little better off in 1932–3 had somebody got his box away from him. He might not have sighted his target or his victim so readily, but here at Blackpool, in 1948, it cleared also the atmosphere and when, at long last, George had got his schneiderian membrane to behave, the three of us fell to discussing the old days in a reminiscent manner. There was no bitterness. I had taken many on the ribs from Larwood and Voce in those bodyline days, but all that was forgotten as we recalled the players of those days and the many incidents – for incidents happened in the bodyline series every other minute.

One has not to talk long with Larwood to realize that he is still embittered over those days. I don't think it is with the Australians, but rather with those English officials who were glad to have him and use him before bodyline became ostracized, and then, conveniently, put him aside. He finds that impossible to forgive. Like the prodigal son, he would have been welcomed home by the MCC in 1935 and had all forgiven, but Larwood is a man of strong beliefs. To satisfy all and sundry, the MCC wished Larwood to apologize to them. Had he done that, like Voce, he would have been chosen again for the Australian tour of 1936–7, but Larwood could not see that he had anything to apologize over and so he remained adamant and went out of the game under a cloud.

He did not say so, but I gathered that he considered himself badly treated, and many who know the story of those bodyline days will agree with him. With us, he recalled only the happy memories of the most distressing tour in cricket history, though when we talked of Bradman I detected again the same old glint of battle I had seen in his eye when I had faced up to him as a batsman.

'When I bowled against Bradman,' he said, 'I always thought he was out to show me up as the worst fast bowler in the world. Well, I took the view that I should try and show him up as the worst batsman. But, laad, he was a good 'un.'

We fell to looking through his photographic albums and the reminiscences among the three of us came thick and fast. His eldest daughter (and Larwood has five beautiful daughters, the youngest between our legs on the floor) had just begun to take an interest in cricket, and only a few days before Larwood had got out his souvenirs to show her, and they included innumerable balls with silver rings about them describing how in many places he had performed grand bowling feats.

Larwood made some pretty shrewd observations about batsmen. He reeled off the names of famous batsmen who, he considered, couldn't play the hook stroke and were thus at a disadvantage against him. The cricket world would be amazed if I repeated the men he named but, like Keith Miller, the Australian, he considered himself fully entitled to prove their weaknesses with bouncers. But how the wheel has now turned full circle! Here, in 1948, under Bradman, the Australians exploited the bouncers to the full (though without the packed leg field of Jardine), and members of the Nottingham County Committee, the same committee which was forced to apologize to Woodfull and his team in 1934 because Voce had bowled bumpers, now admonished their own spectators for barracking against Australian bumpers. The cricket world, surely, is as crazy and as inconsistent as the outside one.

It was with difficulty that we induced Larwood to come with us to a cricket game for charity which we were playing on the Blackpool ground. He compromised to the extent of promising to come down after afternoon tea. He had not seen either the 1934 or 1938 Australian teams in action. He had not seen his C.-in-C., Douglas Jardine, since Jardine had played in his benefit game in 1935. He had not seen this present Australian team in action, though he had a hankering to see Lindwall bowl. He could not remember the last time he had seen a game on his old home ground, Trent Bridge. Cricket had lost all its appeal for Larwood.

He came to the charity game, forced into it, we thought, by his family, who liked to see him with old associates. He told me there a story I loved. It was about Sir Pelham Warner and myself and concerned the bodyline tour. It happened during the Adelaide game, where feeling was tremendously high, and where Woodfull used strong words to Warner over the tactics of the MCC team. That story ran quickly to the press, and Sir Pelham, jumping to conclusions because I was a pressman, wrongly blamed me for the breach of ethics.

'As we were going out to field in your second innings,' said Larwood, 'Sir Pelham said to me, "Larwood, I will give you a pound if you bowl Fingleton out quickly." If you remember, I did, and when I came off the field Sir Pelham was waiting there at the door with a pound note in his hand.'

I will never forget that ball. It was the best ever bowled to me in cricket. At Larwood's top speed, it changed course in the air from leg and, continuing on that course, pitched about the leg and middle stump and took the off bail. It was absolutely unplayable. A batsman never minds being dismissed by a good ball, even for nothing, as I was that day.

'Ah, well,' said Larwood, 'those days are gone for ever, but here's a pound note. Let's all go and have a drink and we will say it is on Sir Pelham.'

There were times, during the Australian tour of bodyline, when Larwood thought the game not worth the candle. He knew abuse. The tumult was overpowering, the work of fast bowling hard. He has a very sensitive side to his nature and often wondered whether it was worth it, but then he allowed his mind to revert to his coal-mining days before he played cricket and that was sufficient. Strangely, on that tour, his stomach revolted against food. He found that beer, with his occasional pinch of snuff on the field, gave him all the sting he wanted. From the Australian viewpoint, it gave him more than enough, but he will always be remembered in Australia, tactics of that MCC side apart, as the Prince of Bowlers.

It was a coincidence that very day that Larwood should have received from Australia a long letter from a youth on the art of bowling. It was an interesting letter, asking for advice. It was fitting, even though this lad had never seen Larwood bowl, that he should have written to such a one for advice, though I smiled to myself as I read this delightful piece of youthful folly: 'Do you think, Mr Larwood,' wrote this ardent theorist, 'that you might have been a better fast bowler if you had begun the swing of your right arm from lower down?' As if any Australian would have wanted Larwood to be better than he was, but perhaps the oddest thing of all about this letter was that it came from Bowral, home town of Bradman. How quaint if Bowral, through Bradman's greatest antagonist on the field, should produce another Larwood!

When we parted we had extracted from him almost a half-promise that he would come to Old Trafford and see and meet the Australians. He wanted to meet O'Reilly; he wanted to see Lindwall particularly, but Larwood never came. I think the inside of an English first-class ground contained too many sad memories for him. He deserved better of the game; he deserved better, particularly, of English cricket because, in tactics, he was only a cog in the wheel. He was, for a certainty, the only bowler who quelled Bradman; the only bowler who made Bradman lose his poise and balance, departing from his set path of easeful centuries into flurried and agitated movements.

I left Blackpool glad that I had seen Larwood, and I think that he, for his part, was pleased again to meet an Australian cricketer, the first since the field of battle in 1932–3. There is something tragic about his finish in cricket and the fact that he wishes to have no ties with the game now at all. It is interesting, too, to look back to those days of 1932–3 and reflect what time has done for the central figures, Bradman and Larwood. The game has been over-kind to one; unkind to the other, but that has ever been the ways of cricket. It is a game, mostly, for batsmen, and I thought of all this as I left Larwood on the note, of all things, of migration. He thinks hard these days of bringing his lovely family of five daughters to settle in a country which once flamed from end to end over his bowling. That, surely, must be the oddest thought of all – Larwood settled in Australia! But he would be doubly welcome. Australia has never held anything against Larwood.

*   *   *

Either side of the Second World War, the England batting was dominated by Denis Compton and Len Hutton. They were alike in achievement and commitment, but dissimilar in personality and technique. Hutton was a taciturn (some would say dour) Yorkshireman, who rarely smiled and always kept his own counsel. Although he possessed a wide array of strokes, he did not often unwrap them in the Test arena. Compton, by contrast, was a cheerfully spontaneous character whose warm and outgoing personality made him loved by schoolboys and opponents alike. He was also an inventive strokemaker who played all the shots in the book, and some that are not there besides. A natural sportsman, he also played soccer for Arsenal and, on occasion, for England.

I have chosen an account of Compton's first-class debut and an epitaph on Hutton's retirement, written by two close contemporaries of the cricketers.

E. W. SWANTON
Compton Arrives (1948)

Just before Whitsun 1936 I played in a match in the Minor Counties' Championship at Folkestone between the Second XIs of Middlesex and Kent. After about half an hour on the first morning the Middlesex position was distinctly awkward, for we had lost four of the best players for round about a dozen, the writer having gone in first and been a spectator of one disaster after another from the bowler's end, and, I dare say, having had little of the bowling himself. There was a strong, chesty fellow doing the damage, I seem to remember, called Cole, perhaps helped by that early freshness in the pitch that one generally finds near the sea.

At this point there entered a juvenile figure with an oddly relaxed way of walking, somewhat loose round the knees and with a swaying of the shoulders, inclined to let his bat trail after him rather than use it as a stick in the usual fashion. As he had to pass me I thought a word of encouragement would not be out of place, and murmured something about playing up and down the line of the ball and there being nothing to worry about. My new companion thanked me politely, and very soon started pushing the ball round the field with every appearance of ease, and running up and down the pitch rather more quickly than his ponderous partner found comfortable. To within a run or two a hundred were put on for this fifth wicket, each of us just missing his fifty. Such was my introduction to Compton (D.).

When I went back to Lord's after the match R. W. V. Robins was anxious to know how it had gone, and whether anyone had distinguished himself. I told him I had been playing with the best young cricketer I had ever seen, and when I mentioned his name he said he was just going to the nets with G. O. Allen to look at some of the younger members of the ground staff, and that there was a place going for one of them in the Middlesex side against Sussex next day.

I can see a cynical smile registering on the faces of a hardened raconteur or two at this point. One has told the story often enough. It has been a stock-in-trade of several talks on cricket, to British and Australian soldiers, to schoolboys, and so on. It is easy to be certain of the truth of any incident one has narrated frequently, as one knows when one endures the hardy annuals of one's friends and notes how details are apt to change colour until the picture becomes very different from its original.

All that can be said then is that to the best of my belief I told the Middlesex captain that this was the finest young cricketer I had ever seen; nor does there seem any great merit in the remark, for Denis at eighteen (his birthday had occurred the preceding week) was already showing those excellent gifts of eye and balance which now distinguish him from even the best of his contemporaries; technical gifts and also gifts of temperament, for he was very soon commanding situations more momentous than our little affair at Folkestone.

In his wisdom, and with Allen's warm approval, the Middlesex captain chose Denis to play in the Whitsuntide match against Sussex. There was insight in this, for though he had made some runs against Kent Second XI, Denis had no substantial record to urge his preference over several others more mature and experienced. He had not even been selected for the match preceding that against Kent. The highest of his three innings in the Minor Counties' Championship the summer before had been 12.

Great cricketers on coming into county cricket more often than not have made distinctive beginnings, either successful or spectacularly the reverse. Patsy Hendren began his career with a duck; Hammond was bowled by Gregory for 0, and, in his second innings, by Mailey for 1; and Woolley has described how in his first match he twice dropped Johnny Tyldesley, who went on to make 295, took 1 for

103, and scored 0, before in Kent's second innings he redeemed himself with an innings of 64. But Hobbs made 88 in his first match for Surrey and 155 in his second; A. C. MacLaren and A. P. F. Chapman are among those who began with hundreds.

Denis Compton's innings in the match against Sussex in 1936 will be remembered by many loyal watchers at Lord's, for it took place on Whit Monday before a big crowd, and the circumstances of it were exciting. On the Saturday Sussex had made 185, Parks (J. H.) having been caught by Compton (D.) off the bowling of Smith (J.), and Parks (H. W.) having been caught by Allen off Compton.

Compton says there was nothing specially notable about his first catch in first-class cricket; Allen, on the other hand, declares that the catch which gave Compton his first wicket was a skier taken as he ran diagonally backwards from mid-off, and was one of the best he ever caught: which, if his memory is accurate, implies, of course, that it was a very fine catch indeed.

On the first evening, against Tate, who in 1936 was still well capable on occasions of the old destructive burst at the beginning of an innings, Middlesex lost four wickets for virtually nothing, and the Monday morning was occupied in a struggle for the lead on the first innings. The end of the batting order read: 9, G. O. Allen, who was going in late having dislocated a finger; 10, Compton; 11, Smith. But this was about the period when the recipe for almost any Middlesex crisis was to send in Jim Smith. Just before one o'clock, therefore, in loomed the vast Smith, and proceeded to cleave the air, and sometimes the ball, being, as *Wisden* records, especially severe on Wensley, whose off breaks were just the giant's handwriting. Smith being out for a highly valuable 28, Denis came in last to join Allen at quarter past one, Middlesex needing 24 for first innings' lead.

Tate bowled from the pavilion end, and as the young man passed England's captain-designate he was given an eminently sound piece of advice: 'This chap comes off much quicker than you expect. Whatever you do, play forward.' 'Yes, sir.' The first ball was a beauty, pitched to a length on the off stump. Denis played back, and it flew an inch over the middle stump into Cornford's hands.

Allen, so he recalls, and I do not doubt him, expressed himself pretty forcibly. Denis said, 'I'm sorry, sir, I'll do better in a minute.' He did do better, to the extent of seeming completely composed. The score crept up until at lunch Middlesex needed only 12. Afterwards these 12 came, and some more for good measure; finally it

was Jim Parks, not the deadly Tate, who had Denis lbw, the stand
having by then realized 36.

Three Middlesex matches at Lord's followed this one, against
Notts, Northants, and Yorkshire. Denis played in all of these, and
before the last of them there was no question of his place in the
team being in danger. He made 26 not out and 14 against Notts,
0 and 87 against Northants, and 26 and 1 against Yorkshire, all in
low-scoring matches. In the Notts match he showed more confidence
than several of the side against Larwood and Voce. In the Northants
match, now promoted to No. 7, he joined Walter Robins in the
second innings when five wickets had fallen to those two dangerous
bowlers Clark and Austin Matthews for 21 runs, and between them
they put on 129.

It was during one of these two matches, when he was batting
with his captain, that he hit either Voce or Clark for two stirring off
drives off successive balls up to the top of the ground. While the
fielder was fetching the ball a conversation took place between Denis
and his captain on these lines:

'You know what to look out for now, don't you?'

'No, sir.'

'Well, he'll bounce one at you.'

'If he does, I shall hook him.' The short fast one came down,
and it was duly hooked with considerable violence into the Mound.

Such a remark, made in another way by a young cricketer, might
have suggested a large head. But no one who has known this particular young cricketer has ever entertained the slightest suspicions
on this score. I quote the incident as illustrating his naively confident
approach to the game. It was utterly natural.

Three weeks after his first appearance, and in his sixth county
match, Denis made his first hundred for Middlesex in the return
against Northants at Northampton. On the third morning Middlesex
led by 3 runs on first innings with five wickets left, and the plain
need was for some more runs with all possible speed. Three wickets
fell at once, but then, to quote *Wisden*'s report: 'By perfect timing
Compton drove, pulled, and cut with remarkable power, and took
out his bat, with fourteen fours as his best strokes, in one and three-
quarter hours. He and Sims put on 76 for the ninth wicket and there
followed a remarkable last partnership of 74 with Peebles, who by
sound defence stayed while Compton scored his last 60 runs.'

All witnesses agree with what a blending of cool judgement and brilliant stroke play Denis set about the bowling on this June morning. He has always revelled in partnerships with tail-enders and it is appropriate that the bulk of his first century should have come in a stand for the last wicket. It would have been fitting, too, if his innings should have led to Middlesex snatching a victory, but this they could not quite do, a thunderstorm stopping the game when Northants had lost eight wickets in their second innings.

There were no more hundreds that season, but several near-misses. We find Denis scoring 81 out of 131 added with Hulme in just over an hour at Lord's against Gloucestershire, and 87 and 96 at Maidstone against Kent, batting for less than two hours in each innings. At Hove in the Bank Holiday match against Sussex he got 80 in an hour and a half; at Lord's against Hampshire 77 in an hour and a quarter. In his last match before rejoining the Arsenal staff for football he reached his thousand runs, finished second to Hendren among the regular Middlesex players with an average of 35. He had been given his county cap (surely the youngest ever to receive it!) and had been jumped from the Third Class on the Lord's Staff to the First.

It was no ordinary thing for a cricketer of eighteen to come into the game and straight away produce such batsmanship as Denis showed in '36. And his attractive method was not the only one, for though by nature a beautifully free striker of the ball, he could become sound and rigid in defence if he decided that that served the occasion best. No wonder that at the end of the season Sir Pelham Warner described him as 'the best young batsman who has come out since Walter Hammond was a boy'.

Only one other circumstance connected with Denis's first season need be recorded here, and it is, I think, disclosed for the first time. When the MCC team to tour Australia was chosen in August there was no small support in committee for his inclusion. Indeed, if G. O. Allen, who was already appointed captain, had been in favour of his going, he would very probably have been chosen: and I venture the opinion that if Allen could have known his man as well then as he soon came to do he would have been happy to take him. As it was, he felt, reasonably enough, that there were considerable risks involved in introducing to the singularly bright light that is always shining on an English team in Australia one so young and inexperienced. Thus might Denis have gone to Australia a full ten years before he did; and, if he had gone, there is little doubt, considering the misfortunes of that side, in spite of its so nearly winning the Ashes, that he would have had his chance in a Test match.

Actually, when he did first play for England in 1937, he was the youngest Englishman to do so, and one of a distinguished company of four who have appeared before their twenty-first birthday, I. A. R. Peebles, J. N. Crawford, and 'Young Jack' Hearne being the others. And when Denis made his century at Nottingham in 1938 he was almost but not quite the youngest cricketer to play in a Test between England and Australia: Archie Jackson, who was to die so tragic a death, and Stan McCabe, both of them players of a brilliance comparable with his, had been a month or two younger.

ALAN ROSS

Hutton Departs (1955)

Self-sufficiency, I suppose, is one of the true marks of the artist, and Hutton has been self-sufficient as a cricketer to the point of often seeming disinterested.

Like probably all men who can do one thing better than anyone else in the world, he seemed at moments unutterably wearied by it. The context of Hutton's cricket, the bleak decade when he almost alone in England – Compton and Bedser were allies – preserved its dignity, has been such that grace and levity seemed almost excluded as indecencies.

Compton, born under a warmer star, has combined all these attributes, as it were in defiance. His genius is romantic and individual. Hutton has never made such an appeal; his art has existed within precise technical limits. It would have been as unthinkable for Hutton the man to step outside the figure of Hutton the batsman as it would have been for Nijinsky suddenly to assert his own personality while dancing the Faun.

It is in precisely this subservience of the personal to the impersonal, this sacrificing of the imp of human impulse to the demands of situation, that classicism consists. Hutton has been the embodiment of so many classical ideals – discipline, restraint, concentration, correctness and elegance of execution – that he came to be thought of as an abstraction, infallible and incapable of improvisation. But he

was neither of these things. In 1948 he conquered majestically a
fallibility against fast, hostile bowling; in 1946–7 in Australia he
showed, when forced to it, powers of improvisation never hitherto
suspected, of an order of which only the greatest are capable.

It was known, of course, that he could play every stroke – except
perhaps the hook, but then the hook is a luxury and Hutton's
technical vocabulary, though complete, was spare in character –
but he showed flashes during his great post-war seasons, flashes as
rewarding as his own smile, the lightening of his eyes, that he took
pleasure in playing the rarer, more dangerous ones. Only, however,
when necessary; it remained an axiom of Hutton's batting that
economy was all, that flourishes were an indulgence and no part of
perfection, no matter how esoteric and complex perfection may be
adjudged to be. 'I refrain from saying too much,' he wrote to me
not long ago, 'I am Yorkshire bred and born you know, I have bought
a drink but not too often.'

In his youth, he was, in fact, as near infallible as a great player
can be: he was so, by cutting down on, by almost completely elimina-
ting, risk. Cardus, in one of his most memorable essays, 'Hutton and
Hobbs and the Classical Style', has written: 'He is perfect at using
the dead bat – rendering it passive, a blanket of a buffer, against
which spin or sudden rise from the pitch come into contact as though
with an anæsthetic.' This defensive resourcefulness, based on a perfect
and calculated technique, was certainly part of his genius: he made
no moves that were not absolutely certain of success. His strength
and superiority were likewise in his preparations, in his asceticism,
his conservations of energy, his power of withdrawal till the right
moment. He had the single-mindedness which Bradman also possessed, which enabled him to be solitary and to convey through the
rigours of his own self-communings an air of nobility. He inspired
admiration, rather than love, but that was his birthright, rather than,
I suspect, his wish. The age and the situation created his character,
and he respected them as forces to which the wise man bows assent.

Unexpectedly, but logically, he came to captain England: and to
new problems he brought the same professional skill, the same
monastic care as he had previously devoted to the problems of
batting. Batting now became the lesser thing, indulged in with no
less responsibility, but with greater abstractedness, as if his mind was
on deeper strategies. His captaincy on the field was as evidently
controlled and rehearsed as used to be his every innings, though it

had limitations and obscurities. Nevertheless, he was a successful, as well as a lucky, captain, and his record against Australia will remain for everyone to see.

Whatever criticisms can ever be laid against him, he never spared himself; he seemed often on the point of exhaustion. I remember saying to him at Sydney that I should like to see him play a handful of innings in which, free of worry, he could bat 'just for fun'. He nodded thoughtfully. At Leeds last summer, when he was already out of Test cricket, he turned to me and said: 'A hundred or two will put me right, a few runs', and he looked up quizzically, as if he found them strange words to say, 'made just for fun.'

It seems we shall have to do without the fun. We shall not again in serious play watch the beautiful ease of his stance at the wicket, the tugging of the shorter left arm at the cap peak, the thoughtful walk, toes slightly turned out, between the overs, the barometric sounding of the pitch. His mannerisms are part of contemporary cricket. A writer, a painter, however, live on through their work: a cricketer leaves only statistics and memories. Hutton's statistics require no repetition. But I shall remember, among many things about him, the unique drama of his last great Test innings at Lord's against Australia. He had, not long before he went in to bat, put down three catches, none easy nor greatly difficult either, and some unkind mockery had greeted him each time he subsequently stopped the ball.

When he went out to open the England innings with Kenyon, he looked even paler than usual, a frail, feverish magnetic figure, with an audience more critical than fond watching him walk to where Lindwall performed his tigerish preliminary antics and Miller lazily fondled the shining red ball. I felt then he would make nought – or a hundred. He made 145, a flawless innings. He cut exquisitely, drove gorgeously square, flicked the ball off his legs as it swung late into him. Next day the Members rose to him, and so they should have done. It was a peculiarly Huttonish triumph.

'I am writing this at 3 a.m., unable to sleep because of the pain down my right leg' – so he wrote to me in a letter this autumn. 'In the real dark night of the soul,' observed F. Scott Fitzgerald, the American chronicler of the Jazz Age, 'it is always 3 o'clock in the morning.' Well, it would not have been worth it, not just for a season or two's fun: so Hutton has retired. Fun after all is a by-product; what went before was much more important. In so far as a game can produce great moments in life, Hutton has contributed to more of them probably than anyone else of his generation. For these, Leonard, thank you, as for much else; and Good Luck.

Can Nothing Be Done?

Can nothing be done for J. B. Hobbs
To make him sometimes get out for blobs?
Or is he doomed for some dreadful crime
To make centuries till the end of time?
An eminent Harley Street specialist
Says that a nervous action of wrist,
Combined with a lesion of eyes and feet
Which is rapidly growing more complete
Through long indulgence without restraint,
Has at last become an organic complaint,
And only a rest in a nursing-home
And elbow-baths with electric foam,
Or using a bat of exiguous size
And wearing a bandage over the eyes
And batting left-handed after tea,
Can uproot this obstinate malady.

Hobbs went to be 'psychoed' the other day,
And the psychoanalyst said to him 'Pray,
Can you remember in early youth
Some terrible shock? Now tell me the truth.'
And Hobbs remembered at last and told
How, when a boy of four years old
And a naughty boy, he was rather fond
Of chasing ducks in the farmer's pond;
And once he chased a particular duck
So far away from its native muck
That it failed at last in wind and leg,
Sat down on the grass and laid an egg;
And Hobbs, triumphant, without alarm
Brought back the egg to show at the farm,
Expecting, of course, to be praised and thanked;
But he wasn't: he got severely spanked.

And the psychoanalyst, looking wise,
Said to Hobbs, who had tears in his eyes,
'It is easy to see how the complex grew
Till a duck became a terror to you.
What you ought to do is go and slay
A covey of wild ducks every day,
Or go and see Henrik Ibsen's play,
Or keep a duck for a household pet,
And dine upon duck's-egg omelette.'

The MCC have at last been moved
To try, if his health is not improved,
To lift from the mind of Hobbs its load
By adding these words to their legal code
Where the ways are mentioned of getting out,
Which do very well for us, no doubt:
'Excepting Hobbs, who must always be given
Out by the Umpire at eighty-seven.'
(A rhyme like that, which is painful to me,
Seems sound, of course, to the MCC.)

But, suppose the amendment does not pass,
Hobbs will be no better off, alas!
Hobbs will go on with both arms aching
For ever and ever century-making.
Unless he follows the doctor's advice,
Or uses a bat without any splice,
Or slippery boots without any nails,
Or ties an invisible thread to the bails,
He will go on for ever enduring the rigours
Of reaching the three ineffable figures.

Can nothing be done for J. B. Hobbs
To make him sometimes get out for blobs?

                                        'EVOE'

FROM
MILLER
TO
TENDULKAR

One of the most popular sides in cricket history was the Australian Services team of 1945. Assembled at the conclusion of the Second World War, this side toured England, India and Australia, spreading joy and cheer, the games they played signalling the end of death and deprivation.

The most charismatic of these ex-Servicemen was the fighter pilot Keith Ross Miller. In the fifth of the 'Victory' Tests, played at Lord's, Miller hit a rapid-fire 185, including a six off Jim Laker that landed in the commentator's box. He had previously been only a batsman, but when the team's opening bowler went home he took the new ball himself. For a decade after 1945 Miller was the leading all-round cricketer in the world. He was also a man with film-star looks. We carry here a tribute to Miller by Ray Robinson, the premier Australian cricket writer of his generation, a widely travelled reporter who wrote for major newspapers in his homeland and in England and India as well. As the *Oxford Companion to Australian Cricket* has remarked, Robinson's skill lay 'in providing the cultural, personal and statistical context of his subjects so that his portrayal of cricket and his players had a great breadth'. These talents are in evidence in this essay, as indeed in Robinson's other contributions to this anthology.

RAY ROBINSON

Touch of a Hero (1951)

Long before Keith Miller gets near the wicket you can tell that something extraordinary is going to happen. The erect set of his capless head on his square shoulders, the loose swing of his long legs, the half-smile on his handsome face and his general ease of manner all signify that no ordinary cricketer approaches.

Then there is the crowd's greeting. In weight and duration the applause may be no more, often less, than Bradman was accustomed to receive as tribute to the weight of his run-getting, the duration of his innings, the skill of his batting and the dramatic crescendo of his scoring. The ear detects different qualities in the applause for Miller. It contains so much pleasurable expectation, as if the hands are clapping, in some kind of morse of their own: 'This will be good.' But the keynote is a shriller sound – the whistling of the boys. Especially at Sydney or Melbourne, it swells to a joyous volume not heard since Jack Gregory came out to play in the years after World War I. It is a sign that here is the youngsters' hero. The place these two strapping adventurers of cricket won in the hearts of the keenest watchers present is not to be earned by enough runs to pack a warehouse, or an average like a skyscraper, or enough wickets to fill a quarry. It is a place involuntarily given them by those who have enjoyed seeing them bat and bowl and catch more excitingly than anybody else, unless it has been Constantine in his inspired moments.

To young eyes, quickest to perceive the things that make cricket, Miller is as an Olympian god among mortals. He brings boys' dreams to life. He is the cricketer they would all like to be, the one who can hit more gloriously and bowl faster than anybody on earth. When Neville Cardus called him a young eagle among crows and daws Miller was not a champion playing out of his class; sharing the field with him were the elect of the world's two greatest cricketing countries, Bradman, Hammond and bearers of other famous names, Compton and other men of personality.

Masculine as Tarzan, he plays lustily. Style suffuses his cricket with glowing power, personality charges it with daring and knocks bowling and conventions sky-high.

Since World War II Miller has made his mark on pavilion roofs across half the earth. He was not clear of his teens when the war began; before long it hid from view a youth from Melbourne High School who at eighteen had scored 181 against Tasmania in his first innings in first-class cricket and, just twenty, overcame the difficulties of Grimmett's bowling in making 108 against South Australia in his fourth match in the Sheffield Shield competition. As a flying officer of twenty-five he gave up piloting Mosquitoes in 1945 to become the mainstay of the Australian Services' batting. As such, he seldom lifted the ball in the Victory Tests, but towards the end of the season he began coping with coping-stones and other upstair targets around

English cricket fields. In his 185 for the Dominions he drove England's bowlers to seven spots among the buildings enclosing Lord's ground. *The Times'* own R. B. Vincent, discriminating and droll, began to wonder whether Lord's was a big enough ground for such terrific hitting. The first and furthest six crashed into the top-tier seats between the towers of the pavilion. Next morning one with less carry struck the southern tower, above the broadcasters' eyrie. They were among the highest blows Lord's pavilion had felt this century, though they left intact the all-time record by an earlier exile from Victoria, Albert Trott, who in 1899 drove a ball over the hallowed edifice. Miller lifted his overnight total by 124 before lunch on the last day of the match. Only such an innings as his 185 could have won the game. A week later he opened his forty-inch chest at Manchester and hit eight sixes in a hundred against an English XI . . .

Miller's forward play is unrivalled in splendour. He is the grandest player of cricket's grandest stroke, the drive. Left shoulder and elbow lead his body in unison with the thrust of his left foot towards the ball. As a thermometer responds to the sun's warmth, the height of his backswing varies in accordance with his estimate of the ball's quality. If he judges it to be coming within range of his matchless drive his swing is as full as a six-footer can keep in control throughout its menacing arc; his hands extend back to neck height and cocked wrists point the bat skyward. At the moment of impact straight arms transmit the energy of true-lined shoulders to whipping wrists. Usually the ball is close to his front pad before the bat smashes through and onwards in the direction the shot has taken. To put the kernel of his style in one sentence, he wields the straightest bat with the greatest power. When Miller springs a stride or two forward both feet grip the pitch for the drive as firmly as when he advances only the front leg, and the purchase they obtain forces his knees inward.

Distinctively his own is a rhythmic lunge with leg and bat seemingly moving together towards the ball, and his body bowing into the stroke as if giving it a benediction. This is more noticeable because nothing like it has been seen in an Australian since the back foot began to rule Test batting in the 1930s, and even before that no stylist made quite the same motion. To me, Miller's lunge is the truest gauge of his form. When playing well, he delivers it as positively as a boxer's classic straight left, whether he drives at boundary finding strength or extends himself to the limit to kill a testing ball in its tracks. If he is out of touch, good bowlers draw him into it too often; the lunge becomes overborne as he stretches to a ball he should have jumped to, or perhaps gone back on. Instead of being a firm anchor, his back leg drags across the crease as a shuffling extra line of defence. Sometimes balance fails him and he props himself up with his right hand or sprawls, full length, on both hands, like a physical culturist doing the body-press – as when he was stumped off Hollies in the Oval Test, 1948.

In this manly athlete's straight-bat strokes force is harnessed to a line as classic as a Corinthian column, but it bursts into full view, unrestrained, when he lets go for a hit to leg. His left side leads so strongly into the blow that the follow-through screws his clean-cut frame into spiral shape; he looks as if a willy-willy* has spun his body around, as if he would revolve if it were not for his staying right foot, twisted over on its outside by the blockhole. No other batsman puts such plunging power into a pull or similar swinging leg hit. (For the like, you have to see American baseballers.) After adding its part to the speed of the bat, his right arm sometimes gets left behind; the hand slips off, like a wheel from a racing car careering around a bend. When this happened as he hit the accurate Toshack's left-arm bowling for three sixes in one over it looked as if he swept the ball over the leg fence of the Melbourne ground with one hand. Watching the ball cannoning about the vast concrete stand, Ponsford (who fielded against Woolley, Constantine, Chapman and all the other famous hitters between the World Wars) said Miller's strokes were the most powerful he had ever seen. Miller made things so warm in his 153 that every time he shaped to hit Toshack to leg people in the ringside seats got ready to duck behind the fence's iron pickets . . .

The one-sided Test rubber in 1946–7 presented little challenge to Miller's imagination to bring forth such stirring innings as his side's need had produced for the Services. Yet his 79 in the first Test contained the most high-bred batting of the match, and his six over long on to the roof of the members' citadel was the longest ever hit on Brisbane's Woolloongabba ground. His 79 runs and 7 wickets for 60 in the first innings were a record opening double for Anglo-Australian Tests.

After the Englishmen opened on Adelaide Oval with their highest

* A spiralling cyclonic wind, so named by West Australian Aborigines.

Test score of the season, 460, Miller responded with the most glorious innings of the rubber. The shutters were hardly down on the fourth morning when he hooked the first delivery of the day, a no-ball, over midwicket for six; only a player with his relaxed readiness could have done business so instantly. The ball soared high over girls depositing lunch bags and patting cushions into place, unaware that the proceedings had opened. It descended smack in front of the vice-regal box – a six almost subversive. Sunshine gleamed on Miller's hair and his circling bat as his front-of-the-wicket shots explored the outskirts of the 208-yard-long field and he cut with such downright style that the ball often ricocheted shoulder high past the slips. His batting, distinguished and dictatorial, threatened the bowlers with utter subjection. To save them, Yardley resorted to spreading six fieldsmen around the leg field and bowling on the leg stump. Australia's position made the stakes too high for Miller – for all the slice of gambler in his make-up – to take risks trying to smash the accurate leg-theory. Later, when the tail end was reached with Australia still behind, he put aside the curb, and the crowd laughed at the unprecedented sight of four longfields strung across the northern reach of the oval. Two attempts were made to catch him – one chance was so hot that the fieldsman dropped it as if it were a radioactive chunk from Bikini – but when Australia's last wicket fell Miller was unconquered for 141, and he had seen his team through to a lead of 27.

Australia's next crisis came on the fifth day of the low-scoring final Test at Sydney, when the Englishmen were within touching distance of victory. Though favoured by luck in a dropped slip catch which enabled Bradman to go from 2 to 63, the Australians were struggling on a pitch responsive enough to make Bedser and Wright difficult for the best batsmen and almost unplayable by the rest. The pair looked capable of rooting out the lower division in a few overs. Only one batsman remained with technique adequate for the task – Miller. Down came a couple of snorters from Bedser which leaped from the pitch like fast leg breaks; tense onlookers in line with the wicket gasped as the tall batsman survived them. In a do-or-die situation Miller tossed his head and struck back, not with desperate slogging but by singling out balls of lesser menace and daringly using his reach to drive them over the eager ring of fieldsmen. While hours of strain had everybody else keyed up, he was enjoying himself. He rolled in a half-somersault to complete a cheeky run. When his partner, McCool, made the winning hit for three Miller stole a stump after running two, carried it with him on the last lap, then gave it to England's top scorer, Compton, fulfilling his promise to get Denis a souvenir. Writing of those Tests, ex-wicketkeeper B. A. Barnett said: 'Miller is undoubtedly Australia's most attractive batsman, as well as cricket personality.'

After the 1947–8 season in Australia, India's captain, Amarnath, summed up: 'Miller is Australia's best batsman as far as style is concerned, though, of course, none can compare with Bradman for making runs.' In Miller's 86 for an Australian XI at Sydney the Indians saw that he was a sportsman of sensitivity as well as a batsman of style and strength. He came in soon after Bradman and for a while seemed likely to steal the show from the older man. Then, seeing that Bradman was heading for his hundredth century, Miller eased himself into the background, leaving the captain a monopoly of the limelight on such a memorable day. On the same ground in the same season Miller raced to 100 against Western Australia in 88 minutes, and his full 170 included three of the longest sixes ever seen at Sydney. One crashed high up the back wall of the alley between the pavilion and the Noble Stand. But some of us were not happy about the way the ex-Victorian's cricket was being burned at both ends. If his pleas to be spared from regular fast bowling received any consideration in the Test seasons against England and India they were outweighed by eager desire for victory. His labours as one of the chief bowlers prevented him from approaching his batting with a fresh mind and untapped energy. The flame of his batsmanship was not burning with the same purity. The power was still there – he could hit as distant a six as ever – but he was tending to become a swash-buckling on-side hitter instead of a distinguished batsman with unrivalled hitting capacity as one of his qualities. The feet, ankles, shins, knees and thighs of such uncommon batsmen as Miller are among cricket's rarest possessions, far too precious to be tarnished and squandered in the dust and potholes of the bowling crease.

His bowling has been chock-full of life and personality, and full of shocks for batsmen – some of them nasty shocks. He gathers momentum in a much shorter run than other fast bowlers, shorter than Wright takes for a slow-medium googly. Nine loose-jointed strides are usually enough, sometimes fewer. He is the only Test-class bowler with such a flexible approach, and the only one I have seen drop the ball as he ran, scoop it up and deliver it without a trace of the interruption. Once he bowled in odd boots, one size nine and a borrowed ten, because the stress of fast bowling had broken his own. After his short run Miller generates pace with such a convulsive body effort that it is a wonder his back and sides have not troubled him more often. His delivery is high-handed (in more senses than one), especially for his in-dipper. Not satisfied with late swerve either way, break-backs and a wide range of pace changes, he rings in a leg break or a round-armer now and again. Batsmen find it hard to understand Miller's bowling. Some of it is well over their heads.

We came to expect one like that whenever he was hit for four. That indignity stung the same combative streak in him as a bowler that a crisis did as a batsman (I preferred to see him hit the roof when he was batting). Tossing back his mane like a mettlesome colt with dilated nostrils, he would stride back, giving a hurrying clap to the fieldsman and thrusting out his hand to command a quick return, in eagerness to get at the batsman again. Rushing up, he would fling down a bumper that made the batsman duck penitently; or occasionally it would be an exaggerated full toss instead. For the most frequent bouncer in post-war cricket he seldom hit a batsman – the ball usually bounded too high – but such moments transformed him from hero to villain, and he has been hooted at Nottingham, Madras, Perth, Adelaide, Brisbane and other points east and west. How much of his apparent anger was simulated only those close at hand could tell. As he ran up Miller did not always look at the batsman, and once started to bowl without noticing that the umpire's arm barred his path because the striker was not ready. When he almost collided with it he changed in a flash from his bowling action to shake the umpire's outstretched hand. His personality abolishes the boundary and brings the crowd into the game with him. Thinking Miller's bowling for a Combined XI against the Englishmen at Hobart lacked its usual devil, a Tasmanian shouted: 'Let 'em have the lot!' Loudly enough to be heard beyond the boundary, Miller answered: 'Quiet!' lifting a cautioning finger in the direction of the barracker.

* * *

With Lindwall, Hassett and others, Miller formed part of Don Bradman's all-conquering side of 1946–8. Another linchpin of that team was the wicketkeeper Don Tallon. Tallon kept beautifully to all types of bowling and, although competition for the 'best-ever wicketkeeper' slot is fierce (Godfrey Evans, Bertie Oldfield and half a dozen other names come to mind), he was up there with the best. What is less in dispute, perhaps, is the claim that this essay by Ray Robinson is the finest portrait by a writer of a stumper.

RAY ROBINSON

Much in a Name (1951)

Tallon! The very name brings to mind an eagle swooping on its prey. The lean, hardbitten Queenslander's presence has made batsmen feel they are being attacked from two directions, that they are as much in danger of being torn down from behind as of being overcome by the visible foe at the bowling crease. No other man within my memory's span has kept wicket with such intensity and brilliance – the efficiency of an Oldfield or a Strudwick, heightened by a verve that was not in their make-up and extended by a taller man's reach. Don Tallon has been as ravenous for victims as Duckworth; less obviously only because he seemed actuated more by an implacable inner hatred for batsmen than the bouncing hostility of the Lancashire man. As with Bradman among batsmen, Tallon has combined the skills of more than one keeper. He alone exceeded 300 wickets before he played 100 first-class matches.

Paganini's wizardry on the violin caused superstitious folk to say the devil guided his fingers. Tallon is the Paganini of wicketkeepers. You see this first in the mystic passes his gloves make before the bowler begins: he gives occult signals by wriggling his fingers; with elbows close to his body he draws his hands sinuously down in front of his chest. He stands nearer the stumps than the others – stands guard over them, alert as a sentry, left foot behind the middle stump. As an outlet for nervous energy his feet smooth down the already level ground. He puts his wrists against his hips, then wipes his forehead with the strip of bare forearm between gauntlet and shirt-sleeve. Taking the peak in both hands, he resettles his cap on his curly, brown head, tugging it nearer his eyes. He stretches his shoulders, hitches his trouser waistband, stoops halfway, then folds like a pocket knife until legs, thighs and body seem all one piece, balanced on level feet. Though rather tall, he squats nearer his heels than the others, with elbows outside his knees. He raps the earth with his fists, makes a final pass before his face with open gloves, and peers past his forefingers before he poises his hands in front of his shins as the bowler runs up. He crouches there, motionless, until his eyes read the ball's secret.

Often scenting a wicket before the batsman becomes conscious of danger, he whips into position in readiness for the victim's mistake. His footwork is full of short, quick steps, his legs rarely straddle wide. He is a master of the sway and the lean to keep eyes and hands true to the ball's course – so much so that he looks as if most of his close-up keeping could be done with a book under each armpit. His glovework is full of wristy curves, convex for the knee-high ball, concave for the skidder. He is as fussy about his hands as a pianist. The wicketkeeper is the nerve centre of the field; when Tallon is there it is a highly strung nerve. As the ball approaches he often jams his tongue into the right corner of his mouth. When the bat denies him the ball he goes through the taking action just the same, bringing his hands back like a chef drawing a tray from an oven. The ball that seems certain to bowl the batsman causes most keepers to stand upright to acclaim the happy sight; embarrassment and four byes usually result if it misses. If the stumps stop the ball from coming to Tallon, as like as not he will catch one of the flying bails.

In his leathery face, tanned by the Queensland sun, his hazel eyes almost disappear amid a network of wrinkles – the result of days staring along baking wickets in shimmering glare, enough to cause mirages to appear at the other end. A sardonic-looking smile occasionally creases his lean cheeks, accompanied now and again by a laugh that sounds hard and dry. Strangers don't find him easy to talk to. He walks to his position with an air of brooding concentration. Sparely built and lithe (5 ft 10½ in and 11 st 4 lb), he could be a dismounted boundary rider, accustomed to hours of solitude on some vast cattle station in Western Queensland. Behind the stumps he is a man of two words: 'How's that?' (When Tallon came in to bat in Sir Donald Bradman's testimonial match and played nowhere near an off-the-wicket ball, every fieldsman joined in a prearranged appeal.)

Tallon fits exactly the picture of the Australian cricketer – sun-dried, hard and efficient – formed by many English people who don't get to know the men personally.

In stumping or running out batsmen from balls taken wide he has sometimes ripped a stump out of the ground, as if his gloves really did have talons. When a batsman clumps down on a yorker he darts around as if to wrench the ball from under the bat. His clamant appeals have been bad for batsmen's nerves; they burst from him, demanding satisfaction; often he holds the ball on high as proof. Refusal is a wounding injustice.

Events made Tallon what he is, toughened the outer man. Of four brothers who learned the game on a back-lawn wicket prepared by their father, Les Tallon, Don was the most gifted, though Bill became an inter-state player too. At thirteen, Don was chosen in the Queensland schoolboys' team, at fourteen he was peeping over full-size pads as he kept in 'A Grade' matches with the men in Bundaberg's Hinkler Park (named after the aviator, another famous son of the sugar-and-rum town, 217 miles north of Brisbane). At sixteen the boy from Bundaberg played for Queensland Country against the Englishmen in 1933 and stumped Sutcliffe for 19. At seventeen he was in the state eleven. He became regular state keeper at Christmas, 1934, went to work in a Brisbane motor car company's store. His keenness laid him open to criticism for too frequent and too dramatic appealing, to convince Brisbane umpires (so southerners said).

In three more years his swiftness and safety had won him first place in the estimation of the cricketers whose opinions matter in these things: bowlers. Some bowlers in other state teams used to say they wished they had him out there in the middle with them. Secondarily, he could out-bat all other Australian keepers. The brilliance of his 193 against Victoria in 1936 set all Australia talking.

Omission from the 1938 tour of Britain put him in a ferment of bewilderment and frustration. It hurt him like a kick in the face. Some professed to know (Lord knows how) that each of the three selectors had Tallon's name in his original pair – D. G. Bradman (South Australia), Walker and Tallon; E. A. Dwyer (NSW), Oldfield and Tallon; W. J. Johnson (Victoria), Barnett and Tallon – but that the Queenslander was crushed out in the final squeeze. I have reason to doubt that he was on all three lists, but I believe he would have been chosen had he been keeper for one of the older cricketing states. Oldfield, swallowing disappointment himself, lamented the omission of the younger man. Fishing for reasons, some said it must have been because Tallon stood back to medium-pace opening bowlers. (The bowler most concerned, Geoff Cook, and the keeper both knew that the best chance of wickets off Cook's pronounced outswingers was by catching; while the ball was new Tallon stood back to make dead sure of them; he stumped a number off Cook when the ball was older.) Another theory was that he lacked experience in taking spin bowling, whereas his rivals were familiar with Fleetwood-Smith, O'Reilly, Grimmett and Ward. None of the explanations was adequate. War was approaching – he might never achieve his lifelong ambition to play for Australia in England. He feared that his only chance had been wrongly denied him. Men's hands were against him.

After that, Tallon gritted his teeth and set out to show how wrong his omission had been. Between then and his disappearance into the Army I believe he reached the highest pitch ever attained by a keeper. He had the satisfaction, a bitter satisfaction, of setting up a series of records. In the season of 1938–9 he evicted 34 batsmen in Queensland's six first-class matches – figures no other keeper has approached in an all-Australian season; four times in ten innings at least 6 men fell to his deft glovework. At Sydney he caught 9 and stumped 3 NSW batsmen to equal Edward Pooley's world record of 12 in a match for Surrey, which had stood for seventy years. At Brisbane he dislodged 7 Victorian batsmen in an innings to equal another world record by Smith, Farrimond and Price. He passed 100 wickets for Queensland in thirty-two matches – remarkable in a team lacking a regular leg-spin bowler, a wicketkeeper's best friend. His hands were so unsparing that batsmen became resigned to the fate awaiting a trailing toe or a touch with the bat. Before the Hitler–Hirohito war stopped first-class cricket he scored a hundred before lunch (in ninety minutes) against NSW, and is the only batsman to have achieved the feat at Brisbane.

This superb keeper had to wait until he was thirty before he played in a Test match, in 1946 in New Zealand. By then, Queensland had gained the googly bowling of Colin McCool from NSW. Tallon welcomed him suitably with six catches and stumpings in their first match together. The pair became an outstanding combination. Their first united effort against Englishmen yielded four stumpings and two catches in the match and brought Tallon's total for Queensland to 170 wickets in fifty games in which he had worn the gloves. When he missed stumping Edrich off Cook, broadcaster Jack Fingleton broke the staggering news to listeners by saying: 'A most astonishing thing has just happened . . .'

Though Tallon was an automatic choice as Australian keeper, he had a sleepless night before the team for the first Test against England was announced. This shadow of doubt had pursued him ever since his pre-war omission from the tour of England; his fellow players' reassurances could not banish the fear that he might be denied his rightful place, as in 1938.

Never has a Test field been so dominated by a keeper as the Sydney ground when England batted in December 1946. The toss had given the Englishmen first use of the wicket. Tallon would not fit into the widely accepted part of a keeper passively waiting in the background for crumbs; he asserted himself as startlingly as a suit of armour striding forward from its corner to carve the joint. The scorebook credited the keen Queenslander with six victims in the match; to watchers it seemed more like sixteen. He menaced the batsmen incessantly from the rear; he beset them from the sides, darting and pouncing, and from above, with triumphant leaps.

Hutton (39) drew back near his leg stump and glanced an off-spinner from Ian Johnson. Instantaneously, a white apparition appeared in the path of the ball and suffocated at birth a stroke destined for fine leg. The speed of it all was ghostly, but once the ball had sunk into his gloves Tallon showed that he was flesh and blood by holding it aloft and dancing a few exultant steps. No other keeper possessed the anticipatory agility to make the catch in the way he did. Nine runs later Compton (5) leaned forward to drive a leg break which McCool pitched outside the off stump. When ball and bat met, Tallon was a yard outside the off stump ready, as the ball spun away, for any chance of a stumping or a snick. But the bat's edge sped the ball wider, into short slip's territory. Over his shoulder Tallon saw it strike Johnson's chest and fall. Spinning half around and diving backward, he shot his right glove under the ball as it neared the ground. It all happened so quickly that Tallon was rolling on the grass, with his left hand flung up in appeal, before we comprehended what he had achieved. Even after witnessing it, such speed of mind and action seems incredible. Only the world's greatest keeper could have done it. Two runs later he caught Hammond (1) off another leg break from McCool, and the back of England's innings was broken, the Ashes lost.

In his hour of triumph Tallon was hurt. Trying to save a ball from Miller which swung wide to leg in England's second innings, he had to stretch, and his left little finger was dislocated. He ran to the dressing room, a masseur jerked it back into place, and he resumed. Before lunch next day Fred Freer's faster ball worsened the trouble; Tallon wrung his hand in pain. The injury dimmed his brilliance in the next two Tests – in fact, a risk was taken in playing him while the finger was tender – but in the final Test he added six more scalps to his belt. Oldfield and he are the only two keepers who have taken 6 wickets in an Anglo-Australian Test twice. Tallon became the first to remove 20 batsmen in a rubber (16 caught); Oldfield and Strudwick, 18 each, had shared the record for twenty-two years. Tallon's innings of 92 at Melbourne, besides being highest Test score by an Australian keeper against England, contained some of the most polished stroke play seen in the rubber. His 35 wickets in first-class matches beat his own record for an Australian season.

India's captain, Amarnath, who entered international cricket in 1933, said after the 1947–8 tour of Australia that Tallon was the greatest keeper he had seen.

Before he got to Britain at last, at the age of thirty-two, Tallon underwent an operation on his tonsils, but he kept wicket so impressively that he was chosen one of *Wisden's* Five Cricketers of the Year. Watching him, Duckworth told me: 'He gets smoothly to balls that would have had me scrambling. In fielding the ball with gloves on he is the cleanest I ever saw.' Yet England did not see him at his superlative best; he touched it several times, but without the match-after-match consistency of his pre-war peak. The 1948 summer was too chilly for the Bundaberg sport-storekeeper. As the Australians were travelling through a village one asked: 'Where's the King's Arms?' Tallon grunted back: 'Around the Queen, in this weather – if he's got any sense.' Midway through the season he had to break from his lifetime habit of wetting his chamois inner gloves. On a misty May day at the Oval, the first time Lindwall let himself go in England, the fast bowler came galloping out of the fog like Dick Turpin's ghost. One ball whizzed over a batsman's shoulder; Tallon sighted it late, just had time to throw up one hand to save his face. He ripped off his glove and shook his hand in the air to cool it. His right middle finger was bruised. In the second Test a dive for a leg ball from the fast bowler damaged his left little finger again and it was X-rayed.

Australia's dependence on fast and fastish bowlers in 1948 kept Tallon mostly in the backstop position and limited British crowds' opportunities to see his close-up mastery, his stumpings of camera-shutter speed and precision – often only one bail flicked off. In the third Test, still worried about his little finger, he and the fieldsmen at square leg and point all were convinced that he stumped Compton (35) off Ian Johnson in England's first innings. Umpire Frank Chester's decision went against them. Disconsolate as a bear with a sore paw, Tallon squirmed down into position again: in such a moment he missed the absent McCool's calming 'Take it easy, Joe', from first slip. Twice in the last three-quarter-hour that evening and once next day he dropped Compton; two of them were little more than finger-end touches, low and wide, in dull light, but Tallon was savagely self-critical.

When the stumping of Compton was disallowed I looked through binoculars from Old Trafford's rooftop press box but could see no clear line on the pitch; the crease was a dark mass of roughened turf, cut up by players' boots. It would ease the umpires' task if the creases were repainted at every interval. Not that this would guarantee freedom from error. Keeping wicket for Brighton (Victoria) between the wars, Roy Hayball appealed for a stumping but was refused. Chatting after the match, he said to the umpire: 'That must have been a very close thing.'

The umpire: 'It was. His toe was on the line.'

Hayball: 'But on the line is out!'

The umpire: 'Ah, but this was a very wide line.'

After his unlucky Test at Manchester Tallon's left little finger, injured in another plunge for a fast ball in the Middlesex match, was so painfully puffy that he could not play in the fourth Test. On his reappearance in the final Test one of his three catches gave Londoners something to marvel at: his rapid sidesteps and falling capture of Hutton's leg glance, with the back of his left glove to the ground.

When the fast bowlers swung the ball too far to leg for his footwork and dive to reach it, Tallon often lay outstretched in disgust, on his left elbow, seemingly heedless of how the ball was retrieved from the boundary. Sometimes, through glasses, he appeared to be easing his feelings with pithy comments which a lip-reader might have identified as predominantly in words of four and five letters.

A memory of Worcester is McCool's cold hand letting slip a leg ball which was still a high full toss when it came to Tallon's gloves, all aquiver with surprise. Next, a wide to the off took the keeper on to his knees; he stared at the bowler with the air of one who would demand an explanation later. Next over McCool lured Kenyon forward to a flightier leg break and Tallon stumped him in a manner showing that all was forgiven.

In readiness to take returns from the field he stoops behind the stumps, every time. He motions with his hands (like a conductor calling his orchestra to their feet) to request outfielders to throw above the bails – but not when the fielder has been Neil Harvey, Hassett or Archer. In Test matches he has grumbled at Loxton for shying at the stumps; he has even had the temerity to rebuke his captain, Bradman, for this – in front of the Lord's crowd, too.

Tallon was not available for the 1949–50 tour of South Africa. On the shorter trip to New Zealand he saved Australia in the unofficial Test by getting 7 wickets and making 116 (seven sixes) with batting few men could equal. What pleased him more was that his hands came through unhurt.

For all his high-pressure intensity in the fight, Tallon has humour. Only three of the seventeen Australian players bound for England in 1948 took part in the ship's fancy-dress parade; Tallon was one, a villainous Arab with wide-apart teeth. In his first Test at Lord's he fooled Compton into running hard by preparing to take a return when nobody was throwing. At Aberdeen his response to an in-accurate leg break was to signal a wide (overriding the umpire) and to insist on being given a chance himself to show how leg breaks ought to be bowled. At Derby, on the morning after the team celebrated having won the Ashes outright, freakish hot weather had many tongues hanging out as left-handed Denis Smith made a new record for the county against Australia in a century partnership with Arnold Townsend. Seldom have eyes been cast more longingly at drinks than at the tray which Don Tallon, as twelfth man, carried on to the ground. Like survivors of a cross-desert trek by the Foreign Legion, the players drooped listlessly about the wicket, too far gone to take a step towards the approaching succour. Halfway out Tallon stopped, laid the tray on the grass, knelt behind it and beckoned: 'Come and get it.' The crowd of 10,000 saw the humour of it, but the captain was not amused. He sternly commanded the grinning twelfth man to bring the tray to the middle, and reproved him with 'This isn't a circus.'

*   *   *

Lord Harris, an English aristocrat who once played a bit of cricket, claimed that 'it is in the matter of patience that the Indian cricketer will never be equal to the Englishman'. This remark, offered at a time when India was still undivided, was calculated to produce both Sunil Gavaskar and Hanif Mohammad. The little Pakistani's classical technique and monumental patience are analysed in this essay by Ray Robinson. Note that it was published before the most remarkable of all defensive innings, Hanif's 337 against the West Indies at Bridgetown in 1957–8. That knock was spread over 970 minutes of playing time. Watching Hanif bat from a palm tree high above square leg were a group of Bajan boys. As the afternoon sun rose higher, one of them could no longer stand it. Delirious from the heat, from Hanif's relentless *thook thook* and doubtless from a steady intake of palm wine, the boy fell off the tree and landed on his head some forty feet below. He was taken to hospital, recovering consciousness twenty-four hours later. Inevitably his first words were 'Is Hanif still batting?' The answer, alas, was in the affirmative.

Ray Robinson
The Original Little Master (1956)

When Hanif Mohammad comes in to bat for Pakistan there appears to be little more of him than a sun helmet, a pair of pads and a dark shadow in between.

Hanif is only sixty-three inches high but, like the girl in *South Pacific*, every inch is packed with dynamite.

Somewhere in the darkness under the helmet's brim two brown eyes focus with burning intensity on the ball approaching through the heat-shimmering air. The helmet tilts forward as his head goes down to watch the last feet of the ball's bounce from the baked wicket to the bat. Every line of his neat figure denotes the concentrated attention to the ball necessary to score a double-century at seventeen or any other age.

By habit, Hanif Mohammad touches his helmet, crouches and goes through the motion of making a cross over his chest before he stoops to face the bowler. Pakistan's captain, Abdul Hafeez Kardar, reads these signs as evidence that Hanif's mind is engrossed in batting. Whenever the lad misses this routine his skipper becomes apprehensive. Hanif's boyish good humour is silenced by the serious business of staying in to make runs. His mien is studious yet not laborious. Nothing the ball does seems to disturb his manner of taking his time in all things on and off the field.

Before he had a helmet, Hanif Mohammad wore a red cap with a camel crest, the emblem of the high school, Sind Madressah Tul-Islam, in Karachi, on the delta of the River Indus. A pitiless sun would be turning the school's red tile roof into a griddle as a dozen pupils emerged from the black oblong which the doorway's shade formed in the yellow stone wall. They played cricket on matting spread over a mixture of gravel and clay. In one game Hanif batted nearly seven and a half hours for 305 not out – an inter-school tournament record which stood for only a year before wristy Ikran Elahi surpassed it by dashing off 317 before tea.

Hanif is the youngest of three sons of a Junagadh hotel keeper. He was born in Manavadar on the fourteenth day of Ramzan, 1353 AH (or 21 December 1934, by the white man's reckoning). Manavadar is in the Ranji country but Hanif's father, a member of the Sunni Muslim sect, migrated to Pakistan after the separation from India. Hanif's eldest brother, Wazir Mohammad, also played for Pakistan in England in 1954 and two years earlier made 104 not out against India's West Zone at Ahmadabad. The middle brother, Raiis Mohammad, nineteen, just missed selection for the same tour.

Hanif's coach was Abdul Aziz, a former All-India wicket keeper, who played against Jack Ryder's Australian team in the unofficial Test at Calcutta in 1936. Abdul Aziz believes in coaching from the feet up – to encourage a youngster to move to the line of the ball to make his stroke. He noticed that Hanif played back too much and tended to spoon the ball to the on side. Abdul showed him how to defend his wicket playing forward as well as back. The shy boy said little, just looked at Abdul and listened closely to every word. For an hour each morning Abdul taught him how to place his feet to drive and to hook. At thirteen Hanif learned how to change from an intended forward stroke to a square cut. His off strokes, notably his drives, are now his best and are likely to improve further when he has more than nine stone to put behind them and has perfected their placing.

At 16 years $10^{1}/_{2}$ months Hanif Mohammad appeared in first-class cricket. Without preliminary, he found himself representing his country and wearing the green blazer with the golden crescent, star and eagle on the pocket. He was opening batsman and wicketkeeper against England on the park-like Lahore ground, in the Punjab. It was the first of two games against N. D. Howard's team touring the Indian subcontinent. Hanif would have been the youngest Test player ever, but for the fact that Pakistan had not then been granted Test status by the Imperial Cricket Conference. Unused to a grass pitch, Hanif was up against a varied attack by English Test bowlers – the pace of Statham and Shackleton, Tattersall's off spin and the left-arm bowling of Watkins (medium-pace), Hilton (slow) and Carr (googly). For two and three-quarter hours the methodical little Muslim kept them out as he made 26 of an opening partnership of 96 with Nazar Mohammad. As the youngster left the field shouts came from the crowd: 'Bahut khoob!' (Urdu for 'Well done!') As wicketkeeper in this drawn match Hanif stumped opening batsman Jack Robertson off portly Amir Elahi, the comical slow bowler with the antics of a light-hearted Othello.

In Pakistan's second unofficial Test the batsmen walked in across Karachi's outfield of sunbaked mud to the inner grass square around the matting-covered gravel wicket. Instead of covering the pitch only, the brown matting stretched like a runway for the length of the bowler's approach and Shackleton looked like becoming airborne any minute. From the central strip to the boundary the ground sloped more than two feet. The ball flew nastily for the first two days of the match and Statham was at his fastest. When Hanif went in to bat in the last innings the Pakistanis needed 285 to achieve the longed-for glory of their first win against another country. For four hours he bent his young back to the task. His top score of 64, before Howard caught him off Tattersall, ushered his team to victory with four wickets and half an hour to spare. This success – the only defeat inflicted on the Englishmen during their tour – rammed home Pakistan's claim for admittance to the select circle of Test countries. All Pakistan hummed with such delighted remarks as:

'Sab tareef Khuda ki!' (Urdu for 'Allah be praised!')

'School ke larke ke liye bahut bari bat hai!' ('How wonderful for a schoolboy!')

The enterprising Pakistanis followed that up by sending a party of young players to England for coaching at the cricket school run by former Surrey fast bowler Alf Gover. Hanif had fifteen days at the school. After seeing him at the nets Gover said, 'I am not going to try to coach this boy and my tip is that you don't let anybody else try it, either. He has got everything. He is a natural.' Hanif watched all the leading English batsmen, and must have taken an extra-long look at Hutton.

Not in the least surprised by Hanif's triumph on Pakistan's tour of India in the last months of 1952, Gover said, 'All I did was advise him how to make the best of his perfect technique in the middle.' Hanif led off with a century in each innings of Pakistan's first match against North Zone at Amritsar, ancient holy city of the Sikhs, with its beautiful Golden Temple. Batting 4 hours 50 minutes for his 121 in the first innings, he hit 14 fours. He was an hour quicker for his second innings of 109 (13 fours). With those innings, this shock-haired son of the Prophet made himself the youngest cricketer (17 years 42 weeks) ever to score a century in both innings of a first-class match.

On to Delhi for Pakistan's first match as an accredited Test country. India's greatest statesman, Prime Minister Pandit Nehru, was there, watching the greatest bowler to come out of the East, Vinoo Mankad. The sturdy Indian left-hander used all his wiles of flight and spin to send back eight batsmen in Pakistan's first innings of 150. Hanif Mohammad was among them, but not before he had held out four hours and topped the score with 51 on his first appearance in an official Test. Mankad's 13 wickets in the match enabled India to win by an innings. That indignity stirred Pakistani policeman Fazal Mahmood to an answering feat on Lucknow's matting wicket in the second Test. Using his leg-cutters as effectively as handcuffs, Superintendent Mahmood removed twelve Indian batsmen in the match. (Fazal likes dealing in wickets by the dozen, as he showed in bowling Pakistan to their first Test victory in England in 1954.) Hanif's opening partner at Lucknow, Nazar Mohammad, became the first Pakistani to carry his bat through a Test innings, with 124 of a total of 331.

By the Islamic calendar it was the eighteenth day of Safar, 1372 (otherwise 8 November 1952), when Hanif Mohammad walked on to the spacious Brabourne Stadium to open Pakistan's innings against Bombay. Below the airy tiers of the towering concrete stands he looked tinier than ever. In only his fourth innings on a turf pitch, he put in the foundation of a double-century with the care of a stonemason laying the bottom course. An hour went by before he allowed himself the liberty of a late cut for his first four. His only miscalculation was just before lunch, when at 28 he gave a hard slip chance off Bombay's fast-medium bowler, S. W. Sohoni.

For most of the day Hanif quietly backed up three aggressive partners – two hours with stylish Nazar Mohammad, fifteen minutes with brother Wazir (about five years older than Hanif, no bigger, though more daring) and an hour and a half with Imtiaz Ahmed. Imtiaz Ahmed's smile and forceful stroke play have made him a favourite everywhere south-east of the North-West Frontier. Two years earlier on the same ground he hit 31 fours in his 300 not out for the Prime Minister's XI against the Commonwealth XI. At the age of seventeen, Imtiaz and Kardar, twenty, scored centuries together against Australian Services at Lahore in 1945. Some of the fieldsmen, unused to the heat, sank into a torpor during a quiet spell. Vultures soared overhead, as if waiting to pick the bones of the bowlers when they dropped in their tracks. A sudden hit skied the ball and a shout of 'Charlie!' roused Price to action at mid-off. He ran twenty yards the wrong way before he found he was chasing a bird's shadow, while the other Australian fieldsmen collapsed in gurgling heaps.

As Hanif's third partner against Bombay, Imtiaz Ahmed raced to 96 at a run a minute before Rajendra Nath stumped him off a flighted leg break from S. G. Shinde. The sight of his partner missing 100 by four failed to infect Hanif's play with the paralysis of overanxiety as he sought the eight runs needed to complete his own century. It seemed to disturb him no more than the Bombay crowd's barracking of his slow scoring before the tea interval. Soon he off-drove a boundary to raise his hundred, drawing cheers from the throats of his hecklers. At the day's end, five hours of calm concentration had brought him 102 of his side's 303 for 3 wickets.

On the second day Hanif Mohammad replayed himself in with as much care as Australia's Sid Barnes used to take when he set his mind on a big innings. In the first three-quarters of an hour his score crept up by 21 while his fourth partner, all-rounder Maqsood Ahmed, made 61. From the pavilion Kardar twice sent out messages to go for the runs, but Hanif felt he could not do so without risking getting out – the thing he hates most of all. When the second message was delivered he asked, 'Before lunch?', indicating that he regarded the pre-lunch period as one for settling in. Little more than one-third of Pakistan's 366 runs had come from Hanif's bat when Shinde had Maqsood caught at cover by Irani.

Not even a cracked bat could make Hanif leave the crease. He would not change it, for fear of breaking his concentration. When, with the insight of a born record-breaker, he felt the bowling was ripe for plucking on the easy-paced pitch, he hit more fours with the faulty blade than he had before it split. Though the field spread wider, he took the shine out of Shinde, leaving little remainder. In the lunch interval, while devout players spread their mats after noon and prostrated themselves toward Mecca in prayer, Hanif lay relaxing on the massage table.

After lunch Bombay's captain, Rusi Modi, called on the third new ball. Instead of being checked, the run-getting became even faster until Hanif and acting captain Hussain raised the score by 150 in 90 minutes. For the first time his team saw Hanif hooking fast bowling. He raced through his fourth fifty in half an hour, like a schoolboy dashing off the last lines of an imposition, with only one blot – a slip chance at 161. Thanks to his last eighty in 70 minutes he added his second hundred in less than half the time of his first-day 102. Up the pitch raced Anwar Hussain to shake the hand of the young double-century scorer and say: 'Shabash, abhi aghai aur buhat score karna hai' (meaning, 'That's the beginning. There are lots more to come'). The innings was promptly closed at 517 for 4 wickets, a record for Pakistan. Hanif had rebuffed Bombay's bowlers for 7 hours 25 minutes, punctuated by 23 fours, chiefly drives through a wide arc from cover to long on.

His 203 not out, coming within a month of his 121 and 109, caused Indians to dub him Pakistan's wonder boy. His teammates nicknamed him Duleep (after the leading Indian film star). As the young batsman walked off, Skipper Kardar greeted him in English: 'Well done, Duleep! Try to repeat it in the Test.' Unlucky teammates rubbed shoulders with Hanif to change their fortune. The Pakistanis cancelled all evening engagements and held a team dinner . . .

The Brabourne Stadium pitch was in different mood for the third Test. A rare tantrum disturbed its placidity, as if it resented being soaked by a heavy dew then baked by the fiery sun. By taking six wickets before lunch, Amarnath and Mankad put the Pakistanis in desperate straits. When the Indians led by 197, Amarnath declared their innings closed late on the second day, to make the tourists begin their second innings in the last half-hour, after five hours fielding in the heat. The first wicket fell with one pitiable run on the board. If ever a side was doomed it was Pakistan, yet Hanif Mohammad and Waqar Hassan would not recognize the inevitable. In that crucial half-hour of the evening these two ex-pupils of Gover's school were so determined to lose no more wickets that they scored

only six runs between them, though Waqar, solidly built, is usually
as full of strokes as of the spirit for big occasions.

Through leaden-footed hours on the third day the pair strove on,
with a constancy hardly to be expected of two batsmen only seventeen and twenty years of age. Amarnath tried six Indian bowlers
against them – himself, Dani's medium pace, Ghulam Ahmed and
Hazare's off spin, Gupte's leg breaks and the left-hand pertinacity of
Mankad. Mostly it was the left-hander, who a few months earlier
had been hailed in England as Mankad the Magnificent when he
brought off a treble of 72, 184 and 5 wickets in the Lord's Test.
Lunch interval came and went . . . tea . . . still they stayed. The sun
was sinking redly as their second-wicket partnership rose, lifting with
it Pakistan's hopes of averting defeat. When they put on 150, reducing
arrears to 47, the Muslim pair looked like batting throughout the
day without loss of a wicket.

Mankad broke the partnership at 165, when Waqar (65) played a
ball around the corner and Hazare snapped up a catch. With this
wicket Mankad adorned his magnificence as an all-rounder by completing the double of 100 wickets and 1,000 runs in his twenty-third
Test match, four games fewer than the previous record by M. A.
Noble for Australia nearly half a century earlier.

Renewed hope sharpened India's bowling and fielding in the last
half-hour of the day, when Hanif had the nearness of a hundred to
intensify the nervous strain of keeping his wicket intact for Pakistan.
On 96 he cautiously played forward to Mankad, but the left-hander
had deceived him with the pace; at silly mid-off Ramchand grasped
the catch which cleared for India a path to victory always barred
while this lad remained at the wicket. In his innings of about six
hours, Hanif got within ten minutes of batting throughout a full
day's play for the second time in a week – an entry in the annals of
cricket which I never expect to see inscribed in the schoolboyish
hand of a seventeen-year-old . . .

Outside cricket, Hanif Mohammad has held the inter-school badminton championship and his hobbies are music and swimming. He
sat for his matriculation examination before the Pakistan team sailed
to England in 1954. He was 19 years 19 weeks when the tour opened.
A rainy season ruined it, but Hanif passed 1,000 runs in 30 innings.
In the cold and the wet he had to wait two months for his first
century in England; it ended at 140 when he was caught attempting
his twenty-third four. The innings that opened connoisseurs' eyes

widest was on sticky Old Trafford turf, so different from Karachi's mat. Making the ball jump bewilderingly, Bedser, Wardle and Glamorgan off-spinner Jim McConnon, in his first Test, settled Pakistan for 90. Kicking balls are most troublesome for a batsman only 5 ft 3 in, yet Hanif hung on for more than one-third of the total. He dropped many balls at the feet of crowding infielders and he took a number of blows on the body by dropping wrists and bat below those that could not be played safely . . .

Like all batsmen and wicketkeepers, Hanif dearly loves to have a bowl. Knowing this, Kardar gave him the ball and a thrill by letting him open the bowling in the last quarter-hour of a Test at Calcutta. After two overs Kardar took him off to let someone else have a turn, whereupon Hanif told him beseechingly, 'Skipper, after swinging the ball I can turn it from the off!' Somerset folk saw a demonstration of even wider versatility when Hanif switched from right- to left-arm bowling twice in one over at Taunton and with a slow ball from his left hand snared his first victim in first-class cricket.

In the final Test, Hanif's small hand threw the ball that scattered the stumps to run out England's last man, completing a win which sent Pakistanis in astrakhan caps delirious with joy. In their homeland thousands heard the finish on radio sets installed in the bazaars, and Prime Minister Mohammad Ali declared a school holiday. Nobody was more excited than the boys in the seats not long vacated by Hanif Mohammad and his teenage teammates.

*   *   *

The tiny island of Barbados (165 square miles all told) has produced more great cricketers than nations a hundred times as big. Among the very best were the batsmen Everton Weekes, Clyde Walcott and Frank Worrell, born within eighteen months of each other. The story is told of a visiting Archbishop of Canterbury who preached in Bridgetown's St Michael's Cathedral. He began by saying he had come to talk about the three Ws. A huge cheer went up, to become a collective groan when the prelate continued: 'Yes, the three Ws – Work, Witness and Worship.'

Later Bajan geniuses included Conrad Hunte, Wesley Hall and, above all, Garfield Sobers. One of his opponents, Hanif Mohammad, remarked that Sobers 'was sent by God to earth to play cricket'.

Certainly no cricketer, before or since, has been so variously gifted. Sobers was a world-class batsman who could bowl effectively in three different styles, and field superbly at short leg or in the covers. He exuded grace and genius: to watch him walk or put on his pads was to know one was in the presence of a master. One of my own abiding regrets is that I am too young to have seen Sobers in the flesh. But I have watched plenty of him on film. The Australian High Commission in New Delhi had tapes of two of his finest innings – the 132 in the Brisbane tied Test of 1960–1 and the 254 hit for the Rest of the World at Melbourne in 1971–2, which Sir Donald Bradman believed was the best knock ever played in Australia. Twice a year, for five years, I would borrow the reels from the High Commission and screen them at the University of Delhi.

The great C. L. R. James was luckier than I. He grew up on Constantine and Headley, but then moved to the United States in 1938 (where he spent fifteen years) before being deported, because of his political views. James thus missed the best of the three Ws, but returned to civilization (and cricket) in time to catch the best of Sobers.

C. L. R. JAMES

A Representative Man (1969)

The pundits colossally misunderstand Garfield Sobers – perhaps the word should be misinterpret, not misunderstand. Garfield Sobers, I shall show, is a West Indian cricketer, not merely a cricketer from the West Indies. He is the most typical West Indies cricketer that it is possible to imagine. All geniuses are merely people who carry to an extreme definitive the characteristics of the unit of civilization to which they belong and the special act or function which they express or practise. Therefore to misunderstand Sobers is to misunderstand the West Indies, if not in intention, by inherent predisposition, which is much worse. Having run up the red flag, I should at least state with whom I intend to do battle. I choose the least offensive and in fact he who is obviously the most well-meaning, Mr Denys Rowbotham of the *Guardian* of Friday 15 December 1967. Mr Rowbotham says of Sobers: 'Nature, indeed, has blessed Sobers liberally, for in addition to the talents and reflexes, conditioned and instinctive, of a great cricketer, he has the eyes of a hawk, the instincts and suppleness of a panther, exceptional stamina, and apparently the constitution of an ox.'

I could not possibly write that way about Garfield Sobers. I react strongly against it. I do not see him that way. I do not see Hammond that way. I see Sobers always, except for one single occasion, as exactly the opposite, the fine fruit of a great tradition. That being stated, let us now move on to what must always be the first consideration in writing about a cricketer, what he has done and what he does: that is, a hard look at Sobers on the field of play.

For Sobers the title of all-rounder has always seemed to me a circumspection. The Sobers of 1966 was not something new: that Sobers of 1966 had been there a long time. The truth is that Sobers for years now has had no superior in the world as an opening fast bowler.

Here are some facts to substantiate this apparently extravagant claim: which even today many of the scribes (and there are among them undoubted Pharisees) do not yet know.

It is the business of a fast bowler, opening the innings, to dismiss for small scores two or three of the first-line batsmen on the opposing side. If he does this and does it dramatically, then good captaincy will keep him in trim to make short work of the last two or three on the side, so ending with five or six wickets.

In 1964, his last session for South Australia, Sobers, against Western Australia, bowled batsman No. 1 for 12, and had batsman No. 2 caught by wicketkeeper Jarman for 2. Against Queensland Jarman caught No. 2 off Sobers for 5, and Sobers bowled No. 3 for 1. Against the history-making New South Wales side, Sobers had Thomas, No. 1 caught by Lill for 0. He had No. 2, Simpson, caught by Jarman for 0. He then had Booth, No. 4, caught by Jarman for 0. He thus had the first three Australian Test players for 0 each. In the second innings he bowled Thomas for 3.

South Australia's last match was against the strong Victoria side. Sobers had Lawry, No. 1, caught by Jarman for 4; Potter, No. 3, caught by Lill for 0; Stackpole, No. 5, caught by Lill for 5. In the second innings Redpath, No. 2, was caught by Jarman for 0; Cowper, No. 4, was caught by Hearne for 0; Lawry, No. 1, was caught by Jarman off Sobers for 22. (Let us note in passing that in this match against Victoria, Sobers scored 124 and had also scored 124 in the game against New South Wales, the same in which he dismissed the three Test batsmen each for 0.)

It is impossible to find within recent years another fast bowler who in big cricket so regularly dismissed for little or 0 the opening batsmen on the other side.

His action as a pace bowler is the most orthodox that I know. It is not the classical perfection, above all the ease, of E. A. McDonald. Sobers gathers himself together and is obviously sparing no effort (a rare thing with his cricket) to put his whole body into the delivery. The result is that the ball leaves the ground at a pace quite inconsistent with what is a fast-medium run-up and delivery. It would be worthwhile to get the pace of his delivery mechanically timed at different stages, as well as the testimony of observant batsmen and observant wicketkeepers.

There is nothing of the panther in the batting of Sobers. He is the most orthodox of great batsmen. The only stroke he makes in a manner peculiar to himself is the hook. Where George Headley used to face the ball square and hit across it, Denis Compton placed himself well outside it on the off side, and Walcott compromised by stepping backwards but not fully across the hitting, usually well in front of and not behind square leg, Sobers seems to stand where he is and depend upon wrist and eyesight to swish the short fast ball square to the leg boundary. Apart from that, his method, his technique is carried to an extreme where it is indistinguishable from nature.

You see it in both his defensive and offensive strokes. He can, and usually does, play back to anything about which he has the slightest doubt. More rarely he uses a forward defensive stroke. But he never just plays forward to put the bat on the ball and kill it. He watches the ball off the pitch and, even in the most careful forward defensive, plays the ball away; very different from that modern master of the forward defensive, Conrad Hunte. Hunte from the advanced front foot (never advanced too far) plays what Ranjitsinhji used to insist on calling a back stroke. His type of mastery of the forward defensive gives us the secret of the capacity of Sobers to punish good-length bowling on anything like a reasonable wicket. He does not need the half-volley of a fast or fast-medium bowler to be able to drive. From a very high backlift he watches the ball that is barely over the good length, takes it on the rise and sends it shooting between mid-on and mid-off. That is a later acquisition to a stroke that he has always had: to move back and time the good length through the covers.

The West Indian crowd has a favourite phrase for that stroke: 'Not a man move.' That stroke plus the ability to drive what is not a half-volley is the basis of the combination that makes Sobers the orthodox attacking player that he is. His aggressive play is very disciplined, which is shown by his capacity to lift the ball straight for six whenever he feels like it. But as a rule he reserves these paroxysms for occasions when the more urgent necessities of an innings have been safely fulfilled. It is possible that Sobers at times plays forward feeling for a slow ball, more often to a slow off-spin bowler, pitching on or just outside his off stump, going away. But I have to confess that I saw this and remembered previous examples when I was searching for a way in which as a captain I would plan to get him out.

Yet I have seen the panther in Sobers. Not when he opened in a Test and hit Miller and Lindwall for 43 runs in 15 minutes. The balls were just not quite there and this neophyte justly put them away. No. The panther one day saw the cage door open. In 1959–60, MCC visited Trinidad in the course of the tour of the West Indies. In between the match against the territory and the Test match the players of the Test side had a practice game, Hall on one side and Sobers on the other. Ramadhin was on the side of Sobers and Hall bowling to him was extremely careful to bowl not too slow but not too fast and always at a good length: he was not going to run the risk of doing damage to one of the main West Indies bowlers. But when he bowled at Sobers, Hall made up for the restraint enforced when bowling to Ramadhin. He ran to the wicket and delivered as fast as he could, obviously determined not to forgo the pleasure of sending Sobers's wicket flying.

Sobers returned in kind. I have never seen a fast bowler hit back so hard. It was not a forward push, it was not a drive. It was a hit. Sobers lifted his bat right back and did not lift the ball. He hit one or two of these balls to the on boundary, almost straight drives. Hall did not fancy it and bowled faster. Sobers hit him harder.

But in competitive cricket Sobers did not play that way. I saw on the screen shots of the famous century in the first Test against Australia in Brisbane in 1961 and also in the latter part of a day's play at Sydney in the third Test. All have agreed, and I agree with them, that at no time was there anything but orthodoxy carried to the penultimate degree when orthodoxy itself disappears in the absolute. There is no need here to give figures. One episode alone will show what the batting of Sobers can mean not only to spectators but to seasoned Test players. The episode will, I am certain, live in the minds of all who saw it. In a recent series, West Indies were striving to force a win against Australia in Barbados. On the last day with less than an hour to go, West Indies had to make some 50 runs.

Sobers promoted himself in the batting order, and as he made his way to the wicket, as usual like a ship in full sail, the feeling in the crowd grew and expressed itself that if this was to be done, here was the man to do it. But somebody else was thinking the same. Simpson, the Australian captain, put Hawke on to bowl; he himself stood at slip and he distributed the other eight men about the boundary. Obviously Simpson felt that if he left one gap in the field unprotected, Sobers would be able to find the boundary through it. I have never seen or heard before of any such arrangement or rather disarrangement of a cricket field.

Sobers had a look at the eight men strewn about the boundary, then had a look at Simpson standing at slip. He accepted Simpson's homage with a great grin which Simpson suitably acknowledged, altogether quite a moment. And an utterly spontaneous obeisance before the fearsome skill of the super batsman.

Two more points remain of Sobers on the field, his close fielding and his captaincy. Sobers has one most unusual characteristic of a distinctive close fielder. The batsman is probably aware of him at short leg, most probably very much aware of him. But the spectator is not. Constantine in the slips and at short leg prowled and pounced like a panther. Sobers did not. Of all the great short legs, he is the most unobtrusive that I can bring to mind. To Gibbs, in particular, he seems to stand where there is no need for him to move; in making the catch he will at most fall or rather stretch his length to the right, to the left or straight in front of him. But he is so close and so sure of himself that I for one am not aware of him except to know that he will be there when wanted.

His captaincy has the same measured, one might say classical, character. Don Bradman has written how embarrassing it is for a junior cricketer, even a Bradman by 1938, to captain a side containing his seniors. Sobers has had to contend with similar pressures native to West Indies society.

I awaited his handling of the captaincy with some trepidation. Not in any doubt about his strategic or tactical ability, not at all. I could not forget a conversation (one of many) with Frank Worrell, immediately after the return from Australia. We had talked about the future captaincy of the West Indies. Worrell was as usual cautious and non-committal: yes, so-and-so was a good man and capable; and so on. Then, when that stage of the conversation was practically at an end, he suddenly threw in:

'I know that in Australia whenever I had to leave the field, I was glad when I was able to leave Sobers in charge.' The timing, the style of the remark was so pointed that I felt I could push the unlocked door right open.

'He knows *everything*?' I asked.

'Everything,' Worrell replied. For me that settled one aspect of the question. The other I would be able to see only on the field. I saw it at Sabina Park at the first Test against Australia in 1965. Sobers was completely master of the situation from the moment he stepped on to the field, most probably before. He was aware of everything and at no time aware of himself. He was more in command of his situation than the far more experienced Simpson, though he did not have to face the onslaught that Simpson had to face, a problem not only collective but personal, Hall at one end and Griffith on the other. To see in the course of one day Sobers dispatch the ball to all parts of the field with his bat, then open the bowling, fielding at slip to Hall or Griffith, change to Gibbs and place himself at short leg, then go on to bowl slows, meanwhile placing his men and changing them with certainty and ease, this is one of the sights of the modern cricket field. I cannot visualize anything in the past that corresponds to it.

It was jealousy, nay, political hatred, which prompted Cassius to say to Caesar:

> Why, man, he doth bestride the narrow world
> Like a Colossus, and we petty men
> Walk under his huge legs and peep about,
> To find ourselves dishonourable graves.

Certainly in the press box watching Sobers a mere scribe is aware of Hazlitt's 'Greatness is great power, producing great effects. It is not enough that a man has great power in himself, he must show it to all the world in a manner that cannot be hid or gainsaid.' Of a famous racket-player: 'He did not seem to follow the ball, but the ball seemed to follow him.' Hazlitt would not have minded the appropriation of this acute simplicity for Sobers at short leg to Gibbs.

At the end of 1966 Sobers had scored over 5,000 runs in Tests and taken well over 100 wickets. Prodigious! Is Sobers the greatest all-rounder ever? The question is not only unrhetorical. It is unhistorical. Is he? I do not know. And nobody knows. I go further. Alert I always am to the reputation of West Indian cricketers; about this I do not even care. Sobers exceeds all I have seen or read of. That for me is enough, but I keep that well within bounds. There are pedants who will claim that he does not face bowling or batting of the temper and skill of previous generations. The argument errs on the side opposite to that which bravely asserts 'the greatest ever'. Sobers has so far met and conquered all opposition in sight. How can anyone say that if he had met this bowling quartet or that batting trio he could not have conquered them too? My presumption is that he would have dealt adequately with whatever problems he faced. Sir Donald Bradman is reported to have contested strongly Sir Stanley Jackson's dictum that George Lohmann was the greatest of medium-pace bowlers. Sir Donald gave first place to O'Reilly, because O'Reilly bowled the googly and Lohmann did not. Despite the eminence of these two gentlemen I beg to disagree with both. Lohmann had no need to bowl the googly. He had enough in his fingers to dismiss the men whom he bowled at. He needed nothing else. To compare him with other bowlers who had other problems and solved them can lead to missing what really matters and what cries for comparison. And what really matters is this: I believe Garfield Sobers has it in him, has already done enough to become the most famous, the most widely known cricketer of the century and of any century barring of course the Telstar of all cricket, W. G. This is not so much a quality of Sobers himself. It is rather the age we live in, its material characteristics and its social temper.

Let us go back to the weekend, more precisely the Sunday, following the first three days of the Oval Test in 1966. West Indies, in their second innings, had lost wickets and still had to make runs to avoid an innings defeat.

On that Sunday over half the world, was that a topic of discussion? Not at all.

The topic was: would Sobers make 200, vitalize his side and so enable West Indies to win? That he could no one doubted, a situation

that only one word can express – the word *formidable* as the French-
man uses it, vocally and manually.

I borrow here a thought from Sir Neville Cardus. Visualize please.
Not only in the crowded towns and hamlets of the United Kingdom,
not only in the scattered villages of the British Caribbean, people
were discussing whether Sobers would make the 200 or not. In the
green hills and on the veldt of Africa, on the remote sheep farms of
Australia, on the plains of Southern and the mountains of Northern
India, on vessels clearing the Indian Ocean, on planes making geo-
metrical figures in the air above the terrestrial globe. In English clubs
in Washington and in New York, there that weekend at some time
or other they were all discussing whether Sobers would make the
200 required from him for the West Indies to win the match.

Would he? No one knew. But everyone knew that he could. And
this was no remote possibility. It was not even 50–50. It was nearer
60–40. I have never known or heard anything like it, though I suspect
that in 1895 when W. G. approached the hundredth century the
whole cricket world stood on its toes and held its breath. But
the means of communication in 1895 were not what they were in
1966. A man must fit into the expanded technicalities of his age.
Garfield Sobers does. We are the second half of the twentieth century,
heading for the twenty-first, and the word global has shrunk to a
modest measure.

In 1967 I saw Garfield Sobers captaining a World XI at Lord's.
He not only had been appointed. He fitted the position. No one
would challenge either his competence or his moral right to the
distinguished position. I confess I was profoundly moved as he led
his team on to the ground and fixed his field.

I thought of cricket and the history of the West Indies. I cannot
think seriously of Garfield Sobers without thinking of Clifford
Goodman, Percy Goodman. H. B. G. Austin (always H. B. G. Austin),
Bertie Harragin and others 'too numerous to mention' (though not
very numerous). They systematically built up the game, played inter-
island matches, invited English teams to the West Indies year after
year, went to England twice before World War I. I remember too
the populace of Trinidad & Tobago subscribing a fund on the spot
so that 'Old Cons' would not miss the trip to England: and that
prodigious St Vincent family of the Ollivierres. The mercantile planter
class led this unmercantile social activity and very rapidly they themselves produced the originator of West Indian batting, George

Challenor. In 1906 he was a boy of eighteen and made the trip to England. He saw and played with the greatest cricketers England has ever known, the men of the Golden Age. Challenor returned to set a standard and pattern for West Indian batting from which at times it may have deviated, but which it has never lost. That history is a history of its own, going deep, too deep for the present area of discourse.

The local masses of the population, Sobers's ancestors and mine, at first looked on; they knew nothing about the game. Then they began to bowl at the nets, producing at that stage fine fast bowlers. Here more than anywhere else all the different classes of the population learned to have an interest in common.

The result of that consummation is Garfield Sobers. There is embodied in him the whole history of the British West Indies. Barbados has established a tradition that today is the strength, not only of Barbados, but of the West Indian people. But if there is the national strength there is also the national weakness. Sobers, like the other great cricketers of the present-day West Indies, could develop his various gifts and bring them to maturity only because the leagues in England offered them the opportunity to master English conditions, the most varied and exacting in the world. Without that financial backing, and the opportunity systematically to consolidate potential, to iron out creases, and to venture forth on the sea of experiment, there would be another fine West Indian cricketer but not Garfield the ubiquitous. When Sobers was appointed captain of the West Indies he was the first genuine native son to hold that position, born in the West Indies, educated in the West Indies, learning the foundations of his cricket there without benefit of secondary school, or British university. And there he was, just over thirty, with no serious challenge as the greatest cricketer of his generation . . .

In writing about cricket you have to keep an eye on the game, your own eye on the game that is before you, not on any other. Sometimes it is, it has to be, play and players reconstructed in the imagination. Garfield Sobers as a small boy most certainly played cricket barefooted in the streets with a sour orange for a ball and a piece of box or a coconut branch hacked into an approximation of a bat. All of us in the West Indies did that. I have owned a bat since I was four years of age and I do not remember ever being in a situation where I did not own a pair of shoes. But in the early years of this century there were not many, if any, motor cars about, cork balls were easily lost and could be bought only at the nearest small town; and to this day, far less than thirty years ago when Sobers was a boy, from convenience or necessity, future players at Lord's may be seen playing barefooted with a piece of wood and a sour orange in some village or the back street of a small town in the Caribbean. In the larger islands, once you show unusual capacity, people begin to watch you and talk about you. Sobers stood out easily and people have told me that even as a lad he conferred distinction on his club and people were on the lookout to help in any way he needed. In the West Indies the sea divides us and, in any case, when Sobers at the age of sixteen played for Barbados, I could not possibly see him because I was far away in England. Though as a personality he could mean little to me, I read the accounts, as I always did (and always will if I live in Tierra del Fuego). I couldn't help noting that he was only sixteen years old and that he had taken 7 wickets. The scores showed that all were bowled or lbw. Very interesting but no more.

Later, however, I saw what I did not see at the time. In the second innings he bowled 67 overs with 35 maidens for 92 runs and 3 wickets, this when India scored 445 for 9. This was a boy of sixteen, obviously someone that would attract special notice. But in those days Valentine filled the bill for slow left-arm bowling. He took 28 wickets in the series so that one could not take Sobers very seriously as a slow left-arm bowler.

Followed the visit of MCC to the West Indies. Sobers did little for Barbados with the ball, but this youth, it seemed, could bat. His 46 in the first innings was the second highest score and he made 27 in the second. After the third Test, Valentine did not play and Sobers came into the fifth Test, taking 4 wickets in one innings and scoring 14 and 26 not out. So far, very useful but nothing to strike the eye of anyone far away. He goes into the list of youngest Test players. When he played at Kingston he was only 17 years and 245 days.

So far there was to the reading eye only promise, but now against the Australians in the West Indies there could be no failure to see that a new man had arrived. Sobers took only 6 wickets in 93.5 overs. But Valentine in 140 had taken only 5. Ramadhin in 139 had taken the same paltry number. Sobers was second in the bowling averages and in batting, in eight innings, had scored 38.50 runs per innings. One began to hear details about his style as a batsman and as a super slip more than as a bowler. In the last Test in Jamaica he made 35 not out and 64. I was informed that from all appearances he would have gone on to the century in a partnership with Walcott which added 79 runs. Sobers was completely master of the bowling but not of himself. Lindwall with a new ball bumped one short at him. Sobers could not resist the hook and found deep square leg waiting for the catch.

Then came a setback that startled. Sobers went to New Zealand as one of the bright stars of the junior Test players. In four Tests his average was 16 runs and with Valentine doing all that was needed from a left-hander he took only 2 wickets. In first-class matches his batting average was below 30 and in all first-class matches he took 4 wickets: far below the boy who had done so well against the full strength of Australia before he was twenty. But for a West Indies team in Port of Spain against E. W. Swanton's team, Sobers had 3 for 85 and 3 for 49, and made 71, second only to Weekes with 89. New Zealand was a distant dot on the Sobers landscape.

West Indies came to England in 1957 and obviously Sobers was someone I had to see as soon as possible. I went down to Lord's to see the team at the nets but this was my first glimpse of the three Ws and I don't remember noticing Sobers, except for his fine physique. I missed the Worcester match but found myself at Northampton to see the second game. Curiously enough, as he did often that year, he played second fiddle to Worrell, in a stand of over a century of which his share was only 36. But great batsman was written all over him, and I think it was Ian Peebles who referred to him in terms of Woolley. I remember noting the stroke off the back foot that sent the length ball of the pace bowler past cover's right hand. There was another stroke, behind point off a pitched-up fast ball. The ball was taken on the rise and placed behind point to beat the covers, now packed. Here obviously was that rare phenomenon, in cricket or any other form of artistic endeavour, someone new, who was himself and like no one else. There are vignettes in 1957 that are a permanent part of my cricket library. There was an innings against MCC at Lord's in which Sobers came as near as it was possible for him to look like Constantine in that with monotonous regularity the ball flew from his bat to all parts of the field. In the first Test at Birmingham, he made over 50 in little more than an hour and I remember in particular my being startled at the assured manner in which he glanced – I think it was Bailey – from the middle stump to square leg and so beat the man at long leg. The same determination to thumb his fingers at the covers lifted Lock or Laker overhead to drop in front of the pavilion for four; batsmen didn't do these things in 1957.

In the last Test at the Oval West Indies collapsed before Lock and Laker and there came fully to the surface the element of stubbornness which Sobers had shown in the last innings at Kingston in 1955 in his partnership with Walcott, and which I had glimpsed at his batting with Worrell at Northampton. Out of a total of 89 he made 39 and in the second innings out of 86, 42. I believe I saw how famous men of old made runs on impossible wickets. To Laker in particular Sobers played back, always back. When Laker had him playing back often enough, he would drop a ball just outside the off stump going away from Sobers to cut: there was a long list of West Indian casualties to this particular disease which appeared most often in the records as 'Walcott c. Evans b. Laker'. Sobers, however, it would appear was waiting for Laker. Time and again he could get across and cut the ball down past third man.

In a review of the season Skelding, former county fast bowler and now umpire, was reported in one of the annuals as saying that the Sobers he saw in 1957 would be one of the greatest batsmen who ever lived. I could not go quite so far but I have it down in writing of 1958 that if Sobers developed as he promised in 1957, he would be the greatest of living batsmen. So that the 365 which exceeded Hutton's 364 and the tremendous scoring which followed filled out a portrait whose outlines had been firmly drawn. No need to go through 1963. I saw and felt what I expected to see and feel. However, there was one piece of play in the field which I have seen mentioned only in *Wisden* and not commented upon elsewhere. That was his bowling in the Oval Test. The famous feat of fast bowling in 1963 was Wesley Hall at Lord's in the second innings when his figures read 40 overs, 9 maidens, 4 wickets for 93 runs. He bowled during the 3 hours and 20 minutes for which play was in progress on the last day. I believe that on that last day he bowled 35 overs.

Now in the Oval Test Sobers bowled in the first innings 21 overs, 4 maidens, for 2 wickets, 44 runs. I remember these two wickets. He had Bolus caught by keeper Murray (33) and Edrich caught Murray for 25. Hall and Griffith had tried in vain to break that partnership and Sobers, struggling mightily, dismissed both of them well set. In the second innings he did even better; again he dismissed Bolus at 15, again well set, and Dexter when at 27 he seemed poised for one of his great innings. Sobers bowled 33 overs and took 3 wickets for 77 runs. At the time and to this day I measure that performance and Sobers as a fast bowler by his approximation at the Oval to Hall's far more famous feat in the Test at Lords.

There is one episode on the field which for some reason or other sticks in my mind as representative of Sobers. He came out to bat at the Oval against Surrey early in 1963. He came to the wicket and some Surrey bowler bowled him a short ball. It went to the square-leg boundary. A dead metaphor can sometimes be made to live again: that ball went like a flash. As far as I remember the same over saw another ball, short, but this time outside the off stump and rising higher than usual. That ball streaked to the off boundary. Sobers had not scored any runs in the south and everybody including myself believed that here was the beginning of one of the great innings. It was not to be. Two or three balls later he was out to the almost audible lamentation of the crowd, which had been keyed up to a pitch in the belief that we were going to see what we had come forth to see.

Sobers today is a captain and I believe it would be worthwhile to give some hint of what I have been able to detect of the personality behind that play. I do not know Sobers as well as I knew Constantine, George John and Headley and the men I have played with. But there are certain things that one can divine. I saw Sobers in 1957 make 27 at Leeds and then get run out not through anybody's fault but by some superb fielding by Tony Lock. Finer batting it is impossible to imagine and that day nothing was more certain than a century before lunch in a Test. But this is not why I remember that day. What remains in my mind is the fury, the rage of Sobers at having been dismissed when he obviously felt that history was in his hands for the making. His walk back to the pavilion made me think of those hurricanes that periodically sweep the Caribbean. I caught a glimpse, by transference so to speak, of the aggressive drive which expresses itself in his batting and fast bowling. I have already referred to the demonic hits with which he greeted Hall's attempt to bowl him out in a practice game. In the Test which followed that practice game Sobers drove too early at a wide half-volley and was caught for 0. Again on his way back to the pavilion I saw the gleam of the damped-down furnace that raced inside of him. Therefore when I read his detailed protests against what he considers the unfairness of British reporters and commentators in their diatribes against his team of 1966 in general and Griffith in particular, I take it much more seriously than most. The protest is not a formality, or something that ought to be put on record, parliamentary fashion. He feels it personally, as a man feels a wound. I suspect that that is the personality which expresses itself as ubiquitously as it does on the field because it needs room. A man of genius is what he is, he cannot be something else and remain a man of genius.

I think of Sobers walking down the pavilion steps at Lord's, captain of an international cricket team. Sixty years ago it would have been Pelham Warner, another West Indian, and thirty years before that it would have been Lord Harris, yet another cricketer of Caribbean connotation. Whoever and whatever we are, we are cricketers. Garfield Sobers I see not as a fortuitous combination of atoms which by chance have coalesced into a superb public performer. He being what he is (and I being what I am), for me his command of the rising ball in the drive, his close fielding and his hurling himself into his fast bowling are a living embodiment of centuries of a tortured history.

*   *   *

After the Second World War, England suffered painfully from the fast-bowling combination of Ray Lindwall and Keith Miller. Revenge was soon at hand, however, in the shape of Brian Statham, Frank Tyson and Fred Trueman. Only the last had a personality to match. Trueman was a man of supreme self-confidence whose penchant for outré remarks frequently found him out of favour with the Establishment. But he was also an enormously skilled fast bowler. After he retired he joined the BBC's *Test Match Special* team, where one of his colleagues was John Arlott. The following pages are extracted from Arlott's book *Fred: Portrait of a Fast Bowler*.

John Arlott

In His Pomp (1971)

For six splendid years Fred Trueman strode the cricket world with a not unjustified swagger. People's eyes turned to him in a cricket match; he sensed it, and gloried in it. He slouched back to his run mark and, when he paused dramatically before moving in, he had his audience in his hand as surely as the ball; and he knew it. When he squatted on his haunches, relaxed but poised, at short leg, his cap deliberately crumpled on his head, a blade of grass between his lips, nattering at the batsman, he was relishing being what he was and where he was – an England cricketer in a Test match, or a Yorkshireman playing for his county.

When he came to his peak, during Ronnie Burnet's period of captaincy, he was an utterly committed Yorkshire player. Previously there had been doubts; he had been ill at ease with teammates, uncertain of himself and of them. By 1959 only Close, with whom he was on gruffly straightforward terms, and Vic Wilson, whom he then found easy – and an asset as a catcher at short leg – were his equals in seniority. The remainder of the team were his juniors, to whom he was affable. Sometimes those who felt the strain of matches and wanted to be quiet might disengage themselves from conversation; but the old hostility had gone and he was now as much at his ease as his nature was ever likely to allow.

Apart from his natural aptitude, he became a great fast bowler for two reasons. The first was his single-minded determination to be exactly that; the second, his immensely strong body. It was not merely powerful, it was quite phenomenally solid, without observable weakness; and it proved magnificently durable. Like S. F. Barnes, Derek Shackleton and Brian Statham, he bowled himself fit. Dexter's 1962–3 team to Australia travelled from Aden to Fremantle on the *Canberra*, where one of their fellow passengers was Gordon Pirie, who offered to organize physical training for the team. He suggested that Trueman, as a bowler, needed exercises to strengthen his legs. 'My legs?' said Fred. 'They've carried me through over a thousand bloody overs this season – and they've never let England down yet – which is more than can be said about some.' Then, with a cold look overboard, 'Canst tha' swim?' The conversation ended. His legs were like tree trunks; and he bowled himself fit – that is to say fit for bowling, which is a peculiar and unique kind of fitness. There is no known training for a man who, wearing heavy – in this case steel-toe-capped – boots, thick socks, long flannel trousers and a shirt thick enough to guard against chill, has to walk 150 yards, run 150 yards, with six violent peaks of muscular action, in five minutes; rest for five minutes and do it again, and at the same intervals for an hour; then become semi-active and, at any moment, when the muscles have set or while they are still tired, be suddenly called upon to go through the entire routine again. All this may be demanded in the cold of an English spring or the high heat and humidity of Brisbane: and the same amount of applied strength, the same precision, is expected of him in either circumstance. It is an illogical form of activity which may account for the fact that there is no logical form of preparation for it. On the other hand, during his later years, if Trueman had three days off, he needed half an hour's bowling before he was loose.

His approach, though long and menacing, was controlled, its length and rhythm changed at different periods of his career as he sensed the changing nature of his demands from it. Its cohesive quality was to be seen, even at his fastest, in the monumental steadiness of his head and shoulders, which remained as firm during his run-up as if he were standing still. If these rocked it meant that he was weary, about to lose rhythm, length and line; but, despite the weight of the demands put upon him, that rarely happened.

He, Statham and Tyson were a remarkable set of contemporaries: the finest fast bowlers of more than a quarter-century, they were born within eight months – and less than sixty miles – of one another: Tyson at Bolton on 6 June 1930, Statham at Gorton, Manchester, eleven days later; Trueman at Stainton in the West Riding of Yorkshire on 6 February 1931. The only comparable incidence of time, place and quality in cricket history is the birth of Frank Worrell, Everton Weekes and Clyde Walcott within an even smaller area of Barbados in the seventeen months between August 1924 and January 1926.

Statham – 'the Whippet' – the most finely drawn of the three, was also the most accurate – probably more consistently so than any other bowler of his pace in cricket history. Tyson, who entered first-class cricket later and left it earlier than the other two, was, for his brief peak period, beyond all question the fastest bowler in the world. He planned his career, acquired a university degree and went consciously into being a fast bowler, content that he could spend himself in one splendid bonfire of effort and, when the flame died, turn to the security of teaching. Fred Trueman came into county cricket before either of the others and left it after them; he had a career of twenty years as a fast bowler and he expressed himself – or his different selves – in every moment of it. He was the most resourceful, violent and unpredictable of the three: Statham was accurate; Tyson was fast: Fred was everything.

Oddly enough, though Statham formed with Trueman England's longest-lasting fast-bowling pairing; and shared Tyson's great series in Australia in 1954–5 and his destruction of South Africa at Trent Bridge in 1955; the three played only once in the same Test, at Adelaide in 1959, when Tyson had declined from his high peak and, though the other two had better figures, Australia still made 476 and 36 for no wicket and won by 10 wickets. Trueman and Tyson played together in only four Tests – all in Australia and New Zealand in 1958–9 – and in all but one Trueman had the better figures.

Trueman needed a strong body for, lacking Statham's capacity for relaxation or Tyson's cool objectivity, he suffered from the stresses of cricket. Fortunately he was a long sleeper.

Fred Trueman was not a level bowler. He could always be a good one; at times he was lit by the fire of greatness: and the most stirring memories of him recall days when, in face of completely discouraging opposition, conditions and state of the game, over-bowled and ill-supported, he tried harder than any captain could fairly ask, and sometimes succeeded beyond the bounds of reasonable possibility. On the other hand, there were occasions – rare, but undeniable – when he turned it in. A dead pitch could depress him, as it did in the Old Trafford Test against Australia in 1961, when he had figures of 1 for 55 in 14 overs and 0 for 92 in 32 overs. Taking his sweater from the umpire he said to Peter May, 'Let Closey bowl.' May, never strong about Trueman, did put Close on. More often Trueman was moved to the heights: though no one could tell what might provide the impetus . . .

The kindling could be sudden and unexpected. All that anyone knew was that suddenly he was going eagerly back to his mark; there was a belligerent spring in his run, he came over like a storm wave breaking on a beach, and followed through with so mighty a heave that the knuckles of his right hand swept the ground. Where previously the ball had curved off the pitch calf high, it now spat to the hips or ribs: wicketkeeper and slips moved deeper; the batsman, who had seemed established, was late on his stroke; and the whole match was transformed.

This was the essence of fast bowling. Yet it is a mistake to think of Fred Trueman as simply a bowler of speed. It is known that he commanded outswing, inswing, that he had greater control with the yorker than any other bowler of comparable pace in modern times except, perhaps, Lindwall; that he had the knack of hammering the ball into the ground – as Keith Miller and Ray Lindwall in 1953 encouraged him to do – so that he gained not only lift, but also movement off the seam. Indeed, he shared with Lindwall the rare ability to 'do' as much as a fast-medium bowler at fast bowler's speed. On 'green' wickets he shrewdly kept the seam straight and let it do its own unpredictable work. So ball after ball would, by his natural tendency, whip away from the bat and then, suddenly, beyond his control – 'I don't know, so how can the batsman?' – one would cut savagely back into the stumps. Although he could not command that ball it was always possible because of his method.

He was proud when he first took wickets with his slower ball. Batsmen, though, remembered his faster ball: he would seem to be bowling at full speed when suddenly one would come through an unaccountable and undetectable foot quicker, and defeat the stroke. He had, too, something of a dossier system of the batsmen of his experience. He knew their weaknesses and their strengths; those who would push forward and those who would go back to his first ball at them; those who felt outside the off stump; those vulnerable on the leg; the shrinkers and the hookers; all were filed in his memory. He was more subtle than those who did not know him ever realized. He was, in the words of S. J. Perelman about an altogether different person, 'crazy like a fox'. In yet another strength, he believed implicitly that he was too good for any batsman; and sometimes he convinced the best of them that he was right.

Only a few great batsmen could play Trueman when he was 'in his pomp' with consistent confidence and certainty: he would admit May, Cowdrey, Sobers, Walcott – on West Indian wickets – Weekes, Sobers, the two Simpsons – Bobby and Reg – Insole, Washbrook and one man who never appeared in a Test, the resolute Brian Reynolds of Northants. Only the two Simpsons were opening batsmen of Trueman's maturity (Washbrook had by then dropped down the order), for when he was fresh and the ball was new, he probed technique, temperament, courage and speed of reaction with so sharp a point that few regularly passed the examination.

A tendency to bowl too many bouncers remained his weakness. Although he could push a man on to the back foot in anticipation of it and then fool him with a yorker, he did not do it frequently enough. The bouncer was his exclamation mark, and he exclaimed to the end of his career, even when its bounce was as predictable as its incidence.

The temptation to use him was irresistible; he was shock bowler and stock bowler in one; capable of containing a strong batting side in conditions to its liking, always with the possibility that he might bowl them out at the same time.

Even in this period he was not a regular choice for England. He was dropped from the team for the last Australian Test of 1961 – when he admitted the selectors' justification – and did not make the tours of Australia 1954–5, South Africa 1956–7 and 1964–5, India–Pakistan in 1961–2 or India in 1963–4. From the beginning to the end of his career as an international cricketer England played 118 Tests and he appeared in only 67 of them. Thus his record number of Test wickets – 30, an average of over 4.5 a match spread over thirteen years – becomes even more remarkable.

It is striking, too, that Statham played his first Test in the series before Trueman and his last in the one after Trueman finished: and that he played in 70 out of 123 – a slightly smaller proportion than Trueman's. Again the coincidence of their careers is striking: no other English fast bowler endured as these two did: while from other countries, only Lindwall – who also had thirteen years of Test cricket – compared with them.

By 1959, Tyson's ankle injury had slowed him and Fred Trueman was without doubt the fastest bowler in England. So far as the world was concerned the Australians Rorke and Meckiff – whose actions were, at mildest, doubtful – Davidson, Wesley Hall of West Indies and, now that Heine had gone, Neil Adcock from South Africa disputed the title. In England his closest challengers were Brian Statham, Peter Loader – of the dubious bouncer – Harold Rhodes and David White: only Brian Statham for completeness of technique and David White, on his day for sheer pace, cast the slightest doubt on his national title.

So he assumed the mantle of authority with a rare blend of violence, humour, tolerance, experience and brilliance; authority, however, never included conformity; he was not the Establishment's man; he could still four-letter-word himself into trouble, still slash the Establishment with the sharpest edge of his tongue. Sometimes, too, in his impatience, he had to resort to the beamer, dispatched straight at the point between the batsman's eyes; and once, when he was offered even greater violence in return, he not only desisted but doled out a couple of drivable half-volleys by way of compensation. Such generosity was unusual. He normally had bouncers, yorkers

and boxers ready for those – generally southerners and fancy caps –
who were on his grudge list; and Yorkshire can attribute their run
of four championships in the five years of Fred's 'pomp' largely to
the fact that, at the pinch, he could usually summon the knowledge,
resource and application – and, above all, the pace – to remove any
batsman.

It is true of all bowlers, but more so in the case of Fred Trueman
than most, that when he was taking wickets he was never tired; once
he mounted the kill he could not be pulled off. When, in 1960, he
was – for the only time in his career – the first bowler in England
to take 100 wickets, he came to Yorkshire's match with Warwickshire
at Bradford nine short and closely pressed by Jackson for the distinction. On the first morning he went, as usual, into the visiting dressing
room and chatted up his opponents with his latest stories, opinions
and humour, which they accepted with the enjoyment of most teams
who did not live with him six days a week. At about eleven o'clock
he eased himself off the table to go and change with the words 'Oh,
yes, and I only want nine wickets to be first to a hundred – so you
buggers can start drawing short straws to see which one I don't
bloody well have.'

The Warwickshire batsmen were duly impressed; but Yorkshire
won the toss and, after a first day shortened by rain, batted until
the middle of Monday before they declared at 304 for 9. Trueman
emphasized the validity of his boast by having both Billy Ibadulla
and Arnold Townsend taken in the gully from lifters in his first over.
The spinners, Jack Birkenshaw and Don Wilson, worked their way
through the middle of the innings and he had a couple of catches
dropped before he took his next wicket – Jack Bannister, edging to
the wicketkeeper – and, when Warwickshire followed on, he still
wanted six more wickets and he was tiring. Nevertheless, once Cowan
had put out their fellow Yorkshireman, Norman Horner, Trueman
swept away Arnold Townsend, Mike Smith, Billy Ibadulla and Ray
Hitchcock and Yorkshire claimed the extra half-hour. Trueman now
was clearly spent and Vic Wilson told him to take his sweater. He
protested, was allowed another over, which proved little more than
fast-medium – and had another catch dropped – before he came off
in high dudgeon and Birkenshaw took his place. 'I'll never bowl for
Yorkshire again – and don't send me back to leg slip because if you
do I shall drop anything that comes near me – like these bastards
have been doing off me all day'. Five minutes later he picked up a

glorious swooping catch off Barry Fletcher from Jack Birkenshaw's bowling – at leg slip.

As he threw it up he said, 'I'll have another over for that' and promptly bowled John Kennedy. So three wickets were left for the next day and he wanted two of them. When play started late, after rain, Bannister and Geoffrey Hill proceeded with steady competence to bat until lunch and double the score. They even batted on into the afternoon before Cowan bowled Hill and Fred, who had refused to be relieved, launched himself at John Fox. He was flagging now and it was a wide, and not very fast ball – the last of an over – that Fox chased and edged to Jimmy Binks to let in Ossie Wheatley, one of the world's natural No. 11s. Bannister took a single off Illingworth and so – less wittingly – did Wheatley, before Trueman began his twelfth consecutive over of the day. He was weary but Wilson would not have dared to take him off: he was not to be baulked of this easy victim – though it was by no means certain that he could muster the fast, straight ball that was invariably enough for Ossie Wheatley. He gathered himself, rushed in and bowled: the ball pitched short and at no great speed, wide of the off stump; Wheatley went to 'shoulder arms' and let it pass, but he did not do so quickly enough: the ball hit his bat on the backlift and flew between slips and gully for four. While the field shook with laughter Trueman stood, hands on hips, scowling at the batsman. 'Well,' he said, 'that's the first time I've been left alone for four.' Wheatley was not the most gifted or intrepid of batsmen and, while he observed Trueman's exhaustion, he was not certain that he would not now be given a bouncer of greater pace than his batting ability warranted. So, as Trueman moved up, Wheatley began to inch away. The ball proved to be a straight full toss but, in the moment before it would have hit the bails, Wheatley's bat, coming from the opposite direction, demolished the wicket completely and, by a fraction of a second, the dismissal became 'Wheatley hit wicket bowled Trueman 5' instead of 'Wheatley bowled Trueman 5' (his batting average for the season was 4.94). F. S. T. was first to the 100 wickets and the afternoon dissolved in talk and celebration.

*   *   *

Another essay by Ray Robinson, and once more about cricketers from a country other than his own. In cultural and geographical terms New Zealand is very close to Australia, but for too long did the latter nation act as a cricketing big brother. Only one Test, in 1946, was played between the two nations until sanity asserted itself in the form of a three-Test series in 1973. Still, the two countries play far less often than they might – a state of affairs that is a product exclusively of Australian arrogance. Which is why this tribute stands out as a rare example of Aussie generosity to the Kiwi. As I write, and you read, the New Zealand tradition of left-handed batsmanship rests secure in the person of its current captain, Stephen Fleming.

Ray Robinson

Southern Southpaws (1956)

Blindfold me and lead me to a Test ground where a teenage left-hander is heading for a hundred and my first guess would be that he comes from the land of the Maoris. Playing cricket left-handed there has become almost as traditional as rubbing noses. If there is anything in proportional representation, the country between Whangaroa and Raki-ura must carry more southpaws to the acre than sunnier and steadier lands. Either that or they are left in the majority because the right-handers migrate across the Tasman Sea to win the coveted racing cups and otherwise run the affairs of their antipodean neighbours, the Australians. A stocky Canterbury left-hander, Thomas Burtt, spun his slow and accurate way in 1954 to a total of 386 wickets at the age of thirty-nine, thereby erasing about the last surviving NZ record by a right-hander, W. E. Merritt, who bowled leg breaks.

When the New Zealanders began practice on their last tour of South Africa the *Cape Times* gave most of the top of its front page to a picture of five of them in a row like peas in a pod, all shaping up with eyes right, bats gripped tight, left heels to the rear. They were Bert Sutcliffe, New Zealand's gift to the cricket-watching public, young John Beck and Eric Dempster from Wellington, much-travelled Lawrence Miller and Guy Overton, the Otago sheepfarmer – together as characteristic of their country as the lemon-squeezer crown of the NZ Army hat.

Put the clock back some years and other faces would appear in such a left-hand line-up under the black caps with the silver fern emblem. There is the ruddy face of Gifford Vivian, youngest of all Test century-makers. A bank clerk barely eighteen, Giff was unknown in first-class cricket when he made 87 in his first match for Auckland so brilliantly that three months later he was chosen in the first New Zealand team to play Test matches in Britain. Already he was well developed, stood 5 ft 10½ in and weighed 12 st 3 lb. As the youngest cricketer his country ever sent abroad his Test chance came at the age of 18 years 267 days, when a leg injury prevented New Zealand's greatest batsman, Stewart Dempster, from playing against England at the Oval in July 1931. The fast bowling of G. O. Allen, which took 5 wickets for 14 runs in 13 overs, wrecked New Zealand's batting on a rain-affected wicket, but in the second innings Vivian clinched his place by outscoring his older companions with 51.

Having shot rapidly to the top, he did not make the mistake of thinking he had mastered the game of cricket in eight months. Any hint dropped by more experienced teammates was heeded and tested. Every leading English cricketer he met was plied with eager questions. Yet the youngster did not allow older men to flag him down to a cautious speed, as older men are prone to do. His first century in England, 135 against Oxford University, came inside three hours and he caned Yorkshire's bowlers for 101 in 100 minutes, with four sixes and a dozen fours. Next match he took five Lancashire wickets with spinners that floated in with his arm and turned back. He completed the tour with 1,002 runs and 64 wickets in first-class matches two months before his nineteenth birthday.

In his first international match in his own country, 121 days after he turned nineteen, Vivian walked in at Wellington to hit up a round 100 against South Africa. He followed that up by taking 4 wickets for 58 in 30 overs and making 73 in the second innings. For skill and stamina, his is the finest feat on record for a Test teenager – and for temperament, too, because every run he made and every ball he bowled were for a struggling team which, despite his efforts, lost by 8 wickets . . .

Another day Vivian's teammates saw him reach 100 with a six over the bowler's head, then collapse in mid-pitch with a knee cartilage trapped by the bone. In wartime he was aboard the *Georgic*, reported sunk by a U-boat, and nobody knew his fate until one day he opened the door of the family home in Auckland.

By then the baton had been taken in the left hand of Martin Donnelly. It probably changed hands in a low-scoring, rainy Test match at Manchester, where Vivian, 50, and Donnelly, 37 not out, put up the only resistance in New Zealand's second innings of 134. Tom Goddard took 6 wickets for 29. Pitching his off breaks in two patches outside the off stump, he spun out six right-handers for 2 runs; the other 27 were made by the two left-handers.

Unlike Vivian, bare-headed except when there was a trying glare, Donnelly never liked batting without a cap. When his own was mislaid he appeared in some bizarre creations which almost amounted to camouflage. Youngest of the three sons of a farmer at Ngaruawahia (pronounced with the g silent, as in Cholmondeley), Martin Paterson Donnelly used to toddle around the Waikato province of Auckland with his oldest cricketing brother, Harry. Martin knew all about runs before he went to school to learn about the other three Rs at Eltham and at New Plymouth High School. In the high-school nets G. G. Bottrill taught the boys to concentrate on the ball and never play a slipshod stroke even at the feeblest practice bowler.

In his last year at high school, the first Donnelly saw of English cricketers was the terrifying sight of Hopper Read rushing up to bowl for Errol Holmes's team against Taranaki. The waiting batsman could see the soles of Read's boots, all sprigs. Martin survived the onrush of the human harrow but was stranded when he swished at a slow ball that Jim Sims turned the wrong way. Between innings Joe Hardstaff gave the eighteen-year-old country boy this tip: 'If you have difficulty in picking the wrong 'un, play down the wicket as far as you can with a dead bat so that the ball, if nicked, won't carry as far as slip. Do that and hang around and you'll soon find it.' Donnelly did that, and his 49 in the second innings saved Taranaki and staked his claim for the tour of England a year later.

When selection time came he was in poor form but the selectors must have been judges of quality, because they gave places to Donnelly, nineteen, and sturdy, right-handed Mervyn Wallace, twenty. The two under-twenty-one members of the team headed the batting, Wallace with 1,641 runs and Donnelly with 1,414. Once I asked Martin how he accounted for two strangers to English conditions out-batting experienced teammates. His reply: 'Perhaps this is the answer to that one: Youths are so chockful of confidence that ordinary reverses do not throw them out of balance. Only a little success is needed to make them feel right.' Something for selectors to paste in their hats.

Donnelly is the youngest New Zealander to have played in a Test match at Lord's. At 19 years 252 days, he made his Test debut in the same match as Hutton, just twenty-one, and the same year as Compton (seven months younger), and Washbrook, twenty-two. Like Hutton, he began with 0. He tried to sweep the first ball from James Parks and was lbw when it drifted back. It might have been 0 and 0. When Verity bowled in the second innings with two short-leg fieldsmen Donnelly seemed almost mesmerized. A ball rolled from his bat but, instead of starting for his first run in Test cricket, he stood while his partner sprinted up the pitch calling: 'Run! Run! Run!'

Once that was over Donnelly was cool as the summit of Mount Cook. Coolness was needed, because only three wickets stood between New Zealand and defeat. One of them belonged to Jack Kerr, usually an opening batsman, whose chin had been gashed earlier in the game but who came in with two hours to go to save the match. To make sure he did not retreat from the first international fast bowler he had faced on a Test wicket, Donnelly stepped across to the off as Alf Gover delivered the ball. It worked, because the ball was seldom far enough up to find him out and his movement put him in position to hook. Donnelly watched all the bowlers closely for clues to their intentions. As Gover came up with his long run, all knees and elbows, Donnelly detected the shoulder movement that warned of a coming bouncer. It flew near his ears (the smallest in Test cricket) but the left-hander had already taken up position and he hooked hard. The ball grazed Hardstaff's curly hair at short leg before he could duck and reached the boundary before cold sweat came out on him. That stroke gave Donnelly confidence, though England's captain, Robins, crowded the batsmen with infielders and Voce's lively left-arm bowling hit the pitch with four short legs and three slips ready for the slightest error.

The last over came with Kerr (38) and Donnelly (21) still there. With the match saved, the youngster exuberantly flashed a square cut at the last ball and snicked it into Ames's gloves . . .

Clambering from a tank in Italy when the war ended, Donnelly flew to Britain, read history at Oxford for his Bachelor of Arts degree, scored six centuries for the University in his first season and became captain in his second. By playing rugger for England against Ireland (at centre three-quarter instead of his usual position, stand-off half) he joined the few who have attained international rank in two sports. The Maoris of his homeland have produced many fine footballers but they leave it to the paler pakeha to uphold New Zealand's name at cricket . . .

As the only New Zealander (with a West Indian, a South African and eight Australians) in the Dominions XI which beat England in 1945 he played an innings of 133 which is remembered with Keith Miller's epic 185, a few weeks after the first atomic bomb was dropped on Japan. Next year he came to Lord's to make the pavilion ring in praise of his 142 for Oxford against Cambridge at almost 50 runs an hour. Next year even greater acclamation was earned by his even faster 162 not out for Gentlemen against Players, with its wind-up of 50 in 40 minutes. In his last Test at Lord's, in 1949, he set a record for NZ with a chanceless 206 (26 fours), fighting three and a half hours for the first 100, then exacting the last 106 from England's bowlers in an hour less. With those centuries for his university, the amateurs and his country he equalled the three-sided record of a larger left-hander, Percy Chapman, for Cambridge, the Gentlemen and England.

First sight of Donnelly at the wicket gave no promise of the treat to come. He bent at the knees and waist, back far over, stern jutting insultingly towards short leg. His front shoulder twisted around to point wide of mid-on, the elbow poked towards midwicket and his body rocked. He resettled his feet, and his sloping bat tapped the ground restlessly behind his left toecap. Though the bottom hand was an inch or two up the handle, the general impression was of a hunched attitude, more pronounced as body and bat sank lower as the bowler approached.

The moment the ball was bowled there was a transformation. Donnelly came up to play it with ease that charmed the eye. Feet and body glided and turned into position naturally, whether he was cutting, cover-hitting, driving, hooking, flicking the ball off his toes or using his own specialty, a confident nudge wide of mid-on to the boundary. This stroke was a bugbear to bowlers, making them wish for an extra fieldsman, but was not a good shot to play against Bill Johnston's late swing. In playing spin bowling from either side Donnelly drove with less concern for the crease line than any post-war English batsmen except Compton and Edrich in their prime. Strokes made with horizontal or diagonal bat never spared a short ball. His cutting involved fewer of the risky slices expected of left-handers. For short-arm hooks his back foot went close to the stumps, his bat was never far from his waist and his whole body spun into the shot as he cracked the ball to the ground. He swung in English, not Australian, manner at balls outside the leg stump . . .

From Donnelly the baton in New Zealand's southpaw relay passed into the safe hands of Bert Sutcliffe, though sticklers for conventional batting regarded those hands as rather unsafe. This was not because of anything wrong with his strokes except his eagerness to play them. When Sutcliffe strode in to open the innings and began to hook in the first over, orthodox believers felt that he would soon be sent back to his pa (Maori for pavilion). Instead, he has stayed in to make and break more records than any other post-war batsman . . .

Bert comes from Dunedin in Otago province, about the last port of call before Antarctica. He was thirteen when he made his first hundred at Takapuna Grammar School, nineteen when he scored a thousand runs in a season for Parnell Seniors. After two years at Teachers' Training College he went to war. As Sergeant Sutcliffe he put up the highest score, 163, in the battle of El Alamein between an Empire side and a United Kingdom team – a sideline to the main contest in which Field Marshal Montgomery, in his own words, hit Rommel for six out of Egypt. Within two years of the war's end Sutcliffe made himself the first New Zealander to score two separate hundreds against a visiting MCC team, 197 and 128 for Otago at his first sight of Bedser, Voce, Pollard, Wright, Yardley and Edrich. The first innings was marred by two slip chances but at 96 he lifted Pollard over the fence for six. Sutcliffe is probably the only man who has completed his first century against English bowling in such cavalier manner.

When New Zealand toured Britain in 1949 he shattered the accepted doctrine about how innings ought to be opened. Early, he was caught a number of times when he did not connect properly with hooks but, like Harvey, he never lowered his colours. In height, 5 ft 8 in, weight (an athletic 10 st 4 lb), southpaw stance and outlook he is like the Australian, and post-war cricket has been lucky to have two batsmen of such genius flourishing simultaneously. After playing against both, England's Freddie Brown ranked the New Zealander top left-hander. That, in my estimation, was tantamount to awarding him second place to Len Hutton among the world's batsmen. Sutcliffe hits more sixes than Harvey and for his size I doubt whether there has ever been a batsman who could land the ball over the fence so often . . .

Like most people in Africa, India and the West Indies, few New Zealanders ever saw Bradman bat. Sutcliffe was disappointed at missing the sight by a couple of days when the NZ team passed through Sydney in 1949 and had to be content with meeting Sir Donald in mufti. Donnelly, so often Sutcliffe's partner in success, believes that had the Otago left-hander been an Englishman or Australian and enjoyed their greater opportunities he would have outstripped all rivals and have been almost another Bradman. How little patriotism has exaggerated here is shown by Bert's figures and Sir Donald's after the same number of innings:

	Innings	Not out	Runs	Centuries
Bradman (1927–34)	166	15	9,728	35
Sutcliffe (1944–54)	166	10	9,540	29

A significant difference was that Bradman was not quite twenty-six when he played his 166th innings, whereas Sutcliffe was thirty-one. As the first New Zealander to make 2,000 on a tour of England, the left-hander amassed more in a season (2,627) than any other visiting player except Bradman (2,960 in 1930). Sutcliffe's seven centuries on tour are a New Zealand record and include the highest score for a Maori-lander abroad, 243 against Essex. With 100 not out in the second innings against Essex he made himself, at twenty-five, the youngest cricketer to have scored two separate centuries in a match four times. The only batsmen who have done this more often, Hammond (seven times), Hobbs (six) and Fry (five) played hundreds more innings. Hammond made his fourth set of twin centuries at thirty, Fry at thirty-three, Herbert Sutcliffe at thirty-four, Hardinge at thirty-five, Jessop at thirty-seven, Bradman at thirty-nine and Perrin, Hobbs, Hendren and Fishlock in the forties.

Sutcliffe holds the world's highest score by a left-hander in first-class cricket, 385 for Otago against Canterbury at Christchurch in 1952, with 3 sixes and 46 fours. For fifty-one years the record had been the 365 not out by Clem Hill for South Australia against New South Wales at the age of twenty-three. Like Hill, Sutcliffe made his triple-century at the rate of 40 runs an hour. None of the other ten Otago players reached 30. Sutcliffe and Don Taylor (later of Warwickshire) are the only batsmen who have put up two double-century opening partnerships in one match, 220 and 286 for Auckland against Canterbury in 1948–9. Lancashire League clubs angled for Bert but he became professional coach of Otago Cricket Association.

On his passing acquaintance with Australian wickets in 1954 he was an instant and striking success. The New Zealanders played three matches and Sutcliffe scored a century in each – 142 against Western Australia, 149 against South Australia, 117 against Victoria. In Melbourne they are still talking of the centuries by Sutcliffe and his sturdy right-hand companion John Reid, with their refreshing outlook on the art of batting. Only once before had a man made hundreds in his first three matches in Australia – England's Jardine, who had a rather different concept of how to use a bat. The New Zealanders were then on their way home from South Africa, where Sutcliffe topped their batting with 1,155 at an average of 46. Louis Duffus recorded that of 29 sixes by the team, 22 were hit by Sutcliffe (14) and Reid (8). The pair scored four of the side's five centuries, made more than one-third of the total runs and, apart from wicket-keeper Frank Mooney, held most catches (Sutcliffe 15, Reid 11). Reid is the first cricketer ever to have scored 1,000 runs and taken 50 wickets in a South African season. In fact, only two, Vogler and Mansell, had ever coupled 500 runs with 50 wickets.

On this tour the youngest of New Zealand's five left-handers, John Beck, nineteen, missed a Test century by the unluckiest margin, 99 run out, and Lawrie Miller, thirty, touched the lowest point in his cosmopolitan career by making ducks in four consecutive Test innings in mid-season. You'd have thought the New Zealanders would have avoided Miller's bat like a leper's handshake but plump schoolteacher-batsman Murray Chapple borrowed it to open the innings against Western Province. 'I want to see if it really works,' he said. Experimenter Chapple scored 33 runs before Clive van Ryneveld found a hole in it to trap him lbw.

After falling cheaply to Tayfield twice in the first Test, Sutcliffe dropped from No. 1 to No. 4 in the batting order. He stepped up from vice-captaincy to captain NZ for the last four matches after a ball broke a bone in one of Rabone's feet.

Only one bowler has been able to take the initiative away from Sutcliffe and make him give ground, even flinch. He is Neil Adcock, the South African fast bowler, who is 6 ft 3 in and towers over Sutcliffe like a lamp-post over a water-bubbler. The physical contrast does not overawe Sutcliffe – not even Bedser could do that. The first time Sutcliffe met the Transvaal terror several balls beat him but he courageously hooked bumpers off his collarbone. But after painful experiences on two lively Test wickets the New Zealander unashamedly admits that Adcock has troubled him more than any other bowler, including England and West Indies' best. Once Skipper Rabone, though knocked down himself, tried to shield the left-hander by sticking at the dangerous end, like another Woodfull, and bravely refusing singles.

Adcock and Sutcliffe were the central figures in the most sensational drama since bodyline rocked the cricket world twenty-one years earlier. The chief difference was that the batsmen under fire from Adcock's bouncers were not tied to the stake by Jardine's ring of leg fieldsmen.

The scene of the drama is Ellis Park, where half-mast flags mourn the deaths of 151 people in the Christmas Eve train disaster between Wellington and Auckland. At this Johannesburg ground a few years earlier Arthur Morris made his first o in big cricket and Australians facing the Springbok fast bowler Cuan McCarthy on a greentop were within an ace of losing their first three wickets without a run.

The pitch's hard surface has a thicker topcoat of grass on Boxing Day 1953. It is the kind of wicket that adds yards to a bowler's speed, feet to his bounce and inches to his smile of exultation. The South Africans estimate it to be faster – though not by much – than the Sydney wicket on which Lindwall and Miller shot them out for 173. Meeting such a bowler on such turf for the first time in their lives throws New Zealanders into confusion. Quick-flying balls from Adcock bruise several batsmen. One is bowled off his ribs, two collapse beside the wicket and another, Miller, goes to hospital coughing up blood after a blow on the chest. No wonder fast bowling on a greentop tends to make a batsman think of his wife and family!

When Sutcliffe comes in after New Zealand's first two wickets have gone for 9 there is no sign that his thoughts may be straying to his wife and toddlers Gary and Christine back in Dunedin. As usual his fair, curly head is capless. Immediately a ball from Adcock rears towards him he tries to flick it away. It strikes the side of his ducking head with a crack heard all around Ellis Park like a gunshot. Sutcliffe sinks to the turf, one hand pressed to his burst left ear. The other still clings to his bat.

In horrified silence the crowd of 22,000 watch first-aid attendants bring out a stretcher to remove him. Many fear that the blow has killed him. After five minutes Sutcliffe rises on staggering feet, waves aside the stretcher-bearers and is helped from the field by his captain. The ambulance takes him to hospital, where he faints while the injury is being treated. An X-ray is taken and by the time he returns to Ellis Park in the afternoon six NZ wickets have gone for 82. Wicketkeeper Mooney hangs on, doggedly keeping the ball out for more than two hours and rubbing his bruises between overs. Though Adcock is resting after his deadly effort, the New Zealanders hardly look like reaching the 122 needed to avoid having to follow on their innings.

The crowd shouts a hero's welcome as Sutcliffe reappears through the tunnel from the players' rooms deep in the stand. A pad of cotton wool is strapped over his ear. To the fieldsmen he looks dazed. The first thing he does is clout a medium-paced ball for six. The ball's fall over the leg boundary sets the tempo for the most thrilling onslaught on Test bowling since McCabe took his hook and cover drive into retirement. Sutcliffe survives one high chance at 17. When Adcock comes back into the attack the left-hander pushes him to off amid a sympathetic murmur. It swells to applause as a cover hit races for four.

Movement loosens Sutcliffe's ear pad, so at 25 first-aid attendants go out to bandage his head. Looking like a warrior in a battle scene in the gallery of the Palace of Versailles, he saves the follow-on with three wickets to go.

New Zealand's need for runs becomes so urgent that Sutcliffe cannot be content to try for fours. The field's thick carpet of kikuyu takes the pace out of ground strokes. So, if he can measure the ball quickly enough for a full-blooded stroke Sutcliffe goes the limit and smacks it over the wire fence. No slogging at everything, though. Sutcliffe the six-hitter remains Sutcliffe the batsman, his bandaged brow over the ball and a straight bat ready for anything demanding it.

That morning the team had left pace bowler R. W. Blair, twenty-two, in his hotel room overcome by the tragic news that his fiancée, Nerissa Ann Love, ninetten, was killed in the railway disaster. They were to have married a few weeks after Blair, a linotype operator, returned to Wellington in March 1954. So when the ninth wicket falls at 154 it looks like the end of the innings and the players begin to move towards the tunnel. But, with his team in a desperate plight, grief-stricken Bob Blair has come to Ellis Park to help if he can.

Amid a hush, he unexpectedly appears on the field. Walking to meet him, Sutcliffe puts a comforting arm around his bereaved mate's shoulders. As they go to the pitch together the crowd breaks the silence with prolonged applause.

The innings rushes to an end packed with excitement. Sutcliffe lifts his fourth, fifth and sixth sixes off Tayfield in one over. Thousands stand to roar appreciation of each stroke. Blair swings the off-spinner for another six to bring the cost of the over to 25. It is his only scoring stroke. The score leaps by 33 in 10 minutes before Waite stumps Blair off Tayfield at 187.

Sutcliffe remains unconquered. Of New Zealand's 105 runs since his reappearance he has made 80, snatched from the torrent of disaster, with 7 sixes and 4 fours. Johannesburg writer Vivian Granger's tribute: 'The greatest eighty ever made in Test cricket.'

Nobody doubts that. Until Sutcliffe played it, such an innings did not exist outside schoolboys' dreams.

★ ★ ★

The Australian side of the 1970s was peopled by players who acquired a reputation for being mean. When they talked to their opponents, it was usually to ask impertinent questions about their paternity. For all this, they were a bunch of outstanding cricketers. Especially the trinity of Denis Lillee, Rodney Marsh and Greg Chappell. They all came into Test cricket at roughly the same time, and went out of it together. This tribute by Frank Keating illustrates how retirement, and the possibility it allows of seeing a career in the round, often prompts the best writing on sport.

FRANK KEATING

Down Under and Out (1984)

Forthcoming Australian cricket will be distinctly odd. No Test cricket side will ever again be Chappelled, Lilleed, and Marshed.

They left, as they arrived, together. They first played against Illingworth's England side of 1970–1. Thirteen years: an awful lot of Pommie-bashing. They didn't care at all for Pakistanis; they pitied little Indians and provincial New Zealanders; they snarled back, glare for glare, at West Indians; they might well have got on famously with South Africans had they been allowed to play them. But it was Englishmen they loathed.

Forgetting, for a moment, that the word 'cricket' still has, to some, connotations of chivalry, the three of them were quite superlative cricketers. Chappell, ever with an upright, cultured, haughty detachment, scored more Test-match runs than any other Australian – more than Bradman, more than Harvey or Ponsford or Trumper or Woodfull or Walters. Lillee, with the kestrel's cruel eye, the ominous drum-roll run-up and the classic side-on action, took more Test wickets by far than any of history's legendary bowlers – more, by a bulging sackful, than Gibbs or Sobers or Hall, or Trueman or Tate or Underwood. Marsh, squat as a mudlark scrum-half, with miner's forearms and gymnast's sprung heels, dismissed many more Test batsmen than even such revered and glittering glovemen as Knott or Evans, Murray or Struddy, Grout or Tallon or Taylor.

They worked together. When Lillee bowled, the other two took the tandem in turns. The legend 'c Marsh b Lillee' was inked into schoolboys' scorecards almost a hundred times in Test matches – a staggering figure when you realize that history's next double act of bowler and padded henchman at the time was that of Botham and Taylor with 52 – followed, by the way, by such appealing duos as Grout/Davidson (44), and Oldfield/Grimmett (37), one more than Murray/Roberts for the West Indies, and Marsh's separate swagbag with Max Walker.

And if Marsh didn't pouch the nick from Lillee, more often than not Chappell, at slip, would. In his last Test match, a fortnight ago, Chappell beat Colin Cowdrey's record of 120 catches. Half of them were sponsored by Lillee's outswinger.

I saw them first on the Friday of the Lord's Test in 1972. It was 'Massie's Match', when Lillee's Perth clubmate bewildered the English with his massive, gently curling, frisbee swingers in the heavy, clouded, atmosphere. At the other end, the gangling Lillee had looked angry and menacing and fast. That afternoon, England hit back: Australia lost their openers for 7 runs: Greg Chappell, as palely frail and straight-backed as a model girl, joined his shoulder-rolling, gum-chewing, combative captain and brother, Ian. They shored up the innings in a stand of 70-odd, the elder man lecturing the kid between every over. Epic stuff. When Ian went, cursing, the young man – who had not scored a boundary in those first three hours – plonked his left foot down the pitch and dismissed Snow, Price, Greig, Gifford and Illingworth to all points. He went to his century in the last over of the day – and next morning he was joined by the tubby Marsh, who peppered the pickets with 6 fours and 2 sixes in a merry half-hour. They had announced themselves to England.

It was later on that tour that, by chance, I shared a lift with the young Chappell. We sat together in the back of the chauffeured limousine. I started with time-of-day small talk. I received not a single word in reply. When we arrived at his London hotel, the Waldorf, he was asleep. I gently woke him. He got out, and slammed the door without a word to me or the driver. Ever since, I have been in awe, or certainly wary, of his cold-fish disdain. Opponents, too, have been intimidated by his almost sneering silences. Tony Lewis said the other day that he did occasionally punctuate them, as he moved from end to end at slip, 'by letting the batsmen know an atrocity or two about their parentage'. But, for the most part, there seethed a contemplative hauteur.

Lillee and Marsh were always, at least, less sinister, more extrovert, about their Pommie-bashing. On the whole they were carefree confident that their deeds would outweigh their devilry. You dared ask for their autograph. Actually, one fancies that the two of them – at thirty-six, Marsh is eighteen months older – learned their first rudiments in aggro, not from the gangland boss, Ian Chappell, but from the captain who first picked them for the Western Australia state side, Tony Lock, the spiky, competitive émigré to Perth who used to bowl for Surrey and England with Jim Laker. Lock was not even afraid to pooh-pooh the chivalries of public-school cricket within earshot of Peter May.

Lillee's longtime nickname was 'F.O.T.'. Only dear friends dare call him so. It recalls the day, as a stringy colt in his first state season, that he was daydreaming in the deep, picking his nose at deep fine leg. Bellowed the infuriated skipper, Lock, from short leg – 'C'mon, wake up, Lill! Yer an Effin' Ol' Tart!'

Marsh, incidentally, answers to the name 'Bacchus' not because, as he once did, he beat the hitherto unbeatable Douggie Walters in a marathon lager-drinking contest – did I hear thirty-six cans of Swan on a flight from London? – but because there is a place in Australia called Bacchus Marsh. Actually, 'Romney' might have been slightly more original.

Together, F.O.T. and Bacchus have been involved in a few tawdry episodes. They each egg the other on, just as they do when they are concentrating only on the cricket. A few years ago, in Perth, Lillee went out to bat against England with one of his sponsor's experimental aluminium bats. When the England captain, Brearley, objected that it would ruin the ball, Lillee said he was quite prepared to leave the advertising gimmick at that – till Marsh, batting at the other end, insisted that he was quite within his rights to stay. The spoiled schoolboy's sit-down strike lasted fully ten minutes.

Neither of them admits who first came up with the idea to bet *against* their own team at Headingley a couple of years ago. The bookie says it was Lillee. In the last innings, Australia needed only 130 to win at a doddle. Marsh and Lillee secured odds of 500–1 that England would be victorious. England won. Lillee collected £5,000, Marsh £2,500. 'There was no question of us not trying to win the game for Australia,' insists Lillee – and with 17 runs he was the third top scorer. But, for many cricket-lovers in Australia, the stench remains.

Even Marsh, however, thinks Lillee went too far the following winter, when he spitefully kicked the Pakistan captain, Javed Miandad, at the wicket. One day, says Marsh, even Dennis will admit that was wrong. Lillee meanwhile sticks to his original story: 'It wasn't a kick; I just tapped his rump with my boot.'

The following season, against New Zealand, the crucial match reached a marvellously dramatic climax. There was one ball left and New Zealand needed just one sixer to win. Greg Chappell shamefully ordered his bowler to bowl an underarm daisy-cutter all along the ground. It was impossible to hit. The captain's long suspected meanness of spirit was at last fully revealed.

And yet, the great multitude of cricketers enjoy their game when – indeed, because – it is noble and generous and forgiving. Foes must be honoured. And the young Chappell, at the wicket, had a poise and grace and grandeur when he drove through mid-off that had been seldom matched in the long litany of lore. Alas, in a way, but his talent *did* outshine the poverty of his sportsmanship. And as Chappell stood there in the field, glowering grim at slip, next to him would be Marsh, gloved and padded, bouncy, bristling with belligerence and buried in his green cap . . . and, far away, the macho man, Lillee, would lick his right index finger as he turned on his mark; a preliminary stutter into his stride; then the momentum would gather, and so would the gale that billowed the back of his shirt, and so would the noise from the baying throng; now, as the gold chain whirled and glinted, the stride would lengthen, and the batsman would swallow, scared; the cocked grenade would be primed as it pumped away under Lillee's chin; the crowd's tattoo would reach crescendo as, in a feverish jingle-jangle of arms and elbows and legs, out would come the pin in a whirr and a stretch and a grunt . . .

Then Chappell, deadpan at slip, would unbend, Marsh, in the gloves, would return the ball with a smug, sadist's grin, and Lillee would set off back to his mark . . .

Three very missable men, who will very much be missed.

★ ★ ★

International cricket was once dominated by England and Australia. This bipolarity was first seriously challenged by the West Indians, who in the 1960s came to be the acknowledged world champions. Over the next two decades, other countries also started asserting their presence. The Indians, long accustomed to being thrashed overseas, won series in the West Indies and England in a single year, 1971. In 1983 they surprised everyone, including themselves, by winning the World Cup. Two of their cricketers stood out — the opening batsman Sunil Gavaskar and the fast-bowling all-rounder Kapil Dev. They each displayed a sense of self-belief and consistency of form unprecedented in their country's history. They also had a surprising taste for breaking records. The two superstars of Indian cricket are here profiled by two contemporary British writers.

SCYLD BERRY

Gavaskar Equals Bradman (1983)

They stand together now, the 'boy from Bowral' in the Australian bush, Sir Donald Bradman, and the guru of Indian batsmanship, Sunil Gavaskar. In Delhi yesterday, with a scintillating innings against

West Indies, Gavaskar equalled the world record of 29 Test centuries that Bradman has held for over a generation.

At the best of times comparisons are odious, and all the more so when they are made in India's capital at the end of a long hot summer. For a start, how can the opening batsman for one of the weaker countries in the modern era be compared with Australia's No. 3 who batted after Woodfull and Ponsford in the days of yore and spin?

Both giants of the crease are small men. Perhaps, if a conclusion has to be reached, the supporters of either side might agree that the difference between them is the same metaphorically as it is literally: that Gavaskar, at 5 ft 5½ in, falls marginally but perceptibly short of Bradman at 5 ft 6¾ in.

However, by happy coincidence or design, Gavaskar drew level with 'the Don' by means of an innings that was Bradmanesque. He thrashed West Indies' four fast bowlers as Graham Gooch has done, and almost no one else. His hundred yesterday was one of the fastest recorded in Test cricket in terms of balls received – 94 in his case. For contrast, Ian Botham's two epic centuries in 1981 against Australia came off 86 and 87 deliveries.

Gavaskar reached his nirvana with a drive for four through mid-wicket, much as Geoff Boycott did when he scored his triumphal hundredth hundred at Headingley. But dhotis and sandals were flung into the air yesterday afternoon, scattering kitehawks into the bright sunlight, not flat caps as in Leeds. As Gavaskar acknowledged the applause of the thousands present, and of tens or hundreds of millions not present, Viv Richards strolled up from slip to shake his hand, getting to know the man he has to beat.

Gavaskar had to play the exorcist as well. The West Indian fast bowlers, led by Malcolm Marshall, gave India a thorough working-over during their innings victory in the First Test of this series. It was Gavaskar's duty to lead the riposte; and counter-attack he did too, from the first over after Kapil Dev had won the toss, quickly hooking Marshall for four and six.

This was the young, attacking Gavaskar born again, not the careworn defender weighed down by the frailties of his colleagues and the responsibility of captaincy which he held for so long. He was helped by the pitch of course. Delhi's groundsman works for a brewery and knows how to concoct something flat.

So Gavaskar achieved it in style, hard though it may be to define exactly what his style is. He favours neither off side nor leg, front foot nor back. To watch him practise of an evening in the Brabourne Stadium in Bombay, the Lord's of India, where members recline in basket chairs around the boundary safe from the city's din, is to be reminded of the old photograph of W. G. practising in a net in his garden. Both are at home, and monumentally assured. Perhaps it is best to say that, if all living things in India are incarnations, Gavaskar is technical orthodoxy made flesh.

The Indian has taken 166 Test innings to make his 29 centuries (only 13 of them in India), against Bradman's 80. It should be borne in mind, though, that Gavaskar has never had the chance to bat against India's gentle bowling (Bradman did and scored four centuries). Nor did 'The Don' have to face a four-man pace attack, except once, whereas yesterday was but one of many occasions when Gavaskar has had to do so.

Gavaskar reached his fifty off 37 balls, giving his only chance en route to the keeper Dujon off a mishook. He slowed down in his fifties, attained the solid base camp of 62 by lunch, and set off briskly afterwards for the summit.

There was one nervous moment when Holding appealed for lbw but umpire Gothoskar was unmoved (in fact only five Indian umpires have ever been moved to give him lbw – and five abroad). Then Marshall tried to ruffle him with three bouncers from round the wicket: the first was hooked high and safe for four, the second along the ground to the squarer of two long legs, and the third straight between them to tumultuous shouts.

Soon it was his record-equalling century. He doffed the white hat that is his trademark, now fitted with a Brearley-type skull-protector inside. It was only the thirty-fifth over of the innings. Having pulled Larry Gomes for a second six, he was bowled off stump by his arm ball for 121, made off 128 balls in 224 minutes. It was his twelfth Test century against West Indies – Bradman's preference was for England, against whom he made nineteen.

More records are sure to go Gavaskar's way. He now has 8,017 Test runs. Sobers scored 8,032; Boycott has 8,114. By the time Yorkshire's special meeting is convened on 3 December, Boycott is likely to have been knocked off that pedestal too by the insatiable Indian.

JOHN WOODCOCK

Kapil's Devil (1993)

An epic climb has been going on for some time in the cricket world, an attempt on one of the great summits of sport. It involves the Indian all-rounder Kapil Dev and his ambition, before the years overtake him, to beat Sir Richard Hadlee's wonderful record of 431 Test wickets.

In the second Test match in Madras, while making merry against England's toiling attack, Kapil scored his 5,000th Test run. In the Bombay Test he took his 417th Test wicket. From all accounts his spell of seven overs at the start of England's second innings in Madras was much the best piece of quicker bowling in the match.

From this it might seem that only some sudden and serious injury can stop Kapil from reaching the goal he has set himself. The other possible snag is the amount of Test cricket India are likely to play in the near future. They have Zimbabwe coming for one Test next month and are scheduled to tour Sri Lanka and Pakistan later this year; but India and Pakistan must have about as much chance of playing cricket against each other in the present political climate as the Serbs and Bosnians have of enjoying a friendly game of football.

It is no help to Kapil, either, that India have remembered at last that their best way of winning Test matches is, and always has been, through spin. Happily, though, Kapil's form remains good and he is thinking in terms of taking 500 Test wickets, not 432.

He was, by three years, the youngest of the quartet of all-rounders who so embellished the 1980s. Of the others, Hadlee and Imran Khan, now both past forty, are in honourable retirement, and Ian Botham, who is thirty-seven, has accepted I fancy, that even his Test days are done. Kapil, thirty-four last month, has become the father figure of the Indian side.

It would be wrong to see him as a typical Indian cricketer. He is anything but that. Coming from Punjab, he is taller and stronger than the average Indian. He is a Jat, a sect to which the Indian army looks for recruits. This influenced Kapil's developments as a cricketer in two crucial ways. It bestowed on him the build of a fast bowler, and gave him the height and power to drive a cricket ball as lustily as anyone ever did. He bats not so much like an Indian – all eye and magic – as like Keith Miller or Botham, all pomp and derring-do.

Nobody at Lord's for the first Test match of 1990 will forget the manner in which Kapil saved India from following on, though not from defeat. When he was joined by Hirwani, the last man in and no sort of a batsman, 24 runs were needed to make England bat again. After Hirwani had blocked his first ball, the last of an over from Angus Fraser, and before he was bowled by his second, the first of Fraser's next over, Kapil drove four successive balls from Hemmings straight for six, strokes of unimaginable disdain.

In the corresponding Test match eight years earlier, Kapil had scored 89 in 55 balls with hitting of extraordinary violence, where-upon, after being last out with less than an hour of the fourth day left, he took 3 England wickets for 8 runs in 4 overs. Last month in Port Elizabeth, his eighth Test hundred (129 in 277 balls) enabled India to recover from 31 for 6 to 197 for 9 and was described as electrifying.

Kapil is the most explosive batsman India have ever had. It was C. B. Fry's opinion that Indians make the most natural batsmen of all. Sunil Gavaskar, the Pataudis, Ranji and his nephew Duleep, the prolific Vijay Merchant, the elegant Rusi Modi, the intrepid Gundappa Viswanath and countless others bear him out. But they have invariably done so with a gentle, wristy touch, and not savagely in the way that Kapil has: That he has performed such wonders as often as not in a struggling cause, and in an age when the game as it is generally played does few favours to the Indians' innate qualities, enhances his record.

Of his 123 Test matches, 58 have been in India, mostly on pitches that have had little to offer bowlers of his type. Of his 417 Test wickets, 210 have been taken at home, 51 in Australia, 43 in England, 43 in Pakistan, 35 in West Indies, 13 in New Zealand, 11 in Sri Lanka, 8 in South Africa and 3 in Zimbabwe.

For those who like to read something into such statistics, 29.5 per cent of those in India have gone to leg-before decisions and 20.8 per cent of those in other countries. The equivalent figure in Australia is 11.8 per cent.

In pace he has never been up with the Hadlees and Imrans or the Thomsons and Lillees; his success has had much more to do with movement and accuracy than with oppression, and that made it more worrying for him when, two or three years ago, he lost his outswinger. Kapil puts this down to too much one-day cricket, where the narrower interpretation of Law 24 led to his being called for wides that would have passed muster in the conventional game. When he stopped bothering about this, in Australia last winter, the outswinger came back and in five Test matches he took 25 wickets.

In the recent Test at Madras, it was off outswingers, pitched in just the right place, that Kapil had Smith caught at second slip and Gatting missed at the wicket at the start of England's second innings. It was another chance in Bombay, which Gooch edged to the wicket-keeper. Kapil knows, as England's new-ball bowlers seem to have forgotten, that in India it is where you bowl that matters most of all, not how fast.

Already Kapil is the only cricketer to have scored 5,000 runs and taken 400 wickets in Test cricket. It is an astonishing achievement. Wasim Akram, the only other seriously good all-rounder playing Test cricket today, is alone in faint pursuit.

As of now, Kapil's batting and bowling averages are almost identical (29.74 and 30.99, respectively), a state of affairs that nobody could possibly sniff at.

He has the appeal of Severiano Ballesteros, the looks of Omar Sharif, prolific talent, a fine reputation as a sportsman, and a beautiful wife, who runs Dev Features, a syndication agency and their own business.

He is camped within sight of Hadlee's New Zealand flag and destined, I am sure, to plant India's alongside it, and he will do it with style.

We should make the most of Kapil while we can. India have never had another cricketer like him, and quite conceivably they never will.

★   ★   ★

During the same period, the Pakistanis were also making major strides. It was the English game that contributed most to the rise of Pakistani cricket. The recruitment of overseas players by the counties, which started in 1968, allowed such players as Mushtaq Mohammad, Zaheer Abbas and Majid Khan further to develop their technique and tactical skills. They were followed by such men as Javed Miandad,

Imran Khan, and Wasim Akram. By the 1980s the Pakistanis were winning Tests and series with some regularity. The pinnacle of their cricketing success was, however, the conquest of the 1992 World Cup.

The great strength of modern Pakistan cricket has been their bowling. Imran Khan and Wasim Akram were two splendidly hostile swing bowlers. Rather different in style was the moody muezzin's son, Abdul Qadir, who resurrected the dying art of leg break bowling. Qadir (who, unusually, never played county cricket) is profiled for us by the South African journalist Donald Woods. This is followed by an essay on Waqar Younis and his famous inswinging yorker.

DONALD WOODS

Twist Again (1982)

Many old gentlemen of England will have a smile in their hearts today because of the revival of an art they had thought lost for ever.

For years they had lamented the passing of leg spin bowling. Where were the successors to Bosanquet, Mailey, Grimmett, Tich Freeman, Peebles, Faulkner – or even that young feller Benaud? Gone and forgotten, it seemed, was the wristy, back-of-the-hand delivery so hard to control that it was too expensive in this era of limited-over cricket.

Now the lament is no longer necessary, thanks to Abdul Qadir, of Pakistan, who proves with the essence of the risky art of leg spin that he can weave spells around England's best batsmen without squandering runs to buy victims. But never mind the figures. It is the way in which he does his devious work that makes Qadir the embodiment of all the composite characteristics of classical leg spin.

It is, after all, the most subtle and sinister of all the cricketing arts, and it is not for your open-hearted extrovert. To go to the unnatural trouble of screwing the ball out of the back of the hand over a cocked wrist requires a nature both complicated and contrary, as well as a readiness to wrench the shoulder, elbow and other parts of the body into unconventional positions.

Action pictures of the great leg-spinners give some idea of the sheer inconvenience of this method of delivery. Douglas Wright's action was once described as a cross between the barn dance and the swallow dive. Roly Jenkins, by all accounts, did a sort of hornpipe. 'Tiger' O'Reilly grimaced as if in agony, and perhaps he was.

But it gets to you. Dabble in the dark arts of leg spin and your whole approach to life is affected. I knew a schoolmaster so addicted that he seemed unable to walk an ordinary pavement very far without going compulsively into the tangential foot-shufflings and shoulder-shruggings apparently inseparable from preparation to bowl a leg break.

Yet the real leg-spinners are the true princes of cricket, and if they have to do a sort of Mephistophelean deal to reach the top orders of the mystical rite they certainly pay the price.

It seems that Qadir could not be other than a leg-spinner. He even walks like one between deliveries, with his feet apparently magnetized to the turf for preparatory purchase (remember Colin McCool?) and he has the right face, too, one of calculation and conspiracy.

The eyes narrow ominously and the fringe of dark beard hints at brigandage and plunder, not at all like the straightforward yeoman growth of Gatting.

You could imagine that face emerging from the mystic gloom of a Karachi bazaar to whisper dread tidings of deceit in high places and intrigue in the back streets, and the name Abdul is somehow appropriate, hinting at the mystery and magic that is about to be worked on some poor plodding Englishman at the crease.

As is fully to be expected, Qadir goes into a most complicated set of movements to begin his bowling action. He holds his left hand high as if in final salute to the doomed batsman, while his right hand twirls the ball urgently to appraise it of future rotational requirements, then squirts the ball into the upraised left hand while his feet begin a ritual dance on the spot.

The left hand brandishes the ball momentarily, then transfers it back into the right, which is already beginning a series of small circular sweeps as he bounds and gambols into his curving (of course) approach run.

In all this activity his entire body is the mere servant of the cocked right wrist as it sweeps over out of a flurry of wheeling arms to float the buzzing ball at his victim, and so complete is all bodily involvement that even after releasing the ball Qadir twirls after it up the pitch as if urging it on to work its own wickedness, and his bowling arm repeats an echo motion of the delivery to quench itself of every last vestige of spinfulness.

What the ball then does is variously astonishing. Taking on a life of its own, it loops and dips, pitching to spin vastly to left or right or to spear straight on with topspin, and if it raps the batsman's pads Qadir has a range of appeals for lbw – one supplicatory, one accusatory, one challenging and one slyly inquisitive, then the major one, the total and ultimate appeal.

With this one he dances an angry tattoo upon the turf, jumping up and down and uttering fierce cries of the sort that surely terrified whole generations of marauders clear out of the Khyber Pass. At such times Qadir makes John McEnroe seem like a calm exponent of reasoned remonstration.

But ultimately it is his superb art that one remembers, and it is a fitting irony that the torments of the googly which he now inflicts on innocent Anglo-Saxon lads had their origin not in the mystical regions of the East but on the playing fields of England.

Bosanquet knew not what he was visiting upon later generations of his countrymen, but Abdul Qadir certainly does, and as a worthy custodian of the rescued art of leg spin he will surely continue to delight millions with his magic.

MARTIN JOHNSON

A Man with a Secret (1992)

A game of cricket, as any Wednesday-night park player who has almost had his nose torn off by a middle-aged slow-medium dobber will confirm, is entirely dependent upon the prevailing conditions. It can take place on a strip of concrete, or twenty-two yards of suet pudding – but for Pakistan's twenty-year-old phenomenon Waqar Younis it matters little whether it has been prepared by McAlpine's or Mrs Beeton. If Waqar does not care for the pitch, he merely dispenses with it.

Waqar's trademark is a ball that takes about a third of a second to travel from launch pad to target, and swings and dips wickedly late in towards the base of the right-hander's leg stump. In terms of working conditions, England's batsmen are not only entering a hard-hat area, but one that demands a pair of steel toecaps. With this delivery, Waqar not only renders the pitch redundant, but the fielders as well. In one and a half seasons with Surrey he has taken 170 championship wickets in 32 matches, and over 60 per cent of them have either been bowled or lbw. Bowled is the preferable option, as it at least guarantees a batsman a semi-dignified walk off, rather than a hobble back on a set of crushed toes.

The romantic version of Waqar's discovery is that Imran was lying at home in bed with a viral infection when he spotted an unknown youngster on television bowling for United Bank in the annual fixture between the domestic champions of Pakistan and India. Imran, so the story goes, leaped from his sickbed to attend the game, and immediately insisted on Waqar joining his squad for the forthcoming one-day tournament in Sharjah. A more prosaic account comes from Intikhab Alam, the current team manager, who says that the United Bank captain, Haroon Rashid, invited him to watch Waqar bowling in the nets. 'It took me six balls to realize he had everything,' Intikhab says, 'and I immediately told Imran that we had to get him into the squad for Sharjah.'

What is certain, however, is that Imran and Intikhab were instrumental in getting Waqar into the Pakistani squad at the earliest available opportunity. It is their way to throw youngsters in at the deep end, just as it is the English way to issue their own young players with rubber rings and lead them gently into a paddling pool. 'It's mostly to do with the system,' Intikhab said. 'It's amazing, really, but most of our players start learning about cricket at Test level. When we see natural talent, such as Waqar's, we leave it alone. If faults creep in, we put them right, but we never try to coach them into doing things that don't come naturally.'

Cricketers being the suspicious characters they are, there are quite a few around not totally convinced that Waqar's talents are God-given. Mutterings about ball tampering are never far from the surface when one of Waqar's missiles abruptly changes direction at 90 mph. At a press conference on New Zealand's last tour of Pakistan, Martin Crowe produced a ball that, so he intimated, bore not so much the evidence of contact with a cricket bat as a combined harvester.

However, nowhere does a ball get roughed up so quickly as on the parched, grassless turf of Pakistan, and it is a legacy of learning his trade in such conditions that makes Waqar (like Wasim Akram) prefer bowling when the ball is older. There is even a theory that Pakistani sweat (rubbed in to provide the polish on one side) has different properties. Intikhab, as you might expect, will have none of this: 'We know why Waqar swings the ball so late, and at such pace, and it is all to do with the bowler. It is, I'm sure you'll understand, our secret.'

Waqar's talent first came to light as a schoolboy in Sharjah, where his parents were living, although he was not smitten by the game until he watched Imran bowling for Pakistan in a one-day tournament there. He went away and studied Imran's action on video, and their master–pupil relationship is still strong today. Imran attempted to get Waqar fixed up with his old county, Sussex, who probably do not care to be reminded that they went instead for the Australian Tony Dodemaide. Later that year, in 1990, Imran bumped into his former Sussex colleague Ian Greig, then captain of Surrey, and after half an hour of his bowling to Alec Stewart in the Oval nets, Surrey rushed through a special registration to get him into their side for a Benson and Hedges quarter-final the following day.

Waqar's potential to become one of history's finest bowlers is illustrated by his record after only 16 Test matches of 79 wickets at an average of 19.97. Wasim has 154 in 41 matches at 24.37, and by any standards they represent a lethal partnership. David Gower, back in the England squad for Old Trafford, says of Waqar: 'When the ball is so close to a batsman before it starts to move, it is horribly difficult to adjust – and the way he races in to you gives you a hint that something less than friendly is on the way.' Robin Smith, just about the only England batsman who would rather face Waqar than Mushtaq Ahmed, describes Waqar's inswinging yorker as ' . . . the deadliest ball I have faced. However well you might be playing, this ball is always at the back of your mind, and you can never relax against him.'

* * *

One of the most enduring friendships in modern cricket was that between Ian Botham and Viv Richards. This was a friendship that stretched across the cultural and racial divide. They played together for Somerset and against one another in the international arena. Both brought to their sport a spirit of joyous aggressiveness.

Not for them the safety-first tactics so beloved of many of their fellow players.

Botham and Richards hit numerous hundreds in Test cricket. Several of these have been much written about. However I have chosen, for each, a relatively obscure knock, the manner of whose making does nonetheless reveal the personality behind the player. It is hard to think of any other post-war cricketers who contributed as much to spectator satisfaction.

SCYLD BERRY

Botham's Fastest Hundred (1982)

The Nehru Stadium at Indore is typical of the grounds on which England played outside the Test matches. A multi-purpose stadium, it was built with government funds in the early 1960s in order to replace the old sports ground attached to the Raj's principal social club. The same is the pattern throughout India. The private ground that belonged to the British and native elite, where other members of the public were allowed in as much on sufferance as on payment to watch the big matches, has been superseded by a new stadium for the many. It is a transformation which might not be regrettable at all, were not the old grounds such verdant, restful havens of retreat, like country-house estates amid the dust of cities: the Bombay Gymkhana, the Roshanara Club in Delhi, the Poona Club, and in Indore the Yeshwant Club, named after the last Maharajah of Holkar. Some of these clubs have become sad old places, going to seed as gently and imperceptibly as the prince drinking to his memories at the club bar. The paint and whitewash haven't been touched since 1947; photographs and the billiard table grow dustier year by year . . .

Two elements, however, about this Nehru Stadium were distinctive when Ian Botham staged the most outstanding innings of the tour there. One was the statue outside the main entrance. Made of stone and inscribed in Hindi, it aims to immortalize the GOM of Indian cricket, Colonel C. K. Nayudu. In the time of the old princely state of Holkar, Nayudu *was* Indore cricket. Crowds would follow him down the street. He was the first Indian cricketer to have charisma in the eyes of his own people (whereas Ranji had been all the rage in England). His physical toughness is a legend: once he was hit in the mouth by Dattu Phadkar; he swept two of his front teeth off the pitch and carried on batting. Botham did likewise when hit by Andy Roberts during his first season in the Somerset side. Nayudu, having been trained on the erratic surface of coir matting, lived adventurously as a batsman in search of sixes; so does Botham. When Nayudu faced foreign bowling for the first time, that of MCC in 1926, he hit it for 153, including 11 sixes, in 115 minutes. The statue to his memory, a fine one as cricket art goes, does not by all accounts capture him in a characteristic pose: C. K. is allowing a ball to pass by his off stump. But it serves as a reminder of the presiding genius of Indore.

A second peculiarity about the game was that when Botham walked to the wicket on Friday 22 January it was the first time since the tour began over two months before that England had not been watched by a virtual capacity crowd. The Nehru Stadium was less than half full, with barely 10,000 spread out around the terracing. Local officials advanced the reasonable explanation that the succession of four drawn Test matches had taken its toll of spectator interest. Thus there was no great clamour of expectation when Botham went in. A striped squirrel sat on top of the sightscreen undisturbed. The surroundings were relaxed. So was he; and he had already made the promise that he would hit.

When Botham walked out to bat thirty-five minutes after lunch, at 1.25, England had just lost two wickets with their score on 87, as if to prove it was one of the game's misfortunate numbers. Geoff Cook, urgently needing plenty of runs if he was going to make the Test side in Kanpur, had been caught at midwicket for 39; or so the umpire had decided. The fielder Sanjeeva Rao had dived forward at the ball, and the batsman clearly believed he had picked it up on the half-volley. Cook, however, apart from waiting in his crease for the decision, made no sign of dissent, although his partner, Fletcher, shrugged his shoulders and pointed at Rao with his bat. After an idle morning the game had sprung alive. With no run added, Fletcher drove an off break from Gopal Sharma to mid-on, who dropped it. At the next ball Fletcher cut and was caught by the wicketkeeper, who for good measure also knocked off the bails.

Picking up his 2 lb 12 oz bat and jamming on his sunhat, Botham called out to the next man in after him, Taylor, 'You'd better get ready.' On his way to the wicket he had no need to look up at the sun because the sky was its usual cloudless self. He could see in front of him, beyond the stadium, a six-storey hospital donated by the former Maharajah of Holkar. Beside it was the old medical college, with a couple of red-tiled turrets that would not have been out of place in Oxford, next to Keble. To his right through some trees was the squat tower of a brightly whitewashed church: that of St Ann's, built in thanksgiving for the suppression of the Mutiny. The plaques inside still poignantly commemorate: Captain Francis Brodie, Commandant of Cavalry, Malwa Contingent, 'killed by Mutineers at Mulharghur on June 12th 1857 whilst in the fearless discharge of his duty'; 'Ross MacMahon esquire, Civil Engineer . . . whose valuable life in its very prime was cut short in the outbreak at Indore on July 1st 1857'. But not all those commemorated were casualties of war. There is also a plaque to one 'who died from the Effects of a Fall at Polo, aged 29. Erected by his brother officers of the Central Indian Horse.' A cavalier: that is more Botham's style.

He began by playing out the two deliveries remaining of the over by Gopal Sharma, a manifestly keen young off-spinner who had been included in India's twelve for the Madras and Kanpur Tests. At the other end was Gatting, who had replaced Cook and had yet to get off the mark. Bent on a good score to make sure of his place in Kanpur, Gatting saw out a maiden over from Anil Mathur, a left-arm medium-pacer who had swung the new ball sharply and had returned for a second spell at the main-stand end.

Each batsman opened his account with a single in Sharma's next over; then Botham unleashed an off drive that sent the ball skidding through mid-off for four. From this stroke it was obvious, as it had not been before during England's hesitant start, that the outfield was exceptionally quick. Constant games of football and hockey on it, combined with a local scarcity of water, had reduced all but a few tufts to hard-baked earth. Ten runs to Botham off that over, followed by another five off Mathur, confirmed impressions that the going was good, the pitch ideal in pace and bounce, and the batsman intent on belligerence.

Then Botham made the first of only two serious mistakes. Trying to cut Sharma he was dropped by slip, who also could not quite reach the rebound. With 15 to his name at that stage, Botham played out the rest of the over for a circumspect maiden. Thus Botham and Gatting, in their partnership of 137 off 12.2 overs, could afford to allow two of them to be maidens.

In the following over from Mathur Botham stepped down the

pitch and lofted the ball far above the height of St Ann's tower, more to that of a steeple. It was like his shot at Old Trafford against Terry Alderman the previous summer, when he was nearly caught from the skyer to end all skyers by mid-off running desperately back ('I got my angles wrong'); this time too the ball went up even further than it carried. Nonetheless it went for six, a few feet to the on side of straight. Fifteen runs off Mathur's over took Botham's score to 30. Whereupon drinks were brought out, to account for almost five of his fifty-five minutes at the wicket. Botham drank some of the green 'staminade', and repeated the message that the next batsman should be ready to come in any minute.

He did not feel so hot as to remove his sleeveless MCC sweater. Yet the day was warm, though fresh because of Indore's altitude of 1,800 feet; and he was about to perform one of the great feats of hitting. He cut the first ball he received after the drinks interval – an off break from Sharma – to the third-man boundary, off-drove the second for four more and swept the third for six. Like all his sixes it was a minimum seventy-five-yard carry. Off the fourth ball he pushed (in anyone else's parlance 'drove') another single; but here he may have miscalculated as the first ball had been a no-ball, which left Gatting with three balls of the over to play out.

With Botham now on 45, the Central Zone captain Parthasarathy Sharma decided on a bowling change. Removing Mathur from the firing line, Sharma brought on a left-arm spinner, Rajinder Singh Hans, at the main-stand end. Hans was once rated a potential successor to his fellow Sikh Bedi. But his bowling, at least in this match, was poor in direction and suffered from a scrambling delivery. Hans ran up and pushed the ball through enthusiastically: Botham reverse-swept him for four. A single from the next ball brought up Botham's fifty. Given the strike again one ball later, he hit Hans over extra cover for six, then pinched the strike with a single: 61.

At the far, hospital, end Gopal Sharma was still spinning the ball sufficiently to make it drift in the air away from the batsman and maybe turning it, except that Botham had dispatched it towards the boundary long before it had any chance to turn. He swung the first ball of this new over for two, and reverse-swept the next for four more. At the other end Gatting laughed in his beard. His mind went back to the one-day international in Ahmadabad, when he had shared a match-winning partnership with Botham. The joint plan then, as proposed by Botham on his arrival, had been to push the ball around and steadily accumulate the 31 runs required. Thereupon, far from suiting his action to the word, Botham had reverse-swept Doshi and hit two sixes over long on. Now here he was again cheerfully breaking all conventions, but so monstrously gifted he was getting away with it. So Gatting contented himself with giving Botham his head and the strike, which the latter was in any event so intent on keeping that once during this over, after scoring a two, he ran thirty yards past his stumps lest he be called for a third.

Botham, his score 70 when Hans began a new over, made the second of his mistakes when he came down the pitch to the first ball and missed it. So did the wicketkeeper, Ved Raj, as it 'went with the arm' and shot past leg stump for four byes. Nothing daunted, Botham swung a four to square leg and half-mowed, half-carted the next ball for his fourth six, falling away to leg as he did so. It pitched around leg stump and kept going, first with the bowler's arm, then with the bat. At this point Hans, as a Sikh, might have remembered that he carried a dagger with him to deal with just such an attack.

And the fielders all this while? Faced with this hectic activity both on the field and the scoreboard (which was forced to confine itself to registering the tens and forgetting about the digits), they remained enthusiastic, if within certain limits. They did not dive after the ball because it is not the Indian custom to dive on hard bare outfields. But if retrieving the ball from the wire fence around the boundary was their primary function, this they did well.

One fielder, however, made the elementary mistake of straying in a few yards from the boundary at long off when Sharma the captain tried his own occasional off breaks instead of Gopal Sharma's. Botham sent the first ball like a tracer bullet to where long off should have been, only to land safely over the line for six more (safely for the fielder perhaps more so than for Botham). Sharma's next rather stiff and portly off break was swung away to square leg, where two fielders stood politely back to allow each other the honour of catching it; four more. These two incidents apart, the Central Zone fielding was by no means as poor as it might have been under the assault. A cut for two and another single took Botham to 94.

When Botham embarked upon the next over from Hans, the only unexpected feature of it was that he did not reach his century with a six. He certainly tried to by stepping inside a leg-stump ball in order to swing it over square leg, but it took the bottom edge and ran down to fine leg for a mere four. Botham 98, and the next ball was identical in both its delivery and dispatch. Botham therefore had reached his hundred off the forty-eighth delivery he had received. Only Robin Hobbs and Lance Cairns are *known* to have reached three figures off fewer deliveries in a first-class match: 45 in both cases. Two centuries by Gilbert Jessop may have been quicker still, but that is conjecture; and with early scorebooks lost the matter can never be verified.

In terms of time Botham had taken 50 minutes. That put him into equal tenth place among the fastest century-makers (and at least two of those above him had not made their runs in serious circumstances). The drinks interval too had wasted several minutes for him.

If there was any scope left for Botham to open out, he did so immediately on reaching his century. He drove the third ball of Hans's over to long on for six, and heaved the fourth over square leg for another six, his seventh. Hans, shifting his line, pushed his fifth ball through on off stump but Botham stepped back, drove, and with a huge grin sliced it through the absent slips for four more. Twenty-four runs had come off the over so far; Botham might have made it 30, but tried instead to keep the strike by pushing a single on the off side. The ball, however, struck his pad, and the keeper was too quick for him to scuttle through for a leg bye. To this point, off the last seven overs, Botham had personally scored 103.

Gatting meanwhile had done his supporting role immaculately by scoring three singles, to Botham's 118 in all. Then he too hit Sharma the captain for a six over long on, prompting Botham to clap him, not in any way sarcastically. A single to Gatting left Botham with three more balls to face: another four, a miss, and finally a pull drive which sent the ball suitably far into the stratosphere before it descended into deep midwicket's hands.

As he walked off, the Nehru Stadium rose. Gatting led the applause of every player on the field. Suddenly, as Botham reached the edge of the playing area, a piece of orange peel landed and rolled towards him. But even that he scooped up and hit away with his bat, bang off the middle. And he was still wearing his sweater.

Gatting afterwards rated it 'a great, great innings' and thought Botham would never surpass it because 'in England the bowlers would be familiar with him, and anywhere else the fielders are going to be a bit keener'. Underwood, amazed, said that a bowler had to attack Botham's stumps 'but even when he mistimes the ball it could still go for six because he hits the thing so hard'. Willis however, whose sardonic exterior could not quite disguise admiration, felt that Botham could exceed even this effort. 'The Megastar,' he grunted, 'he could do anything, within the next four or five years.'

Nayudu was born in Nagpur on 31 October 1895, so he was already thirty-one by the time he had his first taste of any international cricket. At the age of fifty he made 200 in a first-class match. At the age of sixty-one he was asked to come out of retirement to assist Uttar Pradesh in a Ranji Trophy match against Rajasthan. The Rajasthan attack included Ramchand and Mankad, proven Test bowlers both; but Nayudu still agreed. The story is concluded by Raj Singh Dungapore, who captained Rajasthan in that match:

> The Old Man came in when his side had lost four cheap wickets and Vinoo Mankad was bowling. Now there had always been rivalry between them. It was Vinoo who had suggested to Phadkar that he bowl the bouncer which hit C. K. in the mouth. And in 1952 Mankad had been refused a tour guarantee by C. K., then chairman of selectors, which resulted in Mankad not being a member of the touring party to England.
>
> Vinoo's first ball to the Old Man came in with the arm and had him absolutely plumb leg before, except that the umpire wouldn't give him out. Second ball Vinoo was so furious he bowled a beamer which nearly took the Old Man's head off and went for four byes. Third ball he pitched up and C. K. swung him away for six; Vinoo just stood there and glared, and the Old Man stood there too, his back ramrod straight as it was until the end of his life. Fourth ball C. K. again swung him away for six, another seven-iron shot. He made 84 that day before he was run out, after he had dropped his bat going for a third run.

At sixty-one – and there is no doubt about his age – Nayudu's has to be one of the most remarkable innings in first-class cricket. If Botham seeks more challenges in later life, he would do well to surpass that in the year 2016.

HUGH MCILVANNEY

Black Is Bountiful (1985)

It was a time for going against the tide. While more than 50,000 of the country's most committed football supporters flooded towards one Old Trafford, magnetized by Manchester United's leadership of the First Division, about 1,500 of us straggled willingly into the neighbouring premises of the same name to watch Lancashire and Somerset play a bit of cricket.

Our choice, last Monday afternoon, was much less eccentric than it may have appeared. Vivian Richards was due to bat, and that is something he is capable of doing better than anyone else on the planet.

The setting – spectators scattered in chilled, huddled handfuls around acres of seating under stubbornly threatening clouds – was scarcely calculated to galvanize the spirit. But greatness does not require a quorum. When he came to the crease, his juices were flowing and the tiny audience was treated to one of the most memorable experiences in the whole of contemporary sport: a bravura (i.e. characteristic) century by Viv Richards.

It is unnecessary to report that many of the shots that took the recently appointed captain of West Indies beyond 100 for the sixth time this season (he scored a seventh century three days later to strengthen his position at the top of the batting averages) were breathtaking. Some of the eleven fours in his 120 clattered into the boards almost before the bowler's arm had completed its motion and more than one of his five sixes soared away from a swing of the bat so fluid and flawlessly timed, so outrageously relaxed, that the power imparted seemed slightly eerie.

Yet neither the glittering details of a single innings nor the cumulative wonders he has fed into the record books during the long decade of his pre-eminence in cricket can adequately explain the full effect that Richards at his best has on those fortunate enough to be on hand as witnesses.

Of course, a dramatic physical presence is part of it. A man standing an inch under six feet and weighing upwards of thirteen stone might be expected to look bulkily, perhaps ponderously, solid, but in him grace is as basic as breathing. Just watching him walk slowly to the wicket can be more of a thrill than seeing other famous sportsmen at the height of their performances.

His demeanour at such moments has been described as insouciant, but regal might be nearer the mark. The downward curve of the fine nose, the level gaze, the wide, expressive mouth within the handsome beard – all combine to indicate that if he ever went after the role of an emperor, the price of the second favourite at the audition would be 33–1 and drifting.

Still, even when his looks, his sense of theatre and his dazzling technical brilliance are taken into account, the extent to which Richards can electrify his audiences, the way he can stir responses only rarely touched by sport, remains extraordinary. Maybe the best attempt we can make at identifying the extra factor involved is to suggest that he is a remarkable example of a man able to channel a great deal of a large and intense nature into the playing of a game.

All great sportsmen, once in the arena, make statements about themselves but few achieve the eloquence, the vehemence or the depth of declaration that comes from Richards. When he is in action, you have the feeling that you are being addressed by a big spirit and had better pay attention.

The potency of his aura certainly does not diminish at close quarters. One distinguished cricket writer admits to being enfeebled by extreme nervousness at the mere approach of Richards, even when the Antiguan's mood is obviously benign. It's not just that he exudes the kind of challenging strength that makes the contrived machismo of other athletes come across like the currency of a primary-school playground. His capacity to make those around him crave his approval is out of all proportion to his own remarkable prowess.

When Ian Botham, with whom he has sustained a long and genuinely deep friendship rooted in mutual affection, admiration and spontaneous rapport, said that he did not seriously consider playing cricket in South Africa because he wouldn't have been able to look Richards in the eye, the chances are that Botham was speaking literally.

Richards does not vociferously condemn those who have been part of compromising expeditions to Mr Botha's laager, insisting that each individual must answer to his own conscience. As West Indian captain, he has carefully stayed quiet on the Graham Gooch case and its threat to England's winter tour of the islands, refusing to be drawn when his friend Lester Bird, the Antiguan Foreign Minister, articulated the possibility that Gooch's attitudes would make him unacceptable as a tourist.

The definite impression is that if last week's avowal by Gooch of strong opposition to apartheid clears the way for the Essex man to visit the West Indies, that will please Richards, for it did not take the events of Thursday and Friday at the Oval [Gooch made 196 and David Gower 157 against Australia] to place Gooch and Gower at the head of his personal rankings of outstanding English batsmen. And when he and his team go into battle on their own turf, they don't want any favours in the shape of weakened opposition.

His consistent view is that cricketers who have been drawn from the rest of the world to entertain in South Africa, especially fellow West Indians who have yielded to the blandishments and financial lures, have been systematically 'used'.

'Knowing what the South Africans really think of our people, do you imagine they would offer us that sort of money if everything was right with them?'

His face darkens and he shakes his head in dismissal of the ludicrous thought. Then, suddenly, the frown is swept away by an irresistible smile, the kind that might register on a light meter at a range of a hundred yards. 'Of course, our talents are worth more than they could ever pay – but it's not appreciation of our worth that makes them dangle that money in front of us.'

The fact that his century on Monday was followed by a relentless drip of frustration in the field throughout Tuesday as Lancashire progressed to a comfortable victory might have made complications for an interviewer.

But he was as courteous as he was fascinating and the ultimate effect on a scribbler with a fair amount of mileage on the clock was a profound sense of having been privileged to keep such company. Boxing, and a shared respect for the pride and dignity Joe Frazier brought to that rough old pursuit, gave us a good start.

When I first toured India and Pakistan with the West Indies in 1974–5, I remember that in supporting Frazier against Ali I was outnumbered about 17–1 but I didn't mind. Ali was great but Joe, with his big disadvantages in height and reach, had to be very brave and very special to do what he did. I believe in people who put all their heart into what they do and Joe was like that. I used to feel, 'Here's my man, going out to do a job, to give it his best shot.' They might beat him but they could not break him.

The empathy with Frazier, which has combined with a noticeable facial resemblance to give Richards a series of dressing-room nick-names that are variations of Smokin' Joe, has a first-hand basis. In his teens Richards boxed for his neighbourhood in St John's, Antigua, competing with boys from surrounding districts.

'I still spar a lot at the local gym when I go home to Antigua. It gets rid of my frustrations and it helps me to keep fit. I swim too. We have a lot of wonderful beaches. I hate jogging or running for miles, so I like to swim or go to the gym. I believe in burning up the little bit of energy I do possess. Hitting the heavy bag is comforting.'

His aggression has not always found such innocuous outlets. As a young footballer (he actually preferred that game until an ulti-matum from a Leeward Islands cricket official abruptly clarified his thinking) his rumbustious activities in the back four caused him to be known as The Bull.

'I was inclined to take things into my own hands, to go for a little bit of physical stuff,' he says, grinning at the memory. Looking across at the relaxed sprawl of his wide-shouldered body, in which what he calls his beef is kept hard and flexible by a daily programme of exercise that includes about seventy sit-ups and forty press-ups, it was easy to sympathize with The Bull's opponents.

At that moment, dressed in the whites that always heighten his glow of fitness, with an unextravagant glint of gold on one finger of his right hand, at the wrist and at his neck, he was the picture of a successful young athlete at ease with the world. But his fierce pride in himself and his people can release an element in his personality that is positively volcanic.

'I don't stand rubbish from no one,' he said quietly on Tuesday.

A man has to approach me the right way, then I think I can be fair and decent to anybody. But don't come and put rubbish on me, man. I won't stand that shit from no one. I have lost my cool on numerous occasions and I haven't always regretted it. I was not sorry for what I did on the last West Indies tour of Australia.

There was a bad taste about that series. People like Geoff

Lawson were behaving like school kids. There were racist remarks and some of our guys were badly hurt. It couldn't go on. Eventually Allan Border was involved and Graeme Wood and Steve Rixon, though Geoff Lawson was at the centre of it. In the last Test at Sydney in January somebody said something to me and I totally went wild. I said, 'No use we talk about it here in the game. After the match we can sort this out.'

I was waving and making a lot of rude gestures and some nasty words came out. I took plenty of stick from the Australian crowd and the press but I felt better afterwards. I had to make them aware that we are not idiots. The trouble was serious. We were just waiting for one Australian to get out of hand again and everything would have turned loose. That's how bad the guys felt.

His anger then was thoroughly understandable, but less explosive natures are alarmed by the scale of the rage that can be detonated by the conviction that he has been given out unjustly. It led to him being banned for two years as a teenager in Antigua and while on tour in India as vice-captain of West Indies in 1983 what he did to a dressing room instantly became a legend.

'I didn't get any runs in the first match and I wanted desperately to do much better in New Delhi,' he recalled. 'I was going really well until this ridiculous decision put me out. When I got back to the dressing room all the lunches were laid out and I chucked the bat and the first pot it hit had curried mutton in it, or something like that. All hell turned loose.'

In spite of the serious implications that attended the outburst, he cannot remain solemn when he remembers the curry-splattered scene. The rich voice breaks into a staccato laugh.

However, there is no doubt that captaincy of his country will make him more than ever determined to offer the right example in vital areas.

I always want to behave the way a man should, not to do anything cheap. It is true that in the West Indies you're expected to be more than just an exceptional player. You're expected to present yourself in a particular way, the way you have known since you were a kid in the islands, with the natural panache that means so much in a place where the cricket is so important.

His people, he convinces you, could never settle for any math-ematical representation of greatness in a cricketer. True heroes like Sobers and Worrell had to fill the mind with glorious memories. The Richards career, brimming though it is with stunning statistics, will surely survive in the end as a parade of unforgettable images.

He has his own varied pantheon of heroes, from Nelson Mandela to Frank Worrell to Bob Marley, and he is as loyal to the ideals they embody for him as he is to those nearer to his everyday experience who have an affinity with the emotional essence of his nature.

Botham is one, and another was Peter McCombe from Airdrie, who befriended Richards in the lonely early days at Somerset and had become as trusted as a brother by the time he died of a heart attack in Antigua last year.

Richards says he would never disown a friend and will certainly never turn his back on the many men who grew up with him and are now Rastafarians. 'These people are a lot cleaner in their hearts than most who criticize them, and they are and always will be part of me. I believe totally in a friend.'

He believes also in his obligations to the mass of ordinary West Indians in this country. 'So many of them work in lowly jobs and when we do well on the field they can walk a little taller, and hold their heads up. Whether I'm batting, bowling or fielding, I cannot feel satisfied unless I give every ounce to try and make them proud of me.'

For some time the wonderful eyes that he reveres as the greatest of his God-given gifts have been susceptible to inflammation from a condition akin to cataracts. He bathes them religiously with an assortment of lotions and balms to keep the problem in check.

Vivian Richards, now thirty-three, long ago realized that he had to do a great deal more than look out for himself and his family.

*   *   *

For all the strides taken by India and Pakistan in the 1970s and '80s, it was the West Indies who won Tests most often and most convinc-ingly. They also carried off the first two World Cups. They were led by Clive Lloyd, whose bent frame and thick glasses concealed a strokemaker of savage power and a captain with a Bradmanesque will to win. His formula for success was simple – the batsmen hit hard and the bowlers bowled fast.

With these methods the West Indians defeated all comers, but England more often than the others. Frank Keating now writes of the man who is commonly held to be the greatest of all West Indian fast bowlers, Malcolm Marshall. I note with interest that he has chosen not a 'blackwash' of poor England but, rather, Marshall's demolition of some fellow West Indians in a Shell Shield match.

Frank Keating

Marshall Arts (1986)

'Macho'. The nickname seems sinisterly apt. For, to be sure, out there on the cricket field Malcolm Marshall's machismo is at full throttle as he looks to prove his virility by violent domination. He goes about his work with a cold-eyed, businesslike, unsmiling, scary relish. He seems in a hurry to hurt. It is one thing to be acknowledged by all opposition batsmen as the fastest in the world, quite a different kettle of cower to be the most dangerously lethal. Test batsmen have genuine nightmares about Marshall these days – only their wives wake up with worse sweats.

Suddenly, like a revelation, the game is won or lost and Marshall's features crease in a crow's-feet network of laugh lines. He is much liked around cricket's dressing rooms. People enjoy hanging their hat on the peg next to his. For one thing he whistles only the most cheerful reggae tunes. He is a whole-hearted, keen and confident comrade.

On Monday, in his home-town pavilion at Bridgetown, his infectiously giggling delight bubbled all over as he cuddled, and was cuddled by, his Barbados captain Joel Garner after the two of them had laid Jamaica to waste to bring back the Shell Shield to mighty little Barbados. The Colgate-smiling, hand-slapping glee went on for an hour or so and, of a sudden, the nickname Macho had become convivial, endearing and totally untense. Just as the gold chain around his neck with his name on the pendant did not look half so, well, macho, or not as dangerous as it does when it glints ominously like a hired assassin's gun in the sun – or does when he turns from his mark to scud in on his toes with that short sprinter's hostility and that cruel and nasty narrowness to his eyes.

His loins girded with only a towel, Marshall looks almost ludicrously small-boned and slight; certainly he looks more of a spinner with cunning than a devilish and upsetting fast bowler. Botham calls him the 'skinny wimp'. When you talk to him, even my plump 5 ft 11 in tower over him by at least an inch. To Wes Hall's Larry Holmes, Charlie Griffith's Frazier, Michael Holding's Muhammad, Colin Croft's Foreman, and Garner's, say, Carnera, he looks as small, tiny, loose and angelic as Sugar Ray Leonard at 160 lb. It is dotty to believe that Malcolm Marshall is less than two stone heavier than Barry McGuigan.

For all that, mind you, Marshall is in the whippy physical image of other legends of the fast ball – Martindale, Constantine, Gilchrist and that long-ago founder of the faith and man of the people George John, from some sixty years ago, who was but 5 ft 9 in and, as C. L. R. James said: 'All power is in proportion . . . pace and body action, he hits many a poor batsman on the inside of the knee to collapse them like a felled ox.' This new welterweight is even lighter. Marshall's half-dozen summers so far with Hampshire have delighted him to make it his second home. But in truth Bournemouth's balmy breezes and corporation-imported palm trees patently cannot match his very nature's affinity with the bold primary colours and jangling, carefree good cheer of Barbados.

'Malcolm's real strength', said his captain Garner above the hubbub of Monday evening, 'is that he has never given less than 110 per cent for any side he has ever played for – from school, club, Barbados, Hampshire or with us fellows in the West Indian team. Pulling his weight for the side just means everything to him.' Garner and Marshall slapped hands in a last and poignant intimacy that we hangers-on had no business to dare even understand. On Monday evening they would meet later, sure, for celebration drinks, a little music and much more laughter, but the team was off from the airport first thing in the morning to prepare for this weekend's lap of honour in Guyana so they would, they promised themselves, be early abed.

Now, nattily, crisply and casually dressed, Marshall eases through the throng to rev up his sleek car and go home, perhaps for another change of clothing, for organizing the evening. He revs up at the first traffic light. His countrymen recognize their silky bachelor-boy hero, and shout, 'Hey, Macho, you showed 'em!' or 'You lightnin' man, Macho,' and there was not the slightest tremor of resentment that his cricket was building him one of the loveliest homes on the island.

If the Big Bird, Joel, is the working-class hero's prime minister, then Marshall is very much the one true Minister of Culture. Garner, for instance, has built himself, appropriately, the highest and most substantial house on the very foundations of the wooden shack in which his mother brought him up. There is no surprise, when you delve into it, that Marshall loves Hampshire so. He supposes it might have started as his favourite English county when he was a ragged urchin at primary school. The Barbadian cavalier Roy Marshall was the Southern Counties' most dashing import when the young Malcolm was first at school, and had learned to read.

He would look up Marshall's scores, just because of the same name in the paper. Then, when he was fourteen, the other hero, Andy Roberts, joined Hampshire didn't he? Again he would examine in the *Nation* the English scoreboards every morning. When he first came to England it was almost natural that he joined Hampshire. In his debut game in April 1979 it snowed. Nevertheless, with three sweaters on he took seven wickets when he was not embracing the dressing-room radiator. Sorry, 'ragged urchin' was pathetically romantic. But it is not right. Marshall, they say, was always beautifully turned out for school by his mother and grandmother. First at St Giles primary, where he is now challenging Wes Hall as A1 Alumnus, then at the Parkinson Comprehensive, where he was always immaculate in his khaki shorts and shirt. He was, teachers said last week, a model pupil, a team man.

Like Gary Sobers, from across the way at Bayland, Marshall's was a matriarchal boyhood. When Garfield was six his merchant-seaman father's ship was torpedoed. When Malcolm was still in his cot his policeman father died in a motorcycle accident. Dad had played for the police team. Uncle was a cricketer as well, but it was his grandfather, Oscar, who would bowl to him in the backyard every evening or on the beach on Sundays. The boy loved batting then, and he loves it best now to tell the truth. He would, he admits, dearly enjoy to match Botham, Kapil or Imran as a match-winning Test all-rounder.

It is touching that he gives thanks to the fortune of having a steady apprenticeship as understudy after his Packer-induced introduction to

Test cricket in 1978 after, incredibly, only one first-class game. It followed his debut for Barbados when, just like this week, a set of pallid Jamaicans treated him like sheep for the shearing and his seven wickets got him picked for the tour to India. Marshall was deputy then to the quick quartet and, says Joel, he was always the most cheerful and willing of twelfth men, ready with the drinks, the hot bath and laundry. A few years later Colin Croft sold his soul to South Africa, then Roberts retired . . . now Marshall is in the very pomp of fire and evil on the field. He will be twenty-eight in April, and is possibly still short of his prime.

There was a perfect example of his awesome, awful talent on Monday. It was heightened by the baying of the crowd. It was like they were at an execution. Tyburn stuff. With only an hour left and still six Jamaican wickets to fall, Marshall threw in a startlingly nasty bouncer from scarcely short of a length that reared from his ribs to graze Davidson's helmet and, taking off in a screaming fizz, cleared the gloves of the wicketkeeper standing a pitch length back, though he leaped like Shilton. It went at one bounce for four byes. The next fearsome ball seemed exactly the same length and pitch. This time Davidson, scared and weary, ducked his head to the level of his shins, but the ball skidded straight on, hit the nerve that joined his left bicep to his collarbone. As the batsman writhed in his crease, white-faced, he was given out. Plumb leg before, even from the pavilion it was frightening. Poor Davidson rolled away looking drunk with fear and holding his badly bruised, limp arm.

Marshall cannot explain his knack, except to say he is an athlete, with a supple, rubbery physique. He says he has worked hard to balance himself through his short run-up, so he is always at top speed as he delivers. He looks like Roberts from the ropes, and from twenty-two yards, they say, he has discovered the value of the three-speed bouncer. 'Give them a few first-gear bouncers and they might get confident: throw in three times as fast and they appear in no position to play it: they are not ready.' Purists at the old game of chivalry would say there is something sickening, even sadistic, about Marshall's bowling. He is confident about his defence: 'Simply, I am a professional. I play to the rules. I am lucky to have my fitness and aggression, but I do not lack sense. I am a fast bowler, this is my job; if I bowl dangerously and I'm told I intimidate, then the umpires are empowered to stop me. When they do I will think of bowling differently; till then, I can only play to the best of my ability, such

as it is. I am simply a man who loves cricket and happens to be a
fast bowler, a keen professional and a working man with obligations
to meet and a new mortgage to pay. I am a man who wants to do
his best for himself and his team every time I go to work.'

The first Test in Jamaica is racing towards the English tourists.
Sabina Park will probably be the fastest wicket. Yet Gower has scored
a Test century against Marshall at Sabina. 'I can think of better things
than facing him: he is a brilliant bowler, but it is not very nice,' says
the England captain. Gooch has also hit a hundred against him at
Sabina, 'but he is definitely nasty as a proposition'. Lamb has scored
three hundreds against Marshall in England – 'He bounces you at
will, and Malcolm must be the nastiest of them all.'

Last summer at Taunton Botham walked in at 50 for 5, called
for his white helmet and, though peppered by ferocious stuff from
Marshall, answered fire with fire in a blazing innings of 149 in 106
balls, first dismissing Tremlett and then driving Marshall back with
skimmingly crazy two-iron shots over long on or long off, or hooking
him off his whiskers into the car park over fine leg. Exasperated, that
cold-eyed look and beady fury on his brow, Marshall finally clean-
bowled the blond baron of beef, and then went down the wicket
with the broadest of grins, embraced his opponent, and clapped him
all the way back to the pavilion.

As Botham said earlier this week, as he vanished up into the
Bajan Hills, and into faraway, devious, late-night haunts with his pals
Garner and Marshall: 'Of course we are friends. Malcolm and I relish
the contest. He is a magnificent bowler, but he's a cricketer too. He
is an athlete. I always say to the skinny wimp when I get to the
wicket, "What have you in store for me today?" Malcolm is unquestionably the quickest and most dangerous man about today. He is
no Lillee yet, but he is swinging it and plays it just as hard. But the
point with him is everyone has a laugh and a joke afterwards.'

I asked Marshall if he would remember Botham's Taunton innings
when England faced him in Jamaica this month. 'I am not sure if I
will be selected,' he said modestly, and at that, from the highest
corner of the dressing room, Garner stood up and laughed so much
that Marshall had to join in, giggling, and slapping a few nearby
palms. Macho, sure, but a jolly nice sportsman as well.

★ ★ ★

For my final selections in this section I turn to players still active in the game. In this, the first decade of a new century, there is more international cricket played than ever before. These matches are all telecast live, and frequently to audiences of hundreds of millions. The competition between (and sometimes within) teams is fierce. In terms of class, the batsmen and bowlers yield nothing to their predecessors, and the fielders are hugely superior. From this vast pool I have chosen three truly great cricketers. The first of these is Brian Lara, a little left-hander of supreme skill and a penchant for breaking records, a hero to cricket lovers everywhere and a demigod to his fellow Trinidadians.

MARTIN JOHNSON

King of the Willow (1994)

When Brian Lara finally staggered out from beneath the vast rugby scrum of spectators, film crews and security police that had enveloped him almost before he had raised his bat in triumph, he went down on all fours and planted a kiss on the pitch. This was part emotion at the realization of what he had done, and part relief at the realization that he was still alive. Had he done it in his native Trinidad, where he is comfortably the most idolized figure on the island, they would probably have torn off little bits of him in the desperate search for a souvenir. Lara said afterwards that he planned to 'continue leading a simple life', but that may prove to be far more difficult than making 375 runs in a Test match.

From the moment Lara hooked Chris Lewis for four to move from 365, and joint holder with Gary Sobers of the highest individual score in a Test match, to 369, and alone at the top above the greatest cricketer the West Indies has ever produced, it took six minutes for the next ball to be bowled. Somewhere in the pile of bodies around Lara was Sobers himself, who had spent the morning in the home dressing room, and came out personally to offer his congratulations. 'I could not', Sobers said, 'think of a better person to break my record. He is the only batsman today who plays the game as it should be played – with his bat. He never uses his pads, and it is always a pride and joy to watch him play. I had to break someone else's record [Len Hutton's] to break the record, and records are always there to be broken.'

Lara, 320 not out overnight, officially resumed his innings at 10.05 a.m., but it came as no real surprise that he himself had started batting again – in front of his bedroom mirror – at 4 a.m. 'I woke up, and couldn't get back to sleep for nerves.' His hands, he said, were bathed in sweat.

Before the Test match, Lara played golf with Sobers (who plays off a single-figure handicap) and, having watched him play a few times on this tour, I can confirm that when Lara attempts to hit a stationary ball it is neither a thing of beauty, nor does he manage to make it travel very far in the appropriate direction. At the Caymanas Golf Club in Jamaica, he caused a sizeable logjam on the first tee when his caddie offered him at least five balls before he finally bobbled one past the ladies' tee, but this merely mirrored two things. One, Lara is such a cult figure that no one dared tell him to get a move on, and two, he is as determined to master golf as he has cricket. Give him a year, and he will be giving Sobers a stroke a hole.

Not all humility is 100 per cent genuine, but no one who has had any meaningful contact with Lara has ever doubted that he is totally self-effacing. 'I may have made pressures for myself,' he said, 'but I realize that I am only human, and that all it ever takes to get you out is one ball.' In this match, however, it took England 538 balls before Lara finally thin-edged a drive at Andrew Caddick. Off he went, to be given a hero's reception into the pavilion by his teammates' archway of raised bats. Times have changed, though, and when Hutton made his 364, and Sobers his 365, neither of them was hijacked by a satellite-television interviewer before being allowed to get off the field.

Lara's innings of 12 hours and 46 minutes took him half an hour less than Hutton, but almost two and a half hours longer than Sobers. Sobers was only twenty-one and making his maiden Test century when he set his record in February 1958, and Lara continued the trend of triple Test-match centurions being relatively young. Given the stamina required, it is not surprising, and of the now thirteen triple hundreds, only Andy Sandham and Graham Gooch have done it past their thirtieth birthdays. Sandham was thirty-nine and Gooch on his way to thirty-eight. The major difference between Lara and Gooch was that, while Gooch looked like he had just hiked across the Sahara by the time he had finished, Lara looked as though he could have batted the full five days without any physical distress. The mental strain, however, was overpowering, and it showed when he fretted and fussed for nearly twenty minutes on 347. Angus Fraser, trundling in as big-heartedly as ever, beat him twice in quick succession, and, as he stood in familiarly brassed-off mode in mid-pitch, was moved to engage his opponent in conversation. 'I don't suppose I can call you a lucky bleeder when you've got 347,' Fraser said, which made even Lara blow away some of the tension with a chuckle.

If Lara is mature beyond what will be twenty-five years in two weeks' time, then his partner in a stand of 219, Shivnarine Chanderpaul, possesses an equally remarkable temperament, and no little talent himself. When Lara went into his little phase of playing rash strokes, it was Chanderpaul, a nineteen-year-old in his fourth Test if you please, who came down the pitch to offer fatherly advice. Lara's own father is dead, and the fact that he was not alive to be here yesterday was the one regret Lara expressed after his epic innings. After passing Sandham's 325 to go to seventh on the all-time list, Lara's trademark shot off Fraser, a square cut for four, took him past Gooch (333) and Bradman (334) in one blow, and another four, a cover drive off Caddick, saw off both Wally Hammond (336) and Hanif Mohammad (337). A searing extra-cover drive for four then reeled in Hutton (364) and took him level with Sobers, before that final hook off Lewis. As a scrambled single would have done it, this looked like a risk, but Lara said afterwards: 'I knew he was going to bowl me a bouncer.'

During the pitch invasion, the person conducting the wildest celebration was a Rastafarian waving a placard with the inscription 'Blame It On Sir John Hawkins. Slave Trader.' Whoever Sir John Hawkins might be, this will come as a relief to England's bowlers, who might otherwise have thought they had had a hand in it. Oddly enough, England's first impression of Lara in this series was of a nervous, squinting young man playing Devon Malcolm with such desperate unease in the first Test that one feared for his safety. However, it transpired that he has a film-like impediment on both eyes, which will shortly require a minor operation. So there it is.

Once Lara can see properly, he should develop into a fairly handy player.

B. C. PIRES

Emperor of Trinidad (1998)

Fancying a challenge on the first day of the second (i.e. the first) Test at the Queen's Park Oval, I set out to find someone who would be critical of Brian Lara's debut as West Indies captain on his home ground. All I got was a long walk in the hot sun. It would have been easier to find a Bill Clinton T-shirt in Kenneth Starr's wardrobe. The only criticism of Lara's captaincy that has ever been made in Trinidad is that his appointment did not come directly upon his admission to puberty. 'Someone critical of Lara as captain? Try Walsh,' suggested a barrister in the Errol Dos Santos Stand. 'Not even him,' put in someone else. 'Even Courtney's happy that he's not captain any more.'

Andy Caddick, the England fast bowler, said this week that Brian Lara is not God; Caddick clearly had not taken a straw poll at the Oval. If Brian Lara is not God, he is at least the Pope of Queen's Park. Certainly he is infallible in Trinidad.

Not even when Lara dropped an ankle-high catch with Alec Stewart on 40 did the Trinidadians at the Oval bat an eyelid. A sudden shout went up as the ball carried to Lara and was followed by an even quicker sigh as it tumbled out of the captain's hands. Total silence fell with it, but only for the second or two before a Rastaman on the cycle track under the scoreboard spoke. 'Nobody coulda caught that,' he declared, glaring around him, daring anyone to disagree. Intimidation was unnecessary. No one had even heard him. Everyone was immersed in a personal struggle to transform a dropped catch at a critical point into something positive, if not a sign of genius.

The Rastaman found himself on safer ground a few minutes later when, with Stewart on 45, Carl Hooper dived in front of Lara at first slip, only to drop the catch. 'Damned Guyanese,' said the Rasta, smiling broadly. For the first time an Oval crowd was pleased to see a mistake made: it wasn't the home-town hero.

Anything Lara did was spectacular. Strategies that seemed fairly straightforward were heralded as brilliant. In the over before tea he brought Carl Hooper on to try a change from pace, a tactic my Form 3 physics teacher had suggested to our class captain in our inter-house league in 1973. Graham Thorpe obliged by slashing at a ball and was easily caught behind. A sportswriter (need I say a Trinidadian one?) near me in the press box shook his head in amazement. 'That', the writer pronounced breathlessly, 'is genius captaincy.'

After two sessions of fruitless search for anti-Lara sentiment, I decided to be subversive. If I could not find a volunteer, I would entrap someone. I leaned against a pillar in a stand and struck up an ostensibly casual conversation with a man wearing a 'Brian Lara 375' T-shirt. 'He's put on a bit of weight, hasn't he?' I asked. The man looked me up and down with a sneer. 'Not', he said, 'as much as you.' He walked off.

Undaunted, I went to the merchandise booth and waited for someone to buy a Brian Lara cap. A pretty girl picked one up, looked at it, put it back down. 'Brian's got a bit chubby, huh?' I asked. (His face is no longer boyishly slim, and a detractor, if there were such a thing in Trinidad, would say he may be thickening slightly at the waist.)

The girl studied him closely. 'Well,' she said, 'he's captain now. He must have to go to those cocktail parties and dinners and things. He's got to put on a little weight. He's still gorgeous.'

In the middle, Adam Hollioake got himself run out to the bowling of Jimmy Adams. Brilliant captaincy.

★   ★   ★

Shane Warne is a characteristically extroverted Australian who some judges reckon to be the finest wrist-spinner in the history of the game. During the 1999 World Cup he suffered a rare loss of form. Like Frank Keating, I was also at Lord's when a humble Zimbabwe side took him to the cleaners. Keating's appreciation was written on the eve of the semi-final. Happily, his apprehensions were unfounded. Warne bowled beautifully in this match and in the final against Pakistan, and will ennoble our game for some time yet.

FRANK KEATING

Final Fling for the Fizzer (1999)

Tell you something I have seriously missed this World Cup summer so far: that twangy and combative Oz morale-booster 'Bowled Warney!' or the alternative 'Great one, Shaney!' boldly enunciated by the gnarled and gauntleted old bush-whacker Ian Healy four or five times an over when the true-great leg-spinner was zipping and zapping through his six-pack of fizzing dangers and delights.

Differently good as he is, Australia's one-day wicketkeeper Adam Gilchrist has none of Healy's unsettling partner-in-crime vociferousness. Or perhaps the truth is that Warne's once wondrous bowling has lost all its viperish menace and is nothing much to write home about any more, let alone hail and hosanna so noisily from behind the stumps.

We shall see today in Birmingham. Mind you, it is a terrible thought either way, for Australia are not due to return to England till the summer of 2001, which means that this very day at Edgbaston may well be the last time the cricket lovers of England will ever see Shane Warne displaying his arts and sciences, his angles and geometry, his daring and mischief real or imagined: in other words just strutting his wonderful stuff.

Single-handedly, Warne revived a dodo-dead skill, and resuscitated it with such gay garlands and flamboyant streamers that in just seven years at the century's end he became one of the most crucially influential cricketers of an ancient pastime's whole legend and lore. So relish him while we can, today for sure and possibly at Lord's and the final act and denouement of this larky, thrilling enough little pageant on Sunday.

He has had some depressions of late but last weekend he was full of the joys. 'I just know there are more golden years up ahead,' he said. And sure enough on Sunday, in that narrow-eyed but glistening contest of heroes at Headingley, it was heartening to be among that of-late too often contrary, not to say bovine, Yorkshire throng as they genuflected to their antique and eminent cricketing heritage to acclaim roundly Warne and all his works and pomps.

He had crucially nipped out the middle of South Africa's burgeoning innings just as it was set to blossom in the last-fifteen-overs charge. Springboks were smug indeed on the launchpad at 140 for 1 – when the second and fifth balls of Warne's ninth over of an exemplary spell strangled at birth any cashing-in.

A seemingly help-yourself twirler amiably pitched just outside leg stump to induce Cullinan, having the moment before posted his half-century, to celebrate with a heave to deepest midwicket's cow-corner; the ball took the off bail clean as a whistle. Three balls later captain Cronje was walking back for a duck, jet-dark eyes seething, plumb leg before on his kneeling thigh having obviously misread the googly-to-hoick-over-square-leg for the zooter that comes straight on. Thank you and goodnight.

At the end of his next over, when his highly commendable 10–1–33–2 (not to mention the two dropped catches in his spell) was announced, the crowd again gave lusty vent. Promptly he dropped at backward point a fiercely struck sitter off danger man Klusener. But next over, off Fleming, he hared backwards from extra cover to hold a spectacularly high-quality catch off the same batsman.

At which every one of his ten confrères, even those on the faraway rim of the wide field at deepest long leg or midwicket, fair raced to converge on him in collective acclaim. Warne has always been a mighty popular one-of-the-boys team man and talisman.

In the team hotel in Birmingham on Tuesday the great man was as smiling sunny as the weather outside. You know he is missing home desperately. He and his team have, to all intents, been on the road and living out of suitcases since Christmas and before.

On 19 May, back home in Brighton, Victoria, his wife, Simone, gave birth to their second child, a bonny eight-pound boy called Jackson Shane.

Next day Warne's leg breaks were taking some two-sixer stick from New Zealand's Chris Cairns at Cardiff, and Australia lost the match. 'OK, fair dos. Chris and Roger Twose played great cricket that day and I copped it fair and square.'

He copped it, too, against Zimbabwe: 5 overs for 44 when Neil Johnson crisply clocked him for four fours in an over. 'Fair dos again, the bloke batted brilliantly. Fact is, any spinner puts his talent on the line in one-dayers and he's there to be shot at.'

There were three sixes conceded in an over against India but, as he cheerfully admits, he was probably lucky to get away with three that day, and he suggests there has never been a better one-day batting side than India's and tells you to look up the facts.

Even all those greats who have come after him acknowledge Warne as not only the pioneering rekindler of the faith but, still, as the keeper of the flame. Well, 315 Test wickets has already left behind every other spin bowler in the game's long history. And all achieved in less than eight years. The good bloke's a genius, and you can say that again and again.

There will be a frisson today among the throng when he is called upon. Fearless, confident; the three-pace walk-up, the little judder of a quickstep to his delivery stride and, with a half-smile of devious intent and a half-growl of shoulder-straining urgency, down she floats and/or fizzes: 'Bowled Warney!' 'Great one, Shaney!'

Should the plump, already mighty rich but still affably smiling maestro decide after this World Cup, and after a rest and some contented baby-bonding and Australia's tour to Sri Lanka, to accept a fortune for one summer in English county cricket, then OK, we shall have him again among us, but it will not be the same. He is a one-off.

It was all of six Junes ago (Friday 4 June at Manchester) that Warne dramatically announced himself to England (Gatting b Warne 4). In spite of his certainty of 'many more golden years ahead' it seems probable, all things considered, that we shall not see him again at the peak of his fabulous game.

If such is the case, at Edgbaston today or Lord's on Sunday: many thanks, all hail . . . and farewell.

★   ★   ★

The one batsman who has always dominated Shane Warne is Sachin Tendulkar. In a few weeks in the spring of 1998 he hit four masterful hundreds against the Australians – two in Tests, the other two in limited-over internationals. At the end of it all Warne went to Tendulkar and, in perfect sincerity, asked for his autograph. Later that year another Australian chose to compliment Tendulkar. This was Sir Donald Bradman, who invited the Indian to his Adelaide home on the occasion of his ninetieth birthday. The Don has said that of all the batsmen who have come since, it is Sachin Tendulkar who most resembles him. Here an English and an Indian writer offer their own assessments.

MIKE SELVEY

Sachin of Mumbai (1997)

It was one brief moment in time. The World Cup, India/West Indies in Gwalior, and a single stroke of such exquisiteness that the old maharajah surely would have had it carved in ivory and placed on a plinth. In essence, it was no more than a leg-side flick to the boundary and, in a competition that gorged itself on hitting, might have been worth only transient acclaim. But this was a gem: a length ball from a high-class pace bowler met initially with a straight blade, and then, at the last nanosecond, turned away with a roll of the wrist and such an irresistible alliance of power, timing and placement that first of all it eluded the fingertips of a midwicket fielder diving to his right, and then it did the same to the boundary runner haring and plunging to his left. Skill, technique, confidence, awareness, vision: pure genius, and four more runs to Sachin Tendulkar.

The young man is probably the most famous and feted man in India, outglitzing even the stars of Bollywood movies. With endorsements over the next five years estimated to be worth at least $US75 million, he is also the highest earner in cricket. He has become public property in a country of enthusiasms that can spill over into the fanatical, but has managed to maintain a dignified, mature outlook, remaining aware of his responsibilities while protecting his privacy. When he married Anjali, a doctor and friend from his childhood, he rejected massive sums from satellite TV for live coverage, keeping the ceremony a family affair. He knows his worth, and is wealthy beyond the dreams of almost a billion Indians, but he is not a grabber. His father, a university professor, imparted a sense of perspective and a work ethic.

Tendulkar averages over 50 in Tests and is the supreme right-hander, if not quite the finest batsman, on the planet. He is a focused technician, who offers a counterpoint to Brian Lara's more eye-catching destruction, fuelled on flair and ego. He has, it seems, been around for ever. In the third Test at Trent Bridge last summer, he scored 177, the tenth century of his Test career and his second of the series: yet remarkably, at twenty-three Tendulkar was younger than any member of the England team, with only Dominic Cork and Min Patel born even in the same decade. His figures have been achieved despite a lack of Test cricket, particularly at home. Seven of his centuries had been scored before his twenty-first birthday, a unique record. Had India not rationalized their Test-match programme so much that, prior to last summer, they had played just one three-match series, heavily affected by rain, against New Zealand, in the previous eighteen months, there is no telling what he might already have achieved. With time on his side and a return to a full Test programme, he could prove Sunil Gavaskar right and rewrite the records.

Sachin Ramesh Tendulkar was born in Bombay on 24 April 1973, and, since childhood, has trodden a steady, almost inevitable, path to greatness. He attended the city's Sharadashram Vidyamandir school, where the Harris Memorial Challenge Shield, a competition for under-seventeens, provided the chance to bat for hours. From the age of twelve, when he scored his first century for the school and came to notice as a special talent, he indulged himself. When fourteen, he compiled not-out scores of 207, 329 and 346 in the space of five innings, one of them contributing to an unbroken partnership of 664 with Vinod Kambli, a record in any form of cricket.

He was 16 years and 205 days old when he made his Test debut, in November 1989, in the National Stadium in Karachi – for a young Indian, perhaps the most fiery baptism of all. The following year, at Old Trafford, he hit his first Test century – not a scintillating innings, but an exercise in technique, concentration and application beyond his tender years, which saved a game that might have been lost. Had it come thirty-one days earlier, he would have been the youngest century-maker in Test history. During the winter of 1991–2, he went to Australia, where they still talk in awe of the centuries he scored in Sydney and in Perth.

A few days after his nineteenth birthday, Tendulkar came back to England: to Yorkshire, no less, as the county's first overseas player. It would have been a massive responsibility for anyone, let alone a teenager from India, and it did not quite work. Tendulkar assumed the mantle conscientiously, and posed with cloth cap and pint of bitter, impressing colleagues and supporters alike with his understanding of public relations. But, in the end, he failed to come to terms with the county game, scoring only one century and barely scraping past 1,000 runs in his only season. Hindsight would tell him that it was part of his education, but a mistake nonetheless.

In 1996 he returned to England, a teenage prodigy no longer, but a seasoned Test batsman fit to stand alongside his first hero, Gavaskar. The pair have much in common: Gavaskar was slight of build and, of necessity, a supreme judge of length. Tendulkar, too, is short. There is a lot of bottom hand, but he drives strongly, on the rise, such is his strength of wrist and the control in his hands, while he is devastating off his legs, pulls well and – given good bounce – can cut wide bowling to ribbons. If the delicate and unexpected talents of Sourav Ganguly provided a distraction last season, then Tendulkar's two hundreds in three Tests were ample demonstration of the team's premier batsman leading from the front. The first of them – at Edgbaston, where he made 122 out of 219 – was a stunning display of virtuosity in adversity.

In August, aged twenty-three, Tendulkar succeeded Mohammad Azharuddin as captain of his country. Had he craved it and pursued it with a passion, he would surely have got the job earlier, perhaps even while a teenager. Rather, it was a position that was being held in abeyance until the time was right. His leadership has a firm base of experience to it now. His first Test in charge was against Australia. He made 10 and 0 but India won, just as one almost assumed they would. Some things just seem part of a wider plan.

SURESH MENON

Tendulkar of the World (1999)

At twenty-five, Sachin Tendulkar is like the Taj Mahal. There is nothing new to be said about either. Still, there are two strains worth pursuing. His impact abroad, and what it means to be Bradmanesque. In nearly a decade of international cricket, Tendulkar has done what no other Indian has – ensured that in his fans' minds, there is a split between his performance and that of his country. Even when Sunil Gavaskar was making centuries in lost causes, he didn't evoke that kind of response. It is almost as if fans are saying: 'The result doesn't matter, so long as Tendulkar makes his runs.' In one-day cricket, there's a link between the two – when Tendulkar scores, India wins – hence the prayers of Indian expatriates wherever he plays. But the exclusivity is disappearing. Tendulkar is moving out of the confines imposed by nationality, and is seen as that rare sporting idol, the universal hero. In this he's closer to basketball's Michael Jordan than any cricketer.

The India–Pakistan rivalry is still strong, but even in Sharjah, where it was stifling, some of the intensity has gone. Tendulkar can take the credit for this, for suggesting that a loss to Pakistan is not the end of the world. There is great joy in the Pakistani sections of the crowd at the Sharjah Stadium when Tendulkar is dismissed, but, I suspect much regret too. People come as much to see their country win, as to see Tendulkar bat.

Some Pakistani friends of mine have, without being aware of it, repeated the modern version of Neville Cardus's prayer. Cardus was an Englishman, of course, but he revered the Australian great Victor Trumper. To reconcile patriotism with hero worship he would pray: 'Lord, let Trumper score a hundred for Australia in England's win.'

The ideal solution, thus, for many Pakistani spectators is for Tendulkar to score a hundred and Pakistan to win (leaving patriotism unstretched). In recent years, the most popular Indian cricketers abroad have been Sunil Gavaskar (in the West Indies they sang calypsos about him), Kapil Dev, Bishan Bedi (in England, Jim Laker said his idea of paradise was Lord's in the sunshine, Ray Lindwall bowling at one end, Bedi at the other), B. S. Chandrashekhar (in Melbourne, where he had Test figures of 6 for 52 twice in an India win, they're still trying to figure him out).

These players have been fussed over, loved, respected, but there was always an air of condescension, for they did things that weren't easily grasped. They were oriental stereotypes, with supple wrists and boundless enthusiasm, and an air of mystery. Tendulkar, on the other hand, is easily understood in Anglo-Saxon terms. He can be explained in terms that are English, Australian, West Indian, South African. If Steve Waugh, for example, had a better eye and more strokes, he could be Tendulkar who isn't a stereotype, but demons-rates what's possible if Anglo-Saxon batsmanship were carried to its heights . . .

Over the years, Tendulkar, who gives of his cricketing talent so generously, has learned to hold back as a person. He presents a dignified, statesman-like image to the public. In private he can be fun, and speak unguardedly, but in public he will not put a foot wrong. The cultivated aloofness is a shield any icon must wear against exploitation. That was Don Bradman's fate too. He had to be Bradman at all times, just like Tendulkar has to be Tendulkar at all times. The comparison with Bradman is inevitable. Both acted as the repository for all knowledge of batting available till their time.

Tendulkar is, like Bradman was, a one-stop shop where state-of-the-art batsmanship is on display. You could go to different displays for specifics like the cover drive or the cut or the on drive or the pull – or you could get them all under one roof, as it were, with Tendulkar.

The obverse side of such near-perfection is there's no single shot with which he is associated. Bradman's defining shot might have been the pull; he sometimes finished facing the wicketkeeper at the end of it. But Tendulkar's? The straight drive off the fast bowler with hardly any feet movement? The variations on the on-driving theme? The flat-batted swat through cover? At sixteen, Tendulkar was a finished product, in the manner of Ernest Hemingway, who found his voice at twenty-one and didn't need to work on it. The man Hemingway was indistinguishable from the boy Hemingway.

In Peshawar nine years ago, the boy Tendulkar, then not a serious contender for the one-day series, made 53 from 18 balls hitting leg-spinner Abdul Qadir for 27 runs in one over. The first two sixes cleared the stadium; the third exhibited a perfect marriage of youthful exuberance and mature self-confidence. As Tendulkar stepped out, he realized he was not to the pitch of the ball. He was, technically, beaten – yet went through with the shot, relying on his strong forearms, and a natural sense of timing to see him through.

Compare that with his blistering knocks against Shane Warne last year, or his last innings in Sharjah against a marauding Zimbabwean Olonga. Again, he was beaten by the ball which he hit for six – nothing had changed in a decade, for nothing needed to change. 'The best is yet to come' sort of adage holds true for Tendulkar only statistically. Yes, he will emerge the highest run-getter in either form of the game (Test cricket willing); he will get a double-hundred and more.

He will be using the same mixture, though: only the proportions will be different. 'Tendulkarine' is an adjective awaiting entry into dictionaries.

Watching Benaud Bowl

Leg-spinners pose problems much like love,
Requiring commitment, the taking of a chance.
Halfway deludes; the bold advance.

Right back, there's time to watch
Developments, though perhaps too late.
It's not spectacular, but can conciliate.

Instinctively romantics move towards,
Preventing complexities by their embrace,
Batsman and lover embarked as overlords.

ALAN ROSS

LITTLE
HEROES

Having doffed our hats to the true greats of the game, let us now praise less famous men. Our 'Little Heroes' section begins with a charming recollection of an early tour of England by a side of Australian Aboriginals. A century later another tour was organized to commemorate the first. When the members of this latter side went to meet John Arlott, the great writer and broadcaster remarked, 'I could have taken you for a regular Australian side – except for your manners.'

A. A. THOMSON

Bat, Ball and Boomerang (1958)

The All Blacks of 1905, that formidable phalanx of Rugby footballers from New Zealand, were the first Commonwealth visitors to go by that name, but the title might have been more reasonably claimed by the cricketing 'all blacks', that first visiting side from Australia of thirty-seven years earlier, who, apart from their captain, Charles Lawrence, who was also their manager, were Aborigines to a man. In comparatively recent years, only three Aborigines have played state cricket: A. Henry, 'Eddie' Gilbert and J. J. Marsh, the first two of them for Queensland and the third for New South Wales. Of the three, only Gilbert lent much colour to the game. The two best-known facts about him are: (1) his speed was so furious that he once knocked the bat clean out of Bradman's hands and (2) Learie Constantine hit a very fast ball from him out of the Woollongabba ground at Brisbane. They never found the ball. Knowing Constantine, I fancy it may have reached the Great Barrier Reef.

In the 1860s, however, there were more Aborigines in the game, and in the side that Lawrence brought over there were thirteen.

Lawrence himself was a remarkable cricketer. He played at different times for Middlesex and Surrey, and undertook professional engagements in both Scotland and Ireland. Playing for a Scottish Twenty-two against the All-England XI, he bowled Julius Caesar so comprehensively that all three stumps were knocked out of the ground. I should have thought this hardly physically possible, but the records are firm and clear. He went out to Australia with H. H. Stephenson's team and, when they came home, he stayed on to coach the Albert Club, Sydney's leading cricket combination. It was he who conceived the idea of the tour undertaken by his pupils. The visit, like all early tours, was an effort of private enterprise, and, on Lawrence's persuasion, was backed by four gentlemen of speculative temperament, headed by a Mr Graham, of Sydney.

You can see the portraits of the Aborigines, built up into a composite picture, in the Imperial Cricket Museum at Lord's. They were members of the Werrumbrook tribe, a race then living in Victoria but now extinct, and in its day very different in character from the present-day Aborigines of Northern Queensland, with which modern ethnological research, benevolent social work and the delightful detective stories of Arthur Upfield have made us familiar. Our cricketing Aborigines, it is claimed, were nearer in race to the Maoris of New Zealand, though their photographs hardly seem to support this theory. Frankly, they are not as handsome as Maoris, but nothing could now matter less.

Their photographs show them to be black, bearded and, with one or two exceptions, wiry rather than muscular. Their costume is fascinatingly varied. Some are clad in unexceptionable flannels; others appear to be wearing shorts over their trousers. (Who would presume to be fashion's arbiter in such matters?) Their feet are bare. Only a few bear (or brandish) the simple implements connected with their cricket. Mullagh carries a bat over his shoulder and is well within his rights in doing so, for he was by far the best batsman, not to mention the best bowler and wicketkeeper, in the side; Johnny Cuzens, the second-best bowler, is shown in the act of delivering a deadly ball, and Red Cap, in a solemn manner which he seldom assumed in real life at the crease, is squaring up defensively. All the others are provided with examples of their true native weapons: boomerangs, spears and a curious narrow shield, in shape rather like a pelota basket. Some of them are adorned with gay sashes, just as footballers wear numbers, to distinguish their identities,* and the colours—maroon, pink, yellow, magenta—all added to the brightness of the scene.

Apart from polar explorers, our Aborigines must have become in time the most harassed (or hardened) of travellers. They endured a sea voyage of inordinate length on the *Paramatla*, not the kindliest of ships, but this was no unkinder than what came later. They took up their first headquarters at Town Malling in Kent. Afterwards, they moved into a pub called the Queen's Head in the Borough and seemed to have found London less idyllic but more congenial.

At first, because of a prejudice, not against the colour but against the sheer strangeness of the visitors, the business of planning their fixture list hung fire, but the MCC, in characteristically courteous and helpful fashion, came forward and offered them a game at Lord's. After this became known, fixtures in plenty were showered on them. They might possibly have complained that their fixtures were imperfectly arranged, but no one could say that a total of forty-seven matches was insufficient.

Their first game took place at the Oval. It was not played against the county side, which in those days of H. H. Stephenson, George Griffith and Billy Caffyn would no doubt have been too strong for them, but against an excellent Gentlemen's side, the Surrey Club. The Club, who batted first, eventually won by an innings, but the Aborigines put up a stiff enough resistance to show they had good quality in them. Lawrence, of course, helped to give the side a certain stiffening, but splendid batting in each innings came from Mullagh, whose keenness and success were to last right through the tour.

After this game the Aborigines gave a quite electrifying display of spear and boomerang throwing, the grand finale of which was a contribution by Dick-a-Dick, who allowed five gentlemen of Surrey, including Mr William Burrup, the county's honorary secretary, to pelt him with cricket balls as hard as they could go. It sounds an ungentlemanly thing to have done, but everybody, including Dick-a-Dick, swaying, swinging and dodging fantastically, seems to have enjoyed it.

Several interesting things happened to the Aborigines at the Oval that day. Mullagh, because of his unexpectedly brilliant batting, was awarded a golden sovereign as talent money, formally presented by the Surrey secretary in front of the pavilion. Among those who took

* Except at Cardiff Arms Park, where the mud renders this impossible.

part in the sports with the Aborigines was a lanky young fellow, just short of his twentieth birthday, who had come up from Bristol to try his hand at throwing the cricket ball. In three goes he threw 116, 117 and 118 yards and, at his fourth attempt, he threw the ball 109 yards one way and 104 the other. His name was William Gilbert Grace, and whether he was acclaimed the winner of this particular competition I do not know.

After the game the visitors were joined by William Shepherd, a young member of the Surrey ground staff who had stood umpire for them. He became a valuable addition to the side, helping with the general management, umpiring and captaining the eleven when Lawrence took a rest.

Some 7,000 watched the game and about half of them stayed to see the sports. The Aborigines were subsequently taken to see the Derby at Epsom. They missed Hermit's Derby by a year, but I hope they found the winner at equally long odds.

So they were launched upon their arduous Odyssey which lasted from 26 May until the third week in October, and for sheer strenuousness I can think of nothing to compare with it except the Maori rugger team, brought over in similar circumstances in the 1880s, and condemned to a programme of seventy matches that a galley slave would hardly have considered leisurely. Our Aborigines played 47 matches, won 14, lost the same number and drew 19. It is to their credit that most of their losses were incurred early on, before they had had a chance of getting used to English conditions. Indeed, when you consider the sheer wear and tear of their itinerary, it is highly to their credit that they won any matches at all.

It was the day-to-day travelling that they found most punishing. Nobody knows if any of them when at home had ever followed the Aboriginal custom of 'going walkabout', but their stay in England was one long 'walkabout'. Try to imagine forty-seven uncoordinated journeys, including trips between such far-flung places as Kennington and Keighley, Plymouth and Tynemouth, Brighton and Bootle. Shepherd, a sharp-eyed, good-natured little man, mopped his brow in the fierce heat of England's hottest summer for many years, and wondered why these journeys, so ill-arranged and costly, could not have been put into the hands of some more intelligent wanderer. Why, for instance, had they not consulted George Parr, captain and manager of the All-England XI, who had been touring the cricketing towns for years, and whose knowledge of the tricks of transport might have saved the managers much money and the players much discomfort? Even under these hardships the 'demeanour of the Blacks was most becoming' and they travelled from Rochdale to Swansea and from Swansea to Bradford without a murmur. Perhaps they were sustained and uplifted by the fact that at Bootle a boomerang was swung off course by the wind and decapitated a spectator's tall hat.

For publicity's sake, the circus always put up at the best hotels and, at this distance of time, it is impossible not to be awed by the thought of Bullocky, Dick-a-Dick and Jimmy Mosquito flaunting it in the best hotels in Hunslet, Rochdale and Bootle. This, it was complained, played havoc with the venture's finances.

The two leading accounts of the tour are not agreed upon its financial results. One, quoting the large crowds which the visitors attracted everywhere by their enterprising cricket and especially by their athletic displays, declares it to have been a success. The other authority, our Mr Shepherd, argued otherwise. Indeed, Shepherd, whose business acumen should have stamped him as a Scot or a Yorkshireman instead of a mere Southerner, demonstrated in relentless Micawber-like economic logic how the tour lost £2,000, a deficit which should have been shared by four speculators, but fell in fact most heavily upon the unfortunate Mr Graham of Sydney, who had planked down the money in the first place. This loss, and doubts for the future that it spread, put an end to the plan which Lawrence had conceived of wintering in the South of France and returning the following season. The money risk was too heavy.

Besides a well-patronized game against the MCC at Lord's, in which Mullagh again distinguished himself with both bat and ball, the Aborigines made spasmodic forays into Kent and East Lancashire and had some gruesome experiences at Turnham Green on a truly rural wicket, which consisted wholly of ridge and furrow.

Not all the players enjoyed equal success throughout the tour. Easily the most dexterous was Johnny Mullagh, who made 1,670 runs and took nearly 250 wickets, an impressive season's performance by anybody anywhere. Not content with such an excellent record, he frequently kept wicket as a substitute for Bullocky, the regular practitioner, and took a toll of forty victims, half of them stumped. His bowling was of the old-fashioned honest sort, fast and straight. He reinforced his formidable quality by moving swiftly towards the batsman as he finished his delivery, just as W. G. habitually trotted towards silly mid-off. The result was that a surprising number of batsmen found themselves first mesmerized and then caught and bowled. An even bigger number were run out by his swift, deadly aim.

Johnny Cuzens, another remarkable athlete, came next highest among the records both for batting and bowling. His bowling action was not unlike that of some other bowlers we could name; it was, they say, 'of the windmill description'. His deliveries were menacingly fast and bumpy and the manner in which he exploited the relaxed rule about raising the arm above the shoulder is just nobody's business. Conservative old gentlemen who had muttered darkly about the thin end of the wedge were beginning to say: 'I told you so', but the authorities were past worrying about this now. Overarm bowling had come to stay. Johnny Cuzens also made his 1,000 runs and took his 100 wickets and was probably the side's best sprinter. It was his habit to run barefoot until the solicitous Mr Shepherd had a pair of special running pumps made for him in Sheffield. On the third day of the last match of their tour Cuzens was challenged by an anonymous sprinter from the north. Shepherd, who suspected some jiggery-pokery in the wager, was disposed to frown on the challenge, but the tourists' London host happened to be William Holland, proprietor of the old Canterbury music hall, who was full of admiration for his guest. Holland was a man of large ideas and was what we should now call publicity-minded. He once proposed to place an outsize carpet, value at £1,000, in the vestibule of his music hall and was undeterred by the suggestion that patrons would only spit on it.

'Fine,' said he. 'We'll advertise in the papers: "Come and spit on our £1,000 carpet".'

Nothing could stop him from offering to put a fiver on Johnny Cuzens and, almost before Shepherd could open his mouth in protest, the race had started. Cuzens sent his supporters' hearts into their mouths by being slow off the mark and subjected them to something near thrombosis when, halfway down the track, he kicked off one of his running pumps. But from that instant he moved like the wind and slipped past his rival. As he breasted the tape he was engulfed in the warm embrace of his chief backer, who, true to the open-handed tradition of the music hall, pressed both stake and winnings into the runner's hand.

Bullocky was a courageous wicket keeper with a granite frame and would have kept just as boldly unarmed by pads or gloves. He was also a stubborn bat, sometimes exasperatingly so, and had one heroic innings of 64 not out at Hastings which would have done credit to the last of the Saxons.

The rest of the Aborigines, though keen fielders and good sportsmen, were fair-to-indifferent performers with bat and ball. One of their drawbacks (if drawback is the right word) was that they showed a certain rashness in hitting and something more reprehensible than rashness in running between the wickets. To such a degree was their judgement at fault that on the tour there were nearly sixty run-outs. Is this, you may well ask, a record? Twopenny, despite the fact that his sash was drab in colour, was a hearty smiter of what we should now call the 'Jim Smith' school, and performed a feat which I do not think either Grace or Bradman ever achieved: he once hit a 9 (repeat nine) all run and without benefit of overthrow. I hope that news of this feat can be kept from Messrs Wardle and Trueman, who might spend the rest of their active (and otherwise blameless) lives in striving to emulate it.

The Aborigine named Sundown played in only two matches and, despite rival historic claims, must have been the original hero of the legend: 'In the first innings he made one and in the second he was not so successful.' There is an air of Odyssey about the thought of a man travelling right round the world (once round the Horn) for the pleasure of making one run. What is even odder is that he had never made a run in a match before the tour and that he never made a run when he got back home. It is no cliché to say that he never 'troubled the scorers'. Poor Sundown. Or should we say: 'Happy Sundown'? Perhaps it is better to travel hopefully towards the supreme ambition of breaking your duck than to arrive, and he remains a magnificent example of hope and endurance to all the worst batsmen in the world. (Was he by any chance a bowler or a good fielder? And it is interesting to ponder on the stroke that brought him the one historic run: can it, for instance, be proved beyond question that the shot was intentional?) The triumphs of Peter were much more spectacular. His tale of 42 matches was studded with 17 ducks. Old Jemmy Shaw of Notts never did anything half so clever. Even among the bowlers who took more wickets in their careers than they scored runs, this remains an impressive

achievement. I doubt if even Eric Hollies could show so proud a
record.

... Our Aborigines could all throw the spear and boomerang, but
Charley Dumas was outstanding. He had been a champion in his
own land and was undoubtedly paramount here. Great crowds came
to see him hurl the slender stick almost out of sight and apparently
keep it voyaging, rather like an antipodean sputnik, by remote
control. Gaping, spectators would see it return, slowly and, as it
seemed, deliberately, to make a perfect three-point landing between
Charley's bare feet. In the last fifty years much has been learned
about the control of aircraft and missiles from the ground and the
science of aerodynamics has few secrets, but much of the mystery
of the boomerang remains. Some newspapers suggested that more
people came to see Charley Dumas' bravura performance than to
see the cricket and, although this is not strictly true, Dumas had a
large following.

The master of the Australian stockwhip was Jimmy Mosquito,
the brother, in spite of their different names, of Johnny Cuzens.
Jimmy was demonstrably inferior to Johnny as a cricketer and a
sprinter, but with the stockwhip he displayed the same touch of
wizardry as did Charley Dumas with the boomerang. Between lunch
and the resumption of play Shepherd introduced a pretty ritual.
Outside the pavilion he would stand with a shilling in his outstretched
fingers and Jimmy, with a nonchalant crack of his eighteen-foot lash,
would flick the coin clear. This performance was repeated two or
three times and then Shepherd would toss the shilling to Jimmy as
his prize. From the knot of spectators who had gathered to watch
this little game, one man after another would come forward, waving
his shilling and inviting Jimmy to flick it out of his hand. By the
time the bell rang for resumption of play, Jimmy's pockets were
bulging with shillings. But his ethical standards remained high. After
his haul he always returned his partner's decoy shilling.

The poverty of some of the visitors in cricketing skill had probably
a basic cause in the state of their health, for which the English
climate may be held responsible. Fine and warm as was the
English summer of 1868, it was not so dry as summer, or even
winter, in their own Australia; several of them suffered from chest
complaints and one of them died. King Cole was taken ill during the
match at Hastings and was sent up to Guy's Hospital, where he died,

as Fred Grace was to die twelve years later, from congestion of the lungs. Some fragments of a rambling elegiac poem mourned him sadly and this, along with his photograph among his comrades in the museum at Lord's, are all we have to remember him by:

> Now run out for nought in the innings of life
> By the grave of the good he is sleeping;
> Yet sad are his comrades, though reckon they well
> How safe is their mate in our keeping.

A sad and sincere effort, but I do not think poor King Cole would have liked that 'run out for nought'. Though kindly meant, it seems a distressing commentary on human effort.

An odd point about the Aborigines was that on their return home, though two or three of them turned out in state cricket, none of them achieved any success. Johnny Mullagh, by far the highest of them in capacity, played happily in good club cricket, and when he died at the age of fifty he was buried in his club blazer. There is a splendour in his epitaph: 'He was a cricketer to the core.'

★   ★   ★

As more countries were granted Test status, and as they began playing more frequently against one another, the English County Championship began to lose its significance. Now, when the average county match attracts a crowd of a dozen pensioners and their dogs, it is difficult to recall the extreme passions that the championship once commanded. Local loyalties were deep and fierce, and local characters abounded. Much energy and skill once went into the portrayal of cricketers who played for county rather than country. Reproduced here are three essays on characters in the counties, written (by chance) by three *Guardian* men.

JOHN ARLOTT
Rough Diamond (1953)

Tom Wass, the cricketer, died a week or two ago [27 October 1953] in Sutton-in-Ashfield, the village where he was born. He was seventy-

shire, he had still the initial fire to take their first eight wickets for 19 runs in 14 balls.

The men who bowled at Trent Bridge have always had to take the task seriously, and Tom Wass's fitness was a pressing matter in his winter. He spent an hour with a punching bag every morning and he followed the hounds, often as far as twenty miles in a day, twice a week all through his 'off' season.

From the pavilion at Trent Bridge, he watched the county games as a forgotten player in the 1930s until, during the past few years, he became something of a legend. Up there on the roof he held court in the eternal cloth cap set straightly upon his head, a collar looking two sizes too large for his neck, which had become stringy with age, and wearing a loose jacket which drooped about his craggy bones.

The men who had played with him would climb slowly up the two flights of stairs to see him. As he came back into his heroic own, much of his earlier hardness seemed to drop from the old man, and, if he was never really expansive, there was perhaps more of social uncertainty than of unfriendliness in his silences.

'Tom were roogher'n moast,' said Tom Oates, and the bowler himself once told me, 'Ah feared nowt.' His batting was almost useless, and *Wisden* said of his fielding – when according him selection as one of its Five Cricketers of the Year in 1908 – 'When an easy catch goes to him the batsman has a feeling of hopefulness until he sees that the ball has been safely held.' So his bowling was his cricket and his living; perhaps that was why he gave so little away. In fact, his economy was always careful, like that of most of his fellows. The £3 a week of the Edwardian professional left little room for extravagance, and in the effort to economize on their match money many of them had arrangements with the players of opposing counties to save hotel bills by housing one another on a 'home and out' basis.

It was a strange irony which brought together in such a bargain A. E. Knight, the Leicestershire all-rounder, who was a fervent Salvationist, and the big 'roogh' miner who bowled with such fury that he needed beer to give him something to sweat out, and who unloaded his emotions in words as hard as his bowling. For years, the dressing rooms cherished the story of Albert Edward Knight, given a camp bed in the Wass family bedroom, and, saying his prayers within the hearing of his host, closing with 'Please, Lord, let me make a century tomorrow. Amen.' There was, they say, a creaking of the springs of the Wass bed, Tom fell upon his knees, introduced himself to the Almighty as one whose voice might not be well known in those regions, but who was the Nottingham fast bowler and who prayed that he might be allowed, upon the morrow, to 'bowl beggar out for aught'.

He followed the hounds for many years in those strong black boots of his. He had a good run, and would, I fancy, relish the thought that, like many a fox of those distant winters, he has gone to his Nottinghamshire earth.

NEVILLE CARDUS

Robinson of Yorkshire (1934)

A few summers ago I arrived at Bradford an hour or two late for the first day of a match between Yorkshire and Middlesex; I got mixed up with a train connection round about the wilds of Low Moor. As soon as I reached the field my eyes went straight to Emmott Robinson, like the eyes of the lover to the beloved. At once I saw that something was wrong with the man. Middlesex were batting, and the scoreboard said 128 for 2. 'What's been doing?' I asked a man in the crowd, using the vernacular. 'Nowt,' he said, 'nowt but slow play – and Emmott missed Hearne when he was fower.' Hearne was now 57 not out; Emmott Robinson walked across the wicket between overs with his head down. He was a man who took Yorkshire cricket seriously. That day at Bradford he did not look up until, at four o'clock, he bowled Hearne all over his stumps. Just before he achieved this desire he appealed for leg before wicket against Hearne, appealed with all his heart and soul and lungs. I happened to be watching the game from behind the bowler, with glasses fixed on Hearne. I saw that Hearne's legs were not quite in front, and involuntarily I murmured, 'Not out.' Immediately I felt that somebody was observing me. I turned round and saw a typical Yorkshireman eyeing me from my feet to my head. 'And what's the matter with thee?' he asked.

All Yorkshiremen are like that at cricket, and Robinson summed them all up in himself. When Yorkshire were playing Lancashire at Old Trafford a season or two ago they somehow found themselves in a dreadful hole on the third afternoon. With only a draw to play for, they had lost five wickets at half past three; they were hundreds of runs behind. In came Robinson, and he fought the good fight. For two hours and more he defended, bat and pads and all. Ten minutes before close of play, when Yorkshire had but two wickets in hand, Robinson died the hero's death – lbw. He waited a while after he saw the umpire's finger go up, waited on the off chance that some mistake had been made. Then he proceeded to depart. You could not say he was not going, was not definitely moving in Time and Space from one point to another. The retreat was masterful; it was a strategic withdrawal. Alas! the scheme miscarried, through the incredible impulsiveness of Waddington, who rushed to the wicket, ran yards down the pitch and was stumped. Lancashire won first innings points with two minutes to spare.

Months afterwards, in the depth of winter, I was in Yorkshire at a dinner. Who should be sitting next to me but Emmott Robinson? (He ordered a cup of tea after the dinner, saying that he thought coffee 'were no good' for anybody after a meal.) I had forgotten the match at Old Trafford, and Waddington's rashness. But the wound was still bleeding for Emmott. 'Think of it,' he said. 'Gettin' stumped wi' t'match in that state.' He paused, and then, looking at me terribly, he said, 'I'd 'a' died first before they stumped me.' He meant it; Emmott meant everything he ever said about cricket, or did about cricket, in all his life. He once told me how Derbyshire were put out by Yorkshire at Chesterfield for 86. 'But,' he added, 'they should never 'a' got them. Townsend were missed before he scored. They should never 'a' got them.' He was referring to a match that had taken place six years ago. 'Never mind, Emmott,' I said, in the hope of consoling him, 'it all happened a long time ago.' He smote the table with his fist. 'It's no matter,' he answered, 'they should never 'a' got them!' He will die in that belief.

No cricketer has played the game with more than Robinson's grand passion. He was one of the richest characters in the game's great seasonal comedy. He bowled the finest outswinger of his period; he could use the new ball with more venom than any other bowler. He loved what he called a 'green wicket', and at the beginning of a match it was a joy to see him inspecting the turf, pressing his fingers in it, feeling it and talking of 't'texture' like a shrewd buyer of cloth testing material. He could tell you exactly what the wicket would be doing at half past four. Yorkshire once batted the whole of the first day against Surrey and made 400 for 6. On the Sunday the weather broke. Yorkshire continued their innings on the Monday while the wicket was slow and gradually becoming difficult. Everybody was asking when Yorkshire were going to declare. I watched the morning's first hour in the Yorkshire dressing room, and Emmott and Major Lupton and I sat and talked. The game at this stage was not particularly interesting and we talked of many things. Suddenly a ball jumped up; Emmott was in the middle of a sentence. 'Aye, and I told him' – then the ball jumped – 'I told him (call 'em in, Major), I told him . . .' Robinson missed nothing.

He was not in technique a cricketer of extraordinary gifts, but by taking thought he added yards to his stature. He bowled as though nothing in the world existed at the moment but the batsman at the wicket's other end; he would gather up all his loose energy and hurl himself at Makepeace as though at an object detestable. I remember how once he defeated Makepeace's bat with a glorious swinger, and appealed for leg before. It was the last ball of the over, and when the umpire said 'Not out,' Robinson stood still, not comprehending, baffled at the inadequacy of justice in the world. So upset was he that he ran to his wrong place in the field. Against Worcestershire on a certain occasion he decided to field 'silly point' for M. K. Foster, who was in form and hitting the ball hard. 'If I were you,' said Foster solicitously, 'I'd move back a little, Emmott.' And Emmott simply remained where he was and said, 'Get on with thi lakin', Mr Foster.'

Cricket was Emmott Robinson's mission; Yorkshire was his religion. Only once did he ever forget himself. He was saving a match with Rhodes, and against Lancashire, of all counties. Over after over Robinson stonewalled. Suddenly, for no reason whatever, he made a magnificent late cut towards third man off Richard Tyldesley. He was so taken out of himself by the brilliance of the stroke that he stood there, transfixed. And when at last he returned from the world of aesthetic contemplation to the world of things as they are, Wilfred Rhodes was on his doorstep. Emmott was run out by the length of the pitch. No doubt he has not forgiven himself to this day, and no doubt he never will. He and Rhodes were the brains of the great Yorkshire team of their conquering period. I can see the two of them now, watching Roy Kilner flashing his bat at Macdonald's pace. Roy Kilner was incorrigible; the Yorkshire grimness could not be taught him. Humour would creep in with Kilner, even on an

August Bank Holiday at Sheffield. I can see him trying to cut Macdonald, with his cap all a-cock over his eye. 'Hey, look at him!' said
Emmott to Wilfred. 'He'll never get sense, never get sense.'

Robinson seemed to be made out of the stuff of Yorkshire county;
I imagine that the Lord one day gathered together a heap of Yorkshire
clay and breathed into it and said, 'Emmott Robinson, go on and
bowl at the pavilion end for Yorkshire.' He looked the old soldier,
with his lined face and fine grey hairs. He shambled about the
field with his trousers loose. You were getting ready to see them fall
down altogether when he would remember them in time. His feet
were noble. And thrive he did though bandy. I loved the man, and
the crowd loved him, because he did his job with all his heart. His
cricket was of a kind that could never be estimated by the averages,
by statistics; it was an activity that came out of his own being. Of
ordinary cricketers there is little to be said when they are not doing
well; on such occasions we overlook them. Robinson was always in
the game passionately; indeed, it was in moments of frustration that
he was at his most impressive. He had an eloquent droop of the
body in his hours of impotence. You see, he expected to take a
wicket every ball. Lancashire and Yorkshire matches, and perverse
umpires, silvered his head. Often have I looked at his fine keen face
and loved the lines in it, graven by experience. He enriched the
nature of cricket, put into it the humours of the soil, invested it with
character. Like Tom Emmett, he belongs to Yorkshire for all time.

DAVID FOOT

Character in the Counties (1998)

There was for years a defiant reluctance on my part to accept that
cricket wasn't always full of sunshine. Those of us blessed, even
blinkered, by a consuming romantic regard for many aspects of sport
are apt to take it badly when we at last discover that the clouds can
hang heavy over the dressing rooms and that cricketers can be as
contentious, unendearing and egregious in temperament as the rest
of the human race.

I clung to the uplifting image, from my idolatrous school days,
of Wellard and Andrews, Somerset's bronzed giants and fast bowlers,
coming weary and contented off the field at the close of play,

brotherly arms round each other's shoulders, ready for a shared, strong pint and happy talk of a day's work well done. In a country boy's naivety, I noted that Bev and Dar Lyon opposed each other in the Gloucestershire–Somerset Bank Holiday matches and supposed that family feeling on those occasions carried the good-humoured exchanges that I watched amid the buttercups on my village green. What I didn't know was that the Lyons, unlike in demeanour and philosophy, were apt to bare their teeth, for the duration of the match at least, in competitive sibling zeal and rivalry.

My cricket-watching was mostly limited to the West Country. I saw what I wanted to see. Gimblett rattled the sight screen in the first over; I was in awe of his daring and knew nothing of his despair. Hammond was a Bristol prince, wondrous in his deeds, and I assumed there was always congenial banter among the courtiers. One of my first, hard, lessons in sporting realism came, I remember, when Bill Andrews confided in that subjective way of his: 'Those Gloucester-shire players really were a miserable lot of sods. I'd poke my head round the door of the dressing rooms and, apart from Reg Sinfield, I didn't seem to get any kind of greeting.'

Bill was of course the definitive Somerset partisan. Was he being hard on his traditional West Country opponents? I arrived in Bristol in the mid 1950s, having by then rid myself, by the daily disciplines of my chosen craft, of at least the outer layer of cricket's incessant romanticism. My kindly sports editor told me how difficult the revered Wally had been immediately after the war, and that there was a certain cold rigidity about the Gloucestershire hierarchy.

This I was to discover for myself. Basil Allen, master of foxhounds and belonging to the old social tradition as captain, had just gone. So had Sir Derrick Bailey, a quaint choice, and Jack Crapp, a quiet, delightful man but misplaced leader. George Emmett was the next captain. He was a small man with a strong, leathery face and a military manner that reflected his background. He frightened a few of the young pros and maybe did them good. But I never saw him smile in the surrounds of the county ground. He was a martinet, making the rules as assertively as any amateur. Away from the ground I got on well with him, taking surreptitious looks at the wrists which mocked his size and magically created the most exquisite of boundaries.

By now I was coming to the demoralizing conclusion that cricket

wasn't all fun. Those relaxed faces and twinkling eyes on the treas-
ured cigarette cards, stacked with past issues of *Radio Fun* alongside
my cosy cottage bed, had apparently deceived me all the time. I
began the painful business of intensifying my research with as much
dispassion as I could muster. There was, as a starting point, the case
of Herbert Tremenheere Hewett.

He had been an early hero of mine. It wasn't just the grandeur
of the name or the fact that he was born just outside Taunton. I
knew he'd gone to Harrow and gained a blue at Oxford. Such things
were of minimal interest in my youthful imaginings. But I did keep
for years a faded print of him and Lionel Palairet, standing self-
consciously in front of the scoreboard at the county ground on the
day they scored 346 for the first wicket, against Yorkshire. It's still a
Somerset record. The stand, in 1892, took not much more than three
and a half hours. Hewett, the pugnacious left-hander, was then
bowled by Bobby Peel.

I came to acquire all the most inconsequential, meaningless things
about him: that he was known as 'The Colonel', that he was meant
to go in for law, that he picked his teeth. Such relative trivia vied in
my undimmed affection with the statistics. I assumed he was a fine
captain; I knew he could drive, or more so pull, as well as anyone
around in the West in those late-Victorian days (Grace and a few
dozen others were not part of my self-chosen sporting education). It
never occured to me there might be something odd about the fact
that he played no more than fifty times for his county and then left
abruptly.

The truth came to me gradually. Herbert Hewett had been
notorious in the Taunton dressing room for the acerbity of his
tongue, the dogmatic nature of his opinions and the hypersensitive
way he reacted to any critical observation. He could win games for
Somerset by his powerful, exciting stroke play. But he also had a
penchant for snatching up his belongings and leaving the ground in
a huff when something offended him.

He was very angry indeed about the manner he was blamed for
the fiasco in 1893 when the Australians came to Taunton, were told
conditions were unfit for play and went off for a picnic on the
Quantocks instead. The umpires, under pressure – as hundreds of
angry spectators waited impatiently for admission – reversed their
decision, and play started in late afternoon. Hewett was the scapegoat, or so he considered, and he never forgave the county. He

appeared to sulk when it was his turn to bat and gave his wicket away. Soon after that, he had resigned.

My natural sympathies were with him for a long time. I saw him only thumping his fours through midwicket. Why not blame the rest of the Somerset committee or the umpires? Yet I was to discover that there was often fire in his nostrils. Two years after he left the county he was asked to lead an England side against Yorkshire in the Scarborough Festival. It was quite an honour for someone who had almost been forgotten.

Just as for the visit of the Australians two years before, there was too much rain. The umpires looked at the puddles and said play was impossible. Hewett was more flexible this time. He accepted that the festival crowd wanted some cricket at the appointed hour but was overruled. The spectators turned on him. Explanations could doubtless have been given in the public prints the following day. Hewett had no intention to wait around. He changed and left the ground. F. R. Spofforth, 'The Demon' no less, took over.

Was I, as a lad, needlessly selective in my reading habits? I simply took for granted that there could be no better life than that of a county cricketer. I was seduced by the iridescent caps, the freshly creased cream flannels, the observed ritual, the civilized applause; above all, the aesthetic beauty of the game. It left no room for malice.

But alas, it was there all the time. The counties' history books have since revealed the extent of peevish attitudes, pettiness, mean-spiritedness and even fisticuffs. In Victorian and Edwardian England, the poor old pros were paid badly and often drank too much. Theirs was a claustrophobic, frustrated world. Merit was apt to be squeezed out by social clout. Weary professionals were over-bowled and sweated in the outfield. At night, in the nearest sawdust bar, they occasionally got on each other's nerves.

There are tales of exchanged blows, most of them wisely undocumented. It is unlikely that many of the haymakers were in the class of the one the Aussie captain Clem Hill delivered at the expense of fellow selector Peter McAlister. Committee-room folklore suggests that moment of summary justice found plenty of approval.

Threats to suspend fixtures with other counties were not unusual. Ask Yorkshire and Lancashire. And, of course, any side which had Archie MacLaren and Walter Brearley around at the same time could expect a few ructions. The handsome MacLaren was no favourite of mine because of the 424 he dared to score against my native county. Based on geographical allegiance and little else, I labelled him a self-opinionated authoritarian. But I knew he moaned a good deal, at times pedantically, and once refused to go on with a match against Middlesex at Lord's over allegations of pitch damage. Once he huffed so much, too, that he was on the point of walking out on Lancashire to join Hampshire. As for the excitable Brearley, he bowled full tosses at Gloucestershire after one unseemly row. And, more dramatically than MacLaren, he was always threatening to resign.

Who was the most tetchy first-class cricketer of all? Bob Wyatt, with his lugubrious features and taciturn approach, looked it. Shortly before he died, I was lucky enough to spend a day with him in his Cornish home. He was unwell, but the charm was boundless. We stopped for a tea interval: buttered toast and raspberry jam, served ritualistically by Molly, his devoted wife. 'Bob had this reputation of being bad-tempered, I can assure you it was misplaced. The thing was he had this kind of permanent scowl on his face,' she told me.

I wasn't present when Viv Richards made his unscheduled call at the press box at the Recreation Ground, St John's, when he should have been leading out the West Indian team. I was around when Ian Botham made an impulsive diversion towards a taunting spectator, after being dismissed in a Somerset match. Momentarily I feared for the consequences. 'Both' was at a low point and the shot had been that of a neurotic batsman; my sympathies were with him entirely. It was right that the insensitive fan was made to apologize.

His contemporaries, players and scribes, cited Sydney Barnes as 'a very difficult customer'. He stood erect and intimidating, in expression alone. We ceaselessly argue, however skimpy the evidence he chose to give us of himself as a county bowler, that he was the best of all. He articulated his worth and one didn't question it. S. F. Barnes was a respected rather than loved man.

We could all compile lists of prickly cricketers, our judgements in many cases influenced by a personal experience or relayed tale. Some of the Middlesex players retained reservations about Walter Robins. It should have been a cordial occasion when the England team left for the 1959–60 tour of the West Indies on the banana boat from Avonmouth. The press had been invited to wish the party, which included local boy David Allen, *bon voyage*. For some obscure reason, the manager, Robins, wasn't enamoured of the idea. He was in a bad temper, and the memories for me of that tour were affected by that needless rebuff. The reporters were hustled off the boat, without explanation, work undone. It seemed to me poor psychology and poor manners on the manager's part. Why were we asked on board in the first place?

The lack of joy is something I continue to resent. It conflicts too drastically with the game that, in my innocence, I cherished so much. During the 1950s, when I first found myself regularly covering first-class cricket (and asked for nothing more from my profession), it bothered me when players recurrently nominated Surrey as their least favourite county. This was the Surridge era. They were winning a great deal and I suspected an element of envy. Then I saw them up close. They were noisy; several of their bowlers were excessive in the tone of their challenges. And I went off them.

The captains, Surridge and then Peter May, would have justified that combative edge. But I remember one specific match involving Surrey on a lovely day under blue skies. For me there was no sunshine at all. Have any of us, I suppose one must ask, the right to ignore the vagaries of the human condition and hope for a permanently warm-hearted weather report?

* * *

Another county cricketer now, altogether more obscure than the ones previously celebrated. But this one gave his name to one of the most famous of all fictional characters. As the son of the man who 'discovered' Jeeves, Rowland Ryder is ideally placed to write about him.

ROWLAND RYDER

The Unplayable Jeeves (1995)

In the late summer of 1910, my father, then Warwickshire secretary, was on a walking holiday in his native Yorkshire and stayed one night in the village of Hawes. Using his murderous cut-throat razor, he had mistimed a stroke while shaving; a visit to the local doctor was necessary. The doctor, having dealt with the cut, prescribed a visit to the afternoon's cricket match, and here, on the lovely ground at Hawes, my father saw a young cricketer whose effortless grace as a bowler told something of his potential. At the end of the innings he said to him, 'How would you like to play for Warwickshire?' That was how the Jeeves saga began.

In those days there was a two-year qualification period in force, so in 1911 – when Warwickshire won the championship for the first time – he played no first-class cricket. In 1912, the year of the Triangular Tournament, he played for Warwickshire against the Australians. He failed with the bat, making 1 (run out), and o, but did better with his bowling, taking 2 for 35. 'Tiger' Smith gave him his first wicket, snapping up the obdurate Kelleway.

The seasons 1913 and 1914 were to be Jeeves's years of glory.

In 1913, playing in his first championship game at Edgbaston, against Leicestershire, he made 46 and 23. Opening the bowling with F. R. Foster he took 3 for 24 and 5 for 37, playing a major part in his team's victory. This early-season promise was fulfilled. His fast-medium deliveries, with their lightning speed off the pitch, yielded a rich harvest: 106 batsmen, including J. B. Hobbs, were victims to his flowering genius. He was top of his county's bowling averages, his wickets costing 20 runs apiece.

In 1914 Percy Jeeves went from strength to strength. Playing for the Players against the Gentlemen he took 4 for 44, his scalps including those of Spooner and Fry. Michael Falcon, who played in the match, had vivid memories of Jeeves's deliveries biting into the soft pitch, and throwing up pieces of turf – 'I said "Hullo, here's someone!"' In the last match that he ever played at Edgbaston, he took 5 for 52 in Surrey's first innings, clean bowling Surrey's opening batsmen, Tom Hayward and Jack Hobbs. He was showing marked ability, too, as an aggressive middle-order batsman; in a lively 70 against Yorkshire he hit one bowler out of the ground and into the Edgbaston road. Chief of all, it was expected that he would develop into a bowler of world class.

Percy Jeeves became engaged to Annie Austin, younger sister of George Austin, the Warwickshire scorer. When war broke out against Germany, Jeeves joined the Warwickshire Regiment, and was killed in the battle of the Somme on 22 July 1916. Annie Austin, who lived into her eighties, never married.

What is the connection between these two who share the name Jeeves, the inimitable butler – 'Not the yellow spats, sir' – and the splendid bowler? After forty years the question that had often been vaguely in my mind took definite shape: had P. G. Wodehouse chosen the name as a result of seeing Percy Jeeves in the cricket field?

In 1967 I had adapted *The Code of the Woosters* into play form and was producing it at a school in Norfolk, and during the same period I was also writing a feature article for *Wisden*, 'Warwickshire the Unpredictable'. It seemed at that time that I was perpetually face to face with Jeeves. Was there a connection? After all, Conan Doyle got the name for Sherlock Holmes from a Derbyshire cricketer named Shacklock; could not Wodehouse, who was in the Dulwich XI of 1900, have followed a similar course?

If anyone knew it would be the Master himself, so I looked up his address in *Who's Who* and wrote to him, asking if he had named Jeeves of the Junior Ganymede after Percy Jeeves of the Warwickshire Cricket Club. Back came the reply from Remsenburg, Long Island, almost in less time than it takes to say 'How's that?':

> Yes, you are quite right. It must have been in 1913 that I paid a visit to my parents in Cheltenham and went to see Warwick-shire play Gloucestershire in the Cheltenham College Ground.
>
> I suppose Jeeves's bowling must have impressed me, for I remembered him in 1916 when I was in New York and starting the Jeeves and Bertie saga, and it was just the name I wanted. I have always thought till lately that he was playing for Gloucestershire that day. (I remember admiring his action very much.)

Warwickshire did, in fact, play Gloucestershire at Cheltenham in 1913: Percy Jeeves took 0 for 43 in 17 overs, and 1 for 12 in 7 overs – evidently bowling without the luck that even the best player needs, but bowling well enough for P. G. Wodehouse to remember his action three years later.

Excited at the news about Jeeves, I took the liberty of sending PGW a Warwickshire tie. In a delightful letter of acceptance he wrote that the tie was much admired in the family and that it is 'the only one I wear nowadays'. Naturally, I thought that this statement was simply an example of Wodehouse's courtesy. However, when Michael Davie went out to the States to interview him for the *Observer* colour supplement in connection with PGW's ninetieth birthday, it was interesting to see from the photographs that he was indeed wearing the Warwickshire tie. Michael Davie noticed that the

tie was a little worse for wear, having been singed in places by
embers from the Master's pipe. Hearing of this, Leslie Deakins, the
Warwickshire secretary, sent him another tie, which was pleasantly
acknowledged . . .

He wore the Warwickshire tie for the remainder of his life; he
sported it at his ninetieth birthday celebrations and, when he received
a second one from the Warwickshire secretary, he had virtually
become an honorary member of the club that played its home
matches only an hour's drive from the Cheltenham ground where
he saw the inimitable Jeeves.

*   *   *

Our next set of essays rehabilitates local heroes who, but for chance
or history, could very well have become great stars. C. L. R. James
writes of a Trinidadian batsman whose followers experienced an
unspeakable sadness when he failed on his only tour of England.
Matthew Engels remembers an altogether atypical English opener, a
striker of fours and sixes, whose career was ended early by accident.
In writing of the unfulfilled hopes of Dik Abed, Dale Slater also
indicts the system of apartheid, which prohibited the emergence of
black and coloured cricketers of talent. Finally, Philip Snow writes
lovingly of an untrained but gloriously effective Fijian hitter, who in
a more globalized world would have set Lord's alight.

<h1 style="text-align:center">C. L. R. JAMES</h1>

The Most Unkindest Cut (1963)

Wilton St Hill. In my gallery he is present with Bradman, Sobers,
George Headley and the three Ws, Hutton and Compton, Peter May
and a few others. To them he is a stranger. But when he takes his
turn at the mythical nets they stop to look at him and then look at
one another: they recognize that he belongs. That, however, is what
I have to prove. I am playing a single-wicket match on a perfect
wicket against a line of mighty batsmen. But great deeds have been

done under similar conditions. This is my opportunity to make history. Here goes.

W. St Hill was just about six feet or a little under, slim, wiry, with forearms like whipcord. His face was bony, with small sharp eyes and a thin, tight mouth. He was, I think the expression is, flat-footed and never gave the impression of being quick on his feet. His first, and I believe his greatest, strength was judging the ball early in the flight. When in form he could play back to anything, including George John at his fastest. He never got in front in advance, but almost as soon as the ball was out of the bowler's hand he had decided on his stroke and took position. No one I have seen, neither Bradman nor Sobers, saw the ball more quickly, nor made up his mind earlier. Time; he always had plenty of time. From firm feet he watched the ball until it was within easy reach and only then brought his bat to it with his wrists. He never appeared to be flurried, never caught in two minds. With most of his strokes the only sign of tension or effort was the head very slightly bent forward on the shoulders so as to assist the concentration of his eyes riveted on the ball. But you had to be near to see that. I do not remember any more frightening sight at cricket than John running, jumping and letting loose at his terrific pace, and St Hill playing back as if he had known he would have to do so long before the ball was bowled and was somewhat bored by the whole business. You felt that he was giving the ferocious John legitimate reason to hurl the ball at him or take him by the shoulders and shake him. In all his strokes, even the most defensive, the ball always travelled. I have taken people who knew nothing at all about cricket to see him and as soon as they saw this easy, erect, rhythmic back stroke to the fast bowler they burst into murmurs of admiration. His right toe was always towards point, left elbow high and left wrist as a fulcrum.

Playing so late, he preferred to score behind point and behind square leg. His famous stroke was the leg glance. It is a modern fetish that long leg makes this stroke only decorative and I was glad to see Burke's leg glance in 1956 repeatedly beat long leg standing on the boundary. For wizardry Ranjitsinhji's leg glance, when he crossed the left foot over towards point and flicked the ball to fine leg, comes first. St Hill's leg glance was of the same unnatural stamp. To a ball a little over the good length on the middle or middle and leg he advanced the left leg a short distance straight at the ball, so that if he missed he was lbw for sure. With the leg almost straight and his body bending slightly over it from the waist, he took the ball as it rose from the matting and wristed it where he chose towards the leg boundary. From accounts and photographs it can be seen that Ranjitsinhji had to make a sharp twist of the body as well as the wrist. St Hill bent forward slightly from the waist and flicked his wrist – that was all. He never followed round with the right foot. He put the ball where he pleased and John, being the finest bowler, was, of course, the chief sufferer. Describing his play in 1928, *Wisden* of 1929 says in one place that he showed fine strokes on the off side and in another that he was strong on the leg side. When Wilton was 'on the go' that depended entirely on the bowler. My negative memory may be at fault here, but I do not remember ever seeing a batsman standing straight, waiting for the shortish rising ball and as it passed flicking it between the slips. He didn't cut these down. He merely touched them and then pulled the bat away. That seemed sufficient to send them flying to the boundary.

The short fast ball of ordinary height he could get back to for a slash behind point, but he preferred to cut late. The finest of all his cuts was the late cut off the slow bowler, to beat first slip and yet give third man no chance. To save that four on a fast ground third man would have had to stand on the boundary behind second slip, which would have been both ridiculous and useless. All that it would have meant was his running like crazy back to the usual position. One afternoon at the Queen's Park Oval in 1926 Percy Holmes, fielding at deep third man and on the boundary behind the bowler, gave a great exhibition. St Hill had him running now thirty yards for the on drive and then the other way for the off drive. But it was the late cuts to third man that gave Holmes the most trouble. He couldn't anticipate the stroke. We had a wonderful time with Holmes, asking him if he had ever seen in his life strokes like those. The little Yorkshireman never relaxed for an instant and chased each ball like a hare, but he had time and strength to talk to us and admire this superlative batting. Each time St Hill made a stroke we could see Holmes smile as he ducked his head to chase the ball.

I never had enough of talking to St Hill about this late cut. In so far as it was explicable, his secret was that he never timed the ball from the pitch, as I have seen great batsmen do and get out. He did not lie back and lash across, as George Cox used to do. He didn't hammer the bat into the ground as Frank Worrell does (one of the great strokes of our time). He took up position early, watched the ball well on its way and then launched his wrists into the stroke.

This modern theory that the leg glance does not pay is a fetish, first because you can place the ball, and secondly if you can hook then the life of long leg is one long frustration. St Hill did not hook by preference to long leg. (None of us used the modern theory of getting outside the ball first. We faced the ball square so that if you missed it hit you.) He seemed merely to step inwards and swish the blade across the flight so that when it hit the ball it was pointing at the bowler. The ball went past the square-leg umpire like a bullet. If the square-leg boundary was blocked he might move over and, leaning towards point, flick over his shoulder. But there was no catch to long leg. The ball dropped twenty or thirty yards from his bat. He was completely master of the on side. He played the back glance as well as his own special. To bowlers experimenting around his leg stump he sometimes upset all calculations by waiting until the ball was almost on him and making a late on drive, almost all right wrist with practically no follow-through. The ball went between mid-on and the bowler to the boundary, making monkeys of all the fieldsmen on the leg side.

So far he was all grace, all elegance, always there long in advance. But there was a primitive hidden in him. If a fast bowler blocked his leg glance – it was no use putting short legs for he kept the ball down, *always* – or sometimes for no visible reason, all this suavity disappeared. He stretched his left foot down the wicket and, with a sweep that seemed to begin from first slip and encompassed the whole horizon, smashed the ball hard and low to square leg. Sweep is not the correct word. It was a swing, begun when the ball was almost within reach, and carried out with a violence that seemed aimed at the ball personally, to hit it out of sight or break it into bits.

One afternoon I bowled the first ball of a match which swung from his leg stump past the off. He played forward at it and missed. Full of eagerness and anticipation, I let loose the next as fast as I could, aiming outside the leg stump to swing into him. Out came his left foot, right down the pitch. He seemed to be waiting for hours for the ball to reach, and then he smashed it to the square-leg boundary. Root could get the ball to swing in British Guiana, and in 1926 he was at the height of his form. St Hill made 75 for the All West Indies XI and when the players came back they told us that when St Hill was batting, Root's short legs were an apprehensive crew. They were concerned with him, not he with them. I have seen a bunch of short legs cower when a batsman shaped at a loose one, but kept my eye on Tony Lock and saw him bend at the waist a little and face it. Time enough to dodge when he had seen the stroke. You couldn't do that with St Hill's stroke because no fieldsman could sight the ball off that ferocious swish.

His off drive to a fast bowler was of the same ferocity. He used to tell me that on the fast Barbados turf wicket all you had to do was to push forward and the ball went for four. He would outline the stroke and even though we might be standing in the street under a street light, his left elbow, and even the left shoulder, would automatically swing over and the right wrist jerk suddenly and check. His body would be curiously straight, but the head would be bent over the imaginary ball and his eyes would shine. On the matting, with its uncertain rise, he put the left foot well over, the toe usually pointing to cover, not to mid-off. He took the bat so far back, at the end of the back lift it was parallel to the ground with the blade facing the sky. From there he swung with all he had and smashed the fast ball through the covers. A minute later he would be standing almost as if back on his heels (with his head, however, slightly forward) playing the ball back along the ground to the bowler, often as if he were not looking at it. In moments of impishness he would move his feet out of the way, drop the bat sideways on the leg-stump yorker and disdain even to look at the ball racing to the boundary. But this I have seen him do only in friendly games, though I have been told that in earlier days he would do it even in competition matches, and Constantine, who played with him in the Shannon side for years, writes of it as a habit of his. One of his regular phrases in talking about a batsman was 'on the go'. He would say, 'When Challenor is on the go . . .' or 'When Hammond is on the go . . .' For him batting began only when a batsman was 'on the go'. All the rest was preliminary or fringe. I have seen no player whose style could give any idea of St Hill's. The closest I have read of is the Australian boy, Jackson, and perhaps Kippax.

His play has come to mean much in my estimate of the future of cricket. One afternoon, some time in the 1920s, Griffith, the Barbados fast bowler, was bowling to St Hill from the pavilion end at the Queen's Park Oval in an inter-colonial match. Griff was bowling fast, and this afternoon he was almost as fast as John. The ball hit on the matting, and then, s-h-h-h, it plumped into the hands of the wicketkeeper standing well back. All of us noted the unusual speed. Griff was as canny then as he was in England in 1928, and in fact there could never have been a fast bowler who so disliked being hit and took so much pains to avoid it. Griff would not bowl short to St Hill on the matting wicket: he knew he would be mercilessly hooked. He kept the ball well up, swinging in late from outside the off stump to middle and off or thereabouts. The field was well placed, mid-off fairly straight, short extra cover to pick up the single, deep extra cover, deep point for accidents, the leg side well covered. Griffith had his field set and he bowled to it. That was his way. He was as strong as a horse, he always bowled well within himself, and he would wait on the batsman to give him an opening. He didn't know his St Hill.

St Hill watched him for an over or two while we shivered with excitement tinged with fear. We had never seen Wilton up against bowling like this before and he was surely going to do something. (One thing we knew he would not do, and that was in any way hit across the flight of a pitched-up ball.) Soon he countered. With his left shoulder well up, almost scooping up the ball, his body following through almost towards point, St Hill lifted Griff high over mid-off's head for four. Griff moved away a bit and then came back again to be sent hurtling over mid-off's head once more. He dropped mid-off back. St Hill cleared mid-off's head again. *I am pretty sure he had never had to make that stroke before in his life.* But he was 'on the go' and if to remain on the go required the invention of a stroke on the spot, invented it would be . . .

The West Indies selectors left St Hill out of the 1923 team. It did not come as a sudden blow. There were two or three trial matches. He failed in them and they left him out. If they had decided to ignore the trial failures not a soul would have said anything. But they left him out and it was as if a destined Prime Minister had lost his seat in the elections. He maintained his usual silence and it was not the sort of thing I would have raised with him. The blow shook him badly, he was a man of exceeding pride, and it is my belief that he never fully recovered from it. I expect that is one of the differences in temperament that make for success or for failure. As for us, his friends and admirers, that wound was never to heal.

This is what we believed. The great West Indian batsman of the day, before the 1923 tour, was Percy Tarilton, not George Challenor.

Challenor was his superior in style, and the Barbados masses worshipped him. But Tarilton stood first in reliability and solidity. Next to these two was D. W. Ince, a white left-hander, also from Barbados. British Guiana had another white batsman, M. P. Fernandes. This was the traditional order, a line of white batsmen and a line of black bowlers. Joe Small had made for himself a place as a batsman which could not be denied. Joe was enough. They didn't want any more. Further, Joe was an inoffensive person. St Hill was not in any way offensive. Far from it. But he was not friendly.

As we pursued our notes and observations after the dreadful event, some of us went further. We became convinced in our own minds that St Hill was the greatest of all West Indian batsmen and on English wickets this coloured man would infallibly put all white rivals in the shade. And they too were afraid of precisely the same thing, and therefore were glad to keep him out. We were not helped by the fact that in our heart of hearts we didn't know exactly how good he was. We hadn't seen an English team since 1912, and it was only after Challenor's unqualified success in England in 1923 that we had reliable standards to go by. We terribly wanted to say not only to West Indians but to all England, 'That's our boy.' And now we couldn't. On performance Small rivalled St Hill. But Joe never aroused the excitement that Wilton did.

We were neither mean nor vicious. If Challenor had failed to score in every innings of the trial matches we would have protested loudly against any idea of his exclusion. If through loss of form Challenor or Tarilton could have been included only by dropping St Hill we would have made faces but we would have swallowed the dose. Furthermore, the case was not at all simple. Jamaica had to have so many, British Guiana had to have its share. We would have been hard put to it to say whom to leave out. We burned our fingers badly in that very tour. Griffith had made his reputation as a fast bowler in 1921. Griffith had had a secondary education, called nobody mister except the captain, H. B. G. Austin, and had the reputation of being ready to call anybody anything which seemed to him to apply. When the team was selected Griff was out, and an unknown, a bowler at the Austin nets, had been chosen instead. To us it seemed that here was another flagrant piece of class discrimination. But the unknown bowler was soon to make himself known and never to be forgotten. In his first match against Sussex he took 10 for 83, in his second against Hampshire, 7 for 85, in the third against Middlesex,

9 for 120. This silenced us and when the English newspapers came the chorus of praise showed that in preferring Francis to Griffith, Austin had made a judgement which should have its place in history, for in 1923 Griffith was very, very good, as good if not better than he ever was after.

Finally the man whom we chiefly blamed, H. B. G. Austin, could point to West Indies cricket and say with far more justification than Jack: 'This is the house that I built. I know what I am about. I chose young Constantine when on the record most of you would have left him out.' That was true. Few would have been surprised if Constantine had not been selected in 1923. But we were sensitized, on the alert for discrimination. In fact I was so upset and for so long that my friends pointed out to me that in my copies of the *Cricketer* I was underlining everything said against the West Indies team.

We had to shut up on Griffith. But St Hill's omission remained in our minds. He recovered and in 1926, when the Englishmen came, he was, as we have seen, second to none in the West Indies. He scored heavily in the 1928 trials and came to England. The rest should be silence. He was a horrible, a disastrous, an incredible, failure, the greatest failure who ever came out of the West Indies. I have heard authoritatively that he would not change his style and he has been blamed for it. I don't think he could even if he had wanted to. He was not the type, and after 1923 something had hardened in him. In 1930, when the MCC came again, the eagle had clipped his own wings at last. He stood up for four hours and made a patient century. An English commentator said he was very experienced and showed defence. Of course he had defence, he had always had it. But when he was 'on the go' it was the bowler who needed defence, not he. He died in 1957, and I was sorry I had not yet written this notice of him as I had always planned to do. I think he would have liked to read it. Who knows? He might even have said something about it.

One question will remain with every cricketer who never saw him: How good was he exactly? Doesn't your memory enshrine a striking figure with an enhancing haze? Perhaps. But I don't think so. Around about 1910 St Hill was a boy of about eighteen. In those days Stingo was the club of bowlers, with George John and six other bowlers, all internationals or intercolonials, men with reputation and with records. Against them St Hill played an innings of which nearly fifty years later Constantine writes as follows:

He was smoking as he walked out; he took his stance, still smoking, glanced idly round the field, then threw away his cigarette. George John – also now gone to the 'great divide' – one of the most formidable fast bowlers who ever handled a ball, thundered up at the other end and sent down a red lightning flash, atomic if you wish – but the slender boy flicked his wrists and the ball flew to the boundary faster than sound. The next ball went the same way. The boy batted from his wrists, he never seemed to use any force. I don't believe he had the strength even if he so desired. His was just perfect timing. Wilton St Hill became famous later, but I never saw him or anyone else play a more heart-lifting innings than he did that day.

Of an innings played in Barbados eighteen years after Constantine writes in a similar strain. Constantine played and bowled with Francis from 1923 to 1933, all over the West Indies, in England and in Australia. Never, he says, did he see any batsman hit Francis as St Hill hit him, and this was in a trial match on which depended his selection for the English tour. We have heard Lord Harris. I can multiply these testimonies. I shall give only one more. Before their first-class season began the 1928 West Indies team played a two-day game. This is what *The Times* correspondent was moved to say:

> ... W. H. St Hill, who can be relied upon to provide the entertainment of the side. He is very supple, has a beautifully erect stance and, having lifted his bat, performs amazing apparently double-jointed tricks with his wrists and arms. Some of those contortions are graceful and remunerative, such as his gliding to leg, but some are unsound and dangerous, such as an exaggerated turn of the wrist in cutting. He will certainly play some big and attractive innings, but some others may be easily curtailed by his exotic fancy in dealing with balls on the off side.

How I treasure that notice: The critic had caught St Hill's quality even in that brief innings. He stood beautifully erect and still and flicked the ball away like a conjuror. His apparently exotic fancies were exotic only when he mistimed them, as he did so often in 1928. Between 1910 and 1926 they were in perfect control by those amazing double-jointed wrists and arms and never more so than on big occasions. For the general, I can sum it up this way. No one batting at the other end could ever have overshadowed him. Of that I am quite certain, and of very few can that be said. It was against the finest bowlers, John, Francis, C. R. Browne, Root, that he was at his best.

For myself, I stick to the technical. He saw the ball as early as anyone. He played it as late as anyone. His spirit was untameable, perhaps too much so. There we must leave it.

MATTHEW ENGEL

A Great Fat Man (1983)

I ought to remember where I was when the news came, as with Kennedy's assassination or the outbreak of war. But to be honest I have no recollection. It was 23 May 1969, and I must have been doing my A Levels. The details of those have been successfully blotted out of my mind since then. The accident in which Colin Milburn lost his left eye and his career must have been thrown out with them.

I do remember that the sinking-in process took longer than usual. Most of us were fooled a little: by inapt comparisons with Pataudi, who played on with his right eye gone; by the wave of hopeful press coverage from the hospitals; by Colin's own quite outstanding bravery. I also remember feeling that if so freakish an injury (why couldn't he just have broken a leg like normal people, for heaven's sake?) could end his career, then it was the saddest possible news for English cricket. Fifteen years on, that thought gnaws at me all the more. Colin Milburn might not have been the greatest cricketer of his generation, but he was, beyond question, the cricketer we could least afford to lose. And we lost him.

I was not and am still not an unbiased observer. Insofar as I ever grew up, I grew up, between bouts of boarding school, in Northampton in the 1960s. This was a bizarre period in English history for many reasons, and one of its minor oddities was that, very briefly, Northampton became the most successful sporting town in the kingdom. In 1965 Northampton Town FC were promoted for their first and only season in the First Division; the rugby club had the best record in England; and the county, after sixty generally disastrous years of first-class cricket, missed the championship by four miserable points. The cricket team was not only good – we had the best and most exciting young batsman in England.

What's more, he was a friend of mine. Well, more like a friend of a friend actually. But he would recognize me and pass the time of day and take an interest. I had never spoken to a real cricketer before, unless he was donating or withholding his autograph, except for the time Lindsay Hassett burnt my hand with a dog-end (and he had retired long since so no one was very impressed about that). It even fell to Colin to coach me at the Easter nets, which he did without losing his temper. On the basis of this flimsy acquaintance I gave up autograph-hunting as infra dig for a friend of the famous. I realized later that Colin was friends with pretty well everyone in Northampton. That turned out to be one of his problems.

Like so many Northamptonshire cricketers, he belonged to the place only by the curious historical fluke that this insignificant and apathetic town (with little else to offer except a reasonably quick train to London) had first-class cricket while County Durham, which unlike Northamptonshire was somewhere non-cricket people had heard of, did not. Colin had arrived via Burnopfield Junior School, Annfield Plain Secondary Modern, Stanley Grammar and Chester-le-Street in the Durham Senior League (all faraway places with strange-sounding names but places with which Northamptonshire kept in touch), because Ken Turner, the secretary, had offered him ten shillings a week more than Warwickshire. This transaction achieved slightly more notice than the acquisition of most young batsmen: Colin had achieved a sort of public notice as a seventeen-year-old schoolboy when he made 101 for Durham against the 1959 Indians. He even got a special mention in the Editor's Notes in the 1960 *Wisden*, amid sections headed 'Yorkshire's Professional Captain' and 'Welcome South Africa'! There was also the fact that he was, as *Wisden* put it, 'a well-built lad' or, to put it another way, fat.

The fat was the first of his trademarks, and the most unconventional. He had always been a tubby boy. In the cold winter of 1963, just as he was becoming established as a county player, he fought against it furiously and went down from eighteen stones to nearer sixteen. Thereafter, though his weight was a regular talking point every April and continued to bother selectors – official and armchair ones – of a certain cast of mind, I think it bothered him less. I often wonder how he might have batted had he slimmed down to fit the popular perception of what a cricketer should look like. His batting style was the second and most important of his trademarks, and it must have derived from the first, since so often all his tonnage went into the shot. Yet I don't think there was anything essentially unconventional about his batting. Memory plays odd tricks. I remember the crashing hook, of course; I remember the booming drive, hit most often past a helpless cover point; yet in the mind's eye I can most easily recall that great bulk leaning forward, ever so correctly, to prod away a ball he did not fancy.

The difference between him and everyone else is that he would hit a 50–50 ball, that anyone else would leave or block, and hit it with immense force. Not every time. There is another potent memory: his return to the old and grubby Northampton pavilion, red-faced and as near as he ever got to angry, after a daft nick to first slip or something when in single figures. For us kids, the day moved on to a lower plane. But the good days were electric and if he got past 20, he rarely stopped before 70.

Years later, after the accident, I umpired a village benefit match in which he thumped harmless bowling all over the place for about an hour and I was able to watch at close quarters the visible signs of how he made up his mind what to hit. It occurred to me then that his secret had not been his bulk, nor his technique, nor even the quickness of his poor, damned eyes but the speed of his reflexes. How else could an eighteen-stone near non-runner come to break the Northamptonshire catching record, which he did, in 1964, with forty-three catches, almost all at pre-helmet short leg?

Those reflexes were never infallible. Nor was his judgement, and sometimes the good days were well spaced out. In 1965, five years after he joined Northamptonshire, he went into the final match still short of his 1,000. Gloucestershire were at the County Ground and Northamptonshire needed to win to be champions. It rained on the first and last days and the fact that Milburn made 152 not out in three and a half hours to get his 1,000 made no difference whatsoever, except to soothe the pain.

That was the beginning of the end of Northampton, Sparta of English sport. The Cobblers had just started their First Division season, though it would be almost another three months before they would win a match. The rugby team went through years of mediocrity. And the county still have not been champions. But

the blazing three-year summer of Colin Milburn's life was just about
to start. The following year was the one in which many championship matches had their first innings restricted to 65 overs. It was one
of those early, faltering attempts to enliven the three-day game in
response to the success of the Gillette Cup. Colin did not need
livening up, but the system suited him very nicely. He began 1966
with two centuries in his first three innings, scored 64 for MCC
against West Indies, then made 171 at Leicester with Alec Bedser
watching. On the Sunday he was in the Test team. Basil D'Oliveira
was also in the twelve for the first time (though on that occasion he
did not play) and I remember being hurt and puzzled by the 'Hello
Dolly' headlines. Milburn did play and soon was being overshadowed
by no one.

Nine Test matches – that's all he had time for. He changed four
beyond recognition, though it is true that England did not win any
of them: a lively but chancy 94 as England went down to that very
strong West Indian team, with Sobers, Hall and all, at Old Trafford
on his debut; the 126 not out in the next Test at Lord's to save the
game (only Colin would save a game by scoring an even-time
century); the amazing, fighting 83 at Lord's against the 1968 Australians on a bad wicket; and the final 139 at Karachi the following
year, of which more anon.

There would have been time for more but the selectors kept
dropping him. Barely a month after the 126 he was gone. He failed
in the third Test at Trent Bridge then made 71 for once out at
Headingley. I suppose that must have been the game when he was
booed for his fielding. I remember it happening somewhere, and
only a Headingley crowd could be that crass. At any rate, he was
gone the next week along with Cowdrey, the captain, and half his
team to make way for the Brian Close era. In that wonderfully
vengeful mood that brings out the best in some cricketers, Milburn
went to play for Northamptonshire at Clacton and scored 203 not
out – a century before lunch, another before tea and a new county
first-wicket record with Prideaux, who made an occasional contribution (both got 0 in the second innings). That year, he was the first
to 1,000, scored the fastest century, hit the most sixes and only
missed 2,000 because of a broken finger. There was no tour for him
to be left out of, so he spent his first happy winter playing for
Western Australia.

He had a more moderate year in 1967. He played in two Tests

but his best score was 40 at Edgbaston the morning Kunderan had to be given the new ball for India, having taken three wickets in his life. Nonetheless he scored the fastest century of the summer (78 minutes this time, four minutes quicker than the previous year) and was picked to go to the West Indies. When he got there, he started slowly, lost out to Edrich for the first Test and became a spare part.

It was quite clear that a good many influential people did not regard Milburn as a business cricketer. After his Lord's 83 the next year ended in a catch on the deep midwicket boundary, one of the selectors commented sourly 'What a way to get out.' He was injured after that and did not return until the Oval-D'Oliveira-Underwood-mopping-up Test, after which he was left out of the South African tour party. Since someone else was also left out, Milburn again found himself overshadowed by D'Oliveira and there are plenty of people around who still believe Milburn's omission was the dafter.

But the curious thing was that Milburn had plenty of detractors in Northampton as well. He had loads of friends. In some cases the same people were in both categories. The County Ground crowds, such as they are, on both the football and cricket sides have long had a fairly well-deserved reputation for sourness. I think the town was much happier when 1965 was over and its teams stopped all this winning nonsense; we could all go back to being happily miserable again. And much of the moaning was at Milburn. There was something not right about all that boozy joviality. Why couldn't he settle down and live and play boringly like you are supposed to do? And poor old Ollie did not seem able to shut them all up by going out and playing one of his really great innings. They always seemed to come somewhere else, somewhere exotic like Lord's or Clacton. Northampton had to be content with some very, very good ones.

Perhaps the greatest of all came that November, even further away. As soon as England left him out of the squad for their non-existent tour to South Africa, Western Australia rang to invite him back. On a fearsomely humid day at the Gabba in Brisbane Milburn went out to open the batting. At lunch he was 61 not out and, rather out of character, complaining; there was so much sweat seeping through his gloves that he could hardly grip the bat. After lunch, the weather cooled a fraction; Milburn went berserk. In the two-hour afternoon session he scored 181. Even Bradman never approached that. He was out the over after tea for 243 and apologized to his teammates. It may not have registered with everyone in Northampton, but for some of us just hearing about it was something.

He was on a Perth beach with (so the story goes and it is almost certainly true) a couple of birds and a good many beers when, three months later, he got the message that England needed him to reinforce the party for the substitute tour of Pakistan. It is generally held among cricketers that Perth is a better place to be than Dacca and the feeling among the England party at that stage of the tour was, by all accounts, that they should fly out to join Milburn rather than the other way round. But he flew in via one of the most convoluted routes in the history of aviation, and the team summoned up enough energy to give him a guard of honour at the airport and con him into believing that there was no room at the Intercontinental with the other lads and so he would have to stay in a dosshouse next to a swamp.

His very presence had brightened the tour. When they moved to Karachi for the final Test, Milburn was picked and played his last, biggest and probably greatest Test innings, 139 on a dead-slow mud pitch at Karachi. As at Northampton, as with the England selectors, he was not wholly appreciated – the crowd were too busy rioting to take much interest. But, as the game was abandoned after the gates were smashed by the crowd, it was generally agreed that whatever else had gone wrong for English cricket that winter – and pretty well everything had – at least Milburn had now emerged as a genuine Test batsman, and not just a slogger.

The summer of 1969 marked the start of the Sunday League which, genuine Test batsman or not, might have been designed for Milburn's personal use. He began the season with 158 against Leicestershire and played his part in a Northamptonshire win over the West Indies. His selection for the first Test was now not even a matter for discussion. And then it happened.

I was a schoolboy still and cannot be certain that all the smiling pictures were not just a front for the camera. But the sister-in-charge said his manner never changed in his eleven days in hospital, the hospital management committee singled him out in their annual report ('his infectious good humour and indomitable spirit raised morale throughout the hospital') and in the years since I have still not glimpsed whatever sadness lurks behind the mask.

Four years later, when he made his brief and abortive comeback, I was just starting to make my way as a cricket writer in Northampton and was close enough to pick up the jealousy among some of the Northamptonshire players who thought he should not be playing. The comeback did not fail by much – with his little bit of medium-pace bowling, he was almost good enough to play county cricket – but the glory had departed and he knew it.

There is a curious historical parallel. After the last match of the 1936 season the two Northamptonshire openers, A. H. Bakewell and R. P. Northway, were returning by car from Chesterfield. Bakewell had scored 241 not out and had almost taken Northamptonshire, the bottom county, to victory over Derbyshire, the top county. Bakewell had played six Tests, three fewer than Milburn. The car crashed, Northway was killed, and Bakewell, who hovered near death for several days, never played again. Thereafter he lived a shadowed and apparently sad life. Colin Milburn spent a good deal of the time (too much, said all Northampton) after his accident in his old corner spot at the bar of the Abingdon Park Hotel, always with a happy group, in shadow, but obviously not in sadness. Then, quietly and suddenly, he left Northampton and returned to County Durham. There are still booze and birds but no marriage and, for a man past forty, no obvious purpose. He has been doing this and that. He still comes to the odd London do. He still smiles. We still chat.

He might yet find his *métier* on the radio. His occasional commentaries have been shrewd and funny and generous, because he does not believe no one else can play. Please may he find his way. His indomitable spirit did not only raise morale at the hospital; it lit up my youth.

Postscript

Colin never did find his way again. On 28 February 1990, seven years after the above piece was published, Colin Milburn collapsed and died in the car park of a county Durham pub. He was forty-eight, a shade younger than I am now. Ian Botham was one of the pallbearers at his funeral. Someone once suggested to me that had he lived until 1992, when Durham became a first-class county, he might have got the job and purpose he craved most desperately. Maybe. He lives on in the memory of everyone who ever met him or watched him hit a boundary.

Matthew Engel

DALE SLATER

Abed and Apartheid (1993)

Suleiman 'Dik' Abed was born in Cape Town in 1943, the last of four brothers in a famous sporting family. The National Party was yet four years from power, and apartheid – racism elevated to an organizing principle – no more than a nasty twinkle in the Broederbond's eye. Still, racist iniquities abounded in South Africa. Among disadvantaged communities, such as the Cape Coloureds, improvisation was the key to life. Thus Dik learned his rugby on gravel, and his cricket on matting and worse.

In a way, though, Dik was lucky, for trails were being blazed ahead of him. In 1950, the separate Coloured, Indian and Black cricket boards amalgamated to form the South African Cricket Board of Control (SACBOC). Thirty years of segregated cricket were thus thrust aside, among non-whites at least, for though there was no impediment, legal or otherwise, to their joining the process, whites chose to ignore these moves toward integration. Thus in 1951 the first Dadabhai Trophy tournament drew together representative teams from all but the white community. The tournament was seen as a stepping stone to the selection of a team representing all sections of non-white South African cricket. Ongoing negotiations to find a suitable opponent were taking place. By 1953, when the Board announced the imminence of a touring team from Kenya, Dik's two eldest brothers, Salie ('Lobo') and Gesant ('Tiney'), were reckoned certainties for the South African side.

In the event, the tour by the Kenya Asians did not take place until 1956. In the intervening period, SACBOC had applied for full membership of the ICC, a move which was blocked by the South African Cricket Association. The historic first-ever Test, played on matting at Hartleyvale, a Cape Town football ground (Newlands had been refused them), saw Salie Abed in the side as keeper. Dik, then twelve years old, was there to see South Africa, under the captaincy of Basil D'Oliveira, cruise to a six-wicket victory.

Gesant had to wait until the second Test to win his colours. But in that match he proved his all-round worth scoring 54 in the middle order as South Africa piled up 377 first innings runs, then taking three vital wickets as the Kenyans, chasing 286 to win the match, fell in the end only 39 runs short. With the rain-ruined Durban Test drawn, the series was won 2–0. South Africa's non-white cricketers had served notice of their talents against a side which included, in Shokoor Ahmed, formerly of Pakistan, at least one international.

In 1958 history was made again when the SACBOC side went on a return tour of East Africa. Again, D'Oliveira was skipper. Again, both Salie and Gesant were included in the party but Dik's third brother, Ghulam, by now a stalwart of the Western Province and South African Malay sides, just missed selection despite a Dadabhai Trophy hundred. According to D'Oliveira, this was the proudest touring team ever to leave South Africa.

They were to return with one of the proudest records too. The tour's opener, against the Kenya Asians, brought their only defeat. East Africa had in the last three years been the recipient of tours by powerful sides such as the Pakistan Cricket Writers' Club (under A. H. Kardar, and including Hanif Mohammed, Imtiaz and Zulfiqar Ahmed and Waqar Hassan), the Indian Sunder CC (with Mustaq Ali as captain, the legendary left-arm all-rounder Vinoo Mankad, and other internationals in Nari Contractor, Jasu Patel, Pankaj Roy, and Tamhane) and Freddie Brown's MCC (featuring Mike Smith, Peter Richardson and John Warr). Yet, as the South African team steamed through the rest of its sixteen-match itinerary, demolishing Kenya twice and a combined East Africa XI along the way, the hosts were to say of their visitors that they were 'as strong a team as any that has visited us'.

Back home things were changing, and not for the better. As, throughout the 1950s, apartheid legislation had begun to bite, so the exodus of talented black people into exile had begun. There were political figures such as Oliver Tambo, writers such as Con Themba, Alex La Guma, Bloke Modisane, Dennis Brutus, and Es'kia Mpahlele, musicians such as Hugh Masekela and Miriam Makeba.

Internally, black opposition expressed itself in campaigns of passive resistance to which white South Africa responded with massive force. In 1960, the Sharpville massacre showed the shape of things to come, and aroused the outrage of the world. 1961 saw white South Africa's response: the severing of Commonwealth ties by the declaration of Republican status. The Treaty of Vereeniging which ended the Boer War in 1902 effectively broke liberal opposition to racism in South Africa. Britain acquiesced thereby in the sacrifice of black aspirations in order to cement unity between English- and Afrikaans-speaking whites in South Africa under the flag of the Empire. Blacks were formally removed from the Common Voters' Roll after the 1910 Act of Union, and liberalism destroyed as a credible political force within South Africa. Now, by cutting contacts, white South Africa sought to minimize liberal pressures from the world at large.

The move was to backfire in the long run as the world turned the tactic back upon them in the shape of the boycott. Meanwhile, white intransigence was radicalizing black opinion. In 1963, Umkhonto We Sizwe, the armed wing of the ANC, was formed. And the movement into exile gathered pace. From the world of sport, Albert Johanneson, Leeds United's flying winger, Green Vigo, a rugby-league legend, and of course, Basil D'Oliveira.

D'Oliveira's rise to fame is well known. He tells in his book how, in order to develop a technique serviceable in first-class cricket, he had first to unlearn everything he'd learned on the 'Burma Road' wickets of South Africa. Yet even this is not the true measure of his achievement. For D'Oliveira's rebellion was against his third-class status both as a cricketer and as a man. In the early 1960s, county cricket had not yet emerged from what C. L. R. James ten years before had diagnosed as 'the Welfare State of Mind'. Only a handful of men seemed able to transcend the limitations of ambition and outlook which had become the uniform of county batsmen. There was Dexter when the mood took him, there was Graveney, there was Ollie Milburn. And then along came Dolly. England fell in love as much with the spirit of the man as with the man himself.

In D'Oliveira's wake came an influx of coloured cricketers from South Africa to the English leagues. Cecil Abrahams, whose son John would one day captain Lancashire, spent fifteen years in the leagues. Others were John Neethling, Desmond February, Rushdi Majiet, Owen Williams and Dik's brother Ghulam, who came at first to play rugby league and stayed to play cricket as both amateur and professional for Rochdale, where he still lives. In 1967 came Dik Abed himself, when, on the strength of a recommendation from D'Oliveira, who thought him a potential Test player, Lancashire League club Enfield signed him as their pro.

That year, outside South Africa for the first time ever, and in competition with such names as Johnny Wardle, Charlie Griffith and Clive Lloyd, the twenty-three-year-old Abed proved his mettle with 70 wickets at 13.23 and 358 runs at 21.99. It was a good enough beginning for mid-table Enfield to ask him back. Though they didn't yet know it, they were taking him on for a decade. The following year Abed really made his mark with 120 wickets and 600 runs as Enfield stormed away to the title. Another league title would follow in 1971, but before that Abed was to get as close as he ever would to playing first-class cricket.

His 1968 form was enough to persuade Surrey that perhaps Tom Reddick, the ex Notts and long-time coach in South Africa, was right when he said that in county cricket Abed would get a hundred wickets a season and plenty of runs too. White South Africa aside, no one, least of all Dik, could possibly have begrudged Basil D'Oliveira a single atom of his fame. Yet in some ways it must have been easier for Dolly as a trailblazer: certainly his move into the ranks of county cricket was not hindered by the romance of his story, and the accompanying publicity. By the time Abed's chance came, the romance had faded with the novelty. And counties around this time were short on patience anyway: they preferred to sign ready-made stars from overseas. Abed scored 215 runs at 71.66 and picked up a few wickets in two trial games for Surrey seconds. They told him they were looking for a bowler. A month later he took seventeen wickets for Warwickshire's reserves against those of Nottinghamshire and Leicestershire. He was told he hadn't got enough runs. He must have wondered just what he had to do.

What he did was to carry on the only way he knew. Enfield was famous for its local showers, which somehow always fell on Dill Hall Lane, and always on a length. Abed, renowned for his accuracy, would hit that length time and again. Photographs show him in delivery stride, perhaps a touch open-chested, though with right arm high enough to conjure fast-medium devils from the Dill Hall pitch. If subtle variations of pace and swing were not enough, he also possessed a wicked leg-cutter, which no less a judge than Neil Hawke called the best in Lancashire.

Winters he would return home to play for Roslyns, South Africa's premier non-white club, and coach. In 1970 he caused no end of a panic at Newlands when he applied for press facilities to cover the Springboks' first Test against Australia. Since the press box was zoned white, it was illegal for Abed to enter it. He had to make do with a specially reserved seat at the front of the non-white Railway stand.

The fourth Test of that series would be the last South Africa would play for over twenty years. Included in the Springbok side for that Test was Pat Trimborn, who had played against Abed in the

Lancashire League the previous season. Trimborn's figures had been 407 runs at 27.13 and 90 wickets at 10.34, while for Enfield Abed had 424 at 22.31 and 105 wickets at 10.40 each. The two had never played against each other in South Africa and never would. These figures aside, no comparison was possible. Yet, as if by magic, the South African selectors could tell them apart, could divine in those figures some mark by which to distinguish an international from a player not good enough, apparently, for even a single first-class game.

In 1971 Jack Cheetham suggested that Abed was one of two non-white players (left-arm spinner Owen Williams was the other) who should be asked to accompany the Springbok team to Australia. This announcement came out of the blue: the SACA had not thought to consult SACBOC. Predictably then, the plan died, as did the tour itself. Abed will not be drawn on whether he would have accepted such an invitation. But if his reports on the 1970 series are anything to go by – in which he is scathing about any principle of selection but that of merit established in open trials – he would have refused.

In October that same year, around the time the touring team would have been leaving for Australia, Abed married Janny Visser, a Dutch girl he had met two years before on holiday in Greece. The decision to marry effectively forced him into exile from South Africa: since Janny was white, their marriage would have been illegal in the country of his birth.

Dik Abed continued to play for Enfield until 1976, when he felt the time had come for a change. 'It is a very sad day for us indeed,' commented Enfield secretary Alan Higson as Dik announced his retirement. In ten years with the club, the devils of Dill Hall Lane had brought him 969 wickets, and 5,528 runs. Moreover he had proved himself a model professional as well as an excellent coach. No wonder he was pronounced 'irreplaceable'.

Dik moved to Holland, where he now lives with Janny and their children, Rasool and Anissa, and manages a sports complex in The Hague. He is active in Dutch cricket and will tour South Africa in March 1993 with the national side, the tour being part of the Dutch preparations for ICC tournament to be held in Kenya in 1994.

Of events in South Africa he says, 'The changes taking place ... at the present time have come at least forty years too late for a lot of non-white cricketers who no doubt could have made the grade, given the opportunities and facilities.' If the faintest trace of bitterness underlines the sorrow in those words, it is the bitterness of one who sees the frustration of whole generations exemplified in his own.

PHILIP SNOW

The Fijian Botham (1959)

Bula. A simple enough name. Comfortingly so, as Polynesian ones go, for unaccustomed eyes. Its pronunciation is just as simple: it tones in, broadly speaking, with the surname of Field Marshal Sir Redvers Buller.

It was just as well for New Zealand, this simplicity: for it became a household and headline name throughout that country.

Back in its native Fiji, Bula is one of the common words meaning 'Hello', 'How do you do' or 'Greetings'. During the war, when the Islands were glad to be swamped by divisions of Americans and New Zealanders just ahead of the Japanese, it was the first word the troops learned.

It has further meanings, 'Life' and 'Alive'. And it is in that context that it relates to this subject. For Bula's name is properly: Talebulamaineiilikenamainavaleniveivakabulaimainakulalakebalau. Which is in itself as brief a version as can be of a long story recording for posterity that a certain Fijian named Ilikena returned alive from the hospital at the village of Nakula on Lakeba Island in the Province of Lau. The Ilikena who returned in such good shape was father of eight children, one of whom inherited his father's name of Ilikena, and was also, as is customary, given a second name, from the Bible, Lasarusa (Lazarus). Fijians invariably have a third name: it might derive from anywhere. Well, our hero's final name told the story of his father's return from hospital in the briefest manner possible, even if it was a little over-exact, geographically speaking . . .

Not all Fijians have quite such episodic names. The few who do happen to have them cannot claim distinction in other respects.

Bula is the finest batsman produced by the Fijian people. When he was seen in New Zealand in 1948, on the first overseas tour ventured on by the All-Fiji team for fifty years, the experts judged him to be of the very highest class in that country, which was stronger then, with Wallace, Donnelly, Sutcliffe (at his best, which was magnificent), Hadlee, Cowie, Burtt and Rabone, than it is now.

So highly was he thought of that, when New Zealand was beginning to bring its thoughts seriously to bear on forming its team for what proved to be its most successful visit to England a year later, Walter Hadlee asked me whether Bula might feasibly be a candidate for the New Zealand side. We looked together into the rules. It seemed that if Fiji did not play any internal first-class cricket its players were eligible to play for the nearest country of first-class standard, which was New Zealand, a thousand miles distant. It was thought, however, that his selection might raise difficulties within New Zealand itself: the argument could reasonably be offered that New Zealand ought to be able to pick its side wholly within its own shores, even though its resources are slender. Nevertheless, the existing law did provide for the possibility. But it was really never more than an academic possibility: it was evident that Bula, although he would have been delighted to have had the wider experience in England and despite the jovial companionship and the complete lack of colour-consciousness of his New Zealand touring colleagues, would have been too homesick too early.

For, along with his simple name, he is also an uncomplicated character. From the obscurity of cricket in the Fiji Islands the name of this humble villager, who had in that year 1948 been born twenty-six years earlier in a house of total thatch looking like a haystack with one or two openings for doors, was, overnight as it were, on everyone's lips in New Zealand; in its four-letter form it was called after him everywhere – on trains, buses, trams, ships and aeroplanes.

He acknowledged it all with an impressive modesty. Many were the times when he was invited to broadcast his views on big cities, European women, climate, civilization and life in general: each time he would no more than smile gently (this would have been a tremendous hit on television if New Zealand had had it) and with his boldly carved lips enunciate carefully: 'Shorry. I do not speak English good enough. Very shorry.' . . .

Quiet and self-contained, Bula's modesty lies deep. He has no ambitions, except a tour of England. He knows his skill at cricket, but the knowledge has never unbalanced him: never was there less suspicion of side about a man. When he was hitting his enormous sixes, and so many of them, captains of opposing sides in New Zealand told me after the matches that there was never the slightest sign of emotion on his face. Straightening up somewhat from a rather crouching stance, he would half pull, half drive the most guileful spinner in one fluent, powerful, majestic motion clear over the stand. No glimmer of satisfaction on his face, no trace of response to the acclamation of the crowd, no comment.

He would flick some dust off his bare feet or peer at his battered bat. With his great stretches forward, his shin-high *sulu* (white skirt) would float out above the top of his pads: he would tuck it back and prepare to deal wholesomely with the next ball – if possible, over the head and upstretched hands of the extra boundary fielder just put there.

In a tour lasting two months, he had twenty-nine innings and scored a thousand runs in them. It is a far call from 1,000 in May, and there is nothing very heroic about the same number of runs absorbing May and June, or any other two months. Bula's distinction was that all his innings were exhibitions of systematic and scientific big hitting for a side making its way against established teams. It was the first time he had batted on grass. It was a lot of runs also for the son of a man who had fifty years earlier played in a one-innings contest between all the men and boys of two villages, fifty-three a side, all fielding, and had been one of the 104 batsmen in the two innings that day to fail to score.

Bula's greatest innings was against the first-class Province of Canterbury captained by Hadlee and including the Test players Mac-Gibbon, F. B. Smith and Leggat, and Hitchcock, the Warwickshire player. The Christchurch press lauded it as one of the most satisfying exhibitions of batting ever seen: this compliment embraced international sides back to Parr's All-England XI of 1864. The match was played on the best three consecutive days for cricket I remember – each day richly golden, almost too sensuously so for cricket purposes, with a haze over the hills looking beyond Port Lyttelton, the gentlest of breezes playing in the stands, and a big crowd exulting in the rare spectacle of figures in gleaming white shirts and skirts, with noble heads of hair, shiny bronze legs and bare feet flashing in the sun, brilliant white teeth radiating natural goodwill in the dignified features of the Pacific Islanders.

Bula, at No. 3, scored 63 in the first innings: there were four great sixes, all over a high faraway stand, and six thumping fours with so much air in them as to qualify almost for two more runs each. In the next innings, Fiji had to make 354 to win, a formidable task for a Fijian team. Bula went in at 7 for 2. It all depended on him; much of the batting on the tour did. He made his way out

again, his enormous bare calves bulging between the pad straps, to
the wicket, with a gait which is half roll, half lope, like a big-seated
footballer. Something of Compton's gait about his, but with longer,
raking strides and more of a heavy thrust forward like Wooller's. He
put his left foot right down the wicket to meet each ball, this time,
with the responsibility all his, using what has subsequently become
recognized as the Bailey prod with the straightest of bats. Unpredict-
ably, without the flicker of an eye, he would make the same deliberate
movement, but this time it would not be to suffocate the ball by
prodding but to assassinate it by lambasting it into some quiet street
lying in the shade of the stand. He made 120. His effort brought Fiji
to within 36 of the 354 required. And as soon as we had lost, he was
first down, in response to the crowd's usual request for South Sea
songs, to the front of the pavilion. There, in the circle formed by
the team, his voice was the most harmonious. Fijians have fine
voices, excelled only perhaps by Maoris and Tongans. Lauans are
part-Fijians: as one of them, Bula's singing derived extra quality from
the mixture . . .

In the first two matches of the tour he gave his autograph in full
in his habitual elegant copperplate. But he soon realized that if he
continued to do this there would be time for little else on his tour.
So it became 'I. L. Bula'. The press and scoring-box had taken the
same line of least resistance much earlier.

His autograph was naturally more in demand than any of ours,
or, at times it seemed, than all of ours put together. Despite his
repute, I could not quite understand this, as in my own collecting
days the object had been to obtain a comprehensive set of autographs
of all members of a side. I suspected that Bula's signature was being
obtained several times over to be used as a powerful swap on the
autograph market, but I think the explanation was really that Bula
was so much on the field (always in the short and hectic fourth
innings which Fiji invariably batted in) that he was just not available
for the purpose as much as the rest of us. Whatever the cause, he
would always be a good last in our bus or train, having been besieged
by the hunters up to the last minute (where they all came from, I
do not know: there was at this time a polio scare in New Zealand
and children were advised to avoid crowds); and we would always
leave to choruses of children calling out their esteem and affection
for Bula, who would wave politely back, not without a look of
embarrassment towards the rest of us. Some words lend themselves

splendidly to being called out. 'Bula' is one of them. My lasting impression of farewells to strings of New Zealand towns is to the strains of 'Boo-lah', 'Boo-lah' . . .

Bula would come back into the pavilion from practically deciding the turn of a game against a major province with a noble and hard-hit 80 which had aroused spectators to a high degree of excitement. After a shower he would suggest with a kind word to one of the Fijians dropped or rested from the side and sitting on the floor behind the *yaqona* bowl that he might relieve him from the humble task of serving the *yaqona*. Here it is necessary to explain that no game would begin in the morning or go throughout the day without the ceremonial South Sea drink *yaqona*, or *kava* as it is more generally known in the Pacific, being prepared continually in a large bowl presided over non-stop by whichever three Fijians had not been selected to play. This would be served to the two Ratus (Princes) Cakobau, descendants of the former cannibal King Cakobau of Fiji, who were skilled members of my side, and to myself and any visitor to the pavilion adventurous enough to try it. There is a way of serving it governed by convention: a Fijian in a crouching position politely offers it in his two hands and then softly claps, squatting back on his haunches. It was a strange experience, this. The enthusiastic applause which had accompanied Bula's return to the pavilion had scarcely died down: its echo would seem to be taken up a few moments later by the hero himself stepping from the darkest corner of the dressing room and clapping softly as he offered us the *yaqona*, while the twelfth man, relieved from being custodian of the *yaqona* bowl, strolled around the ground in his Fiji blazer eager to bask in a little reflected limelight.

And then there was the time when officials of the Waikato Cricket Association presented him on a railway-station platform with a ball inscribed in silver to mark the District of Waikato's appreciation of two of the hardest-hit innings ever seen. Bula had no English at his command for such an occasion. His 'Thank you, Shir' to the president was all he could muster. He entered the train, walked up the central corridor which New Zealand coaches all have, crouched in it level with my seat and, with his smile in which shyness and equine teeth rival each other for prominence, offered his magnificently won ball to me. I was very touched. But I wish I had accepted it, even if only temporarily, for on the last night of the tour it was stolen out of his suitcase in an Auckland hotel. He was deeply upset, not because he had wanted to show it off to his family on his return, but because, unworthy as he regarded himself as the recipient of such a gift, to his unworthiness he had added incompetence in looking after it.

The great virtue about him was his dependability, a characteristic rare and refreshing in a Fijian. He was always there for everything; not least he seemed to be always at the wicket, surprisingly so for a spectacular bat. But he was judiciousness itself in picking out the right ball to pull for his great sixes: almost never did he fail when going for them. Part of his secret was due to exceptionally rapid footwork: he would put his leg out as far as Sheppard. He had no back defensive shot, but a later change of plans in his general forward technique would result in a very good cut.

What little coaching he had had was from Viliame Tuinaceva Logavatu, himself an uncoached player and as the only Fijian to have exceeded a 200 in an innings (and to have done it twice) the best native player never to have played outside Fiji, and from Ratu Edward Cakobau (who had played for Auckland and in Oxford Trials): this combination gave him a happy mixture of orthodoxy and unorthodoxy, but based in each case on hitting hard and straight. There was a shade of Constantine about him, and also a touch of Hammond about his very robust off drive all along the ground. But in general impression he was more perhaps like Gimblett, that much underestimated bat, than anyone else. Bula's average on the 1948 tour was nearly 40: by outside standards this is not lofty, but (a) Bula knew nothing about averages, and (b) half of his innings were under orders to get, say 60 in 15 to 20 minutes. There were many such situations in the fourth innings, desperate efforts against the clock. Bula then went automatically and willingly in first: it was do or die. If he failed, we had to be careful. He almost always saw us there, but was frequently out in the last over or so before we were quite home, usually having scored 40 in 15 minutes or something of the order of 3 runs a minute. He was the sort of runner between the wickets who covered the pitch in half a dozen effortless and deceptively fast strides, so that not all his runs were by monumental sixes, but in these circumstances included the galling but safe pushes off his legs in the act of having advanced almost halfway up the pitch.

He happened also to be about the best fieldsman in an eminent fielding side. He specialized in fielding at deep long on, the position over which his own hits so frequently soared. During the Canterbury match, Hadlee and MacGibbon were in the middle of a powerful partnership when Hadlee, playing with less restraint than I remember from seeing him on English tours, made a big drive out to Bula off a googly of mine – to be dropped, to everybody's surprise, by Bula who did not have to move a foot. Not long after, MacGibbon also made a tremendous hit at my googly, more across it this time. Bula had to run flat out, *sulu* flying, his bare feet scorching the grass, for yards along the boundary. He took this catch, infinitely more difficult than the one he dropped, with consummate ease while still rushing along at top speed. He allowed himself a broad beam on his honest, light-brown face, and a typical Fijian emotion for his previous somewhat expensive slip in dropping Hadlee, by kicking with his bare instep the ball from deep square leg, where he had taken the catch, past the wicketkeeper across the other side of the ground to third man.

I have said that, as captain of a team, one either does not or should not have heroes in one's own team. The truth is, although there were other splendid players and characters of all kinds in this unusual touring team, that, so far as I was concerned (I can admit this now, but I could not, obviously, at the time), Bula was in the heroic mould because he carried a guarantee of success and popularity for my team as a whole without causing any envy within the team. What more could a captain ask for? I was frequently his partner at the other end – a very passive one. As he would thump the ball back dangerously close to my head and we ran, he would smile softly, chuckle huskily, with the ends of his mouth curled right up and murmur as we passed, 'Shorry, saka' ('Sorry, sir'): his sibilants when speaking English, but not Fijian, were always slurred. He had to say sorry in English: there is not an equivalent in his language.

Not many minutes later the score would have grown, by his efforts alone, quite handsomely, and he would perhaps be striding back to the pavilion with his loping, rolling, heavy-footed stride, head hung modestly down, before running embarrassedly up the pavilion steps to a clamour of applause, back into a corner of the pavilion to crouch and serve out the *yaqona*.

I shockingly overworked him. He was so much of a match-winner and so much the man of the tour whom the crowd wished to see in the breadth and length of New Zealand that I could not rest him from any match in the whole tour.

Fiji is the latest country to have first-class status: Bula is its most spectacular player. Not a little of this achievement for a tiny country of 300 islands, with a mostly unsophisticated and much scattered population no larger in total than that of Leicester or Coventry, is, therefore, due to him. He went again to New Zealand in 1954 and had some splendid innings, including another hundred against Canterbury. He took more catches than anyone. But he was not really quite himself, even if in quite a few New Zealand eyes he was still something of a hero. There was a reason for this. In 1951, his younger brother, Asaeli Waqabaca, a most promising player who was too young to tour in 1948, but was a certainty for further tours, was returning with the team of the capital, Suva, from a visit to an island stronghold of cricket, when the launch carrying the team collided with another in a passage through the coral reef. He was sunning himself on the gunwale: alone of all the passengers thrown into the sea, he was never seen again.

As in triumph, so in grief, Bula was restrained and dignified. Waqabaca was his favourite brother: he regarded him as a better all-round cricketer than he could ever be. He accepted gravely the whale's tooth which my *matanivanus* (herald) presented on my behalf in sympathy as custom requires. His fine long face was mourning, but you had to know his face and have studied it for long to read this, just as you would have to know him well to detect (if you were also quick and close enough) when he would at the last moment be deciding on a six instead of a smothering prod.

There was a public ceremony on Albert Park the next Saturday afternoon, when all eight teams playing on this spacious ground assembled halfway through the afternoon round the flagstaff under the Suva Association's flag at half mast. I was in the middle of an innings in one match and in pads when the adjournment was made for me to say my tribute to Waqabaca. Bula was also halfway through an innings of another match and in pads. As he listened his head was bowed: his bearing outwardly serene, well under control, with a nobility Fijian commoners seem to have in as much measure as do their very regal chiefs. I expected that bearing of him, but I think I would have been disappointed in him as a person if he had been so ironclad as to be able to ride the catastrophe completely, as if it had never happened, although one knew how devoted he had been to his brother. One doesn't know for certain, of course, but I believe that the shock had its effect on his play. As I have said, he went to New Zealand a second time and was a relative success. When the

West Indian team passed through Suva in 1956, Bula gave a glimpse again of his timbre against Dewdney, Ramadhin, Valentine, Sobers, Goddard, Atkinson and C. Smith: in a low-scoring match (neither side made 100) he was top scorer and helped Fiji to win. But his play seemed ever after the disappearance of his brother to have lost its masterly assurance, the distinguished sparkle, the unforced, totally natural, zest.

Bula is now a clerk in the Native Lands Commission: he spends most of his time entering other Fijians' names in the landowners' register in his copperplate style. He still plays and scores runs, by local standards a lot more than anyone else. He has five daughters, also a lot more than most people by any standards. He is thirty-seven, and this year it seemed as though a possibility was arising that he might be seen in this country contributing a little brightness to an overcast Old Trafford day or startling the pigeons on the Lord's boundary with the silence of a bare-footed approach or making sure that slow left-handers would not have the audacity to bowl without a fielder out. When it seemed likely, my friend in the Islands, Harry King (a Sussex man and until recently secretary of the Fiji Association) wrote to tell me that Bula had said that he could think of nothing he would like more than to come to England where he could learn how to play *real* cricket. He was modestly surprised when he was told by Harry King that many of his English countrymen thought that *real* cricket was the way Bula played it.

Of course, the truth cannot be concealed that his modesty can at times be almost maddening: he is too retiring, for instance, to coach, and too much the Fijian of no standing, in his own estimation, to take a hand in helping the administration of the game along a sensible course of action in the Islands. As it is, a tour of England by Fijians will not take place now – or, sadly, in the future, at least during his short remaining time as a player – for reasons which unfortunately could not be further from what I. L. Bula in his essential Fijianism of the finest order represents.

★   ★   ★

In the lore of the game, the cricketing schoolmaster constitutes a category of its own. At home, in England, there were once numerous gifted masters who turned out for their county in August, when their schools went into recess. Abroad, in the colonies, the most effective missionaries of sport were often teachers in the public schools set up on the model of Eton or Rugby. It was one such master, Chester McNaughten, who taught the game to the great K. S. Ranjitsinhji at his school, Rajkumar College, in Rajkot.

At his best, the schoolmaster taught his pupils about cricket and life, about the craft of the game as well as the values that underlay it – namely discipline, fairness and teamwork. Both aspects are nicely illustrated in Sujit Mukherjee's recollection of the Jesuit priest who taught cricket at St Xavier's School, Patna. This is followed by an essay by Cardus on a schoolmaster whose passion for the game was unfortunately not equalled by his skill.

SUJIT MUKHERJEE

A Jesuit in Patna (1996)

One of the enduring enigmas of my association with Father Cleary is that I can never make up my mind about how good he really was as a cricketer. While I was in school it did not seem there could be a better or more complete cricketer than he anywhere in the world. My yardstick was, of course, the standard of cricket I saw being played only in my home town. That he did not score a century and/ or bag ten wickets in every match he played in Patna cannot be a measure of his abilities. Even if he were capable of such feats, by character and by vocation he would have been averse to attempting them. He played in a match, if not as a man of God, certainly as a preceptor of the game – always playing not so much for his own good or even for the good of his team but for the greater good of cricket itself. I am pretty sure that, having chosen to be a Jesuit priest, he abjured any other kind of ambition not connected with his vocation. When the Reverend David Sheppard made or attempted a comeback to England's Test team, I remember wondering whether, had Father Cleary aspired to and got the right breaks, he would have ever made it to the Indian Test team of the mid-1930s, contesting C. S. Nayudu or S. Amir Elahi for a place. The road to such eminence would have been laid through the Pentangular contests – would he have played for the Europeans or the Rest? – and through Ranji

Trophy matches. People who ought to know in Jamshedpur have told me that during his playing days he could have walked into the Bihar team any time he liked, had he made himself available for selection. I have no doubt that, had he gained wider cricket fame, many of us in St Xavier's would happily have converted to Christianity if only he asked us.

A schoolboy's judgement of a cricketer cannot be of much value, less so when that schoolboy had nothing better to judge by than the cricket played in a backwater of the game. Even here Father Cleary's performance in terms of runs scored and wickets taken was not out of the ordinary. Many of his pupils must have surpassed him. Except once, I never saw him pitted against better opposition than what Patna could afford in those days. This was a two-day match with a visiting side from Jamshedpur, probably the Cricket Club of Jamshedpur, played on the Engineering College ground. I remember the location clearly because I was sitting behind the goalpost at the northern end and one of Father Cleary's drives came whistling over it. He seemed to have no difficulty in dealing with the visitors' bowling (which must have included a future Bihar captain, Bimal Bose, at least) and hit up 30-odd runs fairly soon before he was bowled. He also ran somebody out at the striker's end from mid-off and leaped to a marvellous caught-and-bowled for one of the four or five wickets he took in this match. This must have been in 1943 or 1944, and he fully justified my conviction at the time that he was the best all-rounder playing then in India. Happily, this belief has never been tested and, since it was never disproved, I may as well hold it till my dying day . . .

I should remember him better as a bowler because I kept wicket to him in my last two seasons at school. It was a job that came to me more or less by default, there being no other aspirant in the school those days. (Later, the school provided several wicketkeepers to the Patna University team, at least two to the Bihar State team, and very recently S. Saba Karim has toured the West Indies with the national side.) It was a job made more onerous by the worry of letting Father Cleary down by muffing a catch or fumbling a stumping chance off his bowling. I did both, quite regularly, but never heard again about them from him because he knew much better than anybody else that I was anything but a born wicketkeeper. He and I worked out a signal by which, when he pulled up his shirt collar while walking back for his run-up, I would know that the next delivery would be his faster ball and quietly retreat several steps from my already not very close position several yards behind the stumps. This used to be quite fast, from the way my hands stung within schoolboy-size wicketkeeping gloves. Generally I took this right-handed in order to make sure that it stayed – thereby violating a fundamental principle of wicketkeeping, namely, that both hands should be employed – and between overs I sometimes examined my reddening palm (and telling myself, from my reading knowledge, that I should use a piece of raw beef inside, or is that for a black eye?). Mercifully, the good Father bowled this infrequently, perhaps once every three overs or so, and I was spared permanent damage. Even more rare, perhaps one every three matches or so, was his googly – a real secret weapon, a *brahmastra*, preserved carefully for use only when nothing else would do. Or maybe I only imagined it was rare, because I never learned to spot it and he may have bowled many without my recognizing them. In his tactical tip to leg-spinners (I aspired to be one for a couple of seasons) he always advised cautious and sparing use of the googly, so that its surprise effect does not dissipate. Also, he warned that apprentice leg-spinners who get too fond of the googly sometimes lose their leg break. I seized upon this warning thankfully a few years later to explain away (to whoever cared to listen) my failure to develop into a leg-spinner. I had learned to bowl a googly first and could turn it on any wicket, but never mastered the leg break. The few that ever turned did so without any contribution on my part. In this I had sorely failed my mentor.

Father Cleary was mainly a leg-break bowler, but alternated with off breaks, and bowled both quite briskly. Off an eight- to ten-yard springy and beautifully balanced approach, he bowled practically at medium pace, with the ball snapping up smartly from the matting wickets on which I kept to him. Had his cricket career developed amid more specialized circumstances, he would probably have cut back on speed and flighted the ball more. By the time I saw him he was an all-purpose bowler – for example, he used the practically new ball for our school team – and this was another waste forced upon him by his situation. As the shine went off, two to three leg breaks per over were the usual quota, pitching on the stumps and going away, sometimes fetching snicks which I dropped or slip-fielding team-mates muffed. To my boyhood sense of cricket, his pitching on the stumps was a waste, more so when the catches he provoked were not accepted – why didn't he pitch outside the leg stump and aim at hitting the stump outright? This, he explained, not in terms of his own bowling but while instructing aspiring leg-spinners, would be far more wasteful because the batsman had bat as well as pad to deal with the leg break pitched outside the leg stump and may not need to play the ball at all. Whereas by pitching on the stumps, the leg-spinner compelled the batsman to use the bat, whether in defence or in attack, and thus enhanced the chance of his losing his wicket. Watching cricket at higher levels in later years, it has always seemed strange how leg-break bowlers and left-arm spinners assiduously bowl outside the off stump all day. If they had passed through Father Cleary's hands, they would have bowled at the stumps and got on with the job . . .

Father Cleary's playing days gave over soon after I left school, but he remained on the scene as umpire and selector for a few more years. For a few more he continued to coach St Xavier's boys, but the increasing complications of an intestinal ailment finally forced him out of any sustained physical effort. I did not watch this decline and thus can easily remember him better on the field than off it.

The brightest such memory is of the day in 1944 when St Xavier's nearly won the Sifton Cup. That a school team should have been competing at all in this tournament had made enough history. This was Patna's only 'open' cricket tournament – that is, open to all teams, not merely to colleges or only to club sides – run on knockout lines, and it generally fetched an outstation team or two. No school had ever before participated in this tournament, much less reached the final – which we did at only our second attempt. We ventured to participate partly because we could draw upon Father Cleary, also upon another cricket-playing cleric (Father Mackessack), and a lay teacher (Mr Kennedy) more feared in the boxing ring and on the football field. But also, there was no other tournament then in which we could participate, and I don't think we were at all aware of any presumptuousness in challenging college teams or adult, club sides. Our opponent in the final that year was Science College and the match was played on their ground – which to us in those days was the nearest thing to a Test ground. We batted first and were out for a little over 100, but they did no better and lost about eight wickets for somewhat less. Father Cleary must already have taken five or six wickets when one of the tail-enders – Kiran Mitter, to be exact, who was in the team (I later came to know) more for his enthusiasm than for his ability – made a desperate heave at him and away the ball soared over wide mid-on. The nearest fieldsman – again I remember the name, Sourin Ghosh, whose football was better than his cricket – set off in chase, overshot the mark, turned around and just managed to catch the ball near one of the flag sticks marking the boundary and ran across the line. In any class of cricket it was a great effort and we began yelling in joy, but a much greater hubbub arose from college supporters sitting under a tree nearest to the spot. They claimed that the catch had been made outside the boundary line. Now the college captain came out and demanded justice of the umpires. The one at the bowler's end, who had nearly joined our applause for the catch, solemnly walked to the spot, came back to consult his colleague, then broke our hearts by declaring the hit to be a six. We did not know how to protest, and, even had we known how, with Father Cleary present we could not have protested. But all fight was knocked out of us, not by the batsman but by that umpire. A few more swipes and the match was irretrievably lost.

Some of my teammates wept that evening, others uttered foul swear words out of our teachers' hearing, a few planned to murder the umpire. As I cycled back from the ground in a bunch with Father Cleary, he was already talking about the next season. That day, I think, I grew up a little more, and not only in the cricket sense.

Two years later, when the last 'All-India' cricket team to visit England was announced, some of us thought Father Cleary should have been selected instead of C. S. Nayudu or S. G. Shinde or C. T. Sarwate or all three – such was our faith. With India's political independence approaching, we even thought of conferring Indian citizenship upon him by giving away one of ours – such was our innocence. For all we knew, he had always been a citizen of India.

NEVILLE CARDUS

A Shastbury Character (1956)

Richmond was master of mathematics at Shastbury, and he played cricket passionately and statistically. He kept a record of every one of his innings, written down in ledgers of leather binding, carrying the inscription: 'H. Richmond. Cricket. 1893.' And so on. The first volume began much further back. He was grizzled grey in 1912, a little man squarely built with a ragged moustache and keen, kind eyes. When he was not in form, that is to say when he was not making runs, he would walk through the Shastbury streets absent-mindedly and sometimes he was obviously worried. He was, of course, a bachelor.

His stance at the wicket dated him as decisively as an early Victorian shilling. He stood legs astride, with the upper part of his body bent at an acute angle, and even then he appeared to be placed at quite a distance from the line of the bat, wicket to wicket. His left arm suggested an inverted letter V; his bat was scrupulously straight and held upright defending the middle stump so exactly that the bowler might well believe that he could see the off and leg stumps. He played off a stationary right foot, the left one going up in a sort of prance. If the ball came in from the off, he played back this way. One day in the nets I advised him to put his right foot and pad over the wicket and try to get behind the ball to play over it with the break. No; he wouldn't 'stick' his legs in front. 'That Nottinghamshire fellow – Shrewsbury – began it all. This leg-before pest. What's a bat for?' He made this statement in May 1913.

When he was in the field and the other side batting, he could tell you the score in detail at any minute, each batsman's contribution and the analysis of each bowler. He remembered everything. Seldom did he need to refer to his ledgers if any performance of his own was in question; he made an error on one occasion only, as far as I can remember. In a conversation after net practice he confessed that he had made a pair of spectacles once only in his life and that his second o was given to him by a 'shooter' from Woof while playing in a game against Gloucestershire Club and Ground. Next day he corrected himself, having consulted the ledger for the appropriate year: 'No, it wasn't Woof; it was Paish.' But he'd given us the right date.

On a good pitch he was, for all the 'openness' of his stance, hard to get out. He watched the ball all the way, played extremely late, seldom lifted the bat from the ground and was content to get runs by taps through the slips. After he had scored 10, he would remove the pad on his right foot and give it to the umpire; after he had scored 20 he would remove the pad on his left foot and give it to the umpire; after he had scored 30 he would take off the glove of his left hand and give it to the umpire; and arriving at last at the total of 40 he would take off the glove of his right hand and give it also to the umpire. He wore cricket shirts with sleeves the lower half of which could be detached; after the completion of his 50 he would detach both and give the removed parts to the umpire. One afternoon 'Ted' Wainwright, the senior cricket professional, was umpiring and he had not seen Richmond before; it was Ted's first season at Shastbury. As he called for a boy to come from the pavilion to take away his share of Richmond's discarded accoutrements he was overhead to ask: 'What does this little feller look like when he's med an 'undred?'

On a Saturday night in 1912, strangely hot in a season of rain, I was sitting up late in my lodgings at Cross Hill. All afternoon we had umpired, Ted and myself, in a game between the First XI and the Masters. Ted had gone to bed, tolerably drunk. Towards eleven o'clock our landlady came into the sitting room to say a gentleman had called to see Mr Wainwright. I went to the door and there was Richmond. I told him that Wainwright was asleep. 'I'm terribly sorry to disturb you at this time of the night,' he said; 'in fact, I've been to bed myself but I couldn't sleep. You see, Cardus, I'm bothered about Wainwright's decision today – he gave me out lbw to a left-arm bowler from round the wicket. Now, I'm not of course doubting Wainwright's judgement but as you know I never stick my legs in front of the wicket; and the main point I'd like Wainwright to explain is how can a left-arm bowler get a man out lbw from round the wicket on a plumb pitch?' He asked me if I could possibly go and see Wainwright, wake him up and get his point of view. There was nothing else for it; obviously Richmond was in danger of a sleepless night. So I took courage and, after some trouble, brought Wainwright temporarily back to consciousness. I jogged his memory about the afternoon's doings in general and his Richmond judgement in particular. 'Silly old b—;' he said, turning his pillow over: 'tell 'im ball coom back inches and would a' knocked off stump to 'ell.' Then he went to sleep again. But Richmond was satisfied. 'I didn't see the ball turn, but no doubt that was my fault.'

It was the custom at Shastbury for the First XI to go into the nets every Monday, Wednesday and Friday from a quarter to one until a quarter to two – that is, until mid-June set in and the House matches began. The practice was strenuous, especially for the professionals, who were supposed to keep the attack challenging all the time. After a particularly gruelling session on a sweltering Monday, Ted and I were resting at the open windows of the professionals' dressing room at Shastbury, still in our flannels and enjoying our pipes (Edgeworth was one shilling an ounce then, and a Dunhill pipe seven shillings and sixpence), while we looked over the shimmering cricket field, stretching away to the distant Wrekin. Suddenly Richmond knocked at our door and came forward. He had been dreadfully out of form for a month and on the previous Saturday had been clean bowled first ball while opening the innings for the Shropshire Gentlemen. 'Would you please give me a net for half an hour or so?' he asked. Wainwright consented, and Richmond went away to change into flannels. I was furious. 'He knows he has no right to ask for a net after School practice,' I protested. 'Doan't argue,' said Ted. 'Coom on and get it over. There'll be half a crown for thi, anyhow.' I told him I didn't want a half a crown. 'It's the principle,' I argued. 'Well,' said Ted. 'If tha doesn't want to bowl at 'im, tha knows what thi can do?' 'No – what?' "It 'im in cobbles.' 'Oh, don't be a fool, Ted – come on then, let's go and have it done with.' Besides, I was too young to know what he meant by 'cobbles'. As luck would happen, the nets had by this time of a dry summer become worn and dusty. Richmond duly appeared in the brown canvas shoes he invariably wore for the purpose of practice. His bat was very yellow and bound in two places with twine. Wainwright's first ball pitched outside the off and just missed the leg stump. 'Coom forward – it were well up enoo', sir.' Then Richmond studiously went through the correct movements to an invisible ball of the same kind; once or twice he went through them, lost in contemplation. He was beginning to play with some certainty of touch when one of my off breaks pitched on a very bare spot, came back like a knife, and sped upwards at an acute angle smack on to Richmond's bladder. And he never wore a protector or 'box'. He bent double with a stifled groan; but before we could get down the wicket to render first aid he drew himself erect and waved us away. But he decided he had better not continue practice today. He tipped us and apologized for putting us to inconvenience. 'But', he said, in reasonable extenuation, 'it *was* a beast of a ball, wasn't it?' Then he added, 'And it would have missed the bails by inches.'

After he had departed and we were alone again in the professionals' dressing room, Wainwright chuckled richly. 'By gum,' he said. 'Tha's a seight better bowler than Ah thowt. Anybody as can 'it batter in cobbles when he likes is a bit of all right . . .' In vain I protested that I had hit Richmond's bladder by accident. 'Tha's tellin' me,' replied Wainwright; and this was probably the first really relevant use of the term.

*   *   *

We turn now to some gentle debunking, to sketches written in mischief but not malice. Alan Gibson writes of how he grew up on tales of Ranji and Duleep, and then encountered an Indian prince – the skipper of a touring team, no less – who could not play cricket for toffee. N. S. Ramaswami writes of the mystery spinner Jack Iverson, who destroyed the England batting in the Ashes series of 1950–1. Two years later he toured India with a Commonwealth side. Ramaswami chooses however to remember not Iverson the bowler but Iverson the batsman and fielder.

ALAN GIBSON

The Unmasking of a Dashing Oriental Star (1982)

19 May 1982. Fifty years ago I saw the Indians play at Leyton. I can tell you the date: it was 28 May, my ninth birthday – no, I tell a lie, because there was no play on the Saturday, but I had a chance of watching them on the Monday and Tuesday.

Our house overlooked the Leyton ground and on the Saturday, as a birthday treat, I had been allowed to go in, paying sixpence, to watch from closer quarters. It was a disappointment that there was no play, after numerous consultations, but I can remember several things about the rest of the match, though by then I was only surveying it from the balcony at home.

I had bought a scorecard (twopence, a stiff price we thought) and conned it eagerly. No. 1 in the Indian side was described as H. H. Porbandar, with an asterisk to show he was captain. When India went in, after bowling Essex out for 169, their No. 1 played some handsome strokes.

We had some romantic ideas about Indian cricket at that time, because of Duleepsinhji, and the Nawab of Pataudi, and vague folk memories of Duleep's uncle, Ranji. So, although neither Duleep nor the Nawab were available for the Indian party, we expected magic.

When the Indian No. 1 was so dashing, I thought that this Porbandar was going to be another oriental star.

'Cor, old Porbs looked good,' I said to my friends. I wondered what the H. H. stood for. 'Arry? my friends suggested, or 'Erbert? I cannot swear to this, but I do believe I suggested 'Orace, because I knew he was something foreign.

Alas! I discovered later that though Porbandar had played in that match, he had not batted, and that the No. 1 who had played the strokes was Naoomal Jeeoomal – or words to that effect (even *Wisden* was uncertain in its transliteration of Indian names in those days). Naoomal played three times against England and averaged 27, so he cannot have been too bad. He made 1,300 runs in that 1932 season, 1,500 in all matches. So I had seen a pretty good innings; but it was a disappointment that he had not been Porbandar.

H. H., I also discovered, stood for 'His Highness', and the full title was 'The Maharajah of Porbandar'. *Wisden* of 1933 described his appointment as captain of the Indian side (there had been touring sides from India before, but this was the first to be granted a Test match) in these terms:

> Some little difficulty was experienced with regard to the captaincy, and after one or two disappointments the choice fell upon the Maharajah of Porbandar ... For reasons apart from cricket, the necessity existed of having a person of distinction and importance in India at the head of affairs, and it was almost entirely because of this that Porbandar led the team.

(Did anyone murmur anything about sport and politics?)

Wisden continues: 'No injustice is being done to him, therefore, by saying that admirably fitted as he was in many respects for the task, his abilities as a cricketer were not commensurate with the position he occupied.'

I checked Porbandar's figures for the tour:

At Pelsham, v. Mr T. Gilbert Scott's XI (not first-class):
   b R. S. G. Scott 0; b Owen Smith 2.
At Hove, v. Sussex: b Tate 0.
At Maidenhead, v. Mr H. M. Martineau's XI (not first-class):
   b Lowndes 2.
At Cardiff, v. Glamorgan: b Jones 2.
At Cambridge, v. the University: c Titley, b Rought-Rought 0.

He did not play again after the Cambridge match in the second week of June: at least, I can find no trace of it in *Wisden*, which nevertheless attributes 8 runs to him in all matches (average 1.14). Where are the missing runs? I can agree with their verdict on first-class matches (2 runs, average 0.66), but there is a problem here which I feel the Society of Cricket Statisticians should immediately investigate. There is no record of his bowling or taking a catch.

That is not all there is to say about the Maharajah. The tour was difficult, experimental, and it passed off happily. India ('All-India' as the team was then called) did well and, though they lost the only Test match, it was not before they had given England a shock or two. E. W. Swanton wrote that Porbandar 'made a creditable success of keeping his men a happy and united party'. It was also graceful, if inevitable, for him to step out of the side.

That it was not so easy to captain an Indian side in England was shown on the next tour, in 1936, when the amiable Vizianagram ('call me Vizzy', he used to say in the commentary box) struck trouble, and Amarnath, the best all-rounder, was sent home. In a later book Swanton refers, rather unkindly, to Porbandar's 'fleet of white Rolls-Royces', but also states that he had made only two runs on the tour – 'from a leg glance at Cardiff, I seem to recall'.

Fifty years later, with cricket between England and India still going on, I think we owe a salute to him. Porbandar – the state – produces limestone, which, according to the *Encyclopaedia Britannica*, 'is used for buildings in Porbandar without mortar, and is said to coalesce into a solid block under the influence of moisture'. Well, the limestone still holds, and he applied his touches of moisture in those early days.

8 June 1982. It was a pleasure at Edgbaston to meet Robert Brooke, the editor of *The Cricket Statistician*, who has solved the Porbandar mystery, of which I wrote in these columns some weeks ago, and which has perplexed a number of correspondents. Brooke has confounded *Wisden* and demonstrated that the Maharajah did make two more runs, equalling his highest score, in a match, twelve a side, against Blackheath in 1932. This confirms his tour average, for all matches at 1.14. He still holds the record for a touring captain.

N. S. RAMASWAMI

Iverson and the Lesser Arts (1953)

Of the prowess of Jack Iverson as a bowler there is little new to be
said now. But his batsmanship and fielding are facts worth recalling.
Iverson the batsman was a wondrous sight. He was a tail-ender to
the manner born. He stepped into the ground from the pavilion like
a portent. This advent should have been signalized by massed bands
of the I(ndian) A(ir) F(orce), the Navy and the Army, with the
delighted spectators in the background taking up the chorus. With
his wide and white Australian hat flapping about his ears, he made his
steady way to the crease, holding his antedilluvian bat on his shoulder.

This bat was not the least part of the pageant that was Iverson
the batsman. It looked hoary with age, discoloured, perhaps breaking
at the edges. Tradition had it that it was the implement with which
its owner had defied the mighty bowlers of England. An unsenti-
mental man would perhaps have cheerfully abandoned it to the
fireplace. But not the least pleasing of the Australian's qualities was
his devotion to it.

Iverson had, of course, nothing of the graces of a Hammond or
a Hutton. But it is an error in aesthetics, as Browning has demonstrated, that only the pretty or the beautiful is style. Ugliness, if it is
commanding and can impose itself on imagination despite the latter's
instinctive abhorrence of it, is no less to be prized. Perhaps one did
the estimable Iverson injustice by calling his style ugly. It was not so
much that as ungainly, which, of course, is not the same thing.

This remarkable batsman scorned to take 'guard'. He did not in
the Madras 'Test' with the Commonwealth team. Before planting
himself at the crease, slightly leaning on his bat (when the fear arose
that it might break under his accumulated weight), he surveyed the
field benignly. Perhaps in his heart he chuckled at the foolishness of
those three hopeful fieldsmen who had drawn near to him and eyed
his tall, lanky frame with ill-concealed hope.

Iverson was a noble example for tail-enders. Some tail-enders are
convicted tail-enders. They bat as if on sufferance and not by their
prerogative. Should their partner presume to steal the strike, they
aid him with ill-concealed eagerness. It was reserved for Iverson to
uphold the dignity of the class.

The factor which governed Iverson was his sense of humour. There was always a smile about his mouth. He was a kindly man to whom cricket, for all the honours it had bestowed on him, was still only a game. He was not overawed by the supposed dignity of Test matches. He was always free to be himself. I thought that his extraordinary grip in bowling was his way of showing his genial contempt for the pomposities and puerilities with which some aspects of the game have unfortunately been afflicted.

Iverson the fieldsman was an equally rewarding phenomenon. He was one of the few players I have seen who did not object to being considered slow and slovenly. It was in consonance with his attitude to the game that he would not put himself out in chasing an errant and wayward ball. Should it have the thoughtfulness to come to his hands straight, he would throw it to the wicketkeeper with indescribable dignity. Therein he acknowledged his sense of its nature of accommodation. Should it, however, have the impudence to evade him and career to the boundary with unseemly haste, he would follow it more in sorrow than in anger. Not for him the exaggerated efforts of a Pheidippides; after all, his object was nothing so notable as announcing to an expectant Athens the glorious victory of Marathon, but only the recovery of a contumacious piece of leather.

Iverson's progress after the erring ball could not unfairly be compared to a Republic Day procession. With grace and measured steps he followed it, perhaps resolving in his mind deep philosophical thoughts of the Original Sin which must be inducing even an inanimate object to behave in such an extraordinary fashion. When Iverson was embarked on the recovery of the ball, the entire field held its breath. The only man of equanimity was the fieldsman, whom the bowler was regarding with a glare, the captain with exasperation, and the batsmen with gratification. But a sense of the ultimate value of things will teach everybody that the runs which may or may not have been lost by what would conventionally be described as Iverson's slowness matter little in comparison with that wondrous picture, Jack Iverson in pursuit of a cricket ball.

* * *

In cricket, as in other team sports, the crowd maketh the game. Only more so. For the slower pace at which the game is played, and its frequent interruptions, allow for more intelligent crowd participation than soccer or rugby or basketball. Each ground has its resident wit, who attends every match, offering vocal and pungent comments on individual players. Arguably the most famous of all such barrackers was Yabba of Sydney.

RICHARD CASHMAN

The Celebrated Yabba (1984)

There is no question that by far the most celebrated and legendary barracker of the era was Stephen Harold Gascoigne (1878–1942), better known as Yabba, who was as much a part of the game at Sydney as the players themselves. When he took up his seat, usually by the fence in front of the scoreboard, hundreds of Hillites gravitated towards this born entertainer. Yabba was no less than the Hill's own expert commentator: he added to the excitement, relieved the tension and helped the crowd to participate actively in the game. He was also unofficial coach and mentor to the players.

Yabba was born in Redfern but in his adult life hawked rabbits around Balmain in his pony and cart – he supposedly acquired his name from a corrupted version of his call, 'Rabbo, wild rabbo.' He was a large man, just under 1.82 m (6 ft) and around 89 kg (14 stone), with a fleshy face and close-cropped hair which was usually covered by a felt hat or a cloth cap. He had a 'coarse and penetrating voice' which rose above the 'nondescript yells' of lesser lights. Carol Badcock, who was based in Adelaide for part of the 1930s, recalled that such was the power of his voice that it could be heard over the radio commentary. Yabba arrived at the game with his lunch and a couple of bottles of beer but he seldom drank more than that. He rarely missed a major match and was a regular follower of grade cricket: he knew the game intimately. No one knows when he established himself as Sydney's No. 1 barracker – some have claimed that he was prominent before the First World War – but there is no doubt that between the wars he 'stepped forward from the ranks of the chorus', as Ray Robinson put it.

A number of Yabba's comments were variations on themes which

had been called out many times before but with Yabba they were
sharper and more pithy. When a slow batsman scored after a period
of inaction he yelled: 'Whoa there! He's bolted.' Then when a bowler
strayed too far from the stumps he delivered a classic, and much-
repeated, comment: 'Your length is lousy but you bowl a good
width.' On another occasion he advised New South Wales captain
Herbie Collins to declare when a new batsman had added only five
runs in half an hour and the side had passed 500 runs: 'Hurry up,
Herbie, declare the innings before he gets set and scores a century.'

Yabba differed from the run-of-the-mill barracker in that his range
of comments was much wider and was based on a very close knowledge of the game. When the Nawab of Pataudi remained scoreless
for half an hour he advised the umpire, who was a gas-meter
inspector: 'Put a penny in him, George, he's stopped registering.'
Then there was another occasion when an umpire had to hold his
hand aloft for some time waiting for the attendant to move the
board: 'It's no use, Umpire; you'll have to wait till playtime like
the rest of us.' Because he knew the game so well, Yabba's comments
were fairer than most other barrackers'. When a Sydney grade crowd
laughed when a North Sydney tail-ender had his middle stump
smashed first ball Yabba consoled the dejected batsman: 'Don't worry,
son. It would 'a bowled me.' According to the *Sydney Morning
Herald* of 17 December 1934 Yabba was also reluctant to join in the
patronizing remarks made to women cricketers in the first international match at the SCG (New South Wales v. England, 1934).
When the teams were late to return after lunch there was a stream
of comments such as, 'Shake it up with your powder puff in there,
girls!' and 'Don't get impatient, old chap. Women are never on time
these days. Anyway, it's a woman's privilege to keep a gentleman
waiting.' One spectator then turned on Yabba and yelled, 'Hey, Yabba,
why ain't yer yowling?' Yabba replied, 'Why should I? The ladies are
playing all right for me. This is cricket, this is. Leave the girls alone.'

Yabba was not only a celebrity, he was also the subject of a
Cinesound newsreel. When Jack Hobbs played his last match in
Sydney the members of the Hill chipped in to buy him a testimonial,
an ornate boomerang: when Hobbs walked round the Hill to receive
his gift he asked for Yabba and then shook hands with him – the
one-time critic of barrackers acknowledged the No. 1 barracker. After
Yabba died the NSWCA stood in silence before its next meeting in
memory of a man who probably added not only to the entertainment

but also to the very size of the crowd itself. Recently Yabba has achieved another distinction, an entry in the *Australian Dictionary of Biography*, and joins a select band of Test cricketers – a minority of them – who have been similarly honoured.

An Englishman's Crease

I've been standin' 'ere at this wicket since yesterday, just
    arter tea;
My tally to date is eleven and the total's an 'undred an'
    three;
The crowd 'as been booin' an' bawlin'; it's booed and it's
    bawled itself 'oarse,
But barrackin', bawlin' an' booin' I takes as a matter of
    course.
'Oo am I to be put off my stroke, Mum, becos a few 'ooligans
    boos?
An Englishman's crease is 'is castle: I shall stay 'ere as long
    as I choose.

It's not when the wicket's plumb easy that a feller can give
    of 'is best;
It's not 'ittin' out like a blacksmith that wins any sort of a
    Test.
The crowd, they knows nuthink about it; they wants us to
    swipe at the ball;
But the feller 'oo does what the crowd wants, I reckon 'e's
    no use at all.
'Oo am I to be put off my stroke, Mum, becos a few 'ooligans
    boos?
An Englishman's crease is 'is castle, I shall stay 'ere as long
    as I choose.

HUBERT PHILIPS

MATCHES

We begin our selection of great matches with the epic 1882 Test which inaugurated the 'Ashes'. Ralph Barker's essay is a masterpiece of historical reconstruction (he was, of course, born years after the match took place). It is based on a close reading of dozens of old newspapers, yet has the immediacy and detail of an eyewitness report.

RALPH BARKER

The Demon Against England (1967)

It was the first and only Test Match of the 1882 season, and only the second ever played in England, and it excited enormous interest. On the first day 20,000 people paid a shilling each at the turnstiles, and several thousand more filled the privileged seats of the small pavilion and low-roofed, single-deck grandstand. It was the biggest crowd ever known at a cricket match. The Australians had had a highly successful tour, beating the Gentlemen and all the leading counties, but losing – without Spofforth – to the Players. If it was felt that they were showing signs of staleness – of the three matches lost, two, the Players' match and the game against Cambridge University Past and Present, had been in the previous three weeks – no one doubted that they would be at their best to meet the challenge of a representative England XI. The side had been chosen by a team of selectors led by Lord Harris, and eight of the Australian team had forecast it correctly. Everyone was agreed that, with fast bowler Fred Morley unfit and another fast man, Crossland, left out through a suspect action, it was the strongest eleven England could field. Against them the Australians had just about their best side apart from off-spin bowler George Palmer, who was suffering from a strain. Another injured tourist, batsman P. S. McDonnell, might also have got into the side had he been fit. However, England were thought to be invincible at full strength on their own wickets, and in spite of universal respect for Australian skill and temperament it was generally felt that England were certain to win.

The first day's play, on a rain-affected pitch, produced a succession of shocks and a pittance of runs. The Australians won the toss and batted badly; they were dismissed in two and a quarter hours for 63, their lowest score of the tour. England failed to gain the expected big lead and were all out just before the scheduled close of play for 101, 38 in front. In a low-scoring match, though, it might prove a useful lead. England bowled 80 four-ball overs, the equivalent of 53 six-ball overs, and the most successful bowlers were Barlow, left-hand medium, 5 for 19 in 31 overs, and Peate, left-hand slow, 4 for 31 in 38 overs. Both men bowled 15 maidens in their first 20 overs. For Australia, Spofforth bowled throughout apart from a change of ends and took 7 for 46.

Most of the spectators were Londoners and they were soon home; some who came from a distance camped outside the ground. The Australians drove back to their hotel, the Tavistock in Covent Garden. The match was the climax of the London season, and many of the grandstand spectators went on to the Savoy Theatre, where Richard D'Oyly Carte was presenting a new opera by Gilbert and Sullivan. As an added inducement D'Oyly Carte offered cool air and a freedom from asphyxiating vapours during the heat of summer. 'These remarkable results', he claimed, 'are obtained by the use of electric lighting in the place of gas.' This, in the London of the 1880s, was unique.

Unfortunately for D'Oyly Carte, the heatwave had ended and the weather had broken up completely. Temperatures were abnormally low, well down into the fifties, and there was plenty of cool air for everyone.

Next morning the barometer was still falling. It rained heavily and persistently, increasing to a downpour by ten o'clock. There was no covering of the wicket, and prospects of play looked poor. Yet thousands and thousands of Londoners were converging on Kennington Oval, by horse bus, by hansom cab, by train, and on foot, undeterred by the weather, so that a constant stream passed through the turnstiles. The vast open spaces of the Oval were rapidly filling up. It was an unforgettable sight, the green, sodden arena, murky under a lowering sky, completely enclosed by drab, mackintoshed humanity, anonymous and almost invisible beneath a jungle of umbrellas.

Shortly before eleven o'clock the sky cleared, and towards midday came a hint of sun. But the air was still cold. The ground had meanwhile become a vast amphitheatre, with nothing visible outside the actual playing area except people. They threw off their raincoats and sprawled on top of them on the turf, they crammed the seats, they stood behind in ranks six or seven deep, they crowded on to the artificial mounds at the back. They peered in little clusters from every window overlooking the ground, they even perched on the rooftops. Play had been due to start at 11.30, but they waited dumbly and patiently, their long silence enhancing the effect of their full-throated roar when the two white-coated umpires appeared at five minutes past twelve.

The Australians had already earned a reputation for fighting back from adversity. But their two opening batsmen could not have been less alike in temperament and method. The diminutive Bannerman was the stonewaller, the hardest of all the Australians to get out. The broad-shouldered Massie liked to hit. The Australians had doubted Massie's ability to succeed on the slower English wickets, but he had been the success of the tour. Only he and W. L. Murdoch, the Australian captain, had passed 1,000 runs for the season.

Hornby, the England captain, began with Barlow from the pavilion end. The ground was still very wet, unfit for cricket in the opinion of many, the run-ups being slippery and the ball quickly deteriorating into a cake of soap. Barlow had to get a groundsman to dig the mud out of the bowler's footholds so that he could fill them with sawdust. Bannerman cut Barlow's second ball firmly for two, then snicked the next one through the slips for two more. Barlow swore under his breath and ground his teeth in vexation. George Ulyett, the Yorkshire fast bowler, opened from the gasworks end, and Massie drove his second ball hard to the off, his favourite shot. Maurice Read just cut it off before it reached the boundary, but the batsmen ran three. The wicket had rolled out easily, and Massie was determined to attack the bowling before the pitch deteriorated.

Massie took guard to face Barlow. He was unable to get the first three balls away, but he drove the fourth square to the off for four. Ulyett bowled Bannerman a maiden, and then Massie forced Barlow in front of square leg for three.

Ulyett and Barlow quickly adjusted themselves to the conditions

and settled into a length. Twice Ulyett beat and nearly bowled
Massie, and twice Barlow found the edge of Bannerman's bat. But
in Ulyett's fifth over, after Bannerman had stolen a single to Hornby,
who had injured his arm and couldn't throw, Massie pulled the fast
bowler to square leg for four, putting 20 up in 20 minutes. He
followed this with a towering drive off Barlow high to long on for
another four. The crowd applauded each hit, but they were ominously silent in between. They desperately wanted to see some wickets
fall before the arrears were knocked off. England would have to bat
last on a damaged pitch.

Ulyett could get nothing out of the wet turf and Hornby substi-
tuted his fellow Yorkshireman Peate. Peate bowled a maiden to
Bannerman. The situation called for a double change, and Studd
came on at the pavilion end for Barlow. Massie drove him at once
as he had Barlow before him, high to the on for four. Next ball
another hard drive was brilliantly fielded by the bowler. Peate bowled
Bannerman another maiden, but Massie took a single off Studd, and
that was 30 up. Peate now had to bowl to Massie, and he could not
keep him quiet. Massie stepped in and drove him straight for four,
and followed this, when Hornby adjusted his field, with a magnificent
off drive towards the gasometers for his sixth four. That was 38 in
35 minutes and the arrears knocked off without loss.

Bannerman kept up his barn-door defence while Massie went on
hitting. It seemed that Hornby could do nothing to shift either man.
But at 47 he brought on Barnes, the Notts medium-pace bowler, for
Studd, and Massie hit his first ball high and straight to Lucas in front
of the pavilion. To everyone's chagrin except the Australians', Lucas
dropped it. Massie had then made 38.

The 50 went after 40 minutes. There had been nothing like this
rate of scoring in the match so far.

Massie was still prepared to hit the ball in the air. For Peate,
Hornby stood deep at long off, twenty yards in from the long
gasworks boundary, but Massie soon landed the ball over his head
for another four. If Hornby had been standing on the edge it must
have been a catch, but he hadn't credited Massie with such strength.
Peate had to come off, and Hornby tried his sixth bowler, A. G.
Steel. Massie reached his 50 out of 61 in 45 minutes, and in Steel's
second over he carried the score past the Australians' entire first
innings total, still without loss. The time was one o'clock. The wicket
was beginning to dry out a little, and Steel was getting some turn

from leg, the first bowler, in Massie's opinion, to get any movement from the sodden pitch at all. Everyone else had cut straight
through. Massie decided that he'd better knock him off, and he raised
his bat to swing at the first ball of Steel's next over. The ball was
leg-stumpish and looked like one to hit, but it was Steel's faster ball
and Massie came down too late. The leg stump went down to
thunderous applause as the crowd relieved their mounting frustration.

66 for 1, last man 55. Massie had hit 9 fours, 2 threes, 3 twos,
and only 7 singles. It was one of the best attacking innings ever
played.

That the Australians meant to go on hitting if they could was clear
when the massive George Bonnor, 6 ft 6 in tall and acknowledged to
be the biggest hitter in the game, came in next in front of Murdoch.
But Hornby now made a shrewd move. Although Steel had done so
well, he replaced him after one more over with Ulyett. Off the fast
bowler's fourth ball, Bonnor was clean bowled middle stump. 70 for 2.

Bannerman fell at the same total, caught at cover by Studd off
Barnes, to the accompaniment of another great outburst of cheering.
This brought the two best Australian batsmen, Murdoch and Horan,
together. Ulyett had done his job, the run-up was still difficult, and
Hornby at once brought back Peate, Ulyett having bowled only one
over. Murdoch hit Peate for four, but the slow left-hander turned
one away from Horan, and Grace at point took an easy catch.

Giffen came in next, and Grace moved in closer, hands outstretched before him. Peate bowled the identical ball, Giffen reached
out but failed to smother it, and again Grace pouched the catch.
79 for 5.

The bearded Blackham came in to stop the hat-trick. Another
beard was almost sitting on the bat, but Peate tried a little too hard
this time to produce the unplayable ball and it dropped short enough
for Blackham to pull it for four. 83 for 5, though, was a deplorable
setback from 66 for 1. The advantage gained in that wonderful
opening stand was gone. With five wickets to fall the Australians
were only 45 in front. There followed a determined attempt at
consolidation by Murdoch and Blackham, who added 20 runs
together before a sharp shower drove the players in. The time was
a quarter to two, and lunch was taken.

After a break of an hour the game restarted. Peate continued
from the gasworks end, and the last ball of his first over kept low

and found the edge of Blackham's bat. Lyttelton took the catch and the Australians were 99 for 6.

Next man in was the twenty-one-year-old S. P. Jones, the youngest player on either side. Murdoch put up the hundred with a single to leg, and Jones cut Barlow, in his second spell from the pavilion end, for a two and a four in the same over. Then for the next nine overs the run-getting almost subsided as Murdoch, playing with the utmost caution and determined to set England a formidable task, monopolized the strike. He took only seven runs in this period, and then, with the score at 113, came the incident which so incensed the Australians.

Murdoch skied a ball from Barlow towards a vacant space at square leg and the batsmen ran. Lyttelton raced after the ball, threw off a glove, and aimed at the batsman's wicket, but Jones had backed up well and was easily home. Grace strode forward to gather Lyttelton's throw. As he did so, Jones, after grounding his bat, left his crease to pat down some spots on the wicket. Grace immediately removed the bails.

'How's that?'

Jones was young and inexperienced and it was possibly foolish of him to leave his crease before Grace had thrown the ball back to the bowler. But he had grounded his bat, and there was no suggestion that either he or Murdoch was attempting another run. The appeal was made on technical grounds only – the ball had not come to rest in the wicketkeeper's or the bowler's hand, so strictly it was not dead but still in play.

Umpire Thoms, at square leg, was the man on whom the decision rested. The laws of the game gave him no alternative.

'If you appeal for it, sir – out.'*

Murdoch expressed his disapproval openly at the wicket. That Grace was within his rights was not disputed, but his action was seen as sharp practice and a dirty trick. It might be within the laws of the game, but it wasn't cricket.

Those who knew Grace and played regularly with or against him would have taken more care. Grace was accused of taking advantage of the inexperience of youth, but no doubt he felt it would teach the young fellow a lesson. He was thoroughly pleased with himself and

---

* Thoms afterwards denied saying this and stated that his reply had been monosyllabic – 'Out'.

was quite unmoved by the general show of disapproval. No doubt he himself would have accepted such a dismissal without bitterness, and called himself a fool.

Psychologically it was the end of the Australian innings. They had no stomach for it any more. Spofforth was soon out, and Murdoch followed. His innings, too, had a somewhat unsatisfactory end. Garrett hit Steel hard to the off and the batsmen ran two. Hornby was seen to be about to pick up the ball, and, since his injured arm would prevent him from throwing, Garrett called for a third run. Meanwhile Studd, seeing the danger, had backed Hornby up. Hornby passed the ball quickly to Studd, who flung it at Lyttelton, and the wicketkeeper removed the bails with Murdoch still out of his ground. It was an adroit piece of work, but very hard luck on Murdoch. His patient 29 had held the Australian innings together after Massie's fall.

The Australians were all out at 3.20 for 122, leaving England only 85 to win, with almost a day and a half to get them. It was an easy task.

The manner of Jones's dismissal, however, had given the Australians a cause. There was deep despondency in the dressing room, but it was dramatically dispelled by Spofforth. His confidence was infectious, and it was now that he uttered one of the most famous phrases in the history of cricket.

'This thing', he said, 'can be done.'

It is worth examining just how formidable a task it was that faced the Australians. The England side was stacked with batting. First there was W.G. himself. In the previous Test match at the Oval two years earlier he had scored 152, and he was still beyond comparison as a batsman. There were Hornby and Barlow, the Old Trafford run-stealers of the Francis Thompson poem. There was George Ulyett, one of the best all-rounders of the day, whose scores in the Test series in Australia the previous winter had been 87, 23, 25, 67, 0, 23, 149 and 64, and who had been top scorer in the first innings. Maurice Read, of Surrey, and W. Barnes, of Notts, were two professional batsmen who had already scored heavily against the Australians, including a partnership of 158 in the Players' match only three weeks earlier, when Read had made 130 and Barnes 87. C. T. Studd was the most successful batsman of the year and the only man to score two centuries against the tourists. Then there were two more great amateur batsmen in A. P. Lucas and A. G. Steel. Even the wicket-keeper, the Hon. Alfred Lyttelton, was a batsman in his own right who had opened the innings against the Australians and made good scores against them. These four amateurs, Studd, Lucas, Steel and Lyttelton, had been members of the Cambridge Past and Present side that had beaten the Australians ten days earlier. Only the No. 11, Peate, was not an accomplished batsman of the highest class.

Yet Spofforth insisted that it could be done.

The fluctuating fortunes of the day had already played havoc with the emotions of the crowd. For one man, indeed, the excitement had proved too much. When the Australian innings ended, forty-seven-year-old George Spendler, of Brook Street, Kennington, who was seated on the terraces, complained of feeling unwell. He got up, and almost at once fell to the ground, suffering an internal haemorrhage. He was carried to a room next to the pavilion and examined by several doctors, but already poor George Spendler was dead.

Hornby had handled his bowling with real insight and tactical skill; but writing down his batting order in a manner that would please everybody was clearly beyond him. In the first innings he had solved the difficulty to some extent by relegating himself to No. 10. Now he rightly resolved that he must lead the side from the front. He must open himself with Grace.

Spofforth began at his fastest from the gasworks end, forcing Blackham to stand back for the first time in the match. The time was 3.45. Unless England batted very slowly, the likelihood was that they would win well before six o'clock, the scheduled close of play.

Spofforth had slept very little the previous night, rehearsing ways of getting this formidable phalanx of batsmen out a second time. Now, as he bounded up to bowl from his curiously angled run, starting several yards to the offside of the batsman, he seemed with his sinister visage and sinuous figure to have converted the science of bowling into a black art. Several times he bounced the ball deliberately straight at Grace – the first recorded instance of intentional bodyline bowling in Test cricket – but the wicket was still slow and Grace was unperturbed. Spofforth reverted to his normal pace in England of fast-medium, at which speed he could get much more work on the ball, and Blackham stood up close. Knowing how closely Grace always watched his hand, Spofforth wrapped his fingers round the ball in all kinds of odd ways, trying to disguise his intentions. And always he carried the threat of that immensely fast ball, delivered with no apparent change of action.

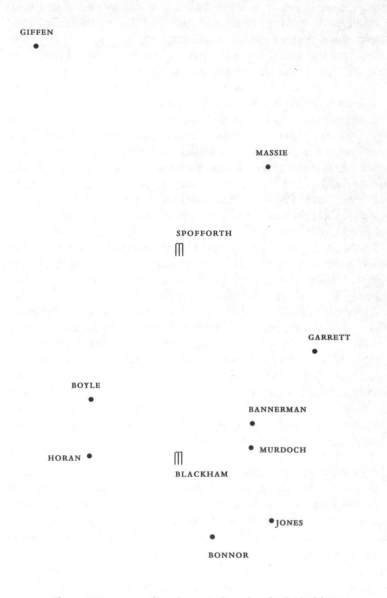

SPOFFORTH'S FIELD AT THE OVAL, 1882

GIFFEN

MASSIE

SPOFFORTH

GARRETT

BOYLE

BANNERMAN

HORAN   MURDOCH

BLACKHAM

JONES

BONNOR

These positions were adjusted to suit the styles of individual batsmen

It was a magnificent sight to see Spofforth bounding up to the wicket and into that final leap, the match in the balance, faced by the ponderous, upright figure of W. G. Grace. Close in at silly mid-on stood Boyle, ready to pounce on any ball that the batsman failed to keep down. Behind the batsman's back stood Horan at short leg. Bonnor and Jones were at slip, Murdoch and Bannerman together at point. Six men close in on the bat. Garrett was at cover, Massie at mid-off, with Giffen the only outfielder at long on, a carefully set snare for any batsman who swung at Spofforth's slower ball.

But the runs began to come. Garrett, fast-medium with a high action, bowled from the pavilion end, and Hornby set the score moving with a single. Grace broke his duck next ball, and two more singles came from Spofforth's second over. Grace was very nearly caught and bowled by Garrett, and then Hornby cut Spofforth sweetly for four. The score had reached 15 after eight overs when Spofforth clean bowled Hornby with a break-back, hitting his off stump. That left 70 to win.

Barlow, the best defensive batsman in England, came next. The second ball he received was very similar to the one that bowled Hornby. Barlow was good enough to get an inside edge, but he could not keep it out of his wicket. 15 for 2.

Everyone had said that the Australians would be bound to make a fight of it. But an England defeat had not seemed even remotely possible. Now, as Ulyett joined Grace, the crowd began to wonder. In the next few minutes, however, the tension was quickly relieved. Grace drove Garrett for three and Spofforth for two, and then took seven runs from Spofforth's next over, driving him to leg in confident style to the accompaniment of loud and almost frenzied cheering. The score reached 30 for 2. Spofforth tried everything – topspin, checkspin, break-back, cut and swerve, with every variation of pace imaginable, but Grace and Ulyett were equal to all he could offer. 'I'd better try the other end,' said Spofforth.

Spofforth went down to the pavilion end, replacing Garrett, and Boyle took over at the gasworks end. It made no difference. Both batsmen went on hitting hard and freely. Ulyett did not always look safe but he was lively and aggressive, while Grace was evidently determined to stay there until the match was won. The 50 went up after 55 minutes, and England were coasting home; 35 to win, Grace and Ulyett well set, and six high-scoring batsmen to come. Book-makers in the crowd were offering 60–1 against an Australian victory.

The wicket seemed as dead as ever. But there was no sign yet that the Australians had given up. Right from the start they had bowled and fielded with tremendous zest and keenness. In spite of their disappointments they had recovered their natural good humour. And in spite of their hopeless situation they seemed not to suffer from nerves. Blackham was still standing up to Spofforth, ignoring the risk of giving away byes. He was only able to do it because of their agreed signalling system.

Spofforth ran up to bowl to Ulyett, eight paces, arms wind-milling, then the final high action, the bicep almost brushing the ear. It was the really fast one. Blackham saw the signal, but Ulyett didn't spot it. He picked it up fairly early, but the ball skidded through and he got a touch. Blackham took the catch low down outside the off stump and England were 51 for 3.

Ulyett had put on 36 valuable runs with Grace, restoring England's impregnable position. Now he made way for Lucas. 34 to win.

This thing can be done, said Spofforth again. This thing can be done. And he was admirably supported by Boyle. It was Boyle, indeed, who took the next and vital wicket. He held one back, Grace drove hard and a little too soon and didn't quite middle it, and Bannerman took the catch at mid-off. A yard higher, a yard to left or right, and it would have been four runs. Instead it was 53 for 4, last man 32.

With their champion gone, the crowd began to think the same way as Spofforth. I told you so, they muttered, through lips that were almost blue with cold, I told you so. These Australians are never beaten. They watched in agony as the Australians gathered together in animated clusters, already apparently scenting victory. But surely such a thing was impossible. 32 to win, and 6 good wickets still to fall. No – defeat was impossible.

Lyttelton came in to partner Lucas. England mustn't lose another wicket just yet. Both men played with grim concentration. Lyttelton just managed to deflect Spofforth's faster one off his stumps, and the batsmen scampered three lucky runs. Then he hit a two and two singles, putting the 60 up. The time was a quarter to five. An hour and a quarter still to go, a whole day tomorrow, and only 25 to win.

The ground had dried sufficiently for Spofforth and Boyle to get more and more movement and life out of the pitch, but Lyttelton and Lucas held firm. Lucas took a single, and then Lyttelton turned

Spofforth neatly to long leg for four, bringing the score to 65 and leaving only 20 to win.

Spofforth and Boyle now tightened up and put on the full pressure. The ball seemed impossible to get away. As maiden over followed maiden over the tension grew unbearable. The crowd lapsed into a heavy silence, and the tinkling of hansom cabs along the Harleyford Road could be clearly heard. The remaining batsmen, watching through the closed windows of the committee room, shivered with a mixture of cold and fright. Every cricketer knows what it is like to wait for his knock in a tight corner when he can't keep warm. A. G. Steel's teeth were chattering; he could not keep his jaw still. Barnes's teeth would have been chattering too if he had had any, but he wore false teeth and had taken them out.

At this crucial point, Hornby decided to change his batting order. Everything he had done so far in the match had been right. He had followed his instinct, and he was bound to do so again. C. T. Studd was next man in, Studd, the man with the highest average against the Australians that season. But in the first innings Studd had been bowled by a Spofforth breakback for 0. Hornby decided to put Steel, his Lancashire colleague, in next, to promote Read, who had carried out his bat for 19 in the first innings, to put Barnes in after Read, because these two had done so well together in the Players' match, and to hold Studd in reserve at No. 10. If all else failed, surely Studd would pull out something special to make sure of the match.

Studd, waiting with his pads on, felt so cold that he asked the Surrey secretary for a blanket. With this wrapped around him he marched up and down the committee room in nervous agitation, still shivering with cold.

Few cricket grounds can have equalled the drear, chill atmosphere of the Oval that afternoon. From the small brick pavilion the players looked out on a leaden, sombre scene that the light and the weather had drained of all colour. Surrounding the cockpit of the playing area was a panorama of grey, relieved only by the low white sight screen at the far end of the ground. To the left of the sight-screen rose a tiered wooden stand whose occupants, exposed to the elements, huddled together for warmth. To the right of the sight screen a marquee was almost hidden amongst the throng of people. Behind rose the three-headed monster of the gasworks, ugly and strictly functional, dwarfing the tall chimneys of the riverside factories at Lambeth. Even the brick façades of the occasional cluster of houses that broke up the skyline, with their varying elevations and outlines and their dingy, backstreet drabness, seemed to stare on the scene with a cold indifference.

Meanwhile a war of attrition was being enacted in the middle. For twelve consecutive overs there were neither runs nor wickets. Sooner or later there must be a lapse of concentration on the part of one of the batsmen, or one of the bowlers must tire. Lucas was anchored at the far end, facing Spofforth, Lyttelton was opposed to Boyle. Whose nerve was going to break first?

At length Spofforth could stand it no longer. Everything that he could bowl to Lucas was met with the straightest bat in England, and at the end of the over he consulted with Murdoch. His idea was that he might break up the partnership if the batsmen changed ends and he could get a bowl at Lyttelton. It was arranged that if the batsmen had still not scored a run by the last ball of Boyle's next over, Boyle should give the batsman a single, even if this meant a misfield. Lyttelton in fact played the last ball to Bannerman at mid-off, Bannerman let it slip through his fingers, and the batsmen took one.

It was a bold move, because it broke the tension of that sequence of maidens and left England with only 19 to win. And it bore no fruit at first, Lyttelton defending with equal skill and stubbornness. Four more maiden overs followed before Spofforth at last beat Lyttelton with a ball that just took the top of the middle stump. 66 for 5.

One man in the crowd found to his astonishment that during those 17 overs for 1 run he had gnawed halfway through his umbrella handle. Even the hands of the scorers were unsteady, and their fingers trembled. There was half an hour left for play. Next man in was A. G. Steel.

Bowling from the pavilion end, Spofforth had achieved a position of strategic value. As each new batsman came in he had to pass Spofforth on his way to the crease. Each man was treated to so searching and baleful a stare that the existing nervousness was multiplied threefold. Horan, at short leg, was close enough to see the strain written on the batsmen's faces. Cold and nerves had induced a deathly pallor, and their lips were ashen grey.

Spofforth ran up to bowl to Steel. The light was beginning to deteriorate, Spofforth had the dark background of the stands behind him, and he bowled his fastest at Steel. Somehow Steel kept the ball out of his wicket, but he looked ill at ease. At the other end, though, a late cut by Lucas off Boyle yielded four runs and brought a tumultuous cheering from the crowd. They too were shivering and were greatly relieved to have something to applaud. 15 to win. Once again Spofforth ran up to bowl to Steel. The action was the same, but this time Spofforth held the ball back, Steel played a shade too soon, and there was Spofforth halfway down the pitch, almost on top of the batsman, to snap up the catch. 70 for 6.

Another tremendous cheer from the Oval crowd announced that their favourite Maurice Read was coming in next. Spofforth ran up to bowl. The applause had hardly subsided when amid further terrific excitement it was seen that the wicket was broken and that Read was on his way back to the pavilion, clean bowled first ball. That was 70 for 7.

Defeat now stared England in the face, yet there was still some batting to come, enough surely to knock off a paltry 15 runs. Lucas was well set, Barnes was in next, Studd had been held in reserve, and even Peate had been known to make a few runs. If they kept their heads they must still win.

Spofforth tried a fast yorker on Barnes first ball, but Barnes came down on it hard and drove it to the on for two. It was the first score off Spofforth for ten overs. Next ball Spofforth for the first time beat not only the batsman but the wicketkeeper as well, and the ball ran down towards the sight-screen for three byes. That was five runs off two balls – nine to tie, ten to win.

It was the first time Blackham had faltered. The nerve of these two men, bowler and wicketkeeper, in ignoring the narrow margin of runs and going all out for a win, scorning to play for safety, amazed the crowd. There was no one to cover Blackham, yet apart from Spofforth's first over he had stood right up over the bails the whole time, a constant nagging threat to each batsman.

Lucas had batted for an hour on a wicket that was taking more and more spin. Earlier in the innings Spofforth had sometimes turned the ball six inches. Now he was sometimes turning a foot.

If Murdoch was frightened of anything it was that someone would have a go at Boyle. It wanted only two or three hits to finish the game. But the medium-pacer, bowling round the wicket and running across the batsman from leg to off, was extremely hard to attack. Murdoch felt anyway that there was nothing he could do now but leave things as they were, and he breathed again when Boyle bowled a maiden to Barnes.

Spofforth had now become virtually unplayable. In his last six balls he had got rid of Lyttelton, Steel and Read. Each wicket had freshened him, giving him new energy and life. He ran up to bowl to Lucas. Somehow Lucas scrambled the first three balls away, but the last one turned from outside the off stump and Lucas could only deflect it into his wicket. England were 75 for 8.

C. T. Studd was next, the man whom Hornby had kept back for this moment. He divested himself of his blanket and strode briskly out to the wicket, nervous undoubtedly but glad of the chance to get to grips with the situation at last and warm himself up. For the moment, though, he was deprived of the strike. Over had been called, and Boyle was now bowling to Barnes.

Boyle was one of the great length bowlers, with a genuine movement from leg. Although he had taken only one wicket, his contribution had been almost as important as Spofforth's. Indeed he had been even more economical, bowling 19 overs for 17 runs. And even now, when he might have been forgiven for keeping the ball outside the off stump, he went on attacking the wicket. His second ball was right on a length, and straight. Barnes had to play at it, it lifted, and he was caught by Murdoch at point off his glove. 75 for 9.

Peate, the last man in, was sipping a glass of champagne in anticipation of victory. When he saw that Barnes was out and that it would be up to him he drained his glass and made his way out to the wicket.

'Leave it to Mr Studd,' called Hornby. The advice was echoed on all sides. But Peate was a character, with ideas of his own about batting, and he was determined to finish the match in true tail-ender's fashion with the minimum of hits. With his first shot he horrified the crowd and sent them into ecstasies at the same time by hitting right across the line and pulling Boyle to leg for two. If he had caught hold of it properly it would have been six. For good measure he darted out of his crease again, trying to persuade Studd to attempt a suicidal third run. Studd stayed where he was. One more ball and they would have to face Spofforth.

7 to tie, 8 to win. It could be done in two hits.

In vain did Hornby and the other England players exhort Peate, from the vast inaudibility of the pavilion, to keep his end up and let Studd do it. The last ball of Boyle's over was just right – well up, and straight. Like all hitters, Peate liked them straight. He swung massively – and missed. An awful groan swept round the Oval when it was seen that Peate had been bowled.

The black horde of spectators remained for a moment immobile, half-paralysed into complete, incredulous, stunned silence. Even the press were too overcome to write or telegraph their copy. One hardened Oval habitué lay slumped over the back of his seat. Alcock, the Surrey secretary, thought he had another death on his hands, and he shook the man by the arm. The man stared up with a glazed look, then slumped back. 'I don't know whether to cry', he said, 'or be sick.'

C. T. Studd, scorer of two centuries that year against the Australians, had been left stranded. He had not faced a single ball.

It was nearly a quarter of a minute before the crowd recovered and burst on to the field like the fragments of a bomb to intercept and cheer the Australians. All day the crowd had been strictly partisan. Now they forgot their intense disappointment in their wild enthusiasm for the victors, and especially for one man. Spofforth had taken 7 wickets for 44 runs and 14 for 90 in the match and the crowd chaired him off the field and up the steps into the pavilion. Such scenes have been repeated at the Oval many times, but no one who saw this one ever forgot it.

The inquests have gone on for eighty-odd years and no doubt they will go on for ever. Certainly Australia had the best of the conditions on the second day. For the first hour the bowlers had trouble with their footholds, the wicket was easy and the ball was greasy. Some thought Hornby should have tried to delay the start still further. But the point is that Hugh Massie took full advantage of the conditions and played a great innings. Australia's subsequent misfortunes, and especially the dismissal of Jones and Murdoch, wiped out their advantage, and the game seemed all over when England were set only 85 to win.

Spofforth said afterwards that the wicket could not have suited him better; but he thought that if England had chanced their arm they must have won. Murdoch thought the same. It was a case of too much batting, with no one accustomed to going in at a crisis at 8, 9 and 10. All the England players agreed that they should have won. 'Well, well,' piped Grace, extracting a morsel of glee from the gloom, 'I left six men to get 30-odd runs and they couldn't do it!'

The final comment came from Peate, the Yorkshire left-hander.

When asked why he hadn't concentrated on defence and left the scoring to his illustrious partner, he made the priceless remark that reeks of Yorkshire and characterizes Peate for all time.

'Ah knew ah could play old Spoff,' he said, 'but ah couldn't trust Mr Stood.'

★ ★ ★

Neville Cardus reported and wrote on the game for thirty years. The match he chose as his 'ideal' was played between the old enemies on the most sacred of grounds. It showcased attacking batsmanship, skilful slow bowling, and superb fielding. An Indian prince made a dazzling debut for England; an Australian commoner coolly put that effort in the shade. Bradman himself thought his 254 to be the best of all his innings. Before the summer began, esteemed judges had predicted that he would be an utter failure on English wickets – you see, he played with a cross bat.

NEVILLE CARDUS

The Ideal Cricket Match (1956)

FIRST DAY

If some good fairy were to ask me to pick out one match of all I have seen, to relive it as I lived it at the time when it happened, my choice would be easy: England v. Australia at Lord's in June 1930. I was at the prime of forty years then, fulfilled in work and happy in home, love and health, the mind still unstaled, yet critical enough. This game could be laid up in heaven, a Platonic idea of cricket in perfection. It was limited to four days and finished at five o'clock on the closing afternoon; 1,601 runs were scored and 29 wickets fell. Bradman batted in a Test match at Lord's for the first time, scoring 254 in his first innings. England batted first and made 425, but lost by 7 wickets. Glorious sunshine blessed every moment's play. London was at its most handsome; 1914 forgotten and 1939 not yet casting a shadow for all to see. I can still catch the warmth and the animation of the scene, feel the mind's and the senses' satisfaction. I can see

Grimmett bowling, his arm as low as my grandfather's, his artfulness as acute; and I can still see Chapman as he played one of the most gallant and dazzling and precarious innings which has ever cocked a snook at an Australian team ready and impatient to put to rout and ruin an England team apparently in the last ditch, the ghost about to be given up.

In the two teams were some of the greatest players of history, names already classic or legendary: Hobbs, Woolley, Hammond, Duleepsinhji, Hendren, Tate, Woodfull, Ponsford, Bradman, Kippax, McCabe, Victor Richardson, Oldfield and Grimmett. From one of the boxes near the grandstand, K. S. Ranjitsinhji looked on; and the fact that he was present in the flesh relates the match more even than the heroism and splendour of the actual cricket to the realm of the fabulous past. Only twenty-six years ago? It is hard to believe. Every department of cricket was seen at its best during this match; fast bowling, slow bowling, spin; all varieties of batsmen from Woodfull and Bradman to Duleepsinhji; with wonderful fielding everywhere.

Sutcliffe was unable to play, and when Chapman had won the toss and England's first innings was about to begin, the vast crowd saw Woolley walking to the wicket with Hobbs. Not since 1921 had Woolley gone in first for England, though he had taken part in thirty Test matches against Australia. And how he opened the England innings now! – the cricket at once seemed as though ignited by the radiant sun. Woolley's strokes were as brilliant, as much a matter of nature as the rays dazzling the field from the blue sky. Wall attacked at a superb pace, supported by the virile dangerous fast-medium swing (both ways) of Fairfax, from whose bowling Hobbs was soon and most courteously caught by Oldfield, a wicketkeeper who, judging by his quiet charm of manner, might well and always have kept wicket in the kid gloves in which he was married. The overthrow of Hobbs cast no gloom over the morning's sheen as Woolley cut and pulled, combining power, poise and felicity. He scored 41 in half an hour; his strokes changed Lord's and a Test match into Canterbury with all the tents and bunting and white wine.

Fairfax changed over to the pavilion end. His first ball rose to cutting height. Woolley lay back, lifted up his tallness and cut hard. We looked to the boundary, and the fieldsman at third man ran in in anticipation; but Wall at backward point scooped up a catch, though the impact of the ball against his hand sent him reeling back.

This, though we did not know it yet, was the match's leitmotif; we shall see how the same kind of catch marked the great climax of the last afternoon. Duleepsinhji and Hammond batted for England with the scoreboard announcing the loss of Hobbs and Woolley for a mere 50. Though Hammond was forced to the defensive and Duleepsinhji likewise, none of us suffered anxiety. England were bound to get ample runs on a fast pitch during a dream of a June day.

But on this occasion, at Lord's in June 1930, Grimmett bowled Hammond, luring him out by flight, defeating him by spin. A few weeks before this, at Trent Bridge, Grimmett on a lovely wicket for batsmen, had shown us spin bowling unparalleled; in half an hour he deceived and drew into his web Hammond, Woolley and Hendren, each put under his influence by hypnotic flight – then the poison of spin performed the dispatch. There has never been a cleverer slow leg-break bowler than Grimmett. He is not really properly described as a leg-break bowler, because the term usually suggests a certain inaccuracy of length. So I shall here call Grimmett a length bowler, a meticulous length bowler, who had control over leg spin and googly: he was a little man, with a shining dome of intellect or cunning, who ran a few nimble steps to deliver the ball, as though on the velvet of a cat's paws. And his arm, not above the shoulder, could toss the ball along an arch of wicked temptation; or send it along with a subterranean deceit.

This day he cudgelled his brain vainly for hours. Duleepsinhji and Hendren used quick feet, making strokes while the ball was coming to them. In half an hour 50 runs flowed over the field, or cracked and thundered when 'Patsy' hooked. This also was a Golden Age. Sunshine and applause, the cricketers' flannels catching the bloom of the day . . . Ripe and red in the face with contentment, the crowd greeted England's 200 for 3 wickets, whereat Hendren hit a long hop from Fairfax into young McCabe's hands at long leg; Hendren greedy for his fifty was out for 48 and came home to the pavilion with his face more or less concealed by the width of his smile. As a fact, England's innings hereabout suffered unexpected indecision. Chapman and Allen failed, so the score 239 for 6 was not good or safe enough. Tate was next man in and as he walked through the Long Room on the way to the wicket he saw me sitting on a table; at once he flourished his blade, envisaging a scythe-like cut, and said to me, out of the corner of his mouth, as though in confidence, 'Batsmanship!' Just that and nothing more. He went

forth, splay-footed, to join the elegant Duleepsinhji and lost no
time before he was driving and heaving the confident Australian
bowlers all over the place. He and 'Duleep' added 98 in 70 minutes,
Tate's share 54. As England's total arrived at the full tide of 400,
Duleepsinhji allowed his freedom of stroke play to run to licentious-
ness; and towards six o'clock he was caught by Bradman from a
reckless hit to the off side. He had made 173 in his first Test match.
He was in a position to enjoy himself, wasn't he? When we review
the match as a whole, seeing the end in the beginning, 'Duleep's'
impetuousness, so near to close of play, must be counted as a major
contribution to England's defeat. His illustrious uncle the Jam Sahib,
'Ranji' himself, severely reprimanded him for carelessness when he
reported himself to the enpurpled box at the end of the innings. At
close of play, England were 405 for 9.

SECOND DAY

Next day, Saturday, the sun outshone the glory of yesterday and the
crowd at Lord's sat in an eternity of content. Woodfull and Ponsford
began Australia's innings with grim protective vigilance. Australia
had lost the first match of the rubber at Nottingham; now they went
in facing 425 and possibly a wicket inclined to get dusty. Woodfull
and Ponsford made only 30 in an hour: 'Playing for a draw already,'
said more than a few irritated patriots, who naturally wanted Ponsford and Woodfull to get out, or assist in the act of their own
downfall. Australia's score reached 100 just after lunch, for none; the
time of day was half past two. At a quarter past three the score was
150 for none, Ponsford 77, Woodfull 70. It was at this point in the
proceedings that King George came to Lord's and was presented on
the field of play to the cricketers. From the first over after the King's
departure from the scene, bowled by White, Ponsford was caught
by Hammond in the slips. He 'followed' a wide ball. There is no
doubt that Ponsford's wicket should really have gone to His Majesty's
credit. At half past three, when Australia were 162 for 1, Bradman
walked to the wicket, taking his time. He drove his first ball smack
to long off, and when he had finished the stroke he was near
enough to the bowler to see the surprised look on White's face; for
until this instant minute no batsman had dreamed of running out to
drive White; in fact several very famous English cricketers had assured
me that to drive White on the half-volley was an act scarcely compre-

hensible in terms of skill or common sanity. The advent of Bradman on this Saturday of burning English summer was like the throwing of combustible stuff on fires that had been slumbering with dreadful potentiality. Nearly every ball was scored from. Bradman ran yards out of his ground to White and belaboured him; White was obliged to pitch short and then Bradman cut him to ribbons. After tea a massacre, nothing less. Never before this hour, or two hours until close of play, and never since, has a batsman equalled Bradman's cool deliberate murder or spifflication of all bowling. Boundaries everywhere – right and left and in front. The bowler helpless and at Bradman's mercy even as he ran to bowl. He reached 100 in one hour and three-quarters, with 13 fours. At 5.20 Australia's score was 300 for 1; at 5.30 it passed 350. Tate was wildly cheered when he sent a maiden to Bradman. But the England attack was entirely at a loss; not to get Bradman out – that wild hope had gone long since – but just to stem the flood of his boundaries. There were not enough fieldsmen available; Bradman found gaps and vacancies in nature. Ten minutes before half past six, Woodfull was stumped pushing out to Robins's spin; and it is a mistake to think that he was a dull, unlovely batsman. His stiff arms and short lift-up of the bat distracted the attention of casual onlookers from the prettiness of his footwork. It is a compliment to Woodfull that he did not sink into anonymity, or invisibility even, while Bradman at the other end of the wicket played the most brilliant and dramatically incisive and murderous innings of his career, and played it without turning a hair. At half past six Australia's total was 404 for 2; and Bradman, in little more than two hours and a half had made 155, not once exerting himself, every shot dead in the target's middle, precise and shattering; an innings which was beautiful and yet somehow cruel in its excessive mastery.

THIRD DAY

In constant sunshine the third day began and ended, but it had in it little of brightness or pleasure for English cricket. The Australians devoted themselves to the twin-souled cause of consolidation and attrition. Bradman abstained from gaudy hits; he and Kippax began the morning as though Australia's position in the match still needed cement in the foundations. Neither batsman seemed likely to get out, except through some error gross and inexplicable. Bradman, like

Kippax, waited for the loose ball, punished it mercilessly without going beyond the safe scope of known and practised technique. No wickets fell before lunch; Australia were then 544 for 2; and after lunch Bradman and Kippax resumed activity or operations exactly where they had left off at half past one. Somebody in the press box asked if King George was expected at Lord's again, and I added the hope that he would bring the entire Court with him. The scalded bowlers worked in shifts waiting for the mistake Bradman or Kippax would surely make in God's good time; and at ten minutes to three Bradman lifted a ball from White into the air – the only ball he raised an inch from the ground in all the length and magnitude of his innings. Chapman ran yards on the off side, and held the catch. Bradman scored 254 in five hours and a half; on the third day he made 99 in three hours, playing with a comfort which told us that he was for reasons of policy not moving along at a quicker or more murderous speed. Kippax soon followed Bradman to the pavilion's refreshing shade. He tried to cut White and played on. His 83 pleased the eye of the connoisseur all the time.

Here happened the ferocious Australian onslaught which for hours had been in sinister preparation. McCabe, Richardson, Oldfield treated the England attack sardonically; every ball was hit somehow, in the air, on the ground, into the crowd, 56 in 25 minutes. The declaration by Woodfull at the total of 729 for 6 was regarded by everybody present not only as an act of policy but also of Christian charity. One of the scoreboards patriotically declined to register the number 7. Australia's innings had lasted ten hours and ten minutes; England were destined eight years later to take revenge for this monstrous spawning and spoliation; but we could not know this on the glorious summer's day of our discontent at Lord's in 1930. A sad day it was to the end. Hobbs and Woolley, when England went in again 304 behind, scored 45 in half an hour by means of strokes good and strokes not so good. Grimmett immediately discovered spots on the wicket, the same wicket which only a few moments earlier had suggested a batsman's field of a cloth of gold. Hobbs walked down the pitch and prodded it. When Bradman left his crease it was always to prod the bowling. Grimmett coaxed Hobbs forward and bowled him with a leg break. He placed a silly mid-on under Woolley's nose. As a retaliation Woolley hit Grimmett square and trod on his wicket while doing so. Apparently fearing the presence of the 'silly' mid-on, Woolley pulled his stroke farther round than he would have done if no 'silly' mid-on had been in his way; he was obliged in consequence to move back on his stumps in order to shorten the ball's length. Craft as well as misfortune contributed to his undoing. At half past six, England's 98 for 2 definitely announced that Australia were on the verge of an astonishing and illustrious victory.

FOURTH AND LAST DAY

At the end of this great and enchanting match, I sat on the Green Bank at Lord's, hurriedly writing my description of the day's play just after five o'clock. I could begin my article for the *Manchester Guardian* in no better way than this –

> There is a passage in *Tom Jones* where Fielding, having got his plot terribly complicated, calls on all the high Muses, in person and severally, for aid; because he tells us, 'without their guidance I do not know how to bring my story to a successful conclusion'. As I write this report, I feel also the need of inspired and kindly forces. The day's play, in the old term, beggars description . . .

England had virtually lost the match by noon; in the last hour of the afternoon – my God, they nearly won it back. And they lowered the flag only after being forced to submit by sheer odds. When twelve o'clock chimed from the clock covered with ivy at the nursery end England were 147 for 5; Hobbs, Woolley, Hammond, Duleepsinhji and Hendren out; and the Australians were 157 ahead and another innings in hand. Grimmett was at his exercises again, wheedling his victims out, by slow flight which hovered before the crease, the ball an Ancient Mariner's eye, fixing the batsman on the spot, until it span with the noise of wasps. Now, as we could hear the England innings splitting on its beam ends, Percy Chapman came in. Before making a run he spooned Grimmett to midwicket, totally confounded by flight. The chance was the easiest ever offered to fieldsmen in a Test match. The ball hung obligingly, waiting to be caught. Two Australian fieldsmen dithered – and the ball fell harmlessly to earth between them. I can see at this distant hour and in the distant place where I am writing these lines the wild incredulous stare of Grimmett's eyes; and I think I can hear also a slightly demented laugh. Chapman proceeded to play an innings fantastic and audacious, with skill half blinded by hazard and gallantry. G. O. Allen helped him staunchly in a stand which, coming as it did after the impotence of Hammond and Hendren, seemed absolutely secure, once Chapman had discovered that he could kick Grimmett's breaking-away ball (the 'googly' to Chapman's left-handed bat) with his legs and pads; he then proceeded to kick and frustrate it by pedal movements which were scarcely related to any known formulated footwork. At lunch Chapman and Allen were still not out, England 262 for 5. And all Lord's wondered and hoped . . . could the match after all be saved? Alas, after the interval, Grimmett's straight ball ensnared Allen, but not before the sixth wicket had added 125 in 95 minutes. Allen's courage and trustfulness in a straight bat played forward entitles this innings to an immortal place or chapter in the Foxe's Book of Martyrs of Cricket. Chapman's cricket was played as though in a strange dimension of unreason with a method in all the apparently inverted science. Some of his strokes, technically to be counted and described as mishits, seemed somehow to have the power and certainty of strokes made and directed from the bat's true middle. With a combination of pushwork with his pads and a delayed forward lunge, he upset Grimmett's tactics in the very first stage of his innings, when England's position was at its worst. Grimmett was obliged to pack the on side and pitch his leg break – off break, of course, to Chapman – wide to the off stump. But as soon as Chapman had obtained a 'sight' of the ball, he repeatedly pulled Grimmett round, square or to long on, or in spaces between these two points. No cricketer entirely speculative could hope to hit Grimmett hard and often simply by flinging his bat through the air. Chapman pulled Grimmett for six, pulled or drove him for six three times. In an hour he scored 69. A mighty straight drive from Grimmett lifted the astonished, happy crowd to the height. This was Chapman's hour; he was in a beatitude. His bat performed wonders and it was as if he did not know it was performing wonders. He sent a ball into the deeps of the packed multitude on the Mound stand. Seldom has an innings in a Test match stirred a crowd to such jubilation as Chapman inspired now; it was a jubilation in which people saw visions and experienced unwonted impulses towards perfection. We should probably have to refer to Jessop's rout and rape of the Australians at the Oval in 1902 to find an equal to Chapman's century at Lord's in 1930. His 121 was made out of 207 in two hours and a half; and England in a second innings, broken of back halfway, survived to achieve a total of 375. A run-out, which threw away White's wicket when he was defending safely enough with Robins at the other end, no doubt had a subtle and far-reaching influence on the result of the match, a result that was not reached in the matter-of-course way expected by the Australians and everybody else at all interested.

At ten minutes to four, Woodfull and Ponsford walked confidently into the sunshine to compile the nominal 72 needed for victory. Against Tate and Hammond, Ponsford batted as though intent on getting all the runs himself. Two fours from Tate set him in excellent motion. Woodfull then sent a severe chance of a catch to Duleepsinhji at mid-on; and an over or two afterwards Robins, who had found a spot at the pavilion end, bowled Ponsford beautifully. Bradman, in next, was as usual slow in his progress to the wicket; the crowd remained, of course, to see him bat. People who had seen his first innings told those who hadn't exactly what they thought he would do to finish off the game. He scored a non-committal single before he lay back and cut Tate ferociously, a great stroke cracking in the air like gunshot. It disturbed the pigeons. Thousands of eyes flashed to the boundary. Chapman was in the 'gully', standing in his favourite position as the ball was bowled, legs apart, arms semi-folded, left elbow resting on the top of the right hand. As Bradman made the stroke, Chapman bent down, picked up the ball an inch from the grass, threw up a catch beyond belief, and assumed his usual upright stance, legs slightly apart, left elbow . . . and so on. The roar of the crowd expressed ecstasy and incredulity simultaneously. I was watching the match at this point in the company of Sir James Barrie, in front of the Tavern. As Bradman departed from the crease, on his way back to the pavilion, Barrie spoke to me, saying: 'Why is he going away?' 'But surely,' I said, 'surely, Sir James, you saw that marvellous catch by Chapman?' 'Oh yes,' replied Barrie. 'I saw it all right. But what evidence is there that the ball which Chapman threw up into the air is the same ball that left Bradman's bat?'

Spin by Robins ensnared Kippax, caught at the wicket by Duckworth with a terrible noise and yelping. Australia 22 for 3. Could England . . . but nobody dared tempt Providence by asking. Young McCabe the next batsman was met by Woodfull, who spoke to him. Robins lost his length; McCabe plundered 13 in an over, settling the account and issue. As the cricketers came from the field, the light of a glorious June afternoon shone on them; it shines on them yet. A victory in four days won in the face of a total of 425; England, though needing 304 to save defeat by an innings and though down and out at noon on the last day, in the fourth innings of a dusty

Lord's wicket, forced Australia to sweat and strain at the finish. It was the match of everybody who played in it. Victor and vanquished emerged with equal honour; and the chief laurel crowned the fair perspiring brow of A. P. F. Chapman. The match of every cricketer's heart's desire.

★ ★ ★

From Lord's Cricket Ground we move to an obscure venue in the north of England. The Lancashire League has always featured some bitterly contested matches. Each team is made up of ten workaday players, young and old, and one well-regarded 'professional'. In this particular match the professionals were two of the immortals. The man writing of their clash, although then unknown, is now regarded as one of the greatest of all cricket writers.

C. L. R. JAMES

Barnes v. Constantine (1932)

Sydney Barnes is generally admitted to be the greatest bowler cricket has yet seen. I had a glimpse of him the other day in action. He is fifty-nine years of age (the date of his birth given in *Wisden* is incorrect). Yet the man is still a fine bowler. It was an experience to watch him.

To begin with, Barnes not only is fifty-nine, but looks it. Some cricketers at fifty-nine look and move like men in their thirties. Not so Barnes. You can almost hear the old bones creaking. He is tall and thin, well over six feet, with strong features. It is rather a remarkable face in its way, and could belong to a great lawyer or a statesman without incongruity. He holds his head well back, with the rather long chin lifted. He looks like a man who has seen as much of the world as he wants to see.

I saw him first before the match began, bowling to one of his own side without wickets. He carried his arm over as straight as a post, spinning a leg break in the orthodox way. Then he had a knock himself. But although the distance was only a dozen yards and the ball was being bowled at a very slow pace, Barnes put a glove on. He was not going to run the risk of those precious fingers being struck by the ball. When the preliminary practice stopped he walked in, by himself, with his head in the air, a man intent on his own affairs.

His own side, Rawtenstall, took the field to get Nelson out. League sides will sometimes treat the new ball with Saturday-after-noon carelessness; not so Rawtenstall. Ten of them played about with an old ball: Barnes held the new. He fixed his field, two slips close in and the old-fashioned point, close in. Mid-off was rather wide. When every man was placed to the nearest centimetre Barnes walked back and set the old machinery in motion. As he forced himself to the crease you could see every year of the fifty-nine; but the arm swung over gallantly, high and straight. The wicket was slow, but a ball whipped hot from the pitch in the first over, and second slip took a neat catch. When the over was finished he walked a certain number of steps and took up his position in the slips. He stood as straight as his right arm, with his hands behind his back. The bowler began his run – a long run – Barnes still immovable. Just as the ball was about to be delivered Barnes bent forward slightly with his hands ready in front of him. To go right down as a normal slip fieldsman goes was for him, obviously, a physical impossibility. But he looked alert, and I got the impression that whatever went into his hands would stay there. As the ball reached the wicket-keeper's hands or was played by the batsman, Barnes straightened himself and again put his hands behind his back. That was his procedure in the field right through the afternoon. Now and then by way of variety he would move a leg an inch or two and point it on the toe for a second or two. Apart from that, he husbanded his strength.

He took 7 wickets for about 30 runs, and it is impossible to imagine better bowling of its kind. The batsmen opposed to him were not of high rank, most of them, but good bowling is good bowling, whoever plays it. Armistead, a sound batsman, was obvi-ously on his mettle. Barnes kept him playing; then he bowled one of his most dangerous balls – a flighted one, dropping feet shorter without any change of action and, what is so much more dangerous, pitching on the middle wicket and missing the off. Armistead, mag-netized into playing forward, had the good sense to keep his right toe firm. The wicketkeeper observed Armistead's toe regretfully, and threw the ball back to Barnes. Up to this time Armistead had relied almost entirely on the back stroke. It had carried him to where he was without mishap. A forward stroke had imperilled his innings. Behold there the elements of a tragedy, obvious, no doubt, but as Mr Desmond MacCarthy says, the obvious is the crowning glory of art. Armistead played back to the next ball. But he couldn't get his bat to it in time. Barnes hit him hard on the pads with a straight ball, and the pads were in front of the wicket.

He went from triumph to triumph, aided, no doubt, by the terror of his name. When Constantine came in I looked for a duel. Constantine was not going to be drawn into playing forward. Barnes was not going to bowl short to be hooked over the pavilion, or over-pitch to be hit into the football field. Constantine also was not going to chance it. For on that turning wicket, to such accurate bowling, who chanced it was lost.

Constantine jumped to him once, and a long field picked the ball up from the ground, where it had been from the time it left the bat. Barnes bowled a slow one, that might almost be called short. It pitched on the leg stump. Constantine shaped for the forcing back stroke. The field was open. But even as he raised himself for the stroke he held his hand, and wisely. The ball popped up and turned many inches. Another ball or two, and again Barnes dropped another on the same spot. It was a sore temptation. Constantine shaped again for his stroke, his own stroke, and again he held his hand; wisely, for the ball broke and popped up again. So the pair watched one another, like two fencers sparring for an opening. The crowd sat tense. Was this recitative suddenly to burst into the melody of fours and sixes to all parts of the field? The Nelson crowd at least hoped so. But it was not to be. Some insignificant trundler at the other end who bowled mediocre balls bowled Constantine with one of them.

After that it was a case of the boa constrictor and the rabbits, the only matter of interest being how long he would take to dispose of them. But, nevertheless, old campaigner as he is, Barnes took no chances. Slip would stand on the exact spot where the bowler wanted him, there and nowhere else. When a batsman who had once hit him for two or three fours came in, Barnes put two men out immediately. As soon as a single was made, the outfieldsmen were drawn in again and carefully fixed in their original positions, although the score might be about 50 for 8 or something of the kind. Barnes had lived long enough in the world of cricket to know that there at any rate it does not pay to give anything away. Nelson failed to reach 70. As the Rawtenstall team came in, the crowd applauded his fine bowling mightily. Barnes walked through it intent on his own affairs. He had had much of that all his life.

Constantine, running seventeen yards and hurling the ball violently through the air, began sending back the Rawtenstall batsmen. One, two, three, wickets and bails flying every time. Forth from the pavilion came Barnes. He faced the West Indian fast bowler. He was older than Constantine's father and the wicket was faster now. Barnes got behind the ball, the pitched-up ball, and played it back along the pitch to the bowler. He judged the ball quickly and so got there in time. He kept his left shoulder forward and that kept the bat straight. He played the slower bowlers with equal skill, and whenever there was a single to be taken he took it. He never lost one, and he was in difficulties to get into his crease once only. 'Yes' and 'No' he said decisively in a deep voice which could be heard all over the ground. His bones were too stiff to force the ball away. But his bat swung true to the drive and he got over the short ball to cut. He stayed there some 40 minutes for 10, and as long as he was there his side was winning. But Constantine bowled him behind his back. Barnes satisfied himself that he was out, and then he left the crease. He came in slowly amid the plaudits of the Nelson crowd, applauding his innings and their satisfaction at his having been dismissed. Courtesy acknowledged the applause. For the rest he continued as he had begun, a man unconsciously scornful of his milieu. After he left, Rawtenstall collapsed.

Since then, Barnes has taken 5 for a few and startled Lancashire a few days ago by taking 9 for 20. In the years to come, it will be something to say that we have seen him.

⋆   ⋆   ⋆

As player and reporter, J. H. Fingleton had a range of experience that exceeded even that of Neville Cardus. One must therefore take seriously his choice of the finest Test he had known. With typical modesty, he does not tell the reader that he made top score in his side's first innings. This Australian touring side did not contain Bradman (who was unavailable) but it did have three peerless slow bowlers – Grimmett, O'Reilly and Fleetwood-Smith.

J. H. FINGLETON

The Best Test I Have Known (1958)

I've seen some very exciting Test matches and I've seen some pretty dull ones (especially during the past few years when captains have been parsimonious in their outlook on the game), but as Tests 'viewed' cannot possibly compete with Tests 'played', from the viewpoint of personal interest, I'm going to plump very solidly for a Test in which I played. That Test produced two of the greatest innings of this century, and other critics, with no personal part in the game, might also consider this particular Test the best they ever witnessed. Even though it finished in a draw!

The time was late December 1935. Victor Richardson's team of Australians had won the first Test against South Africa in Durban, and, although the Springboks a few months earlier had taken the series from England in England, they were deep in the depths of despondency as the second Test came due at the Wanderers' Ground, Johannesburg.

It had been a sad homecoming for them. Jock Cameron, a champion wicketkeeper, one of the hardest and most scientific hitters known to modern cricket, and a prince of good fellows, was stricken with enteric fever on the voyage from England and had died. This cast an immediate blight over the tour and, in addition, Grimmett and O'Reilly, possibly the best spin-bowling combination known to Test cricket, had driven a feeling of inferiority into the Springbok ranks. Tremendous bowlers, these two, completely unlike in their tactics. You could bat for two hours against the two masters and not get a loose ball. Often, as I crouched at short leg with Vic Richardson, driving home still further the threat of O'Reilly in particular, I felt pity for the Springboks as I saw their creased looks of intense concentration and worry.

Fleetwood-Smith was the third of the spinning trio. He, being a left-handed googly bowler, was entirely different from the others, but every batsman had moments of anticipation against him. He was likely to bowl the best batsman in the world head, neck and heels (as he did Hammond once on a true pitch in Adelaide in 1937), and yet every now and then you would get a loose ball from 'Chuck'.

Our batsmen were in fine shape, we had Oldfield behind the

stilts, and our fielding was said to be up to our highest standards. This, I suppose, was because we had more than a fair sprinkling of young chaps and because, too, we would regularly spend some two hours at fielding when net practice was over. We had the zest of young fellows who knew that to get the best out of a game you must put all you have into it. We loved the exhilaration of living and being on a cricket tour. And we were happily led by a chivalrous warrior, Vic Richardson.

Well, then, to Johannesburg on this late December morning of 1935. Though we had been walking over the provincial sides, the South African enthusiasts were sure there was something better around the corner. Many families from Durban, Cape Town and the outlying veldts breakfasted outside the Wanderers' Ground that day, waiting for the gates to open.

Herby Wade won the toss, gave a happy signal to his dressing room, and a hearty cheer ran around the ground. First blood to South Africa.

Elation, however, soon turned to dejection. Ernie McCormick (one of the richest wits in the game and the most delightful of teammates) was in his best fast-bowling form that morning. He did not share the feeling of those athletes who are distressed by the high altitude of Johannesburg, 5,700 feet above sea level. The ball behaves differently compared with sea-level grounds, and many a fieldsman, shaping for a catch in the outfield, will find the ball carrying further in the rarefied air, only to finish over the fence.

McCormick, this day, was as fast as any bowler I have known. He had two other similar spells – one at Brisbane and one at Lord's, both later – and he revelled in the conditions of this fast pitch. At lunch, South Africa were 6 for 78, their backs and hearts broken. McCormick, at one stage, had these figures: 9–4–26–3. And then came Grimmett to rub it in, as usual.

I can well recall the anguished 'Oh!' that circled the ground when McCormick sent spinning the leg stump of Dudley Nourse, certainly South Africa's greatest batsman of modern times. Nourse was then in his middle twenties, of average height, splendidly built, and the son of Dave, who, himself, had hit his Test centuries for the Union and was to make a half-century against us in Cape Town towards the end of the tour.

'Dudley will get us out of this mess,' the crowd had hopefully murmured as he swung through the gate, a picture of fitness and confidence. But Nourse could not put his bat on McCormick, who, apart from his great burst of speed, was swinging the ball late from the leg. So to lunch, with the locals in a state of dejection – but we enjoyed ours!

The Springboks doubled their score after lunch but were all out for 157. O'Reilly had thundered into the breach and, bowling his leg breaks and bosies to an impeccable length from his height of 6 ft 3 in, he tied the batsmen into many an awkward knot.

We came to bat just after tea and by stumps that night were ahead with seven wickets in hand. Brown and I were having a happy tour and put on a century opening partnership at better than a run a minute. McCabe was forcing it home in his own brilliant manner when he was dismissed right on time.

The South African newspapers, I remember, told a doleful tale next day. It was in this innings that I remarked to Richardson, who had taken my customary New South Wales position of silly short leg to O'Reilly, that I would like more fielding work to do. 'Come and join me,' said the bright Victor, and along I went to make a double leg trap. The two of us, up so close, had many a narrow escape from decapitation, but we pegged the batsmen down for O'Reilly. It was strange, therefore, knowing what risks we were taking, to read next morning that we 'were being unsporting in fielding so close to the batsman'. The batsman had the solving of that little problem all in his own hands!

It was a docile, glum crowd next morning – but not for long. Chud Langton, one of the best medium bowlers I have known, soon got to work on a perfect pitch and under a cloudless sky. He knocked back Richardson's stumps; he baited Chipperfield in the fine-leg trap; and, with us having last use of a pitch not long laid, we began to have some apprehensive thoughts of what this bowler would do to us on a wearing pitch in the fourth innings.

Darling, a spectacular left-hander who never gave the grass much chance to grow under his feet or in the direction of his drives or pulls, was in great form. So, too, was Oldfield, as neat with the bat as the gloves. From 5 for 174 we shot up to 5 for 209. 'Getting out of the woods,' we told ourselves as we watched from the pavilion. But then came one of the most brilliant pieces of fielding I have ever seen. Oldfield hit a ball hard and wide of mid-off and called. Darling came on. Langton threw out his right hand at top speed, gathered the ball, wheeled, and threw the stumps over. Darling was out by a foot to as thrilling a piece of fielding as one could ever hope to see.

The crowd began to chortle again. In the next five minutes – through the medium of Bruce Mitchell – they went crazy with excitement and joy. Mitchell was a grand opening batsman and a very safe slip field, though in the Brisbane Test of 1931 he gave himself the most awesome nightmare for the future by dropping Bradman three times off Neville Quinn before he was 20 – and the Don made 226! Mitchell was also a very fair bowler of leg breaks, walking just two steps to the bowling line, and in one over on this hectic day he took 3 wickets for 3 runs. No wonder the spectators became almost hysterical with excitement.

The stands were crammed when play recommenced after lunch. This Wanderers' Ground, since taken over for extension of the railway yards, was in the heart of the city and spectators flocked there during the lunch hour.

Mitchell's bowling again made us reflect. If he could turn like this on the second day, what could we expect on the last? No doubt the Springboks were thinking: 'If Bruce can turn like this, what will O'Reilly and Grimmett do?'

There must have been some feverish planning in the Springboks' dressing room, and it was soon obvious what the policy would be. They had decided that this was their day. The portents were clear and they would continue to attack.

As a true captain should, Herby Wade came first to practise what he preached. No leader from behind was Wade.

Spurred on by his first-innings success, McCormick bowled again as fast as human could, but this time he lacked accuracy. Twice in his first over wide balls went for boundaries. There was a yell when, in the second over, point misfielded and Siedle went for a run. Wade shouted 'No', Siedle jammed on his brakes, turned – and narrowly beat the throw home. Exciting stuff!

In his second over, Wade beautifully hooked McCormick twice for four. Then came another thrilling pull for four. Siedle also got two fours in the one over from O'Reilly, one a powerful pull, the other a scorching straight drive. Forty came up in 30 minutes. Richardson made quick bowling changes. It was tense, dramatic cricket. Grimmett came on. Wade thought there was turn where there wasn't, the ball came straight and fast with topspin, and out he went, lbw. Grimmett, the fox of cricket, smiled broadly. He loved to see batsmen play where the ball wasn't.

Grimmett and Fleetwood-Smith bowled four successive maiden overs. And now a hush fell over the crowd, only the crack of bat against ball breaking the expectant silence.

Rowan had come to the crease. Siedle, remembering Wade, played for a straight one which broke – and 'tinkle, tinkle' went his bails. Grimmett, as he was wont to do, clasped his arms and smiled again – expansively. 'You old fox, Clarrie,' we said, as we thumped him on the back. His grin of delight, when such things happened, was one of the sights of the cricket field. He loved to diddle a batsman out.

Rowan, the 'Talkative' (so called because he kept up a running conversation with bowler, fieldsman and keeper all the time he batted), was kept defending as hard as he talked.

'Wasting your time there, Vic,' Rowan would say as he played a dead bat to O'Reilly. 'I hope you see home again, Fingo,' he said to me as he crashed into a no-ball from O'Reilly and Richardson and I dropped to the ground as if in an air raid.

Richardson had the decisive, if not the final, word. 'There's your passage ticket, Eric,' said Vic as Rowan feverishly played where the ball wasn't against Grimmett and up went the umpire's finger as Grimmett spun round, index finger aloft, and put the question.

'I'll get you next Test,' hissed the irrepressible Rowan as off he went.

So we had fought back again, thanks to Grimmett, whose figures at this stage read: 10–4–20–3. Wonderful bowling.

Mitchell came at No. 4 this time and Nourse No. 5. Nourse was not himself. Even so early in the tour we had considered that his weakness, if he had one, was against pacy bowling. Richardson must have thought hard as Nourse came to bat. McCormick should have come on immediately for Nourse, but Grimmett couldn't be taken off and Fleetwood-Smith was also on the spot. It was a difficult decision. Richardson went on with spin.

Nourse batted as if in a nightmare. He stabbed feverishly, his footwork indecisive. Mitchell thumped two fours off Fleetwood-Smith and another in the next over, but Nourse just couldn't get the ball away. He was, of course, facing a 'pair' and he had the large crowd as uncomfortable as himself – as one feels uncomfortable when watching somebody in distress.

Grimmett was teasing Nourse unmercifully, but eventually, after

playing four maidens, Nourse got him past cover for four. He had
been 25 minutes getting off his 'pair'; but now was to come one of
the greatest innings in Test cricket, and perhaps the greatest ever
played by a Springbok on his home soil.

Nourse found himself immediately. He stroked now with precision and confidence, and there was a great yell from the crowd
when, at the end of Fleetwood-Smith's next over, Richardson tossed
the ball to McCormick. This purgatory of spin bowling, said the
crowd, was over at last. Thrilling and admirable as it was, it was too
uncomfortable to watch. Here, now, was McCormick!

The crowd hadn't heard Richardson say, as he tossed the ball to
McCormick, 'Grum, Drong.' A team on tour – a good team, that is
– works like a machine and two contractions of nicknames were
enough to suggest that there was no spell yet for Grimmett. McCormick, ever the wag, swung his bowling arm several times – and then
threw the ball to Grimmett. Mitchell, who could hit when in the
mood, tucked Clarrie away for three fours in that over. The crowd
loved it.

So to tea, with South Africa 3 for 132 – Mitchell 28, Nourse 14.

'Stoke yourself up, Drong,' said Richardson to McCormick at tea.
'You look like having a long lease of that top end.'

'And about time, too,' chipped in Grimmett. 'You ought to be
ashamed of yourself, leaving all the hard work to young chaps like
me!'

'Who said you were coming off, Grum?' said Richardson, ban-
tering Grimmett, as he always did. 'You've just started to bowl. And
no more experiments with Bruce Mitchell, either. Get stuck into
him.'

McCormick paced out his long run after tea. In that very first
over Nourse snicked one that flew high to the clutching hands of
the jumping Chipperfield and Richardson in the slips. Luck was
with the batsman, and the ball went through, untouched, to the
fence. The crowd gasped in relief.

Then came a three and a two through the slips, upon which
Richardson gave McCormick more slips, until he had five in all.
Nourse accepted the challenge and once, twice, thrice he cut McCormick through the massed slips to the fence. The crowd roared with
glee and then shouted approbation in the next over as Nourse calmly
ignored every ball from McCormick, all teasingly outside the off

stump with the slipsmen crouched, their tense fingers expectant for the catch.

Nourse overtook Mitchell in the thirties, forced Grimmett superlatively off his toes for four, picked McCormick square for four, and then on-drove him for four. Fast, anticipatory fielding by Darling saved another four. Then came O'Reilly, to curb Nourse with four successive maidens. Nourse broke the sequence by drawing back to his stumps, standing tiptoe, and crashing O'Reilly with a short-arm backswing between Richardson and myself. To the fence, again – and we withdrew a yard.

Up came Nourse's fifty in 90 minutes, with eight fours. Take out his abortive first 25 minutes and his fifty came in 65 minutes. Not even Cyril Walters had treated Grimmett and O'Reilly like this in the preceding year in England.

Nourse surged on, his feet twinkling, his bat scourging. Out and back, out and back, his body never still, never retaining its initial position of the stance. Mitchell, like the sensible man he was, withdrew into passive obscurity.

Nourse almost went at 65, Fleetwood-Smith getting one hand to a hefty pull off Grimmett. Next ball, Nourse savagely hooked Grimmett for four, where there was no fieldsman.

The new ball came at 210. McCormick had four slips but Nourse got him through immediately for four. Oldfield snapped Mitchell up off McCabe (134 minutes for 45) and Nourse had made 76 of the 129 partnership – a partnership which redeemed the reputation of South African cricket because it quelled, for the first time, the great Australian spin attack.

Still Nourse sailed on. Off four successive balls from McCormick, he took 11 with two successive fours out through the alert off-side field – drives in the classic manner, timed to perfection, the bat swinging against a stiff left leg and the ball sounding off the bat like a sweet chime.

Nourse stood at 98 as the last over came. 'Dudley, Dudley, Dudley!' chanted the wildly excited natives in their special stand on the far side of the ground. I went down near them, to field on the fence, and there saw a mass of dark faces, with white teeth gleaming in anticipation of Nourse's hundred that night. On the opposite side of the ground, no noise came from the whites. They sat like monks in contemplation.

The garish day finished at last, with Nourse still 98 and still not out. The Springboks were 161 ahead – with six wickets in hand. We could, we told ourselves in the pavilion that night, lose this game. But what an innings from Nourse!

We were to find next day that the innings had barely begun. As Nourse came in with Dooley Briscoe, a sharp nor' westerly was stirring up dust, and O'Reilly and Grimmett inspected happily the now very worn patches at both ends. This was the first time this pitch had been used. It had stood up well to all the pounding feet but now it was breaking.

Nourse, immediately and majestically, moved to his century with a push for two off Grimmett. The crowd rose to him. O'Reilly was troubling him, the big fellow spinning and jumping the ball up smartly from the turf, but Nourse eventually got him square for four and then thumped him to the off for another four.

The sun was blazing and Nourse, too, warmed up, peppering our hands on the off side. It was exhilarating to be in the middle of this and Billy Brown, Darling and I, on the off side, pitted our wits and our speed against Nourse, trying to anticipate his shots, trying to manoeuvre him away from the strike. We were earning our biltong!

Gradually Nourse became dominant. He hit Grimmett off for Fleetwood-Smith; he took 7 in successive balls from O'Reilly; he drove Fleetwood-Smith straight for four; he murderously pulled him. Then, in the 160s, he hopped into Fleetwood-Smith, missed, was stranded, and Oldfield, for once, didn't pick the turn of the ball. It was the left-hander's bosie, deceiving batsman and keeper, and Nourse scrambled back as Oldfield fumbled.

Nourse hooked O'Reilly for four and Nicholson hit him high into the pavilion for six. At lunch the score was 5 for 370, Nourse 179.

Dark clouds came up during lunch and the mineral-laden sky looked ominous. The light was now bad and rain came. For 15 minutes we were off while a swarm of natives covered the pitch. Fleetwood-Smith took the ball and a handful of sawdust. Three times, off successive balls, Nourse hit him to the leg boundary. A single then, and Nourse was 200 in 276 minutes.

Now Nourse began to loft the ball. He hit Grimmett back over his head while Nicholson went and Langton came. Langton hit Fleetwood-Smith for six and Nourse now surged boundaries in all directions until it became a flood. He swept past all South African records, and, on this worn pitch against some of the greatest spinners ever, he humbled us well and truly.

Richardson tried to control the game, but it was no use. 'Got any ideas, Chuck, about Dudley?' he said once to Fleetwood-Smith.

'Yes,' said that bowler, 'Shoot him.'

We just had to wait until the end of Nourse came.

It came at last, McCormick brilliantly catching him at point. A. D. Nourse, c McCormick, b McCabe – 231. This score should be entered in the cricket book of all time, in letters of gold.

Nourse hit 36 fours and batted for 298 minutes. As we were leaving the field for tea we lined up to meet General Smuts. 'I, too,' he said with sparkling eyes, 'have done some hectic chasing in my time!'

Bob Crisp (then a journalist, now a farmer in England) had a merry 35 and the innings finished for 491. It was the Australians, now, who were dragging the chain.

Vic Richardson was the best possible captain to play under. He never stood over his men, but jollied them along and gave them credit for knowing the game. No long string of tedious orders from Victor.

'Now then, you two,' he said as Brown and I padded up, 'work it out for yourselves in the middle. It's going to be tough. I'll leave it to you.'

We needed 399 to win on a fourth-innings pitch, and at the rate of almost a run a minute. As we had managed only 250 in the first innings, 399 was something stiff.

'G'luck, Nugget,' I said to Brown as we walked towards the middle, with me to take strike.

'Same to you, my friend,' said Brown with a smile.

'One thing, Bill,' I said, 'is that "Buster" Nupen would have made our job much harder here.'

Bill Brown nodded in agreement. We had been regaled since our arrival with tales of how great a bowler Nupen *had been* on matting pitches. Now that turf had come to all South African Test pitches Nupen had been put aside – and that was a consoling thought as Brown and I went out to bat. The truth was that Nupen was a great spin bowler on *any* pitch!

You would never wish for a better opening partner than Bill Brown. He always came at your call, you could rely on his, and he never hogged the strike. His smile, however, was a little wry. We both had an idea it was going to be hard going.

It was not Bill's day. Nicholson soon snapped him up behind off

Crisp. Then came Stan McCabe, with his quick walk, always anxious to start proceedings. Stan was a bad 'pavilion waiter'. He had much waiting to do with Ponsford and Bradman in England in 1934, as they piled up huge partnerships, and he was always pleased when his job commenced.

Nourse had been superlative in his final stages, but now McCabe began to play, from the very beginning, every bit as wonderfully as Nourse had done. He batted with effortless ease. He never lunged; he always stroked. He was built very much like Nourse – medium height, solid, square shoulders – and there was a definite similarity between their styles. McCabe had whippy, powerful wrists and he was a master of placement.

It was 4.20 o'clock on the last day but one, with Australia 1 for 17 and the light wretched, with dark black clouds looming for the certain storm, and the pitch thoroughly unreliable. But in 40 minutes McCabe never made a false step, stroke or error of judgement. In 40 minutes he made 51–40 of them from boundaries.

I left it all to McCabe. At 4.55 the light was shocking. It was a ticklish position for us. We still had a long way to go and we knew that we had a very long tail. Stan was vice-captain and we had a midwicket conference.

'I can hardly see the ball,' said Stan.

I smiled. 'No foolin'?' I said.

'Well, you mightn't think so,' said McCabe, in his modest, shy manner, 'but I've got my work cut out to see it. We have all day tomorrow. This is a good start. I think we had better give the light a go.'

'Umpire,' I called, 'how is the light?'

We got the appeal immediately and left the field 1 for 85, of which McCabe was 59.

'Well done,' said Richardson, as we got in, 'you did the right thing. I didn't want to lose another wicket tonight.'

This last day should have been a battle all the way against the clock as well, yet inside an hour, on a turning, dusty pitch that was a bowler's dream, McCabe tore the Springbok attack to tatters. Sometimes the ball would rear and turn amazingly, but McCabe was either right out or right back, and every time he played a stroke he seemed to find a gap in the field. My orders were to hold tight and leave it to McCabe.

Our hundred came up in 85 minutes, with boundaries coming

from McCabe at an almost incredible rate. He ran to his own hundred in 90 minutes. An appeal was made for a slip catch, but the umpire was with McCabe.

With the total 194, Mitchell spun one off the dust round my legs and just flicked the leg bail. I had made 40 in a hard struggle to keep out shooters and big and sudden breaks – which made McCabe's innings at the other end seem like a crazy dream to me. He had made 148 of our partnership of 177.

The Springbok attack was well tamed, but not beaten. McCabe's wicket was the one they wanted. If they could get him, they reasoned, the other Australians should be easy.

Darling came to give McCabe support, and to see the 200 go up in 166 minutes. McCabe ran to 150 in 145 minutes and at lunch he was 159. He had made his century before lunch, joining Trumper, Macartney and Bradman in achieving this feat.

At lunch we were 2 for 217. The clock, too, was beaten. But, though we now looked certain to win, we knew that this match could well be over in an hour.

The light, after lunch, was as murky as a tunnel. In the distance, vivid flashes of lightning lit the sky, and now the prospect was certain rain.

A new ball was due and McCabe and Darling had to fight hard. McCabe got a high one luckily through slips and then, in quick succession both he and Darling were dropped in the slips.

McCabe brought up the 250 in 199 minutes, but Darling, who had commenced delightfully, was now hard put to it to sight the ball. Thunder was crackling and erupting and the forked lightning was almost frightening to behold. McCabe snicked one again into the slips and Robertson, diving, failed to hold it.

Then came an historic appeal. Herby Wade, from the field, appealed against the light! The umpires agreed, the players came off, the rain tumbled down, and in fifteen minutes the pitch was under water. We Australians were only 125 off victory, with three hours left for play.

So ended what I still think was the greatest Test I have known. It had every ingredient of exciting, fighting Test cricket, with the fortunes changing almost hourly. The bowling, the fielding, the tactics were always interesting, and in Nourse's 231 and McCabe's 189 not out (he hit 29 fours) it gave cricket two of its greatest innings ever.

Said Wade at the finish: 'It has been a wonderful game of ups and downs, both sides being on top at different periods. The Australians were definitely on top when bad light and rain brought the close. The game was played in the best spirit. These Australians are a splendid lot of cricketers. I want to congratulate McCabe on his classical innings and Grimmett on his great bowling.'

Said Richardson: 'Unfortunately, a very fine finish was nipped in the bud by bad light and rain. The South Africans fought back splendidly in their second innings and set us an almost herculean task to collect 399 runs on a dusty, wearing pitch; but it is a pity that, despite McCabe's individual record Test score and a very fine knock by Fingleton, which set us well on the road to accomplishing that task, finality was not reached.'

In retrospect, I think it best that the game ended as it did. Both sides deserved to win: neither side merited defeat.

★   ★   ★

Three years after Fingleton wrote about the 1935 Johannesburg Test, he was made to relegate that match to 'second-best' status. Open to revision, as the best scholars and writers must be, he wrote a book on the 1960 Brisbane Test called *The Greatest Test of All*. That work I heartily commend to the reader. However, for this anthology I have chosen to include instead an account by a man who captained one of the sides in that singular match. Like Fingleton, Richie Benaud was a trained journalist who wrote every word that appeared under his name.

RICHIE BENAUD

The Last Day at Brisbane (1962)

233 to win and 310 minutes to play . . . In retrospect, surely the most nerve-racking 310 minutes of all time . . .

I made a bad start at the ground. When I walked through the gate and along the side of the pavilion to the dressing rooms I could see white flowers dotting the turf; clover flowers. It was obvious that the ground hadn't been mown this morning.

*I ask for a mowing but the curator tells me there was a heavy shower
just after seven o'clock and he hasn't been able to get the mower on
the ground . . . now he hasn't time to do it. Short of getting the
mower and doing it myself it seems that the grass will not be mown
today. I don't s'pose it matters a great deal really, we'll only have a
bit over 200 to make.*

So I thought at the time – but how wrong can one be?

It was a dismal morning for Australia. With only one run on the
board, Simpson was caught at short leg off Hall. The fast bowler
landed the ball short and for some reason Bobby went to duck
instead of swaying away from it as he had been doing. When he
changed his mind, and tried to play a stroke, it was far too late. All
he could do was push the ball weakly to short leg. Harvey made 5
before he was out to an absolutely brilliant catch by Sobers at slip,
and we were 2 for 7 . . . bad but not irretrievable, for the next man
in was O'Neill.

Just two years before I had seen this brilliant player massacre the
MCC attack on the last day of the first Test to give victory to
Australia. Now Norm was in fine touch again, for his near double-
century in the first innings had given him confidence, so I settled
down to watch him take this West Indies attack apart.

'Have a look and then thrash them!' was the only advice I offered
as he went out. But he just couldn't do it this time, and neither
could Col McDonald, who battled till lunchtime for a handful of
runs.

Hall called the tune for almost the whole of this pre-lunch session,
and the West Indies were completely on top. We had taken over an
hour for less than 30 runs and from lunch we had to score at the
rate of nearly 50 runs per 100 balls to win the game. But we had
eight wickets left, and I thought we still had the chance of victory
in the remaining two sessions.

Lunch nowadays at the Brisbane Cricket Ground is a pleasant
affair. Unless of course you happen to be one of the not-out batsmen
who 'just don't feel like food', or the captain of the side, who spends
most of the time preoccupied, calculating runs per minute and runs
per over.

The batsmen come off the field weary from concentrating and
sweaty from the steamy tropical heat that had brought the early-
morning showers.

'What about it, Benordy?' O'Neill wanted to know. 'What do you reckon about the scoring?'

'We're going much too slow,' was McDonald's comment. 'Sorry, but they're bowling pretty well out there.'

'I know they're bowling well,' I said, 'but we'll have to step it up a bit if we want to get there . . .' and mentally realized that it was very easy to say that but not quite so easy to carry it out against Hall with his pace and length of run.

'Just see what you can do and watch the short ones . . . we want to win this one,' was all I said as Norm and Colin went out to resume after lunch.

Immediately they went berserk against the big Barbadian, and took 28 from four of his overs. The main run-getting came from O'Neill, who took 3 fours and a three from him.

But O'Neill and McDonald were suddenly dismissed within a few balls of each other, the former in trying to cut Hall and the latter bowled by Worrell. Favell made only 7 before being caught off Hall (a little unluckily, for he tried to hook and the ball flew from glove to short leg).

We were 5 for 57 and most of the afternoon left to play. The situation didn't look too good.

Mackay and Davidson added 35 of which 'Slasher' made 28 in pretty good style, too, before he tried to drive Ramadhin's leg break and was bowled. I passed him on the way out, and he managed a wry grin as he said: 'Sorry – she turned a bit.' Now the only names left on the scoreboard were Davidson and Benaud – the two batsmen in – Grout, Meckiff and Kline. Five names between defeat and victory for Australia, and mine was one of them.

It's a lonely feeling to walk on to a Test arena to do battle with eleven players from another country. Lonely as you walk to the centre with the thousands of eyes focused on you from the stands – the twenty-two eyes of the opposition fixed on you as you near the stumps. Lonely . . . exciting . . . and challenging for both the batsman himself and the opposition. I hadn't made many runs lately but if ever they were to come along, today would be the best time I could possibly imagine.

Ram's bowling and Val's on the other end, I thought. They're very good . . . but not as good as they used to be, although the little fellow has probably got his tail up from bowling 'Slash' . . . forget it and

concentrate . . . concentrate . . . concentrate. Don't do anything
silly . . . but keep your head down and concentrate. You can bat better
than any of these jokers can bowl . . . but concentrate!

You feel better once you're right out in the centre and not many
of the thousands watching anxiously would guess that you're nervous
all the same. Perhaps a little quiver of the bat as you ask for leg
stump and the urge to shuffle the feet a little before facing up to the
first ball, but apart from that you're OK. Just that empty feeling in
the pit of the stomach as Ram gives that little skip before his flurry
of shirt sends the ball on its way.

The first one hit the middle of the bat but the second produced
a cry of anguish as it skirted to top of middle and off and flashed
past Alexander for wonderful runs – byes. Davo at the other end
was steady as a rock but took his chance to capture 5 runs from
Valentine's next over. I'd got the strike again and was still on 0 . . .
never had a half-volley looked so good and I smashed it away to the
cover fence as the clock showed tea time.

There were 92 runs on the board . . . and 6 wickets down . . .

I sat with Davidson at tea in the players' section and we were
joined by Sir Donald Bradman, who was obviously enjoying himself.
He said what a wonderful game it had been over the four days and
that today was building up to a great last session.

Then he added: 'What are you going for, Richie – a win or a
draw?'

'We're going for a win, of course,' I replied.

His answer was a direct 'I'm very pleased to hear it.'

Later I realized what a good thing it was that the Chairman of
Selectors had spoken as he did at the team meeting . . . that he was
obviously completely against any ideas of playing for a soulless
draw . . . but there was little chance to think of that at the time.

With Davidson, I had to concentrate on trying to get the 123
runs still needed in even time if we were to win. As we walked back
on to the field neither 'Davo' nor myself had any knowledge that
we were to play a part in one of the most fantastic cricket sessions
of all time.

Davidson had already performed heroically in the match . . . 11
wickets for 222 runs from 55 overs and a near half-century when we
batted in the first innings. Now as we followed the perky Kanhai
and quiet little Joe Solomon on to the field he was needed again.

What will happen when he's not around to bat, bowl and field for Australia brings a furrow to my brow . . . but on 14 December 1960 he looked as dependable as ever as he strode to the wicket, his shoulders thrown back, and bat tapping the turf as he went. He didn't say much . . . we'd already discussed the plans of taking short singles and thrashing at anything loose . . . and then more and more short singles.

They'll crack, if only we can get the pressure on them. Pressure and more and more pressure and they must crack . . . they've done it so often before.

But, although this was the same team as they'd had before, they had a leader this time . . . a great player in his own right, a shrewd tactician and a man who had the respect and liking of his side . . . and of the opposition, too. A great cricketer this Worrell . . . a great cricketer in every sense of the word. A quiet man with a sense of humour, and a throaty laugh, the sort of man one cannot imagine falling into panic.

The play immediately after tea went magnificently with short singles coming apace and the occasional four keeping the scoring rate about a run a minute. We added 50 in around even time, with ones turned into twos and half-runs turned into quick singles. Davidson played two hooks from Hall that I can still see as if they were happening now. The second hit the ground a foot or two inside the fence and was a glorious stroke. Despite all this, however, we still had to push the scoring rate along to keep up with the one a minute needed for victory. Worrell changed his bowlers and put Hall in cotton wool for the new ball. Sobers, Valentine, Worrell, and Ramadhin all bowled but with little impression and gradually the game was tilting our way.

There was great tension around the ground. Not out in the centre, where the players remained cool, keeping the simmering excitement of the game within bounds, but in the crowd there was a frenzy that I hadn't seen before at a cricket ground. Spectators hushed to the delivery of each ball and then would come the shaking burst of excitement – or a long sigh if nothing happened.

The new ball had the crowd simmering . . . they had expected it, but now that it was here it was a new device to put them on the edge of their seats. In the dressing rooms players who would think nothing of being in a similar situation to the players if on the field,

were shaking like schoolboys at their first match ... and twenty
minutes later I was suffering the same emotion ... but out in the
centre it was all so different.

> *Come on now, concentrate, I thought. Wes has got the new ball ...*
> *but don't worry about it ... just play it like the old one. You've got*
> *27 to make in half an hour ... so just get your head down ... this'd*
> *be a hell of a game to win after being in such trouble.*

Worrell also had a pretty good grip of the game in the middle.
During this tense period, when lesser men and skippers would have
panicked, he ruled with an iron hand.

'Relax, fellas and concentrate ... come on now, concentrate,' he
would exhort.

Joe Solomon was to achieve a moment of some fame in the
second Test in Melbourne when he was given out through his cap
dropping on the wicket, and 67,000 spectators rose to his defence ...
but his real fame came a few weeks earlier on this beautiful Brisbane
afternoon.

The clock above the scoreboard showed ten to six and Australia
needed 9 runs ... just 9 runs. Sobers bowled a ball down the leg
stump and a little push to the onside made it 8 runs to go ...

> *Solomon was a bit slow getting to it – watch for another one there,*
> *Alan.*

A single to Davidson and I had the strike again. The ball pitched
down the line of the leg stump ... again I pushed it wide of Solomon
at forward square leg and called for 'One'. But this time Solomon was
on to it in a flash and in the same action threw from side-on to the
stumps. The bails were scattered as Davidson vainly tried to make
his ground at Alexander's end. The West Indians were jubilant. But
I was far from jubilant. It was a bad call ... a dangerous call. Even
if Solomon hadn't hit the stumps Davidson would have been out by
a yard with Alexander crouching for the return.

It was tragic but it had happened and I did some harsh
thinking ...

> *Come on now, concentrate ... don't let's have any more run-outs.*

Grout came in, played two balls and took a quick single off the
second-last ball of Sobers's over ... the second-last over of the day
and of the match. Try as I might I couldn't get the last one away to

take strike to Hall's last over and Wally was left with the job at the bottom end.

Hall took the ball in his hand and slowly paced back to his mark. The mark was a long, long way from the batsman, nearly out to the sight screen, and just before he turned for his run-up the players in the dressing room and on the patio in front of the room had a much better view of him than the crouching batsman. He's a tall man, almost ebony in colour, with flashing white teeth that light his face when he smiles. He has broad shoulders, and a lithe bouncing run to the wicket, gathering himself in as the popping crease approaches, to explode in what seems a flurry of arms and legs as he hurtles the ball at the opposing batsman. He likes an occasional drink and singing calypsos . . . but he dislikes batsmen.

As he walked back to the mark there were four minutes to go – this was definitely the last over.

Grout had the strike in this last over of the most memorable of cricket matches, and waiting in the pavilion were bowlers Meckiff and Kline, waiting in case they were needed to make the last 6 runs for victory from those eight balls from Hall.

Meckiff had spent the early part of the innings at the back of the dressing room, but as the score mounted he and Kline either sat on the edge of their chairs or paced up and down near the windows, to watch the game. Grout had prefaced his arrival at the crease by some nervous chain-smoking, and when Davidson was dismissed had searched desperately for his batting gloves . . . only to find he was sitting on them! Now he was facing the first ball of this last vital over from 'Big Wes'.

I watched, every nerve tense . . .

Just push a single, Wal . . . anywhere will do . . . Get an edge . . . off the pads . . . anything . . . but we must have a single so I can have the strike.

We got it, too, but in a painful way. Wally was struck in the solar plexus, a crippling blow, and the ball fell at his feet. It had hardly hit the ground before I was on my way without calling. Wally saw me coming and made off down the pitch holding his stomach . . . an agonizing single to be sure.

Five to win and seven balls to go . . . I thought. One four will do it just one four . . . concentrate . . . concentrate.

Next ball . . . it was a bumper. Surely no one in his right mind would bowl a bumper at that stage of the match . . . but it was a bumper delivered with every bit of speed and power the big fella could muster. I tried to hook . . . trying for the 4 runs that would have all but won the game. The only result was a sharp touch on the gloves and Gerry Alexander's victory shout as he caught me.

Have you ever tried so hard to do something . . . concentrated so desperately that everything else was pushed out from your mind . . . and then seen it disappear in a fraction of a second? Then you'll have some idea of how I felt as I passed Grout at the other end and said: 'All yours, Wal . . .'

He merely lifted his eyes and muttered: 'Thanks very much!'

Now it was 5 to win – and six balls left.

Meckiff played the first ball and missed the second and the batsmen scampered for a single as the ball went through to Alexander. A bye . . . brilliant thinking from Grout . . . and near heart failure for the spectators as Hall grabbed the return and hurled it at the stumps at the bowler's end. Valentine just managed to get behind the ball and save it from 4 overthrows. This was almost too much for me. I leaned across to Jackie Hendriks and whispered: 'What's wrong with Wes, Jackie? He can throw much harder than that.'

Grout had the strike now, and someone near me muttered: 'Please bowl another bouncer, Wes . . .' Wally is one of the best hookers in Australia and we needed only 4 to win.

Evidently Grout also expected a bouncer for he got into position to hook only to find the ball was of good length. He misjudged his shot and it skewed off the top edge straight to Kanhai at backward square leg.

Kanhai set himself under it as the Australian players watched. But in a flash Wes changed direction and was hurtling towards the now dropping ball. It was a nerve-racking sight, even for the Australians who didn't have time to realize the implications of Hall's charge.

Someone gasped: 'Wes! No Wes!' Too late! Next moment the ball was whisked away from Kanhai's steady hands and fell to the ground.

The dressing-room patio was sheer chaos. All restraint disappeared and players shouted and assured one another that this was the end . . . they couldn't take any more.

Just 3 runs needed – only 3 more. Meckiff trusted to a five-iron shot from the next ball, hitting 'outside in' and the ball flew to the midwicket boundary.

Watching from the patio we lost the ball in the setting sun but the batsmen were scampering up and down the wicket, determined to get the 3 runs needed for victory in case the ball didn't hit the fence. It didn't . . . the ball stopped a foot or so short of the boundary – a curse on that uncut clover! – and was picked up by Conrad Hunte.

Of all the minor miracles that took place on this day I give pride of place to this one. Hunte was about eighty yards from the stumps when he picked up, turned and threw in the one action. I couldn't see the ball . . . all I could see was the blurred throwing action to my right and the batsmen turning for three. For Grout to be run out the ball had to go directly to Alexander . . . not to the right or left but directly to him . . . thrown on the turn and from eighty yards. It was a magnificent throw and as Alexander swept the bails from the stumps Grout was hurling himself towards the crease . . . but still a foot out of his ground.

The game was tied, with two balls to go! One run to win . . . and last man Kline joined Meckiff.

Hall bounded in to bowl the second last ball of the match to Kline. He knew he must be deadly accurate . . . the only way to prevent the batsman getting the run that would mean victory for Australia was to bowl at the stumps . . . to spreadeagle them if possible.

There was not much sound on the ground at that moment, and even less as Hall let the ball go. It pitched in line with the middle and leg stumps and Kline played it with the full face of the bat to forward square leg.

The crowd screamed as the two batsmen set off on the winning run. They crossed as Joe Solomon was just about to gather it in both hands . . . he picked up as Meckiff got to within about six yards of the safety of the crease. Solomon the quiet one . . . good and dependable . . . the sort of man for a crisis. Was there ever a more crisis-like moment in a game of cricket than this?

There surely could never have been a better throw. The ball hit the stumps from the side on with Meckiff scrambling desperately for the crease. Umpire Hoy's finger shot to the sky and there came a tremendous roar from a crowd of 4,000 . . . who sounded like

twenty times that number ... greeting the end of the game. A
TIE ... the first in Test history.

★   ★   ★

The World Cup final of 1996 was much more than a 'sporting'
contest. The previous winter the Sri Lankans had toured Australia,
where they faced racist taunts. Their best bowler, who had passed
the scrutiny of rule-makers the world over, was called for throwing
by an Australian umpire. Earlier in the World Cup the Australians
had refused to play in Sri Lanka, saying the island was not 'safe'
enough. Asians, always touchy about these things, took this as a slur
on subcontinental hospitality. To show that the emerald isle was safe
for cricket at least, a combined Indo-Pakistan team stood in for the
absent Australians. With this background, it was ordained that Sri
Lanka would play against Australia in the tournament's final. Our
report comes from an American writer who learned to love the game
in exile in England.

MIKE MARQUSEE

David Slays Goliath (1996)

The teams lined up on the field for the national anthems, the
Australians in canary yellow with green lettering and the Sri Lankans
in deep blue with yellow lettering. I had become accustomed to the
garish pyjamas but the music was an unwelcome innovation, another
sop to the jingoists. The Australian anthem was played first, followed
by another tune which nearly everyone at the ground assumed
belonged to the Sri Lankans. It took me a moment to realize why
the theme sounded so familiar. It was 'Nkosi Sikelele Afrika', the
song of the liberation movement and now of the new, democratic
nation of South Africa. I turned to the lone South African in our
wing of the press box. We shared a bewildered look. When 'Nkosi'
finished, the Australians trooped off casually, but the Sri Lankans
remained in place, waiting for their anthem. After an embarrassing
silence the loudspeakers crackled with 'Namo Namo Matha' ('Hail

Motherland'), and the opening rites were concluded. As this bungled celebration of national identity was enacted, I surveyed the stadium. The boundaries and the stands were festooned with the insignia of multinational corporations: Coke, Shell, Visa, Philips, Fuji, National Panasonic, ICI. Whatever happened in the field today, *they* had already walked off with the true spoils of the World Cup.

Sri Lanka's itinerant cheerleaders, the veteran Percy Abeysekere and his young apprentice, Lionel, had made the journey from Colombo, thanks to corporate benefactors. Throughout the match, they ran ceaselessly to and fro with their giant Sri Lankan flags, cheered by the Pakistani fans. There were small islands of Australian support, but they were engulfed in a sea of Sri Lankan enthusiasm. The afternoon was overcast and breezy and the brilliant colours of the lion flag, gold and crimson and orange and green, fluttered in luminous streams. Because of the rain, the verges of the outfield were sodden and the boundary rope had been drawn in. It was as if the organizers had dropped a school playing field into the middle of a vast modern arena. The short boundaries, I reasoned, would benefit Sri Lanka, with their penchant for hitting over the top in the first fifteen overs.

Ranatunga won the toss and invited the Australians to bat. This had been his policy throughout the World Cup, and he persisted with it at Lahore, despite the fact that no team batting second had ever won the World Cup. He had been under pressure to play an extra bowler, but he kept faith with all seven of his batsmen. The Sri Lankan brains trust, guided off the field by manager Dav Whatmore, born in Colombo but raised in Australia, remained confident that they could outscore any other team. The match began on schedule at 2.30 p.m. The general stand was half empty; the long queue was still working its way through the gates.

This was the fourth time I had seen the Sri Lankans play in this World Cup and I had grown more attached to the side and its diverse personalities with each exposure. In the field, they were a charming *mélange* of willowy youth and portly experience. The two Sri Lankan pace bowlers, Vaas and Wickremasinghe, tried to harry the Australian openers, but on this flat pitch anything short stood up and asked to be hit. With a meaty bat, Taylor dispatched the quick bowlers square on both sides of the wicket. Although Mark Waugh, thus far Australia's outstanding World Cup performer, was out early, clipping Vaas into the hands of Jayasuriya at square leg, the Australians seemed unperturbed. Ponting, helmetless, slashed Vaas to cover off the front foot. Then, with a sweet flick of the wrist, he deposited a short ball from Wickremasinghe high over midwicket. Taylor continued to cut and drive crisply, and when spin replaced pace in the fourteenth over the score had already reached 79 for 1. My heart sank. The Australians looked like a well-oiled tank rolling to victory. What foolishness to think that the odds would be overturned, yet again, in this World Cup.

Luckily, Ranatunga and his men did not suffer such dark thoughts. Although Taylor and Ponting continued to take runs freely off the spinners, the Sri Lankans remained vigilant in the field, and Muralitharan and Dharmasena kept their nerve while searching for the right length on a pitch just beginning to turn. The Australians passed their hundred in the nineteenth over. In the press box old hands predicted a total of not less than 330. This first innings had begun to seem like an academic exercise. The real drama would come later, watching the Lankans do what they do better than anyone in one-day cricket history: chase outlandishly large totals . . .

Ranatunga juggled his spinners. Jayasuriya replaced Murali and De Silva came on for Dharmasena. The boundaries dried up, though Taylor and Ponting kept the score moving by pushing for singles and posted a 100 partnership off only 110 balls. At the halfway stage, after 25 overs, they had reached 134 for 1, a strong position. Shortly after, De Silva induced the first and only false stroke of Mark Taylor's innings: the ball flew off the top edge to deep square leg where Jayasuriya, running around at full tilt, took a difficult catch. The day before the final, he had been named 'Player of the World Cup' and presented with a new Audi (breathlessly described by Tony Greig as 'state of the art German automotive technology'). It was a popular choice. Batting, bowling, fielding – the man had seemed irrepressible, injecting the spirit of the playground into the over-wrought arena of global cricket. Now he popped up again, and the crowd was delighted. Sri Lankan flags fluttered.

Ponting, frustrated by his slow progress to 45 off 73 balls, tried to make room to run the ball down to third man but was deceived by De Silva's gentle turn. He lost his balance, missed and was clean bowled. In an attempt to knock the spinners off their line, Taylor sent in Shane Warne. At Madras, in the quarter-final against New Zealand, the ploy had worked. Warne's big hitting had stolen the momentum. But this time Taylor and Warne were out-thought by

Ranatunga and Murali. As Warne went on to the front foot to turn
the off-spinner to the leg side, Murali pushed a faster ball through
to the keeper, Kaluwitherana, who whipped off the bails even as the
batsman completed his forward lunge. A huge cheer greeted Warne's
dismissal. Steve Waugh was the next victim of spin strangulation.
Shaping to flick Dharmasena to the leg side, he sent the ball flying
off the leading edge high and deep over the bowler's head. De Silva,
running from mid-on, judged the catch perfectly and leaped in
delight; only three years before, he had been omitted from the Sri
Lankan side after failing a fitness test. At the end of the thirty-fifth
over the score was 170 for 5.

Stuart Law and Michael Bevan now faced the Lankan spinners.
Bevan was listed on the scoreboard simply as 'Michael', a Pakistani
payback for the countless times their names had been muddled by
commentators abroad. These two had saved Australia from ignominy
in the semi-final. Both were powerful and determined players, and
expert at the one-day art of controlled acceleration. But their
opponents were inspired by the clatter of Australian wickets. Earlier
the Sri Lankans had been watchful, as if waiting for the prey to
enter the trap. Now they scurried around, clapped and called to each
other, responding with alacrity to Ranatunga's constant adjustments.
In his second spell, Murali gave the ball more air and it turned and
bounced disconcertingly. Suddenly it was impossible to pierce the
field. The crowd emitted a continuous happy roar, which rose and
fell every time a ball was bowled and every time a fielder intercepted
a shot. I could not have been more wrong about the short boundaries.
In their first five overs at the crease together, Bevan and Law managed
to score only 8 runs. When Law pulled Dharmasena for six in the
forty-third over, it was the first Australian boundary in seventeen
overs. Soon after, he tried to slash a wide ball from Jayasuriya and
only succeeded in spooning to De Silva in the gully. Bristling with
belligerence, Ian Healy, the most experienced wicketkeeper in the
Cup, joined Bevan at the crease. De Silva tossed the ball in the air
like an expert angler dangling a fly in front of a trout's nose. Going
for a big hit off the front foot, Healy played around the ball and lost
his off stump. At the end of the forty-fifth over the score was 205 for 7.

Dharmasena and Muralitharan, the front-line spinners, had
completed their quota of overs, but Ranatunga decided not to bring
back his seam bowlers, Vaas and Wickremasinghe. Throughout
the Cup, he had relied on his part-time slow bowlers to frustrate the

opposition, and he did so now, calling on Jayasuriya and De Silva to finish off the innings. Thanks to Bevan's improvising, the Australians put on 33 runs for the last five overs without losing any more wickets. Jayasuriya beat him through the air, but Kaluwitherana fumbled the stumping. In the field, the Sri Lankans maintained the pressure. Even the rotund Ranatunga threw himself full-length to cut off a single, and Wickremasinghe redeemed his patchy bowling by steaming across the turf to stop Bevan's reverse sweep reaching the rope. Murali, fast on his feet, with a swift pick-up and hard, accurate throw, performed wonders in the deep. In the forty-ninth over Bevan made room to strike a leg side delivery high over extra cover. It was a strange inside-out shot which he repeated off Jayasuriya in the final over; these were the only two boundaries in his innings of 36 not out off 49 balls.

To have restricted the Australians to 241 for 7 after their brilliant early dash for runs was an achievement. But was 241 still too many? A run rate of 4.84 per over would not normally be a daunting target for this Sri Lankan side, but the Australians had successfully defended a smaller total against the West Indies at Chandigarh. The consensus in the press box was that the Sri Lankans would fall short. On a turning wicket, the Australians could call not only on Shane Warne but on Mark Waugh and Michael Bevan. All three turned the ball away from the left-hander, and the Sri Lankan side was packed with left-handers. Everything, it was said, would depend on Jayasuriya and Kaluwitherana, the opening batsmen. An early onslaught of the type they had made famous in the course of the Cup would enable Sri Lanka to mount a challenge. An Indian friend shook his head sadly and sceptically: 'They won't get it. Not on this pitch. Not under floodlights. Not against Australia. Not in a World Cup final.' And no team batting second had ever won the World Cup. . .

The Australians took the field to a mix of cheers and boos. In the second over, Jayasuriya tipped the ball to third man, took a single, then set off on a second run. The television replay showed that McGrath's throw from the deep had beaten him by a millisecond. The Australian bowlers ran in at full tilt, seeking quick wickets, and Kalu looked nervous. In the sixth over he pulled Fleming to Bevan at square leg. For the second successive match, the feared Sri Lankan openers had destroyed themselves in a wanton fit. It was 23 for 2 and I was despondent. Surely no team could stage a miraculous recovery from early disaster twice in succession: 241 suddenly seemed a formidable total. When an edgy De Silva nearly ran himself out backing up too far I wondered if the Sri Lankans were finally going to crack.

McGrath's line and length were unerring during his first spell, and Gurusinha and De Silva contented themselves with playing their shots off the less consistent Fleming. In Australia, De Silva, frustrated by the umpires and upset at the allegations, had fared poorly with the bat. He had averaged more than 50 in the World Cup so far but now he faced, for the first time in the competition, a well-rounded attack and an aggressive captain. Taylor brought Warne on and the field in for the eleventh over. The aerial route and the short boundaries beckoned, but De Silva kept the ball along the ground. He cut Warne late with a full swing of the bat, then opened the blade to stroke the next ball backward of point. The last ball of the over was a googly. It took the inside edge of De Silva's bat, barely missed the stumps and somehow evaded Healey's grasp. My heart skipped a beat. A furrow appeared between Warne's bleached eyebrows.

In Calcutta, De Silva mastered the Indian attack and the ball was his to do with as he willed. In Lahore, conditions (and the opposition) were more awkward. The dew on the field was heavy and scoring required luck and perseverance. In an attempt to step up the run rate, Gurusinha and De Silva embarked on quick singles, but the tactic seemed to put more pressure on the batsmen than the fielders, who pounced eagerly to cut off the drives and flicks. Warne, mixing googlies and leg breaks, tied down Gurusinha. De Silva cut and drove through the narrow gaps. His 360-degree field awareness seemed uncanny. After 15 overs, Sri Lanka had reached 71 for 2, level with the asking rate. Gurusinha lofted Mark Waugh over mid-off, where Fleming skidded past the ball, which ran to the boundary – the second difficult chance the Australians had missed.

A huge roar erupted from the bank of seats to our right. Javed Miandad had been spotted. After a moment, he rose to acknowledge the cheers. He clearly loved the adoration and would miss it desperately. The crowd's love was his bulwark against all the demeaning insults he had suffered, both abroad and at home. The evening was mild and a gentle breeze ruffled thousands of Sri Lankan flags. It would take a painter to capture the scene: the particoloured crowd dense and delighted, clapping and whistling, revelling in the sheer joy of big cricket under the floodlights.

Gurusinha finally got hold of Warne in the twenty-first over. He belted a short ball through mid-on to take Sri Lanka past their hundred, then struck a steepling straight six with a cross-batted tennis-style forearm. This laconic bear of a batsman exudes lazy strength. Warne, flustered, bowled a no-ball, flat and wide. Two overs later, the two batsmen reached their fifties. Shortly after, Gurusinha lifted Bevan against the spin high to deep midwicket, where Law cupped his hands in front of his face, waited patiently for the descending ball – and dropped it. Was he too casual or too nervous? Delighted with the error, the spectators hooted and waved their Sri Lankan flags. They were beginning to believe in a Sri Lankan victory. But a voice inside me warned, 'Remember Chandigarh, remember Calcutta.' In the thirty-first over, Reiffel spotted Gurusinha charging down the wicket and knocked his off stump out of the ground with a full-length ball. The Nalanda Old Boy had scored a measured and invaluable 65 runs off 99 pressure-primed balls.

When Ranatunga came in the game was still to be lost or won. The Sri Lankans needed 95 runs off 19 overs, with 7 wickets in hand. Ranatunga was off the mark gliding Reiffel behind for a single. Taylor brought Warne back into the attack, to a chorus of boos and whistles, and stationed himself menacingly at slip. Watching Ranatunga, Warne and umpire David Shepherd standing together at the non-strikers' end, I reflected that despite modern training regimes this could still be a game for rotund men. Warne's over yielded only one run. As in the Australian innings, the boundaries, though temptingly close at hand, remained frustratingly out of reach. Warne's second spell of three overs went for only 7 runs. The Australians were fighting back, covering the outfield and blocking scoring shots, but De Silva and Ranatunga, who between them had appeared in more than 300 one-day internationals, retained their poise. Both sides still believed they could win the match.

The two Sri Lankan veterans ran more singles that night in Lahore than they had in the whole of the rest of the tournament. De Silva, who had begun imperiously, retrenched in the middle overs. At this point, I confess I seemed to be the only person in the press box who thought Sri Lanka could lose. The Australian pressure was relentless and the batsmen seemed adrift, huffing and puffing up and down the pitch. I could not bring myself to believe that what I had so much wished to see was happening in front of my eyes. But the wisdom of the Sri Lankan captain and vice-captain became apparent in the fortieth over, when they ran four singles and struck two boundaries off Mark Waugh, unsettled by the left-hand–right-hand combination. That left 50 needed off 10 overs. Ranatunga and De Silva had calculated their assault to the decimal point.

Taylor brought back Warne for his final spell in the forty-first over. A couple of quick wickets now and the Sri Lankans could still be in trouble. De Silva chose this moment to assume command. He deftly cut the leg-spinner behind for two, drove an off-stump ball cleanly to the deep for two more, before swinging to leg for a single. In the next over, elbow high and head still, he caressed Reiffel through the covers. Then he leaned forward and turned his wrists to dispatch a ball on middle stump crisply through midwicket. A Mexican wave circled the ground.

Warne's final over, the forty-third of the Sri Lankan innings, was the Australians' last chance. Enveloped by a deafening cacophony of derisive whistles, the leg-spinner wheeled in for the last time in the 1996 World Cup. De Silva pushed him gently for a single. Then Ranatunga, as if to prove his claim that Warne was an 'overrated media hype', danced down the pitch to drive the ball fiercely through the air. It flew through the bowler's clammy hands and bounced into the sight screen. Annoyed, Warne unleashed a full toss, which Ranatunga, in a rare display of muscularity, pulled for six. The next ball the Sri Lankan captain slashed high towards long on for two more runs. Warne seemed unable to fathom what had happened to him: 12 runs had come off the over. The dew on the grass made the ball wet, but I suspect that was only one reason for the Australian's loss of control. Had Ranatunga's gamesmanship struck home? Had the Sri Lankan captain intuited that the bulky, brazen Australian was thin-skinned? Suddenly Sri Lanka needed only 17 to win with overs and wickets in hand. I began to relax.

Both Ranatunga and De Silva clipped the hitherto dominant McGrath for fours in the next over. De Silva reached his hundred with a leg glance to the boundary and raised his arms aloft. He was embraced by Ranatunga. After years of being patronized by the big cricket powers and persecuted by their home board, these two savoured their joint moment of triumph. After all the hoopla about Lara, Tendulkar and Mark Waugh, it was Aravinda De Silva who turned out to be the batsman of the tournament. De Silva's century in Lahore was less domineering but more demanding than his effort in Calcutta; eschewing pyrotechnics, moving with dainty but decisive footsteps, he had proved himself a master of the one-day art. Now he cover-drove Reiffel to level the scores. The crowd clapped

in rhythm, building in crescendo as McGrath ran in to bowl. Ranatunga ended the match by repeating the stroke with which he had
got off the mark, gliding the ball with minimum effort to third man
for four, a reminder of the relaxed hedonism of Sri Lankan cricket
at its best. Clearly, Ranatunga remained a man who believed there
was no reason to run when you could walk.

The Sri Lankan players dashed to the middle and engulfed the
two batsmen. Even Gurusinha smiled, at last. The cricketers were
followed by a mob of spectators, politicians, cameramen and journalists. Where were the 7,000 policemen said to be on duty? Where
were the heavy-handed security officers who had kept the denizens
of the general stand out of the ground till halfway through the
Australian innings? As so often in this World Cup, the police were
absent when they were most needed. As the floodlights burned
through the thickening mist, the military band struck up a victory
march. Keeping their ranks tidy, they presented the only element of
order in a scene of chaos. The Sri Lankan players tried to regroup
for the presentation ceremony; Benazir Bhutto, bereft of protection,
made her way through the crowd to the podium. Percy ran in manic
circles with his giant Sri Lankan flag. The crowd was on its feet,
raining prolonged, heartfelt applause on the winners, and chanting
'Allah illah Allah illah' (an Islamic invocation which had recently
become popular at Pakistani cricket grounds). The Muslim League
loyalists packed into one of the patrons' enclosures booed the Prime
Minister as she presented the trophy to Ranatunga and the outsize
man-of-the-match cheque to De Silva. The mist turned to rain and
quickly soaked everyone on the field but did not hinder the
impromptu dancing in the middle. In the mayhem several Sri Lankan
players were knocked down and the World Cup winners' cheque
was picked from Ranatunga's pocket. Later it was cancelled and
replaced by Pilcom, who topped up the pot with an additional
US$100,000; the disparity between the millions they were raking
in and the relatively derisory prize money had become too embarrassing.

The 97-run match-winning stand shared by De Silva and Ranatunga was a masterpiece of cricket nous. Together they had outwitted
Taylor, nullified Warne, and made the 7-wicket victory look easier
than it was. In this low-scoring battle of nerves it was those notoriously hard competitors, the Australians, who had cracked first, while

the Sri Lankans just kept playing cricket. Ignoring the sledging that had distracted them in the past, the Lankan middle-order batsmen kept their minds on the target. They made errors. There were alarms. But after every mishap they picked themselves up, brushed themselves off and got on with their accustomed game . . .

I had been rewarded for betting on my hopes. But the reward was not quite what I had expected. The element of personal vindication was dwarfed by an almost physical sense of sharing the satisfaction the Sri Lankan victory had given to so many people in so many places for so many reasons. As I indulged in a celebratory sundae in one of Lahore's excellent ice-cream parlours, I studied the beaming faces of the city's trendy, well-heeled youth. All of us, here and across the subcontinent, had supped from this World Cup. Internationalism is sometimes dismissed as an abstract, unreal creed, but I knew from experience, not least my experience during the World Cup, that it could be as intimate, profound and sustaining as any national identity. And it has this advantage: it places no restrictions on your growth. It has no limits. Later, I went to bed in a kind of post-coital buzz. My romance with subcontinental cricket had been consummated.

Critics in England derided the 1996 World Cup as inefficiently organized, excessively commercial, corrupted by politicians and besmirched by the bad behaviour of overly nationalistic host-country fans. All of this, they argued, was symptomatic of south Asian society, a place quite unfit to host an event of this kind. Within months, however, the same features disfigured the Atlanta Olympics. Clearly, whatever was wrong with the World Cup was wrong with global sport in general. As for me, I loved the World Cup. In spite of self-serving officials, vulgar profiteering and ugly zealotry, the tournament had proved a success – a giant, subcontinental festival of cricket whose impact could be seen in roadside *dhabas*, college hostels, bazaars, buses, trains, *maidans* and all the other locales where the 'unofficial' culture of cricket is forged. I felt privileged to have enjoyed such a wide-angle view of this epic saga. Players and journalists complained about having to travel to far-flung venues, but the sheer scale of the Cup was part of its fascination. Travelling from city to city, constantly crossing not only the borders of states but those of language, religion, culture, I was afforded countless glimpses of my fellow human beings in all their variety, as well as a ripening insight into our essential oneness. This was the deceptively modest grail at the end of my quest: that cricket can be unifier or divider, symbol of solidarity or 'war minus the shooting'. It's up to us.

The One-Way Critic

Upon the groaning bench he took his seat –
    Sunlight and shadow on the dew-blessed grass –
He spread the *Daily Moan* beneath his feet,
    Hitched to his eye an astigmatic glass,
Then, like a corncrake calling to an owl
    That knows no answer, he began to curse,
Remarking, with an unattractive scowl,
    'The state of Cricket goes from bad to worse;
Where are the bowlers of my boyhood's prime?
    Where are the batsmen of the pristine years?
Where are the fieldsmen of the former time?'
    And, as he spoke, my eyelids filled with tears;
For I, perhaps alone, knew they were dead,
    Mynn an old myth, and Hambledon a name,
And it occurred to me that I had read
    (In classroom) 'All things always are the same';
So, comfort drawing from this maxim, turned
    To the myopic moaner on the seat;
A flame of rage, not pity, in me burned,
    Yet I replied in accents clear and sweet –
'There *were* no bowlers in your boyhood's prime,
    There *were* no batsmen in the pristine years,
There *were* no fieldsmen in that former time' –
    My voice grew firm, my eyes were dry of tears –
    '*Your* fathers cursed the bowlers you adored,
    Your fathers damned the batsmen of your choice,
Your fine, ecstatic rapture they deplored,
    Theirs was the ONE-WAY CRITIC's ageless voice,
And their immortal curse is yours today,
    The croak which kills all airy Cricket Dryads,
Withers the light on tree and grass and spray,
    The strangling fugue of senile jeremiads.'

I ceas'd; and turn'd to Larwood's bounding run,
And Woolley's rapier flashing in the sun.

R. C. ROBERTSON-GLASGOW

STYLES
AND
THEMES

The repugnant politics of the men who once ruled South Africa meant that that country's cricketers never got a chance to play against sides other than the 'white' ones. West Indies v. South Africa, say in 1966, or India v. South Africa, five years later, would verily have been a contest for the championship of the world. What we all missed was brought home when blacks and whites happily played together for the Rest of the World sides of the early 1970s. One magic day at the Oval in the summer of 1970, Garfield Sobers and Graeme Pollock scored 100 runs in partnership. At this time they were the two best, as well as the two most graceful, batsmen in the world. Their genius prompted this essay by J. H. Fingleton, which seeks to answer the question: Why is it that left-handers are so much more attractive to watch?

J. H. FINGLETON

The Brilliance of Left-Handers (1972)

Is it an advantage to be a left-handed batsman? Apart from Richards, of South Africa, it is impossible to refute the argument that the most brilliant batting in recent years has come from the left-handed Sobers, Pollock and the West Indian Lloyd. Considering their small-ness in numbers, it is remarkable that left-handers have been so prominent down the years. In other days, there was the great Frank Woolley, of Kent and England, and Ransford and Hill of Australia. Bardsley, also of Australia, and Mead, of England, were heavy-scorers but they weren't in the same brilliant class as the three named above. Percy Chapman and Jack Gregory were exciting, swashbuckling left-handers and in recent years have been the exuberant Donnelly, New Zealand, and Harvey and Morris of Australia. Left-handers, all of them!

When Sir Donald Bradman saw Graeme Pollock for the first time in Perth, in October 1963, he said Pollock could well make in all ways the success of the Springbok tour. Pollock had just hit a century (18 fours) in 88 minutes. Sir Donald doesn't lightly enthuse. His patronage, like that of royalty, is not widely distributed and he proved prophetic about Pollock. He hit at Sydney and Adelaide two of the most scintillating Test centuries seen in Australia.

Those with memories mellowed in cricket said Pollock was Frank Woolley all over again when they saw Pollock hit 122 in Sydney. Many recalled how the tall man of Kent – Pollock is also over six feet – flowed forward to the kangaroo-bounding fast bowling of Jack Gregory and clobbered the ball through the off against the picket fence. Old men are apt to say, in deference to their own generation, that they will never see the like of so-and-so again; but before Pollock in Australia we had seen Sobers, who scaled even higher heights than Woolley.

Nobody in cricket has given me more sheer delight than Sobers. His brilliance has been breathtaking. For the West Indies and South Australia, for which state he played for a number of Australian summers, he has played many of his greatest innings in Australia and the classical ease of his stroke-making recur readily to memory. One day in Sydney, on his first tour of Australia, he moved forward to play Meckiff off the front foot. Of a sudden, he went into reverse and off the back foot, with a cross bat, he hit Meckiff wide of mid-on for a huge six. This stroke was unsurpassed in its brilliancy of conception and execution. Meckiff was no slouch in pace and only a genius could so quickly and completely change the whole nature of his stroke.

In his last innings in Sydney, for an MCC side, I saw Woolley hit a double-century, but he never hit with more power on the off than Pollock did in his Sydney Test century. One cover drive off O'Neill was unforgettable. It travelled, one thought, almost with the speed of light to the boundary. In this innings of 122 – and Pollock was then only nineteen years of age – he hit one mighty six to leg, square, and with thirty yards to spare over the fence. He scorched 19 fours, most of them on the off. He interspersed his off boundaries with some hefty sweeps to leg yet one thought the leg side was not his strength. Benaud fished for him often in this innings, with several near nibbles, but there wasn't a chance to hand until he reached 104.

His 122 was exactly half his side's total when he was dismissed and he retired to an acclaim seldom heard on a cricket field.

Pollock's second fifty was hit in 57 minutes and this rich glut of strokes was shown on a pitch which, only some seven months before, was denounced by both English and Australian Test batsmen as an impossible one on which to play strokes!

Several weeks later in Adelaide, Pollock sent 22,000 spectators into rhapsodies as he played an even more brilliant innings. The Australians had struggled over 450 minutes for 345 runs. It wasn't thrilling to watch, and Pollock's first fifty in 86 minutes was like a sea breeze in a heatwave. His second fifty almost took the breath away. It took him only 40 minutes! Sitting in the pavilion, Gary Sobers was one of the spectators who rose to their feet to applaud Pollock back.

Once again, as in Sydney, Pollock specialized in off-driving, in a lazy, languorous manner that sent the ball whizzing away. But he also pulverized Benaud and Simpson with his smiting to leg. Pollock differed from Sobers significantly in his footwork. Sobers rarely danced down the pitch, as I remember him, but this day Pollock went yards down the pitch to both Simpson and Benaud. He hit Benaud far and wide over midwicket for six; he went even better against Simpson, hitting him for two sixes off successive balls. Several years before, Les Favell had hit Alf Valentine, of the West Indies, for two successive sixes in Brisbane's unforgettable Test.

All Pollock's sixes were hit towards Adelaide's cathedral, just outside the ground. 'Murder in the cathedral,' murmured Bill O'Reilly. Pollock also hit two successive balls from Simpson for four so that he hit 22 runs off four successive balls. No wonder the crowd roared! I saw old-timers in Nip Pellew, Stan McCabe and Clarrie Grimmett stand with the thousands to acclaim Pollock that day. His century was chanceless, carving the Australian attack into small pieces. It is given to few to inject such enthusiasm and enjoyment into a crowd.

In writing at the time that Pollock was Frank Woolley all over again, I had an analytical look at Pollock and wrote this:

> As soon as one looks at Graeme Pollock at the crease, one begins to think of how he could be improved. His stance is an ugly one. He holds his short-handle bat at the bottom of the handle. As he stands well over six feet, he has to pop his

posterior in the air to fit in everything and he forms an ugly, elongated, upside-down figure of S as he stands awaiting the ball. In such a stance his head is far away from his feet. He cramps himself, one feels, on the leg side and, indeed, he is cramped on that side and, if he has a weakness, it is just behind square leg. But suddenly his stance is immaterial as he blazes forth with ferocious, fiery off drives that surge across the turf.

Pollock was only nineteen when I wrote this. He proved in Adelaide that he was almost as strong on the leg as on the off, and in subsequent innings against Australia in South Africa Pollock has shown that it is merely a toss-up which is the better batsman when Sobers and Pollock are both at their top.

I have never tired of singing the praises of Gary Sobers. So many times to me he has been absolute batting perfection. Nor is that all. He has been an amazing fieldsman, taking wonderful catches in the slips and throwing the stumps down from the field, and he is the best all-round bowler the game has known. I once described his bowling as being like a packet of mixed dried vegetables – something of everything – and, indeed, there has not been a type of left-hand bowl that Sobers has not used. In 1968, in Australia, he was worried by a piece of floating bone in his right shoulder. It hurt him, oddly, to bowl his over-the-wrist spinners. After three overs of fast bowling in the Brisbane Test, Sobers turned to slow, orthodox spin, breaking from the right-hander's legs, and took 6 for 73 off 37 overs . . .

I have seen Sobers play immortal innings and strokes not reminiscent of any other batsman. So, too, with Bradman, McCabe, Compton and Hammond. They displayed an individual flair in playing strokes that one could recognize immediately in one peep after rounding a pavilion corner. I have watched Sobers many times and thought he had only one chink in his armour – he doesn't always pick the bosie, which is strange for a man who bowls a perfect one himself.

I saw Sincock turn him inside out one day at Port of Spain with a bosie and the hysterical motions of a man who thought the ball was going the other way were a strange suggestion of clay. Nor did he pick Gleeson in Sydney one day in 1968, a snick going to slip. This incident was notable in two ways: first, the mistaken judgement of Sobers; and, secondly, the incredible whooping war dance that Lawry did on the pitch at Sobers's downfall.

Strangely, as I wrote earlier, Sobers was not extravagant in his footwork. When Barry Richards faced up to Gleeson in South Africa, he waltzed down the pitch before Gleeson had bowled and hit him for 4 fours in one over. This showed a blatant disdain for Gleeson's ability to turn the ball, but Sobers always played Gleeson from the crease in Australia, and with suspicion. His footwork, then, was confined; but it was impeccable in the crease and his batting was helped by a long reach.

Davidson (and here was another mighty left-handed smiter of the ball!) was a better user of the new ball than Sobers. Davidson was the best left-handed user of a new ball I have seen. Voce bowled a more dangerous bouncer than Davidson or Sobers and I think Fleetwood-Smith was a better over-the-wrist spinner than Sobers. Fleetwood was faster through the air and also spun the ball more. Bradman often mauled Fleetwood and, had they been pitted, would have done the same to Sobers. Spin didn't worry the Great Man and his footwork would have quelled Sobers's spin at the outset.

But you don't measure Sobers's bowling against a Bradman. There has never been another bowler like Sobers. The Australian Bill Johnston, one of the most delightful characters ever to tread a cricket field, was another splendid left-hand bowler with the new ball but neither Davidson, Voce nor Johnston could bowl spinners. I once advocated the thought in the London *Sunday Times* that Sobers was not only the greatest all-round cricketer of all time, but there was nobody else even to approach him. Sir Donald Bradman later also expressed the same opinion.

There is an abiding memory of the centuries I have seen Sobers hit. In retrospect, there never seemed a period in them when he didn't look like hitting a century. Some centurions struggle, go slow and fast in patches, have their lucky streaks, possibly bog down in the nineties and emerge, at last, gasping at the three-figure mark. There was nothing like this about Sobers. He just flowed on and on, his technique and stroke play on a pedestal.

His best shots were the two most spectacular and most productive – the drive and the pull. In the drive, he had a full flow of the bat and, like Pollock, he possessed an intuitive genius that enabled him to cleave the fieldsmen on the off side. There was no stroke he could not play. He could cut – Martin Donnelly says later that few left-handers cut – and square-cut and force majestically off his toes. This requires the very epitome of timing. I have written in another place of his very own inspirational stroke when he stood tiptoe, as if in defence, only at the very last fraction of time to swivel his body and send the ball screaming past square leg. This stroke was pure genius.

Sobers was a complex study when he came to Australia in 1968, coming from a heavy county season with Nottinghamshire. His cricket appetite was clearly jaded. He made touring history by not playing for his own country in the opening game at Kalgoorlie. I met him, during that match, at the Australia Open golf in Perth and there was no mistaking where his sporting interests had been diverted.

He played in the second game, making a superlative century, but he omitted himself from the third game, in which the West Indians were beaten by a combined team. The team manager, Mr Gaskin, was a hearty concurrer. He concurred with Sobers dropping himself, he said, because it was wrong for the West Indians to depend too much upon Sobers. My own thought was that the place of a touring skipper at the beginning of a tour is on the field, to build team spirit and confidence.

Sobers played at Adelaide, against South Australia. The West Indians put up such a woeful display that Sobers summoned them behind closed doors and tongue-lashed them. Mr Gaskin again concurred. The things that Sobers had said, commented Mr Gaskin, needed to be said. It might have been thought that somebody needed to say a few direct things to the skipper, pointing out that his approach to the tour was not all it might be. Although one who had been through the mill could recognize the signs with Sobers. He had gone stale with too much cricket in England. It was no longer a game to him: it was hard work, and he had to drive himself.

It was not surprising, therefore, that Sobers should have turned often to the golf course for relaxation. He played golf at every opportunity and several times on the eve of a Test, when he surely should have been at the nets with his fellows, even if only watching. His team lifted itself against Victoria and New South Wales but then Sobers went back on his tracks. Instead of going to Brisbane for the last first-class match before the Test, he returned south to Melbourne 'on business'. This, too, met with Mr Gaskin's approval.

The West Indies hit rock bottom against Queensland, but their splendid win over Australia in the first Test saved Sobers and the team management much criticism. They took too much for granted in that victory. In no time, they sloughed again and, finally, were no match for Australia, losing the series 1–3.

I don't think Sobers likes the responsibility of being captain. Unlike Frank Worrell, altogether a different personality who was always with his 'boys', Sobers is a loner. Some of his men grumbled that he left them too much to themselves. Manager Gaskin said Sobers didn't attend the nets before the third Test in Sydney because he was having treatment for his corns. Those corns didn't stop Sobers from having eighteen holes of golf that same afternoon!

I often saw Sobers on the cricket field going through the motions of a little wedge golf shot. Obviously, he found on the golf course the mental relaxation denied him on a cricket field. He continually wore a frown on the field (one saw it through binoculars) and, when taxed with not bowling himself enough in Adelaide, replied wearily: 'I am not a cricket machine.'

For all his frowns, for all his worries, for all his apparent cricket staleness, Sobers still managed to hit two peerless Test centuries in Australia in 1968. One was in Adelaide, 110 in 132 minutes with 2 sixes and 15 fours; the other in Sydney, 113 in just over two hours, with 20 fours. In Adelaide he batted in his now customary position of No. 6 and ran out of partners. He fell in trying to keep the strike. It took a lot to budge him from that No. 6 position.

Sobers cast a spell over the Australian attack in each innings but in each case his century was too late to give full value to his side. He came to bat at Adelaide at 4 for 107; at 3 for 30 in Sydney. A century innings from him in either city at No. 3 or No. 4 would have had much more effect upon his side's innings.

Sobers has now hit 25 centuries in 86 Tests (I can't accept those matches in England in 1970, hastily arranged when the South African tour fell through, as Test matches, which, surely, are between one country and another). Bradman leads with 29 Test centuries. Hammond has 22, Harvey and Sobers each 25, Sobers passing Barrington in Sydney. Sobers again hit his peerless form in England in 1970 but retention of keenness will be a big factor if he is to pass Bradman's 29. The cricket yoke is beginning to tell on Sobers.

I like to recall Sobers in that thrilling over at Swansea in 1968 when he hit Malcolm Nash for 6, 6, 6, 6, 6, 6 – over long on, long on, long off, midwicket to the on, long on, midwicket to the on. Two hits went right out of the ground. This was a world's record for an over in a first-class match. Nash was philosophical about it.

'I suppose I can gain some satisfaction from the fact that my name will be permanently in the records book,' he said. He wanted to have the ball mounted – but it never came back the last time Sobers hit it out of the ground.

And so I return to the original theme of this chapter – is it an advantage to be a left-handed batsman? Is driving easier for them than a right-hander? Or, and this is a point which gave me much thought, are some left-hand batsmen really stronger in the right hand and does this give them an advantage in driving in that their top hand, the main driving one, is the right hand? Golfers, right-handed ones, know how important is the left arm and hand in the drive and how abortive the stroke becomes if there is too much right hand, and too soon, in the shot.

Pondering on this, I wrote to Graeme Pollock, Gary Sobers and Frank Woolley in England, asking them pertinent questions. Pollock and Woolley were good enough to answer immediately and with most interesting information. I spoke at length with Arthur Morris and Neil Harvey in Sydney and, after speaking with Martin Donnelly, he was good enough to put his magnificent thoughts on paper. Gary, not surprisingly, didn't get around to answering!

Pollock agreed with me that left-handers excel in the drive and, in his own case, says he has an advantage in that his top (right) hand is the stronger one. He plays every single-handed game right-handed. He writes right, throws right, plays tennis right but as soon as the two hands are required, such as in cricket and golf, he goes left-handed. But Sobers, Pollock writes:

> is left-handed in everything he does. This is probably the reason for his strong on-side play off the back foot, where his left hand dominates.
>
> Left-handers are probably fortunate because most bowlers tend to move the ball away from us. This gives you lots of room in which to play your shot, whereas with the ball coming into the body you are inclined to become cramped. It is said that left-handers are weak outside the off stump, but this is only natural because of the terrific concentration of bowling directed at this side of the wicket.
>
> The same can be said for right-hand batsmen when facing a left-arm quick bowler from over the wicket. How many right-handers are suspect outside their off stump to this type of

bowler? Left-hand batsmen have to contend with this angle of attack for 90 per cent of their batting time. The biggest bugbear for left-handers is the rough outside the off stump from the third day onwards of a Test. Off-driving then has to be treated very carefully. Only when the ball is right up can the shot be played with any confidence. This is the reason why all left-handers like to bat first because this eliminates for a while the problem of rough outside their off stump.

Graeme Pollock's views are most interesting and I am indebted to him for so lucidly explaining them – even though brother Peter is the journalist!

Neil Harvey writes right-handed, bowled right, kicks with his right foot and plays tennis right-handed. This suggests he is a more natural right-hander than a left one. When it comes to two-handed action (including wood-chopping, he said with a wide grin), he goes left. His right did the work in the drive but his left in the cut, square cut and the pull and he was most proficient in all these strokes.

I asked him which eye was stronger. Martin Donnelly had put to me the interesting and intricate theory that the left-hand side of the brain dominated the right eye, which seemed to give the left-hander another advantage, but Harvey, now bespectacled, staggered me by saying he was weak in both eyes. 'Ever since I was fourteen,' he said, 'I have seen strange shapes. I could never read the scores on the board. Our Australian team in South Africa once had their eyes tested and only Drennan had worse sight than mine. The specialist said to me, "Who leads you out to bat?"'

Harvey had one thing in common with Sobers. He, too, had difficulty at times in picking a bosie. Bill O'Reilly told me the tale of how Fred Johnston, the New South Wales slow bowler, once had Harvey completely at sea with his bosie when Harvey was playing for Victoria. 'Hutton told me', said O'Reilly, 'that Johnston was the best slow bowler never chosen by Australia for England. And many not as good were chosen. He said he would have got over 100 wickets there every time he toured.'

I am glad that story came from O'Reilly because I was responsible for Johnston going from Canberra into big cricket in Sydney. I asked O'Reilly whether he would mind if I used this story. 'Do what you like with it,' said the affable O'Reilly. 'I would remind you of the story of the judge who received an anonymous letter one morning while his case was part-heard. As the court assembled, the judge fixed its members with a stern eye and told them he had received an anonymous letter that morning. "It ill-behoves me," said the judge, "sitting where I am now, to say what I did with that letter, sitting where I was then.'"

Frank Woolley wrote me as follows:

I don't think left-handers are fortunate in being left-handers. My experience was that more right-hand bowlers can make the ball move in the air into a right-hander and away from a left-hander, which is the most difficult ball to play. Also, a left-hand batsman has to cope with the bowler's rough and particularly in my time on a 'sticky' wicket. These, with covers being used, are no longer known in the game.

Because of the bowler's rough, a cover drive was always difficult for a left-hander, or so I found it. My left hand was always the main force in my batting. My right hand, for me, was only a steadying hand, just with my thumb and first finger, which allowed the bat to go straight through. But I am not left-handed in all things. I write right-handed, eat right-handed, play billiards right-handed and pick up most things with my right hand.

At eighty-three, Frank apologized for what he described as his scribble. He said his right hand was full of arthritis. I thought his writing magnificent!

Martin Donnelly, as rich a character as he was an all-round sportsman, wrote me an enthralling letter on the subject. He is a left-hander in all things – writing, eating, playing tennis, throwing, shooting and kicking.

You ask which was my 'motive or power hand'. I am not certain that these are the same. I would regard my left hand as the power hand because this is the one that puts most power into shots, whether off- or on-driving, slashing behind point (I almost said 'cutting', but few left-handers I saw really played the cut shot properly) or in hooking or pulling. However, the top hand, in my view, must always be the control hand and the guiding hand. You might even call it the motivating hand – in all shots. It must be primarily responsible for the arc through which the bat moves up and down and in so doing must harness and direct the power hand (i.e. the bottom hand), which is the hand that dictates speed and power. This is the hand with which the bat is moved in executing any stroke.

To my mind, the golden rule in batting is that the top hand should have at *all times* not only a firm but a tight grip on the bat and this grip should never be changed or relaxed in the playing of any stroke (either defensive or offensive). Clearly, the hands work together, but basically, as I see it, the top hand must be the control hand, the bottom one the power hand.

On the eye question, I checked with an eminent ophthalmic surgeon who said there was no basic rule about eye dominance and certainly gave no support whatever to my hopeful, but embryonic theory about the right eye being dominant in left-handers and the left eye dominant in right-handers. However, we did establish that M.P.D. is left-eye dominant. Incidentally, the simple test on this one is to point your index finger at a focused object on a wall and then to close each eye in turn. The eye that sees the finger in line with the object is the dominant eye as opposed to the one which throws the finger off to the left or right.

I hope not too many right-handers find, as I did when I tried this test, that their right eye is the stronger one. If a right-hand batsman's shoulders are not allowed to come round too far to the bowler, thus giving him what is known as a two-eyed stance, the left eye does much more work in batting for the right-hander than the right one!

Martin Donnelly was also a magnificent footballer, capped for Oxford and England. Only the war and his later studies at Oxford prevented him being an All Black. Stewart Harris, the Australian representative of the London *Times*, who has an office next to mine in Parliament House, Canberra, remembers Donnelly with awe playing against Harris's Cambridge side. Harris said Donnelly was the most brilliant handler of a football at five-eighth he remembers. Modestly, Donnelly says his Oxford half-back, Ossie Newton-Thompson, threw a perfect dive-pass, which, says Donnelly, enabled him to get moving quickly and play well away from the forwards. He observed that when he played for England against Ireland, Ireland, 22–3, had their greatest victory to that date over England!

Donnelly and I once figured in an unfortunate incident in a club

game in England. He bowled little – he says he bowled a ball that
spins at the bowler's end and goes with the arm at the other end –
and we both detected a sniff on the face of the batsman when
Donnelly was given the ball. The batsman was E. W. Swanton and,
as I recall it, he was plumb lbw to Donnelly's first ball, which was as
straight as a barrel. As umpire, I didn't hesitate. E. W. S. gave one
of his most noted stares down the wicket – but he had to go! Both
Donnelly and I were members of the Arab Club, of which E. W. S.
was founder. We are both still members!

Arthur Morris is left-handed in everything, and left-footed also.
He says his left hand was definitely stronger – and his left eye
also stronger. 'I don't use my top hand very much in batting,' Morris
told me. 'I think I drove mostly with my shoulders and wrists, but I
didn't drive in any pronounced fashion, neither to the off nor on.
I think I was more a square player and forcing them off my toes.'
And, I might add, an exceptionally good player, too.

There is the case for left-handers, as I see it, although it is to be
noted that some of the famous left-handers don't agree on all points.
What can be agreed upon, however, and especially when remembering their meagre numbers, is that left-handers have been far
more outstanding in brilliancy in recent years than their right-handed
fellows.

Pondering that, I wondered whether left-handers might not profit
from having the right hand the top one on the bat when I reflected
that many golfers consider the top left hand to be the dominant one
in a right-hand golfer. Golf can teach batsmen a great deal in driving.
So many batsmen are bottom-hand conscious and I can think of no
better illustration than Bobby Simpson. Simpson played golf off
scratch and he possesses a glorious golf swing, fluid and full. Yet,
when he came to batting, his bottom hand was the dominant one
and he never drove as freely as nature equipped him to do. I think,
in the main, this was brought about by the period in which Simpson
played. He, with others, saw a vacancy in the Australian Test team
for an opener and, in making himself into an opening batsman,
Simpson concentrated upon defence and so used his bottom hand
more than the top one.

Yet, if there is anything in my theory, why are there so few
prominent left-hand golfers? I asked Gary Player this once and he
said he could recall only one, Bob Charles. Arnold Palmer said
Charles was not the only left-hander in tournaments, only the best

known, but he could not name any others. Palmer said it was a matter of statistics, that a smaller number of left-hand players were willing to dedicate themselves to the game, but he looked a little blank when it was pointed out to him that there were a large number of champion left-handed tennis players, Laver and Roche, to name two. Many would contend that Laver has been the greatest tennis player of all time.

Palmer says definitely that golf is a right-hander's game and that courses are made exclusively for right-handers. I wonder would the mighty Jack Nicklaus have hit them even further had he turned about and got even more punch out of his right hand as the top one? The prospect is mind-boggling!

Several of us had dinner one night with Gary Player in Canberra and he advanced the theory that golf was the most difficult of all games to play. I couldn't agree with him. Golf is a forward game, with every shot played the same way with obvious variations in power and technique yet with the backswing invariably the same, differing only for an intentional slice or pull and that only in a slight degree. The ball is never played backwards – and the cut and the glance are two of the most telling strokes in cricket – and the cover drive, one of the most brilliant strokes in cricket, would correspond to the golfer's nightmare – the socket or shank!

Yet, in the drive and the use of the top hand, golf, I repeat, has an important message for all batsmen because the drive is the very foundation of good batsmanship. It is the safest of all shots because the bat comes to the ball full face, minimizing risks; it pays the richest dividends in runs scored and, finally and most importantly, it has a demoralizing effect upon bowlers. No bowler, and particularly a fast bowler, likes to be driven. A bowler is encouraged when he sees a batsman cutting or deflecting, taking risks, but no bowler likes to be consistently driven. It is then that he tends to drop the ball short so that the drive, as I see it, is the dominant stroke in batting. It paves the way for the other strokes.

It is their ability to drive that makes Sobers and Pollock two such brilliant batsmen. Whether nature has given them an advantage over right-handers is something to be pondered. All that remains for me is to express my thanks to so many brilliant left-handers for telling me so much about themselves.

★   ★   ★

For the English, the summer of 1948 was not a happy one. The less partisan fans could, however, glory in the classic technique of one of the world's greatest new ball bowlers. Ray Lindwall's action was the spur to this meditation on fast bowling by John Arlott. In 1948 there were no English exemplars in sight. But, as previously noted, Lindwall and Miller were soon to be answered by Statham, Trueman and Tyson.

JOHN ARLOTT
Fast and Furious (1949)

On Friday 25 June 1948, spectators at Lord's Cricket Ground saw the contemporary inheritor of a great tradition. On that day Ray Lindwall, of New South Wales and Australia, showed himself to be in direct line of descent from the great classic fast bowlers.

He bowled from the pavilion end, running fifteen rhythmic, gradually lengthening and accelerating paces to the wicket. Perhaps he delivered the ball with his arm lower than the nicest technical purism would approve, but he bowled fast indeed. He 'moved' the new ball away from the bat in the air and, by dint of delivering from the extreme edge of the crease and by virtue of his body action, he sometimes made the ball come in to the batsman off the pitch. With him, however, as with his great predecessors, the destructive agent is speed. Three English batsmen, two of them long enough at the crease to be seeing the ball well, were clean bowled by sheer speed. Or the ball was pitched that dangerous fraction short of a length about the line of the off stump, the batsmen were unable to decide whether or not to play the ball and, in their indecision, edged a catch to slips or the wicketkeeper – the second classic method of dismissal by fast bowling. The ball rose sharply from the pitch, it was upon batsman after batsman before his feet or bat were in proper position for a stroke. Lindwall was successful – more than successful enough to justify the tradition to which he belongs before the eyes of English cricket.

That tradition is more than 150 years old, for before 1800 the famous underhand fast bowler, Brown of Brighton, was said to have bowled a ball which beat bat, wicket and wicketkeeper, passed through long stop's coat and killed a dog on the other side. But the first of the line with characteristics obviously in common with Lindwall was Alfred Mynn, 'the Lion of Kent' of the 1840s. Six feet tall and sixteen stone in playing trim, Mynn bowled in the days when it was illegal to bowl with the arm higher than the shoulder. G. F. Watts' drawing of Mynn bowling shows his arm swinging round the barest legal fraction below the shoulder, but his action was smooth and he controlled the ball. Mynn made fast bowling the ambition of every young cricketer in the country – and that threw up a generation of fierce slingers who were positively dangerous on the rough pitches of his day. This was the school of bowlers curbed by Pilch and Felix and whose successors were finally thrashed into extinction by W. G. Grace. Nevertheless there were among them good bowlers, particularly after the introduction of overarm bowling. *Scores and Biographies* says of John Wisden that his bowling was 'very fast indeed and ripping'; Jackson, Tarrant and Freeman of Yorkshire, too, were bowlers too fast for any batsman's comfort.

They led to the classic fast bowling. That is, in short, an attack designed to hit the stumps or compel the catch to slips or wicketkeeper by the speed of the ball bowled to a length or just short of a length. The great fast bowlers have had a fairly long run and a smooth high delivery. Some, like Mold of Lancashire and Gilbert of Queensland, have bowled off a short run-up, but they have been suspected of throwing. There have been fast bowlers, too, with a low action, usually described as 'slingers', but they lack the steeply hostile 'rise' from the pitch which distinguishes the great fast bowlers.

In the last decade of the nineteenth century, fast bowling in English cricket reached its finest flowering. Then, Tom Richardson and Lockwood of Surrey and C. J. Kortright of Essex overshadowed many of their contemporaries who were yet very fast bowlers indeed. At any other period Kortright must have taken an automatic place in any England eleven but such was the greatness of Richardson and Lockwood that he did not play in a single Test match. From their day until 1939 there were fast bowlers in England. And if in 1939 the standard was already falling, there were then ten bowlers in England faster than any in the country today.

Australia had run parallel with us. From that Ernest Jones who bowled through W. G. Grace's beard, to Gregory and Macdonald who swept through the post-war English cricket of 1921, Australia had produced the men who bowled fast in the classic manner. Macdonald returned to England to play for Lancashire – and to be a model of the way to bowl at speed – through many an English season. The West Indians Constantine, Griffith and Martindale, the New Zealander Cromb, and the South African Kotze, maintained the tradition in the other countries of cricket.

Yet, when, on that dull June day of 1948, Lindwall, carefully nursed for months to such a peak, bowled really fast, he bowled to batsmen to whom true fast bowling was a misty idea in the recesses of memory.

There have been somewhat similar phases in both English and Australian cricket in the past, but none quite so pronounced. When Gregory and Macdonald destroyed the best of English batting in 1921, they were only slightly faster than bowlers then bowling in county cricket. There were at least eight bowlers in England then who *forced* the wicketkeeper to stand back – today no county wicketkeeper need do so except for convenience in making catches off swing bowling. When Larwood, Voce, Allen and Bowes won the Test series of 1932–3 in Australia under Douglas Jardine, Australian cricket had, in the Aboriginal Eddie Gilbert, a bowler faster than any of them. It was the method of its employment rather than the speed of their bowling that defeated the Australian batsmen.

In England in 1948 there was no bowler bowling at the speed of Gover of Surrey immediately before he retired in August 1947 – at the age of thirty-nine. Pritchard of Warwickshire, quite fast in 1947, has often found it possible to reduce his pace to fast-medium and still bowl successfully in terms of taking wickets cheaply.

What has happened to English fast bowling? Will it ever revive?

Before we can offer any reply to these questions we shall be wise to look back to the days of Tom Richardson, to examine the problem of the fast bowler. Tom Richardson was a strong man, he had a magnificent physique and he loved bowling. He would walk, on the morning of a match, from Mitcham to Kennington Oval with his cricket bag on his shoulder and then cheerfully bowl all day. Yet Richardson, for all that mighty moustache, was done with first-class cricket by the time he was thirty-three. Lockwood's career ended when he was thirty-six. Richardson and Lockwood were professionals. Kortright took less than 100 wickets in first-class cricket in the scattered matches he played after he was twenty-nine: he was an amateur.

Fast bowling is not economical for a professional cricketer: he cannot afford to bowl fast and finish in his early thirties when he might be a batsman and play until he is forty-five. Notice how many of England's fast bowlers were amateurs during the inter-war years, when young men were considering the economic aspect of their careers. Fast bowling may be spectacular sport but it is poor business.

Even apart from its financial aspect, it is doubtful if fast bowling is as rewarding in itself as it once was. The so-called bodyline bowling was practised by bowlers, but it was dictated by the batsmen. On perfect wickets nowadays, fast bowlers may bowl their hearts out. If they aim at the stumps the batsmen play them defensively. When the ball has been pitched just outside the off stump, in the classic manner, for slip catches, the modern batsmen have merely raised their bats above their shoulders, put their pads in the line of the stumps and allowed the ball to sail harmlessly past. The fast bowler's opening spell, when he is fresh and the ball new, is short: he cannot afford to waste it. So the bowlers, in effect, decided to give batsmen something they must play. So they bowled the ball which runs into the batsman and denied him reliance on the pitch of the ball by slipping in an occasional bumper. This type of bowling was, historically speaking, an automatic development of cricket. Thus bowlers *made* batsmen play their keenest bowling – an aim with which it is difficult not to sympathize.

I talked, only a few days ago, with C. J. Kortright, who is often said to have been the fastest of all bowlers. In my innocence I said to him, 'How often did you bowl a bumper?' 'Oh, never,' he said, 'never – we didn't need to; you see batsmen in my day would always play the balls we bowled outside the off stump except wides, we didn't need to *make* 'em play.' That batting, of course, was the classic reply to classic fast bowling. The bowler bowled on or outside the off stump – daring the batsman to pit his off-side strokes, which are the most handsome strokes in the game, against the bowler's pace. But modern batsmen have plumped for utilitarian methods and fast bowling has become less glorious than of old.

So there is little profit, either in cash or glory, in fast bowling today. Again, food shortages do not tend to produce bowlers with the bonus energy demanded by fast bowling. The war restricted coaching and the development of young cricketers. Many young men of the good physique and good heart essential in a fast bowler gave their lives in a contest grimmer than a Test match. So England is short of fast bowlers who might bowl out the Australians or even give English batsmen practice against speed such as that of Ray Lindwall.

But, as Ray Lindwall moved in silky momentum to the crease and swept away the English batting at Lord's, he set foot in England an idea which cannot but prove heady to youth.

Up and down the country small boys at cricket on school playing fields, odd grass patches, or side streets, gripped a ball, struck poses and said, 'I'm Lindwall.' Then they propelled the ball wildly towards a nervous batsman at the other end. This virus in the young will undoubtedly lead to broken windows, probably to bruised shins, even to black eyes. It may also produce in England a great fast bowler of the class of Ray Lindwall. There may be a gap of a few years before that bowler, in his turn, runs up to bowl in a Test at Lord's, but in him the tradition will remain unbroken.

★　★　★

Fast bowlers hunt in pairs, it is said; but so do opening batsmen. There have been many famous partnerships, and in my opinion the best of them all was the Bajan firm of Gordon Greenidge and Desmond Haynes. This essay by Ian Peebles recalls some older openers.

IAN PEEBLES

Opening Batsmen (1958)

'Opening batsmen,' said my friend, a man of judgement in sporting matters. 'A couple of dull dogs, sent in to discourage the opposition.'

This was a surprising pronouncement to me, as I have always regarded opening pairs as the glamour boys of cricket. Not for them the long, anxious wait followed by the solitary walk to meet an already established bowler. They enter the freshly cleared area shoulder to shoulder like royalty, with eleven retainers going before to make arrangements for their welcome. When famous, their names become linked together as closely as Rolls and Royce or Negretti and Zambra, lending them all the stability and grandeur of an old-established firm of lawyers. Think of a few of the 'old firms' – Gunn and Shrewsbury, Tunnicliffe and Brown, Hobbs and Sutcliffe, Woodfull and Ponsford. Could any commercial venture have flopped with a title such as one of these?

But opening the innings is not all a bed of roses, or should we say Nottingham marl? It calls for special qualities of technique and judgement rather beyond those of the rest of the batting order, for the first partnership is the keystone on which will largely depend the pattern of things to come.

The opening batsman need never be dull, but he must be sound. The new ball in the hands of the expert can be made to do strange and diabolical things and, while every batsman will sometime meet it, shine and swing are the opener's stock in trade. If there are any shortcomings in the mechanics of his craft they will be exposed in no time, for the new ball moves fast and late, calling for special vigilance and treatment. Not the least important refinement is the art of leaving it alone. You may have seen Hobbs or Hutton pull the bat away so late in the stroke that it looks as if they had been beaten. They haven't, but practice and reflex have detected a last-second deviation from the pitch.

Apart from physical ability, the start of an innings calls for sound assessment of a number of points. State of the wicket, time factor, and the type and extent of the bowling resources will determine whether to be a 'dull dog' and dig in or to launch a blitzkrieg and seize the initiative right away. The crafty campaigner may nurse one bowler in order to keep another off or shield a partner vulnerable to some particular form of attack. The unselfish Bill Woodfull, affectionately called 'the worm killer' in his own country, would sniff around for the chief danger of the day, and then manœuvre to stay opposite it until his less certain but more brilliant colleagues were well in. Some of us can remember the superb bluff of Jack Hobbs, which in 1926 succeeded in convincing the Australians, and everyone else, that a sticky Oval wicket was really an ordinary slow one.

The first-wicket man must also have physical courage. Nothing is more stimulating to the nervous system than a bright hard new ball received on thumb or thigh from a fresh Larwood or Lindwall off a fresh green wicket. With the increase of discretion and the decrease of vision, this quality has occasionally been known to wane. One distinguished and mature county No. 1 made no bones about it. If the name of Larwood or Macdonald appeared on the scoresheet he had a three-day attack of flu, which he doctored on the local golf course. And Bobby Abel, on being taxed with a slight reluctance in facing the fearsome Kortright, sensibly replied that he was a married man with a family, and there were lots of other bowlers in England.

With the destinies of their side so heavily depending upon them, it is logical that Nos. 1 and 2 have produced many picturesque characters. My own favourite opening batsman will ever be George Gunn, whose talents as a musician were reflected in his loftily detached attitude at the crease. One feels that he and his fellow pianist Pachman would have made most amiable companions. What records he would hold had he been mathematically instead of musically minded no man can say. Some years ago at Edgbaston he mentioned to Bob Wyatt as he took guard that his committee thought he might make some more runs, so he was going to make a hundred, which he did at his leisure. Second innings he casually observed that there had been some criticism of his century as being too slow, so this one was going to be a bit quicker. It took an hour and a half. I myself remember the evening at Lord's when he abruptly terminated a dazzling innings at 95 on the grounds that his side were now all right and he would rather like to sit and watch the game with his wife. When Leicestershire, in an experiment with time, advanced the lunch hour to two o'clock he deposited the ball neatly into a delighted bowler's hands at precisely one-thirty, remarking that this was his accustomed lunchtime.

In broader vein were the eccentricities of the impish George Brown of Hampshire, who once advanced to attack Larwood and Voce with a crash helmet surmounting his majestic stature. Alan Fairfax likes to tell of him opening the innings for his county against the Australians when he received the raconteur's first ball, of adequate pace and length, with a blow of such unorthodox violence that it narrowly missed a tram some distance outside the square-leg boundary. Knowing the striker, I'd wager that this gesture was prompted by a motorcyclist's deep-rooted aversion to trams rather than the solemnity of the occasion, of which he was probably quite oblivious.

There is also Charlie Harris, who when absorbed in his play seems transported far from his immediate surroundings. His partner of many years' standing complained mildly one morning at Lord's that for two hours he had been addressed from the further end by a rich variety of English Christian names, not one of which bore any resemblance to his own, which happens to be Walter.

There was Victor Trumper, perhaps the greatest legendary figure in cricket, whose gentle unselfish character contrasted so strongly with the ruthless brilliance of his play. Herbie Taylor, master of the mat and full of mercurial and unexpected theory, is remembered among the truly great, over all of whom presides the mighty figure of 'W. G.' himself. They say that when he had written Grace at No. 1 he would make known his further wishes by telling the rest of the side at what number they would COME in.

But most moderns would unhesitatingly point to Jack Hobbs as the greatest opening batsman of their times, with Hobbs and Sutcliffe as the greatest pair. Of the immortals, Hobbs is perhaps the only one of the moderns whom it is not possible to fault in certain circumstances. His astonishing technique was adaptable to every variety of wicket, and the more trying the conditions the greater the disparity between his performance and the next best. The extreme pace of Cotter, Gregory and Macdonald he met with serene confidence and, as he bowled rather good swingers and googlies himself, these held no mystery for him.

In the iron determination and tireless concentration of Herbert Sutcliffe he found an ideal foil, and the understanding between the two seemed to be almost telepathic. Do you remember the singles they used to trot which would have strained most legs and nerves to bursting point?

Since the war there have been many good pairs, but none seem to have been associated long enough to become crystallized into a family business, though the early dissolution of Messrs Barnes and Morris was probably a mercy for visiting firemen. In this country post-war county cricket has so far been too transient and short-lived to produce anything so established as Makepeace and Hallows – but the names of Hutton and Lowson scan very nicely.

* * *

Cover has always been a vital fielding position, its importance further enhanced in one-day cricket. John Arlott writes of the famous cover fielders in the history of the game; characteristically, he ranges across

the globe in search of candidates. Would that he had lived long
enough to watch and write about Jonty Rhodes!

JOHN ARLOTT

Not One to Cover (1970s)

'Not one to cover' is a seriously cautionary comment in more circles
than one. In cricket it is the batsman's warning to his partner that
the fieldsman at cover point is too good for them to expect a single
from a stroke in that direction. Cover is potentially the villain or the
hero of any fielding story. His specific task is to nullify the most
romantic of all strokes, the cover drive: on the other hand, he has
the opportunity to be the most spectacularly graceful fieldsman in
the game.

Strictly speaking – certainly in the firm opinion of any captain
who does not himself field in that position – there should *never* be
one run from a stroke to cover. Yet, in practice, there often is. Jack
Hobbs – who understood the tactic so well because he fielded there
himself – used to 'bait' the opposing cover point. First he would play
a series of checked strokes to him: hit hard the ball would reach the
fieldsman too quickly to allow a single: but 'checked' – played gently
– there was time for the batsmen to run one while it was travelling
to him. Then, having lured him in too close, Hobbs would unleash
the fully powered stroke, placed wide of him and too fast to be
stopped, for four runs. It was a joke Jack always appreciated, but
cover points never did.

Cover does, of course, make catches – skiers and horribly
awkward swirlers from mishits, and stinging skimmers from full-
blooded drives only fractionally mistimed – but he is predominantly
a run-saver. Nyren, speaking from the wisdom of the Hambledon
cricket of almost 200 years ago, wrote that the fieldsman posted 'to
cover the middle wicket and point' needed to know 'the exact spot
where the two runs may be saved, and that where the one run may
be prevented' – the perfect posing of a problem no one has ever
managed to solve all the time.

Nevertheless, for the man eager in temperament and fast on his
feet, it is the most exciting of all positions: he could probably excel
in the deep but, at cover, the challenge is not to save the four or the

two, but to save the one: he is as deeply involved with every ball bowled as any close catcher, for even the defensive stroke which trickles the ball out on the off side may give the chance of a quick single in his direction.

Nyren says he must 'play from the pitch of the ball, and the motion of the batsman so as to get the start of the ball' and 'learn to judge the direction in which the batter, by his position and motion, will strike the ball, and whether high or low, hard or gently, and before it is struck, he should be off to meet it'.

There is never 'one to cover' against a man who meets that demand. The first of them was Vernon Royle, good enough to play for Lancashire in 1873 straight from school while, as an attacking bat, he once finished second in the Lancashire averages: but his great fame was as a cover point. He was ambidextrous, vitally important there since the right-hander's cover drive always tends to curl to the left. The enduring tribute to him was reported from a Roses match. Tom Emmett, that shrewd Yorkshire character, was batting when his partner pushed a ball out to cover and called for a run. 'Nay, nay', said Tom, indicating Royle. 'Woa, now, there's a policeman theer.'

Many of the finest cover points, because of their speed of reaction and certainty of hand, have been translated and posted close to the wicket, like A. O. Jones – who invented the gully position – Percy Chapman, Patsy Hendren and Keith Miller. But Gilbert Jessop, the legendary hitter, who also opened the bowling for England against Australia, fielded there all his life and C. B. Fry, in his analysis of the playing methods of the great, picked him as the pre-eminent fieldsman. Jessop was stockily built and, crouched in anticipation, he was valuably near the ground. As he moved in to pick up, his right arm was in position to swing back and his left foot was lifted so, the instant the ball entered his hand, he was ready to throw in. His throw involved no hint of the 'wind up' which gives batsmen the crucial extra moment of running time. He saved the fractions of a second, so often decisive in a run-out, by throwing from the elbow down, largely by a flick of the wrist, so that the running batsman, accustomed to the often laborious mechanics of the throw from the deep, was beaten for speed.

From the deep, however, Jessop employed a different, more shoulder-powered, but still low, throw. In 1905, the Australians played Surrey at the Oval on the same three days as were allotted to the Middlesex–Gloucestershire match at Lord's. In the county game

Middlesex were soon in trouble on a bad pitch and Gloucester, captained by Jessop, took an advantage by the end of the first day. On the second day the then Prince of Wales – president as well as landlord of the Surrey club – and his two sons arrived to watch play at the Oval in the afternoon, soon after the county began their second innings. It had been arranged that W. G. Grace should sit with His Royal Highness, as well as the chairman, Lord Alverstoke, and, since Surrey were batting, Lord Dalmeny their captain joined the company. Late in the day Hayward struck a ball wide of mid-on to the boundary in the distant – Harleyford Road – corner of the ground, a vastly long hit. Suddenly the ball came back out of the crowd in a fierce, low arc, plumb into the wicketkeeper's gloves. 'Middlesex must have lost,' said 'W. G'. 'How do you know that, Doctor?' asked Dalmeny. 'Only Jessopus could have thrown that ball,' answered the 'Old Man'. He was right. Jessop, unable to bat because of a knee injury, had left the rest of the Gloucestershire side to make the 14 runs they needed to beat Middlesex and gone to take a sight of the Australians. His cab put him down at the Vauxhall corner gate and he walked in just as Hayward's stroke took the ball into the crowd: and, to W. G. at least, the arc of his throw was unmistakable. We may hope the heir to the throne was suitably impressed by the 'Old Man's' expertise.

In that match at the Oval, Jack Hobbs opened the innings for Surrey. The critics of the time, though impressed by his batting, criticized his apparent slackness in the field and, always a model professional, he set out to rectify the fault. Quick-footed, neat and controlled in movement, intelligent in approach, within a couple of years he made himself into one of the finest cover points in the history of the game – so that there was never 'one to cover' when Jack Hobbs was there. For a time, however, he 'kidded' batsmen that there was. He would move in slowly, allow them to take a few runs and then, as they assumed the single, he pounced. In eleven matches of the 1911–12 tour of Australia, he ran out fifteen batsmen from cover. His accuracy was such that, under pressure and with only one stump to aim at, he would whip all three out of the ground.

As a rule, though, he did not take that risk of overthrows: if the minutest margin of time was left to him, he threw not merely to the wicketkeeper, but slap into his gloves. His friend Herbert Strud-wick who for years kept wicket in the same Surrey and England sides, said, 'Jack threw so hard that, if I hadn't taken it, it would have smashed my ribs: at first I used to be a bit alarmed until I realized that it was always going to hit my gloves just over the stumps.'

As the years went by Hobbs ran out fewer opponents: one could observe those he did bring off, his catches and his stops; no one could count the number of runs his reputation saved, runs batsmen *might* have taken but did not dare to attempt because Hobbs was there.

In the days before bowlers set out to close the off side, when the old masters of slow left-arm tempted batsmen to drive into the covers, the post of cover point was even more highly specialized than now. Indeed, Middlesex thought it worthwhile to include S. H. Saville for his cover fielding alone: and Jim Hutchinson, whose career batting average was under 19, and who was a negligible bowler, held his place in the Derbyshire XI for a decade for his value.

Some great men fielded there occasionally. Sir Learie Constantine, surely the greatest of all fieldsmen, was often needed for his close catching but he was pre-eminent at cover point as anywhere else.

The classic Australian cover was Syd Gregory, whose successors were Tommy Andrews and, briefly, before he moved to short leg, Victor Richardson. But their cricket produced a whole succession of players whom memory recalls as all of the same physical mould, of no more than average height, wide-shouldered and tapering down to neat, quick feet: all of them would run and pick up into the long, low accurate throw which marks the great Australian outfields – men like Vernon Ransford, Johnnie Taylor, 'Nip' Pellow, Sir Don Bradman, Neil Harvey, Jack Fingleton – all of whom fielded at cover often enough to demonstrate outstanding ability.

Other leading Englishmen in the position between the two wars were Percy Chapman – with the dual advantage of being left-handed and having the strength and timing to throw accurately and fast when off balance, but who soon became a specialist at silly point – Eddie Paynter, Jack Davies and the bubbling Jack Stephenson, an entertainment in himself. At one point in the middle 1930s Middlesex, for the slow left-arm and leg-spin bowling which they always favoured, could set an arc of superb cover fieldsmen – George Hart, Joe Hulme, Walter Robins and 'Tuppy' Owen-Smith – from short third man round to extra cover, and still have John Human in reserve and the elder master, Patsy Hendren, standing at slip.

In the post-war years the standard has been maintained by Cyril Washbrook, unmistakable as he prowled the covers, cap tilted, shoulders hunched and wary; Reggie Simpson, slim, poised and graceful; the Indians Gul Mahommad, Adhikari and Gaekwad; Athol Rowan of South Africa, Martin Donnelly and Brunty Smith, New Zealand; Alan Rees of Glamorgan and, when he could be spared from the near position, 'Tiger' Pataudi.

Now, though cover point is no longer considered so important as twenty years ago, and when cricket standards are said to be deteriorating, the game has produced two men as fine as any who ever filled the position: arguably, indeed, the greatest, Colin Bland, the Rhodesian, has so studied and practised the movement of stop, pick up and throw that he seems to blend the three in a single ripple of movement, and his accuracy is amazing. The West Indian Clive Lloyd hardly looks an athlete, for he stoops and shambles: but he moves like a great cat and throws, on balance with whip, off balance with a kind of push, so that he is as fast in reaching and returning the ball as anyone we have ever known.

Still the wise batsman must often say to his partner, 'It is not one to cover'.

★   ★   ★

Cricket is a game of subtlety, but nothing excites the passions more than the elemental force with which a ball is hit over the ropes. I once saw Viv Richards hit five sixes in a day at the Ferozeshah Kotla, the last out of the stadium, literally all the way from New Delhi to Old Delhi. Later I saw, if on television, Kapil Dev smash four sixes in succession to save the follow-on in a Lord's Test. These men were heir to an ancient tradition. For, as Gerald Brodribb now reminds us, the big hit and the big hitter long antedate the modern bat and the one-day game.

GERALD BRODRIBB

The Big Hit (1961)

A swirl of great swarthy arms, the sweep of a bat, and a joyous crack as the ball went up and up, high over the deep fielder, rising still over the holiday crowd, and then plummeting down with a crash on the roof of the court house, some 120 yards away. It was Maurice Tate – Hastings – 1924 – some luckless Hampshire bowler – the first six I ever saw. As I watched from the top of a car, the ball rattled down off the steep roof, and fell almost at my feet. I might perhaps have retrieved it, might perhaps have thrown it back daringly on to the field, but the moment was too overpowering. It was enough to feel that – even though I was so young – the very nearness of the ball had put me right into the game; cricket was mine, now and for ever. Not mine only, for the whole crowd was buzzing with talk and smiles; the great 'Oo-ah!' as the ball had rocketed up had given way to a murmur of delight. Without the reaction of the crowd that great six would have signified nothing. It instantly linked the spectators with the game, took them right on the stage and gave most of them a moment to be long remembered.

A hit over the ropes counts six, but the difference between a six and a four is out of all proportion to the numerical difference. Most people go to a county match in the hope of seeing the ball hit hard and high. There is beauty in the curve of the flight, delight in the sound of a full-blooded hit, and an engaging element of danger. 'Mind out, here she comes!'; the crowd eagerly makes a path for the ball; but someone will try to stop it or even catch it. 'I caught you out twice today,' said a perfect stranger to A. E. R. Gilligan, as he walked down the street one evening. Gilligan was puzzled until the stranger explained that the catches had been made somewhere up in the grandstand. Gilligan had hit his sixes, and the memory of two of them will remain with that spectator as long as he lives. For a moment of time he was playing *in* the match, with all barriers lifted. A similar thrill must have been enjoyed by the spectator in a Currie Cup game in South Africa who off two consecutive balls made catches of sixes hit by Winslow off Tayfield's bowling.

Though some batsmen give the impression that the crowd does not matter, might just as well not be there, the spectator has paid his money and expects to see some live cricket in return. W. G. Grace fully realized the good influence keen and satisfied spectators could have upon the game. In 1899 he wrote:

> There is no doubt that big hitters draw crowds and delight spectators, who would sooner see an hour of spirited play than spend an afternoon watching the most perfect slow batsman compiling runs in monotonous singles . . . Say what you will,

the cricket-loving public likes lively batting, and for this reason, that is, for the good of cricket, I think hitters should be encouraged. Moreover, if there were more hard hitters, there would be fewer drawn games.

I know nothing more exhilarating than the feeling that the spectators are on the *qui vive* and eagerly watching every ball, and it is because I realize that spectators are always in this mood when a notorious hard hitter is at the wicket that I say: 'Encourage a young batsman who has a disposition to hit out.'

An orthodox method may be important, especially for those of limited natural ability, but in the end it is the results which matter. I always like the story of the boy who was being coached by an old pro, who bowled him a good ball which the boy hit hard and high into the distance. 'Just look where your foot is,' reprimanded the pro, who considered that the ball should have been treated with respect. 'And just look where the ball is,' replied the boy, not perhaps tactfully, but with some measure of justification.

If you are a hitter, the great thing is to win the name of 'scientific' hitter, which simply means someone who looks at the ball when he hits and shows some judgement in choosing the right ball. What a pity no one thought of calling Bonnor 'a scientific hitter', and then everyone would have been satisfied. Though some bowlers really do object to being hit about – one Yorkshire bowler is said to have murmured that it was 'sheer murder and not cricket' when F. T. Mann hit him twice running to the top seats of the Lord's pavilion – most of them join in spontaneous admiration when a batsman makes a really fine hit off their bowling. I can well remember Ian Thomson, of Sussex, hitting a ball from Lock over the screen at Hove in 1957 and the bowler clapping him for doing so, and it was a sight almost as pleasant as the hit itself. Townsend of Warwickshire once made a very fine hit in the opposite direction at Hove off the bowling of James Langridge, and he writes: 'I always remember Jim striding down the wicket, and saying to me, "Well hit!"' as the ball sailed away towards the entrance gate. I believe that such applause from 'the enemy' is largely confined to sixes, and not even the best of turf-clinging fours will often produce it.

Sir Pelham Warner, whose cricket experience is unrivalled, said that the best match he ever saw at Lord's was the England v. Dominions one of 1945. It was packed full of splendid hitting and produced more sixes than almost any match at Lord's had ever done. From the expert observer down to the casual visitor the big hit is regarded as something excellent and worthwhile; E. V. Lucas sums up the whole matter very neatly in his famous poem:

'You must keep them on the carpet,' is the counsel of the pro,
'And don't ever leave your ground,' he adds, and all agree 'tis so.
Yet even from the pedant what a deep ecstatic sigh
When the batsman jumps to meet one, and a sixer climbs the sky.

When big hits flow in profusion the whole game blooms like some exotic flower and the effect is almost intoxicating. I know no better description of this than Ronald Mason's account in his *Batsman's Paradise* of a day he spent at the Oval when he was aged twelve; the match was Yorkshire (Champion County) against the Rest of England:

Fortune favoured the two left-handers on that day; and, I have since thought, a relaxed carelessness on the part of the two bowlers, Rhodes and Kilner, whom in normal conditions no one hit with impunity. But the Fates were with the batsmen, and it was the last game of the season (15 September 1924, I shall remember the date all my life) and the bowlers' fingers were perhaps September-weary, and the left-hander's spinner to the left-handed batsmen encouraged a gladsome sweep to leg with the break – and altogether we were presented with such conditions as never before or since concatenated so gloriously; and these two beautiful left-handers, Woolley in a roseate dream of willowy motion and Chapman in a great muscular charging flourish of strong limbs in their pride, collected 50 runs off these tremendous bowlers in exactly seven minutes by the clock. Woolley's right foot, again and again, planted itself lengthily down the wicket as he swung lazily with the break; Chapman, all of him, came swinging out in delight with his bat flourishing high – and time and again the ball soared splendidly over the crowd, out into the road, under the gasometer. I can still hear the joyous crack, still rise with the excited crowd around me as the ball sails above our heads, join in the high squall of delighted cheering, wave on wave of it, and down comes Chapman again and crack comes the ball once more into our midst. I felt, innocent and inexperienced as I was, a sense of tremendous exultation. It was elementary, charity-match stuff; but it affected me as no incident at any cricket match has ever affected me, before or since. For the rest of the day I felt breathless, dizzy, almost ill; the ordinary world seemed unreal. But for years later, literally years, the memory of those moments (which Woolley and Chapman have probably forgotten; I doubt whether I can say the same of Rhodes) recurred to me and, curiously enough, steadied me at times when steadying was what I most needed.

A big hit is not only memorable to those who saw it, but regarded as worth recording by cricket correspondents. Glance through any columns of cricket reports, and consider the headlines. Here are a few from miscellaneous papers of the 1930s:

'Voce Hits Ball into Hotel Bar' – *Daily Express*.
'Gigantic Hit by Hammond' – *Sussex Daily News*.
'Budd's One Stroke – Six – ' *Morning Post*.
'R. H. Moore Hits Two Great Sixes' – *Daily Telegraph*.
'A Great Hit by Voce' – *The Times*.
'Wellard's Giant Sixes – Hits Ball into River' – *Daily Telegraph*.

A big six must then be regarded as something to be reported, and indeed the purpose of this piece is to place on record and in some detail the hitting feats of those whose particular talent has glorified the game.

Scorebooks and histories give the details of runs gained and conceded, but the individual great strokes which provided such pleasure to all those who saw them soon become lost in the mist of memory; some exceptional ones may be lucky enough to blossom into legend and grow with the passage of time, but in the end they fade into oblivion as though they never had been. It is surely unjust that such glories should meet with such a fate, while the score-sheets that contained them linger on, like skeletons. I hope by recounting the feats of the great hitters to recall the joys they must have produced, and perhaps to remind batsmen of today what seemingly impossible feats have been achieved.

It is easy enough to appreciate the joyous feelings of those who have witnessed the great hits. It is sometimes forgotten that the man who makes them is also provided with intense pleasure. Though this pleasure is sometimes evident, there are not many batsmen who have been able to express their feelings in words. We are lucky though to have something which Jessop wrote in 1899 on the subject of hitters and spectators. He wrote:

The man who hits always possesses one consoling thought in success or failure, that with him goes the sympathy of the great majority of spectators. Most of them maintain firmly that 'It is better to have hit and missed than never to have hit at all.'

A few old-fashioned theorists still shake their heads sadly, and endeavour to look disgusted when the ball crashes into the pavilion clock or disappears into the neighbouring gardens, but I suppose I cannot be wrong in saying that even these in their hearts are not especially saddened by the sight, while for the more ordinary sportsman, the men who have just come to see some fun, and the younger people of both sexes, the spectacle causes unqualified enthusiasm.

Playing to the gallery in all sports is one of the most offensive forms of diseased vanity, and to hit simply in order to extort applause would indeed be a lamentable method of seeking cheap popularity. But it cannot be denied that there is some satisfaction in feeling that you are giving pleasure to the vast throng surrounding the field of play, that they are glad to see you appear, rejoice when an incompetent fielder gives you another life, are saddened when you retire to well-deserved obscurity. And even if the fates prove unfavourable, and your first ball, designed to disappear beyond the boundary, screws stupidly into the arms of extra cover, and you retire dejectedly into the pavilion for an ignominious 'blob', it is some slight satisfaction to feel that there is scarcely one who is not sorry for your departure. 'He did his best to make things lively,' they amiably remark, and even cheer your retiring figure, in a kind-hearted attempt to inform you of their appreciation of your effort . . .

But remember that the object of each player is to do the best for his side regardless of the crowd; that we who are hitters hit because we are most use doing this, and those who play a stonewall game do so because they are most use doing that, and that all have equal right to participate in the finest sport, whether they cause interest to the spectators or whether they cause indifference.

This is the fullest statement ever made by a great hitter on his approach to the crowd, and their sympathy with a batsman who is obviously willing to hit the ball. It was ever thus, as we learn from this verse written over 130 years ago on the great Fuller Pilch, then in his 'promising' days:

> At present his batting's a little too wild,
> Though the 'non-pareil' hitter he's sometimes been styled,
> So free and so fine, with the head of a master,
> Spectators all grieve when he meets with disaster.

Some batsmen will remember some particular hit to the end of their days. Paul Winslow's hit at Old Trafford in 1955, for example, when he reached his first Test century with one of the biggest hits ever seen on the ground, and waved joyfully to his fellows in the pavilion to include them in his delight. Herbert Sutcliffe well remembers the six with which he completed his first century in first-class cricket. He writes:

> In the match at Northampton in 1919, I remember that Holmes's score stood at 98, when my score was 94. George Hirst, who was sitting in the pavilion, then said, 'He ought to hit a six now.' The next ball enabled me to do what Hirst hoped I would do. I went out to it, got properly hold of it and it soared over long off to clear the boundary by about forty yards, and pitch on the tennis courts. Probably one of the biggest hits I have made. The thrill stayed with me for a long time – there is a touch of it now when I think of the shot – but the hit was one I should not have attempted had there not been a race with Percy for the pleasure of scoring our first hundred for the county.

Sutcliffe also recalls the innings at Bradford against Gloucester in 1932 which gave him his hundredth hundred in first-class cricket. It contained many sixes, of which he writes:

> I know the eight sixes I hit at Bradford when I made my hundredth hundred gave me great joy and I always have a similar feeling of joy when I see a batsman hit a six whether he is playing for us or against us.

Other batsmen have stated the pleasure they have had in making a big hit. K. S. Ranjitsinhji, who could hit a very long ball when he

wanted to, wrote: 'A big drive, clean and true, gives a satisfaction
that cannot be expressed in words.' J. H. Wardle says: 'There is no
joy in the world like the "tonk" in the middle of the bat that sends
the ball flying over the ropes for six. There is no more beautiful
sight than to see it soaring; if you are the batsman, that is. If you
are the bowler, it is not so hot.' Wardle was a somewhat cross-bat
swiper, and in the course of an innings at Lord's when he made
several huge hits to leg, one purist is said to have remarked that
Wardle's batting was 'agricultural', to which a Yorkshire supporter is
said to have replied: 'Yes, perhaps, but bloomin' fertile.'

Many writers have attempted to describe the sound of a well-hit
ball; about which Dean Hole, who was once a keen Notts supporter,
wrote:

> I maintain that there are few more blissful emotions than those
> which were ours when, having hit the billet with precision and
> power, we heard it whizzing through the air, saw our adversary
> gazing at it like a retriever at a partridge which begins to tower,
> and started to add runs to our score . . . I have myself played
> some beautiful though simple airs on the flute; but I have never
> heard any music, home-made or foreign, so sweet as the song
> of the billet.

Robin Marlar says that he can still remember the whizz of a ball
which a West Indian hit off his bowling out of the ground at Hove,
and, for all his many great bowling performances, he considers that
his 'proudest cricket achievement' was when he hit a ball from Lock
into the distant Vauxhall stands at the Oval.

It is then no wonder that the six-hit has such glamour, and the
element of risk adds to it. In 1928–9 Australia lost a Test match
to England by a handful of runs when Blackie was caught on the
edge of the boundary. 'I was going to make a six to give the boys
something to remember,' he said regretfully. 'It did look such an
easy one.' Sometimes batsmen have been egged on by promises of
reward for sixes hit in Test matches, and when cricket was resumed
in 1946 it was suggested that there be an annual prize for the batsman who hit the greatest number of sixes in a season. Though
other annual awards are now made, nothing has yet been given for
six-hitters. I do not think there would be anything unseemly in
encouraging batsmen to go out for hits which produce such lasting
pleasure, for the pleasure does linger on. Consider this story of

lay down luxuriously to await the next batsman's arrival. The shouts which greeted his feat were to him but distant whispers, but his beautiful reverie was disrupted by the arrival of a breathless mid-on.

'Throw it in, you old fool,' bellowed this emissary. 'It's a no-ball, and they've already run seven.'

Many may know this story in some shape or form, but this is, I believe, the true and original version. Essex were in the field late in the afternoon when a batsman hit a full toss right out of the meat of a well-swung bat. The ball sang down on square leg out of the low sun like a jet fighter going into the attack and, taking him smack dab on the cap badge, knocked him flat on his back. While the rest of the field rushed to the rescue, that incomparable man Charlie McGahey went up to the remorseful striker and said in conversational tones, 'Cigar or coconut, sir?'

One of the most spectacular misses it has been my lot to see was made by 'Hopper' Levett of Kent, who essayed to catch Jim Smith. The stroke was a prodigious one, and so faultlessly vertical that it was really unnecessary for the wicketkeeper to claim it as his as he set about his task. This he did by revolving round and round the wicket in taut circles. With arched back and imploring hands held before his painfully upturned face, it only wanted a voodoo drum to complete the scene. He had gone round about five times when his cap fell off, and several times more when he suddenly realized that the ball was about to arrive at the opposite side of the circle. Seeking a short cut to this point, he lurched into the castle and went down with a crash of bails, pads and stumps, closely followed, by way of an emphatic full stop, by the thud of the arriving ball.

It took quite some time to restore order. Someone then callously suggested that if 'Hopper' hadn't interfered, the ball would have descended on top of the middle stump and the batsman would have been out 'played on'.

Ponder these things next time the ball is a pinprick in the sky and the cry is raised, 'Yours, Reader!'

* * *

Like the wicketkeeper, the umpire must be in the game at all times. Like the wicketkeeper again, he is a man who is noticed only when he errs. Unlike the wicketkeeper, however, he is on the field when both sides bat. Given the stress and the strain, it is a wonder that there are so many volunteers. The prince of cricket writers celebrates the rarely celebrated adjudicators of the game.

NEVILLE CARDUS

The Umpire (1934)

The umpire at cricket is like the geyser in the bathroom: we cannot do without it, yet we notice it only when it is out of order. The solemn truth is that the umpire is the most important man on the field; he is like the conductor of an orchestra. If first slip misses a catch, the error involves only a personal fallibility; we say 'Hard luck!' and first slip begins again. If the umpire falters, everybody in the game is drawn into the range of mortal frailty; we do not say 'Hard luck!' to the miserable man in the white coat; we even add to our gloating over his fallibility the imputation of stupidity or of malice prepense. If a batsman misses a half-volley and is bowled, the crowd laughs or, at the worst, calls the guilty one an ass. But the umpire who errs as obviously as that is likely to be regarded as unfit for his job. His fallibility can be reported at Lord's; nobody reports to Lord's the cricketer who in the excitement of the moment runs his partner out.

All day long, ball after ball, the umpire must keep his mind intensely on the game. The players are free to enjoy relaxations. Some of them indulge in a good sleep while their side is batting. When rain falls and stops play, the cricketers can forget the match for a while. The umpire enjoys no release from responsibility; until the match is over, or until weather causes an abandonment, he is obliged to watch, watch, watch – either the play or the pitch or the groundsman. The amount of concentration he is expected to perform every day is almost an abuse of human endurance. What a great country this would be if every man, whatever his station, concentrated half as much on the smallest detail of his work as an umpire is compelled to do, from high noon to dewy evening of a cricket match!

The umpires are the Dogberrys of the game. We see them as essentially comic characters. Whenever a batsman swipes to leg, and hits the umpire in the small of the back, how the crowd roars! If the wind blows the hat off the umpire's head, laughter holds sides. The reason for the humour which comes out of the activities of the umpires is a matter of deep psychology. For the simple fact is that no man can sustain with dignity the semblance of infallible judgement. Man is born to sin and error; and when he wears the robes of virtue and wisdom and law and infallibility all rolled into one, the gods infect us with their merriment.

'How's that?' shrieked the whole field when a batsman was brilliantly thrown out. 'Wait a minute,' answered the umpire. 'Who did it?'

It is, of course, to country cricket that we must look for the really comical Dogberry of the crease. I remember Old George, in the days when we used to go on a jolly tour through Shropshire. The custom was for each side to bring its own umpire, and at the beginning of every match old George made a point of meeting the other team's umpire, over a glass of ale in the pavilion.

'Now, look' 'ee 'ere,' he would say, 'it is for yew to luke after yewre business, and oi'll luke after mine!'

Once on a time a cricket match was about to be played between two village clubs of long and vehement rivalry. An hour before the pitching of stumps a visitor to the district walked on to the ground and inspected the wicket. He was greeted by an old man, a very old man. The visitor asked for information about the impending battle, and the ancient monument told him.

'Is your team strong in bowling?' asked the visitor.

'Ay sir, not so bad,' was the answer.

'And who gets most of your wickets?' asked the visitor.

'Why sir, oi do,' was the reply.

'Heaven,' said the visitor, 'surely you don't bowl at your time of life?'

'No, sir, oi be the umpire.'

But in the highest realms of county and Test cricket the umpire, though frequently the source of humour, is seldom allowed to share in it. A crucial blunder might mean an end to his livelihood. He deserves all the help he can possibly be given. Is not his job difficult enough in itself without the addition of embarrassments which are the consequence of our hastiness and temper? I appeal to every lover of the game to think of the umpire always, to bear always in mind that, like the backwoods' pianist, he is doing his best – in threatening circumstances.

English cricket today is fortunate to be under the supervision of umpires as fine and courageous and clever as Arthur Morton (a rich character), Frank Chester, Hardstaff – to name but a few. Chester is a joy to watch; he delivers his decisions sometimes with immense irony. I have seen him signal a snicked boundary by means of a gesture of regal disdain, as though to say, 'What a stroke! I am compelled by the law to rule it worth four; but I reserve the right to say what I think about it.'

I have seen Chester give a batsman out with a finger suddenly pointed to heaven, dramatic in its announcement of ruthless finality. And I have seen him turn his back on a bowler's manifestly absurd appeal for leg-before-wicket – turn his back with the air of a man consigning another to some place outside the pale of all sense and decency.

Arthur Morton is not so spectacular; he believes in the conservation of energy. But county cricketers know well, and revel in, his comments at the wicket, many of them delivered out of the corner of the mouth. 'I wish you'd keep quiet,' he once said at the agony of a Lancashire and Yorkshire match; 'it's like umpiring in a parrot house.'

Parry is the umpire who bends himself into a right angle for every ball when he is standing at the bowler's end; he takes on this terrible burden of physical discomfort so that, as he thinks, he can get a better sight of the ball in a leg-before-wicket mix-up. Merely to look at him for an hour is to go home suffering from lumbago. They all of them are worthy of our applause, the men who serve the game by standing – and waiting for the end of the long, long day.

*   *   *

There comes a time when all players must leave the stage. Some choose their moment of departure, going when the fans ask 'Why?' rather than 'Why not?' Others are forced out, the failure of form or the advance of age leading to non-selection. Whatever the manner of exit, it is always a deeply poignant moment for player and follower. This essay by an Australian about three departing Englishmen is one of my favourites.

J. H. FINGLETON

Cricket Farewells (1955)

Twiddling the peak of his cap, as is his wont, Len Hutton walked from the Sydney ground and into the pavilion depths just as the workman on the balcony above hauled down the MCC flag for the last time.

Behind Hutton came Compton, surrounded, as he invariably was in Australia when play ended, by a doting band of the British merchant service who unfailingly convoyed him from the field and then, after depositing him at the dressing-room door, just as unfailingly convoyed themselves in the general surge to the members' bar. And behind Compton came Evans, his red-faced gloves tucked under his right arm and his left consolingly about a small boy who, like his ilk, thinks time and place of no autograph consequence.

In short time the pavilion had swallowed them all up and the sad thought grew that possibly no Australian ground will see again Hutton, Compton and Evans. In such a way did Grace, Trumper, Ranjitsinhji, the Gregorys and all the brilliant rest pass from cricketing sight. There is a moment in every cricketer's life when he's seen; another moment and he's no more, nor ever will be again.

Lord's could not comprehend in 1948 that it had seen Bradman for the last time. Thousands stood on the grass in front of the pavilion and called for their hero. They found it hard to leave a sunlit scene where so often he had made the hours immortal; they found it harder to believe that he had gone from their sight for ever. So also with Hobbs in Australia in 1929. On his last day in Sydney he walked the full circuit of the ground with Noble while the crowd rose to him, singing 'Auld Lang Syne', and the Hill presented him with a birthday fund.

Hutton and Compton for a surety won't be seen again in Australia. Evans might be, because keepers go till their knuckles grow callous, and Strudwick and Duckworth became as familiar on the ship's run to Australia as the Galle Face at Colombo.

Those who thrive on statistics will say that Hutton did this and that on our various grounds; that Compton once got two Test centuries in an Adelaide game, and that Evans knew peerless

stumping days in addition to batting often with pronounced entertainment and success.

Others, however, will have richer memories.

Of Hutton here I will always recall the sheer brilliance of *the*
perfect innings he played in Sydney nine years ago. It didn't pass 40
but it ran the gamut of the whole batting art. I see him again in his
own elegant manner driving Lindwall straight and to the off; glancing
– and he knew no peer in glancing – and forcing Miller, and all the
time fiddling with his cap just before he settled down to the crease
or cradling his bat as he ran. Those movements were part of Hutton.
That classical innings gave me an imperishable memory.

Compton, like the majestic Hammond before him, has known
some of his greatest and some of his poorest days in Australia. The
latter are soon forgotten. Those who know genius will always carry
the mental picture of Compton smacking the ball fine to leg as only
Compton could; of the sheer beauty and thrill of his cover drive
and hook; of his impish run out before the ball was bowled and,
sometimes, his scamper back like a schoolboy caught helping himself
to jam.

In Melbourne, once, when that weird bowler 'Wrong Grip'
Iverson (who flicked off breaks off his second finger with a leg-
break action) was befuddling the Englishmen at their first meeting,
Sheppard, who had been doing best of all, walked down the pitch
and asked skipper Compton whether he (Sheppard) shouldn't change
from defence to attack. 'Go on as you are, David,' said Compton,
who had been in the most abject bother. 'Leave the antics to me.'

Evans, always tremendously vital, will live as the man who stood
undaunted over the stumps to Bedser – as Strudwick did before him
to Tate at his greatest.

Rich characters, all of them, fading from the scene, but their
memories will remain. There is poignancy in thinking we will see
them no more, poignancy and regret. When the last flag had long
been furled I looked up from my press work and saw in the gloaming
a man in civilian clothes treading the pitch as if a pilgrim in Mecca.
He walked, at last, towards the pavilion and then turned 'and took
one long and lingering look, and took a last farewell' before he, too,
went into the pavilion for the last time. It was Alec Bedser.

*   *   *

Another evocation now – more cheerful perhaps, and of a living ground rather than departing players. A writer born in India, educated in England and now resident in the United States explains why Lord's will always be the loveliest place to watch a cricket match.

TUNKU VARADARAJAN

To Lord's with Love – and a Hamper (1995)

At no other ground is the light so tautly drawn; nowhere else is there green of such deep and clenched perfection; and in no other place where cricket is played is the air as flecked with feat and fable. That is why I love Lord's.

I loved Lord's early, before I learned to love most other things. As a small boy at boarding school in the Rajasthan desert in north-west India, with transistor pressed to small left ear, I heard John Arlott speak and Brian Johnston, too, of the sloping ground, and of old Father Time with his scythe and wicket.

I moved to England in 1979, and in the years since – spent first as sloppy London schoolboy, then at university down the M40, and lastly as settled Anglophile 'incomer' – I have missed the Lord's Test match only once, in 1991. Yet even then, on holiday in Guyana; I kept in touch with St John's Wood by sharing short-wave radio and rum with men who loved Lord's and its game almost as much as I do. 'Lord's is where even the baddest cricket look full and sweet,' said a man called Bacchus in a bar in Charity, on the Essequibo coast. He may never have been to Lord's, his grammar may have been toasted on some eccentric flame, but there was a truth in the tidy Guyanese compliment, to which I clinked my glass of the best Five Star.

Now, as Michael Atherton's men make white-flannelled war against Richie Richardson's West Indians at Headingley, I prepare myself once more for a pilgrimage to Lord's, where the summer's next and most important Test match will soon be played. 'The Tavern is noisy and vernacular,' wrote Cardus in his *English Cricket*, in 1945, 'with London spread outside.' The pavilion may no longer be 'a chapter out of Galsworthy', but the place boasts still a cavalcade of English character. Preparing to watch cricket at a venue such as this is a taxing examination of the senses and, as with all examinations, the student is advised to ready himself beforehand.

Some of us need no such counsel: guided by instincts which kindle themselves awake at the merest hint of a Test match, the mind surrenders to the sweetest tension. As a boy, I spent many nights before a match – sometimes five or six – in a sleepless and fragile accounting of possibilities. Would Ajit Wadekar win the toss? Would Gavaskar survive Andy Roberts's opening spell? Please, please let Chandrasekhar be fit to baffle the Englishmen with his googlies and topspinners and leg breaks. If only Bedi could get Tony Greig early with his arm ball. Let it not rain; whatever happens, let it not rain.

Older now, I still cannot sleep or wake or work as gently as I would like in the days before a Test match. A vivid series of images, shots, wickets and shouts takes over every idle moment, as if from the Revd Cotton's cricket song:

> Here's guarding and catching, and throwing and tossing,
> And bowling and striking, and running and crossing . . .

Test cricket's pace and style may have altered, and the cricketers are now mostly younger than I am, but the game is still dependent more than any other on the character and idealism of its players. 'Character and idealism': such strange and awkward words today, but those who watch cricket know them well, and understand their import. Those who watch cricket are aware of other truths: in accounting for a day at a Test match one must account also for all the other senses.

Sitting on a hard seat beyond the boundary allows me not just to watch and marvel at balletic play, to record scores and statistics, and to commit pure strokes to memory, but to eat delicious food and drink chilled wine and beer, to smoke strong cigarettes and share stronger observations with people who begin the day as strangers but who linger with you at stumps 'in the westering sunshine, reluctant to return to the world' (as Cardus puts it) after the last flash of flannel has departed.

Ever since I acquired control of such things, I have made sure that I take with me to a Test match those provisions which are essential for a day given over totally to pleasure. As a small boy at my first Test match at Delhi in December 1972, when England, under Tony Lewis, beat India by six wickets, my grandmother packed for me a small boy's lunch: bread spread thickly with jam, packets of potato crisps, bananas and several bottles of sticky Gold Spot. My brother and I were also given a few rupees to buy warm peanuts in their shells from the hawkers who roamed from stand to stand, shouting loudly and getting in people's way.

Jam sandwiches gave way gradually to better and more stylish food. With each passing Test, I began to associate my evolution from novice spectator to older hand with the food and drink which I brought to the ground. Yet it was not until my first Test at Lord's that I grasped the full richness of possibility that can rest in a lunch basket. On this occasion, a man and his wife sat next to me, drinking cold champagne and eating neatly sculpted sandwiches of salmon, tongue and Parma ham as India were bowled out for 96 by Botham, Lever and Hendrick. I nibbled on a lunch (I will not reveal what it was) that was, by comparison, as paltry as India's batting had been. Only my hero, Gavaskar, made a score of 42, I think, before he was caught behind, off Gooch of all people. My dejection must have been apparent to my neighbours, because they offered me some of their lunch. It was not my first glass of champagne, but it was my first tongue sandwich.

I have eaten many more since then, my Brahmin palate having acquired an unlikely taste for beef. Basking in the new-found beauty of Lord's that day I learned a simple truth: however compelling the play, a poorly assembled lunch can ruin a day at the Test match. Now I take to Lord's only those things which are fit to be eaten and drunk at a ground of such sovereignty. What best accompanies the cricket at a Lord's Test match? Just as one would not dream of drinking Coke with crab or Liebfraumilch with sweetbreads, one must ensure that, while the eyes and mind feast on a Lara or an Ambrose, the mouth receives only that which is in some sort of harmony with the game. I believe that heavy food is not appropriate: however delicious it is in the eating, food that lulls one to sleep should not be taken to a Test match. Small parcels of food are best, easy to pack and convenient to share with neighbours.

There is as much pleasure in turning to the man next to you and offering him a slice of your Spanish omelette on bread, or whatever else you have brought, as there is in the exchange of Jesuitical observations. And, over the years, I have received a cornucopia of goodies in return: Jamaican patties, Trinidadian roti, biltong, crab pie, samosa, shrimp sandwiches, quail's eggs, even Chilean empanadas (from an Australian who married a girl from Valparaiso, divorced her, but still retained his love for her food). This year I will take small pitta-bread parcels, some smeared inside with black olive paste and stuffed with mortadella, others filled with Pecorino Romano and Serrano ham. I will drink, I think, some chilled sauvignon – Cloudy Bay, perhaps, or Poggio alle Gazze, if I can find any in London. And for tea time I might take a box of Indian sweets from Drummond Street, to be eaten with strong black coffee and rum from a hip flask.

Part of this feast I will share with agreeable neighbours. A Lord's Test makes one generous. There can be no generosity, however, towards those who will, with their transistor radios and mobile phones, drown the hollow sound of wary bat on ball; or those who would, by the waving of their flags and banners, introduce at Lord's a tribal taste to which the place is just not suited. Cricket is played in a variety of places, to a flock of styles and values, yet at Lord's it must be played and watched as it has always been done.

Of course I love Lord's because of its light, its green and its air. But I love it most of all for the quietness of its passion and the soft culture of its observation. In this, we must resist all wanton change. John Arlott wrote the following words on cricket at Worcester, and I imagine sometimes perhaps too fondly in the present day their echo at Lord's:

> Like rattle of dry seeds in pods
> The warm crowd faintly clapped;
> The boys who came to watch their gods,
> The tired old men who napped.

> The members sat in their strong deckchairs,
> And sometimes glanced at the play,
> They smoked and talked of stocks and shares,
> And the bar stayed open all day.

These are old-fashioned thoughts, of course, but Lord's is an old-fashioned place.

★   ★   ★

For the truly great, there is always life after cricket. Sometimes after death, too. Alan Ross writes of the continuing presence in his home town of Ranji, 'the prince of a small state, but the king of a great game'. This is followed by a shrewd analysis of the Bradman legend by a fellow Australian.

ALAN ROSS

The Presence of Ranji (1982)

It is, naturally, at Jamnagar that the presence of Ranji remains most evident. Although the princes have long since been stripped of their titles and their privy purses – within a score of years all Ranji's predictions came to be fulfilled, though whether for the general good or ill is a matter of opinion – in many princely states the trappings, if not the reality, of power survive. Nawanagar was never anything but a minnow in the large pond of princely India but Ranji, by his own prestige and his progressive management of industry and agriculture, saw that it counted for far more than its size might have warranted. Fifty years after his death Jamnagar is still recognizably his city. Cattle may wander beside the bazaars or be parked like motorcars outside the arcades of Willingdon Crescent but the job of clearing and cleansing, that was Ranji's first priority when he became ruler, has not been undone.

The four main palaces of Jamnagar still remain, externally, much as Ranji left them. They may be the habitat of birds and bats, like the enclosed and highly decorated City Palace, or of pet animals, bucks, antelopes, gazelles, like Ranji's preferred Bhavindra Vilas, or simply shuttered and empty, except for the rare cold-weather visitor, like the multi-domed Pratap Vilas Palace, or used as a government guest house like Vibha Vilas Palace; but whatever uses, or disuses, they are put to, they stand within their palace walls – the locked gates attended by Arab guards – as stately and resplendent as ever they did.

The grounds, alas, are scarcely kept up and gradually their handsome outbuildings – stables, garages, badminton and racquet courts – are being disposed of or converted. It is ironic that the huge and magnificently ornate Pratap Vilas Palace, which Ranji himself had built, should have received as its first guests his own mourners.

Within, the palaces reek of desertion, though their long corridors are still swept and a residue of ancient palace servants, a dozen or so in all, emerge sleepily from compounds or pantries to preserve the illusion of occupancy.

It is in Ranji's own room in the Jam Palace – the room in which he died – that the illusion is most devotedly fostered. Nothing here has been disturbed since Ranji's body was carried from it. The bed with its silver headboard is made up, and propped against the pillow lies a portrait of the Jam Saheb in ceremonial dress. On a bedside table Sir Pelham Warner's photograph, inscribed 'To Ranji, the greatest batsman of my time, from his sincere admirer and friend "Plum", December 1912', bears witness to Ranji's farewell season in English cricket. Popsey's cage is there, and many portraits; a row of cricket bats the colour of rich tobacco; old uniforms and turbans.

The heart of the room is not the bed but the locked glass cabinet beside which, on a shelf, stands the romantic alabaster head, in the art-nouveau style, of a beautiful young woman. The cabinet itself contains such items as a letter from George V's secretary commiserating on the King's behalf on the loss of Ranji's eye; Ranji's glasses and cigarette case; his medals and Orders; his half-hunter on its gold chain, a miniature silver bat, a lighter; rings and cuff-links and pins; pieces of jewellery.

On the highest of the three shelves Ranji's passport, the photograph in Indian dress with turban and eyeglass, lies open: Caste/Rajput; Religion/Hindoo; Indian home/Nawanagar; Profession/Ruling Prince; Place and date of birth/Sarodar 10 Sept 1872; Domicile/Nawanagar; Height 5 ft 9; Colour of eyes/Dark brown; Colour of hair/Black/grey; Visible distinguishing marks/Smallpox marks on the face.

On the right of this, the six glass eyes which took their turn in Ranji's face are lodged in two satin-lined cases, marked 'G. Muller, 8 New Oxford Street'. For nearly a third of his life the socket of Ranji's eye had each night to be bathed by his doctor. During his years at Jamnagar, Dr Prosser Thomas later recalled, he had made efforts to establish a clinic in the city. Always, though, Ranji would mischievously summon him from his work to make up a four at bridge. Until the last days the ritual of replacing the eye and washing the eye socket were the only tasks the doctor was allowed to perform.

There are still two servants alive at Jamnagar who have looked after the Jam Saheb. In their old age they carry out their shadow duties, materializing silently on bare feet, much as if His Highness were still alive. They attend and guard his room as if it were a shrine, allowing nothing to be moved.

For all that, Ranji's room is not a solemn place, simply the bedroom of a much loved and revered ruler who, in his day, happened to be a great cricketer. His trophies and personal effects are all around and, though the sun streams through the shutters over the marble corridors outside and the hyenas and peacocks screech, within all is shuttered cool.

'When a person dies who does any one thing better than anyone else in the world,' wrote Hazlitt, discussing the fives player John Cavanagh in his famous essay 'Indian Jugglers', 'it leaves a gap in society.' That was certainly true of Ranji. Elsewhere in the same essay Hazlitt wrote, again about Cavanagh: 'He could not have shown himself in any ground in England, but he would have been immediately surrounded with inquisitive gazers, trying to find out in what part of his frame his unrivalled skill lay' – and that was true of Ranji too.

His effect on people was not confined to cricketers. The sculptor Eric Gill observed in his *Autobiography*, published seven years after Ranji's death:

> And while I am thus writing about the beauty and impressiveness of technical prowess I cannot, for it made an immense difference to my mind, omit the famous name of Ranjitsinhji. Even now, when I want to have a little quiet wallow in the thought of something wholly delightful and perfect, I think of Ranji on the county ground at Hove . . . There were many minor stars, each with his special and beloved technique, but nothing on earth could approach the special quality of Ranji's batting or fielding . . . I only place it on record that such craftsmanship and grace entered into my very soul.

GIDEON HAIGH

Sir Donald Brandname (1998)

The Australian sporting public is notoriously fickle, bestowing and withdrawing devotion in a blink, apt to forget even the firmest of favourites within a few years of retirement. Yet the flame of Sir

Donald George Bradman, seven decades since he first made headlines, has never burned brighter.

No public appearances are expected for his ninetieth birthday on 27 August: almost a year after the passing of his beloved wife, Bradman finds them strenuous. But his continued health will be the subject of front-page encomiums, and feature in evening television bulletins: an annual vigil for some years now. Whatever the tribulations of state, cricket-fancying Prime Minister John Howard will convey congratulations.

Never mind that the youngest people with clear recollection of Bradman the batsman are nudging sixty themselves, for his feats appear to be growing larger, not smaller, as they recede into antiquity. In the last decade, the cricket-industrial complex has produced a trove of books, memorabilia albums, videos, audio tapes, stamps, plates, prints and other collectables bearing the Bradman imprimatur, while the museum bearing his name at Bowral continues deriving a tidy annuity income from licensing it to coins, breakfast cereals and sporting goods. 'He is the symbol of Australian cricket,' says Steve Waugh. 'The heartbeat; the inspiration; the image of all that is good in sport and life in general.' In other words, the perfect marketing tool: Sir Donald Bradman is become Sir Donald Brandname.

In some respects, it has been ever thus. Mention of 'the Don' in Australia has never been mistaken for a reference to *The Godfather*. Little bits of his legend can be found everywhere. Australian state capitals boast twenty-two thoroughfares named in Bradman's honour (Victor Trumper has eight). Australians corresponding with the Australian Broadcasting Corporation do so to post office box number 9994: Bradman's totemic Test batting average, a pleasing notion of the Australian Lord Reith, Sir Charles Moses. A newspaper poll last year found that Bradman was the Australian most respondents wanted to light the flame at the 2000 Olympics: at ninety-two, it would be a feat to rank with anything he accomplished on a cricket field.

Today, however, cachet implies cash. A Bradman bat from 1930 changed hands at Philips in London last year for £21,732, a lifesize Bradman bronze at Christie's in Melbourne for $65,000 six months ago. A second collecting institution has opened in his honour at Adelaide's Mortlock Library. There has been yet another reissue of Bradman's 1958 instructional bible *The Art of Cricket* and, despite full-scale biographies in 1995 and 1997, three more books are forthcoming: a collection of tributes, a volume on Bradman's 1948 side and a compilation of *Wisden* writings. To paraphrase ABC's *This Sporting Life*: too much Bradman is not enough.

Australians can count themselves blessed that the Don is still with them. It is sixty-four years since newspapers, fearful of his prospects after a severe appendicitis, first felt the need to set obituarists on him. And Bradman was half his current age when he retired from stockbroking after a 'serious warning' from his physician. In some respects, however, Bradman himself has been supplanted in import-ance by Bradmyth. The idea of him is at least as important as the reality. It is odd, but not really surprising, that the best biography of Bradman was written by an Englishman: Irving Rosenwater's stupendous *Sir Donald Bradman*. And, despite the recent proliferation of Bric-a-Bradman, no one anywhere has tangibly added to the sum of human knowledge about the Don in twenty years. The most recent Bradman biography, Lord Williams's *Bradman: An Australian Hero*, is a case in point: of 428 footnotes, 244 referred to four titles, two of them previous Bradman biographies.

At one time, it was Bradman who sought Garbo-like quietude, no less than he deserved after more than four decades as a prisoner of his prowess. Nowadays, though, Australians do just as much to preserve that distance. The last locally-produced Bradman biography – Roland Perry's *The Don* (1995) – had as much substance as a comic strip. The last public interview with Bradman – two hours broadcast in May 1996 by Channel Nine's top-rating current-affairs host Ray Martin on the basis of a corporate donation to the Bradman Museum – was what *Private Eye* used to describe as a journey to the province of Arslikhan.

It may justly be asked what more of the Bradman saga begs understanding. After all, the Greatest Story Ever Bowled To is so beguiling as it is: uncoached boy from the bush rises on merit, plays for honour and glory, puts Poms to flight, becomes an intimate of sovereigns and statesmen, retires Cincinnatus-like to his unosten-tatious suburban home.

But turning Bradman into Mr 99.94 is a bit like reducing Einstein to Mr $E = mc^2$. Read most Bradmanarama and you'd be forgiven for thinking that his eighty Test innings were the sum of him. His family is largely invisible. Precious little exists about Bradman's three decades as an administrator. There is next to nothing about his extensive business career. And no one, I think, has grasped what is perhaps most extraordinary about Bradman: his singularity as a man as well as a cricketer. For his beatification as a national symbol contains at least some irony: he is a strange choice for an acme of Australianness.

For most Australian boys, for instance, participation in sport is a rite of passage, an important aspect of socialization. Yet, if Bradman developed close cricketing pals in his Bowral boyhood, they kept remarkably shtum afterwards. The rudimentary game with paling bat and kerosene-tin wicket in some urban thoroughfare is one of Australian cricket's cosiest images: think of Ray Lindwall and his cobbers playing in Hurstville's Hudson Street, trying to catch the eye of Bill O'Reilly as that canny old soul walked by; or of the brothers Harvey playing their fraternal Tests behind the family's Argyle Street terrace in Fitzroy. Bradman's contribution to the lore of juvenile cricket, by contrast, is one of solitary autodidacticism, his water-tank training ritual with golf ball and stump. As Rodney Cavalier explains in a perceptive introduction to the new *Sir Donald Bradman AC*, Bradman chose to practise alone not because he had no choice, but because he wished to.

That carapace hardened as Bradman reached cricketing maturity, and set him still further apart. Where the paradigmatic Australian male is hearty and sanguine, priding himself on good fellowship, hospitality and ability to hold his alcohol, Bradman was private, reserved, fragile of physique and teetotal. Where the traditional Australian work ethic has been to do just enough to get by, Bradman was a virtuoso who set his own standards and allowed nothing to impede their attainment.

Australia in the late 1920s, moreover, was not a country that seemed likely to foster an abundance of remarkable men. Even that big bridge was still to come. It was a small subsidiary of Empire, with an ethnically and culturally homogenous population of six million. Indeed, we might regard such homogeneity as a precondition to a personality cult like Bradman's: it is hard to imagine a figure arising today with such effortlessly broad appeal.

There were extremes of wealth and poverty in the Australia of Bradman's rise, but social mobility was constrained both by economic hardship and prevailing belief in an underlying social equality. Visiting Australia for the first time in the year of Bradman's first-class debut, American critic Hartley Grattan was amazed by the vehemence of this latter faith: 'Australia is perhaps the last stronghold of egalitarian democracy . . . The aggressive insistence on the worth and unique importance of the common man seems to me to be one of the fundamental Australian characteristics.' As D. H. Lawrence described it in his novel of 1920s Australia, *Kangaroo*: 'Each individual seems to feel himself pledged to put himself aside, to keep himself at least half out of count. The whole geniality is based on a sort of code of "You put yourself aside, and I'll put myself aside". This is done with a watchful will: a sort of duel.'

Bradman, however, was not a 'common man', and he assuredly did not 'put himself aside'. In the words of Ben Bennison, who collaborated with the twenty-one-year-old cricketer on *Don Bradman's Book*: 'He set out and meant to be king . . . To the last ounce he knew his value, not only as a cricketer but as a man.' R. C. Robertson-Glasgow recalled that, at his first meeting with Bradman at Folkestone in September 1930, the Australian was surrounded by piles of correspondence to which he was steadily reaming off replies. 'He had made his name at cricket,' wrote Crusoe. 'And now, quiet and calculating, he was, he told me, trying to capitalize his success.'

The times may have been ripe for such individual aspiration. Certainly, Bradman's benefactors on that tour had no difficulty singling him out for gifts and gratuities, not least the Fleming and Whitelaw soap magnate Arthur Whitelaw, who bestowed a spontaneous £1,000 on Bradman after his Headingley 334. But nothing before or since has paralleled the Caesar-like triumph that Bradman's employer Mick Simmons Ltd organized for him when the team returned to Australia, where he travelled independently of his team and was plied with public subscriptions and prizes in Perth, Adelaide, Melbourne, Goulburn and Sydney.

It was the beginning of a career in which Bradman showed conspicuous aptitude for parlaying his athletic talent into commercial reward. Leaving Mick Simmons Ltd in 1931, he signed a tripartite contract worth more than £1,000 a year with radio station 2UE, retailer F. J. Palmer and Associated Newspapers (proprietor Robert Clyde Packer, grandfather of Kerry). He spruiked bats (Wm Sykes), boots (McKeown) and books (three while he was playing, two afterwards), irked the Australian Board of Control by writing about cricket in apparent defiance of its dictates, deliberated over effectively quitting Test cricket to accept the Lancashire League shilling for the 1932 season, swapped states in 1935 to further his career. At a time when Australian industry lurked behind perhaps the highest tariff barriers on earth, Bradman was the quintessential disciple of the free market.

No dispute that Bradman deserved every penny and more. No question of undue rapacity either. As that felicitous phrase-maker Ray Robinson once expressed it, the Don did not so much chase money as overhaul it. Equally, however, Bradman's approach betokens an elitism uncharacteristic of Australia at the time and not a quality many today would willingly volunteer as a national hallmark.

It was this impregnable self-estimation – not arrogance, but a remarkable awareness of his entitlements – that distanced Bradman from his peers. Some criticisms of the Don by playing contemporaries were undoubtedly actuated by jealousy. All the same, he seems to have been incapable of the sort of gesture that might have put comrades at their ease. In his autobiography *Farewell to Cricket*, he commented: 'I was often accused of being unsociable because at the end of the day I did not think it my duty to breast the bar and engage in a beer-drinking contest.' It is a curious perspective on cricket's social conventions, with the implication, as John Arlott put it, that Bradman had 'missed something of cricket that less gifted and less memorable men have gained'.

Bradman's playing philosophy – that cricket should not be a career, and that those good enough could profit from other avenues – also seems to have borne on his approach to administration. Biographers have disserved Bradman in glossing over his years in officialdom. His strength and scruples over more than three decades were exemplary; the foremost master of the game became its staunchest servant. But he largely missed the secular shift toward the professionalization of sport in the late 1960s and early '70s, which finally found expression in Kerry Packer's World Series Cricket.

Discussing the rise of World Series Cricket, Bradman told Williams in January 1995 he 'accepted that cricket had to become professional'. Yet, as Dr Bob Stewart comments in his recent work on the commercial and cultural development of post-war Australian cricket *I Heard It on the Radio, I Saw It on the Television*, cricket wages declined markedly in real terms during the period that Bradman was Australian cricket's *éminence grise*. When Bradman retired, the home Test fee was seven times the average weekly wage. A quarter of a century later it was twice the average weekly wage. Ian Chappell opined in his *The Cutting Edge* that the pervasion of Bradman's attitude to player pay within the Australian Cricket Board 'contributed to the success World Series Cricket officials had when a couple of years later they approached Australian players with a contract'.

Perhaps these paradoxes of the Bradman myth relate something about the complex Australian attitude to sport. As the Australian social commentator Donald Horne once put it: 'It is only in sport that many Australians express those approaches to life that are un-Australian if expressed any other way.' But, as Bradman enters his tenth decade fit for both commodification and canonization, two questions seem worth asking, with apologies to C. L. R. James.

First: What do they know of Bradman who only cricket know? Surely it's possible in writing about someone who has lived for ninety years to do something more than prattle on endlessly about the fifteen or so of them he spent in flannels – recirculating the same stories, the same banal and blinkered visions – and bring some new perspectives and insights?

Second: What do they know of cricket who only Bradman know? A generation has now grown up in Australia that regards cricket history as 6996 and all that. Where are the home-grown biographies of Charlie Macartney, Warwick Armstrong, Bill Woodfull, Bill Pons-ford, Lindsay Hassett, Keith Miller, Neil Harvey, Alan Davidson, Richie Benaud, Bob Simpson, even Ian Chappell and Dennis Lillee, plus sundry others one could name? Such is the lava flow from the Bradman volcano, they are unlikely to see daylight.

So enough with the obeisances already. Yes, Bradman at ninety is a legend worth saluting. But as the American journalist Walter Lippman once said: 'When all think alike, none are thinking.'

*   *   *

Only one side can win a cricket match. This basic fact is often forgotten by even the most seasoned of men. Cricket writing in present-day England is marked by a tone of nostalgic lament, the decline of the present being set against the lost victories of the past. Australian writers find it difficult to accept defeat, Indian writers even more so. Salutary in this respect is the attitude of the West Indian writer B. C. Pires. When his team lost to England in 1991 and Australia in 1995 the breast-beating was tempered by a healthy admixture of sardonic whimsy.

B. C. PIRES

Coping with Defeat

I: JUNE 1991

If my attention wanders a little more than usual in the course of this column, please forgive me. I am watching what looks more and more like the West Indian demise at Headingley.

Richardson and Dujon are at the wicket. Viv is gone. Gus is gone. Hooper? Gone. Haynes? Gone. Was Simmons in the line-up? West Indies are toppling and all of England is delighted. Richie Benaud, the man on television, has just said, 'We're staying with cricket here on BBC1. *Starsky and Hutch* can be seen at . . . some other time.' England is smelling its first victory at home against the West Indies in twenty-two years and the antics of two television cops are not going to prevent the masses enjoying the execution.

And now Richardson is gone. And it's not even half past two. Have Dujon and Marshall ever had a 278-run partnership? I can't believe this – Marshall is gone. I hardly even saw him come in. How could he have been in and out in the space of two sentences? It must've been done with mirrors. Couldn't he have held on for enough time to allow my heartbeat to subside? If God has seen fit to give England a victory after all this time, why is He rushing the job at the end? Here comes Ambrose. The West Indian hopes are flapping from that gangly frame. Every delivery looks so much closer, so much scarier, when Curtly Ambrose faces it.

The television commentary just switched from BBC1 to BBC2 and Dujon disappeared in the changeover. He was batting on BBC1. Now, on BBC2, there is a batsman wearing a helmet and beard but, on close examination of his face, or cursory examination of his batting technique, I discern it is not him. Dujon must be out, but how did he get there? More, I suppose, of the white man's magic. 137 for 8 Walsh and Ambrose at the wicket. Rain, who normally plays for the other side, is the West Indies' only hope now. The West Indies have pulled off all sorts of amazing comebacks but not one of them has featured Ambrose, Walsh and 150 runs; although, if there ever was to be such a comeback, it would be against England.

But wait. There was a four, yes, a lovely straight drive from the normally wildly flailing Ambrose. Runs. But, more importantly, they are not getting out. Ambrose has been dropped in the slips by Lamb and, as I write, again escapes being caught and bowled by De Freitas. It seems England feels it can afford to allow them two or three goes each, and that raises not a hope but a doubt. Rain will fall, of course, because this is England and this is cricket, but can the West Indian bowlers hold on until it comes?

Hope springs up for a moment, but not as high as the ball one of those tall wankers has just popped into the air . . . and this time the catch is taken. Well, that must be it, surely. Everyone knows it now. Jubilation in Leeds. White men – from Yorkshire – are dancing in the aisles. With no embarrassment. Nor, I observe, rhythm. The crowd is singing in one massive voice, as if Headingley were Wembley. The television commentators have finally thrown caution to the wind and are talking about how victory was achieved. Patterson is only a lagniappe. He can delay the end of the innings by only as long as it takes to adjust his pads and take a 'middle' from the umpire. But he is not even going to face the ball.

There it goes, off Walsh's bat and up, up and away again, in the air long enough for Atherton and Ramprakash to quarrel about who is going to take The Catch That Won The Match. It would be lovely to see Atherton drop it after running halfway across the field, but he takes it in spectacular fashion, running, diving, turning over, coming up with ball in hand and smile in high beam. Where is the England cricket team I knew and loved, the one that could be counted on to select a team of eleven men, each and every one of whom would unfailingly drop precisely that catch?

So that's it, then. It takes only a moment to lose a Test match and there it went, the longest moment in the history of sport. West Indies has lost the match and my column is going to be early, for once. But do I dare leave this room? The entire English male population of London is lying in wait for me, waiting to pounce on my accent. 'You from Trinny-dad?' they will say. 'Get off,' I will reply, or something of a similar nature. Twenty-two years in the build-up and I have to be here for the denouement.

My friend Samantha, English, but very pleasant about it, just looked in to commiserate. She noted the position of my chin, between knees and ankles, and advised me to cheer up. 'It's only a game,' she said. Yeah, Sam, and ballet is only a dance. 'You don't know what it's like to be West Indian and lose a game of cricket,'

I said. 'Well,' she replied, 'look how long we've been losing.' 'It's OK for y'all,' I told her. 'You're used to it. This is very new to us.' She was less sympathetic after that, for some reason. The English! They colonize us for 400 years and then beat us at cricket once every twenty and still cannot figure out why we're upset. They still don't understand our rules. We would rather lose a governor, a job, anything but a match. As David Rudder and C. L. R. James said, this is not just cricket, this thing goes beyond a boundary. But that, it seems, is beyond the pale.

ii: May 1995

Well, I've just watched the first ball of the fourth – last? – day of the fourth Test at Sabina Park. Sheesh! Ian Healy just dropped James 'Jeemee' Adams off the second ball. My heart is in my mouth and the first over isn't even halfway through yet. Jimmy has to bat for two days to save the West Indies.

And now they're putting Shane Warne on to bowl the second over. Isn't it a bit late for the Australians to convince us of this best-bowler-in-the world thing? I mean, we've seen him for the rest of the series. Look, even Winston Benjamin can get a run off him, even with this tension. The first run of the day. Will we have more wickets than runs in the next few hours? My goodness! Winston Benjamin should have been caught off Paul Reiffel. Whew! This is sport?

All good things must come to an end, and it looks very much like the West Indies' fifteen-year domination of world cricket is going to do just that today, perhaps even this morning. No team I can remember ever had a better chance of beating the West Indies: seven wickets to go, still nearly 200 runs to make to reach zero, star batsman gone for the same zero, two full days of play left, not a cloud in the sky and Paul Reiffel bowling like a demon. Thank God for two dropped catches already. Can we hold off the second-most-successful – soon to be the best? – team in the world?

How do you avoid buckling under this pressure? It's not just this game. The world is waiting for these islands to fall. Sports writers everywhere (but here) have been fantasizing of writing about the West Indies losing and composing the most exciting opening sentence of their careers since Viv Richards went. Mike Selvey, cricket correspondent of the *Guardian* (the real *Guardian*, not d' Impostor) fully expected to write his during the third Test in Trinidad, which we won in three days.

But now Jimmy Adams is gone, caught by Steve Waugh, who else? And now it becomes even more difficult to imagine defeat being avoided, or even making them bat again. And Waugh will be man of the series and salt in the wounds. But wait! What is this? Lunch has just ended, television coverage just resumed, and Hooper and Benjamin are both out? Already? Keith Arthurton and Courtney Brown batting? 145 for 6?

The last time I watched the West Indies take licks like this was in 1991, I think, when England won at Leeds. Fifteen years of championship go with defeat but I actually feel better today. At least I'm watching this in St Ann's, on TTT, instead of South London, on BBC1, where every accent I heard was a taunt. And now Keith Arthurton is out for 14 runs, and the bowlers have to make 100 runs to make the Aussies bat again. Arthurton was lbw to a ball that Michael Holding doubted would hit the wicket. It's more like he was out TFW: Time For another Wicket.

And Curtly is the man to come in. I love to see him on TV, but not today. What are these guys going to feel like? Many of them have been on the winningest team in modern cricket. Now they're going to be on the West Indies team that lost. And it's Shane Warne who gets Curtly out stupidly, chipping down the wicket and being stumped. Good thing Shane Warne won't have to bat again. Curtly would be vexed.

And now Courtney Walsh, the man who least deserves to be on a losing West Indies team, comes in to bat. Ah, he's got a run. Thank Heaven's Small Mercies Department for that. And a four, too! Well, if he follows Arthurton's lead, he should hit a six and then be out.

I've just realized that there are two Courtneys at the wicket. Very good, but it would have been better to have a single Brian. It is hard to take this licks. I know there are West Indians who are untroubled today because they don't follow cricket. They're like people who don't like chocolate – I don't know whether I should feel sorry or glad for them. Chocolate and West Indies cricket can make me fat and totally depressed, respectively, but I don't care. Nothing is as sweet as chocolate or West Indies cricket, and I would not want to live without either.

And now Ian Healy has dropped an even easier catch. It's like he doesn't want to leave the ground too early for some reason. Wouldn't it be lovely if Courtney went on to score a century? Oh, this thing called hope that this West Indies team has given us for the last fifteen years that makes me think Courtney Walsh could make a century.

Ah. Courtney's out. So there's just the formality of Kenny Benjamin and the agony of defeat should start. This is what people in Trinidad call a 'whiteman' – where you cut yourself so deeply that you don't even see blood for a while, just the white of your flesh, and then the blood seeps in before your eyes.

OK, there it is, it's over. An ecstatic Mark Taylor lifts the trophy and Richie Richardson comes on TV to say this is the worst Aussie team he's ever played. Why didn't he congratulate the Aussies and warn them that their best team in decades was playing a team in transition, and they ought to enjoy the Frank Worrell trophy while they have it, because we'll have it back for ever next time? Poor Richie. He's Antiguan, you know. Their hearts are in the right place but they usually have their feet in their mouths.

And now I know the reason I've subjected myself to watching the tightening of the coils. It is right that I should watch, that we all should. We've cheered so often in the past. We should take our one blow and shed our tears without blaming anyone. But you know cricket goes to the heart in these parts. I expect many will call the names of Stuart Williams, Sherwin Campbell and David Holford, while invoking those of Dessie Haynes and Phil Simmons. I wish they wouldn't. I'd feel better about the West Indies if we could take this one on our chests, instead of pointing fingers.

*   *   *

From 1960 to 1995 the great rivalry in international cricket was Australia v. the West Indies. For decades previously it was England v. Australia. In 1977, on the occasion of the Centenary Test, a distinguished British journalist asked two great players to choose their All-Time XIs. That was the year Ian Botham first played Test cricket; Shane Warne's debut lay a dozen years into the future. Both men would surely figure in a revision of the exercise.

IAN WOOLDRIDGE

Ashes Dream Teams (1977)

One hundred years ago on 15 March, at one o'clock Australian time in the afternoon, a bearded Englishman named Alfred Shaw turned his back on the ornate pavilions of Melbourne Cricket Ground and ran in to bowl at a moustachioed Australian named Charles Bannerman.

So began a relationship unique in the history of sport. One century later England and Australia are still periodically playing cricket Test matches against one another in the same atmosphere of uncompromising hostility and inherent mutual respect.

Only Armageddon or nuclear holocaust, should there be any difference, will terminate a continuing contest incomprehensible to the outside world in its intensity.

You have to be born either English or Australian to understand that any weakening in the resolve to win would render the whole exercise as pointless as perpetuating a grudge in the wake of defeat.

The mere first 100 years of this special relationship will be celebrated with a single Test between England and Australia starting tomorrow week in Melbourne Cricket Ground.

It is now a vast tiered concrete colosseum, cruel of aspect and devoid of hiding places. The Olympic Games were staged there in 1956 and it is now capable of holding 100,000 spectators, which makes it three times the size of the average Test arena.

To commemorate this genuine Match of the Century we invited two of the most eminent contestants of the first 100 years – Sir Leonard Hutton of England and Keith Miller of Australia – to choose their strongest All-Time XIs to represent their respective countries in a mythical Test. Each was asked to select himself.

Hutton had 318 players to choose from, Miller 250. Neither sought to confuse the issue by considering William Midwinter, the only man who played for each country against the other.

One thing is certain: their choices will generate many heated discussions on such eternal questions as how would Donald Bradman have fared against Wilfred Rhodes, and how is the 125-year-old Charles Bannerman likely to cope with the pace of the 72-year-old Harold Larwood?

Serious students of cricket will be intrigued and possibly alarmed by one fact. Hutton and Miller chose their respective All-Time XIs independently. Neither man chose a single cricketer currently playing the game.

ENGLAND

Sir Leonard Hutton announced his all-time England team with the portentous deliberation of some Bradford electoral returning officer. Then he stayed silent, counting the seconds it took you to spot that five of the eleven were Yorkshiremen.

It wasn't long, but experience warns you against engaging Hutton in the intricate swordplay of cricket theory.

In any case, only one was a contentious selection and Hutton, sensitive to accusations of northern chauvinism, already had the gloves on waiting to defend his choice of Maurice Leyland ahead of Denis Compton, Peter May or the early-or-mid-career Colin Cowdrey.

'Since it's inconceivable that any all-time Australian team would go into the field without Bill O'Reilly,' he said, 'I've picked Leyland as the horse for the course.

'O'Reilly was the best bowler Australia ever had: aggressive, unbelievably accurate to the right-handers. Well, Leyland was a left-hander and he also had the jinx on O'Reilly.

'I remember him saying: "I've got that O'Reilly in my pocket and, what's more, he knows it." I've never heard another England batsman tempt fate by saying anything like that. But it was true and that's why Leyland is in.'

Hutton's de rigueur inclusion gave him the initial problem of where to bat himself. 'It wasn't a big one,' he said. 'Hobbs and Sutcliffe were not only great players of fast bowling but had a magnificent understanding running between wickets.

'I'd be quite happy to go in No. 5, particularly in Melbourne, where opening an innings can be a literally frightening experience.'

After explaining Leyland's presence, he knew that no justification of Walter Hammond's inclusion was required. 'He was simply the best cricketer I ever played with.'

Woolley, towering, commanding and also left-handed to challenge O'Reilly, was a natural. And although there was sorrow that he could not include Godfrey Evans – 'a friend, a marvellous team man and great reader of batsmen's weaknesses' – he chose Leslie Ames as wicketkeeper.

Much of Hutton's own character was revealed by his selection of bowlers. Not only did he require wickets, but he also wanted men who could bat.

'George Hirst was fantastically accurate and could also swing an old ball. What's more, he was a very aggressive batsman.

'It's also impossible to leave out either Wilfred Rhodes or Syd Barnes. They represent genius. Barnes could bowl anything.

'Rhodes was the complete cricketer, a very great bowler who began batting No. 11 for England and finished up opening the innings.'

It was only after much analysis that Hutton chose Harold Larwood as his spearhead fast bowler. Tyson, phenomenally fast, had won him a series in real-life cricket against Australia but Hutton said: 'I think Larwood just had the edge over Tyson for speed. He had the finest action I've ever seen.'

It was obvious that Sir Leonard Hutton had given many hours to his selections.

'I shall probably be criticized for the fact that it isn't a great fielding side,' he said. 'I know that. Given the choice I would have chosen Peter May or Colin Cowdrey as twelfth man as well. But I gather the idea is to beat Australia in Melbourne. It's never easy.'

AUSTRALIA

Keith Miller, inveterate horse-player, party-goer and probably the most glamorous figure ever to play for Australia at anything, immediately renounced the responsibilities of captaincy. It was almost as though he couldn't trust himself to get to the ground in time to toss up.

His team is more controversial than Hutton's, but it is his voluntary decision to play under the captaincy of Sir Donald Bradman that will cause most comment in Australia. They were always seen as incompatible figures and there are many legends of bad blood between them.

'It is quite true', admits Miller, 'that we had a couple of blow-ups during Test matches. One was at Lord's, when I flung the ball back and refused to bowl for him. But that never lessened my respect for him as a captain dedicated to winning, and since this match is against England there can be no other choice.'

Those with some knowledge of cricket may feel that Miller has gambled with his very first selection in his all-time Australian team.

'I probably have,' confesses Miller, 'but I'm a bit of a romantic as well. Obviously there's nobody alive today who ever saw Charlie Bannerman bat, but he faced the very first ball ever bowled in England–Australia Tests and he scored 165 before he had to retire hurt and Australia won by 45 runs. He must have been as tough as nails.

'It's bloody hard choosing Australia's opening batsmen because there have been so many great ones: Ponsford, Woodfull, Barnes, Morris and Bobby Simpson, who was also the greatest slip fielder I've ever seen. It's hard to leave any of them out.

'I couldn't contemplate leaving Ponsford out altogether so I've chosen him to bat No. 4. That means Victor Trumper opens the innings with Bannerman. I never saw Trumper either, but the stories can't all be wrong. Anyway, my father saw him bat and said he was as good as Bradman and that will do me.'

No one would challenge Miller's own selection and few that of Stan McCabe at No. 5. It was while McCabe was scoring his 232 at Nottingham in 1938 that Bradman summoned Australia's players from a dressing-room card game to the pavilion balcony with the words 'Come and watch this. You may never see anything like it again.'

Miller delves back to the turn of the century for Monty Noble, a huge first-generation Australian all-rounder who defeated England little short of single-handed in several Tests with either a batting onslaught or a swing-bowling technique which he had developed as a young baseball player.

His choice of Ray Lindwall, his own new-ball partner and inseparable drinking buddy, as the greatest of all Australian fast bowlers will cause no controversy. Nor will his choice of Bill O'Reilly 'the greatest bowler of any type the game has ever seen'.

'Also I had no hesitation', said Miller, 'about choosing Don Tallon. He was the best batsman–wicketkeeper I've ever seen.'

Miller's final selection, spin support for O'Reilly, caused him his only lost sleep. 'It was a straight fight between a very good friend, Richie Benaud, and Clarrie Grimmett. In the end I decided to go entirely on the evidence of the record books: Benaud 248 wickets in 63 Tests, Grimmett 216 wickets in only 37 Tests.'

*　*　*

Recall the words ascribed to Frederick Spofforth by Ralph Barker: 'This thing can be done.' Five words that constitute the kernel of a cricketing philosophy that is distinctively Australian. Consider a fielder running in to catch a ball forty yards distant and fast dropping to ground; or a batsman at the top of the order, his side following on 200 runs behind on a wearing wicket; or, indeed, a bowler opening the attack with less than 100 to play with, and against a side led by Dr W. G. Grace. The response of the Australian to these rather difficult if commonplace cricketing situations would always be: this thing can be done. John Arlott captures this attitude well. In the forty-five years since he wrote the next piece, the proportion of Tests won against England by Australia has greatly altered in their favour.

JOHN ARLOTT

Australianism (1949)

Why are the Australian cricketers different? Why is a Test match against Australia different from a Test match against any other country? And why do we *feel* that it is different?

Now I am sure it is not only, or even basically, because the Australians are our senior Test opponents. If it were, then South African, West Indian and Indian cricket followers would not have this same feeling about the Australians to a greater degree than about English teams – as they have.

No, it is the quality of 'Australianism' which makes the difference. Historically, 'Australianism' dates from that momentous day at the Oval in 1882 when England twice seemed to have the solitary Test match of that season won, only for Massie, and then Spofforth, to snatch it away – in the face of all cricket probability and eleven great English cricketers. It has gone on through the forty-four Test tours. I remember, as a boy, hearing with steadily growing awe of the two Australian fast bowlers, Gregory and Macdonald of Warwick Armstrong's 1921 team, and how they passed through English cricket like a scourge. More than human those two men seemed to me – almost devilish in their relentless destruction of English batting.

This feeling does not come from regular Australian victory – they have but 64 won tests to our 55 – and, indeed, we have won 21 to their 20 in England. The West Indies have beaten us in two consecutive tours there, beaten us by means of crushing batting, yet we are not alarmed.

How many English cricket followers, I wonder, like me, have anxiously followed Anglo-Australian Test matches by radio or, at vast penny-expenditure, in a series of newspaper 'stop press' columns? When England seem to be winning we have dreaded an Australian recovery – for every Australian seems capable of saving his side – and when the Australians have been on top, then we have felt, in our hearts, that they would never relax. Why?

Australia has had her great players, certainly, but against their Bradman, Ponsford, Woodfull, Miller we can place Hammond, Hobbs, Sutcliffe and Compton. Grimmett and Mailey and O'Reilly took many wickets – but no one of them ever took so many in a single series as Maurice Tate's 38 in 1924–5 in Australia. The Australian fielding has invariably been superb – but remember Jardine's sharks at the batsman's elbow in 1932–3.

No, the difference does not lie in comparative excellence in any department of the game but in the whole Australian *attitude* to cricket. Australian cricket is not the same game as English cricket. Why should it be? The Australians come from a country at the opposite end of the world, their setting is different, their very atmosphere is different. Certainly their speech, their laws, their cooking, their manners are not the same as ours – why should they be? So it follows that, if Australian cricket were no more than an imitation of the game in England, the Dominion would be less the fine country it is. Australia has its own character and that character is in its cricket, because *Australian* cricket is part of the life of those people.

Now this difference, this 'Australianism', is not always admitted by those who follow cricket in England. Some try to pretend that there is no difference between the cricket of the two countries. Others, overconscious of the difference, have tried to capitalize it with stories of 'crises' and 'controversies' which ignore the essential humanity of the difference.

Let me try to capture that difference for you in one game. On the Saturday of Whit weekend of 1948, the Australians made 721 runs in a day against Essex. On Whit Monday Essex came out to bat: the Australian bowlers were at them like tigers. Miller bowled as fast and as grimly as he had done in all the tour, the fielding was as tight as in a Test match. There was going to be no nonsense about 'giving Essex a chance' even in the face of that appalling Australian total.

Soon Essex were struggling – before lunch they were more than struggling, they were being smothered. Things were grim indeed when Ray Smith came in. Five Essex wickets were down, one batsman, Bailey, was unable to bat because of injury, and the first fifty was still not on the board. Toshack was bowling from the railway end – medium pace left arm over the wicket. Sydney Barnes at silly mid-on was so close to the batsman that if Ray Smith had held out his hat at full arm's stretch and Barnes had reached out his hand the two would have touched. Ray Smith has in him a blend of courage and gaiety that cannot be quelled even by a deficit of almost 600 runs and a Test attack against him. Almost at once he drove a ball from Toshack past Barnes' ear like a bullet for four. Barnes looked at him undisturbed – 'You cain't drive me away,' he said. Square, self-reliant and grim, he put his hands on his knees and glared at the batsman. In Toshack's next over Ray Smith hit a half-volley straight on to Barnes' foot – whence it ricocheted to the boundary! Barnes did not say a word. Smith had scored 25 when he received another half-volley from Toshack. Here was his chance to drive away this suicidal fieldsman – whose very presence was like a curb upon a batsman's play. Ray hit that ball with a swing like a flailsman's – straight at Barnes. Barnes put up his hands to the ball – it forced them apart and struck against his chest – as it bounced off he darted out his right hand and caught it! Ray Smith, caught Barnes, bowled Toshack – 25. As Ray looked at him unbelievingly Sydney Barnes said, 'I told you you cain't drive me away' and he casually tossed the ball back to Toshack.

In the Essex second innings Pearce and Peter Smith made a stand of 133 but they had to fight every run. The Australians bowled and fielded seriously and unsparingly to the last Essex wicket, and they won by an innings and 145 runs. They never gave away a run, never relaxed, the field was always placed as tightly as it would stretch round the batsman. The Australians play their hardest and they expect their opponents to do the same, then, they say, in effect, the result is absolutely accurate.

So far, so good, we know where the Australians stand, we know where we stand. But, unless we are prepared to play as hard as the Australians then we ought not to play Test cricket against them. There has long been a custom in much English cricket for the batsman to 'give the bowler a chance' after he has scored a hundred. An Australian batsman merely takes guard afresh after the first hundred: of Bradman's 108 scores of over 100, 37 – more than a third of them – have also been over 200. Again, we expect that, in Test matches, where the bowling and fielding combination is stronger, batsmen will not score so heavily as in ordinary county or state matches – but Barnes, Bradman, Miller and Morris have higher averages in Tests than in ordinary games!

The Australians set out to win Tests. They start at the bottom, they train their youngsters hard. The young Australian cricketer fights for his place in grade cricket – often against seasoned Test players. And the Australians trust their young men early with great Test-match responsibilities. There is a single-mindedness about their cricket – Lindwall, Loxton and Miller gave up football in the preceding Australian season to be certain of being fit for their tour of England. Several doctors sat on a consultative board to decide whether Toshack was absolutely fit to make the trip. Recall, too, that there is no full-time professionalism in Australian cricket and that many of the men making an English tour are saved financial loss only by their (uncertain) tour bonus. They draw no pay from their jobs in Australia and their pocket money for the tour is much less than their normal wage. There are strict rules against players being accompanied by their wives, against their broadcasting or writing. They are here to play cricket and they are not to be diverted from that purpose.

We in England can learn from them. Some of our players have already done so – it was Hutton who took fresh guard after his first hundred to go on and break the record for a Test innings at the Oval in 1938. Godfrey Evans batted 100 minutes for 0, doggedly partnering Denis Compton in the fourth (Adelaide) Test in 1946–7. Denis Compton is a great batsman when all depends on him – but sometimes, when things are going well, he seems to relax as the Australians never do.

We are faced with Australian batting, bowling, fielding, captaincy – and 'Australianism'. 'Australianism' means single-minded determination to win – to win within the laws but, if necessary, to the last limit within them. It means that where the 'impossible' is within the realm of what the human body can do, there are Australians who *believe* that they can do it – and who have succeeded often enough to make us wonder if anything is impossible to them. It means that they have never lost a match – particularly a Test match – until the last run is scored or their last wicket has fallen.

*   *   *

In the scattered islands of the Caribbean, cricket is more than a game. It has been, indeed, the vehicle of anticolonialism and cultural assertiveness. Dozens of small nations, each with its own army, flag and seat in the United Nations, come together as 'the West Indies' for the purposes of cricket. The social significance of sport was brilliantly captured in the title, contents and conclusions of C. L. R. James's *Beyond a Boundary*. I reproduce here a review of that book, published when the book appeared and written by the young V. S. Naipaul. In the essay that follows, the novelist J. B. Priestley, a Yorkshireman, marvels at the fluid grace of the great Garfield Sobers. This tribute was written at the end of a summer in which Sobers led the West Indies to a 3–1 win over England. In the five Tests he himself scored 722 runs, took 20 wickets, and held 10 catches.

V. S. NAIPAUL

The Caribbean Flavour (1963)

'Who is the greatest cricketer in the world?' The question came up in a General Knowledge test one day in 1940, when I was in the fourth standard at the Tranquillity Boys' School in Port of Spain. I saw it as a trap question. Though I had never seen him play, and he was reported to live in England, no cricketer was better known to me than Learie Constantine. Regularly in the *Trinidad Guardian* I saw the same picture of him: sweatered, smiling, running back to the pavilion bat in hand. To me the bat was golden: Constantine, in a previous General Knowledge test, had proved to be 'the man with the golden bat' as, earlier, he had been 'the man with the golden ball'. But now – the greatest cricketer? I wrote, 'Bradman.' This was wrong; the pencilled cross on my paper was large and angry. 'Constantine' was the answer to this one too.

The teacher was a Negro, brown-skinned, but this is a later assessment and may be wrong: to me then, and for some time afterwards, race and colour were not among the attributes of teachers. It is possible now to see his propaganda for Constantine as a type of racialism or nationalism. But this would be only part of the truth. Racial pride pure and simple in the victories of Joe Louis, yes. But the teacher's devotion to Constantine was more complex. And it is with the unravelling of this West Indian complexity that

C. L. R. James, politician, pamphleteer, historian, former cricket correspondent for the *Manchester Guardian*, is concerned. He has done his job superbly.

Beyond a Boundary, like Nirad Chaudhuri's *Autobiography of an Unknown Indian*, is part of the cultural boomeranging from the former colonies, delayed and still imperfectly understood. With one or two exceptions, a journalistic reaction to his material – cricket – has obscured the originality of Mr James's purpose and method.

Since 1950 the newspapers have perhaps made us too familiar with calypsos at Lord's. For West Indians, as one cricket writer says, the game is a carnival. But what a game to choose for a carnival! It is leisurely, intricate, difficult to appreciate, its drama often concealed or curtailed; and the players stop for tea. Soccer, swift, short and brutal, would have been more suitable; or baseball, or bullfighting. But cricket has been chosen; and the conclusion must be that we are dealing with more than the picturesque. Consider just what cricket means to the West Indian: in Trinidad, with a population of 800,000, 30,000 can go to a Test match on one day. Consider the mixed population. Here is Mr James describing the cricket field of his school in the 1910s:

> We were a motley crew. The children of some white officials and white business men, middle-class blacks and mulattos, Chinese boys, some of whose parents still spoke broken English, Indian boys, some of whose parents could speak no English at all, and some poor black boys who had won exhibitions or whose parents had starved and toiled on plots of agricultural land and were spending their hard-earned money on giving the eldest boy an education. Yet rapidly we learned to obey the umpire's decision . . . We learned to play with the team.

Racial generalizations – about certain people being good at ball games – won't help. There has been no West African cricketer; the only Chinese cricketers of standing have come from Trinidad; and, though the fact is seldom noticed, white West Indians have produced more first-class players per thousand of their population than any other community anywhere. Consider now the history of the islands: slavery until 1834, indentured labour until 1917. And then consider the cricket code: gentlemanliness, fair play, teamwork. The very words are tired and, in the West Indian situation, ridiculous, irrelevant. But they filled a need. In islands that had known only brutality and proclaimed greed, cricket and its code provided an area of rest, a release for much that was denied by the society: skill, courage, style: the graces, the very things that in a changed world are making the game archaic. And the code that came with the game, the code recognized by everyone, whatever his race or class, was the British public-school code:

> I learned and obeyed and taught a code, the English public-school code. Britain and her colonies and the colonial peoples. What do the British people know of what they have done there? Precious little. The colonial peoples, particularly West Indians, scarcely know themselves as yet.

Twenty years ago the colonial who wrote those words might have been judged to be angling for an OBE or MBE. But Mr James, who is over sixty, has a background of Marxism (he was a prominent follower of Trotsky) and African nationalism. He was the first of the emigrant West Indian writers; and his first book, published in 1933, was *The Case for West Indian Self-Government*. Self-government has more or less come to the West Indies; Sir Learie Constantine is now the Trinidad High Commissioner in London. The West Indies, captained for the first time by a black man, did great things in Australia in 1960–1. A quarter of a million people came out into the streets of Melbourne to say goodbye to the cricketers: West Indian cricket's finest moment, which Mr James sees as something more. 'Clearing their way with bat and ball, West Indians at that moment had made a public entry into the comity of nations.' It is a success story, then, that Mr James has to tell, but an odd one, since it is also the story of the triumph of the code. To Mr James Frank Worrell is more than the first black West Indian captain: 'Thomas Arnold, Thomas Hughes and the Old Master himself would have recognized Frank Worrell as their boy.'

This is the last sentence of Mr James's book, and this is his astounding thesis. To dismiss it would be to deny the curious position of the West Indies and West Indians in the Commonwealth, to fail to see that these territories are a unique imperial creation, where people of many lands, thrown together, 'came to maturity within a system that was the result of centuries of development in another land, was transplanted as a hothouse flower is transplanted and bore some strange fruit'. Stollmeyer, Gomez, Pierre, Christiani, Tang Choon, Ramadhin: the names of West Indian cricketers are sufficient evidence. To be a nationalist, Mr James says elsewhere, you must have a nation. The African in Africa had a nation; so had the Asian in Asia. The West Indian, whatever his community, had only this 'system'; and my fourth-standard teacher could only grope towards some definition of his position in the world by his devotion to Constantine.

It is part of the originality and rightness of Mr James's book that he should have combined the story of his development within the system with his view of West Indian political growth, and combined that with sketches of West Indian cricketers he knew and watched develop. In the islands the cricketers were familiar to many; they were as much men as cricketers. So they emerge in Mr James's pages, but even so they remain touched with heroic qualities, for their success, as with Constantine or Headley, was the only type of triumph the society as a whole knew. And their failure, as with Wilton St Hill who, achieving nothing in England in 1928, remained all his life a clerk in a department store, bitter tragedy.

How did Mr James become part of this 'system'? He was born in a small Trinidad country town at the turn of the century. His father was a teacher. Yet slavery had been abolished only seventy years before, and 'Cousin Nancy, who lived a few yards away, told many stories of her early days as a house-slave.' Already, then, the slave society had been transformed, its assumptions destroyed; and this rapid transformation must be regarded as part of the West Indian good fortune. The family was not rich, but for the young James, as for every boy in the island, there was a narrow way out. Every year the government offered four exhibitions to one of the two secondary schools. There a boy could get a Senior Cambridge Certificate, which would ensure a modest job in the civil service. He could do more: he could win one of the three annual scholarships. With this he could get a profession in England, come back to Trinidad, make money and achieve honour. The form of promising boys was studied as carefully as that of racehorses; the course, from exhibition to scholarship, aroused island-wide interest and excitement.

James won his exhibition. He came from a house with books. Preparing for his exhibition, he became a 'British intellectual long before I was ten, already an alien in my own environment'. But he was ready for the public-school code of the Queen's Royal College, staffed for two generations by Oxford and Cambridge men. 'Our masters, our curriculum, our code of morals, *everything* began from the basis that Britain was the source of all light and leading, and our business was to admire, wonder, imitate, learn.' It was not hard. The colony might be ruled autocratically by Englishmen, but there was as yet no National Question and, within the school, no race question. 'If the masters were so successful in instilling and maintaining their British principles as the ideal and norm it was because within the school, and particularly on the playing field, they practised them themselves . . . They were correct in the letter and in the spirit.' They were also not competing with any other system. Today, he says, these teachers with their 'bristling Britishness' would be anachronisms. But was it possible to reject them then? Was it possible for Mr James, forty years later, at a public meeting in Manchester, to accept Mr Aneurin Bevan's sneers at public-school morality? As it was, however, the playing fields of Queen's Royal College undid Mr James. Cricket possessed him; he did not win the scholarship. But he had educated himself 'into a member of the British middle class'. In 1932, with the encouragement and help of Learie Constantine, he came to England. And he has been a wanderer ever since.

To me, who thirty years later followed in his path almost step by step – but I only watched cricket, and I won the scholarship – Mr James's career is of particular interest. Our backgrounds were dissimilar. His was Negro, puritan, fearful of lower-class contamination; mine was Hindu, restricted, enclosed. But we have ended speaking the same language; and though England is not perhaps the country we thought it was, we have both charmed ourselves away from Trinidad. 'For the inner self,' as Mr James writes, 'the die was cast.'

In our absence the static society we knew has altered. Secondary education is free. Not three, but more like thirty, scholarships are given each year. With the new nationalism and confidence, the public-school code has become as anachronistic as the masters who taught it. What new code will be developed in a society so clearly British-made? Cricket is no longer a substitute for nationalism. Has it then served its purpose, and will it die in the West Indies as it has died (in spite of Dexter, in spite of the Lord's Test) in England? Trinidad, we must remind ourselves, has produced no major player since Ramadhin, discovered in 1950. It would be interesting to have Mr James's views. In the meantime let us rejoice over what he has given us. *Beyond a Boundary* is one of the finest and most finished books to come out of the West Indies, important to England, important to

the West Indies. It has a further value: it gives a base and solidity
to West Indian literary endeavour.

J. B. PRIESTLEY

The Lesson of Garfield Sobers (1966)

I seem to have spent a lot of time, this summer, sitting in front of
the TV watching Garfield Sobers. Always I have stared at him out
of a mixture of apprehension and admiration. He frightened me and
enchanted me by turns. Batting, bowling, fielding, captaining his side,
he seemed to be pronouncing, often with a grin, the doom of the
England XI. More than once – in the bitter hours facing defeat – I
wished he would sprain a wrist or turn an ankle. But even so,
admiration came seeping through these mud walls of partisanship.
And it was not only his feats with bat and ball that compelled my
applause; it was his style and manner, the way he carried himself,
the way he moved.

There is none of the chin-up-chest-out nonsense about Sobers.
He isn't one of your stiff-necked athletes. He carries his head slightly
forward, as if eager to swing the bat or deliver the ball and so break
another record, and he seems to ripple towards the wickets. All is
loose, easy, instant and powerful. And if I were coaching young
cricketers – though I must add here that I think some of ours have
been over-coached and so torment themselves wondering what is
the correct stroke to play – I would show them films of this great
cricketer, asking them to note his posture and movements, his avoid-
ance of unnecessary effort and strain, the whole cat-like style of the
man.

I don't know what happens now in military training, but I do
know that the way we were taught to carry ourselves in 1914 and
early 1915 was utterly and damnably wrong, the worst possible
preparation for what we were called to endure later at the front.
Nothing was loose and easy, minimizing effort and strain. It was as
if we were being drilled to go on guard at Buckingham Palace, not
to survive long night marches, to carry heavy coils of barbed wire
up slippery communication trenches, to go raiding across no man's
land. I realize that today's army is far more sensible than the one I

knew (it could hardly be less), but it might be helpful, even today, if somebody in charge of training took a good look at Garfield Sobers.

But while we remain with the body I am like a hippopotamus trying to describe a leopard, so now I turn with relief to the mind. This doesn't mean – please, *please*, everybody! – that I imagine that my own mind has the loping ease and then the instant power of a Sobers in the field. What it does mean is that I believe there is a mental equivalent of the Sobers style. And indeed we can choose as an example a member of his own race, for I have always liked the story of the old coloured woman who was asked how she had been able to cope with her own troubles and also help many other people. She replied: 'I wear my life like a loose garment.'

Alan Watts, in his latest book, *This Is It*, asks us to laugh with him at that stern and quite idiotic imperative so often read and heard in America – *You Must Relax*. Here are hundreds of thousands of nice conscientious people, already staggering under a load of *musts*, who are now faced with yet another and perhaps final *Must*. Clenching their teeth and straining every nerve, they have to relax. I have spent weekends with such people, all wearing special casual-living clothes and doing *fun things*, relaxing so hard that it must have been a pleasure to get back to work again. And all this of course is the opposite to wearing life like a loose garment. It is as if a Garfield Sobers arrived on the cricket field wearing a strait-jacket.

Never be afraid – I am advising the young now; their elders are hopeless – of any accusations and taunts of being *half-baked* and *woolly-minded*. These come from the kind of people who would tell a Sobers to pull himself together, to keep his chin up and his chest out. They have minds that can never be loose and easy. They are stiff-necked in all their opinions and conclusions. They carry their intelligence rigidly, never allowing it to amble and lope, so that it is strained and tired before it has been asked to do anything in particular. And England – and I mean England because I can't speak for Scotland, Wales, Ulster – is crammed with such people.

This may seem a surprising statement. But then, so far as we have any idea of ourselves at all, we have the wrong idea. We are deceived by superficial appearances and what we read in the papers, which are always looking for the picturesque and the grotesque and so offer us tiny minorities as typical examples. Because we are shown young men with long hair in fancy dress, because we think the housepainters took it easy and the chaps mending the road appear to be idle, we conjure up a disturbing vision of an England full of layabouts, a country going nowhere except to the dogs. It is as if, while the actual weather gets wetter and worse, we are mentally and spiritually ambling into some tropical land of *mañana*, all taking longer and longer siestas under imaginary palm trees. But most of this is nonsensical. We are in a mess not because we are too slack but because we are too stiff.

It might be better if we were all going to the dogs, because then at least we would be all going somewhere together. Our trouble is that we aren't going anywhere together. We are no longer a nation at all. We consist of a number of mentally stiff-necked sections, all chin up and chest out. Between these rigid camps there are committees but no real communications. Nationally we are at the opposite extreme to a Sobers on the field, loose, easy, instant and powerful. We are like people standing to attention or doing a goose step, all in the various uniforms of our class or sectional interests. It is no use our politicians exhorting the nation, with a final reference to the 'spirit of Dunkirk'; the nation isn't there, only so many listeners and viewers, so many sectional interests and prejudices.

We can imagine what would have happened to a famous declar- ation if it had been received in the spirit of today. *We shall fight on beaches* would have been denounced at once by the Association of Boarding-House Keepers and Deckchair Hiring. *On landing grounds* – a sharp protest and a threat to strike by the Union of Airline Ground Staff employees. *In fields* – a deputation to the Prime Minister by representatives of the Farmers' Union. *In streets* – agreed by every borough council to be irresponsible and unwarrantable. *And on hills* – bringing about, for the first time, joint action by the Landowners' Association and the National Council of Hikers.

But this won't do, I shall be told, because after all we aren't at war now or in any danger. But we seem to be in considerable danger, even if it isn't of a spectacular sort. Something rather nasty happens to people who insist on living – and living well – on borrowed money. If they don't go bankrupt outside, they go bankrupt inside, where the spirit dwells. We have all met – and afterwards avoided – people trying to live as the English have been trying to live for some time now, people who expect the largest possible result from the smallest possible effort, who say they are boldly facing the future while clinging to every remaining vestige of the past, who want everybody to be united except themselves and condemn all prejudices except those they cherish themselves, who are hopelessly committed to self-deception.

Has this taken us too far from Garfield Sobers? I don't think so. Instead of holding ourselves loose and easy, rippling along, in our thinking, we still insist upon the stiff neck, the chin up, the chest out. We arrive on the field of our national interests like sergeant majors on parade. What we thought the day before yesterday, perhaps thirty years ago, is good enough for today. We turn again to economics when we should be thinking in terms of psychology. We listen to economists whose understanding of ordinary English human nature is almost nil. The recent sterling crisis offered a wonderful opportunity to ask the English (who love drama and are easily bored by routine) to be heroic and self-sacrificing, making a huge common effort, which the English enjoy because it breaks down the class barriers, the shyness and social suspicion, and they feel they can talk to one another without having been introduced. What we like is a national crisis as big and all-embracing as the weather.

But what have we got? Chin up and chest out, that's all. Just enough, no doubt, to put the statistics right, but also just enough to make England a still more unheroic and disagreeable country to live in, a good country to get out of. Nothing stiff has been broken or loosened; nobody will go loping and rippling on to the field. And don't let any Tory take heart from all this. They have always been in the same leaky boat while pretending it was a luxury liner. They are still solidly behind any chest-out 'world power' nonsense, any chin-up 'top table' drivel, any stiff-necked back-to-the-Thirties deflationary moves, with prosperity and joy at the end of long queues at the labour exchanges.

So we arrive on the ground, to play the world, still marching as if on parade, not as a nation but in regimented sections, each shouting old slogans and moving to tunes that have bored the hell out of us for years. We might remember, before making our final protest and then deciding to emigrate, how a man from Barbados came on to our Test-match grounds, so eager and yet so easy, apparently without a stubborn bone or stiffened muscle in his body. Yes indeed, we can learn from Garfield Sobers.

* * *

Now come two lovely meditations by literary-minded and cricket-mad Englishmen. Neville Cardus remembers the spirit of cricket in inter-war England, the game and its characters between the bloody conflicts. A. A. Thomson recalls the continuation of cricket in the English winter, in places and climes far removed from his own cold hearth.

NEVILLE CARDUS

The Spirit of Summer (1949)

For twenty years I went to cricket matches north, south, east and west, and I saw the blossom come upon orchards in Gloucestershire, as we journeyed from Manchester to Bristol; and I saw midsummer in full blaze at Canterbury; and I saw midsummer dropping torrents of rain on the same lovely place, the white tents dropsical: 'Play abandoned for the day.' I saw the autumn leaves falling at Eastbourne. I have shivered to the bone in the springtime blasts at the Parks at Oxford. In a *Manchester Guardian* article I congratulated the keenness and devotion of two spectators who at Leicester sat all day, near the sight screen, from eleven until half past six, in spite of an east wind like a knife. Then, as I was finishing my notice, a thought struck me. 'But', I added in a final sentence, 'perhaps they were only dead.' I have seen English summer days pass like a dream as the cricketers changed places in the field over by over. Sometimes I have seen in vision all the games going on throughout the land at the same minute of high noon; Hobbs, easy and unhurriedly on the way to another hundred under the gasometer at the Oval; Tate and Gilligan at Hove skittling wickets while the tide comes in; Hendren and Hearne batting for ever at Lord's while the Tavern gets busier and busier; at Southampton, Kennedy bowling for hours for Hampshire – Kennedy never ceased bowling in those days; he could always have produced a clinching alibi if ever circumstantial evidence had convicted him of anything:

'What were you doing on 17 July at 4.45 in the afternoon?'

'Why, bowling of course.'

From Old Trafford to Dover, from Hull to Bristol, the fields were active as fast bowlers heaved and thudded and sweated over the earth, and batsmen drove and cut or got their legs in front; and the men in the slips bent down, all four of them together, as though moved by one string. On every afternoon at half past six I saw them, in my mind's eye, all walking home to the pavilion, with a deeper tan on their faces. And the newspapers came out with the cricket scores and the visitor from Budapest, in London for the first time, experienced a certain bewilderment when he saw an *Evening News* poster: 'Collapse of Surrey.' In these twenty seasons I saw also a change in cricket. It is not fanciful, I think, to say that a national game is influenced by the spirit and atmosphere of the period. In 1920 cricket retained much of the gusto and free personal gesture of the years before the war of 1914–18. Then, as disillusion increased and the nation's life contracted and the catchword 'safety first' became familiar and a sense of insecurity gathered, cricket itself lost confidence and character. My own county of Lancashire provided a striking example of how a mere game can express a transition in the social and industrial scene. When Manchester was wealthy and the mills of Lancashire were busy most days and nights, cricket at Old Trafford was luxuriant with MacLaren, Spooner and Tyldesley squandering runs opulently right and left. It was as soon as the county's shoe began to pinch and mill after mill closed that Lancashire cricket obtained its reputation for suspicious thriftiness; care and want batted visibly at both ends of the wicket. Not that the players consciously expressed anything; of course they didn't. But a cricketer, like anybody else, is what his period and environment make of him, and he acts or plays accordingly.

The romantic flourish vanished as much from cricket as from the theatre and the arts. I even reacted against the romanticism in my own cricket writing. The lyric gush, the 'old flashing bat' and 'rippling green grass' metaphors gave way to, or became tinctured with, satire if not with open irony. Hammond no longer inspired me into comparisons between him and the Elgin marbles; I saw something middle-class and respectable about his play, and was vastly amused and relieved when occasionally he fell off his pedestal and struck a ball with the oil hole of his bat, or received a blow from a fast ball on his toe. Bradman was the summing-up of the Efficient Age which succeeded the Golden Age. Here was brilliance safe and sure, streamlined and without impulse. Victor Trumper was the flying bird; Bradman the aeroplane. It was the same in music, by the way: the objective Toscanini was preferred to the subjective Furtwängler.

In an England XI of 1938, A. C. MacLaren would have looked as much an anachronism as Irving in a Noël Coward play.

But the humour of English character kept creeping in, even to Lancashire cricket. And I came to love the dour shrewd ways of these north-country 'professors'; it was true to life at any rate, and not, like much of the cricket of the south of England, suburban and genteel. The Lancashire and Yorkshire match was every year like a play and pageant exhibiting the genius of the two counties. To watch it rightly you needed the clue; for years I myself had missed the point. There is slow play and slow play at cricket. There are batsmen who cannot score quickly because they can't, and there are batsmen who can score quickly but won't. In a representative Lancashire and Yorkshire match of 1924–34, runs were severely dis-countenanced. No fours before lunch, on principle, was the unannounced policy; and as few as possible after. But fours or no fours, runs or no runs, the games touched greatness because of the north of England character that was exposed in every action, every movement, all day. Imagine the scene: Bramall Lane. Factory chimneys everywhere; a pall of smoke between earth and sun. A crowd mainly silent; hard hats or caps and scarves on all sides. Makepeace is batting to Rhodes; old soldier against old soldier. Makepeace has only one purpose in life at the moment, and that is not to get out. And Rhodes pitches a cautious ball wide of the off stump – pitches it there so that Makepeace cannot safely score off it; Makepeace, mind you, who is not going to put his bat anywhere near a ball if he can help it.

Maiden overs occurred in profusion. Appeals for leg before wicket were the only signs of waking life for hours. Often I thought that one day during overs, while the field was changing positions, some-body would return the ball from the outfield and accidentally hit a batsman on the pads, and then eleven terrific 'H'zats!' would be emitted by sheer force of habit. 'Aye,' said Roy Kilner, 'it's a rum 'un is t'Yarksheer and Lankysheer match. T'two teams meets in t'dressin' room on t'Bank Holiday; and then we never speaks agean for three days – except to appeal.' The ordeal of umpiring in a Lancashire and Yorkshire match during 1924–30 was severe. One day at Leeds, Yorkshire fell upon the Lancashire first innings and three wickets – the best – were annihilated for next to nothing. Two young novices nervously discovered themselves together, holding the fourth Lanca-shire wicket, while 30,000 Yorkshire folk roared for their blood; and the Yorkshire team crouched under their very noses, a few yards from the block-hole. By some miracle worked on high, the two young novices stayed in. Not only that; they began to hit fours. One drive soared over the ropes. George Macaulay, the Yorkshire medium-paced bowler (a grand fellow off the field, and on it a tiger with the temper of the jungle) glared down the wicket until his eyes were pinpoints of incredulity and frustration. And Emmott Robinson, grey-haired in the service of Yorkshire and whose trousers were always coming down, an old campaigner who would any day have died rather than give 'owt away', kept muttering, 'Hey, dear, dear, dear; what's t'matter, what's t'matter?' The two novices declined to get out; the score mounted – 40 for 3, 50 for 3, 80 for 3, 100 for 3. At that time the Yorkshire captain was not a good cricketer though a very nice man – an 'amateur' of course; for even Yorkshire continued to observe the custom that no first-class county team should be captained by a professional; even Yorkshire carried a 'passenger' for the sake of traditional social distinctions. But he was only a figure-head; the leadership was a joint dictatorship; Rhodes and Robinson. This day the situation got out of hand; the novices each made a century. One of the umpires told me, after the scalding afternoon's play was over: 'Never again; no more "standin'" in Yorkshire and Lancashire matches for me. Why, this afternoon, when them two lads were knockin' t'stuffin' out of t'Yorkshire bowlers, the row and racket on t'field were awful. George Macaulay were cussin' 'is 'ead off, and Emmott were mutterin' to 'isself, and poor owd captain 'ad been sent out into t'outfield so's 'e couldn't 'ear. At last I 'ad to call order; I said "Now look 'ere, you chaps, how the 'ell do you expect me and me pal 'Arry to umpire in a bloody parrot 'ouse?"'

Roy Kilner, Yorkshire to the end of his days and for ever after, once said that umpires were only 'luxurious superfluities' in a Lanca-shire and Yorkshire match. 'They gets in t'way. What we want in Yarksheer and Lankysheer matches is "fair do's" – no umpires, and honest cheatin' all round, in conformity wi' the law.'

The joke about Yorkshire cricket is that for Yorkshiremen it is no laughing matter. It is a possession of the clan and must on no account be put down, or interfered with by anybody not born in the county. When Hammond was an unknown young player, I went to look at him at Huddersfield one day when Gloucestershire were playing Yorkshire. I had been told he was more than promising. He came to the wicket and began well. I watched from behind the bowler's arm, through Zeiss glasses. Suddenly a ball from Emmott Robinson struck him on the pad, high up. Every Yorkshireman on the field of play, and many not on it, roared 'Howzat!' Involuntarily I spoke aloud and said, 'No, not out, not out'; through my glasses I had seen that the ball would have missed the wicket. Then I was conscious I was being watched; you know how you can somehow feel that somebody behind you is looking at you. I turned round and saw a typical Yorkshireman eyeing me from my boots upward to the crown of my head, his hand deep and aggressively thrust in his pocket. 'And what's the matter with thee?' he asked.

No writer of novels could make a picture of Yorkshire life half as full of meaning as the one drawn every year in matches between Lancashire and Yorkshire. Cricket on the dole; Nature herself on the dole. The very grass on the field of play told of the struggle for existence; it eventually achieved a triumphant greenness. 'Tha can't be too careful.' If it happened to be a fine day, well – 'maybe it'll last and maybe it won't'. And, if things are at a pretty pass all round, well – 'they'll get worse before they get better'. 'Ah'm tekking nowt on trust.' At Sheffield there is a refreshment room situated deep in the earth under a concrete stand. I descended one afternoon for a cup of tea. A plump Yorkshire lass served me and I asked for a spoon. 'It's there, Maister,' she said.

'Where?' I asked.

She pointed with her bread knife. 'There,' she said, 'tied to t'counter, la-ad.' So it was; a lead spoon tied to the premises with a piece of string.

A. A. THOMSON

Winter Made Glorious (1954)

Winter in England is a time of raw, foggy days, of running colds and streaming umbrellas, when a man has practically no friends in the world but his goloshes, and when he has nothing more to look forward to at the end of the day but one small whisky, two large aspirins and a lukewarm hot-water bottle. That is England in winter, and never were time and place more entitled to separation on grounds of incompatibility.

Would it not be wonderful if, by the stretching of a finger, by the mere turning of a vulcanite knob, you could be transported from the murk and the mud of the city streets to a land of cloudless turquoise skies, emerald-green velvet turf and clear air dancing and shimmering in the heat haze? Wonderful, perhaps, but not impossible. Turn on the radio and listen. If you listen at the right time, you will discover that cricket will be going on in one of many sunny climes and a welcome voice will be telling you about it. You may not always like what he tells you. The facts may be grim for England. But the facts of life are grim anyhow. That is not the point.

The voice could conceivably come from Brisbane, Bombay, Barbados, or from any one of a score of blessed plots in Australia, South Africa, India, New Zealand or the West Indies. (Whatever evil tidings may have come from Sabina Park, Kingston, Jamaica, it will still be an enchanted ground under the shade of green palm and blue mountain.) These places lie in the happier southern hemisphere; all, that is, except India and the West Indies, which are near enough to the equator for hemispheres not to matter. Blue sky, golden sun, green turf; all this and cricketers' heaven, too, except that in some places the ground is not green but brown and the pitch is a tightly stretched matting. As if that made any difference, except to the naughtier bowlers . . .

Long before the birth of radio and, solemn thought, of its attendant Arlotts and Alstons, cricket under a less wintry sun lived and had its being and men went out from England to do battle under fairer skies than those that hang over Lord's in winter or Old Trafford in summer. All good things must have a beginning, and the first Test match, the very first Test that ever was, took place at Melbourne in 1877. To be fair the month was March and the English winter should have been nearly over, but the records tell us that it was a bad year and gentlemen in England then abed must have snuggled down tightly under the blankets while they thought that somebody or something was warm, 12,000 miles away.

The Australian side on that day in 1877 contained a few names that you will naturally remember. Charles Bannerman, elder brother of the other Bannerman (Alec) who stonewalled his way through five tours in this country; Midwinter, who afterwards came to England and played for Gloucester; D. W. Gregory, first of a whole gaggle of Gregorys; and the stumper J. M. Blackham, owner of cricket's fiercest beard (always excepting W. G.'s), the toughest appendage since that of Blackbeard the Buccaneer. The English team contained names which are still freshly remembered, at least in the north country; five of them were Yorkshiremen: Happy Jack Ulyett and Tom Emmett, the two most famous of the old Yorkshire players; Allan Hill and Andrew Greenwood, who came, you will remember, from Lascelles Hall; and Tom Armitage, the stout fellow who, in the New Zealand floods, had carried the lady across the river on his back. The captain was James Lillywhite, Junior, the Sussex pro, which shows that Len Hutton was not his country's first professional captain. Besides Lillywhite and his five Yorkshiremen there was Harry Jupp, the Surrey batsman who had to keep wicket because Ted Pooley had been left behind in New Zealand, and Alfred Shaw, the renowned Notts slow bowler. Somebody had to bowl the first ball in any Test, and this honour fell to Alfred himself, for whom it was claimed that he never bowled a wide or a no-ball all his life. Bannerman hit the first run; he also hit 164 more. Somebody is said to have missed him before he scored, but why should I tell you who it was? Historians are now giving even Richard III the benefit of the doubt. The bowlers could not get Bannerman out, though his partners fell regularly by the wayside, until a nasty break-back ball from Ulyett suddenly rose and hit him on the hand. Into retirement he had to go . . .

Bannerman's score amounted to two-thirds of the whole and the crowd collected 165 sovereigns, one for each run. When England went in, they never quite caught up. Jupp scored the first half-century ever made for England, but nobody else produced any fireworks until Allan Hill, the handsome fellow from Lascelles Hall, carried his bat for a truculently hammered 35.

In the second innings the English bowlers were too much for the Australians and nobody could make anything of Alfred Shaw and Ulyett. Bannerman, his hand in bandages, scored only one run. When England went in to get 154, which did not seem too difficult, they fared just as badly. Kendall took 7 for 55, and a swashbuckling 38 from Ulyett was the best contribution to an inadequate English total of 108. So Australia won the first Test match and that is how it all started.

The first Test in South Africa was played in our winter of 1888–9, also a winter of rough weather. Playing on the charming ground at Port Elizabeth, the English team was hardly formidable as an international side, but it was nevertheless too strong for an infant South Africa, and who do you think was the English captain? A tall, slim undergraduate named C. A. ('Round the Corner') Smith, who was named partly after his bowling action and partly after a character in Surtees. C. A. Smith lived another sixty years, achieved a well-deserved knighthood, and (solemn thought) taught Hollywood cricket and court etiquette, in that order. He took 5 wickets for 19 in the South Africans' first innings, and they simply did not know which corner he was bowling round. England won by 8 wickets, although nobody but Bobby Abel made a respectable score. A fortnight later there was another Test, also on a very pleasant ground, at Cape Town. Abel made his usual century, but England's innings victory was due not so much to this as to the slightly fantastic bowling of Johnny Briggs, who in the two innings took 15 wickets for 28 runs. Repeat: 15 for 28. And 14 of them were clean bowled. There can never have been such hitting of the stumps before or since, even by Schofield Haigh.

What of those other English winters? It was in the same period – 1929–30 – that the first away Tests were played not only against the West Indies, but also against New Zealand. On 11 January to 16 January 1930, an English eleven under the Hon. F. S. G. Calthorpe played the West Indies on the lovely Barbados ground at Kensington Oval – I said *Kensington*. There was some tall scoring by Sandham for England and, for the West Indies, by Roach and George Headley of the panther-like spring, who made the first of his many centuries. (At the age of forty-four he was brought back to the West Indies by public subscription to take part in the 1953–4 Tests against England.) This was Constantine's first Test at home, though he had, of course, visited England the previous summer and achieved 'the double'. In the West Indies his batting and bowling for once fell short of the spectacular, but he made four of those incredible catches by which the quickness of his hands perennially deceived the eye.

In New Zealand, at Lancaster Park, Christchurch, an English eleven which included Woolley and Duleepsinhji, got seven New Zealand wickets down for 21 runs, mainly through some sensational bowling by M. J. C. Allom, who laid the foundations of a fairly easy victory for his side by taking four wickets in five balls.

The first Test played in India began at Bombay four years later and saw centuries by B. H. Valentine on one side and L. Amarnath on the other. There was also some fine attacking bowling by Maurice Nichols and Mohamed Nissar. In the end England won without great difficulty by 9 wickets, but it was the beginning of a shining period which gave English cricket lovers the pleasures that came from playing against or watching Merchant, Mankad, Hazare and Umrigar.

If I were asked to think of a match which, beyond many others, truly made winter glorious, I would recall Bobby Peel's match at Sydney in December 1894. I did not see it, because it took place round about the time I was born, but there are times when I have *felt* that match, just as I have *seen* the 1893 Yorkshire v. Lancashire match through the eager eyes of Uncle Walter. At Sydney England faced the mountainous task of following on against an Australian total of 586, and it is to their credit that they fought back with tenacity. The first hero was Albert Ward, the man whom Uncle Walter saw catch Ulyett off the last ball of that Lancashire v. Yorkshire game. Ward made 100 and there were several forties; even so, Australia were set only 177 to win, and they started off with cheerful confidence. On the evening of the fifth day they were 113 with only two wickets down. It was in the bag. There was a clattering thunderstorm during the night, and when Bobby Peel and Johnny Briggs went down to Sydney Oval in the morning to look at the wicket the sun was shining fiercely. Bobby dug his toe into the turf and exclaimed with gleeful wickedness: 'That's for me!' The third wicket fell at 130 and the whole of the rest of the Australian team put on only 36 more. Five of the last six wickets fell to Peel, and England, after following on 261 behind, had won by 10 runs.

> Now is the winter of our discontent
> Made glorious summer by this sun of York . . .

At any rate, I think the sons of Yorkshire have done their share.

*   *   *

In our last selection from his work, Neville Cardus writes of the suggestiveness in the names of individual players. All of us develop likes and dislikes based purely on the sound of a cricketer's name – this before we have a proper understanding of the game itself. One of the first cricketers I admired was J. Van Geloven, the exoticism of whose name concealed his modest record for Leicestershire. I came across him in the *Wisden Cricketers' Almanack* for 1965, a book given to me when I was seven. *Wisden* is, of course, a comprehensive book of names – and of much else besides. What the fat yellow book contains, and where it might lead you, are the subject of our final essay, by a man who followed cricket and read *Wisden* for more than sixty years.

Neville Cardus

What's in a Name? (1948)

Mr E. V. Lucas has somewhere written a charming essay on cricketers' names, and such is my annoyance at not having thought of the theme first that (without Mr Lucas's permission) I now borrow it and use it myself. Why should I not? In music, composers have never had scruples against stealing subjects from one another for their variations. Besides, many years ago, long before Mr Lucas's writings on cricket came pleasantly into my life, I pondered frequently the question of the poetic justness of the names of cricketers. I used to choose my 'favourite' batsmen on the strength of an agreeable name, much as ladies pick a winner at Ascot. I was, even while a schoolboy, as convinced as Mr Shandy would have been that a cricketer's surname possessed an enormous influence one way or another upon his skill, nay upon his very destiny. When Hobbs first played for Surrey I would have none of him. 'No man ever has or ever will do good with a name like that,' I said, adding, 'Hobbes, maybe, but not Hobbs.' My Shandean theory was, of course, rather shocked by the quick movement of Hobbs to fame; I consoled myself with the reflection that there must be exceptions to every rule.

One afternoon I remember running out of school to get the latest news of the Lancashire match. In those years Lancashire cricket meant more to me, perhaps, than anything else on earth. One afternoon I escaped from school eager about Lancashire, who were meeting Worcestershire – a rare side that year, with the Fosters, Ted Arnold, Burrows and Wilson. I bought a newspaper and turned to the scores on the middle page inside. I never could as a boy – and sometimes cannot yet – muster up courage enough to plunge headlong to the 'stop-press'; news had to come to my apprehensive young mind gradually. Inside the paper, which I opened cautiously, I learned that Worcestershire were 67 for 6 and all the Fosters out. These tidings of joy sent me confidently to the 'stop-press'. And there, what did my incredulous eyes read? 'Worcestershire 152 for 6, Gaukrodger not out 82.' I decided on the spot that (a) this was outrageous and absurd, that (b) Gaukrodger was an impossible name for a cricketer, and that (c) with such a name he ought never in this world to have been permitted to score 19, let alone 91. From that afternoon, until Gaukrodger passed into honourable retirement, I regarded him (or rather his name – which amounted to the same thing) with open derision. 'Gaukrodger!' I would murmur. And to this present time I have remained unshaken in the view that 'Gaukrodger' was a heathen-ish name for a cricketer; I am glad he never played for England.

There is, I am aware, a sophistical argument which tries to persuade us that only by force of mechanical association do we begin to regard a great man's name as part and parcel of all that we feel about his personality and genius. I admit this notion can gather support from the way the ridiculous monosyllable 'Hobbs' has, with the passing of time, come to sound in many ears like a very trumpet of greatness. But my strong opinion is this: Hobbs has conquered in spite of his name. It would have crippled many a smaller man. 'What about Trumper?' asks the scoffer. 'How can you fit in a name like that with the destiny of a glorious cricketer?' And again do I freely confess that at first glance 'Trumper' seems a name not at all likely to guide anybody towards sweetness and light. But Trumper's Christian name was Victor; the poetry in 'Victor' neutralized the (let us say) prose in 'Trumper'; had Trumper been named Obadiah he could scarcely have scored a century for Australia against England before lunch – as Trumper rapturously did at Old Trafford in 1902.

The crowd in the shilling seats will bear me out that there's much power for good or for evil in a cricketer's name. Consider how the crowd instinctively felt, when Hendren began his county cricket, that the man's Christian name of Elias was all wrong – not only that, but a positive danger to his future. The crowd looked at Hendren's face, his gigantic smile; also at his admirable batting. Then they pro-nounced to themselves 'Elias'. And they looked at Hendren once more and, to a man, they agreed that that 'Elias' was not true . . . They called him 'Patsy' – even as they called Augustus Lilley 'Dick'.

Mr Warner has invented a sort of rainy-day pastime for cricketers; you have to pick a 'World XI' to play a side from Mars. I always select my 'World XI' on the principle that a handsome name is a harbinger of handsome achievement. And herewith I publish my 'World XI' – every man chosen with no reference at all to form, but simply because he carries a name which, if not actually poetic, has suggestions which are far from those of unlovely prose:

Grace
Shrewsbury
Darling
Noble
Warwick Armstrong
Knight (A. E. or D. J.)
Lilley
Rhodes
Flowers
Mead (W., of Essex)
Blythe.

Perhaps I ought to go a little into my choice of 'Rhodes'. It is not exactly musical in sound, or, as a word, poetic or picturesque. But it is redolent of the ancient Aegean, the Dorian Hexapolis, and the Colossus of Chares. Besides, I am prepared to go to any extreme of subterfuge and sophistry to get Wilfred into my 'World XI'. 'Tennyson' is a name of handsomer aspect at first glance than 'Rhodes' – which really is a hideous word, if only we could look at it with fresh eyes. But as a cricketer Tennyson

> . . . altogether lacks the abilities
> That Rhodes is dress'd in.

Against my XI of delectable names I would like to see opposed the following team, which might be called 'The Onomatopoeics':

Hobbs
Fry
Studd (C. T.)
Gunn (W.)
Brown (J. T.)
Hirst
Trumble
Boyle
Briggs
Sugg
   and (of course)
Gaukrodger.

My XI's inevitable victory would demonstrate once and for all that there is plenty of virtue in a name – among cricketers, at any rate. Could Grace conceivably have been Grace, known as W. G. Blenkinsop?

ROWLAND RYDER

The Pleasures of Reading Wisden (1995)

As my father was secretary of the Warwickshire County Cricket Club from 1895 to 1944, it is not altogether surprising that the game was a frequent topic of conversation at the family meal table: cricket was our bread and butter.

Reaching double figures in the early 1920s, I naturally heard a good deal about the achievements of Hobbs and Sutcliffe and, in the cricketless winters, learned from my father, and from the yellow-backed pages of *Wisden*'s, about Grace and Spofforth; 'Ranji' and Fry and Jessop; Blackham and Lilley; and, of course, 'My Hornby and my Barlow long ago'. I knew about the cricketing giants of the past before I had learned about Gladstone and Disraeli; looking back on those days of enchantment, and with all respect to those eminent statesmen, I have no regrets.

We had in our living room a formidable Victorian bookcase, its shelves protected by glass shutters. In one of these shelves, over-spilling into a second, were editions of *Wisden*'s, in strict chrono-logical order – and woe betide anyone who took out a copy and put it back in the wrong place: a bad school report might on some rare occasion be forgiven, but to cause havoc in the thin yellow line – that was another matter.

It was always a red-letter day for me when our stock was increased by a new volume, Father announcing 'I've got the new *Wisden*'s!' with the same quiet pride that Disraeli – whom I eventually did get to hear about – would have announced that he had secured shares in the Suez Canal. My excited request to peruse the magic pages was always countered by my father with dark allusions to homework; but the reply deceived neither of us, for we both knew that he wanted to read *Wisden*'s first.

We all have our foibles about the Almanack. For each, of course, his own county. We study our own side's home matches times without number, paying scant attention to the achievements of the other counties. Sir Arthur Conan Doyle, who played for the MCC and for Sussex, who had 'WG', as one of his victims, and who wrote 'The Missing Three-Quarter', might well have written a cricket detective story, entitled, say, 'The Missing Mid-On':

'Did you not observe, my dear Watson, that in the library were thirty-seven editions of Wisden's?'

This makes Watson forget the Afghan campaign. 'By heavens, Holmes, then the man was possibly interested in cricket?'

'More than that, my dear Watson. I noticed that in all these editions the home matches of Loamshire were heavily thumbed. This put me on the scent of the miscreant . . .'

Sherlock Holmes, in any case, is not unconnected with Wisden. In the Births and Deaths section of earlier editions will be found the names of Shacklock, F. (Derbyshire, Notts and Otago), and Mycroft, Thomas (Derbyshire), who inspired Conan Doyle to use the names Sherlock and Mycroft Holmes for his detective stories. Perhaps Sir Arthur played against them: certainly the line 'Doyle, Sir A. C. (MCC) b. May 22, 1859' appeared for many years in Wisden's. A shame that space could not be found for the famous though fictitious Raffles in the Births and Deaths. He would enjoy being on the same page as Ranjitsinhji.

For each, too, his favourite editions of Wisden. If I were permitted to take eight editions of the Almanack with me to some remote island, I would find the task of selection an extremely difficult one. To choose the first half-dozen, recording the most absorbing of the England v. Australia Test-match series, would be a tricky enough problem in all conscience.

What of the final pair? The first of all the Wisden's? – the current issue? – the copies recounting Warwickshire's championship triumphs of 1911 and 1951? – the 1915 edition, in which batsmen were laconically recorded as 'absent' during the fateful first week in August? – how does one choose two from these?

But if on my desert island I could have one Wisden and one only, then there would be not the faintest tremor of hesitation: I would plump for the issue of 1903, recording that superb vintage year (1902) when the Australians came over with Darling, Trumper, Noble, Clem Hill and Warwick Armstrong, and when, during the course of the series, the English selectors could actually leave out G. L. Jessop, C. B. Fry and Ranjitsinhji.

This, the fortieth edition, informs us of marquees to be bought for £10, tents for £5, lawn-tennis nets for five shillings, Lord Harris eulogizes Bartlett's 'repercussive' cricket bats, on sale at prices varying from nine and six to a guinea. Cricket balls on sale for tenpence, leg guards for three and six. Peru House Private Hotel, Russell Square (for convenience, quietude, comfort and economy) offers Bedroom and Meat Breakfast for four and six.

The real feast, of course, is provided in the Test-match accounts. Of the first Test match, played at Edgbaston, on Thursday, Friday and Saturday, 29, 30 and 31 May, the *Wisden's* chronicler writes most evocatively, and many authorities have since considered that the England team in this game was the greatest ever to represent the Mother Country – A. C. MacLaren, C. B. Fry, K. S. Ranjitsinhji, F. S. Jackson, J. T. Tyldesley, A. A. Lilley, G. H. Hirst, G. L. Jessop, L. C. Braund, W. H. Lockwood, W. Rhodes. *Wisden's* reports that

> A beautiful wicket had been prepared, and when MacLaren beat Darling in the toss for innings, it was almost taken for granted that England would make a big score. In the end expectation was realized, but success came only after a deplorable start, and after the Australians had discounted their chances by two or three palpable blunders in the field. Fry was caught by the wicketkeeper standing back in the third over; a misunderstanding, for which Ranjitsinhji considered himself somewhat unjustly blamed, led to MacLaren being run out, and then Ranjitsinhji himself, quite upset by what had happened, was clean bowled, three of the best English wickets being thus down for 35 runs.

England recovered and finished the day with 351 for 9, Tyldesley scoring 138 and Jackson 53. Owing to rain the game did not commence until three o'clock on the second day:

> Some people expected that MacLaren would at once declare the English innings closed, but acting, it was understood, on Lilley's advice, he decided to let his own side go on batting for a time, so that his bowlers might not have to start work on a slippery foothold. He declared when the score had been raised to 376 and then followed one of the chief sensations of the cricket season of 1902, the Australians being got rid of in less

than an hour and a half for 36, Trumper, who played fine cricket for seventy minutes, alone making a stand.

Trumper made 18. Wilfred Rhodes returned the extraordinary figures:

O	M	R	W
11	3	17	7

In 1961, when Australia were batting against England once again at Edgbaston, I had the privilege of meeting Wilfred Rhodes, sole survivor of the twenty-two players in that struggle of 1902, and observed that we sorely needed his 7 for 17.

'Ah, yes,' said Rhodes reflectively, 'you know how we got them out, don't you? We changed over!' Len Braund, who made an immortal slip catch to dismiss Clem Hill, had bowled one over to allow Hirst (3 for 15) and Rhodes to change ends. Following on, the Australians had scored 8 for no wicket at close of play.

Writing in *Wisden's*, 1936 ('Trials of a County Secretary'), my father has this to say about the third day:

Torrents of rain fell overnight, and at 9 a.m. the ground was a complete lake. Not a square yard of turf was visible and play was, of course, out of the question that day. The head groundsman agreed; I paid off half my gatemen and dispensed with the services of half the police. It proved to be a 'penny wise pound foolish' action. The umpires arrived; the players arrived – the captains were there. I have never known any men more patient, more hopeful than those umpires and captains. They just sat still and said nothing most effectively. At two o'clock the sun came out and a great crowd assembled outside the ground. What I hadn't thought of was that two umpires and two captains would sit and wait so long without making a decision. The crowd broke in, and to save our skins we started play at 5.20 on a swamp. The game ended as a draw with Australia 46 for 2.

The second Test match, says *Wisden's*, was 'utterly ruined by rain', the third 'a severe disaster for England', who lost by 143 runs. Of the last agonizing over in the fourth Test, when England had nine wickets down and needed 8 to win, *Wisden's* relates: 'Tate got a four on the leg side from the first ball he received from Saunders, but the fourth, which came a little with the bowler's arm and kept low, hit the wicket and the match was over.'

For the fifth Test match Ranjitsinhji was left out. England, set 263 to win, were saved by G. L. Jessop with possibly the best innings of his life. 'He scored,' says *Wisden's*, 'in just over an hour and a quarter, 104 runs out of 139, his hits being a five in the slips, 17 fours, 2 threes, 4 twos and 17 singles.' Hirst and Rhodes, the last pair, scored the necessary 15 runs to win. It was of this occasion that the apocryphal story 'We'll get them in singles, Wilfred!' is told. *Wisden's*, preferring accuracy to romance, records: 'Rhodes sent a ball from Trumble between the bowler and mid-on, and England won the match by one wicket.'

Yorkshire's victory over the Australians, who were dismissed for 23 in their second innings, is described as 'a big performance'; an Australian victory over Gloucestershire is chronicled in a burst of Edwardian prose – 'the Colonials had no great difficulty in beating the western county in a single innings'; and of a match against Surrey we are told 'Trumper and Duff hit up 142 in an hour and a quarter' – this against Richardson and Lockwood. The historian is chatty and informative about the match with Cambridge University. 'So greatly were the Australians weakened by illness that they had to complete their side by playing Dr R. J. Pope, a cricketer, who it will be remembered, appeared several times for H. J. H. Scott's eleven in 1886. Dr Pope came over from Australia for a holiday mainly to see the cricket, and was a sort of general medical adviser to the eleven.' Anyway, he made 2 not out.

The 1923 edition contains the saga of the Warwickshire v. Hampshire match at Edgbaston; surely the most extraordinary game of county cricket ever played. Warwickshire, batting first, were out for a mediocre 223 on a good wicket. They then proceeded to dismiss their opponents in 53 balls for 15. The analyses of Howell and Calthorpe speak for themselves:

	O	M	R	W
Howell	4.5	2	7	6
Calthorpe	4	3	4	4

Hampshire followed on, and lost 6 wickets for 186. However, as *Wisden's* observes, 'Brown batted splendidly for four hours and three-quarters and Livsey made his first hundred without a mistake.' Brown made 172, and Livsey 110 not out; Hampshire made 521, bowled

Warwickshire out for 158 and won by 155 runs. 'The victory, taken as a whole,' says *Wisden*'s, 'must surely be without precedent in first-class cricket.' And has there been anything like it since?

Not long ago I had the good fortune to discuss the match with the late George Brown in his house at Winchester where, appropriately enough, a framed scorecard of the conflict hung in the hall. He contended that Hampshire should have been out for 7 in their first innings, explaining that 'Tiger' Smith, while unsighted, had let a ball go for four byes, and that Lionel Tennyson was missed at mid-on, the ball then travelling to the boundary.

The chief joy of reading *Wisden* is also the chief snare – once you have picked up a copy you cannot put it down. How many wives have become grass-widowed on account of the limp-covered, yellow-backed magician it is impossible to say. If a teasing problem crops up – when was W. G.'s birthday? Who captained the Australians in 1909? Who won the championship in 1961? – then 'I won't be a minute,' says the cricket enthusiast, 'I'll just look it up in *Wisden*', and he disappears in search of his treasures. And, of course, he isn't a minute: he may be away for an hour or for the rest of the day. He may even never return.

There is one thing that you can be quite certain of in 'looking it up in *Wisden*' and that is that you will pick up a whole miscellany of information before you find the thing you have been looking for.

Suppose, for instance, that you want to look up the match between Kent and Derbyshire at Folkestone in 1963. You pick up your *Wisden* for 1964, open it at random, believing firmly that the problem will be solved in a matter of seconds, and you find yourself confronted with a Lancashire–Yorkshire match at Old Trafford.

The result is a draw. Forgetting now altogether about Kent and Derbyshire at Folkestone, you next turn up the Table of Main Contents to see if you can find out how Yorkshire and Lancashire have fared over the years in their Roses battles. On skimming down the Table of Contents, however, you come across a heading about Test Cricketers (1877–1963). This immediately starts you off on a new track, and you turn to the appropriate section to find how many cricketers have played for their country. The names Clay, Close, Coldwell, Compton, Cook, Copson leap up at you from the printed page: memories of past Test matches dance in bright kaleidoscopic colours before you. *Wisden*, you feel, is as exciting as a Buchan thriller. The word 'Buchan' leads logically enough to Midwinter.

Midwinter – of course! – now, didn't he play for England v. Australia, and also for Australia v. England? Research confirms that such was indeed the case. You look him up in Births and Deaths; but this entails searching an earlier edition. At random you select the issue for 1910; and sailing purposefully past an offer on page 3 of a free sample of Oatine (for Men after Shaving) you find that Midwinter, W. E., was also a regular player for Gloucestershire and for Victoria. Meanwhile, you have hit upon another Test-match series.

In the first of this series of Tests England were trying out a twenty-six-year-old opening batsman named Hobbs (Cambridgeshire and Surrey). He made a duck in his first innings, but did better in the second. 'England wanted 105 to win, and as it happened, Hobbs and Fry hit off the runs in an hour and a half without being separated.'

There are now two tracks that lie ahead. You can follow the Australians on their tour, to find that they won the Ashes but came close to defeat against Sussex and Somerset, and also played some unusual sides – Western Union (Scotland), South Wales, two rain-ridden draws against combined Yorkshire and Lancashire elevens, and, towards the end of the tour, Mr Bamford's eleven at Uttoxeter. The other track, of course, is the golden trail of the Master's 197 centuries.

Wisden's attractions are endless. A county cricketer of former days recently told me how much he enjoyed browsing over the Public School averages 'so that I can see how my friends' sons are getting on'.

Even the briefer obituaries are always interesting to read and, when occasion demands, amusing – as surely obituaries should be. To return again to the 1903 edition, we read of the Reverend Walter Fellows, described in Scores and Biographies as 'a tremendous fast round-armed bowler'. For Westminster against Rugby (1852) he took a wicket in the first innings and 6 in the second. However, in the course of so doing he bowled 30 wides, 'thereby giving away as many runs as Westminster made in their two innings combined'. In 1856 he hit a ball 175 yards 'from hit to pitch . . . In 1863 he emigrated to Australia, and joined the Melbourne Club the following year. He was interested in the game to the last. Height 5 ft 11 in, and playing weight as much as 16 st 4 lb.'

And again, in the 1961 edition there is the superb obituary of Alec Skelding. Of the many selected tales *Wisden* recounts of him, perhaps this is the loveliest: 'In a game in 1948 he turned down a strong appeal by the Australian touring team. A little later a dog ran on to the field, and one of the Australians captured it, carried it to Skelding and said: "Here you are. All you want now is a white stick."'

Wisden is indeed better than rubies. *Wisden* is an inexhaustible goldmine in which lies embedded the golden glory of a century of cricketing summers. In the 1964 edition (page 1024) we read the brief statement '*Wisden* for cricket.' I think that sums it up.

A dream I have every so often begins in an unfamiliar station where I have to change trains. I arrive in the morning, and the connection is in the early afternoon. After leaving my bags in the waiting room I set off in search of a second-hand bookstore. With the aid of an auto-rickshaw driver I find one. The shop is dimly lit, and with closely packed shelves. The owner is there, somewhere, but no words are exchanged. I must search this place thoroughly before I return to my train. Eyes racing, I espy a faded spine with 'Cardus' written on it. The book is taken out and I turn the pages, to find that this is the first (1949) edition of the *Autobiography*. I turn to ask its price – and am woken up.

As a little boy, Neville Cardus' autobiography was for me indeed a forbidden fruit. I first encountered the work in my aunt's house in Delhi. The books in the house were all in one room, occupied by my Oxford-educated cousin. He was to me what Robert was to William in the Richmal Crompton stories – a lofty elder sibling who forbade me from coming near his cigarettes, his books or his girl-friends. His mother, who worshipped him, had also warned me off his room. My cousin went to work but my aunt stayed at home, and in any case I was a timid child. I entered the room only rarely and fleetingly: altogether, I must have fingered the *Autobiography* for a mere five or ten minutes.

I had never before seen a book by Neville Cardus. But I knew already that he was the Don Bradman of cricket writers. I must have read of him in one of the first books I owned, Keith Miller's *Cricket Crossfire* (the two were friends, for the fast bowler, like the scribe, had an abiding passion for classical music). He also peeped in and out of the works of A. A. Thomson, two of whose books my father had found for me in a bookstore in Delhi's Connaught Circus. Thomson was an accomplished writer himself, at his best in remembering the Yorkshire cricketers of his boyhood. From him I learned that a lover of cricket must find a club or county before he finds a country.

For a middle-class cricket-mad boy in the India of the 1960s, building a library was much like assembling an innings on a bowler's wicket – a run from here and a run from there, and no easy pickings. Some books from England found their way to the local stores, but they were always extravagantly priced. In the time it took to save money to buy them, the pound had grown twice as strong against the rupee. Easier to obtain were the ghosted autobiographies which Indian publishers were willing to commission or reprint. That is how I got the Keith Miller, and that is how I came to read – and reread – Denis Compton's *End of an Innings* and Syed Mushtaq Ali's *Cricket Delightful*. Even so, I could tell literature apart from propaganda, the first-hand evocations of A. A. Thomson from the carelessly remembered achievements of the star as retold by his ghost.

I grew up, to discover the second-hand bookstores. These included the pavement sellers in Delhi, a town I went to study in, and the charming Select Bookshop in Bangalore, a town I visited every summer to see my grandparents. My collection got a ferocious fillip in my second year at university, when Delhi hosted its first World Book Fair. The fair was held at the new Pragati Maidan (loosely translated, 'The Grounds of Progress'). My pocket money had increased – my father had recently been awarded a promotion – while an adoring (and cricket-playing) uncle unilaterally offered an additional fifty rupees a month. It was the capital at its most glorious: winter, the sun out, a clear view of the Purana Qila, and the music of the great shehnai player Bismillah Khan. Walking through the fair, I came upon a shop with rows upon rows of cricket books. (This was Prabhu Book Service of Gurgaon, known to all foreign historians of India.) The books had once belonged to a couple named Indumathi and Piyush Diwan. They were many and various, and had the owners' names stamped on the first page. I bought several autobiographies of older cricketers (Lord Harris and S. M. J. Woods, among others), Pelham Warner's history of Lord's Cricket Ground, and more of the sentimental studies of A. A. Thomson. Unhappily, I did not have the money at hand to buy C. B. Fry's classic book on batsmanship. To my surprise, there weren't any books by Neville Cardus. It seems that the Diwan heir who sold away the family jewellery knew the worth of that particular design.

It was also at the 1976 World Book Fair, but at an open stall outside the main hall, that I picked up a reprint of C. L. R. James's *Beyond a Boundary.* It cost me four rupees. I had already read the book (a copy lay in my college library), and have read it almost every year since. It must surely be the greatest work written on any sport. It has spawned an extensive and mostly tedious critical literature, which I have no wish to add to. Suffice it to say that years later, when my first child was born, and I returned from the hospital to an empty home where the enormity of the event hit me, I read, as consolation and stimulation, my favourite chapter from *Beyond a Boundary.*

The James was the only volume I retained when in 1980 I disposed of my cricket books. I had begun a PhD in sociology in Calcutta, and converted to Marxism. Books were property, and property (I now understood) was theft. Besides, cricket and other sports were pursuits that kept the masses away from the class struggle. Sensibly, I did not sell the collection but identified a suitable person to give it to. This was Mudar Patherya, a talented young cricket writer then with the *Telegraph* of Calcutta. I met him, briefly explained the collection's strengths, and obtained his consent to paying the freight charges from my home in northern India. For 750 rupees Mr Patherya came into the possession of what might have been among the most hard won of all cricket libraries.

As it happened, in a year or two I was rid of Marxism and had returned to cricket. In Delhi on a research visit, I found the National Archives closed on account of a festival. Returning to my uncle's, I switched on the television and found that a Test match was on and that my boyhood hero, G. R. Viswanath, was batting on 60 not out. Watching cricket led, inevitably, to once again reading about it. The habit had proved impossible to kick.

In rebuilding my library, I now knew which books were worth having and which ones could be ignored. I also had more money – money of my own. Through my work, I came to travel more within India, thus to draw upon the shaded stalls of Bombay's Flora Fountain, as well as the shops that come up every Sunday on the sands of the Sabarmati River, under Ellis Bridge in Ahmedabad. I also came to travel overseas and visit the specialist second-hand cricket bookseller, a species unknown in my country. I have spent money at J. W. McKenzie's shop in Surrey and Martin Wood's in Kent, and also (my own favourite place) in Roger Page's store on

Tarcoola Drive, in MacLeod, a suburb of that great cricketing city Melbourne.

There remain some gems from the original holdings that have not yet been replaced. Meanwhile, Mr Patherya himself has abandoned cricket. After writing two or three books on the sport, he has become a successful trader in stocks and shares. On my next visit to Calcutta I must make a bid for his (or my) collection.

I shall now enumerate, for the benefit of the reader, fifty fine books on the game. To choose a cricket eleven is to invite dispute, and so it is with a cricket library. Asked by a friend which ten books he should buy to begin his collection, A. A. Thomson answered, 'John Nyren's A Cricketer's Tutor, Altham and Swanton's A History of Cricket and any eight of Cardus.' I have five times as many slots to play with, and yet, the first two of Thomson's recommendations do not figure in my list at all.

I will begin with authors rather than titles, with the acknowledged masters of cricket writing. James presents no problem, since only two books have appeared under his name: Beyond a Boundary, which was first published in 1963 – the year Frank Worrell led his West Indian side on a triumphant march through the grounds of England – and Cricket, a collection of fugitive pieces lovingly put together twenty-three years later by his assistant, Anna Grimshaw. Jack Fingleton wrote more books, but two clearly stand out: his first-person account of bodyline, Cricket Crisis (1946), and The Masters of Cricket (1958), a collection of portraits of contemporaries and heroes. His compatriot Ray Robinson wrote half a dozen books of roughly equal worth. If one cannot have them all, one might make do with Between Wickets (1946), a fact-filled analysis of cricket between the wars, and his last book, On Top Down Under, a cheerful roam through the careers of the men who have captained Australia (first published in 1976, this book reappeared in 1998, updated by Gideon Haigh).

What then of Cardus? He certainly wrote more than eight books, but I am not an Englishman, and must set against his undoubted genius the claims of geographical correctness. Perhaps one can allow him three. The Autobiography, of course, and with it The Essential Neville Cardus, also printed in 1949, the essays chosen with care by his publisher, Rupert Hart-Davis. Reprinted here are pieces from his books of the 1920s and '30s – Cardus at his freshest: anecdotal, worshipful and breathless. To go with it I would recommend *Close of Play* (1956), a more meditative and, dare one say, mature work.

Sports literature is dominated by biographies and autobiographies, the former of uneven quality, the latter not often written by the person whose name appears on the title page. Lives of great cricketers published in recent years are long on gossip and short on analysis. Things were once otherwise. I think for example of Gerald Howat's 1975 biography of the first great black cricketer, Learie Constantine, a book which subtly weaves anecdote with social history, or of Irving Rosenwater's study of Don Bradman (1978), a dispassionate and heavily numbered analysis of the record-breaking batsman. Alongside Rosenwater one could read, and buy beforehand, *Brightly Fades the Don* (1949), Jack Fingleton's account of Bradman's remarkable last tour of England.

The Don was the most phenomenal of all cricketers, possibly excepting W. G. Grace. In England, where there is a perennial interest in Victoriana, there is a fresh book on Grace published almost every year. I prefer to all of these the warm remembrance of Bernard Darwin. *W. G. Grace*, printed in 1934, is written by a supreme stylist who made his name writing about another sport (golf). The modern cricketer who has resembled Grace in the expansiveness of his personality is surely Frederick Sewards Trueman. John Arlott's *Fred: Portrait of a Fast Bowler* (1971) is a wonderful evocation of the bowler and man, by one who spent much time with his subject in pub and commentary box. Three other lives by English writers shall go on to my short list – David Foot's *Harold Gimblett* (1982), a Somerset man writing with love and despair about a tormented Somerset hero; Leslie Duckworth's *S. F. Barnes* (1970), the life of a truly great bowler who chose to play in the obscurity of the leagues rather than for Lancashire and England; and Simon Wilde's *Ranji: A Genius Rich and Strange* (1990), a superb warts-and-all recollection of the Indian prince who played for Sussex and England.

The finest of all cricket autobiographies is unquestionably Arthur Mailey's *10 for 66 and All That* (1958), the tale of a lowly mechanic whose playing skills allowed him to meet kings and prime ministers and to befriend Sir James Barrie and Neville Cardus. Mailey was a natural wit and a gifted artist (the book carries his illustrations), and had strong views on the game besides. Not as strong, however, as the views of Bill O'Reilly, another in the long line of Australian googly bowlers who have made mincemeat of English batsmen. His

Tiger: Sixty Years in Cricket (1985) is unsparing in its criticisms of the modern game. But it also contains lovely memories of life and sport in the bush, including a chapter (reproduced in this anthology) on O'Reilly's first encounter with Don Bradman. Among the English contributions to this genre I shall select Bill Bowes's *Express Deliveries* (1958), which is reliably known not to have been written by a ghost. This is an account of professional cricket as seen by a hard-boiled Yorkshireman whose first job was as a net bowler at Lord's. Add to that Ian Peebles' *Spinner's Yarn* (1977), by a contemporary of Bowes who came from further north (Scotland), and whose route to Test cricket lay instead through The Parks at Oxford.

Some of the best memoirists have been less than world-class players themselves. R. C. Robertson-Glasgow's *46 Not Out* (1948) displays in abundance the love for the game of a fast bowler who appeared, if not with a great deal of success, for Oxford University and for Somerset. It must be read alongside Bernard Hollowood's *Cricket on the Brain* (1970), by a celebrated cartoonist and former editor of *Punch*, who played in the tough northern leagues and for Staffordshire in the Minor County Championship. Rounding off this group is Sujit Mukherjee's *Autobiography of an Unknown Cricketer* (1996), about life in a complete cricketing backwater, the eastern Indian state of Bihar.

Mukherjee's principal reputation lies outside cricket, as a literary historian. Two other men of letters who adored cricket – although they played it with even less distinction – were Edmund Blunden and Ronald Mason. Blunden's *Cricket Country* (1944), published in the depths of war, is a joyous exercise in escapism. Mason's *Batsman's Paradise* (1955) is likewise a moving personal account of what the game and its icons meant to a bookish English boy.

To move now from the idiosyncratic to the encyclopedic, from books that foreground one person to those that pretend to a greater comprehensiveness. If one is looking for a single-volume history of cricket, then Altham and Swanton, I am afraid, must give way to Rowland Bowen's *Cricket: A History of its Growth and Development throughout the World* (1970), a magnificently learned work which is less Anglocentric and far richer in sociological insight. Those of a more technical bent should supplement Bowen with Gerald Brod-ribb's *Next Man In* (first published in 1952, then in an updated edition in 1985), which is a delightful look at the origins of the game's laws and customs.

In terms of player strength and commercial robustness Australia has been, for some time now, the leading cricket nation of the world. The recently published *Oxford Companion to Australian Cricket* (1996) presents an authoritative and always readable account of the game in that country. There are no comparable books, I fear, on other lands, but their partisans can make do with the *Wisden Book of Cricketers' Lives* (1986), compiled by Benny Green from the obituary section of the great almanack, a little outdated, but with 8,614 entries nonetheless. Collective biography is also how one would describe David Frith's book *The Fast Men* (1975; revised edition 1977), with its companion volume on *The Slow Men* (1984). I recommend these strongly, for the author probably knows more cricket facts than any man alive, and because in these books he celebrates cricket's underpaid proletarians. Batsmen are the glamour boys of the game, who are paid more, profiled more, and rewarded more. When Len Hutton was knighted, back in 1956, Arthur Mailey congratulated him but added, 'I hope next time it is a bowler – the last one to be knighted was Sir Francis Drake.'

For the visually minded, I commend *Cricket Cartoons and Caricatures* (1989), by George Plumptre, and *The Art of Cricket* (1983), by Robin Simon and Alastair Smart, both of which range deep and wide and reproduce their selections well. Alas, there is no comparable book on cricket photography (a casualty, one suspects, of royalty payments). Also worth possessing is *Lord's and Commons* (1988), edited by John Bright-Holmes, which focuses exclusively on cricket fiction. *Wodehouse at the Wicket* (1998), edited by Murray Hedgecock, shall be placed next to it. This brings together all that the master humorist published on cricket, prefaced by a superlative introduction by the editor.

Of the many anthologies preceding this one, I can bring myself to recommend Alan Ross's *A Cricketer's Companion* (second enlarged edition 1979), compiled by a man who was born in India, who played cricket for Oxford, who wrote his first book about Australia, and who is a notable poet besides. Ross, whom some reckon to be the last great cricket writer, published in 1999 a selection of his writings over four decades, called (after a line of Tennyson on the county of Sussex) *Green Fading into Blue*.

Ross chooses, in his old age, to privilege his identification with Sussex. The county has been to him what Lancashire once was to Cardus, or Yorkshire to A. A. Thomson. For an Indian, himself living in a vaster and altogether more diverse land, what is truly amazing about English literature is its love of place. The flowers, trees and rivers, so much smaller and less colourful, are written about with a detail and emotional intensity absent in our own literature. Happily, cricket has been a prime beneficiary of English localism. In 1946 Dudley Carew wrote *To the Wicket*, a delightful ramble through the counties and their cricketers. Then in 1961 A. A. Thomson published *A Cricket Bouquet*, another lovely book, whose seventeen chapters end with all-time county elevens. A quarter of a century later Tim Heald brought out *The Character of Cricket*, which differed only in focusing more on the atmosphere of county grounds rather than on their players. The most celebrated of these grounds is the subject of Pelham Warner's *Lord's: 1787–1945* (1946), written by one who captained Middlesex and England – the former to the County Championship, the latter to an Ashes victory in Australia – founded the *Cricketer* magazine and was (need it be said?) president of the MCC as well. No one knew Lord's better than Warner. His book is suffused with love and knowledge; it is the one volume currently with Mr Patherya I most wish I had back with me.*

Eight places remain, and I shall fill them with some of my own favourites. *Great Australian Cricket Stories* (1982), edited by Ken Piese, is a massive collection of tales epic and small. Alan Gibson's *The Cricket Captains of England* (1976) wears its research lightly; it is almost as informative as, and possibly better written than, the comparable book by Ray Robinson. Gibson's *Growing Up with Cricket* contains memories of cricket played and cricketers watched in Essex and Oxford; the tone is urbane, the wit dry. By contrast the style is extravagant and the stories are risqué in Michael Parkinson's *Cricket Mad* (1969), set in Yorkshire, and another well-thumbed book of mine. Another most readable book by a fan is Rowland Ryder's *Cricket Calling* (1995), written in his eighties by a man who grew up in Edgbaston Cricket Ground (where his father worked), and whose memories stretched all the way back to Warwick Armstrong's 1921 Australian side.

Among biographies, I can offer Ashley Mallet's *Grimmett* (1993), a good Australian spin bowler remembering a better. The finest book on the loveliest of cricket arts is probably Trevor Bailey and Fred

---

* After this book went to press I did pick up a copy from a pavement stall in the Madras locality of Luz.

Trueman's *The Spinners' Web* (1988), which chronicles the varying styles and achievements of the slow bowlers the authors watched or played against (Bailey certainly wrote his sections; Trueman possibly spoke his). I am allowed, I think, to end with a fellow countryman writing about other fellow countrymen. Sujit Mukherjee's *The Romance of Indian Cricket* (1968) pays proper tribute to a generation of great Indian cricketers always ignored abroad and since superseded at home by the Tendulkars and Gavaskars.

Fifty is a number whose cricketing significance is restricted only to the pyjama game. But eleven is too few, and a hundred would take too much time – and stretch the budget. The list offered here is the product of a lifelong addiction and a deeply felt cosmopolitanism. My experience may even be unique; I know no one else who has had to build his collection of cricket books twice over. Happily, the second one is still growing. When we first discussed this anthology, my publisher gifted me the very scarce first edition of *Beyond a Boundary*. To hurry me up, he then sent a copy, in its original dust jacket, of Cardus's *Second Innings*. The work is now done, and he still owes me the *Autobiography*.

Ramachandra Guha

The Bowler's Epitaph

To Cricket's shrine I offer'd, day by day,
Pace, length and spin, swervers that 'ran away';
For Cricket I threw Tennis down the drain,
Abjur'd my mashie – abjuration vain;
For England's game I bowl'd on English muds,
Bowl'd, to a field of never-bending duds;
Heard, while the catches dropp'd, the river's call,
The pop of Bass, the punt-pole's sleepy fall;
Beheld, each Over, Slip's unpleasing face,
And wonder'd why Short-leg was not in place;
Till God, who saw me tried too sorely, gave
The resting-place I ask'd – a Bowler's grave;
O thou, whom chance leads to this nameless stone –
Come with a baffl'd trundler, or alone;
By Wides, No-balls, by Extra-Covers stout,
By l.b.w.'s, miscalled NOT OUT,
One last APPEAL. Let fall a kindred tear
O'er Bowler's dust. A broken heart lies here.

R. C. ROBERTSON–GLASGOW

Acknowledgements

Every effort has been made by the publishers to contact the copyright holders of the material published in this book but any omissions will be restituted at the earliest opportunity.

John Arlott, 'Cricket at Worcester: 1938', from *Horizon*, July 1943.

Alan Gibson, 'Great Men Before Agamemnon', from Gibson, *The Cricket Captains of England* (Cassell, 1975). Attempts at tracing the copyright holder were unsuccessful.

C. B. Fry, 'The Founder of Modern Batsmanship', from Fry, *Life Worth Living* (1939: reprint Michael Joseph, 1986).

Bernard Darwin, 'Genial Giant', from Darwin, *W. G. Grace* (1934: reprint Duckworth, 1978).

Ray Robinson, 'The Second Most Famous Beard in Cricket', from Robinson, *From the Boundary* (Collins, 1950).

J. H. Fingleton, 'Never Another Like Victor', from Fingleton, *Masters of Cricket* (1958: reprint Michael Joseph, 1986). Attempts at tracing the copyright holder were unsuccessful.

Bernard Hollowood, 'The Greatest of Bowlers', from Hollowood, *Cricket on the Brain* (Eyre and Spottiswoode, 1970).

Ian Peebles, 'The Colossus of Rhodes', first published in the *Cricketer* magazine in 1967 and reproduced with their kind permission.

Ralph Barker, 'The American Lillee', from Barker, *Ten Great Bowlers* (Chatto & Windus, 1967).

Neville Cardus, 'The Millionaire of Spin', from Cardus, *Full Score* (Cassell, 1970). Attempts at tracing the copyright holder were unsuccessful.

R. C. Robertson-Glasgow, 'Three English Batsmen', from *Crusoe on Cricket* (1966: reprint Michael Joseph, 1985).

Ronald Mason, 'Imperial Hammond', from Mason, *Batsman's Paradise* (Hollis and Carter, 1955).

W. J. O'Reilly, 'Young Don Bradman', from O'Reilly, *Tiger: Sixty Years in Cricket* (Collins, Sydney, 1985).

J. H. Fingleton, 'Brightly Fades the Don', from Fingleton, *Brightly Fades the Don* (1949: reprint Michael Joseph, 1986). Attempts at tracing the copyright holder were unsuccessful.

C. L. R. James, 'The Black Bradman', from James, *Beyond a Boundary* (Hutchinson, 1963).

J. H. Fingleton, 'My Friend, the Enemy', from Fingleton, *Brightly Fades the Don* (1949: reprint Michael Joseph, 1986). Attempts at tracing the copyright holder were unsuccessful.

E. W. Swanton, 'Compton Arrives', from Swanton, *Denis Compton* (Sporting Handbooks, 1948).

Alan Ross, 'Hutton Departs', from Ross, *Cape Summer and the Australians in England* (Hamish Hamilton, 1957).

'Evoe', 'Can Nothing Be Done?' first published in *Punch*, 29 July 1925, here reprinted from David Rayvern Allen, editor, *The Punch Book of Cricket* (Granada, 1985).

Ray Robinson, 'Touch of a Hero', and Ray Robinson, 'Much in a Name', both from Robinson, *From the Boundary* (Collins, 1950).

Ray Robinson, 'The Original Little Master', from Robinson, *The Glad Season* (Sportsmans Book Club, 1956).

C. L. R. James, 'A Representative Man', from James, *Cricket*, edited by Anna Grimshaw (Allison & Busby, 1986). Reprinted by kind permission of Allison & Busby, London.

John Arlott, 'In His Pomp', from Arlott, *Fred* (Eyre and Spottiswoode, 1971).

Ray Robinson, 'Southern Southpaws', from Robinson, *The Glad Season* (Sportsmans Book Club, 1956).

Frank Keating, 'Down Under and Out', originally published in *Punch*,

reprinted in Keating, *Long Days, Late Nights* (Unwin, 1984). Copyright © *Guardian* and Frank Keating 1984.

Scyld Berry, 'Gavaskar Equals Bradman', originally published in the *Observer*, here reprinted from Scyld Berry, editor, *The Observer on Cricket* (Unwin, 1988).

John Woodcock, 'Kapil's Devil', originally published in *The Times*.

Donald Woods, 'Twist Again', originally published in *The Times*, here reprinted from Marcus Williams, editor, *Double Century: Cricket in The Times* (Collins, 1985).

Martin Johnson, 'A Man with a Secret', originally published in the *Independent*, here reprinted from Andrew Green, editor, *Can't Bat, Can't Bowl, Can't Field: The Best Cricket Writings of Martin Johnson* (Collins Willow, 1997).

Scyld Berry, 'Botham's Fastest Hundred', from Scyld Berry, *Cricket Wallah* (Hodder & Stoughton, 1982).

Hugh Mcilvaney, 'Black Is Bountiful', originally published in the *Observer*, here reprinted from Scyld Berry, editor, *The Observer on Cricket* (Unwin, 1988).

Frank Keating, 'Marshall Arts', from Keating, *Sportswriter's Eye* (Queen Anne Press, 1990).

Martin Johnson, 'King of the Willow', originally published in the *Independent*, here reprinted from Andrew Green, editor, *Can't Bat, Can't Bowl, Can't Field: The Best Cricket Writings of Martin Johnson* (Collins Willow, 1997).

B. C. Pires, 'Emperor of Trinidad', from the *Guardian*. Copyright © *The Guardian* and B. C. Pires 1998.

Frank Keating, 'Final Fling for the Fizzer', from the *Guardian* 1999. Copyright © *Guardian*.

Mike Selvey, 'Sachin of Mumbai', from *Wisden Cricketers' Almanac* 1997. Copyright © *Guardian* and Mike Selvey.

Suresh Menon, 'Tendulkar of the World', from *Outlook* magazine, New Delhi.

Alan Ross, 'Watching Benaud Bowl', reprinted from Ross, *Green Fading into Blue* (André Deutsch, 1999).

A. A. Thomson, 'Bat, Ball and Boomerang', from Thomson, *Odd Men In* (1958: reprint, Michael Joseph, 1985).

John Arlott, 'Rough Diamond', originally published in *The Spectator*, reprinted in *Arlott on Cricket*, edited by David Rayvern Allen (Collins, 1984).

Neville Cardus, 'Robinson of Yorkshire', from Cardus, *Good Days* (Jonathan Cape, 1934).

David Foot, 'Character in the Counties', originally published in *Cricket Lore* magazine. Copyright © the *Guardian* and David Foot 1998.

Rowland Ryder, 'The Unplayable Jeeves', from Ryder, *Cricket Calling* (Faber and Faber, 1995).

C. L. R. James, 'The Most Unkindest Cut', from James, *Beyond a Boundary* (Hutchinson, 1963).

Matthew Engel, 'A Great Fat Man', from *Cricket Heroes* (Queen Anne Press, 1983) copyright © Matthew Engel 1983.

Dale Slater, 'Abed and Apartheid', published in *Cricket Lore* magazine.

Philip Snow, 'The Fijian Botham', from *Cricket Heroes* (Phoenix Sports Books, 1959).

Sujit Mukherjee, 'A Jesuit in Patna', from Mukherjee, *Autobiography of an Unknown Cricketer* (Ravi Dayal Publishers, New Delhi, 1996). Copyright © Sujit Mukherjee 1996.

Neville Cardus, 'A Shastbury Character', from Cardus, *Close of Play* (Collins, 1956).

Alan Gibson, 'The Unmasking of a Dashing Oriental Star', originally published in *The Times*, here reprinted from Marcus Williams, editor, *Double Century: Cricket in The Times* (Collins, 1985).

N. S. Ramaswami, 'Iverson and the Lesser Arts', from Ramaswami, *Winter of Content* (Swadeshimitran Press, Madras, 1967).

Richard Cashman, 'The Celebrated Yabba', from Cashman, *'Ave a Go, Yer Mug!* (Collins, Sydney, 1984).

Hubert Phillips, 'An Englishman's Crease', reprinted from Alan Ross, *A Cricketer's Companion* (second edition: Eyre Methuen, 1979).

Ralph Barker, 'The Demon against England', from Barker, *Ten Great Bowlers* (Chatto & Windus, 1967).

Neville Cardus, 'The Ideal Cricket Match', from Cardus, *Close of Play* (Collins, 1956).

C. L. R. James, 'Barnes v. Constantine', from James, *Cricket*, edited by Anna Grimshaw (Allison & Busby, 1986). Reprinted by kind permission of Allison & Busby, London.

J. H. Fingleton, 'The Best Test I Have Known', from Fingleton, *Masters of Cricket* (1958: reprint Michael Joseph, 1986). Attempts at tracing the copyright holder were unsuccessful.

Richie Benaud, 'The Last Day at Brisbane', from Benaud, *A Tale of Two Tests* (Hodder and Stoughton, 1962).

Mike Marqusee, 'David Slays Goliath', from Marqusee, *War Minus the Shooting* (Mandarin, 1996).

R. C. Robertson-Glasgow, 'The One-Way Critic', from Robertson-Glasgow, *The Brighter Side of Cricket* (Arthur Baker, 1933).

J. H. Fingleton, 'The Brilliance of Left-Handers', from *Fingleton on Cricket* (Collins, 1972). Attempts at tracing the copyright holder were unsuccessful.

John Arlott, 'Fast and Furious', from Arlott, *Concerning Cricket* (Longman, Green and Co., 1949).

Ian Peebles, 'Opening Batsmen', from Peebles, *Talking of Cricket* (Sportsmans Book Club, 1955).

John Arlott, 'Not One to Cover', reprinted in *Arlott on Cricket*, edited by David Rayvern Allen (Collins, 1984).

Gerald Brodribb, 'The Big Hit', from Brodribb, *Hit for Six* (Sportsmans Book Club, 1951).

Ian Peebles, 'Ballooners', from Peebles, *Talking of Cricket* (Sportsmans Book Club, 1955).

Neville Cardus, 'The Umpire', from Cardus, *Good Days* (Jonathan Cape, 1934).

J. H. Fingleton, 'Cricket Farewells', from *Fingleton on Cricket* (Collins, 1972). Attempts at tracing the copyright holder were unsuccessful.

Tunku Varadarajan, 'To Lords with Love – and a Hamper', from *The Times*, 1994. Copyright © *The Times*.

Alan Ross, 'The Presence of Ranji', from Ross, *Green Fading into Blue* (André Deutsch, 1999).

Gideon Haigh, 'Sir Donald Brandname', first published in *Wisden Cricket Monthly.*

B. C. Pires, 'Coping with Defeat' (in two parts), originally published in *The Trinidad Guardian.*

Ian Wooldridge, 'Ashes Dream Teams', *Daily Mail*, 1977, here reprinted from Roy Peskett, editor, *The Best of Cricket* (Hamlyn, 1982). Copyright © *Daily Mail* 1977 and reprinted with kind permission of the author.

John Arlott, 'Australianism', from Arlott, *Concerning Cricket* (Longman, Green & Co., 1949).

V. S. Naipaul, 'The Caribbean Flavour', from *Encounter*, September 1963.

J. B. Priestley, 'The Lesson of Garfield Sobers', from *The New Statesman*, 9 September 1966. Copyright © New Statesman 1999.